TAX
HANDBOOK
2008–09

ZURICH
TAX
HANDBOOK
2008–09

A. Foreman and G. Mowles

PEARSON EDUCATION LIMITED

Edinburgh Gate
Harlow CM20 2JE
Tel: +44 (0)1279 623623
Fax: +44 (0)1279 431059
Website: www.pearsoned.co.uk

This edition first published in Great Britain in 2008 by Pearson Education

© Zurich Financial Services 2008
www.zurichadvice.co.uk

The rights of A. Foreman and G. Mowles to be identified as authors
of this Work have been asserted by them in accordance with the
Copyright, Designs and Patents Act 1988.

ISBN: 978-0-273-72143-7

British Library Cataloguing in Publication Data
A CIP catalogue record for this book can be obtained
from the British Library

Typeset by 30
Printed and bound in Great Britain by Clays Ltd, Bungay, Suffolk

The Publishers' policy is to use paper manufactured
from sustainable forests.

KEY CHANGES INTRODUCED BY THE FINANCE ACT 2008 AND RECENT COURT DECISIONS, ETC

Chapter 1 Introduction

- What's new for 2008 and 2009? See 1.2

Chapter 2 Self-assessment

- Changes to the filing date for 2008–09. See 2.1.2

Chapter 3 HMRC and you

- Shorter enquiry window for HMRC from next year. See 3.3
- HMRC introduces facility for advance rulings. See 3.8.3

Chapter 4 Employment income

- Advisory fuel rates change from 1 July 2008. See 4.4.9
- New scale rates for company cars. See 4.5
- Exemption from benefit in kind charge where overseas holiday home is held in a company. See 4.8.6

Chapter 5 Share incentives

- Foreign domiciliaries and not ordinarily resident brought within the charging provisions from 6 April 2008. See 5.3.3
- EMI limit increased to £120,000. See 5.5
- Definition of qualifying company excludes companies with more than 249 employees. See 5.5

Chapter 6 Self-employment

- New restriction on sideways loss relief for non-active sole traders. See 6.7.8

Chapter 7 Income from UK property

- Reduction in writing down allowances for integral building plant. See 7.7.4
- Changes in rates of agricultural buildings allowances and industrial buildings allowances. See 7.7.5 and 7.7.6

Chapter 8 Savings income

- Tax credits for foreign dividends. See 8.10.9
- Increase in rate of retention tax from July 2008. See 8.10.4

Chapter 9 Other income

- New rules on distributor funds. See 9.7.1

Chapter 12 Capital gains tax

- CGT exemption increased to £9,600. See 12.1.1
- Taper relief and indexation abolished from 6 April 2008. See 12.11 and 12.12

Chapter 15 Computation of business profits and capital allowances

- First-year allowances for small businesses. See 15.2.9
- First-year allowances for medium-sized businesses. See 15.2.10
- 100% first-year allowances for refurbishing business premises in disadvantaged areas. See 15.2.14
- Abolition of ABA, IBA and hotel balancing charges and allowances. See 15.2.20, 15.2.21 and 15.2.22

Chapter 16 Capital gains tax and business transactions

- Entrepreneurs relief. See 16.8

Chapter 17 Tax and companies

- Rate of corporation tax reduced to 28%. See 17.4.2
- Small companies rate increased. See 17.4.3
- ECA tax credits. See 17.17

Chapter 21 Outline of VAT

- New registration threshold. See 21.4.1

Chapter 25 Pensions

- Pensions annual allowance increased to £235,000. See 25.1.4

Chapter 27 Life assurance

- Discounted gift schemes. See 27.10

Chapter 29 Inheritance tax and individuals

- Transfer of unused nil rate band to spouse. See 29.5.1
- No IHT relief for debt. See 29.11.6

Chapter 30 The taxation of trusts

- Trustees, not the settlor, are taxed on capital gains from 6 April 2008 where the trust is a settlor-interested trust. See 30.2.1 and 32.14.6
- Certain trusts may qualify for CGT entrepreneurs relief. See 30.2.4

Chapter 32 Anti-avoidance

- HMRC loses the *Arctic* case but the Government plans legislation to counter income-splitting for FA 2009. See 32.5.3
- Foreign-domiciled shareholders in non-resident companies may be taxed on the company's capital gains from 6 April 2008. See 32.16.1
- Foreign-domiciled beneficiaries now subject to capital gains tax on capital payments from non-resident trusts. See 32.17.9

Chapter 33 Residence status

- Days of arrival may be counted for the 183-day test. See 33.2.2

Chapter 34 Income and gains of foreign domiciliaries

- £30,000 special charge. See 34.2
- New rules on remittances. See 34.3
- Irish income may now come under the remittance basis. See 34.12

Chapter 35 Being subject to two tax regimes

- Use of offshore companies to hold overseas property. See 35.4.4

Chapter 36 Some special types of taxpayer

- The green taxpayer. See 36.18

Chapter 37 Charities and not for profit organisations

- Transitional supplement to Gift Aid repayments. See 37.1.7
- New limits for benefits to Gift Aid donors. See 37.1.16

Chapter 38 Stamp duties

- Clampdown on abuse of provisions for Islamic alternative finance. See 38.2.9
- Group relief loophole blocked. See 38.2.13
- Anti-avoidance rules on partnerships. See 38.2.16
- Relief for zero carbon new homes. See 38.2.21

Chapter 40 Tax tables

- Increased personal allowances matched by reduction in the increase in the basic rate band make up for the abolition of the 10% rate of income tax from 2008–09

Readers can access the accompanying website:

www.pearson-books.com/zurichtaxhandbook

for relevant and up-to-date changes that occur throughout the year between Budgets.

CONTENTS

PREFACE

The prime purpose of this book is to enable you, the reader, to understand how the UK tax system applies to your own situation, especially in relation to what is expected of you in terms of reporting and payment of tax, and to identify situations where it may be possible for you (possibly with professional advice) to save tax. This involves our setting out the basic principles and at the same time providing commentary on problem areas and opportunities for saving tax. We reproduce the relevant pages of Revenue forms, cross-referenced to the relevant sections of the text, and explain ways in which readers may obtain further details from Government publications. The advice given varies from the basics of filling in the forms to interpretations of the often overly-complicated British legal system.

We also provide detailed information aimed at professionals whose daily work brings them face to face with our complex tax system – accountants, solicitors and company secretaries – and we refer them to other reference material, especially the material provided by the Revenue for professional advisers via its website and its *Tax Bulletin* newsletter.

This book is very much a team effort and we believe that this helps to make it more useful and relevant. Readers can e-mail any of us with queries and suggestions (see pp. xxi–xxiii).

We must again record our thanks to Linda Dhondy, our editor.

Tony Foreman and Gerald Mowles

CONTRIBUTORS

Anne-Marie Boden is an employment taxes and reward manager at PKF (UK) LLP. She has 20 years' experience in tax investigation work, including PAYE audits of large businesses, Government departments and charities. She also specialises in employment-related securities, including the arrangements in respect of expatriates. She has a wealth of experience in the negotiation of settlements with HMRC and is well versed in its new risk based approach. E-mail anne-marie.boden@uk.pkf.com

Dale Butcher is a personal tax manager for PKF (UK) LLP in Guildford. He deals with wealthy individuals, owner-managed businesses, professional partnerships and Lloyd's Underwriters. He is a member of the Chartered Institute of Taxation. E-mail dale.butcher@uk.pkf.com

Sarah Campbell is a corporate tax manager in PKF and specialises in direct tax issues for charities and the wider not-for-profit sector. E-mail sarah.campbell@uk.pkf.com

Viran De Silva is a corporate tax manager with PKF (UK) LLP in London. He has advised clients ranging from owner-managed businesses to multinational groups. His expertise covers corporate as well as personal tax, in particular, advising on maximising capital allowances, group reconstructions and demergers, company sales, purchase of own shares and capital gains tax planning. E-mail viran.desilva@uk.pkf.com

Bryan Fernandes is a tax manager in the Guildford office of PKF (UK) LLP. He specialises in providing tax advice to medical practitioners and GP partnerships. He trained with the Inland Revenue and is a member of the Association of Tax Advisers. E-mail bryan.fernandes@uk.pkf.com

Philip Fisher is a partner with PKF (UK) LLP and heads the employment tax and rewards team. He has a particular interest in share schemes and expatriate issues. He is a regular contributor to the taxation press on employment tax issues. He is also the author of *Employee Share Schemes* and was, for a number of years, editor of *Income Tax & NIC for the Employed*. Philip is a consultant editor of this book. E-mail philip.fisher@uk.pkf.com

Tony Foreman has been a PKF partner since 1988. He specialises in personal tax planning. He has served on the ICAEW's Tax Technical Committee and is the author of a number of books on taxation and personal financial planning. He is a joint editor of this book. E-mail tony.foreman@uk.pkf.com

Mark Francis is a trust manager with PKF (UK) LLP and has dealt with trusts throughout his career. He has in-depth experience in all matters relating to trust and estate taxation, administration and accounting. Mark is a very active member of STEP (Society of Trust and Estate Practitioners). E-mail mark.francis@uk.pkf.com

Patricia Goldie is a manager with PKF (UK) LLP and specialises in employment taxes. She started her career with the Inland Revenue, where she worked in employer compliance, and has since worked for several accountancy firms across the UK. Patricia currently deals with all issues in respect of PAYE and NIC, from compliance through to planning and PAYE investigations. E-mail patricia.goldie@uk.pkf.com

Peter Harrup is a partner in PKF (UK) LLP's Ipswich office. He specialises in personal and corporate tax for owner-managed businesses. The services he provides to clients include the most tax-efficient ways of holding property. Peter also advises clients concerning the purchase and sale of businesses, the use of share schemes and offshore tax planning. He is a member of the Chartered Institute of Tax and a chartered accountant. E-mail peter.harrup@uk.pkf.com

Jon Hills is a tax partner with PKF (UK) LLP in Guildford. Jon has more than 30 years' experience as a tax practitioner and has specialised in share schemes and other employee incentive arrangements. He is a fellow of the ICAEW and also a member of the Chartered Institute of Arbitrators. E-mail: jon.hills@uk.pkf.com

Gordon Hopkins is a tax manager in PKF (UK) LLP Ipswich. He qualified as a chartered tax adviser with the firm in 1999. He advises a wide range of family-owned businesses on compliance and tax planning issues. E-mail gordon.hopkins@uk.pkf.com

Peter Jun Tai oversees the provision of tax services in the Guildford office of PKF (UK) LLP. Dealing with a wide range of businesses in the industrial, commercial and professional sectors, he has accumulated considerable experience in identifying and tackling problems in a practical way. Peter's expertise covers corporate, employee and personal tax and this allows him to develop solutions that balance the aims and needs of the company and investors. E-mail peter.juntai@uk.pkf.com

Tony Millward is a senior consultant at The Financial Planning Group. Tony covers all areas of financial advice with a focus on developing personalised investment strategies and retirement planning. Tony has worked in specialist financial planning teams in accountancy firms, is an economics graduate from the University of Bath and holds the DipPFS with the Personal Finance Society.

Colin Murrell is a corporate tax manager in the Guildford office of PKF (UK) LLP and specialises in dealing with private client and corporation tax issues. He is a member of the Chartered Institute of Tax. E-mail colin. murrell@uk.pkf.com

Gerald Mowles was formerly a personal tax manager with PKF London. He has since qualified as a US Enrolled Agent and specialises in US tax and its interaction with UK tax. Gerald is a partner with BBL (UK) Services LLP. He is a joint editor of this book. E-mail gerald@ukservicesllp.com

Robert Newey is a solicitor and a fellow of the Chartered Institute of Taxation. He has 20 years' experience of VAT, and has done a good deal of litigation in that field. He also works on a wide range of business and international tax issues and drafts employee benefit schemes. He is a member of the Chown Dewhurst Tax Group. Email newey@robertnewey.com

Sue Parr is the tax librarian and research officer with PKF's National Tax Directorate. Her main role is the provision of information to the professional tax staff in the firm; she is also responsible for PKF's tax library. E-mail sue.parr@uk.pkf.com

Hilary Sharpe is a tax partner in PKF (UK) LLP in Manchester. Hilary qualified as a chartered accountant in 1989 and has specialised in the taxation of owner-managed businesses ever since. Her experience includes capital tax planning and shareholder issues in respect of buying and selling businesses together with all aspects of company taxation. E-mail hilary.sharpe@uk.pkf.com

Nicholas Tarrant is managing partner of Ball Baker Leake LLC in New York. Nick left the UK in 1985 after qualifying as a chartered accountant and was made a partner of the New York firm he now manages in 1990. Since leaving the UK Nick has also qualified as a CPA. Nick leads the personal financial management department and oversees asset protection and planning for individuals, trusts and families of high net worth. E-mail ntarrant@ballbaker.com

Simon Webber is a director based in PKF (UK) LLP's Guildford office. He specialises in corporation tax and tax planning for owner-managed companies, their directors and shareholders. Simon also advises clients on corporate reorganisations, employee incentives and share schemes, and the tax implications of buying and selling companies and businesses. He is a member of the Chartered Institute of Taxation and the Chartered Institute of Taxation. E-mail simon.webber@uk.pkf.com

Mike Wilkes is a personal tax specialist and a partner with BBL (UK) Services LLP. He trained with the Revenue and a leading firm of chartered accountants. Mike has particular expertise in international tax planning for individuals. Until recently, he was responsible for PKF London's personal tax department, which deals mainly with owner managers, directors, expatriates, foreign-domiciliaries and high net wealth individuals. E-mail mike@ukservicesllp.com

ABBREVIATIONS

ABA	agricultural buildings allowance
ACT	advance corporation tax
AGM	annual general meeting
AIM	Alternative Investment Market
AMAP	authorised mileage allowance payments
AMT	Alternative Minimum Tax
APPP	appropriate personal pension plan
ASB	Accounting Standards Board
ASP	alternatively secured pension
AVC	additional voluntary contribution
BES	Business Expansion Scheme
BPR	business property relief
CGT	capital gains tax
CIS	Construction Industry Scheme
CNR	Centre for Non-Residents (formerly FICO)
COMPS	contracted-out money purchase scheme
COP	code of practice
CO2	carbon dioxide
CPO	compulsory purchase order
CTO	Capital Taxes Office
CVS	Corporate Venturing Scheme
CY	current year
DCMS	Department of Culture, Media and Sport
DETR	Department of the Environment, Transport and the Regions
DPTC	Disabled Persons' Tax Credits
DTA	Double taxation agreement
DWP	Department for Work and Pensions
ECJ	European Court of Justice
EIS	Enterprise Investment Scheme
ELS	Electronic Lodgement Service
EMI	Enterprise Management Incentive
ESC	extra-statutory concession
EU	European Union
FA	Finance Act
FICO	Financial Intermediaries and Claims Office (now called Centre for Non-Residents)

FID	Foreign Income Dividend
FIF	Foreign Investment Fund
FIFO	first in first out
FOTRA	Free of tax to residents abroad
FRS	Financial Reporting Standard
FRSSE	Financial Reporting Standard for Smaller Entities
FSAVC	free-standing AVC
FURBS	Funded Unapproved Retirement Benefit Scheme
FYA	first year allowance
g/km	grammes per kilometre
GAAR	General Anti-Avoidance Rule
GWR	gifts with reservation
GP	general practitioner
HMRC	HM Revenue & Customs
HP	hire purchase
IBA	industrial buildings allowance
IHT	inheritance tax
IHTA	Inheritance Tax Act
IO	Integrated Office
IR(C)	Inland Revenue (Charities)
ISA	individual savings account
IT(E&P)A	Income Tax (Earnings & Pensions) Act
IT(T&OI)A	Income Tax (Trading and Other Income) Act
LEL	lower earnings limit
LIFO	last in first out
LLA	long-life asset
LLP	limited liability partnership
MAPA	Members' Agents Pooling Arrangement
MBO	management buy-out
MSC	managed service company
NCDR	non-corporate distribution rate
NICO	National Insurance Contributions Office
NICs	national insurance contributions
NSB	National Savings Bank
ODCQ	Office for the Determination of Contribution Questions
OEIC	Open-ended investment company
pa	per annum
PAYE	Pay As You Earn
PEP	personal equity plan
PET	potentially exempt transfer
PILON	payment in lieu of notice
pm	per month
PPR	principal primary residence
PPS	personal pension scheme
PRAS	pensions relief at source

PRP	profit-related pay
PSA	PAYE Settlement Agreement
PSO	Pension Schemes Office. Now called the SPSS
pw	per week
QCB	qualifying corporate bond
R&D	research and development
RAC	retirement annuity contract
RCA	Readily convertible asset
REIT	Real Estate Investment Trust
RPI	Retail Prices Index
S2P	State second pension
SA	self-assessment
SAYE	save as you earn
SDLT	stamp duty land tax
SDRT	stamp duty reserve tax
SERPS	State earnings related pension scheme
SIPPs	self-invested personal pensions
SLA	statutory lifetime allowance
SLC	Student Loans Company
SME	small or medium-sized enterprise
SMP	statutory maternity pay
SP	statements of practice
SPA	statutory personal allowance
SPSS	Savings, Pensions Share Schemes Office
SSAP	Statement of Standard Accounting Practice
SSAS	small, self-administered schemes
SSP	statutory sick pay
TA	Income and Corporation Taxes Act
TCGA	Taxation of Chargeable Gains Act
TDO	Tax District Office
TESSA	Tax-Exempt Special Savings Account
TMA	Taxes Management Act
TSO	Taxpayer Service Office
UEL	upper earnings limit
UN	United Nations
USM	Unlisted Securities Market
UURBS	Unfunded Unapproved Retirement Benefit Scheme
VAT	value added tax
VATA	Value Added Tax Act
VCT	Venture Capital Trust
WFTC	Working Families' Tax Credits
WTC	Working Tax Credit

INTRODUCTION:
PRINCIPLES OF TAX PLANNING
AND HOW TO USE THIS BOOK

This chapter contains the following sections:

Introduction and review of recent changes

(1) Introduction.
(2) What's new for 2008 and 2009?

Managing your tax affairs

(3) General strategy.
(4) Planning points if you are employed.
(5) If you are thinking of becoming self-employed.
(6) If you are already in business.
(7) Investments and capital gains tax.
(8) Business tax and finance.
(9) Managing your investments and your family's financial affairs.
(10) Tax issues if you are non-resident or have a foreign domicile.

Good housekeeping

(11) Ensure that all important deadlines are kept.

INTRODUCTION AND REVIEW OF RECENT CHANGES

1.1 INTRODUCTION

Why would you want to read a book on tax? Almost certainly because you want to have a better understanding of how taxes are assessed and administered in general, and how they can be made as painless as possible in your particular case. We intend this book to empower you so that you can deal with the annual task of filing your self-assessment tax return (or instruct a professional), stay on top of your tax obligations and identify tax planning opportunities.

Any reference book can easily become just a miscellany of facts and figures. There is a particular danger of this here because the UK tax system has developed in a piecemeal way. A new set of specific rules and regulations come in every year and are superimposed on last year's version. The cumulative effect of this process is to make things incredibly complicated and, in so doing, obscure any coherent structure which reflected the reasons why that particular aspect of the tax 'system' was originally designed.

With all this in mind, we have split this book into six parts so that you can more easily distinguish the chapters that are particularly relevant to you:

Part 1: The self-assessment process

The first part of this book deals mainly with the practical aspects of filing your annual tax return.

We also look at how you deal with HM Revenue & Customs (HMRC) and its various offices. (When we refer to the Revenue in this book we mean HMRC – the merged Revenue and Customs bodies.)

As we go through various aspects of self-assessment, we identify some tax saving possibilities. The Revenue will always give good advice on your obligations to file forms and pay taxes but it is not within its remit to tell you how you might save taxes and avoid unnecessary filing.

Part 2: Business tax and finance

This part covers aspects of the UK tax regime of which you need to be aware in your business life, especially if you are running your own business. For example, how business profits are computed, capital gains tax as it affects business transactions, getting relief for financing costs and your duty to act as an unpaid tax collector by withholding tax and paying it over to the Revenue. You need to know the specific filing obligations that apply to you as a sole trader, a member of a partnership or LLP, or shareholder in a company.

There is another aspect on which we have increasingly focused in recent editions. It is important when you are in business to plan ahead, not least in relation to your ultimate exit from the business on retirement. At regular intervals in this book, we recommend that you take professional advice. Saying this is not ducking the issue; the best course of action for you can only be ascertained when the full facts have been established. But as in so many matters, the facts often speak for themselves when you ask the right questions.

Part 3: Tax and wealth planning

Apparently we are all getting older and wealthier (according to the Office of National Statistics) and in recognition of this we have put together several chapters that concentrate on how you can build up capital and increase your wealth. The chapters cover matters such as:

- tax privileged investments (eg ISAs, EIS investments, VCTs);
- the tax treatment of life assurance policies;
- pension schemes;
- some ways of reducing capital gains tax;
- inheritance tax;
- the taxation of trusts;
- passing on your family business.

Part 4: Anti-avoidance legislation

We all want to keep tax down to the minimum but unfortunately successive governments and the Revenue have constructed a series of barriers and traps to ensure that the UK Exchequer is not diminished (a kind of fiscal Maginot Line). This part of the book deals with areas of taxation on which you would normally consult a tax accountant or lawyer. Our intention is to make you aware of the pitfalls in certain wealth creation tax schemes and to give you a strong indication when you might stray into areas where you need specialist advice.

Part 5: Residence, domicile and international matters

The chapters in this part cover international issues arising out of an individual's residence and domicile status.

Part 6: Other tax payers and taxes

Finally, we deal with miscellaneous tax matters and some taxes that do not fit easily into any one section. An example of this is stamp duty, one of the UK's oldest taxes given new teeth by the introduction of SDLT in the Finance Act 2003.

1.2 WHAT'S NEW FOR 2008 AND 2009?

Twice a year, in the autumn statement and spring Budget, the Chancellor makes our life more complicated or more interesting, depending on whether your outlook on life is that the glass is half full or half empty. The following is a brief overview of changes introduced in the 2007 and 2008 Budgets, which will take effect in 2008–09 and 2009–10.

Personal income tax

Personal income tax allowances were increased broadly in accordance with inflation initially. The headline from the 2007 Budget was the reduction in basic rate tax from 22% to 20% from 6 April 2008. However, it took a year for the penny (or to be more precise the tuppence) to drop in that the 2p reduction would be financed by the abolition of the 10% band. In the end, the Government had to increase the personal allowance to defuse the row. It balanced the books by limiting the increase in the basic rate band so that taxable income in excess of £34,800 is taxed at 40%.

Self-assessment

Following the Carter review, the dates for filing the self assessment return are being changed. These changes have come into operation for the 2007–08 return. People filing online will still have until 31 January following the end of the tax year to file, but paper filers will only have until 31 October to file (see 2.1). But even if you file a paper return after the deadline, there will be no penalty provided that you settle all your tax by 31 January 2009.

Another change for 2007–08 onwards affects the Revenue's Enquiry Window, ie the period during which HMRC can start an enquiry into a self-assessment tax return. Previously, the period ran for 22 months from the end of the tax year; going forward it will run only for 12 months from the date the return is submitted. This will be a real incentive to file earlier for those of us who wish to achieve finality on our tax liabilities.

The Revenue has been given considerable additional powers to obtain information.

HMRC will in future be able to accept payments by credit card, but with the merchant's fee being passed on to the taxpayer.

10% tax credit on foreign dividends

Individuals who own less than 10% of the shares in an overseas company can now claim a tax credit in respect of dividends received (see 8.10).

New restrictions on loss relief

The FA 2008 contains provisions that restrict the ability of sole traders to set losses against their other income. These restrictions apply where the sole trader devotes less than ten hours a week to the business. See 6.7.8.

Enterprise Investment Scheme

The maximum amount that may qualify for 20% income tax relief has been increased from £400,000 to £500,000 for 2008–09 (see 24.5.8).

Residence

The legislation now provides that a day in which an individual is present in the UK at midnight counts as a UK day for the purposes of determining residence (except that if the individual is in transit, it will not be so counted), see 33.2.3.

Foreign domiciliaries

A raft of changes applies to 'non-doms' from 6 April 2008 – in fact these changes really amount to a completely new tax regime for some foreign domiciliaries (see Chapter 34).

Capital gains tax

The annual exemption for 2008–09 is £9,600.

Taper relief and indexation, with all their complexities, were abolished with effect from 6 April 2008.

As from 6 April 2008, the calculation of capital gains has been greatly simplified by the introduction of a single 18% tax rate with a mandatory rebasing of all assets held prior to March 1982 to their March 1982 value.

A new entrepreneurs relief is introduced to appease taxpayers who have lost out with the abolition of the 10% rate on the disposal of business assets. In broad terms, the relief will give an effective rate of 10% on the first £1m of qualifying gains.

Inheritance tax

The threshold at which an estate falls liable to inheritance tax has been raised to £312,000 for 2008–09 and will be further increased over the next three years to £350,000. Also, an additional nil rate band can be claimed if the deceased's spouse had died without fully using his nil rate band. This means that a person who dies in 2008–09 may have a combined nil rate band of as much as £624,000. Although this may sound quite a large amount of money, individuals with property are well advised to look at IHT and will planning because once the value of your estate exceeds the threshold, the tax rate is a flat 40% (see Chapter 29).

Charities

A transitional relief for charities applies for Gift Aid donations. A donation made after 5 April 2008 is deemed to be a net payment after the donor has deducted 20% basic rate tax. The charity can now claim an additional 2% as well as repayment of the 20% basic rate tax. This transitional relief is available for the years 2008–09 to 2010–11.

Business taxes

Once again, the 2008 Budget contains changes that overall are revenue-neutral but which will result in gainers and losers.

The rate of corporation tax has been reduced to 28% from 1 April 2008 but this is being paid for by the introduction of a new, and much less generous, capital allowances regime.

The rates of allowances on plant and machinery have been reduced, once again with effect from April 2008. In addition to changes in the rates and initial allowances, the Chancellor has also decided to simplify capital allowances by abolishing certain categories under which capital allowances are given. To some extent this represents retrospective legislation as a person who purchased a new factory in (say) 2005 will find that industrial buildings allowances will cease in 2011 rather than continue until 2030 as would have been expected at the date of purchase.

Overall, the gainers will be companies such as banks, which will benefit from the 2p reduction in corporation tax and lose relatively little in terms of capital allowances. Manufacturing companies may well be worse off in the future.

The rate of R&D tax credits for SMEs has been increased from 150% to 175% from 1 April 2008. A new tax credit applies for companies that are entitled to ECA allowances (see 17.17).

What didn't change for 2008–09

Following the outcome of the Arctic Systems case (see 32.5), legislation was expected to be introduced in respect of income-shifting, which would not only introduce a form of transfer pricing (the concept that any transaction should be done at arm's length or market value) for married couples but also for other related or connected parties. Following protests, this legislation was deferred for one year for more consultation. A small victory for commonsense.

People who work for themselves

The first decade of this century has been marked by a running battle between contractors and HMRC and this has continued with the introduction of anti-avoidance legislation aimed at individuals using managed service companies to reduce their tax burden. In a pincer movement, the increases to the corporation tax rate for small companies will eventually eliminate most of the benefit from using personal service companies to reduce tax (see 20.4).

The lower rates of capital allowances will affect unincorporated businesses, which will not benefit from the 2% reduction in corporation tax.

MANAGING YOUR TAX AFFAIRS

Managing your tax affairs and planning ahead are inextricably connected: you cannot plan in an effective way unless you are on top of your responsibility to file returns and you are aware of the deadlines.

1.3 GENERAL STRATEGY

There is no simple solution to the question of how to pay less tax – if only there were! And there are plenty of ways of going wrong and increasing your tax problems. However, you should not go too far wrong if you bear in mind the following advice:

1 Carry out some background research

Your tax affairs need to be taken seriously. It is important to fill out your tax return in a meticulous way. You should carefully read the notes issued with the tax return and, if there are areas on which you are not quite sure, you should seek advice, either from the Revenue itself by calling the Self-Assessment Helpline number 0845 9000 444, or from a practising accountant.

2 Deal with your self-assessment return issued in April 2008

You need to submit your 2008 Self Assessment tax return by either 31 October 2008 (paper filers) or 31 January 2009 (online filers), and settle your outstanding tax by 31 January following the tax year. If you fail to do this, you automatically become liable for interest and penalties.

3 Check on back years

Mistakes do happen, and in the past you may have failed to claim all the allowances to which you were entitled. You should therefore carry out a periodic check or 'audit' to ensure that you (and family members, eg your minor children or elderly dependent relatives) have claimed all the tax allowances and reliefs to which you are entitled. If you find that mistakes have occurred in relation to 2002–03, you need to file a repayment claim by 31 January 2009. If you do not, the overpaid tax will be lost to you forever.

4 Steer clear of tax evasion

Arguably this should be point number 1.

Before you commit yourself to any course of action, make sure that you would be happy for all the facts and documentation to be laid out before the Inspector of Taxes. If a scheme or arrangement relies on non-disclosure, you may be getting involved in tax evasion. People who are found out become liable for interest and penalties and are sometimes prosecuted.

Tax evasion is illegal; tax avoidance is legal but may still lead to problems with the Revenue (see below).

5 Take professional advice

Unless your affairs are extremely straightforward, you could probably do with a financial 'health check' from time to time, ie a discussion with an accountant or tax adviser to go over your affairs to look at how you might improve your situation and pay less tax. A good accountant should be able to more than cover the fees charged by pointing out ways in which you can reduce personal taxes or avoid penalties.

If your affairs are more complex, you probably need to take professional advice regularly. It also makes sense for a tax accountant or adviser to take over the detailed work of preparing your tax return, agreeing payments and making sure that deadlines are not missed.

6 Plan ahead

Part of practical tax planning is to anticipate what could change in the future. For example, it may be that you are likely to sell your present home in two or three years' time when you reach retirement. If you have let the property in the past, you need to look into the position now to see whether there could be a CGT charge when you sell it and, if there is a potential problem, what steps you might take to avoid it. If you are going to sell your business when you retire in a few years' time, you need to find out what tax may be payable and what you can do to reduce this.

7 Take all taxes into account

It is important to be aware that steps you might take to avoid income tax may have CGT consequences, or vice versa. For example, you may be able to get a tax deduction if you set aside part of your home for work. However, if a couple of rooms are set aside exclusively for business purposes, this may affect your main residence exemption and could result in a CGT charge when you sell the property. There may well be ways in which you could both have your cake and eat it, but you need to look into the fine detail of the rules concerning the main residence exemption.

There are also many situations where you should find out the VAT and stamp duty consequences before taking steps that will reduce the tax on your business profits: one example of this is transferring an investment property to a company.

8 Be flexible

It makes no sense to invest in a savings plan because the return is free of tax if the plan is not suited to your personal requirements and the capital is tied up for, say, ten years. You should bear in mind that circumstances may change. It may therefore be unwise to put all your spare investments into a trust for the benefit of your children if your own situation might change for the worse. In recent years, many individuals have suffered unexpected demands on their capital and some people are now regretting that they gave away capital that they thought was surplus to their requirements.

9 Do not forget the rules may change

Tax legislation is subject to a review at least once a year in the Chancellor's Budget. At one time, it was possible to obtain income tax relief for all interest payments. When the law was changed, individuals were given relief for a transitional period on existing borrowings. Nevertheless, the withdrawal of interest relief came as a serious blow to those who had come to depend on it. Another example is where the rules on non-resident trusts were changed in 1998 and individuals who had created such trusts found that they could be made to pay tax on the trustees' capital gains even though these gains might not be paid out to them. Before you carry out any tax planning that will affect your situation in future years, put down on paper how much the various tax reliefs are worth to you and the extent to which you could rearrange your affairs if the law were changed and the reliefs curtailed or abolished.

Court decisions constantly result in changed interpretations or sometimes the Revenue simply decides to interpret the legislation in a different way. It could be unwise to rely too heavily on tax breaks afforded by the present rules. A recent example is the Revenue's attack on situations where husband and wife took out profits from a company in the form of dividends and the spouse who contributed most to the business took an unrealistically low salary (see 32.5.3). The Revenue suddenly picked up on this and demanded extra tax for past years, which the people concerned had thought to be settled.

10 If it sounds too good to be true, it probably is ...

All professional advisers complain that clients invariably know someone who assures them that, quite legitimately, he is paying virtually no tax at all. Be wary of advice given over a 'gin and tonic': very often, the individual himself does not understand all the ramifications of his own affairs. Worse still, some of the schemes put forward often turn out to involve evasion (which is illegal) rather than avoidance. Even where there is some substance to what is being said, your friend's or colleague's situation may be quite different from yours. For example, someone who advises you that he pays no tax on his earnings from work carried out outside this country may have a foreign domicile (see Chapter 34) and so be entitled to reliefs that are not available to you as a UK domiciliary.

11 Bear in mind the anti-avoidance provisions

One definition of tax avoidance is that it involves 'really smart people doing things that would be absolutely dumb if it were not for the tax advantages.' Unfortunately, this (and the previous) Government do not see the funny side. The tax legislation now contains extensive anti-avoidance provisions intended to make sure that you cannot save tax by carrying out transactions in a roundabout way. In particular, much legislation is aimed at preventing a person from converting interest income into capital gain. There are also provisions aimed against the use (or, to be more specific, the abuse) of settlements. In the main, you will be assessed on income arising to trustees of a settlement if you created that settlement and there is any way in which you, your spouse or partner, may benefit under the settlement.

If you are considering taking steps for tax planning that you hope will help you to escape tax, but that are contrary to the spirit of the legislation, you need to take a particularly close look at the anti-avoidance provisions. This is a situation where it is normally necessary to take professional advice.

12 Artificial tax avoidance schemes are likely to be challenged

Taxpayers are under no obligation to arrange their tax affairs in such a way that they maximise their tax liability. Indeed, Lord Tomlin stated in the Duke of Westminster case that:

> Every man is entitled if he can so order his affairs so that the tax attaching to them ... is less than it otherwise would be. If he succeeds in ordering them so as to secure this result, then however unappreciative the Commissioners of the Inland Revenue or his fellow taxpayers may be of his ingenuity, he cannot be compelled to pay an increased tax.

However, the courts have drawn a distinction between acceptable tax planning and unacceptably artificial avoidance and the Government has increasingly employed this distinction. Dawn Primarolo summarised the Government's policy on 1 April 2004 as follows:

> the Government takes steps to close down tax avoidance schemes ... where they create economic distortions, provide commercial advantages over compliant taxpayers, redistribute tax revenues in an unfair or arbitrary manner, or represent an abuse that conflicts with or defeats the will of Parliament.

Using unacceptably artificial avoidance schemes could be playing with fire. The Government has naturally encouraged the Revenue to challenge tax avoidance schemes with the utmost vigour. It has just reinforced HMRC's information powers by requiring tax advisers to register tax avoidance schemes. Someone who uses a tax scheme must therefore expect wide-ranging and searching questions from the taxman. If there is significant money at stake, you are likely to be dragged through the courts. If you lose in the High Court, you will normally have to bear the Revenue's legal costs on top.

Furthermore, the FA 2004 introduced income tax and capital gains tax charges that operate retrospectively (see pre-owned assets (32.7) and trusts and main residence exemption (32.13)). Another threat of such retrospective legislation was given in the December 2004 mini-budget. This is a trend that further tips the balance of risk-v-reward against tax avoiders.

See also the *Ramsay* doctrine (32.19) on the way that the courts have ignored purely artificial steps inserted for tax avoidance purposes.

If you have used a tax avoidance scheme in the past, you should seek professional advice to ensure that the year concerned is now closed (see 3.3.9 on the Revenue's powers to issue a discovery assessment where facts were not fully disclosed). If the scheme is still being challenged, you need an up-to-date prognosis as to the chances of the Revenue succeeding.

1.4 PLANNING POINTS IF YOU ARE EMPLOYED

Whether you are a company director, a senior executive, a manager or an ordinary employee, there are all manner of ways you may be able to reduce your tax liabilities.

1.4.1 Claim expenses

It is important to claim all allowable expenses (see 4.3). There are fixed deductions for workers in certain industries (eg nurses, dental nurses, midwives and radiographers can claim £70 pa, uniformed police officers can claim £55 pa and pharmacists £45 pa without having to produce any receipts). If you have to belong to a professional institute, the subscription is normally an allowable expense. If you are required to provide certain equipment yourself (eg a fax machine at home), make sure you put in a claim for the expenses associated with it, and claim capital allowances. If you have to use your own car for business trips, consider claiming mileage allowance (see 4.4.9).

1.4.2 Keep records

If you are required to travel extensively, especially overseas, keep a note of your itinerary and the main types of expense you incur. By doing this, you will be well placed to answer any queries from the Inspector and you should be able to demonstrate that there is no benefit-in-kind if all the expenses were business related.

Again, if you need to use your own car in the course of your employment, find out whether your employer pays the authorised mileage rates (see 4.4.9). If it does not, or if the mileage payments exceed the authorised rates, you need to keep a detailed note of your business and private mileage so that any benefit-in-kind can be calculated. Under SA, keeping good records is no longer simply a matter of 'good housekeeping' but a necessity (see 3.2.2).

1.4.3 Reduce car scale benefits and consider cash options

The company car rules changed in 2002–03 and the taxable benefit has been increased each year since then. If you have a company car, but your employer would be prepared to give you cash instead, you should check that having the car still makes sense. You need to work out the after-tax value of having a company car and compare this with your after-tax position if you were to run your own car and claim approved mileage allowance when you used it for business (see 4.4.9).

1.4.4 Go for benefits that do not attract NICs

The cost of traditional benefits packages became much more onerous for employers because of the imposition of the Class 1A NICs charge at 12.8% (see 22.1.8). Why not suggest a package of benefits that are not subject to Class 1A, such as approved share schemes?

1.4.5 Other tax-efficient benefits

If you have any influence over the way your remuneration package is made up, take account of the fact that some benefits are more tax efficient than others. For example, it is well worth having an interest-free loan of £5,000 since no benefit-in-kind is assessed whatsoever. Indeed it may be worth considering the idea of a loan above this limit as the tax charge may be more favourable than the commercial options. The benefit of having the right to occupy a company flat is often taxed in a favourable way, especially where it originally cost your company £75,000 or less (see 4.8).

1.4.6 Pension schemes

Pension benefits are particularly attractive as they are not normally taxable. If you do not need all your salary to cover your living costs, it may well be attractive if you can reach a 'deal' with your employer so that he makes contributions towards your pension instead of giving you a larger annual pay rise. If your employer has gone to the trouble of setting up a pension scheme for you, make sure that you get the most benefit out of it. Recent changes in legislation also mean that anyone who employs more than five employees may be required by the employees to offer a pension scheme.

Quite separately from this, do carefully consider the merits of making additional voluntary contributions. If you are not in a company pension scheme, you are most strongly advised to start a personal pension scheme or review your retirement planning strategy. See generally Chapter 25.

1.4.7 Share incentives

Company directors and senior executives are often offered an opportunity to acquire shares in their company. However, there are various pitfalls that can apply if you acquire shares through a non-approved scheme (see 5.3), so you need to seek professional advice. You need to plan ahead; for example, there can be situations where you can elect to pay tax upfront on the receipt of restricted shares and this can be a sensible course of action if it results in any future capital growth being subject to only 10 or 18% CGT. Also if you have been given approved share options in the past (see 5.4), consider how you will reap the benefit in a way that involves the least capital gains tax.

Approved schemes offer significant advantages (see Chapter 5). The all-employee share scheme provides total exemption from tax after five years; the Enterprise Management Incentive options are designed to provide larger equity profits that may be taxed at just 10%.

Be especially careful to take advice if you are offered the opportunity to subscribe for shares on a partly-paid basis as an especially unpleasant tax charge can arise on a sale of such shares (see 5.6).

Take advice if you are offered a chance to participate in a management buy-out (MBO) as there are tax considerations (see 10.5.2 and 36.12).

1.5 IF YOU ARE THINKING OF BECOMING SELF-EMPLOYED

1.5.1 Will the Revenue accept that you are self-employed?

The first question to address is whether the Revenue is likely to accept that you are self-employed. If the main thing that you have to sell is your time, and you are subject to supervision in the way in which you carry out your work, the Revenue may well regard you as an employee. It cuts no ice that your contract may state that you are self-employed.

One reason why the Revenue will look into this so closely is that, if you are self-employed, you will be able to claim certain expenses that are not allowable deductions for employees. So you should take all possible steps to ensure that your claim for self-employed status can stand up to scrutiny by the Revenue (see 6.2).

In theory, the risk of the Revenue's reclassifying a self-employed person as an employee lies with the employer. If the Revenue's view is eventually upheld, the employer is liable to pay Class 1 NICs and the Revenue may well require him to pay over the tax that he ought to have withheld under PAYE. Where this happens, the consequences can be disastrous. In law, an employer is precluded from collecting arrears of Class 1 NICs by deducting them from subsequent payments to the individual concerned. In other words, if the employer does not get it right first time round, he cannot correct his mistake later on. Similarly, the primary responsibility for deducting tax under PAYE and paying it over to the Revenue lies with the employer. The Collector of Taxes is normally reluctant to get into time-consuming disputes with the employee and will simply demand the tax from the employer, leaving him to make any adjustment by agreement with the employee.

Nevertheless, most self-employed individuals also have a vested interest in the Revenue's accepting that they are genuinely self-employed. If a dispute arises with someone to whom you provide services, he is unlikely to want to deal with you again in the future, certainly not on a self-employed basis.

1.5.2 Keep the Revenue informed

Once you start to be self-employed, your best interests are safeguarded by keeping the Revenue advised about what you are doing. You are legally obliged to make your existence known to your local tax district by either completing a form available at www.hmrc.gov.uk/startingup or by calling on 08459 15 45 15. New businesses have three months to register with the Revenue for Class 2 NICs or face a £100 penalty. An Inspector of Taxes is like anyone else: he is likely to be more reasonable if he is handled properly rather than irritated by the fact that he constantly has to chase you for information.

There are various other practical matters. You should make enquiries of your local VAT Office to see if you need to be registered for VAT (see 21.4.1). You should also advise the Revenue that you are self-employed and start to pay Class 2 NICs as a self-employed person. You can get advice on this from www.hmrc.gov.uk/startingup or by calling the helpline 08459 15 45 15.

The Revenue issues a starter pack for new businesses, which can be obtained by either visiting www.hmrc.gov.uk/employers or calling 08457 646 646.

1.5.3 Should you employ your spouse?

Depending on the type of business you carry on, it may be appropriate for you to employ your spouse, or even to have your spouse as a partner (see 1.6.4). This may be a particularly good idea if your spouse would otherwise have little or no taxable income. However, if you employ your spouse, do not pay an unrealistic salary. The Revenue is almost bound to challenge a situation where the salary is disproportionate. The Revenue's argument is that you will be due a deduction only for a reasonable rate of remuneration paid to your spouse in return for services and expertise provided.

Do be careful on this; in principle you could suffer double taxation if you get it wrong since your spouse will still be taxed on his or her full salary, even if only part of that salary is allowed as a deduction in arriving at your business profits for tax purposes. Problems could also arise if you are deemed to pay your spouse too little; you should obtain advice on the implications of the minimum wage legislation.

1.5.4 Provide for tax

Finally, when you commence self-employment, do think ahead and make provision for the tax payments that you will need to make over the next 18 months to two years. Get into the habit of setting aside part of your earnings each month so that you will have something in hand to pay the Revenue when the assessments are eventually issued. Under self-assessment, the first tax payment can often be crippling as it represents a payment of tax for your first year plus a 50% payment on account.

Example – 50% payment on account

S becomes self-employed during the tax year to 5 April 2008 and draws up his accounts on a fiscal year basis. He was formerly an employee who paid all his tax under PAYE and was therefore not required to make payments on account. On 31 January 2009, *S* will have to pay a balancing payment for all of the tax due for the year to 5 April 2008 plus a payment on account in respect of the year to 5 April 2009 equal to 50% of the 2007–08 tax.

1.5.5 Take advice on IR35 and managed services companies

If you are setting up a limited company to supply your services, bear in mind that the company may have to pay over PAYE tax on notional salary that you have not actually taken out. The legislation is aimed at individuals who provide their services via intermediary companies (or partnerships) and who would otherwise be regarded as employees of the end customer. The effect of the rules is that your company is required to account for tax on its income from 'relevant engagements' as if that income was your earnings subject to PAYE. See 20.3 on this. The FA 2007 made matters even more complicated by introducing rules to stamp out the use by individuals of managed services companies to avoid PAYE.

1.5.6 VAT

Research the VAT implications relating to your business. Check regularly to make sure you comply with registration requirements (see 21.4.1). The onus is on you to notify Customs & Excise if you exceed the VAT registration threshold. Make sure that you charge VAT where appropriate and allow for VAT in costings. VAT is a transaction tax, not a tax on profit, so forgetting VAT can be costly and putting mistakes right can often wipe out any profit.

1.6 IF YOU ARE ALREADY IN BUSINESS

1.6.1 Keep good records

Much of the above applies to the same extent if you have already been in business for a number of years. In many businesses, some figures have to be estimated (eg the extent to which a trader's telephone bill relates to business, as opposed to private, calls). There is nothing wrong with estimates, but do try to keep some sort of record so that the estimate can be supported if the Revenue challenges it.

You must indicate estimated entries on your SA return. The Revenue may enquire into this and the Inspector may well want to go back to previous years if he later looks into the position and decides the estimate is unreasonable. The main defence against this would be where the Inspector was already on notice about the way the estimates were arrived at.

Keep your records: the Revenue may call for them up to five years and ten months after the end of the tax year. Remember that this applies to all your tax affairs, not just the records relating to your business.

If you are a partner, keep tabs on the partnership's tax affairs. One of the partners (the 'representative partner') is responsible for filing a partnership return and you will not be able to complete your personal return without reference to this.

1.6.2 Do not cut corners on PAYE

Beware of situations where you should withhold tax, especially where you are paying casual or freelance workers whom the Revenue may regard as employees. The Revenue has teams of investigators who carry out regular reviews of PAYE compliance.

1.6.3 Take VAT seriously

VAT is a constant source of problems. Whenever you carry out a major transaction you should ask a VAT specialist for advice. Also, bear in mind that Customs & Excise makes regular control visits to examine accounting records. Penalties can be levied if mistakes are uncovered during visits, so it is well worth having a review carried out in good time for errors to be corrected before a visit.

If you are VAT-registered, you are an unpaid tax collector. Make certain that VAT works for you by taking account of opportunities to improve cash flow, for example try to make your large value sales at the start of a VAT return period. Ideally you should organise matters so that suppliers send you invoices before the end of the return period. Ensure that you take full advantage of recovering input VAT. Consider whether special accounting schemes or flat rate schemes may be best for you (see 21.6).

1.6.4 Remunerating your spouse

Think carefully about the salary you pay to your spouse. If it is less than you have to pay to an ordinary employee, increase the amount (if only to that required under the minimum wage legislation). Consider setting up a pension scheme for your spouse, as your contributions will be tax deductible.

Think also about bringing your spouse into partnership. This is a complex matter on which it is best to seek professional advice that will take account of the nature of your business, and the time, expertise or capital brought to the business by your spouse.

1.6.5 Financing a partnership

There are some interesting possibilities for accelerating tax relief by you and your partners raising personal loans to put money into the firm to enable it to clear borrowings. Suppose your firm makes up accounts to 30 April 2009: interest on the firm's borrowings will be an expense in arriving at 2009–10 taxable profits, whereas interest paid in 2008–09 by the partners on personal loans will be a deduction from their taxable income for 2008–09, so you get your tax relief one year earlier (see 10.4).

1.6.6 Relief for losses

If your business has not been going well and you suffered losses, look into the best way you can get relief. In some cases, you may be able to carry back the losses and set them against your other income (see 6.7). In other situations, the choice open to you is to set your losses against your income for the year of the loss, or against the following or preceding year's income, or carry forward the losses to be set against trading income received in later years. Obviously, it will make a great difference if you take relief in a year in which you will otherwise be subject to 40% tax rather than in a year in which your other income is relatively low and tax relief will be obtained at only 20%.

1.6.7 Pension schemes (see Chapter 25)

It is particularly important for self-employed individuals to provide for their retirement since they qualify only for the basic State pension and not for S2P.

Contributions to a personal scheme are tax deductible. Furthermore, the scheme is not subject to tax of any kind and so the fund is likely to grow at a far faster rate than investments that are subject to tax.

Up to 25% of the fund may be taken as a tax-free lump sum. The balance must be used to provide a pension.

1.6.8 If you are a partner in a large professional firm

Make sure that tax relief is due for interest on loans used to finance your investment in the partnership (see 10.4).

You must liaise with your firm's 'nominated partner' to obtain the information required for your SA return (see 6.4.7). If you incur any expenses, or buy plant and machinery used for the firm's business (eg a fax machine), you must arrange for the appropriate relief to be claimed in the partnership return (see 6.4.7).

Your firm may be considering conversion into a limited liability partnership (LLP) (see 6.5). The tax legislation makes allowance for this. However, there may be other considerations, for example a bank manager or landlord may be happy to take a guarantee from a normal partnership as he knows that each partner is jointly and severally liable, whereas he may not be inclined to accept a guarantee from an LLP, where each partner's liability is limited to their share of the capital. Also the rules regarding interest on qualifying loans can give rise to problems where an investment LLP is involved (see 10.4).

1.6.9 Should you transfer your business to a company?

If your business is going very well, you should consider incorporating your business, ie transfer your business to a company. Some general principles are set out in Chapter 19, but once again this is a matter where you would probably be best advised to consult an accountant or tax adviser. You will also have to consider the new rules in respect of service companies, discussed at 20.4. Another option is to set up an LLP (see 6.5).

1.6.10 If you already have a private company

A key issue is whether it makes sense to take a smaller salary and take the rest of your income in the form of dividends (which do not incur NICs). Another issue concerns the ownership of shares; if shares are held by your wife she may pay a lower rate of tax on dividends. However, bear in mind that the Revenue is looking at these situations much more closely (see 32.5.3).

You should fund your pension scheme to the maximum extent. A small self-administered scheme may have much to commend it if you wish to be able to take loan-backs or have the fund buy a property to rent to your company (see 25.3).

Do you see an opportunity to start a new business or extend your company's existing business to a new location? You could establish a subsidiary company but this may not necessarily be the best approach (amongst other considerations, having two companies may affect your existing company's rate of corporation tax (see 17.4.3)). One way of organising matters, which is worth investigating, is to have a LLP with the members being yourself (and possibly your spouse) and your existing limited company. The terms of the LLP can mean that your company bears most of the risk but you and your spouse are entitled to a share of profits in return for the work that you put into the venture. Your share of the profits should not attract any NICs (assuming that your company remuneration takes you over the limit for class 4 contributions). See 6.5 on LLPs in general.

Do you need to recruit or retain key managers? If so, consider share schemes because these can have great motivational value and (if you take advice) can be taxed more beneficially than cash bonuses and benefits in kind (see 4.13–4.16). Bear in mind that your company may get tax relief for such schemes (see 17.3.2) and you may also qualify for capital gains tax relief on sales to approved employee trusts (see 12.7).

1.6.11 **Plan for retirement and handing the business on**

Finally, do plan ahead, both for retirement and for passing on your business in due course to your family. Try not to leave pension funding until the last few years as this will inevitably make it much more expensive.

Key questions need to be addressed in relation to CGT planning: make sure that you take full advantage of entrepreneurs relief.

Will IHT be payable on your death? It may be possible to arrange matters so that either 100% or 50% business or agricultural property relief will be due, see 29.8–29.9 on this.

See Chapter 31 on passing on a family business.

1.7 INVESTMENTS AND CAPITAL GAINS TAX

Chapters 7–9 explain how various types of investments are dealt with for tax purposes.

We cover capital gains tax in Chapter 12.

Your home may well be your most valuable asset. See Chapter 13 on the detailed rules that determine whether the whole of any gain is exempt when you sell a property which has been your main residence.

1.8 BUSINESS TAX AND FINANCE

We have already touched on a number of issues in passing that affect people in business. However, part of this book is aimed specifically at business people.

The following chapters cover matters that are particularly relevant for a proprietor of an unincorporated business or a shareholder/director in a limited company:

- Chapter 15 Computation of business profits and capital allowances
- Chapter 16 Capital gains tax and business transactions
- Chapter 17 Tax and companies
- Chapter 18 Financing your business
- Chapter 19 Should you operate through a company?
- Chapter 20 Deducting tax at source and paying it over to HMRC
- Chapter 21 Outline of VAT
- Chapter 22 National insurance contributions

1.9 MANAGING YOUR INVESTMENTS AND YOUR FAMILY'S FINANCIAL AFFAIRS

We focus on this subject in Chapter 23.

Relevant issues include the following:

- How can you make best use of investments that carry 'tax breaks'? See Chapter 24.
- How much can you pay into a pension scheme? See Chapter 25.
- How can you take the benefits from your pension scheme in the most advantageous way? See 25.2.
- The technical aspects and advantages of investing in life assurance policies – see Chapter 27.
- How can you keep CGT liabilities down to the minimum? See Chapter 28.
- When is inheritance tax charged and what can you do to save this? See Chapter 29.
- How are trusts taxed? See Chapter 30.
- Passing on your family business – see Chapter 31.
- What are the obstacles to tax saving that arise from the anti-avoidance legislation? See Chapter 32.

1.10 TAX ISSUES IF YOU ARE NON-RESIDENT OR HAVE A FOREIGN DOMICILE

We address these issues in Part 5 of this book.

Chapter 33 deals with questions such as:

- What are the tests that determine whether you will be treated as resident and/or ordinarily resident in the UK?
- How will your income tax and CGT liabilities be affected by your being non-resident or not ordinarily resident?

Chapter 34 deals with issues such as:

- What does it mean to say that someone has foreign domicile?
- How does having foreign domicile affect your tax position?
- Tax planning.

The 2008 Budget introduced changes in the taxation of non domiciliaries that will have a profound effect on individuals who have been resident in the UK for at least seven of the previous nine tax years.

In Chapter 35, we look at considerations for people who are caught up (in varying degrees) in more than one tax regime – something that happens increasingly often now that many of the barriers to travel and individuals relocating abroad have fallen away.

GOOD HOUSEKEEPING

1.11 ENSURE THAT ALL IMPORTANT DEADLINES ARE KEPT

It is pointless trying to arrange your affairs tax efficiently unless you get the basics right and keep your affairs tidy. This means watching deadlines for action (eg paying tax) and making elections.

The most important tax planning deadlines are listed below. Note that this section should be read subject to three cautions:

(1) Most of the deadlines are dates by which a return, claim or election must be received by the Inspector of Taxes, or a payment received by the Collector. A document or payment must be posted at least one working day before the deadline and, because of the danger of postal delays, ideally at least a week.

(2) To keep this checklist to a manageable size, only those deadlines likely to apply to the majority of people have been included; the checklist is not fully comprehensive.

(3) Many deadlines cannot be included because they are fixed by reference to the facts of the individual case. For example, most corporation tax deadlines are fixed by reference to the end of the company's accounting period.

1.11.1 Outstanding deadlines for tax year 2007–08

5 October 2008   To avoid the danger of incurring penalties, individuals with new sources of income in 2007–08 should have notified the Revenue by 4pm today if no tax return has been received.

19 October 2008   Amounts agreed under PSAs due for payment – interest starts to run.

31 October 2008   Paper filers: the self-assessment tax return for 2007–08 needs to be filed by this date if it was issued to you before 31 July 2008

30 December 2008   Closing date for claiming, on grounds of low income, repayment of Class 2 NICs paid in 2007–08 (see 22.2.3)

31 January 2009   Online filers: the self-assessment tax return for 2007–08 needs to be filed by this date.

1.11.2 Main 31 January 2009 deadlines for tax year 2006–07

Personal tax

(1) Claiming a set-off for industrial buildings allowances on enterprise zone investments made in 2006–07 (see 24.8 and 7.7.5–7.7.6).
(2) Electing for the tests for furnished holiday accommodation to be by reference to an average (see 7.5.1).
(3) Claiming relief against income tax for 2006–07 for a loss on the disposal of shares in a qualifying trading company (see 16.2).

Capital gains tax

(1) Claiming that an asset became of negligible value during 2006–07 (see 12.5.9).
(2) Electing to compute all gains and losses on assets acquired before 31 March 1982 by reference to values on that day (possible only where the first relevant disposal which took place after 5 April 1988 occurred during 2006–07: see 12.9.3).
(3) Claiming the special 50% relief in respect of a rolled-over or held-over gain that crystallised in 2006–07 (see 12.9.5).
(4) Claiming a set-off against capital gains assessed for 2006–07 in respect of a loss incurred on a qualifying loan to a trader (see 16.1).
(5) Electing under TCGA 1992, s 138A where an earn-out is to be satisfied by the issue of securities (see 16.9).

Business tax

(1) Claiming that a trading loss incurred in 2006–07 should be set against other 2006–07 income (see 6.7.2).
(2) Claiming that a trading loss incurred in 2006–07 should be set against a capital gain realised in 2006–07 (see 6.7.6).
(3) Claiming that a trading loss incurred in 2006–07 be carried back, where permitted under the 'new business' rules (see 6.7.5).
(4) Disapplying CGT incorporation relief (see 16.6.5).
(5) Electing to treat plant or machinery purchased in 2006–07 as a short-life asset for capital allowance purposes (see 15.2.7).
(6) Electing for post-cessation receipts received in 2006–07 to be taxed for the year the trade was discontinued (see 15.4).

1.11.3 Main 31 January 2009 deadlines for 2002–03

Personal tax

(1) Claiming personal allowances (see Chapter 11).
(2) Claiming relief for interest paid.
(3) Claiming relief for pension contributions paid.
(4) Claiming 'top-slicing' relief in respect of life assurance policy gains (see 27.3.4).
(5) Claiming relief to correct an error or mistake made by the taxpayer that resulted in an excessive assessment being made in the year.

Capital gains tax

Claiming roll-over and hold-over relief in respect of disposals (see 16.3 and 16.5).

1.11.4 Deadlines for next year's diary

19 April 2009	PAYE/NICs payments due at the Accounts Office by today. Interest chargeable after this date (see 20.1).
19 May 2009	Employers who do not file end-of-year returns (on Forms P14, P35 and P38/P38A, CIS36) by today may be fined (see 20.1.7).
31 May 2009	Last date for giving a 2008–09 form P60 to each relevant employee.
6 July 2009	Substantial fines may be imposed on any employer who does not submit Form P9D/P11D (returns of benefits, etc provided for employees) by today (see 4.4.1 and 20.1.8). Details of benefits shown on P9D or P11D forms must be supplied to each employee. Deadline for submission of form 42 covering reportable events under the legislation on employment-related securities (see 5.1).
19 July 2009	Due date for payment for 2008–09 Class 1A NICs (see 22.1.8). PAYE quarterly payment date for small employers (see 20.1.1).
31 July 2009	Second interim tax payment for 2008–09 due (see 2.1.3).

PART 1

SELF-ASSESSMENT

Self-assessment and the 31 January filing deadline are now firmly established in the UK calendar and, although the dates for paper filing of the 2007–08 SA return form will change, the date for payment of tax remains the same. This part of the book looks at the practicalities surrounding the annual chore of filing your form. The section is broken down into the following chapters:

2

SELF-ASSESSMENT

This chapter considers the following:

(1) Self-assessment (SA).
(2) New features of the 2008 SA form.
(3) Online filing of SA tax returns.
(4) Short tax return 2008.
(5) Ten golden rules for dealing with your 2008 tax return.
(6) Common errors.
(7) Providing additional information.
(8) Finding your way around the SA form.

2.1 SELF-ASSESSMENT (SA)

The chances are that if you are going to receive a 2008 SA tax return, you will have received it just after the start of the tax year in April. If you do not receive a form and you had a new source of income or capital gains in the year just ended, you should report this to the Revenue by 5 October 2008. If you have received the form, this must be filed by 31 October 2008. Alternatively if you intend to file online you still have until 31 January 2009 to file.

If you want the Revenue to work out your tax for you or have underpayments collected under PAYE in the following tax year, you need to file your paper return by 31 October 2008. The online filing date is 31 January 2009 and the online system will work out your tax liability, though you will still need to file by 30 December if you want any tax to be collected by a PAYE adjustment in 2009–10 (see Figure 2.1).

Tax notes

Your tax affairs need to be taken seriously. It is important to fill out the tax return in a meticulous way. You should read the notes issued with the tax return carefully and, if there are areas on which you are not quite sure, seek advice, either from the Revenue itself by calling the Self-Assessment Helpline number 0845 9000 444, or from a practising accountant.

2.1.1 An overview of the SA system

Do not be put off by the fact that the form seems complicated: the Revenue has produced a number of helpsheets and your tax office will be only too pleased to clarify anything that is not covered by the notes. Indeed you may even be one of the individuals selected for the simplified forms (see 2.4), which will hopefully make the annual chore a little easier. The SA system is proving to be a great improvement on what went before: a system designed afresh rather than a set of procedures that evolved gradually in a piecemeal fashion over 200 years. For example, you only need to deal with one tax office. Also, you or the Revenue work out the tax that you owe (or are owed) as a global figure, whereas in the past many taxpayers had to contend with several different tax districts making assessments on particular types of income, sometimes from opposite ends of the country.

The Revenue form contains a 'core' section that applies to all taxpayers. Beyond that, there are special schedules that you need to complete only if you have a specific type of income, etc.

The principle is that by completing the form you should work out your own tax liability and settle what you owe by 31 January each year. However, provided an SA return is filed not later than 31 October following the end of the tax year, the Revenue will calculate the amount of tax payable for you.

The legislation contains a number of 'incentives' to ensure that people comply with their obligations. If a person does not file the SA return by the 31 January deadline, he becomes liable for a fixed penalty of £100 (or the amount of tax owing if this is less). If the return has still not been sent in six months later, there is another £100 fixed penalty. If the individual continues to be dila-

Figure 2.1 – Deadlines

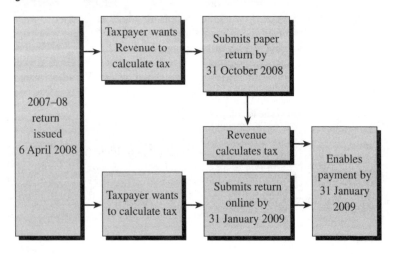

tory, the Revenue may apply to the Commissioners for more penalties to be imposed of up to £60 per day that the return remains outstanding.

The penalties for late submission of the return forms are in addition to surcharges that may be imposed on outstanding tax (see 2.1.3).

Table 2.1 – Diary under self-assessment (continued overleaf)

Date	Who is affected	What happens
6 April 2008	Everybody who gets a tax return	Paper Self-assessment tax return for 2007–08 sent out
31 May 2008	Employees	Employer should have given employee P60 for 2007–08 by this date
6 July 2008	Employees who receive expenses and benefits-in-kind (not covered by a dispensation)	Employer should have given employee details of expenses and benefits for 2007–08 by this date
31 July 2008	Some people: the Revenue will notify in advance where it applies	Second interim payment on account of 2007–08 tax
5 October 2008	People with new sources of income or capital gains arising in 2007–08, who have not received a return	Report to Revenue by now or risk penalty
31 October 2008	Paper filers who want the Revenue to calculate their 2007–08 tax	Report to Revenue by now or risk penalty
31 October 2008	Paper filers who pay tax under PAYE and want the Revenue to collect any tax due (up to £2,000) through their PAYE code during 2009–10	Send in tax return by now
30 December 2008	Online filers who pay tax under PAYE and want the Revenue to collect any tax due (up to £2,000) through their PAYE code during 2009–10	File tax return online now
31 January 2009	Online filers	This is the deadline for filing the online return and paying all the tax due (£100 penalty for those failing to comply)

Table 2.1 – Continued

Date	Who is affected	What happens
31 January 2009	Everybody who had an income tax liability for 2007–08 of more than £500 and less than 80% of liability not accounted for by tax deducted at source	First interim payment on account in respect of 2008–09 tax
28 February 2009	Everybody who has not paid tax due on 31 January 2008	Automatic surcharge will arise
6 April 2009	Start of new tax year, paper filers will receive 2008–09 form	Paper return for 2008–09 will be sent out

If you read nothing else in this chapter read this!

The UK allows taxpayers more time to file tax returns than many other countries. Compare the US where the tax year ends on 31 December and the individual is required to file the return and pay the outstanding tax by the following 15 April. If the UK imposed the same time table, the tax form you received in April would need to be filed in July of the same year, not October or even January of the following year. So what do you do with this extra time? Well, in summary, based on our professional and personal experiences, one in five of you will wait until after Christmas to file your tax form. And a substantial number of taxpayers will wait in line at a tax offices to have their tax forms stamped on the final filing day, come rain or shine; lose tax papers issued during the previous summer; pay interest on missed payments on account; and forgo the option to have unpaid tax collected under PAYE in the following tax year (in effect an interest-free loan) whilst paying 23% on credit card purchases!

Tax notes

Organise your tax papers early and aim to file early to improve your tax position. You can turn this chore into something constructive as a tax return can serve a similar function to an annual set of accounts. Armed with this information you will be better placed to make informed financial decisions going forward.

2.1.2 Provisional figures, estimates and valuations

The maximum time permitted for completion and submission of a return is ten months (ie for 2007–08, 6 April 2008 to 31 January 2009) if you file online. Final figures may not always be available by the submission deadline and therefore it may be necessary to estimate these amounts.

The Revenue's current policy is that it will accept a return (assuming there are no other problems) where the taxpayer has used a provisional or estimated figure and it will not send back a return just because it does not contain an adequate explanation for why such figures are needed or does not give a date for the supply of final figures. However, the omission of such explanation or information will be a factor to be taken into account in deciding whether to open an enquiry into the return. Furthermore, the Revenue also believes that it is possible for the use of provisional or estimated figures to result in an incorrect return for which a penalty may be charged. This might apply where the taxpayer did not take reasonable care when calculating the figures or because final figures could have been obtained before the return was sent to the Revenue.

There will be situations where an estimated figure is submitted that will not be amended in the future (eg where there is inadequate information to reach a precise figure). If the estimate is considered to be sufficiently reliable to make a complete return (eg where it is based on detailed records for a sample representative period in the case of private proportion expenses such as motoring expenses), it is not necessary to refer specifically to the estimate. However, if the figure is not reliable (eg because the records may have been lost or destroyed), the Revenue requires identification of the amounts and an explanation of its calculation.

The Revenue also draws a distinction between estimates and judgmental figures. A valuation at 31 March 1982 for CGT is a good example of a judgmental figure. That is, there is no right or wrong answer, and the figure to be included is basically the taxpayer's best judgment as to the figures, which could be agreed with the Revenue. Again, the Revenue requires identification of, and details about, the valuation. The Revenue has agreed that where no enquiry is made into a valuation within the 12-month enquiry period, and the valuation falls within the range of bona fide valuations that could arise in negotiations between valuers who were fully instructed on the facts, it will not try to reopen the position.

2.1.3 Payment of tax

Having filed the SA return, the taxpayer must settle any tax liability for the year concerned. Of course, some income will have borne tax during the course of the year, either under PAYE or because a self-employed person has made payments on account of his tax liability. If tax is still outstanding after the 31 January payment date, interest is charged and the following surcharges are imposed:

(9) a 5% surcharge on any tax that is unpaid by 28 February after the end of the tax year (a month after the tax fell due);

(10) a further 5% surcharge on any tax still outstanding by 31 July (six months after the date that the tax fell due for payment on 31 January).

> **Tax notes**
>
> Try not to get into this situation but, if you find it impossible to submit your tax return within 30 days of the filing date, make a payment on account of the tax that is owing to keep any surcharge to the minimum.

2.1.4 Payments on account

A person who files an SA return may be required to make payments on account of the tax liability for the current year. Basically, the person should take the total tax liability for the previous year (ie the year covered by the SA return) and deduct CGT and tax withheld at source. If the balance is £500 or more, the taxpayer must make equal payments on account on 31 January and 31 July, which add up to this amount.

Example

> A files a SA return for 2007–08 in January 2009. There is tax to pay of £10,000, but £4,500 of this is CGT. A must pay £2,750 on 31 January 2009 as a payment on account for 2008–09 and must make a similar payment on account on 31 July 2009.

There is also no need to make payments on account if 80% of the liability (ignoring any CGT) is covered by tax deducted at source.

> **Tax notes**
>
> You can apply for a reduction in your 2008–09 payments on account if you have reason to believe that your tax liability will be lower than that for 2007–08, but if you turn out to be mistaken you will be charged interest.

2.1.5 Return amendments by the taxpayer and the Revenue

The taxpayer may within 12 months of the filing date give a notice to the Revenue amending an SA return.

The Revenue may repair an SA return within nine months of receiving it to correct obvious errors of principle, transpositions of figures and arithmetical errors. The Revenue is required to issue a notice of this correction and the taxpayer can then accept the repair or file an objection.

2.1.6 Tell the Revenue to issue a return if you owe tax

A taxpayer who has not received a return form is still obliged to inform the Inspector of any taxable income or gains (other than income taxed under the PAYE scheme, income taxed by deduction at source, and income and gains already assessed) within six months of the end of the year of assessment. Any taxpayer who fails to do so becomes liable to a penalty equal to the tax unpaid at the filing date.

2.2   NEW FEATURES OF THE 2008 SA FORM

The Inland Revenue has highlighted the following areas as noteworthy with the 2008 SA form:

- The return now has three parts that are sent to everyone:
  (1) core return;
  (2) additional information page;
  (3) an insert to encourage charitable giving.
- Personal information is now on page 1 of the main form.
- Fewer questions.
- A new self employment section.
- A self employment short form for where business turnover is less than £64,000.
- Threshold for simplified accounts increased to £30,000.
- Simpler capital gains tax form.
- See new boxes for disclosure of pre-owned assets (see 32.7) and income derived from service companies (see 20.4).

2.3   ONLINE FILING OF SA TAX RETURNS

The Revenue has tried to motivate people over the years to file their tax returns electronically. The benefits for the Revenue are obvious and as stated on Californian state tax returns, no tree wants to grow up to be a tax return! It is advisable for confidentiality that you use your personal computer to file online and that you ensure that you have adequate anti-virus software installed on your machine.

You will also have to register at www.hmrc.gov.uk before you can file and will need the following details to hand:

- your UTR – unique taxpayer reference, which is 10 digits long;
- your national insurance number;
- your postal code.

The site asks also for an electronic-mail address and a password. Once you have successfully registered, an ID number will be generated on screen and an activation PIN number sent in the post.

The following forms can be filed online:

- Self Assessment tax returns SA100, SA800, SA900 and supplementary pages;
- Amended tax returns filed online for 2007–08 onwards.

The following are not available online:

- Non Resident, Companies or Self Administered Pension Schemes Returns;
- Previous year's Self Assessment Tax Return.

The now preferential January 31 deadline still applies for online filing, ie the tax return for the year ended 5 April 2008 must be filed no later than 31 January 2009, but there is an extension to the 31 October deadline for individuals who wish to have payments of up to £2,000 collected via the PAYE code operated against their earnings in the tax year commencing 6 April 2009. For the 2008 SA, the online date is 30 December 2008. If you have missed the 31 October deadline for paper filing it may therefore be worth considering filing online by the December deadline.

Tax notes

HMRC states the advantages of filing online are: 'secure, accurate and you will get an immediate acknowledgement of receipt, plus you should receive a repayment significantly faster if you are owed money. Our Self Assessment Service checks your Tax Return as you fill it in and automatically calculates your tax for you.'!

2.4 SHORT TAX RETURN 2008

The Revenue has tried to make things easier by issuing a short tax return to some taxpayers (see pages 50–53). Issue of the short form is at the Revenue's discretion, ie the taxpayer cannot simply choose to complete the short form. On the other hand, a taxpayer who has been sent the short form has the right to request the long form or file online.

2.5 TEN GOLDEN RULES FOR DEALING WITH YOUR 2008 TAX RETURN

The SA system requires that you carry out certain tasks by fixed deadlines. If you fail to deal with your tax affairs in a business-like way, you will be charged interest and surcharges (and possibly worse).

The SA tax return may still be unfamiliar but is not as difficult as it seems at first glance. A review carried out by the Revenue showed that 30% of returns contained clerical errors that needed correction (eg arithmetical mistakes, figures entered in the wrong columns, etc), but 90% of the mistakes could be readily identified to enable the return to be 'processed' and the taxpayer's details entered on the Revenue computer. The standard ten-page return may need to be supplemented by additional schedules so this is probably your first task: to see if you have been sent all the extra schedules that you will need. The tax legislation can be very complicated but the Revenue has gone to considerable expense to provide detailed notes and helpsheets that accompany the extra schedules and these should enable you to cope with most straightforward situations.

The next thing to take on board is that the Revenue has powers enabling it to check up on taxpayers. Tax officials will be using these powers and will not find it amusing if you are audited and found wanting, even where the shortcomings amount only to carelessness. The Revenue Enquiry Manual makes it quite plain that SA will not be allowed to degenerate into 'pay what you like'. Furthermore, even though there is a set time limit for the Revenue to announce that a return will be audited ('selected for enquiry'), it will be able to reopen back years if the taxpayer has omitted key information (this is called 'discovery': see 3.3.9).

Therefore, you are advised to do the following:

(1) Get organised; start to collect together the information you will need (see Table 2.2).

(2) Do not throw anything away for the time being. In fact, you should keep your 2007–08 records until 31 January 2010 (2014 if you run a business or receive rental income). Remember that the Revenue's policy is 'process now, check later'. The Revenue will be able to open an enquiry into your 2007–08 return by serving a notice within 12 months of the date they receive the SA form – and it will not have to give any justification for doing so.

(3) Do not leave everything until the last minute. There will be an automatic £100 penalty if you are late in filing your return and it will be easier to tackle the return while things are fresh in your mind. If there are any gaps in your records, you may be able to reconstruct them by getting down to the task before the trail goes cold.

(4) Do not send in an incomplete return because it will be rejected. If you had benefits-in-kind, such as a company car, you will need to put down a figure for your taxable benefit: just reporting 'per form P11D' or 'as PAYE' is not acceptable.

Table 2.2 – Information you will need (continued overleaf)

If you are employed:	
Form P60, ie the annual certificate of pay and tax deducted at source	Your employer should have provided this automatically by 5 July 2008
Taxable figures for any benefits-in-kind (company car, cheap loans in excess of £5,000) from your employer	
Details of amounts paid to you as approved mileage payments for using your own car for company business (see 4.4.9)	

Table 2.2 – Continued

If you changed jobs during the year ended 5 April 2008, details of benefits provided by your previous employer	You may have to ask for this
Advice from your employer as to what to report if you received free shares or exercised (or were given) a share option in 2007–08	Speak to your personnel department
If you were self-employed:	
You will need to prepare accounts or have an accountant do this for you. The Revenue requires your details in a set format so that it can use its computer to assist it in identifying cases that should be taken up for enquiry	See 6.1.4
If you have rental income:	
You should keep an analysis of rents receivable for 2007–08 and a note of any bad debts, details of expenditure such as fees paid to managing agents, repair bills and redecoration, replacement of electrical goods and furniture. If you have borrowed to fund your property 'business', the interest should be an allowable expense	Rent charged for 2007–08 will normally be taxable even if you did not receive it until after the end of the year
If you have income from savings:	
Keep a copy of your bank deposit account statements, your building society passbook and dividend vouchers	
If you had trust income:	
You need form R185, which sets out the amount of income paid to you and the tax deducted at source	
If you have made capital gains:	
You will need the stockbroker's contract notes for sales of shares and copies of the sale contract and completion statement if you made real estate sales. If you gave assets to your children you may be liable for CGT as if you had sold at market value so seek advice in such situations	The gains are exempt if they totalled less than £9,200. See 12.1.1

(5) Start to put cash aside now so that you can settle your 2007–08 tax and make a payment on account for 2008–09 next 31 January. If you are short of funds after Christmas you may find yourself exposed to interest (APR currently at 6.5%). Worse still, if you are unable to clear your 2007–08 tax by 28 February, you will be liable for an automatic 5% surcharge (equal to an APR of over 60%).

(6) Consider filing by early. Somerset House has given repeated assurances that filing early will not increase the likelihood of your return being selected for enquiry. On a positive note, the Revenue will collect underpayments of up to £2,000 via the PAYE system if you submit your paper return by 31 October or online by 30 December. This may be much more convenient than having to make a lump sum payment.

(7) Work on the basis that your return will be selected for enquiry. The Revenue will be selecting about 10,000 returns each year randomly; this means there is less than a 1% chance of being selected, but you are considerably more likely to be selected for random enquiry than to win the National Lottery. Tax offices are also expected to check another 30,000 returns with the selection being made on a more scientific assessment of risk of undeclared tax.

(8) Remember to tick the box 20 if your return contains any estimated or provisional figures. It will probably be in your own best interests to give an explanation of how you have arrived at the figures concerned as this may pre-empt queries from the Revenue. It may also afford a degree of protection against the Revenue 12 months after they have received the form and reopening 2007–08 by making a 'discovery assessment'.

(9) Think twice about not drawing attention to any assumptions you have made in completing your return that could be challenged by the Revenue. You do not have to follow the Revenue's line on everything, especially if you receive advice that the Revenue's interpretation of the legislation is open to doubt, but you should not be coy about this. From time to time the Revenue is shown to be wrong, but the Revenue wins more often than it loses and you could be liable for penalties if the courts uphold the Revenue's interpretation and it emerges that you had not put all your cards face up on the table. Bear in mind the recent case of *Langham* v *Veltema*, which is covered at 3.3.9. Consider investing in a certificate of tax deposit to cover exposure to interest if the Revenue challenges your interpretation (see 3.3.10).

(10) Finally, get professional advice if your affairs are complicated. DIY tax returns may be a false economy if your situation is non-standard, however hard the Revenue has tried to explain the rules in its helpsheets.

Tax notes

The HMRC website lists the following tips for self assessment:

(1) Don't be afraid to ask for help.
(2) Keep good tax records each year.
(3) Get started early. There is nothing to be gained from delay.
(4) Make sure your return is complete.
(5) Pay in good time.

Tax notes

Deal with your self-assessment return issued in April 2008. Under self-assessment (SA), you need to submit your tax return either by 31 October 2008 if you file the paper form or 31 January 2009 if you file online and settle your outstanding tax by 31 January 2009. If you fail to do this, you automatically become liable for interest and penalties.

2.6 COMMON ERRORS

In the past, HMRC's Press Office has kindly provided us with a note of the more common errors on the SA form:

(1) Not explaining unusual variations – there is an area on the return that allows you to explain variations. By filling in this section you can avoid follow-up requests for extra information to explain any apparent discrepancies.
(2) Misclassifying expenses – any anomalies may trigger a request for further explanation.
(3) Not including relevant supplementary pages – any supplementary pages indicated as relevant must be sent with the return.
(4) Using rounded-up figures or estimates – these can be a sign that a person's affairs have not been properly maintained and could trigger further enquiry.
(5) Not including actual information on the main Tax Return – it is important to provide specific figures where appropriate on the return itself – reference to supplementary sheets or accounts can lead to delays.
(6) Capital expenditure v capital allowances – another common mistake is entering a client's capital expenditure in the Self Employment section instead of their capital allowances, resulting in a claim to undue tax relief.
(7) Highlighting 'private use' items – it should be made clear where items have been used for private purposes, and the relevant adjustments made to reflect this.

Enabling letters

In recent years the Revenue has taken to issuing what are referred to as 'enabling letters' to self-employed individuals with turnover of up to £150,000. The letters are not enquiries into the tax payer's affairs and do not reflect upon the character of either the taxpayer or tax agent, but can be taken as a warning over common areas of inaccuracies and reporting. The Revenue's objective, in issuing these letters, is to ensure that the taxpayer is aware of their obligations.

Typically the letter will highlight the fact that most formal inquiries result in additional tax due together with interest and penalty charges. The following general points will be made:

- read the SA form guidance notes;
- include all business income;
- claim only actual expenses;
- have records that support both income and expenditure;
- file and pay your taxes on time.

The letter then highlights specific areas where errors are likely to occur when reporting self-employed income.

- **Turnover** – taxpayers should ensure that the gross income received and not the net are shown, eg if you are a freelance self-employed consultant and receive a fee with the deduction of tax, it is the gross figure that needs to be declared. Payments in kind, tips and insurance proceeds for loss or damage to stock should also be included. Conversely, tax credits, business-start up allowance, funds introduced by the taxpayer and proceeds from the sale of a fixed asset do not need to be included.
- **Goods taken from stock** – should be included at normal selling price.
- **Plant and machinery** – the cost of repairing but not buying equipment is an allowable business expenses, although capital allowances may be claimed on the latter (see 15.2).
- **Dual purpose expenditure** – if an expense is for both private and business purposes, it is said to have a duality for tax purposes. If the two elements are inseparable, no tax relief is due (see 15.1.5).
- **Motoring costs** – remember that travel between your home and place of work is not deductible.
- **Business trips** – only reasonable costs are allowable.
- **Cost of home office** – these should be accurately calculated to reflect only that part of the home which is used for business. Remember that home office expenditure is a double-edged sword in that it might give rise to a capital gains tax charge on disposal (see 13.2.1).
- **Salaries** – where paid to the individual these are effectively drawings and not deductible. Any payments to spouses may give rise to the question as to whether any services were performed by the spouse in allowing them as a deduction.
- **Cost of services** – where provided to friends and family these are non-deductible.

2.7 PROVIDING ADDITIONAL INFORMATION

At the end of the SA form, the Revenue has left a number of blank pages for additional information. You may take the view that this is the Revenue's way of giving you enough rope to hang yourself, but in fact it should be grasped as a lifeline. There may be aspects of the form where you or your tax adviser has relied on a certain interpretation of the tax law. The Revenue may not agree with your interpretation but will be unaware of the basis on which you have completed the form unless you draw its attention to this. If this emerges later on, the Revenue may seek to re-open your self-assessment and possibly charge interest and penalties. One way of covering yourself is to make appropriate entries in the additional information box 19 (sometimes referred to as the 'white space'). If you make your assumptions and interpretations explicit, you will protect yourself against the Revenue using its discovery powers (see 3.3.9).

Tax notes

Protect yourself against penalties or discovery assessments by making entries on the tax return in the white space.

2.8 FINDING YOUR WAY AROUND THE SA FORM

When you examine your return, you will see that we have referenced the following questions to this book (see following pages).

What makes up your Tax Return

To make a **complete** return of your taxable income and gains for the year to 5 April 2008 you may need to complete some separate **supplementary pages**. Answer the following questions by putting 'X' in the 'Yes' or 'No' box. ——— Chapter 4

1 Employment

Were you an employee (or director or office holder) or agency worker in the year to 5 April 2008? (Also answer 'Yes' if you received expenses payments or benefits from a former employer in the year.)

If you had more than one employment or directorship, say how many and fill in a separate *Employment* page for each one.

Yes ☐   No ☐   Number ☐

2 Self-employment

Did you work for yourself (on your 'own account' or in self-employment) in the year to 5 April 2008? (Answer 'Yes' if you were a 'Name' at Lloyd's.) If you had more than one business, say how many and fill in a separate *Self-employment* page for each one.

Yes ☐   No ☐   Number ☐

3 Partnership

Were you in partnership? If you were a partner in more than one partnership, say how many and fill in a separate *Partnership* page for each one.

Yes ☐   No ☐   Number ☐

4 UK property

Did you receive any income from UK property (including rents and other income from land you own or lease out)?

Yes ☐   No ☐

5 Foreign

Did you receive any foreign income or income gains (other than from employment or self-employment)?

Have you, or could you have, received (in the widest sense) income, or received a capital payment or benefit, from a person abroad as a result of any transfer of assets?

Do you want to claim relief for foreign tax paid?

You **may** not need the *Foreign* pages if your only foreign income was taxed dividends up to £300, or if you are claiming the remittance basis – read page TRG 3 of the guide before answering.

Yes ☐   No ☐

6 Trusts etc. — 9.10 and Chapter 30

Did you receive, or do we consider you to have received, income from a trust, settlement or a deceased person's estate?

Yes ☐   No ☐

7 Capital Gains Summary — Chapters 12 and 16

Did you dispose of any chargeable assets (including, for example, stocks, shares, units in a unit trust, land and property, goodwill in a business), or have any chargeable gains, or do you wish to claim an allowable loss or make any other claim or election? If yes, read pages TRG 3 and TRG 4 of the guide to decide if you have to fill in the *Capital Gains Summary* page. ——— Chapter 6

Do you need the *Capital Gains Summary* page?

Yes ☐   No ☐

8 Non-resident — Chapter 33

Were you, for all or part of the year to 5 April 2008, one or more of the following – not resident, not ordinarily resident, not domiciled, in the UK, or were you dual resident in the UK and another country? ——— Chapter 6

Yes ☐   No ☐

9 Supplementary pages — Chapter 7

Do you need supplementary pages? If you answered 'Yes' to any of Questions 1 to 8, please check to see if, **within this form**, there is a page dealing with that kind of income etc. If there is not, you will need separate supplementary pages. ——— Chapter 9.1–9.5

Yes ☐   No ☐

If 'Yes', ring **0845 9000 404** and ask us for the relevant page.

*Some less common kinds of income and tax reliefs (not covered by Questions 1 to 8) should be returned on the **Additional information** supplementary pages enclosed in the Tax Return pack.*

Student Loan repayments

Please read page TRG 4 of the guide before completing boxes 1 and 2 ——— 20.1.9

1 If your employer has deducted Student Loan repayments enter the amount deducted

£ ☐☐☐☐☐☐☐ · 0 0

2 If you have received notification from the Student Loans Company that repayment of an Income Contingent Student Loan began before 6 April 2008, put 'X' in the box

☐

Income

UK interest etc. and dividends ———————————————— Cha

1 UK bank, building society, unit trust, etc. interest/amount which has been taxed already – *the net amount after tax*

£ [   ] · 0 0

2 Untaxed UK interest etc. (amounts that have not been taxed at all) – *the total amount*

£ [   ] · 0 0

3 Dividends from UK companies – *do not include the tax credit. Property Income Dividends (PIDs) go in box 15 below*

£ [   ] · 0 0

4 Dividends from authorised unit trusts and open-ended investment companies

£ [   ] · 0 0

5 Foreign dividends (up to £300) – *the amount in sterling before foreign tax was taken off. Do not include this amount in the Foreign pages*

£ [   ] · 0 0

6 Tax taken off foreign dividends (the sterling equivalent)

£ [   ] · 0 0

UK pensions, annuities and other State benefits received ———————— Cha

7 State Pension – *the amount due for the year (not the weekly amount)*

£ [   ] · 0 0

8 State Pension lump sum

£ [   ] · 0 0

9 Tax taken off box 8

£ [   ] · 0 0

10 Pensions (other than State Pension), retirement annuities and taxable triviality payments – *give details of the payers, amounts paid and tax deducted in box 19 on page TR 6*

£ [   ] · 0 0

11 Tax taken off box 10

£ [   ] · 0 0

12 Taxable Incapacity Benefit – *the total amount before tax was taken off*

£ [   ] · 0 0

13 Tax taken off box 12

£ [   ] · 0 0

14 Total of any other taxable State Pensions and benefits

£ [   ] · 0 0

Other UK income not included on supplementary pages

Do not use this section for income that should be returned on supplementary pages. Share schemes, gilts, stock dividends, life insurance gains and certain other kinds of income go on the *Additional information* pages in the Tax Return pack.

15 Other taxable income – *before expenses and tax taken off*

£ [   ] · 0 0

16 Total amount of allowable expenses – *read page TRG 11 of the guide*

£ [   ] · 0 0

17 Any tax taken off box 15

£ [   ] · 0 0

18 Benefit from pre-owned assets – *read page TRG 11 of the guide*

£ [   ] · 0 0 ——— 32.7

19 Description of boxes 15 and 18 income – *if there is not enough space here please give details in the 'Any other information' box on page TR 6*

[   ]

[   ]

[   ]

Tax reliefs

🛈 **Married couple's allowance** (if you or your spouse or civil partner were born **before** 6 April 1935) and other less common reliefs are on the *Additional information* pages, enclosed in the Tax Return pack.

Paying into registered pension schemes and overseas pension schemes ─── Chapter 25

Do not include payments you make to your employer's pension scheme which are deducted from your pay before tax or payments made by your employer. Boxes to return pension savings tax charges and taxable lump sums from overseas pensions schemes are on the *Additional information* pages.

1	Payments to registered pension schemes where basic rate tax relief will be claimed by your pension provider (called 'relief at source'). Enter the payments and basic rate tax
	£ · 0 0

2	Payments to a retirement annuity contract where basic rate tax relief will not be claimed by your provider
	£ · 0 0

3	Payments to your employer's scheme which were not deducted from your pay before tax
	£ · 0 0

4	Payments to an overseas pension scheme which is not UK-registered which are eligible for tax relief and were not deducted from your pay before tax
	£ · 0 0

Charitable giving ─────────────────────────── 10.9–10.11

5	Gift Aid payments made in the year to 5 April 2008
	£ · 0 0

6	Total of any 'one-off' payments in box 5
	£ · 0 0

7	Gift Aid payments made in the year to 5 April 2008 but treated as if made in the year to 5 April 2007 – *read page TRG 14 of the guide*
	£ · 0 0

8	Gift Aid payments made after 5 April 2008 but to be treated as if made in the year to 5 April 2008 – *read page TRG 14 of the guide*
	£ · 0 0

9	Value of any shares or securities gifted to charity
	£ · 0 0

10	Value of any land and buildings gifted to charity
	£ · 0 0

Blind person's allowance ───────────────────────── 11.6

11	If you are registered blind on a local authority or other register, put 'X' in the box

12	Enter the name of the local authority or other register

13	If you want your spouse's, or civil partner's, surplus allowance, put 'X' in the box

14	If you want your spouse, or civil partner, to have your surplus allowance, put 'X' in the box

Service companies ──────────────────────────── 20.3

1	Total amount of any income included anywhere on this Tax Return, derived from the provision of your services through a service company – *read page TRG 15 of the guide*
	£ · 0 0

Finishing your Tax Return

ℹ **Calculating your tax** – if we receive your Tax Return by 31 October 2008, or if you file online, we will do the calculation for you **and** tell you how much you have to pay (or what your repayment will be) before 31 January 2009.

But if you want to calculate your tax ask us for the *Tax Calculation Summary* pages and *notes*. The *notes* will help you work out any tax due or repayable, and if payments on account are necessary.

Tax refunded or set-off

1 If you have had any 2007–08 Income Tax refunded or set-off by us or Jobcentre Plus, enter the amount

£ ⬚⬚⬚⬚⬚⬚⬚⬚ . 0 0

If you have not paid enough tax

Use the payslip at the foot of your next statement (or reminder) from us to pay any tax due.

2 If you owe tax for 2007–08 and have a PAYE tax code, we will try to collect the tax due (up to £2,000) through your tax code for 2009–10, unless you put 'X' in the box

3 If you are likely to owe tax for **2008–09** on income other than employed earnings or pensions, and you do **not** want us to use your 2008–09 PAYE tax code to collect that tax during the year, put 'X' in the box – *read page TRG 18 of the guide*

If you have paid too much tax

We will repay direct to your bank or building society account – this is the safest and quickest method. Tell us where you would like any repayment to be made by filling in boxes 4 to 13.

If you would like us to send some, or all, of your repayment to charity please use the *Giving your tax repayment to charity* form in your Tax Return pack.

4 Name of bank or building society

5 Name of account holder (or nominee)

6 Branch sort code

7 Account number

8 Building society reference number

9 If you do not have a bank or building society account, read the notes on page TRG 19 of the guide and put 'X' in the box

10 If you have entered a nominee's name in box 5, put 'X' in the box

11 If your nominee is your tax adviser, put 'X' in the box

12 Nominee's address

13 and postcode

14 To authorise your nominee to receive any repayment, you must sign in the box. A photocopy of your signature will not do

Tax Return: Page TR 5

44

Your tax adviser, if you have one

15 Your tax adviser's name

16 Their phone number

17 The first line of their address and the postcode

18 The reference your adviser uses for you

Any other information — 2.7

19 Please give any other information in this space

Signing your form and sending it back

20 If this Tax Return contains provisional or estimated figures, put 'X' in the box

21 If you are enclosing separate supplementary pages, put 'X' in the box

22 If you give false information, you may have to pay financial penalties and face prosecution. Please sign and date this form.

The information I have given on this Tax Return is correct and complete to the best of my knowledge and belief

Date *DD MM YYYY*

Signature

23 If you have signed on behalf of someone else, enter the capacity. For example, executor, receiver

24 Enter the name of the person you have signed for

25 If you filled in boxes 23 and 24 enter your name

26 and your address

Finally, please send us your completed form in the envelope provided.

HM Revenue & Customs

Additional information
Tax year 6 April 2007 to 5 April 2008

These pages:
- are for less common types of income, deductions and tax reliefs, and for other information
- if completed, are to be sent back with your Tax Return (but we do not want these pages back if you have made no entries on them, please).

If you think you need to complete them, go to **www.hmrc.gov.uk** or ring **0845 9000 404** and ask us for the *Additional information notes*.

Other UK income ——————————————————————————— 8.4

Interest from gilt edged and other UK securities (and accrued income profits)

1 Gilt etc. interest after tax taken off

£ _____ · 0 0

3 Gross amount before tax

£ _____ · 0 0

2 Tax taken off

£ _____ · 0 0

Life insurance gains ——————————————————————————— 27.3

4 UK life insurance policy etc. gains on which tax was treated as paid - *the amount of the gain*

£ _____ · 0 0

5 Number of years the policy has been held or since the last gain - *whichever is less*

☐☐

6 UK life insurance policy etc. gains where no tax was treated as paid - *the amount of the gain*

£ _____ · 0 0

7 Number of years the policy has been held or since the last gain - *whichever is less*

☐☐

8 UK life insurance policy etc. gains from voided ISAs

£ _____ · 0 0

9 Number of years the policy was held

☐☐

10 Tax taken off box 8

£ _____ · 0 0

11 Deficiency relief

£ _____ · 0 0

Stock dividends, non-qualifying distributions and loans written off ——————— 8.8–8

12 Stock dividends - the appropriate amount in cash/cash equivalent of the share capital - *without any tax*

£ _____ · 0 0

13 Non-qualifying distributions and close company loans written off or released

£ _____ · 0 0

Business receipts taxed as income of an earlier year ——————————————— 15.4

14 The amount of post-cessation or other business receipts

£ _____ · 0 0

15 Tax year income to be taxed, for example 2006-07 *YYYY YY*

☐☐☐☐ — ☐☐

Share schemes and employment lump sums, compensation and deductions

1 Share schemes – the taxable amount – *excluding amounts included on your P60 or P45*

£ · 0 0

2 Tax taken off box 1

£ · 0 0

3 Taxable lump sums – excluding redundancy and compensation for loss of your job – *see notes starting on page Ain 24 and Working Sheet 22*

£ · 0 0

4 Lump sums or benefits received from an Employer Financed Retirement Benefits Scheme excluding pensions

£ · 0 0

5 Redundancy and other lump sums and compensation payments

£ · 0 0

6 Tax taken off boxes 3 to 5

£ · 0 0

7 If you have left box 6 blank because the tax is included in box 2 on the *Employment* page, put 'X' in the box

8 Exemptions for amounts entered in box 4

£ · 0 0

9 Compensation and lump sum £30,000 exemption – *see page Ain 24 of the notes*

£ · 0 0

10 Disability and foreign service deduction

£ · 0 0

11 Seafarers' Earnings Deduction – *the total amount (and give the names of the ships in the 'Additional information' box on page Ai 4)*

£ · 0 0

12 Foreign earnings not taxable in the UK

£ · 0 0

13 Foreign tax for which tax credit relief not claimed

£ · 0 0

14 Exempt employers' contributions to an overseas pension scheme

£ · 0 0

Chapter 5

4.15–4.16

36.13

34.4

4.15–4.16

Other tax reliefs

1 Subscriptions for Venture Capital Trust shares – *the amount on which relief is claimed*

£ · 0 0

2 Subscriptions for shares under the Enterprise Investment Scheme – *the amount on which relief is claimed (and provide more information on page Ai 4)*

£ · 0 0

3 Community Investment Tax Relief – *the amount on which relief is claimed*

£ · 0 0

4 Annuities and annual payments made

£ · 0 0

5 Qualifying loan interest payable in the year

£ · 0 0

6 Post-cessation expenses and certain other losses

£ · 0 0

7 Maintenance payments (max £2,440) – *only if you or your former spouse or civil partner were born before 6 April 1935*

£ · 0 0

8 Payments to a trade union etc. for death benefits – *half the amount paid (max £100)*

£ · 0 0

9 Relief claimed for employer's compulsory widow's, widower's or orphan's benefit scheme – *(max £22)*

£ · 0 0

10 Relief claimed on a qualifying distribution on the redemption of bonus shares or securities

£ · 0 0

24.6

15.5

10.1

24.5

10.13

10.15

10.12

10.2–10.7

8.9

Age related married couple's allowance ——————————— Chapte

Boxes 1 to 5 and, if appropriate, 9, 10 or 11, should be completed by a husband (marriages up to 5 December 2005) or by the spouse or civil partner with the higher income (marriages and civil partnerships on or after 5 December 2005).

Boxes 6 to 8, and, if appropriate, 9, 10 or 11, should be completed by a wife (marriages up to 5 December 2005) or the spouse or civil partner with the lower income (marriages and civil partnerships on or after 5 December 2005) who has **already** claimed half or all of the minimum married couple's allowance.

If you, or your spouse or civil partner, were born **before** 6 April 1935, complete the relevant boxes

1 Your spouse's or civil partner's full name

7 If all of the minimum allowance is to be given to you, put 'X' in the box

2 Their date of birth if older than you (and at least one of you was born before 6 April 1935) *DD MM YYYY*

8 Your spouse's or civil partner's full name

3 If you have already agreed that half the minimum allowance is to go to your spouse or civil partner, put 'X' in the box

9 If you were married or formed a civil partnership after 5 April 2007, enter the date of marriage or civil partnership

4 If you have already agreed that all of the minimum allowance is to go to your spouse or civil partner, put 'X' in the box

10 If you want to have your spouse's or civil partner's surplus allowance, put 'X' in the box

5 If, in the year to 5 April 2008, you lived with any previous spouse or civil partner, enter their date of birth

11 If you want your spouse or civil partner to have your surplus allowance, put 'X' in the box

6 If half of the minimum allowance is to be given to you, put 'X' in the box

Other information

Income Tax losses ——————————————————— 6.7

1 Earlier years' losses – *which can be set against certain other income in 2007-08*
£ · 0 0

3 Relief now for 2008-09 trading, or certain capital, losses
£ · 0 0

4 and tax year for which you are claiming relief in box 3 *YYYY YY*

2 Total unused losses carried forward
£ · 0 0

Pension savings tax charges and taxable lump sums from overseas pension schemes —— Chapter 25

5 Value of pension benefits in excess of your Available Lifetime Allowance, taken by you as a lump sum

£ ・ 0 0

6 Value of pension benefits in excess of your Available Lifetime Allowance, not taken as a lump sum

£ ・ 0 0

7 Lifetime Allowance tax paid by your pension scheme

£ ・ 0 0

8 Amount saved towards your pension, in the period covered by this Tax Return, in excess of the Annual Allowance

£ ・ 0 0

9 Amount of unauthorised payment from a pension scheme, not subject to Surcharge

£ ・ 0 0

10 Amount of unauthorised payment from a pension scheme, subject to Surcharge

£ ・ 0 0

11 Foreign tax paid on an unauthorised payment (in £ sterling)

£ ・ 0 0

12 Taxable short service refund of contributions (overseas pension schemes only)

£ ・ 0 0

13 Taxable lump sum death benefit payment (overseas pension schemes only)

£ ・ 0 0

14 Foreign tax paid (in £ sterling) on boxes 12 and 13

£ ・ 0 0

Tax avoidance schemes

—— 32.20

15 The scheme reference number ——

16 The tax year in which the expected advantage arises - *year ended 5 April YYYY*

Additional information

17 Please give any additional information in this space

Personal details

18 Your name

19 Your unique taxpayer reference (UTR)

Printed in the U.K. by Adare Group 5009987 12/07

 **HM Revenue & Customs**

Short Tax Return 2008
Tax year 6 April 2007 to 5 April 2008

Your Tax Return

This Notice requires you, by law, to make a return of your taxable income and capital gains, and any documents requested, for the year from 6 April 2007 to 5 April 2008.

Before you start to fill in this Tax Return, please read pages 1 and 2 of the enclosed guide to check that it is the right Tax Return for you.

Deadlines
We must receive your Tax Return by either:
- **31 October 2008** - if you are going to send us a **paper** Return, or
- **31 January 2009** - if you are going to file **online**.

Please note the new filing date for paper Returns.

You will be charged a **£100 penalty** if your Tax Return is received after the appropriate deadline. If you pay late you will be charged interest and possibly a surcharge.

To file online, go to **www.hmrc.gov.uk** and under *do it online* select *Self Assessment*.

How to fill in this form
This form is designed to be read by machine - please follow the rules below so that the Tax Return is read correctly.

Use black ink and capital letters | Cross out any mistakes and write the correct information below

ABYPANK

Please round up tax paid: £4,700.21 would be £4701

- Enter your figures in whole pounds - ignore the pence. Round down income and round up expenses and tax paid - it is to your benefit.
- If a box does not apply, please leave it blank - do not strike through empty boxes or write anything else.

Starting your Tax Return

Your personal details

1.1 Your date of birth *DD MM YYYY*

1.2 Your name and address - *if it is different from what is on the top of this page. Please write the correct details underneath the wrong ones, and put 'X' in the box*

1.3 Your contact phone number

1.4 Your National Insurance number - *leave blank if it is shown above as your 'Tax Reference'*

1.5 Capital gains - *if you made a taxable capital gain, or a loss, put 'X' in the box, read page 3 of the guide and enclose your computation and form SA200(CG)*

180000 00456259 001

Employment income

This section is for PAYE earnings – any self-employment income goes in boxes 3.1 to 3.13 ———————————— Chapter 4

2.1 The number of employments you had in the year

2.2 Pay from all employments before tax was taken off

2.3 Tax taken off box 2.2

2.4 Benefits and taxable expenses received – *read page 4 of the guide*

2.5 Allowable expenses

2.6 PAYE tax reference of your main or last employer in the year to 5 April 2008

Self-employment income ———————————————————————————— Chapter 6

3.1 What work do you do? *For example, plumber, book-keeper*

3.2 If you began working for yourself after 5 April 2005, enter the date you began *DD MM YYYY*

3.3 If you stopped working for yourself before 6 April 2008, enter the date you stopped

3.4 Date you made your books up to – *please read page 6 of the guide*

3.5 Class 4 National Insurance contributions. Put 'X' in the box if they are excepted – *read page 7 of the guide*

3.6 Business Start Up Allowance – *do not include in box 3.7*

3.7 Turnover (including any balancing charges). You cannot use this form if your annual turnover was £30,000 or more – *if so, please contact us*

3.8 Expenses allowable for tax (excluding any capital allowances – *they go in box 3.9*)

3.9 Capital allowances

3.10 Profit (box 3.7 minus (boxes 3.8 + 3.9))

3.11 Loss (box 3.7 minus (boxes 3.8 + 3.9))

3.12 Business losses brought forward from earlier years

3.13 Deductions on payment and deduction statements from contractors – *construction industry subcontractors only*

UK pensions and State benefits received

This section is for the pensions and benefits you get – pensions you are paying into go in boxes 9.1 and 9.2——————— Chapter 39

4.1 State Pension – *enter the amount for the year (not the weekly, or 4 weekly, amount)*

4.2 Total of other pensions and retirement annuities before tax was taken off

4.3 Tax taken off box 4.2

4.4 Total of other taxable State benefits

4.5 Tax taken off taxable Incapacity Benefit included in box 4.4

UK interest, dividends and other investment income

Please use the notes on pages 11 and 12 of the guide, before filling in boxes 5.1 to 5.3 —————————— Chapter and 9

5.1	Net amount paid by a bank or building society etc. - *after they have taken off tax*	5.2	Untaxed UK interest etc. (amounts that have not been taxed at all) - *enter the total amount*
	£ · 0 0		£ · 0 0

		5.3	Company dividends (but do not include the tax credits)
			£ · 0 0

UK property

You cannot use this form if your UK property income was £15,000 or more - if it was, please contact us —————————— Chapter

6.1	Income	6.4	Loss
	£ · 0 0		£ · 0 0

6.2	Expenses allowable for tax	6.5	UK property losses brought forward from earlier years
	£ · 0 0		£ · 0 0

6.3	Profit		
	£ · 0 0		

Other UK Income for 2007-08

This section is **not** to be used for the types of income listed on page 2 of the guide

7.1	Other income	7.3	Where does box 7.1 income come from? *For example, commission, tips, locum fees*
	£ · 0 0		

7.2	Any tax taken off income in box 7.1		
	£ · 0 0		

Gift Aid ———————————————————————————— 10.9

8.1	Gift Aid payments made in the year to 5 April 2008 - *read page 15 of the guide*	8.2	Total of any 'one off' payments included in box 8.1
	£ · 0 0		· 0 0

Paying into registered pension schemes or overseas pension schemes ———————— Chapter

If payments to your pension scheme are deducted from your pay before it is taxed, do not include them here

9.1	Payments to registered pension schemes where basic rate tax relief will be claimed by your pension provider (called 'relief at source'). Enter the payments and basic rate tax	9.2	Gross payments - *payments made without basic rate tax relief*
	£ · 0 0		£ · 0 0

Blind person's allowance ———————————————————————— 11.6

10.1	If you are registered blind on a local authority or other register, put 'X' in the box	10.2	Enter the name of the local authority or other register

Married couple's allowance ─────────────────────────── 11.3

Married couple's allowance is only due if you, or your spouse or civil partner were born before 6 April 1935. It is made up of two amounts - a minimum amount (worth up to £244), plus an age related amount. **Read page 17 of the guide.**

11.1	To claim the full allowance, enter your spouse or civil partner's first name	11.3	Your spouse or civil partner's date of birth *DD MM YYYY* - *if older than you and you filled in boxes 11.1 or 11.2*

11.2	If, as a couple, you have already asked us to give all of the minimum amount to you, or your spouse or civil partner, put 'X' in the box	11.4	Date of marriage or formation of civil partnership - *if between 6 April 2007 and 5 April 2008*

Finishing your Tax Return – you may have paid too much, or too little, tax

Please carefully fill in boxes 12.1 to 12.6 to tell us how you would like any repayment to be made. If you also want some of your repayment to go to charity, fill in boxes 12.8 to 12.10 as well. But if you would like all of your repayment to go to charity, just fill in boxes 12.7, 12.9 and 12.10.

12.1 Name of bank or building society

12.8 But if you want only some of your repayment to go to charity, enter the maximum amount we can send

12.9 Enter the charity code - you can get this from **www.hmrc.gov.uk/charities/charities-search.htm**

12.2 Branch sort code

─────── 10.9.3

12.3 Account number

12.10 If you want Gift Aid to apply to the payment to charity, put 'X' in the box

12.4 Building society reference number

12.11 2007-08 tax refunded, already

12.5 Name of account holder

12.12 If you owe tax for 2007-08 and have a PAYE tax code, we will try to collect the tax due (up to £2,000) through your tax code for 2009-10, unless you put 'X' in the box

12.6 If you have entered a nominee's name in box 12.5, put 'X' in the box

12.13 If you are likely to owe tax for **2008-09** on income other than employed earnings or pensions, and you do **not** want us to use your 2008-09 PAYE tax code to collect that tax during the year, put 'X' in the box

12.7 If you would like all of your repayment to go to a charity, put 'X' in the box

Signing your form and sending it back

13.1 Please sign and date this form. If you give false information, you may face financial penalties and prosecution. (If you have asked us to send any repayment to a nominee's account, your signature will be our authority to pay that person.)

The information I have given in this Tax Return is correct and complete to the best of my knowledge

Finally, please send us your completed form. Please do not fold it – keep it flat and use the envelope provided.

HMRC 12/07 5010068
Printed in the U.K. by Adare Group.

3

HMRC AND YOU

'We want you to pay the right amount of tax: no more, no less'

HM Revenue and Customs

Throughout this book we refer to the Revenue and to Customs. The Inland Revenue and Customs & Excise now operate as one department called HM Revenue & Customs (HMRC). The logic, beyond obvious government savings on costs in merging these two bodies, is that they will have what is described as 'a greater customer focus'. What this will mean for the taxpayer, when the two departments have fully integrated, is a single Government department collating and analysing tax data. You have been warned!

This chapter looks at the way in which the taxpayer and the HMRC will interact during the lifetime of your SA tax return and following its submission. We also look at the limits of the Revenue's powers and your rights as a taxpayer.

(1) Understanding your responsibilities and rights.
(2) The tax return process.
(3) Revenue enquiries into tax returns.
(4) What penalties can the Revenue impose?
(5) Remission of tax by the Revenue.
(6) Error or mistake relief.
(7) Codes of practice.
(8) Revenue information and advice.
(9) Statements of practice and extra-statutory concessions.
(10) Complaints and compensation.
(11) Revenue Adjudicator.

3.1 UNDERSTANDING YOUR RESPONSIBILITIES AND RIGHTS

The Revenue is increasingly run more like a business. At the same time, the Government requires it to operate quality management and to assess its efficiency in terms of 'satisfied customers'.

It is the Revenue's policy to help taxpayers understand their rights and obligations, get their tax affairs right and pay their tax on time. Its standards in dealing with the public are explained in its Customer Service Standards. The work must be done thoroughly, timely and cost-efficiently and its staff must get it right first time. Targets are set each year and measured regularly to see if they are being achieved.

What this means in practice

The Revenue expect taxpayers to deal with their tax obligations (filing returns, paying tax, replying to Revenue queries) in a businesslike way, ie conscientiously and in a timely fashion.

In practice, this means that a taxpayer should attend promptly to correspondence from the Revenue and complete tax returns within a reasonable period. If you find there are some aspects of your tax return that are complex and prevent you from completing the entire form, you should contact the Inspector and explain the reason for the difficulty. In return, the Revenue promises to deal with you in a fair and reasonable way and to avoid making unnecessary demands on your time.

3.2 THE TAX RETURN PROCESS

3.2.1 Processing of tax returns

The Revenue has designed the SA return with its own data processing in mind. Returns are normally read electronically or figures are input by people who have little or no tax knowledge. Returns may be submitted electronically and the Revenue has taken great strides over the past few years to make e-filing or filing online a reality. This year sees a further incentive to file online by bringing back the 2007–08 filing deadline to 31 October 2008 for paper filers. Online filers still have until January 31 2009.

The basic principle adopted by the Revenue is 'process now, check later'. The fact that the return is processed does not imply that it has been accepted.

Past experience has shown that many returns need correcting because of arithmetical errors, figures being transposed, amounts being entered in the wrong column, etc. When the Revenue officer identifies such mistakes he issues a notice to the taxpayer advising him of the correction (or 'repair') needed. The taxpayer can object, but if the Revenue does not hear further within three months, the correction is deemed to form part of the return. In recent years HMRC has taken a more pragmatic approach to this process by phoning the taxpayer to discuss any simple amendments that show up on the processing of the forms.

Tax notes

If you receive a phone call from HMRC it is important that you keep a note of the Revenue officer's name, date of call, topic discussed and any agreement made.

Routine checking and making corrections must not be confused with Revenue officers carrying out an enquiry (see 3.3).

3.2.2 Keeping proper records

Because the Revenue operates on a 'process now, check later' basis, you need to keep records to be able to back up the entries on your SA return. The length of time that you need to retain your records depends on whether you have a business or are letting property. If you do, the required period is five years and ten months after the end of the tax year. If you do not have either of these sources of income, the minimum period for retaining your records is normally one year and ten months after the end of the tax year concerned.

3.3 REVENUE ENQUIRIES INTO TAX RETURNS

In the past the Revenue normally had a period of 12 months from the 31 January filing date to issue a notice that it was carrying out an enquiry into a tax return, although this changes for the 2007–08 return, when the window will be 12 months from the date the form is received by your HMRC office; but remember the old rules apply for the 2006–07 tax form.

Tax notes

For 2007–08 the Revenue SA enquiry window changes so that HMRC now has 12 months from the date it receives the form to launch an enquiry.

Once an enquiry is completed, or if no enquiry is opened before the deadline, the position becomes final and the Revenue cannot reopen enquiries into that year unless it can show 'discovery', ie that the taxpayer acted negligently or fraudulently so that key information was withheld from the Revenue. Enquiries can be made into partnership returns under the same rules as apply to individual returns, but any amendments to partnership profits then need to be taken through to each partner's tax returns.

Tax notes

The time limit for enquiries changes with the 2007–08 SA, giving an incentive to file early.

3.3.1 Selection of returns for Revenue enquiries

The Revenue has the statutory power to enquire into any tax return without giving a reason. However, because of its limited resources, it has to be selective.

It is more likely to look into cases where a larger amount of tax is perceived to be at risk; enquiries are also likely to arise in cases where the Revenue's internal procedures require a mandatory review. A number of returns not suspected of being incorrect will also be selected at random each year.

An examination of the Revenue's Internal Enquiry Handbook indicates that Revenue employees are required to review certain returns such as:

- returns filed late;
- returns that include provisional figures;
- cases that involve large capital gains;
- situations where there has been a change in accounting year.

3.3.2 Revenue procedure for enquiries

The Revenue must give written notice that an enquiry is to be made into an SA return. This notice must be served within a strict time limit. For 2007–08, this is 12 months from the date HMRC receives the form. For earlier years the deadline was:

- 12 months after the 31 January filing date; or
- where the return was delivered after the normal 31 January filing date, the quarter date following 12 months after delivery.

For these purposes, the quarter dates are 31 January, 30 April, 31 July and 31 October. Thus, if an SA return for 2006–07 was not delivered until 31 March 2008, the Revenue can give notice that it is starting an enquiry up to 30 April 2009.

The Revenue will not give any reason for having opened an enquiry. However, it should soon become apparent whether it is initially an enquiry into one particular aspect of the return or a full enquiry under which the Revenue requires access to all the taxpayer's records. An aspect enquiry can extend into a full enquiry as the Revenue receives information, so the distinction is not completely clear cut.

The opening of an enquiry is not meant to imply that the Revenue believes that anything is untoward, merely that it is carrying out checks to test the return's accuracy and reliability.

The Enquiry Handbook states repeatedly that Revenue officers should adopt a non-confrontational approach and keep an open mind. The Revenue intends that the opening of enquiries should be less contentious, and that its aim is to develop a more neutral and less confrontational approach in this area. It is acknowledged that the information initially available in the return and elsewhere is unlikely to be sufficient to establish whether the return is incorrect, and even where it appears incorrect it could be that the information is incomplete, misleading or capable of explanation. The handbook advises officers that unless they are reasonably certain that there have been omissions (and often it will not be possible for them to be certain), they should ask the taxpayer in a neutral way whether there is anything more that he has to say, taking account of what has already been said. They should make it clear that no allegations are being made at this point. When the Revenue opens an enquiry, it will issue details of its code of practice (see 3.7), which will be either the full code or a short version in straightforward cases.

3.3.3 Information required

The Revenue is instructed to request informally any information needed, rather than using its formal powers to require the production of the information. A formal notice would, however, be issued for documents in the taxpayer's power or possession if he had refused to co-operate with the informal request or had failed to comply within the specified timescale. Such a notice must allow the taxpayer at least 30 days to comply. Moreover, the taxpayer may appeal to the Commissioners if he thinks that the notice is invalid. If the Commissioners decide that the notice is valid, the documents must then be produced within 30 days of their decision.

The Revenue should only request information and documents that are relevant and reasonably required to determine whether the self-assessment is correct. Its approach varies according to whether the taxpayer is a business taxpayer (ie a taxpayer who is in self-employment or in receipt of income from property). In the case of a full enquiry into the business taxpayer's affairs, the Revenue considers that the following items can be reasonably requested without providing an explanation:

- business records generally;
- cash book, petty cash book, sales and purchase invoices and bank account statements;
- details of how any adjustments by the accountant had been calculated;
- an analysis of drawings;
- details of any balancing figures or estimates used in the accounts.

Private bank statements are not normally required at the initial stage of an enquiry.

Where there is a full enquiry into a non-business taxpayer that is a complex case, officers should seek to verify in the first place the income and gains declared by reference to any third-party information held (eg a form P11D). The information requested directly might then comprise:

- dividend vouchers;
- certificates of loan interest paid;
- form PPCC (a certificate confirming payment under a personal pension scheme);
- a detailed CGT computation;
- a copy of a property valuation;
- an account of the precise use made of a company asset, such as a private plane.

As for business taxpayers, the advice to officers is that they should not ask to see private bank statements at this early stage unless it can be demonstrated that the statements are relevant to the return and can be reasonably required for checking the return's accuracy.

In aspect cases (where the Revenue focuses on just one aspect of the return), the request should, unsurprisingly, concentrate on information relevant to the particular point under review.

3.3.4 Meetings with the Revenue

Taxpayers are not obliged to attend any meeting requested by the Revenue, but are expected to provide promptly any information considered essential to the enquiry. The Revenue believes meetings allow taxpayers to clarify and explain any points that might have been misunderstood, and to ask questions of the Revenue. The taxpayer will be told if the Revenue considers correspondence is an inadequate substitute for a meeting. However, an officer cannot insist that a taxpayer attends any meeting, and his only option in terms of asking questions of the taxpayer face-to-face is to take an appeal to a personal hearing before the Commissioners and put his questions to the taxpayer during cross-examination (assuming the taxpayer is put forward as a witness). The Revenue has confirmed that the taxpayer should be sent an agenda in advance of such a meeting. The March 2002 edition of the Revenue newsletter *Working Together* stated:

> Enquiry staff should provide an agenda covering the main areas for discussion ... It should be case specific but not a detailed list of questions and should not be seen by either party to be exhaustive or restrictive. We would not expect a completely new major agenda item to be introduced at the meeting unless something unexpected is revealed during the course of the meeting.

There is no reason in principle why enquiries should not be conducted entirely through correspondence. Code of Practice 11 commits the Inspector to being mindful of the taxpayer's compliance costs and it may be possible to agree with the officer that matters should proceed by way of correspondence without this being viewed as lack of co-operation on the taxpayer's part. It should be borne in mind, however, that a refusal to attend a meeting might, in certain circumstances, be seen as a lack of co-operation when it comes to assessing penalties in the event that the enquiry reveals an under-declaration of tax.

A request for a meeting can often be taken as an indication that the officer, having considered the information initially supplied, has concluded that there are grounds for doubting the return's accuracy or that there are matters that require further detailed enquiry. Officers are instructed that where irregularities are suspected they would need to consider how to give the taxpayer the opportunity to disclose them and to co-operate actively in quantifying them. Whether the taxpayer does take this opportunity could have a bearing on the level of penalty that might be levied on him or her. Officers are instructed to seek early meetings.

3.3.5 Closure of the enquiry

The legislation does not specify any time limit in which the Revenue must complete its enquiries. However, any taxpayer who feels that the Revenue has had sufficient information may appeal to the Commissioners for them to direct the Revenue to bring the enquiry to an end.

When the Revenue officer who has conducted the enquiry has completed his investigation, he must issue a notice stating this and setting out the conclusions of the correct amount of tax that should be payable for the year in question. Once the notice has been issued, the Revenue is debarred from starting new enquiries in relation to that return.

3.3.6 'Faster Working' enquiries

The Revenue is keen to reduce the time taken to deal with enquiries into business returns and therefore introduced 'Faster Working'. Business taxpayers whose returns are selected for enquiry may elect for Faster Working. This is voluntary for taxpayers, and either side can pull out of the agreement if, for example, the enquiry proves to be unexpectedly complex. It involves setting an agreed but flexible timetable for the enquiry; the total time will vary according to circumstances. The Revenue's aim is for enquiries under Faster Working to be completed within about six months. Leaflet IR162, *A better approach to local office enquiry work under self-assessment*, and Tax Bulletin Supplement to Special Edition 2, provide more information.

3.3.7 If you and the Revenue cannot reach agreement

There will be cases where an Inspector and a taxpayer (or professional adviser) form different conclusions about whether, or how, tax should apply to a particular transaction. In such cases where there is an honest difference of opinion, or even in cases where there is an argument about the actual facts, the Revenue does not have the last word. The procedure for resolving such disputes is to require an appeal to be heard by the Commissioners.

There are two types of Commissioners: General Commissioners and Special Commissioners. The difference lies mainly in the type of disputes that each type of Commissioner is best equipped to deal with. Questions of fact, requiring local knowledge, are best heard by General Commissioners. Special Commissioners are generally lawyers and are normally regarded as more competent to deal with technical issues arising from the interpretation of the legislation.

The Commissioners are an independent body and are not connected with the Inspector of Taxes or the Revenue. Their findings on matters of fact are normally final, but if a taxpayer (or the Revenue) is dissatisfied with his (or its) decision on a point of law, an appeal may be made to the courts. Normally, the appeal is heard by the High Court (Court of Session in Scotland). It is even possible to appeal against decisions by the courts and ultimately the matter may go right up to the House of Lords for a decision.

3.3.8 What happens if the SA return is found to be incorrect?

If the Revenue's enquiry shows that a taxpayer has self-assessed and paid too much tax, the difference is refunded, together with interest (normally from the date of payment). If the enquiry reveals material errors in the taxpayer's favour, he is likely to be charged interest from the 31 January filing date plus a penalty. If the errors revealed in the enquiry were duplicated in previous tax years, the Revenue is likely to raise discovery assessments for those years and to seek interest and surcharges. Penalties may also be imposed where the enquiry reveals under-declarations, which amount to negligence or fraud.

3.3.9 Protection from discovery assessments

Even though an assessment has been accepted, the normal time limit for starting an enquiry has expired and all enquiries have been completed, the Revenue may still revisit the past if fresh information comes to light or if it turns out that the taxpayer had negligently or fraudulently withheld that information. An assessment to collect underpaid tax in these circumstances is called a 'discovery assessment'.

No discovery assessment may be made where the Revenue could reasonably have been expected to identify the point at issue from information provided in a SA return. Moreover, information provided in SA returns for the two previous years is also to be taken into account in this connection. It follows that taxpayers should provide the Revenue with too much information rather than too little to avoid discovery assessments. The provision of business accounts is particularly useful in this context, although the Revenue guidance notes for taxpayers state that it is not necessary to send them.

The case of *Langham* v *Veltema* (2004) STC 544 sheds interesting light on all this. The taxpayer had bought a property from his company and it did not occur to the Inspector that the valuation needed to be agreed. The Court of Appeal held that a discovery assessment could be made as the return should have contained an explicit reference to the fact that the valuation had not been agreed with the Revenue. In December 2004, the Revenue issued guidance on the implications of this case for taxpayers who wish to ensure finality by filing tax returns which draw the Revenue's attention to potentially contentious aspects. See also SP1/06.

An additional form of protection may be secured by obtaining post-transaction rulings (see 3.8).

3.3.10 Consider an investment in a certificate of tax deposit

There is a way of protecting yourself against interest charges that might otherwise arise if the Revenue successfully challenges your tax return.

A taxpayer can make deposits with Collectors of Taxes. A certificate is issued and the deposit is held for the general benefit of the individual until such time as he surrenders all or part of the certificate to cover tax liabilities.

Where a deposit is used to cover a tax liability, interest on overdue tax cannot run from the date that the deposit was made. Deposits are therefore commonly used to cover a tax liability that cannot easily be quantified, for example a capital gain on a sale of unquoted shares where a value at 31 March 1982 needs to be negotiated with the Shares Valuation Division.

Interest is credited from the date the deposit is made to the date it is used (or cashed) for a maximum of six years. The rate of interest is fixed by reference to money market rates and is taxable. Interest is paid at a lower rate where deposits are encashed rather than used to settle tax liabilities.

3.4 WHAT PENALTIES CAN THE REVENUE IMPOSE?

3.4.1 Penalties for submission of an incorrect return

If a taxpayer submits an incorrect return, he is liable to a maximum penalty equal to the difference between the tax charged on the income or gain returned and the true income or gain. Strictly, such a penalty is chargeable only if the taxpayer has been fraudulent or negligent, but the Revenue's approach has always been that the mere fact that the return is wrong proves that the taxpayer must have been guilty at least of negligence. Moreover, the taxpayer is not allowed to blame a third party (eg an accountant) for the error, although he may be able to insist that the accountant reimburses any penalty suffered.

Similar provisions apply for partnership returns; penalties for incorrect partnership returns may be levied on each partner.

3.4.2 Mitigation of penalties for incorrect return

The penalty for an error in a return (including a set of business accounts submitted with a return) is, therefore, a potential doubling of the tax chargeable on the income or gains under-declared. This could be levied in addition to any interest charge. However, the Revenue's practice is to reduce or mitigate the potential penalty by reference to three factors. Taking the maximum penalty as a surcharge of 100%, the possible reductions are as follows:

(1) For disclosure, a maximum of 30% if the taxpayer goes to the Inspector admitting that a mistake has been made and a maximum of 20% if the taxpayer makes a complete disclosure as soon as he is challenged by the Inspector.
(2) For co-operation, a maximum of 40%. 'Co-operation' means, for example, answering the Inspector's questions and providing any back-up documentation within a reasonable time span.

(3) For reduced culpability, a maximum of 40%. For example, nothing will be allowed under this heading if it is clear, even though the Inspector cannot prove it, that the taxpayer set out deliberately to cheat the Revenue. A reduction of perhaps 15–25% will be allowed if the taxpayer has been guilty of gross carelessness and between 30% and 40% where he has simply misunderstood information supplied by a third party (eg where he has entered the net instead of the gross interest received on a building society account).

The usual procedure is for the Inspector to suggest an overall settlement figure to include underpaid tax, interest and any penalty. However, he will also provide a computation showing how the overall figure was calculated and it is open to the taxpayer to argue for a bigger reduction of the penalty element. If the Inspector does not agree, he must submit the case to his Head Office, which is sometimes willing to accept a lower settlement than originally proposed by the Inspector.

Payment by instalments is possible where the taxpayer does not have readily realisable capital, but this will increase the interest (though not the penalty) payable.

Tax notes

Minimise penalties by co-operating fully in an investigation. Don't make matters worse by digging your heels in if you are in the wrong.

New penalty regime

HMRC has introduced a new penalty regime for errors on returns or other documents in respect of VAT, PAYE, national insurance, capital gains tax, income tax, corporation tax and the Construction Industry Scheme for tax periods starting on or after 1 April 2008 due to be filed on or after 1 April 2009.

For self assessment, the first year affected will be 2008–09. Additional information will be provided in next year's edition of this book, but in essence what HMRC is saying is that it expects you to pay due care and attention when providing them with information. Details can be found at: www.hmrc.gov.uk/about/new-penalties/index.htm.

3.5 REMISSION OF TAX BY THE REVENUE

The Revenue's policy, detailed in ESC A19, is to give up arrears of tax that have arisen because of failure by the Revenue to make proper and timely use of information supplied. Remission of tax in this way is normally available where the taxpayer could have reasonably believed that his tax affairs were in order and was notified of the arrears more than 12 months after the end of the tax year in which the Revenue was informed. Alternatively, in the case of an over-repayment, it is available if the taxpayer was notified after the end of the tax year following the year in which the repayment was made.

3.6 ERROR OR MISTAKE RELIEF

Sometimes errors are made against the taxpayer and relief can be claimed against any over-assessment to income tax or CGT owing to an error or mistake in a return. However, relief does not extend to an error or mistake in a claim included in the return. Relief will not be available on the ground of an alleged error in the basis of computation of liability if the return was made on the basis of, or in accordance with, the practice generally prevailing at the time when the return was made. According to the Revenue's internal manuals at IM3751A, the term 'error or mistake' includes errors of omission such as the non-deduction of an admissible expense, errors of commission (eg computational or arithmetical errors), errors arising from a misunderstanding of the law and erroneous statements of fact.

The relief is also available for an error or mistake in a partnership statement where the partners claim that their self-assessments were excessive. If the claim results in an amendment to the partnership statement, any necessary amendments to the partners' individual self-assessments are made by notice by the Board of the Revenue.

Relief may be claimed within five years of 31 January following the tax year to which the return relates.

3.7 CODES OF PRACTICE

The Revenue has published codes of practice (COPs), some of which are examined in this chapter, explaining their approach and procedures in certain areas of work, which set out the legal rights of taxpayers (and the Revenue) and explain what the taxpayer can expect to happen. The COPs (which can be found at www.hmrc.gov.uk/leaflets) include the following:

- COP3   Review of employers' and contractors' records;
- COP8   Special Compliance Office investigations. Cases of other than suspected serious fraud;
- COP9   Special Compliance Office investigations. Cases of suspected serious fraud;
- COP10   Information and advice;
- COP11   Enquiries into tax returns by local offices;
- COP14   Enquiries into Company Tax Returns;
- COP24   Stamp Duty Land Tax Enquiries;
- COP25   Stamp Duty Land Tax;

- COP26   What happens if we have paid you too much tax credit?;
- Consultation Code of Practice on Consultation;
- COP-AT   Anti-Terrorism, Crime and Security Act 2001: Code of Practice on the Disclosure of Information;

3.8 REVENUE INFORMATION AND ADVICE

3.8.1 Revenue rulings on specific transactions

COP10 outlines Revenue practice in giving post-transactional rulings, statutory clearances and approvals, together with interpretations of tax law (in certain circumstances), and provides details of the other information published. Post-transactional rulings are rulings given by the Revenue on the application of tax law to a specific transaction after it has taken place. Such rulings bind the Revenue unless material information was withheld. The scheme requires the following information to be submitted before a ruling can be obtained:

- The taxpayer's name and tax reference;
- Full particulars of the transaction or event;
- A statement of the issue(s) to be considered;
- Copies of all relevant documents, with the relevant passages identified;
- A statement that, to the best of the taxpayer's knowledge and belief, the facts as stated are correct and all relevant facts have been disclosed;
- A statement of the specific point(s) of difficulty giving rise to the ruling request;
- A statement of the ruling requested or suggested as appropriate by the applicant;
- Particulars of sections of the Taxes Acts considered to be relevant;
- Particulars of any case law, statements of practice, extra-statutory concessions, etc considered to be relevant;
- Particulars of any previous discussions or correspondence about the tax treatment of the transaction, or of any similar transaction between the taxpayer and any Revenue office; also, when the taxpayer or his advisers are aware of correspondence on the transaction between any other person and any Revenue office, particulars of that correspondence;
- A statement of the applicant's opinion of the transaction's tax consequence, along with reasons to the extent that they are capable of being supplied.

> **Tax notes**
>
> Make use of the post-transaction rulings procedure before you need to file your return so that when you file that particular aspect has been agreed in advance. For example, you may want to agree the value of unquoted shares at the time that you acquired them if that value determines your tax liability under the employment income provisions. Or if you have sold shares in a private company, you will want confirmation that the whole gain qualifies for business taper relief.

3.8.2 General information available from HMRC

The following information is available from the Revenue:

- Explanatory leaflets, booklets and helpsheets, designed to explain different aspects of the tax system and provide assistance with tax return completion;
- Statements of practice (SPs), which explain the Revenue's interpretation of legislation and the application of the law in practice;
- Extra-statutory concessions (ESCs), which are relaxations providing a reduction in tax liability that would not be available under the strict letter of the law;
- Press Releases, which announce a proposed change in the law, in Revenue practice or other change;
- The *Tax Bulletin*, which provides insight into the thinking of Revenue specialists on technical issues and interpretation of tax law (published every two months);
- Internal Guidance Manuals, which cover the Revenue's interpretation of tax law and the operation of the tax system.

Most of the above information is on the Revenue's website, www.hmrc.gov.uk. Any Revenue Enquiry Centre, Tax Office or the Revenue Information Centre should be able to provide leaflets, booklets, SPs and ESCs and certain items can be obtained through the Self-Assessment Orderline. The website is valuable for not only the large amount of information it makes available, but also in the speed with which it is updated. As well as providing information, return forms (eg SA and employer's forms) can be downloaded and there are specialist areas such as:

- Construction Industry Scheme;
- E-business and e-commerce;
- IR35 regulations;
- Employee Share Schemes;
- Working Families' Tax Credit.

Over the past few years, access to the Revenue's Internal Manuals has increased and at present more than 50 manuals are in the public domain, covering a range of subjects. The manuals are available for reference in Revenue Enquiry Centres or can be purchased from independent publishers. A selection of these manuals is also available at www.hmrc.gov.uk/manuals.

The Revenue's information sources do not have the force of law, but are merely interpretations of the legally binding statute and case law. Therefore, potentially they could be open to challenge through the courts.

3.8.3 HMRC clearance and rulings available from May 2008

HMRC has recently introduced a system for the clearances and advance transactions rulings that it is prepared to offer to 'business customers' and to non business customers in respect of business property relief for inheritance tax.

HMRC has stated that it will provide written advice as to its view on the application of the tax law in respect of the specific event where it can be demonstrated that:

- the business faces material uncertainty;
- the tax issue is of real commercial significance; and
- it arises in respect of legislation introduced earlier than the last four finance acts.

Large businesses and their advisers should approach their normal tax district or failing this: HMRC Clearances Team, Alexander House, 21 Victoria Avenue, Southend-on-Sea, Essex SS99 1BD.

Queries in respect of business property relief and IHT are dealt with at: IHT-BPR Clearances Team, Ferrers House, Castle Meadow Road, Nottingham, NG2 1BB.

In essence, what HMRC is now offering is the opportunity for certain taxpayers and their professional advisers to obtain a degree of comfort in advance of a tax event. Any professional adviser would warn you that HMRC is not bound by any guidance offered unless all relevant facts are disclosed. Also, getting the ruling from HMRC may be a problem if you don't like its analysis of the tax consequences. If you do not follow that ruling when submitting your SA return, you will be bound to draw attention to this.

Checklist for non-statutory clearance applications

HMRC asks that you use the checklist below when deciding which documents to attach to your e-mail application or print and include it as a cover sheet where you post it in. Check that you have included information that is relevant and available for your clearance application and indicate with a tick items that are included. HMRC asks you to follow the order set out in the checklist in your letter and in the way that you group supporting documents.

1. Information about the applicant and the application:
1.1   Name and address of the individual applicant and any existing IHT reference number
1.2   Name and address of the business and relevant business identification e.g. Unique Taxpayer Reference, Company Registration Number
1.3   Details of the interest held by the individual in the business e.g. number and nature of shares held
1.4   Your contact details (if you are acting on behalf of a client) and authority to act for the client
1.5   A brief indication of the subject of the application. Fuller details should be provided under the appropriate headings below.
2. Information about the transaction:
2.1   The reason why the business is undertaking the transaction
2.2   The relevant facts about the transaction, set out chronologically as transaction steps, so that we have enough information to provide the clearance response
2.3   The answer sought – set out your view of the tax consequences of the transaction and the issues you want us to consider
2.4   The proposed date of the transaction if it has not yet happened, and supporting information, such as draft contracts where available
2.5   Any details that are contingent, e.g. on future events or the consent of others
3. Information about the commercial background:
3.1   Explain the significance of the tax result in achieving the desired outcome
3.2   Explain why you chose this form of transaction over another that could achieve the same commercial result, where you have considered alternative forms
3.3   Details of any related clearances (both statutory and non-statutory) including the relevant clearance references where known
3.4   Details of the commercial significance to the business of the issue
3.5   Accounts for the business for two full accounting years prior to the transaction or proposed transaction
4. Information about legal points:
4.1   Outline the specific legislation at issue
4.2   Details of why you believe the application of the legislation is open to possible different interpretations, summary of those possible interpretations, and why the tax consequences are uncertain, including reference to our published guidance or to case law
4.3   Any legal advice you have received and you are content to disclose
4.4   Details of any previous advice you have received from HMRC

(Copyright HMRC)

Once again, professional advice should be taken before approaching HMRC.

3.9 STATEMENTS OF PRACTICE AND EXTRA-STATUTORY CONCESSIONS

It is extremely important that the Revenue operates a uniform interpretation of the tax legislation. This was expressly stated in the Taxpayer's Charter, which committed the Revenue to dealing with two taxpayers in the same way if their circumstances were identical.

In cases where the legislation is obscure, or its precise implication is uncertain, the Revenue publishes statements of practice (SPs). These operate as a shield for the taxpayer rather than a sword for the Revenue. You can rely on the Revenue applying these SPs but they do not affect your statutory rights and, if you believe that the Revenue interpretation is wrong, it is still open to you to appeal to the Commissioners.

The Revenue also publishes extra-statutory concessions (ESCs). These apply in cases where the legislation is quite clear but the letter of the law produces an unreasonable result. In effect, the Revenue recognises that Parliament could never have intended to impose certain tax liabilities, and ESCs are commonsense rules that the Revenue applies so as to avoid an unreasonable result. Once again, the Revenue publishes these ESCs because it recognises the need to treat all taxpayers alike. In general, and unless your circumstances are special, or you are seeking to apply an ESC so as to avoid tax, you can rely on the Inspector of Taxes applying a published ESC if it covers your particular circumstances. FA 2008 has given HMRC specific authority to grant ESCs, following doubts as to their legality arising from the *Wilkinson* case.

3.10 COMPLAINTS AND COMPENSATION

A taxpayer who is not happy with the way he has been treated by the Revenue is entitled to complain. In this first instance, it is recommended that the complaint be raised with the Officer in Charge of the local district before approaching the Director or Controller with overall responsibility for that office. Further details are provided in leaflet COP1. If this proves unsatisfactory, the complaint should be raised with the Adjudicator (see leaflet AO1); failing that, the case could be referred through the taxpayer's local MP to the independent Parliamentary Commissioner for Administration (the Ombudsman).

If the Revenue makes a mistake or causes unreasonable delay, the taxpayer is entitled to an apology, an explanation of what went wrong and, if appropriate, details of the steps taken to ensure the mistake does not happen again. If reasonable and possible, the Revenue will also have the mistake corrected.

The Revenue has a 28-day target for replying to all letters and enquiries; if there is a delay in excess of six months, without good reason, it will give up interest on unpaid tax and pay repayment interest on overpaid tax arising because of the delay. Furthermore, any reasonable costs incurred as a direct result of the delay will also be paid. The Revenue's policy on remitting tax where there has been a delay in using information provided to it is explained at 3.5.

If the mistake or delay is serious, it may be possible to claim additional costs arising from the mistake. According to the Revenue's internal Redress Manual, a serious error is something that no responsible person, acting in good faith and with proper care, could reasonably have done; this would indicate that a non-serious error was a pardonable error, or even an innocent misunderstanding. Although the interpretation of 'serious' is dependent on the facts of each situation, the Revenue considers the following to fall within the definition:

(1) taking a wholly unreasonable view of, as opposed to having a genuine difference of opinion about, the law;
(2) starting or pursuing enquiries into matters that were obviously trivial on the basis of the facts available at the time;
(3) making what would normally be a simple or trivial mistake, but the particular circumstances required more care because the Revenue should have known that such a mistake could have serious consequences.

Even if the mistakes are not serious, reasonable costs may be paid for persistent errors (eg where the Revenue makes the same type of mistake or continues in the mistake even after it has been revealed, unless there is a genuine difference of opinion). If several unconnected mistakes were made in any 12-month period, for the same tax year or for the same period of assessment, this may also be regarded as persistent (eg if an assessment keeps being amended because of new facts, but each time the Revenue gets the amendment wrong).

The reasonable costs that may be paid extend to professional fees, incidental personal expenses, or wages or fees that would have been earned but were lost through having to sort things out. They could also include such items as postage and telephone charges.

In exceptional cases, where a serious error has resulted directly in a significant and unwarranted intrusion into the taxpayer's personal life, the Revenue will consider making a payment as consolation for any worry and distress suffered as a direct result of that error. Significant and unwarranted intrusions may comprise confidentiality breaches, inappropriate use of information, poorly handled investigations and misleading advice or mistakes affecting vulnerable taxpayers (such as those suffering medical or physical illness, emotional trauma such as bereavement, or the elderly). If the unreasonable delay exceeds more than two years, a consolatory payment may also be made. In handling the complaint itself, if there has been significant delay for no good reason or where it has been seriously mishandled, consolatory payments may be made. Unsurprisingly, each case will be considered on its own merits and payments are likely to be in the region of £25–£500.

3.11 REVENUE ADJUDICATOR

If you are dissatisfied with the treatment you receive from the Revenue (or Customs & Excise) you can ask an independent body to investigate your complaint. The matter should be referred to:

The Adjudicator's Office
Haymarket House
28 Haymarket
London
SW1Y 4SP
Tel: 020 7930 2292
Fax: 020 7930 2298
E-mail: adjudicators@gtnet.gov.uk

If this fails you can ask your Member of Parliament to refer the case to the Parliamentary Ombudsman.

EMPLOYMENT INCOME

JON HILLS

This chapter deals with the following matters:
 (1) Basis of assessment.
 (2) How tax is collected.
 (3) Allowable expenses.
 (4) Benefits-in-kind in general.
 (5) Company cars.
 (6) Free use of assets.
 (7) Beneficial loans.
 (8) Living accommodation.
 (9) Miscellaneous benefits.
(10) Share incentives.
(11) Options to acquire gilts.
(12) Options to acquire other company assets.
(13) Golden hellos.
(14) Restrictive covenants.
(15) Redundancy payments.
(16) Golden handshakes, other termination payments and continuing benefits.
(17) Designing a 'tax efficient' remuneration package.

4.1 BASIS OF ASSESSMENT

4.1.1 Introduction

An individual who holds an office or employment is taxed under the Income Tax (Earnings and Pensions) Act 2003, which came into force on 6 April 2003.

Employment income is taxed according to the residence status of the individual concerned. The rules are set out in Table 4.1.

Table 4.1 – Different treatment according to residence/domicile of employee

---

Individual resident and ordinarily resident in the UK: tax is due on total remuneration received (s 15 IT(E&P)A 2003).

Individual resident but not ordinarily resident in the UK: tax is due on total remuneration received (subject to special treatment of foreign emoluments (see 34.2).

Individual not resident in the UK: tax is due on total remuneration received for duties performed in the UK (s 25 IT(E&P)A 2003).

Individual resident but not ordinarily resident in the UK where the duties are performed outside the UK. Tax is due on earnings brought into the UK.

Individual resident and ordinarily resident but not domiciled in the UK where all the duties are performed abroad ('foreign emoluments', see 34.2). Tax is due on earnings brought into the UK (s 26 and s 22 IT(E&P)A 2003).

The remainder of this chapter concentrates on UK resident and ordinarily resident employees who are taxed under s 15 IT(E&P)A 2003 (formerly Schedule E Case I). See Chapters 33 and 34 for the taxation of non-ordinarily resident and foreign domiciled individuals.

4.1.2 Receipts basis
(IT(E&P)A 2003, s 10)

The amount that is assessable for a tax year is the amount of earnings received in that year.

4.1.3 Date remuneration is deemed to be received
(IT(E&P)A 2003, s 18)

Special provisions define the date that an individual is deemed to receive remuneration as the earlier of:

(1) the date when payment is actually made; and
(2) the time when the employee becomes entitled to payment.

In the case of directors, the date can be earlier than above, in that payment is deemed to take place on the earliest of (1) and (2); and

(3) the date that income is credited to the director in the company's accounts or records;
(4) the date when the amount of income for a period is determined; or
(5) the end of a period if the director's remuneration for a period is determined before the period has expired.

The employer is required to operate PAYE when payment is deemed to take place (see 20.1).

4.1.4 **Amounts deducted in arriving at pay**
(IT(E&P)A 2003, s 713)

Contributions made by an employee to an approved retirement benefit scheme and contributions to a payroll giving scheme ('give as you earn') are deducted from an individual's salary in arriving at taxable pay for both PAYE and for assessment purposes. Note that NICs are based on pay before such amounts are deducted (see 22.1).

4.2 HOW TAX IS COLLECTED

4.2.1 Tax deductions under PAYE

All payments of 'emoluments' by a UK-resident employer to directors and employees are subject to Pay As You Earn (PAYE). Emoluments are cash payments (salary, wages, bonus, etc) other than expense payments.

PAYE code numbers

The Revenue issues code numbers that determine the amount of PAYE deductions. Such code numbers are based on the latest information available to the Revenue and are intended to ensure that the amounts withheld under PAYE approximate closely to an individual's actual liability. Nevertheless, deduction of tax under PAYE is provisional in that if the actual liability exceeds the amount withheld under PAYE, the Revenue may collect the balance either by increased PAYE deductions in subsequent years or by raising an assessment. Although the top rate of tax is 40%, the Revenue may issue K codes under which increased deductions may be taken of up to 50% of an individual's pay. The principle behind K codes is that notional pay is added to an employee's actual pay, and PAYE is operated accordingly. This is intended to cover the situation where the benefits-in-kind that are taxable exceed a person's allowances.

What the letters in your code mean

A Basic personal allowance plus one half of the Children's Tax Credit, and the Revenue estimates that you are liable at the basic rate of tax.

H Basic personal allowance plus the full Children's Tax Credit, and the Revenue estimates that you are liable at the basic rate of tax

L Basic personal allowance.

P Full personal allowance for those aged 65–74.

V Full personal allowance for those aged 65–74, plus the full married couple's allowance for those born before 6 April 1939 and aged under 75; the Revenue estimates that you are liable at the basic rate of tax.

Y Full personal allowance for those aged 75+.

T   Any other items the Revenue needs to review in your tax code or if you ask the Revenue not to use any of the other tax code letters listed.

K   'K' followed by a number means that the total allowances in your code are less than the total deductions to be taken away from your allowances. The Revenue publishes a leaflet (P3), which is available from your local tax office or from the Revenue's website and which explains how a K coding works.

BR Tax deducted at the basic rate, currently 20%.

D0 Tax deducted at a flat rate of 40%.

0T No allowances, salary charged at progressive rates.

NT No Tax, usually used for non-residents being paid from the UK.

How HMRC tax code is worked out

Step one

Your tax allowances are added up (in most cases this will just be your personal allowance and any blind person's allowance; in some cases it may include certain job expenses).

Step two

Income you've not paid tax on (for example, untaxed interest or part-time earnings) and any taxable employment benefits are added up.

Step three

The total amount of income you've not paid any tax on (called 'deductions') is taken away from the total amount of tax allowances. The amount you are left with is the total tax-free income you are allowed in a year.

Step four

To arrive at your tax code, the amount of tax-free income you are left with is divided by 10 and added to the letter that fits your circumstances.

As an example, the tax code 117L means:

- you are entitled to the basic personal allowance;
- £1,170 must be taken away from your total taxable income.

Revenue example of how tax code is worked out

How tax was worked out using this tax code for 2007–08

Pay from employment or pension		£21,840
Minus tax free amount for the year		£1,770
Pay on which tax will be paid		£20,070
On £20,070, the tax payable is		
Starting rate 10% on £2,230	=	£223.00
Basic rate 22% on £17,840	=	£3,924.80
So, tax to be paid in the year	=	£4,147.80

4.2.2 Foreign employers unable to operate PAYE

Where a person is employed by a foreign employer that has no place of business in the UK, PAYE is not normally operated. Tax is payable by the employee as if he were self-employed, ie two payments on account based on the previous year's tax bill plus a balancing payment on 31 January following the end of the tax year.

4.2.3 Self-assessment

An employee has until 31 January following the year of assessment to file a return and pay any additional tax due (ie for 2007–08, by 31 January 2009). If the employee wants the tax underpaid (of up to £2,000) to be collected by way of an adjustment in the code operated against his salary, he is requested to file the return by 31 October following the year of assessment (ie for 2007–08, by 31 October 2008). The 31 October filing date is extended to 30 December 2008 for individuals who file their 2007/08 returns online.

Where the taxpayer fails to notify the Revenue and pay any tax due by 31 January, interest penalties and surcharges may arise (see Chapter 2).

4.3 ALLOWABLE EXPENSES

4.3.1 Strict conditions must be satisfied for expenses to be allowed
(IT(E&P)A 2003, s 327)

The rules governing the amounts that may be deducted for tax purposes from remuneration subject to tax as employment income are extremely strict. The legislation provides for a deduction to be made only in respect of expenses that are wholly, exclusively and necessarily incurred in the performance of the duties of the employment or office.

Wholly, exclusively ...

The courts have held that the following expenses are not deductible for employment income purposes because they are not deemed to have been incurred wholly and exclusively in the performance of the employment duties:

(1) meal expenses paid out of meal allowances;
(2) the rent of a telephone installed for business reasons but not used wholly and exclusively in the performance of duties;
(3) the cost of domestic assistance where the taxpayer's wife is employed;
(4) the cost of looking after a widower's children; and
(5) the cost of ordinary clothing.

... and necessarily ...

The situation often arises that the employer has reimbursed the expense because it is regarded as essential. This is helpful, but not conclusive. The Revenue will assess the amount paid to a director or P11D employee (see 4.4.1) but may then seek to disallow the individual's expenditure claim on the grounds that it is not necessary. Two of the leading cases involved reimbursed expenditure by journalists on newspapers and other periodicals. The point at issue was whether reading such newspapers was part, or inherent in the performance, of the journalists' duties. The key point here is that it is not the employer's decision that determines the case. The employer may be fully prepared to reimburse the expenditure but the Revenue may still argue that it fails to meet the very strict guidelines on what constitutes 'necessary'.

... in the performance of the duties

Other expenses were rejected on the grounds that they were not incurred in the performance of the duties of the relevant employment:

(1) employment agency fees (although entertainers specifically are now entitled to claim a deduction for such expenses up to 17.5% of their earnings);
(2) a headmaster's course to improve background knowledge;
(3) an NHS registrar's costs of attending training courses that had to be completed so that he could apply for a position as a consultant (*HMRC v Decadt* [2007] ER (D) 139)
(4) an articled clerk's examination fees;
(5) travelling costs from home to the place where the employment duties were performed;
(6) living expenses paid out of living allowances paid to an employee when working away from home;
(7) expenditure by a rugby league player on diet supplements to improve and maintain his fitness (*Ansell* v *Brown* 2001 STC 1166);
(8) expenses incurred by a supply teacher in keeping a room at her home for preparation of lessons, marking, etc (*Warner* v *Prior* 2003 SpC 353);
(9) expenses incurred by a Civil Servant who was allowed to work from home in Norfolk but was required to travel to the department's offices in Leeds each week (*Kirkwood* v *Evans* 2002 STC 231).

Cases where the taxpayer has succeeded

There have been cases where travelling expenses have been allowed because the courts were satisfied that a person's duties started as soon as he left home. For example, in *Gilbert* v *Hemsley* [1981] STC 703, a plant-hire company director's duties involved him using his home as a base and travelling to various sites. The court held that once he left home he was travelling in the course of his duties. Similarly, in *Pook* v *Owen* (1969) 45 TC 571 a doctor was 'on call' and his duties started once he was telephoned by the hospital to ask him to attend.

4.3.2 Expenses that are allowable
(IT(E&P)A 2003, ss 333–360)

Certain expenses are specifically allowable, such as the cost of professional subscriptions to an approved body that is relevant to the individual's employment (eg the annual subscription to the Institute of Chartered Accountants or The Law Society). Also, flat rate expenses are given to employees in certain industries to cover expenditure on tools, overalls, special clothing, etc.

Tax notes

The Revenue publishes a list of approved bodies whose subscriptions qualify as allowable expenses at www.hmrc.gov.uk/list3/list3.htm.

Despite the very restrictive rules outlined in 4.3.1, you may be able to secure a deduction if you pay interest on a loan used to purchase equipment used by you in the course of your employment (eg a computer or a fax machine at your home that you use for business purposes).

In addition to claiming a deduction for loan interest, relief may be due for expenses such as running costs and (in the case of a fax machine) the line rental. Capital allowances may also be due, subject to a restriction if the equipment is used for private purposes as well as for your employment.

At one time, directors or employees could not obtain tax relief for expenditure on items such as directors' and officers' liability insurance, or professional indemnity insurance. FA 1995 introduced relief for such premiums where they were paid by employees. Moreover, tax relief is also available where an employee has to meet his own uninsured liability.

The relief for insurance or payment of uninsured liabilities is also available to former employees who incur such expenses within a six-year period after the year in which the employment ceased.

4.3.3 Capital allowances for cars

2001–02 was the last tax year for which you could claim capital allowance on a car or motorbike used for work-related purposes.

4.4 BENEFITS-IN-KIND IN GENERAL

4.4.1 Directors and 'higher paid employees'
(IT(E&P)A 2003, s 201)

The legislation distinguishes P11D employees (ie directors and employees earning £8,500+ pa) from other employees. An employer is required to submit form P11D in respect of each P11D employee, who may then be assessed on the cost to the employer of benefits-in-kind received by them. Other employees are normally taxed on benefits only if they are convertible into cash.

An employee will fall within the P11D category where remuneration, together with benefits and reimbursed expenses, is £8,500+ pa. Such employees formerly were called 'higher paid' employees!

Employees are treated as earning £8,500+ if they are remunerated at the rate of £8,500+ pa. For example, a person whose employment began on 1 January 2008 and who had received a salary of £2,000 and reimbursed expenses of £200 by 5 April 2008 would be within the P11D category as the total amount of £2,200 would give an annual rate greater than £8,500.

All reimbursed expenses and other benefits have to be reported on form P11D and count towards the £8,500 limit, even though they may be justified as being for business purposes and ultimately no taxable benefit-in-kind arises, unless a dispensation has been agreed by the Revenue (see 4.4.2).

Directors are normally within the P11D regime, regardless of whether their remuneration reaches or exceeds the £8,500 limit (subject to one exception: see below). Furthermore, individuals who control a company's affairs and take management decisions may be treated as directors, even if they do not hold a formal position with the company and may have another title or job description within the company.

A person remunerated at a rate below £8,500 by a particular company is still within the P11D category if a directorship is held with another company in the same group, or if the total remuneration from group companies amounts to £8,500 pa whether or not any directorships are held. Certain directors are exempt from these rules by virtue of s 168 and therefore are excluded from the definition. To qualify for this favourable treatment, certain conditions need to be satisfied. The director:

(1) must not hold more than 5% of the company's ordinary share capital (holdings by his associates may need to be included as if he held the shares); and

(2) must be employed on a full-time basis (or the company must be a non-profit making organisation); and

(3) must be receiving remuneration and benefits that in aggregate are less than £8,500 pa.

An employer must provide employees with details of the taxable amounts for benefits shown on his form P11D. This must be done before 5 July following the tax year unless the employee had left the firm before the end of the tax year (in which case the employer must provide the information within 30 days of the former employee requesting him to do so). The P11D must include the cost of benefits provided by third parties where they were arranged by the employer.

4.4.2 Dispensations

The Revenue may grant a dispensation so that certain reimbursed expenses need not be reported on form P11D. This clearly is useful in reducing administration and accounting work and, wherever possible, employers should apply for a dispensation. The Revenue will set out expenses covered by it; any expenses not covered must still be reported. Any changes in the method of reimbursing expenses or scales of allowances must be notified to the Revenue.

4.4.3 Benefits-in-kind provided by third parties
(IT(E&P)A 2003, s 265)

It is not uncommon for wholesalers and distributors to offer benefits-in-kind to employees of retailers with whom they do business. Subject to certain *de minimis* rules, such benefits are taxable just as if they had been provided by the retailer himself.

However, non-monetary gifts costing no more than £250 received by an employee or his family from someone other than his employer are generally exempt from income tax. Likewise, no income tax liability usually arises on entertainment that an employee receives from a third party. These exemptions apply only where the gift or entertainment is not provided directly or indirectly by the employer and, furthermore, where it is not provided as a reward for, or in recognition of, specific services done or to be done by the employee.

Where the third party benefits have not been arranged by the employer, the provider must give the employee details of any taxable benefits by 5 July following the tax year.

4.4.4 Benefits for a director's family
(IT(E&P)A 2003, s 201(2))

A fundamental point is that an assessment may arise even though the director or employee has not personally received a benefit-in-kind. A tax liability may arise if the benefit was made available to a member of the director's or employee's household by reason of his employment. The Revenue may argue that substantial benefits-in-kind enjoyed by a director's family are provided by reason of that person's employment even though the recipient may also be a company employee. The Revenue is especially likely to argue this where a director's spouse is employed by the company and receives abnormally large benefits-in-kind for employees of that category.

The legislation defines an individual's family or household as his spouse, children, parents, servants, dependants and guests. Note that this definition does not include grandparents, brothers, sisters and grand-children, although there can be situations where such relatives count as dependants.

4.4.5 Scholarships
(IT(E&P)A 2003, s 213)

There is a general exemption for scholarships, but a scholarship provided to a child by reason of his parent's employment is normally treated as a benefit-in-kind of the parent. The benefit is taxable unless it can be shown that the scholarship was not awarded by reason of the employment and 75% of the scholarships awarded by the fund are awarded to children whose parents are not employed by the company.

4.4.6 Benefits that may result in a tax charge for non-P11D employees

The general rule is that employees not within the P11D category are assessable only on benefits capable of being converted into cash or on any benefits provided through an employer meeting an employee's own personal liability. This principle has been modified to some extent so that, for example, credit vouchers are an assessable benefit even if the employee is not within the P11D category. However, the principle continues to hold good with regard to benefits such as the provision of a company car, free use of assets, beneficial loans, etc. Table 4.2 sets out the position.

Table 4.2 – Treatment of benefits received by non-P11D employees

	Taxable	Non-taxable
Benefits capable of being turned to pecuniary account, ie convertible to cash	✓	
Luncheon vouchers in excess of 15p per working day	✓	
Credit tokens and vouchers	✓	
Transport vouchers (ie any ticket, pass or other document or token intended to enable a person to obtain passenger transport services)	✓	
Living accommodation	✓	
Payment of employees' personal liabilities	✓	
Company cars		✓
Free use of assets		✓
Beneficial loans		✓
Medical insurance		✓

4.4.7 Tax treatment of specific benefits when received by a non-P11D employee

Benefits capable of being converted into cash

Where the benefit is convertible into cash, the measure of assessable benefit is the amount of cash that could be realised. For example, an employee provided with a new suit by the employer would be taxable on its second-hand value.

Credit tokens and vouchers
(IT(E&P)A 2003, s 90)

The taxable amount in respect of credit tokens and vouchers is the cost to the employer of providing them. Vouchers other than cheque vouchers are deemed to be taxable emoluments as and when they are allocated to a particular employee, not when they are used by that employee.

Transport vouchers
(IT(E&P)A 2003, s 82)

Specific legislation was introduced some years ago to ensure that season tickets provided by employers should be taxable. Once again, the measure of the assessable benefit is the cost to the employer of providing the voucher.

Living accommodation
(IT(E&P)A 2003, s 97)

The assessable amount is the greater of the property's gross rateable value or the rent payable by the employer, less any amount made good by the employee. Following the abolition of domestic rates, estimated values are used for new or substantially altered properties. No assessable benefit arises where the employee occupies representative accommodation (see 4.4.8).

Payment of employee's personal liabilities

A liability arises where the employer pays a personal liability of the employee. This would include such items as home heating, lighting bills and water rates, but special rules apply where the employee is in representative accommodation (see 4.4.8).

4.4.8 Benefits not taxable for any category of employees

There are certain benefits that are not usually taxable even when the employee is within the P11D category. The most widely used tax-free benefits are as set out below.

Retirement benefits

Payments by an employer to an approved occupational pension scheme to secure retirement benefits for an employee do not give rise to an income tax liability for that employee. Payments into a non-approved scheme are taxable as additional remuneration for the year that the employer makes the relevant contribution. To secure approval, a pension scheme must be established for the sole purpose of providing 'relevant benefits' (ie pensions, death-in-service payments and widows' and dependants' pensions). In addition, an employee's contributions must not exceed 15% of his remuneration. The pension benefits payable by an approved scheme must not exceed certain limits. Pension schemes are covered in more detail in Chapter 25.

Luncheon vouchers

Non-transferable luncheon vouchers (ie vouchers that are not capable of being exchanged for cash) are exempt from income tax up to a limit of 15p per working day. Vouchers for larger amounts are partly exempt, with the excess over 15p being taxable in full, whether or not the employee is within the P11D category.

Staff canteen and dining facilities

No taxable benefit-in-kind arises where the canteen, etc is used by all staff. Furthermore, the use of a separate room by directors and more senior staff does not prejudice this exemption, unless the meals provided are superior. The Revenue also accepts that facilities provided by a hotel or restaurant for staff to 'eat in' may come within the definition of a 'canteen', provided that the meals are taken at a time or place when they are not being served to the public or where part of the restaurant or dining room is designated specifically as being for staff use only.

Sports facilities
(IT(E&P)A 2003, s 261)

No taxable benefit arises in respect of the use or availability of sports facilities owned by the employer. At one time, no assessment was normally made where an employer took out corporate membership of an outside sports club so that all the employees were able to use its facilities. However, the Revenue's current literature states that the exemption is not available for sports facilities that are available to the general public.

Medical check-ups

The provision of routine health checks or medical screening does not constitute a taxable benefit provided the check-ups are available to all employees or all those employees who have been identified in a health screening as requiring a medical check-up.

Eye tests and corrective glasses

Employers are required by law to pay for eye tests where employees use computer screens. The Revenue does not charge tax in these circumstances, whether the benefit is provided directly or through the provision of a voucher.

Workplace nurseries and crèches

Employees are exempt from income tax on the benefit derived from the use of a workplace nursery provided by the employer. The exemption applies only to nurseries run by employers alone or jointly with other employers or bodies, either at the workplace or elsewhere.

The provision by an employer of cash allowances to employees for childcare, or the direct meeting of an employee's childcare bills by an employer, are at present taxable benefits. From 2005–06, an employer has been able to provide a tax free benefit of up to £50 per week by either contracting with an approved childcarer or providing vouchers that the employee can use to pay an approved childcarer. The limit was increased to £55 pw from 2006–07 onwards.

Pool cars
(IT(E&P)A 2003, s 167)

No tax charge arises by reason of the use of a pooled car. A car qualifies as a pooled car only if all the following conditions are satisfied:

(1) It is available for, and used by, more than one employee and is not used ordinarily by any one of them to the exclusion of the others.
(2) Any private use of the car by an employee is merely incidental to its business use.
(3) It is not normally kept overnight at or near the residence of any of the employees unless it is kept on the employer's premises.

These requirements are interpreted strictly. Note that a car only qualifies as a pooled car for a tax year. There is a danger, therefore, in a car being taken out of pooled use and allotted to a specific employee towards the end of a tax year. As the car now no longer qualifies as a pooled car, any employee who has had the car available for private use during the same tax year may be assessed. So, if the car is ordinarily parked overnight near the home of one of the users, it does not qualify as a pooled car and creates a tax problem for any other employees who use it.

Emergency service vehicles

With effect from 6 April 2004, emergency service workers in the fire, police and ambulance services are entitled to a specific exemption from the benefit charge which might otherwise arise from having to take their emergency vehicles home when on call.

Disabled employees' travel costs

Assistance with travelling costs between home and work is not taxable where it is given to disabled persons. This includes contributions towards the cost of travel by public transport. A car provided for travel between home and work is not taxed where:

(1) the employee is severely and permanently disabled; and
(2) the car has been specially adapted; and
(3) no private use is made other than travel between home and work occupied by the employer.

'Green commuting' facilities

There is no taxable benefit in respect of:

(1) works buses with a seating capacity of nine or more;
(2) subsidies to public bus services, provided the employee pays the same fare as other members of the public;
(3) bicycles and cycle safety equipment made available for employees to get to and from work; and
(4) workplace parking for bicycles and motorcycles.

For employees who may need to shower and change clothes after arriving at the office because, for example, they cycle or run to work, tax is not chargeable on the free use by employees of changing and shower room facilities at an employer's premises, provided they are generally available to all employees. The employer can also provide breakfast on designated 'cycle to work days' without this constituting a taxable benefit.

Late travel

There is an exemption for the cost to an employer of providing transport to get an employee home (after 9 pm) where public transport is not available or it is not reasonable for the employer to expect the employee to use it. The exemption does not apply if the employee has to work late on a regular or frequent basis. There is an overall limit of 60 occasions on which transport can be provided.

The exemption has been extended to cover extra travel costs where car-sharing arrangements temporarily break down. This can include situations where the employee travels home at his normal time (eg where the employee whose car he shares is unexpectedly kept late).

Employees' rail strike costs
(IT(E&P)A 2003, s 245)

There is now a statutory exemption covering the extra costs incurred by employees in getting to work because of a rail strike. The exemption (which may also cover the cost of hotel accommodation near the place of work) means that no tax is payable where the employer meets these expenses.

Homeworking allowance

The Finance Act 2003 has introduced an exemption for payments of up to £2 per week to cover extra expenses where the employee is required to work from home.

Relocation expenses
(IT(E&P)A 2003, s 271)

There is an exemption from tax on certain removal expenses borne by an employer when an employee has to change his residence to take up a new job within the same organisation, or to take up completely new employment. It is not necessary for the employee to sell his former home, but the exemption is available only where it would be unreasonable to expect him to work at the new location without moving closer to it. Abortive costs where a particular purchase falls through can be covered by the exemption provided the employee does eventually move house. The exemption is subject to a ceiling of £8,000 for any one move.

Payments made to compensate employees for losses on the sale of their former houses are regarded as taxable.

The Revenue has published a guide for employees on relocation packages and their tax treatment (IR134, obtainable from tax offices and tax enquiry centres). Sometimes employers provide guaranteed selling prices for the employee's former home, either directly or through a relocation agency. The Revenue published its views on the tax consequences of such arrangements in *Tax Bulletin* May 1994, available from the Revenue Press Office.

Gifts by third parties

The exemption for non-monetary gifts by third parties covered at 4.4.3 applies to all categories of employees.

Long service awards
(IT(E&P)A 2003, s 323)

Awards to directors and employees to mark long service are exempt provided the period of service is at least 20 years and no similar award has been given to the employee within the previous ten years. The gift must not consist of cash and the cost should not exceed £50 per year of service. The exemption also applies to gifts of shares in the company that employs the individual or in another group company.

Awards under suggestion schemes
(IT(E&P)A 2003, ss 321–322)

Provided the employee is not engaged in research work, he may receive a tax-free payment under a firm's suggestion scheme. Making suggestions should not, however, be regarded as part of the employee's job. The size of the award should be within certain limits, ie £25 or less where the suggestion, although not implemented, has intrinsic value. Where the suggestion is implemented, the amount should be related to the expected net financial benefit to the employer. In any event, any excess over £5,000 is taxable.

Use of company computers

From 6 April 1999 to 5 April 2006, employees were able to take up the loan of a computer without being faced with a tax charge. This exemption applied to computer equipment with a value of up to £2,500. The normal benefit-in-kind rules (20% × market value), see 4.6, applied to any excess over £2,500. The exemption was not given if the equipment was confined to directors and senior staff.

The exemption has been abolished for 2006–07 and future years.

Representative accommodation
(IT(E&P)A 2003, s 99)

Living accommodation qualifies as representative accommodation if any one of the following conditions is satisfied:

(1) it is necessary for the performance of the employee's duties that he should reside in the accommodation;
(2) the accommodation is provided for the better performance of the employee's duties and it is customary to provide accommodation for such employees; or
(3) the employee has to live in the accommodation because of a special threat to his security.

The exemption under the first two conditions is usually available only to directors who (together with their associates) hold 5% or less of the company's ordinary share capital and are full-time working directors.

The Revenue strongly resists the application of the third exemption to any but the most clear-cut cases. However, in 2004, the Special Commissioners upheld a claim by the late Lord Hanson that he was entitled to the security exemption.

Where the employer pays for heating, lighting, repairs, maintenance, etc, the representative occupiers cannot be assessed in respect of such benefits on more than 10% of their emoluments of the employment.

The main occupations that satisfy the conditions for exemption are:

(1) agricultural workers living on farms or agricultural estates;
(2) lock-gate and level-crossing gatekeepers;
(3) caretakers who live on the premises for which they are responsible;
(4) stewards and greenkeepers who live on the premises they look after;
(5) managers of public houses who live on the premises;
(6) wardens of sheltered housing who live on the premises;
(7) police officers and Ministry of Defence police;
(8) prison governors, officers and chaplains;
(9) clergymen and ministers of religion, unless engaged on administrative duties only;
(10) members of the armed forces;
(11) members of the Diplomatic Service;
(12) managers of newspaper shops that have paper rounds;
(13) managers of traditional off-licences (ie those with opening hours that are the same as for public houses);
(14) head teachers and teachers at boarding schools who have pastoral responsibility, if the accommodation is at or near the school;
(15) veterinary surgeons who live near their practice so that they can respond regularly to emergency calls; and
(16) managers of camping and caravan sites living on or near the premises.

Retraining
(IT(E&P)A 2003, ss 311–312)

Where an employer pays the cost of a course undertaken by an employee (or former employee) to provide him with skills for future employment elsewhere, that cost can be a deductible expense of the employer, and may not be a taxable benefit of the employee. The employee must have completed at least two years' service. Until 6 April 2005, it was also necessary that the individual had been a full-time employee but the exemption is now also available in respect of part-time employees.

The exemption is normally dependent on the employee leaving his job no later than two years after completing the course.

Sandwich courses
(SP4/86)

Where an employer releases an employee to take a full-time educational course at a university, technical college or similar educational institution that is open to the public at large, payments for periods of attendance may be treated as exempt from income tax. There are various conditions that attach to this exemption:

(1) the course must last for at least one academic year with an average of at least 20 weeks of full-time attendance; and

(2) the rate of payment must not exceed £15,480 (a limit of £15,000 applied up to the 2006–07 academic year).

Where the rate of payment exceeds £15,480, the full amount is taxable; where the amount of payment is increased during a course, only subsequent payments are taxable.

Education and training
(IT(E&P)A 2003, ss 255–260)

No tax charge arises on payments made to a provider in respect of the costs of providing 'qualifying education or training' for a fundable employee. Similar relief is available for payment or reimbursement of any incidental costs incurred wholly and exclusively as a result of the employee undertaking the course. The exemption is available only where participation is available on similar terms to all employees.

'Qualifying education or training' is education or training which qualifies for grants under the Learning and Skills Act 2000 and its Scottish equivalent. A fundable employee is one who holds an account qualifying under the Learning and Skills Act, s 104 or who is a party to arrangements under s 105 or s 106 of that Act.

4.4.9 Expenses relating to directors and P11D employees

This section deals with problem areas that arise regularly in practice where expenses are paid on behalf of directors and senior employees or where the employer reimburses them.

Travelling expenses
(IT(E&P)A 2003, ss 336–340)

Travel between home and the ordinary place of work does not rank as business travel. Where an individual is 'on call' and assumes the responsibilities of the employment upon leaving home, it may be possible to argue that home to work travel is business, not private, travel, but usually this applies only in exceptional cases. Other travelling expenses are not normally treated as a benefit-in-kind so long as the individual has a 'normal place of work' that he attends the majority of the time. The Special Commissioners decided in 2003 that site-based employees of an agency did not meet these requirements (*Phillips* v *Hamilton* 2003 SpC 366).

Where an employee performs incidental duties of the employment at another location and travels there directly to or from his home, the allowable expense is the lesser of the travel and subsistence expenses actually incurred, and the expenses that would have been incurred if the journey had started and finished at the normal place of work.

To secure tax relief on reimbursed travelling expenses, the employee must keep adequate records so as to distinguish business from non-business travel. Ideally, expenses claims to the employer should show the actual cost of such travel and, if the employer is to obtain a dispensation, the Revenue will need to be satisfied that such internal controls exist.

Approved Mileage Allowance Payments (AMAP)

There is a statutory scheme of flat-rate allowances for business mileage that has applied since 6 April 2002. The following rates have been in force since 2002–03 and will apply to future years unless changed by the Revenue.

Cars and vans:	*Per mile*
First 10,000 miles in tax year	40p
Each additional mile	25p
Motorcycles	24p
Bicycles	20p

The employee cannot claim tax relief for interest on a loan used to buy his car.

Tax notes

Where an individual is required to use his own car for business, and he is reimbursed at less than the authorised rates, he can claim a deduction equal to the shortfall. Form P87 is designed to be used by employees who make such claims. You should keep a log of your business travel to back up your claim.

In addition to the mileage allowance payment, an employer can also pay up to 5p per passenger per mile free of tax and NICs for fellow employees carried in the employer's or employee's car or van where the journey constitutes business travel for both driver and passengers. The employee cannot claim any relief if the employer does not pay the passenger rate.

Mileage allowances for business travel in a company car

Where an employer reimburses fuel costs relating to business mileage, the following rates may be paid tax free (rates published 31 May 2008).

Petrol			*Diesel*	
1400cc or less 11.9p	1401cc to 2000cc 14.7p	Over 2000cc 20.9p	Up to 2000cc 12.7p	Over 2000cc 16.8p

If the car uses liquid petroleum gas, the rates are 7.4p, 9.1p and 13p per mile.

It may be possible to negotiate higher rates in particular circumstances (Revenue internet statement 28 January 2002).

Employee car ownership schemes

HMRC has been reviewing employee car ownership schemes that take maximum benefit of the approved mileage allowances and this could lead to a more restrictive approach in future.

Using a bicycle for business

Employees can claim capital allowances on bicycles used for business travel. A tax-free cycling allowance of 20p per business mile can be paid. Where the employer pays less than this rate, the employee can claim a tax deduction for the difference.

Subsistence

The Revenue's view is that it is strictly only the extra costs of living away from home that are allowable. If there are continuing financial commitments at home, the whole cost of living away from home is normally allowed. This concession is not available if the employee has no permanent residence, for example an unmarried person who normally lives in a hotel or club and who gives up that accommodation when away on a business trip. There is a specific exemption where an employee performs his duties wholly overseas and needs board and lodging abroad to do so.

Miscellaneous personal expenses

There is a statutory exemption for employees' miscellaneous personal expenses when they are required to stay away from home overnight on business. This exemption allows employers to meet expenses of up to £5 a night (£10 if overseas). Under the previous rules, incidental personal expenses such as newspapers, laundry and phone calls home were often met by employers but, because relief is only available for expenses necessarily incurred in the performance of the duties, these were liable to tax. Payments up to these limits are exempt, which should reduce employers' compliance costs and simplify their administrative procedures. But if the limits are exceeded, the whole of the expense payment is taxable, not just the excess.

Employees' travel and subsistence

There are special rules covering 'triangular travel'.

Triangular travel

Triangular travel occurs where an employee with a normal place of work travels not between home and normal place of work, but between home and another place at which he is required to perform his employment duties.

Example of triangular travel

An employee usually commutes by car from home in Oxford to a normal place of work in London. This is a daily round trip of 114 miles. On a particular day, the employee drives instead to a temporary place of work in Brighton, a round trip of 120 miles.

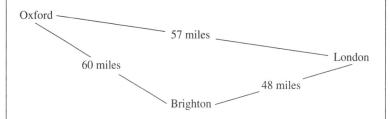

The rules allow a claim for the full mileage cost of 120 miles. It is not necessary to restrict the claim for the normal commuting costs that would have been incurred if the employee had travelled to London.

Of course, nothing in tax is ever as straightforward as this; for example, the Revenue would not allow the cost of the employee travelling to Brighton if he worked there so regularly that it became a normal place of employment. The Revenue's criterion here is that a place of work becomes a normal place of employment if the employee spends 40% of his time there.

The Revenue has issued a comprehensive guide, *Tax relief for business travel*, to employers.

These rules affect employees in employment that involves travel where tax relief is available for travel between home and various places visited. The Revenue will review whether the travelling is 'on the job', as opposed to 'to the job'. Such employees are expected to visit a number of places each day and have no base to which they report regularly. Thus, the definition of 'permanent workplace' may create difficulties where an employee reports regularly to a head office or regional base, say, every Tuesday.

Employees who are based at home may also be affected by these rules. The key issue is often whether the home base is an objective requirement of their duties, rather than a personal choice.

Area-based employees whose duties are defined by reference to a specific area (ie a county) have their tax relief restricted if they live outside that area. Tax relief is due only on necessary business journeys within the designated area or to a temporary workplace outside the area.

There are specific anti-avoidance measures (including a 'necessary attendance rule') that require attendance to be an objective requirement of the duties, and not from personal choice or to claim tax relief. It is also a requirement that any changes to a workplace must be significant in the effect on the journey. The Revenue normally accepts a ten-mile 'common sense' rule.

Site-based employees

A deduction is allowed for the costs of travel to or from any place where attendance at that place is in the performance of the duties of a person's employment. The subsistence costs of site-based employees are also an allowable expense.

Temporary absence from normal place of work

Where an employee is required to work temporarily at a place other than his normal workplace, the deductions for travel expenses described above are available.

Temporary relocation to another office, etc

The Revenue has clarified the circumstances in which employees who are temporarily absent from their normal place of work can claim a deduction for travelling and subsistence expenses. Normally an employee is regarded as temporarily absent from his normal place of work if:

(1) the absence is not for more than 24 months; and
(2) the employee returns to the normal place of work at the end of the period.

If these conditions are satisfied, the employer can pay a subsistence allowance free of tax.

The Revenue takes the view that an individual may also qualify if these conditions are expected to be satisfied at the outset but circumstances subsequently change. Relief is available for the period up to the time when it becomes clear that either condition will be breached.

There are special rules for subsistence allowances given to employees of overseas companies who are seconded to work in the UK for periods of up to two years. While it is not a statutory requirement that the employee is not UK-domiciled, in practice most employees who are temporarily seconded to the UK fall into this category. These rules are dealt with in 34.4.

Overseas travelling expenses
(IT(E&P)A 2003, s 370)

Where some or all of the employment duties are performed abroad, travelling expenses to and from the UK to carry out these duties are specifically regarded as having been necessarily incurred in the performance of the overseas employment. It follows that if those expenses are reimbursed by the employer, no benefit-in-kind arises. Legislative changes have relaxed the rules further so that, while the employee is serving abroad, the employer may pay for an unlimited number of journeys made by the employee to and from the UK without any tax charge arising. However, these journeys must be made wholly and exclusively for the purpose of performing the employment duties.

Moreover, where an employee travels between places where different jobs are performed, and one or more of these jobs are performed wholly or partly overseas, the expenses incurred in travelling overseas are also deemed to be necessarily incurred in performing the duties carried out overseas, so that once again no benefit-in-kind arises. In many cases, there is dual purpose in travelling and a taxable benefit-in-kind arises on the private element. Consequently, where travel expenses relate partly to a foreign holiday taken at the end of the business trip, there would be a taxable benefit-in-kind.

Similarly, a benefit-in-kind may be assessed on some or all of the expense where a spouse accompanies a director or employee and where this is not necessary for business purposes.

The maximum allowance to cover an employee's miscellaneous personal expenses is £10 per night when he is abroad.

A director or employee who travels overseas should be able to substantiate a claim that expenses were necessarily incurred for business purposes by producing details of the expenses and the time spent away from home. A brief itinerary should be available where travel is undertaken within the overseas country or countries. Inspectors of Taxes normally expect that an employer will properly control expenditure, but in certain cases they may wish to see receipted bills or other vouchers.

HMRC has published benchmark scale rates that employers can use to reimburse accommodation and subsistence expenses incurred by employees while visiting various countries. See the HMRC Employment Manual at EIM 05255.

Tax notes

Keep records of your travel costs to avoid arguments with the Revenue. These records should include details of the purpose of each trip and the business undertaken.

Spouse's travelling and subsistence expenses

Where a spouse or other member of the family accompanies a director abroad on a business trip, it will be helpful in satisfying the Revenue that no benefit-in-kind arises if the board of directors minutes its decision that the director should be so accompanied. However, this is not generally sufficient in itself and it must be shown that the spouse, etc was able to perform certain tasks that could not be performed by the director.

It may be possible to show this if the spouse has some practical qualification, for example an ability to speak the foreign language concerned. A relative's expenses may also be allowable where the director or employee is in poor health and to travel alone would be impracticable or unreasonable. Where the individual's presence is for the purpose of accompanying his or her spouse at business entertainment functions, the expenses of the trip may be disallowed in calculating the employer's tax liability under the entertainment legislation, even though the expenses may be allowable in determining the employee's tax liability.

Tax notes

Be prepared for HMRC to contend that the cost of your spouse's travel is a benefit in kind and collect evidence to show that her accompanying you was necessary for business purposes.

Employees working overseas: family visits
(IT(E&P)A 2003, s 371)

Where an employee is abroad for a continuous period of 60 days or more, there is an exemption for amounts borne by the employer in respect of the travelling expenses for visits by the employee's spouse and minor children. The exemption is available for only two journeys by the same person in each direction in a tax year. There is no relief if ultimately the employee bears the expense personally.

Entertaining expenses and round-sum allowances

It is not uncommon for directors or employees to have a round-sum allowance to cover such things as travelling, subsistence and entertaining. In the case of travelling and subsistence, the allowance counts as the director's or employee's taxable income, but a tax deduction may be claimed in respect of any part of the allowance that can be shown to have been spent for business purposes. It is very important to keep records that enable such claims to be substantiated. It may be better to dispense with round-sum allowances and reimburse the director or employee for properly substantiated expenditure, since no benefit-in-kind should then arise.

The situation is more complex for entertaining expenditure. If an employer reimburses entertaining expenditure or pays a round-sum allowance that is specifically intended for entertaining, the expense to the employer is disallowed for tax purposes. The reimbursement or allowance is entered on the director's or employee's P11D, but a deduction may be claimed for expenditure which is for genuine business purposes. If, on the other hand, the director or employee is given a round-sum allowance not specifically designated for entertaining, there is no question of the allowance being disallowed in the employer's tax computation. However, the director or employee would only escape liability on any part of the allowance that could be shown to have been used for business expenditure other than entertainment.

4.5 COMPANY CARS

(IT(E&P)A 2003, s 114)

4.5.1 Car benefits

From 6 April 2002, a more environmentally friendly regime for calculating the cash equivalent of the benefit where an employer provides a car to an employee or member of his family or household was introduced. This is based on the published carbon dioxide (CO_2) emissions figure (in grams per kilometre) for a given car. From 1 March 2001 that figure appears in the car log book. For cars registered between 1 January 1998 and 1 March 2001, the emissions figure can be obtained from a booklet published by:

The Vehicle Certification Agency
1 The Eastgate Office Centre
Eastgate Road
Bristol BS5 6XX
Web page: www.vca.gov.uk

The emissions figure is rounded down to the nearest whole 5g below and is then converted to a percentage using the Revenue table (see Table 4.3). The maximum percentage to be applied to the list price of the car is 35%. The list price is still subject to an overall limit of £80,000.

Diesel cars have a low CO_2 figure but produce other emissions. To maintain an environmental balance with petrol vehicles, the percentage is increased by 3% (up to the maximum 35%), for example if diesel emissions in 2007–08 are 230 grams per kilometre, the percentage is 33% + 2%.

Electric cars are taxed on 9% of list price.

Cars registered before 1 January 1998 do not have a CO_2 emissions figure and the percentage for these vehicles will continue to be based on engine size, but with no discounts for age or business use, as follows:

Engine size (cc)	Percentage of car's price taxed
0–1400	15%
1401–2000	22%
2001 and over	32%

A limited number of cars produced on or after that date will also not have a CO_2 figure and the percentage to be used then is:

Engine size (cc)	Percentage of car's price taxed
0–1400	15% *
1401–2000	25% *
2001 and over	35%

*Plus 3% supplement for diesel cars

Diesel cars

Add a 3% supplement to the relevant percentage scale charge to arrive at the amount of the car's price to be taxed. This is subject to a maximum charge based upon 35% of the car's list price. Some low emission diesel cars are not subject to this addition but this exemption will not be available for cars registered on or after 1 January 2006.

Automatic cars

These have higher CO_2 emissions. However, where an employee is disabled (ie holds an 'orange badge') and can only drive an automatic, the emission figure is taken as that of the 'equivalent manual car', ie the closest non-automatic variant of the car concerned.

Second cars

Second cars are charged at the same rate as first cars.

Table 4.3 – CO_2 emissions: cars registered from 1 January 1998

CO_2 emissions in grams per kilometre				Percentage of car's price taxed
2003–04	*2004–05*	*2005–06 to 2007–08*	*2008–09 to 2009–10*	
155	145	140	135	15
160	150	145	140	16
165	155	150	145	17
170	160	155	150	18
175	165	160	155	19
180	170	165	160	20
185	175	170	165	21
190	180	175	170	22
195	185	180	175	23
200	190	185	180	24
205	195	190	185	25
210	200	195	190	26
215	205	200	195	27
220	210	205	200	28
225	215	210	205	29
230	220	215	210	30
235	225	220	215	31
240	230	225	220	32
245	235	230	225	33
250	240	235	230	34
255	245	240	235	35

Reductions in the scale benefit

The scale figures are reduced where an employee was provided with a company car part way through the tax year, or where he ceased to have a company car. However, there is no reduction where the car was not available for use because of repairs, unless it was incapable of being used for at least 30 consecutive days. Contributions made by an employee towards the cost of the car can be deducted from the list price, up to £5,000.

Tax notes

If you are not using your company car while you are away on holiday, your scale benefit would be reduced if your employer required you to hand back your car for this period so that it was not available for your use.

4.5.3 Private petrol
(IT(E&P)A 2003, s 149)

Since 2003–04, the charge has been calculated by taking the vehicle's CO_2 emissions percentage figure shown in Table 4.3 and multiplying it by £14,400. However, from 6 April 2008, the fuel scale charge is based on multiplying the relevant CO_2 rate by £16,900. The scale figures apply regardless of the amount of private fuel provided. If any is provided, the fuel scale charge is always applied unless the employee reimburses the employer for the full cost. It may be cost effective for the employee to do this so the position should be reviewed before each tax year.

The charge is reduced if the car is not available for part of the tax year (see 4.5.1) or where fuel is not provided for part of a tax year or the employee makes good the cost during part of the tax year.

4.5.4 Car parking spaces
(IT(E&P)A 2003, s 266(1))

The provision of a car parking space at or near the employee's place of work is not treated as a taxable benefit. Where an employee pays for car parking himself, he cannot claim a deduction for those charges.

4.5.5 Private use of company vans
(IT(E&P)A 2003, s 154)

There is a scale charge for employees who have private use of company vans. An employee may be assessed on a standard amount of £3,000 pa (£500 for 2006–07) in respect of private use of a van irrespective of its age and since 2006–07 an additional charge of £500 applies if the employer provides fuel for private use. There is an exemption if the only private use is travel between home and work. Any vehicles in excess of 3.5 tons are exempt from tax altogether (unless the vehicle is used wholly or mainly for the employee's private purposes).

The scale charge is reduced if the van was not available for private use throughout the year.

For 2006–07, the £500 scale charge was reduced to £350 for vans that were four or more years old at the end of the tax year. It was possible for employees to elect to pay tax on a flat benefit of £5 for every day in 2006–07 that the van was made available to them for private use.

Where an employee has two or more vans made available for private use at the same time, tax is charged on the scale figure for each van. The standard amount is reduced pro rata where the van is only available part of the year. As for company cars, a £1-for-£1 reduction is made for any contributions made by the employee towards the private use. Where a van is shared among several employees, the standard amount is apportioned among the employees.

4.5.6 Congestion charge

No tax charge arises where an employer pays the congestion charge on a company car or van. It does apply where the congestion charge relates to a vehicle that is not owned by the employer unless the travel into London was an expense incurred wholly and necessarily in the performance of the employee's duties.

4.5.7 Hands-free phone kit

The Revenue accepts that no additional benefit arises where an employer pays for a hands-free phone kit to be fitted in a company car.

4.6 FREE USE OF ASSETS
(IT(E&P)A 2003, s 203)

A taxable benefit arises where an employer makes an asset available for use by a director or P11D employee. The annual amount is 20% of the asset's market value when it was first made available for use by the employee. Assets that may be involved include yachts, furniture, television sets, stereo equipment, company vans, etc – virtually any asset apart from living accommodation and company cars. If the employer rents or hires the asset for a sum in excess of 20% of its original market value, the higher rental charge is substituted as the assessable benefit. A deduction is allowed for any contribution or rental payable by the employee.

A further charge may arise if the ownership of assets is eventually transferred to the employee. The amount may be determined by either the asset's market value at the time of transfer of ownership or, where a higher figure results, its original cost at the time it was first made available as a benefit for any person, less any amounts already charged as benefits in connection with its availability.

Example – Transfer of assets

A company provides an employee with the use of a yacht that costs £40,000, with the employee paying a rental of £2,000 pa. After two years the yacht is sold to the employee for its second-hand market value of £20,000. The assessable benefit would be:

		Benefit £
Year 1:	£40,000 × 20%	8,000
	Less: rental paid	(2,000)
		6,000
Year 2:	£40,000 × 20%	8,000
	Less: rental paid	(2,000)
		6,000
Year 3:	Cost of yacht	40,000
	Less: benefits assessed in Years 1 and 2	(12,000)
	Amounts paid by employee	(24,000)
		4,000

Where an asset previously made available to an individual is transferred to him (or to another employee) at a time when its market value is still high, it is possible that the total amount charged as a benefit for tax purposes exceeds the original cost. In other cases, the rules may operate to impose a high benefit charge on the transfer of an asset despite its value having depreciated rapidly during the period of use.

Such rules must therefore be considered carefully when planning the provision of an asset for use by an employee or arranging for its transfer to him. It may be that where a tax-efficient remuneration package is desired, transfer of ownership should be avoided where assets have a relatively short useful life.

Example – Ownership of assets

A company provides employees with the use of suits that remain the property of the company. The suits cost £200 and have a useful life of two years, after which they are scrapped. An employee could therefore have an effective benefit of £200, but would be charged tax on only £40 for each of the two tax years.

4.6.2 Assets where this charge does not arise

In the case of a car, the charge is calculated only by reference to the market value at the time that the car is transferred to the employee. Thus if a car had been purchased for £40,000 and after two years the employee buys it for £20,000, a tax charge will arise only if the £20,000 is less than market value.

Similarly, from 6 April 2005 the tax charge on a transfer to an employee of a computer or bicycle previously made available to him or another employee is based only on the market value at that time.

4.7 BENEFICIAL LOANS
(IT(E&P)A 2003, s 184)

4.7.1 Type of loans caught

A charge generally arises for directors and P11D employees on the annual value of beneficial loan arrangements. A loan's 'annual value' is taken as interest at the 'official rate' less the amount of interest (if any) paid by the employee. The official rate is now set annually in advance and is 6.25% for 2007–08 and 2008–09 (previously 5% from 2002–03 to 2006–07). An additional taxable benefit arises if the loan is subsequently written off or forgiven. The beneficial loan provisions can also apply if a loan is made to a member of an employee's family.

Moreover, the Revenue can assess benefits where credit has been involved, even though there may be no formal loan. In particular, a director who overdraws his current account with the company is regarded as having obtained a loan.

Almost all loans by employers (and persons connected with them) are caught as the legislation deems such loans to have been given by reason of the employment. Originally there was only a single exception in that this rule did not apply where the employee was related to the employer and it could be shown that the loan was given for family reasons. Loans made by an employer whose business includes lending money to the general public do not give rise to a charge on the employees provided the loans are made on similar terms to the public.

4.7.2 Beneficial loans used for qualifying purpose

No charge arises in respect of a cheap loan where the money borrowed has been applied for a qualifying purpose, for example to purchase shares in a close company in which the individual has a material interest or where he is employed full time in the conduct and management of the company's business.

4.7.3 *De minimis* exemption

All cheap or interest-free loans made to an individual employee that do not exceed £5,000 are exempt. This figure excludes loans used to buy shares in employee-controlled companies (see 10.6).

4.7.4 **Employee loans written off**

If the loan is written off, the amount forgiven is treated as assessable income for that year even if the company no longer employs the person concerned. The only exception here is if the loan is forgiven on the employee's death.

Some care must be taken if it is decided to clear a loan by making an *ex gratia* or compensation payment to an employee on termination of employment. An income tax liability will arise if the loan is formally written off. However, no liability normally arises if the employee receives a cheque as an *ex gratia* or compensation payment and uses that sum to clear his outstanding loan. It is recommended that professional advice be taken in such circumstances.

4.7.5 **Further information**

HMRC guidance on how loans provided by employers to employees are taxed can be found at www.hmrc.gov.uk/employers/ebik/ebik2/loans.htm.

4.8 **LIVING ACCOMMODATION**
(IT(E&P)A 2003, ss 105–106)

4.8.1 **Introduction**

The income tax charge that generally applies where an employee is provided with accommodation (unless it is representative accommodation: see 4.4.8) depends on whether the property is owned or rented by the employer. In the past, where the employer owned the property, the assessable amount was usually the gross annual value for rating purposes. Despite the abolition of domestic rates, this treatment continued to apply for properties on existing rating lists (see 4.4.7). For new properties and those where there have been major improvements, the Revenue makes an estimate of what the gross annual value would have been had rates continued.

Where the property is rented by the employer, the assessable amount is the greater of the rent paid and the annual value as above. In addition, a charge may arise on the annual value of any furniture and fixtures, and on any occupier's expenses borne by the company such as water rates, decorations, gardener's wages, etc.

An additional charge may arise where the employer paid more than £75,000 to acquire the property. The amount assessable is a percentage of the excess of the property's cost over £75,000. The percentage to be applied is the official rate of interest used for beneficial loans (see 4.7) as at the beginning of the tax year.

Example – Charge on living accommodation in excess of £75,000

For several years a company director has occupied a property owned by the company that has a gross annual value of £2,000. The cost of the property in 2003 was £95,000. The director will be assessed on the following amount for 2008–09:

	£	£
Gross annual value		2,000
Additional charge:		
Cost in 2003	95,000	
Less:	(75,000)	
	20,000	
Assessment on £20,000 at official rate of 6.25%		1,250
		3,250

4.8.2 Properties owned for more than six years

Where the company has owned the property for at least six years, the figure taken into account in computing the additional charge is the market value at the time it was made available, rather than the cost. The actual cost (including improvements) to the employer is still used to determine whether the provisions apply. Consequently, properties where the actual cost was less than £75,000 (including the cost of any improvements) are not within the scope of this additional charge even if their market value exceeds £75,000. Where the actual cost exceeded £75,000, the additional charge is based on the market value.

Example – Charge on living accommodation purchased more than six years ago

In the example in 4.8.1, assume the company has owned the property for more than six years before the director moves in. Also assume that in May 2004, when the director first occupies it, the market value is £191,000. As the original cost of the property exceeded £75,000, the director will be assessed on the following amount for 2008–09:

	£	£
Gross annual value		2,000
Additional charge:		
Market value in 2004	191,000	
Less:	(75,000)	
	116,000	
Assessment on £116,000 at official rate of 6.25%		7,250
		9,250

4.8.3 Possible reduction in taxable amount

It may be possible to reduce the taxable amount where the employee is required to occupy a property that is larger than would normally be needed for his own purposes. In *Westcott* v *Bryan* (1969) 45 TC 476 a director was required to live in a large house so that he could entertain customers. He was allowed a reduction in the taxable amount to cover the relevant proportion of the annual value and the running expenses.

Some care is needed if it is intended to claim relief in this way. This claim succeeded because the house was larger than needed for the director and his family. It would not have succeeded had the property merely been more expensive than he would have chosen. It was also helpful that the company directors had approved board minutes setting out their requirement and the business reason for it.

Where part of the property is used exclusively for work, the taxable amount may be reduced on a pro rata basis. Revenue Helpsheet IR202 (last updated for 2006–07) contains working sheets that enable you to compute your taxable benefits in this situation.

4.8.4 Possible increase in taxable benefit

It is sometimes the case that an employer offers a choice: salary of £x or salary of £y plus a house. In this situation, the difference between £x and £y may be taxed if this exceeds the normal benefit-in-kind calculated along the lines set out in 4.8.1–4.8.2.

4.8.5 Holiday accommodation and foreign properties

Some employers buy holiday flats, cottages, etc for use by staff. In practice, generally the Revenue apportions the assessable amount for the year among those employees who have occupied the property. The assessment can be reduced by letting the accommodation to third parties when directors and employees do not require it.

A practical problem arises with overseas properties. Because there is no rateable value, the benefit is the annual rent that the property would normally command on the open market. However, where this applies, there is normally no additional charge based on the excess of the property's cost over £75,000 (see 4.8.1). An ESC avoiding such a double charge was published on 28 November 1995.

4.8.6 Overseas holiday homes held in a company

It is common for a UK individual who is acquiring a home overseas to set up a company to buy the property. Where the individual is a director, he is potentially subject to the tax charge under section 105 IT(E&P)A 2003. The Finance Act 2008 provides an exemption from this (with full retrospective effect) as long as these conditions are satisfied:

- the company must be owned by individuals;
- the company's main activity must be to own the property, any other activity being incidental;
- the property must be the only or main asset of the company;
- the company is not funded directly or indirectly by a connected company.

4.9 MISCELLANEOUS BENEFITS

Council tax

Where an employer pays the council tax on behalf of an employee, this is normally chargeable as part of the employee's remuneration package, resulting in a charge to both income tax and NICs. The one exception to this is where the employee is a representative occupier (see 4.4.8).

Mobile phones
(FA 1991, s 30)

Tax was charged on a standard amount of £200 pa per telephone where it was used privately. 'Private use' meant making personal calls or accepting reverse charge calls; it did not include receiving normal personal calls. The charge was abolished from 6 April 1999 but from 2006–07 onwards the exemption is limited to one telephone for each employee.

No benefit in kind arises where an employer pays for a hands-free mobile kit to be fitted in an employee's car provided the employer retains ownership of the kit.

Telephone rental

The Revenue treats the full amount of the rental paid by the employer as a taxable benefit-in-kind even though the phone may be partly (or mainly) used for business calls. The decision in *Lucas* v *Cattell* (1972) 48 TC 353 was that the expenditure on rental had a dual purpose (ie that a phone was intended to be used for both business and personal use) and therefore no part of it was allowable.

Liability insurance and payment of uninsured liabilities

FA 1995 provides that employees are not subject to tax on a benefit-in-kind where their employer pays premiums on items such as directors' and officers' liability insurance or a professional indemnity insurance policy. Furthermore, the Act also provides that payment of an employee's un-insured liabilities does not give rise to a benefit-in-kind provided they arise from the employee's work. This is subject to the overriding requirement that the liabilities could have been insured against and this means that those arising from, for example criminal convictions, cannot attract relief.

Medical insurance

The cost of medical insurance is normally assessable on P11D employees. Where the employer has a group scheme, a proportion of the total premiums is related to individual employees. There is an exception in that the premiums are exempt to the extent that they provide cover for an employee working outside the UK.

Club subscriptions

A benefit-in-kind is deemed to arise where an employer pays or reimburses an employee's subscription to a club, even though the employee may only belong to the club to entertain the employer's customers.

In-house tax and financial advice

This is a type of expenditure that the Revenue has ignored in the past, but certain Inspectors of Taxes are now treating this as a benefit-in-kind where the cost can clearly be allocated to particular employees. Similarly, the Revenue will seek to assess directors on a benefit-in-kind where work on their personal taxation affairs has been carried out by the company's auditors, the cost being recovered in whole or in part from the company.

Christmas parties and other functions

The Revenue does not assess a benefit in respect of 'modest' expenditure on a Christmas party for staff, provided the party is open to all staff. The limit regarded as modest in this context is £150 per head. If the cost (including VAT) amounts to £151 or more, the whole amount is taxable, not just the excess. Although this rule is generally attributed to Christmas parties, it may apply to a function at another time of year. The £150 annual 'allowance' can be used to cover the cost of more than one function.

Legal fees

There may be expenditure incurred for the benefit of the company's business but nevertheless is deemed to give rise to a benefit-in-kind. A leading case in this connection concerned a company director who was accused of dangerous driving. It was necessary for the company's business that he should not be imprisoned and the company paid his legal expenses. Although the lawyers engaged by the company were more expensive than the director would have used himself, the expenditure by the company was treated as a benefit-in-kind.

Outplacement counselling
(IT(E&P)A 2003, s 310)

The value of outplacement services provided to employees made redundant is exempt from income tax. Such services may include assistance with CVs, job searches, office equipment provisions and advice on interview skills. The Finance Act 2005 extended this exemption to part-time employees, previously it was restricted to full-time employees.

Goods and services provided at a discount to the normal price ('in-house benefits')

Where employees are allowed to purchase goods or services from their employer, no tax charge arises provided they pay an amount equal to the employer's cost. The House of Lords eventually decided that 'cost' meant marginal, and not average, cost (*Pepper* v *Hart* [1992] STC 898). This will normally produce a significantly lower benefit.

Following this case, the Revenue published an SP with regard to teachers, employees within the transport industry and other employees who receive goods or services from their employer. It stated that the *Pepper* v *Hart* decision means that:

(1) rail or bus travel by employees on terms that do not displace fare-paying passengers involves no or negligible additional costs;
(2) goods sold at a discount that leave employees paying at least the wholesale price involve no or negligible net benefit;
(3) where teachers pay 15% or more of a school's normal fees, there is no taxable benefit;
(4) professional services that do not require additional employees or partners (eg legal and financial services) have no or negligible cost to the employer (provided the employee meets the cost of any disbursements).

Funded Unapproved Retirement Benefit Schemes (FURBS)
(IT(E&P)A, s 386)

Some employers make contributions to a FURBS. The creation of a FURBS must be reported to the company's Inspector of Taxes within three months. For 2005–06 and previous years, the employer's contributions had also to be reported on Form P11D and the employee was treated as if he had received a benefit the cost of which is equal to the amount paid into the FURBS. No such charge arises for 2006–07 and later years. See 25.4 for details.

Making good benefits-in-kind for previous years

The cash equivalent of any benefit chargeable to tax under s 203 IT(E&P)A 2003 is the cost of the benefit 'less so much (if any) of it as is made good by the employee to those providing the benefit'. The Revenue accepts that there is no time limit for making good and, provided the relevant year's assessment has not been determined, there could be some merit in the person concerned taking further remuneration now and using the net cash left to him after PAYE to make good benefits provided for earlier years. This could be a particularly good idea where a director of a family company is faced with an income tax assessment plus penalties and interest in respect of prior year incorrect returns because benefits have not been reported properly.

For beneficial loans, however, the cash equivalent can be reduced by a payment in a later year only if the interest is paid under an obligation that existed at the time of the loan.

4.10 SHARE INCENTIVES

We cover the subject of share incentives in Chapter 5, both from the employee's point of view and from the employer's perspective.

There are many situations where a gift of shares or the exercise of an option gives rise to a liability for the employer to account for PAYE. Where this happens, the taxable income should be included in the figure for taxable pay on form P60.

There are also situations where shares are made available through a Revenue approved scheme and no income tax charge will arise on the acquisition of such shares provided the necessary conditions are satisfied.

In the case of other share incentives ('unapproved schemes'), the employee will need to complete a special schedule to his tax return (Share Schemes).

4.11 OPTIONS TO ACQUIRE GILTS

The treatment of non-approved employee share options was regarded as disadvantageous, but this was because of specific legislation on share options; the rules governing options involving other assets has been quite different. However, the FA 2003 introduced rules that apply to options over other securities such as British Government securities ('gilts') granted after 15 April 2003.

Under the old rules, an income tax charge could arise at the time an option was granted if the option had a market value. However, if the exercise of the option was conditional on the employee achieving demanding performance targets it is arguable that the option had little or no value at the time it was granted. Furthermore, no employment income tax charge would normally arise on the exercise of the option.

The FA 2003 provisions mean that a profit on the exercise of such an option granted after 15 April 2003 will generally be subject to income tax as employment income. Furthermore, the profit will normally be subject to PAYE.

4.12 OPTIONS TO ACQUIRE OTHER COMPANY ASSETS

The treatment of options involving other assets is quite different. An income tax charge may arise at the time an option is granted if the option has a market value. However, if the price at which the option may be exercised is higher than the asset's present market value, it is arguable that the option has little or no value at the time it is granted.

No employment income tax charge would normally arise on the exercise of the option. Furthermore, on a subsequent disposal of the asset there would normally be liability only for CGT on the profit over the amount paid. Although special care needs to be taken where the director or employee is connected (perhaps as a shareholder) with the company that grants the option, this type of option can provide substantial benefits.

Example – Option to acquire assets

A company director, who is not a shareholder, is granted the option to purchase surplus development land owned by the company for £150,000 at any time during a period of ten years. The land has a market value of only £125,000 at the time the option is granted and the option, therefore, has only a small value at that time. When the option is exercised the land has a market value of £250,000 and the director has in effect acquired a capital asset at a discount of £100,000 on its current market value. This discount would not normally be subject to income tax.

4.13 GOLDEN HELLOS

These are payments made to induce a prospective employee to take up employment with the company and are occasionally not taxable. In *Pritchard* v *Arundale* (1971) 47 TC 680, which involved a firm of chartered accountants, a senior partner was approached by a client to leave his practice and become a director of the client's company. In order to induce him to do this, he was given shares in the company that were held to be not a reward for services to be rendered in the future, but an inducement to leave his practice and take up the employment. It was therefore not taxable.

In *Vaughan-Neil* v *IRC* [1979] STC 644 a barrister received £40,000 to induce him to give up his practice and join a company as its 'in-house adviser'. Once again it was held that the payment was not taxable. By contrast, in *Glantre Engineering Ltd* v *Goodhand* [1983] STC 1 a payment by an engineering company to induce an employee of a firm of accountants to join them was held to be taxable.

The principles that emerge from these three cases are as follows:

(1) it must be clear from the facts that the payment is an inducement and not a reward for future services;

(2) the payment must not be returnable if the person does not take up the employment; and

(3) it is probably more likely that the payment will be accepted as non-taxable if the recipient has previously been in practice or self-employed rather than an employee of another company.

Shilton v *Wilmshurst* [1991] STC 88 extended these principles by deciding that a payment made by a football club to a footballer about to transfer as an inducement to him to join his new club was taxable. The House of Lords held that an emolument from an employment meant an emolument for being or becoming an employee and therefore would include a sum paid by a third party as an inducement to enter into a contract of employment to perform services in the future. It was not necessary for the payer to have any interest in the performance of those services.

In *Silva* v *Charnock* 2202 SpC 332, the taxpayer had taken a career break to study for an MBA. Her tuition fees cost her £18,000. After getting her MBA, she took a new job and received a signing-on bonus of £18,000. It was held that this was not taxable as it fell within the exemption contained in TA 1988, s 200B.

4.14 RESTRICTIVE COVENANTS
(IT(E&P)A 2003, s 155)

Where the present, past or future holder of an office or employment gives an undertaking that restricts his conduct or activities, any sum paid in respect of that restrictive covenant is treated as remuneration from the office or employment for the year in which the payment is received. This rule applies even where the covenant is not legally valid. In some cases, valuable consideration other than money is given for the restrictive covenant and in such a situation a sum equal to the value of that consideration is treated as having been paid. The payment may not necessarily come from the employer and so a payment to an employee that was made by a major shareholder in a family company may well be caught under these provisions.

4.15 REDUNDANCY PAYMENTS
(IT(E&P)A 2003, s 309)

A statutory redundancy payment made under the Employment Protection (Consolidation) Act 1978 is exempt from tax, although it may need to be taken into account in computing the tax payable on a termination payment (see 4.16). The Revenue generally treats payment to an employee under a non-statutory redundancy scheme as exempt under SP1/94 where the following conditions are satisfied:

(1) payments are made only on accounts of redundancy as defined in s 81 of the 1978 Act;
(2) the individual has at least two years' continuous service;

(3) payments are made to all relevant employees and not merely to a selected group of employees; and

(4) the payments are not excessively large in relation to earnings and length of service.

In *Mairs* v *Haughey* [1993] STC 569 the Revenue sought to tax a payment made to an employee for giving up contingent redundancy rights. The Revenue argued that the payment constituted an emolument of the employment, but it was held that a redundancy payment is not an emolument and a lump sum paid in lieu of a right to receive such payment is equally not an emolument. This case also cast doubt on the view still generally held within the Revenue that a termination payment is always taxable where the employee is contractually entitled to it.

4.16 GOLDEN HANDSHAKES, OTHER TERMINATION PAYMENTS AND CONTINUING BENEFITS
(IT(E&P)A 2003, s 401)

4.16.1 Introduction

Where a director's or employee's contract of service is terminated, it may be possible for a compensation or *ex gratia* payment to be made that is either wholly or partly tax free provided the employee is not entitled to the compensation under a contract of service and the payment is not deemed to be a benefit under a retirement benefit scheme. Where the individual receives compensation under a term of his employment contract, the Revenue's view is that it is taxable in the usual way. A payment made to a director as compensation for accepting a reduced salary or any other variation of his service contract is not regarded as a termination payment, and the amount received is normally taxable in full. However, the Revenue lost in the recent case of *Wilson* v *Clayton* where an employer was required by an employment tribunal to reinstate an employee and make a payment of £5,060.

The Revenue succeeded in a 2004 case (*Allum & Allum* v *Marsh* SpC 446) in arguing that voluntary payments to outgoing directors were, in fact, no more than a payment for past services and therefore taxable in full as emoluments.

4.16.2 Exemptions from the charge under s 401

There are various types of termination payment that are exempt:

(1) Payments made because of termination of employment through death, injury or disability. Disability covers not only a condition arising from a sudden affliction, but also a continuing incapacity to perform the

duties of an office or employment because of the culmination of a process of deterioration of physical or mental health caused by chronic illness (see SP10/81).

(2) Terminal grants and gratuities to members of HM forces.

(3) Lump sum payments from Commonwealth government superannuation schemes or compensation for loss of career owing to constitutional changes in Commonwealth countries.

(4) A special contribution by an employer into an approved retirement benefit scheme.

(5) A lump sum payment where the employment has constituted foreign service that exceeds the following limits:

(a) three-quarters of the whole period of service;

(b) the last ten years;

(c) one-half of the period of service provided this amounted to at least 20 years and subject to at least ten of the last 20 years of service being foreign service.

(6) 'Foreign' service is defined as meaning a period of service during which the earnings were not taxable because either the individual was not resident in the UK or the 100% deduction was available because the period spent working overseas exceeded 365 days.

4.16.3 Basic £30,000 exemption
(IT(E&P)A 2003, s 404)

Where a termination payment is not wholly exempt, the first £30,000 is normally tax free and only the balance is chargeable. Where an individual receives both statutory redundancy payments and a termination payment, the amount of the statutory redundancy payments uses up part of the £30,000 exemption and only the balance is available to cover part of the termination payment.

4.16.4 Employment includes a period of foreign service

The £30,000 exemption may be increased where the employment has included 'foreign service'.

Example – Increased exemption owing to foreign service

> B was non-resident in the UK from 1986 to 1994. He then qualified for a 100% deduction from 1994 to 1996, so that he was not subject to UK tax on his salary even though he was resident (this deduction was abolished in 1998 – it applied where a UK resident individual worked overseas for a period of at least 365 days). B retires in December 2007 and receives compensation of £80,000. The exemption is found by using the fraction:
>
> $$\frac{\text{Foreign services}}{\text{Total period of employment}} \text{, i.e. in this case } \frac{10 \text{ years}}{21 \text{ years}}$$
>
> This fraction is applied to the amount of the golden handshake after deduction of the £30,000 exemption. The taxable amount would be arrived at as follows:
>
> | | £ |
> |---|---|
> | Compensation | 80,000 |
> | *Less*: 'normal exemption' | (30,000) |
> | | 50,000 |
> | $^{10}/_{21}$ thereof | (23,809) |
> | Taxable amount | 26,191 |

4.16.5 Year for which a termination payment may be taxed

It used to be the case that the time when a termination payment was made did not affect the tax liability because it was always treated as taxable income for the year in which the employment was terminated. However, since 1998–99, it has been the year of receipt that counts and termination payments are taxed as income of the year in which they are received.

4.16.6 Taxation of continuing payments and benefits

Redundancy and other termination settlements often include provisions for payments to be made or benefits to continue after termination. Such benefits are taxable only as they arise. So, both benefits and payments are taxable in the year when received or enjoyed (not in the year of termination).

Example – Benefits-in-kind following redundancy

> M was made redundant on 6 October 2006 and received a lump sum of £20,000 plus a further £20,000 on 6 April 2007. She also continued in the company medical insurance scheme for 18 months at a continuing cost to the employer of £350 in 2006–07 and £650 in 2007–08.
>
> In 2006–07 M received a combined redundancy package of £20,350 that is covered by the £30,000 exemption. The £9,650 exemption balance is carried forward to the following year. In 2007–08 she received the balance of the package of £20,650, of which £9,650 is exempt. The medical benefit of £650 is covered by the balance of the exemption as is £9,000 of the cash payment, leaving £11,000 to be taxed at the basic rate under PAYE.

4.16.7 Certain benefits are not taxed on former employees

(The Employer-Financed Retirement Benefits Schemes (Excluded Benefits for Tax Purposes) Regulations 2007 SI 2007 No 3537)

No charge arises where an employer continues to provide certain benefits after an employment has ceased. These benefits are:

- living accommodation and related benefits;
- non-cash benefits received before 6 April 1999;
- welfare counselling;
- recreational benefits;
- annual parties and similar functions;
- writing of wills, etc;
- equipment for disabled employees.

4.16.8 *Ex gratia* payments

There has been concern that *ex gratia* payments may be subject to tax as unapproved retirement benefits taxable as employment income under IT(E&P)A 2003, s 393. If this charge arises, the £30,000 exemption is not available. The Revenue issued SP13/91 in October 1991 and subsequently has clarified the position. An *ex gratia* payment is normally regarded as a retirement benefit taxable under s 393 only where it is paid in connection with an individual's retirement.

The Revenue has also given the following guidelines on hypothetical situations:

(1) A person who has worked for a company for 20 years leaves at age 54 to take a senior executive position in another company – 'golden handshake'.

(2) A long-service employee leaves to take a senior executive position in another company at age 60 – borderline, probably retirement.

(3) A division of a company is sold and the 55-year-old manager responsible for running it leaves to take a job with the purchaser – 'golden handshake'.

(4) A person in his 50s has a heart attack and is advised by his doctor to leave and seek a less stressful position – 'golden handshake'.

(5) An employee aged 35 is involved in an accident and suffers disabilities that make him unable to continue with his job – 'golden handshake'.

(6) An employee aged 50 leaves to take a job nearer home to nurse her aged parents – borderline, 'golden handshake': if the employee did not take a new job, or was nearer normal retirement age, this situation would be treated as retirement.

4.16.9 Payments in lieu of notice (PILONs)

PILONs have featured increasingly in employment contracts in recent years as employees have tried to formalise their rights and employers have wanted to be able to enforce restrictive covenants and prevent ex-employees using confidential information that they have acquired in the course of their employment. The Revenue set out its opinion in a lengthy article in Tax Bulletin August 1996. In large measure, the Revenue's interpretations have been upheld by the courts (see *EMI Electronics Group Ltd* v *Coldicott*). Also see *SCA Packaging Limited* v *HMRC* [2007] EWHC 270.

The term 'PILON' is sometimes used loosely to include payments to employees on 'garden leave'. This is not correct. An employee on garden leave is still an employee: he cannot take another job until the end of the notice period. All that has changed is that he is not required to carry out any duties. Payments to such an employee are taxable in the normal way and the employer should deduct tax under PAYE.

There are also situations where the employee's service contract actually provides for a PILON, usually at the employer's option. The Revenue's view is that where an employer decides to make a PILON, the payment is made under the contract rather than as compensation for the contract having been broken. As such, it remains taxable in full and PAYE deductions should be made.

Rather more controversially, the Revenue argues that there may be an implied term to an employment contract where an employer customarily makes PILONs. This is common in certain industries (IT, stockbroking, asset management) where the last thing an employer wants is for an employee who is serving out a notice period to have continued access to confidential information or to clients. You should take professional advice if you are an employer who has a history of regularly making PILONs.

Virtually the only circumstances in which you can be completely confident that a PILON will be treated as a golden handshake (see 4.16.1) is where the payment is a 'one-off' exception to your normal rule, and there is no reference to the possibility of such a payment in the service contract or related documents such as the staff handbook. In this situation, the first £30,000 is normally exempt from tax.

4.17 DESIGNING A 'TAX EFFICIENT' REMUNERATION PACKAGE

Where an individual has a real degree of influence over the way his total remuneration package of salary and benefits is made up, the following should be borne in mind.

(1) Pension schemes are very tax efficient.
(2) Approved share options are treated more favourably than non-approved options.
(3) The legislation on benefits-in-kind still leaves some scope for manoeuvre.
(4) Golden handshakes are not always taxable.

4.17.1 Advantages of pension funds in general

There can be no better medium to long-term investment than a pension scheme. The fact that pension schemes are not subject to tax internally because of the funds' exemption from UK income tax and CGT, combined with the facility to take one quarter of the fund as a tax-free lump sum at retirement, means that the overall return will almost certainly beat any comparable investment. Furthermore, an employer's contribution does not attract NIC.

4.17.2 Employer can contribute up to £235,000 pa

An employer can make contributions of up to £235,000 pa provided that the contributions do not take the employee's pension fund over the lifetime allowance (see 25.1.2). This allowance is £1.65 million for 2008–09.

4.17.3 Employee shares

With CGT at 18%, an employee share scheme can form part of a very attractive benefits package. However, close attention needs to be given to the rules on special shares (see 5.6). Bear in mind the election under 5.7.7 where shares have only a small initial value as it could be well worth accepting a modest income tax charge upfront in order to ensure that the capital appreciation will be subject only to CGT.

4.17.4 Approved share option schemes

The tax treatment of an individual who exercises an approved share option or receives shares via an approved profit-sharing scheme is significantly better off than someone who benefits via an unapproved arrangement. Basically, no tax charge arises on the exercise of an approved share option provided that the necessary conditions have been observed (see 5.5.4).

The conclusion must be that wherever an individual has a choice, he should normally participate via an approved rather than a non-approved scheme.

The other approved schemes introduced in FA 2000 must also be borne in mind, especially the EMI scheme (see 5.6).

4.17.5 Tax efficient benefits-in-kind

Despite the Government's long-term intention to remove any discrimination between the tax treatment of benefits-in-kind and cash remuneration, there are still certain benefits-in-kind that are treated favourably for tax purposes. If a person is a company director, or someone else who has a degree of say in the way his remuneration package is made up, significant tax benefits can be secured by a judicious choice of benefits-in-kind.

Company cars or cash allowance?

You need to check that you will be better off with a company car as opposed to receiving a cash allowance with which you can buy your own car and then charge for business mileage at the flat-rate mileage allowances (see 4.4.9).

It may pay to buy your company car

Because of the high rate of depreciation in the first year, it may be advantageous for a director to arrange for his company to purchase a car with a view to its being sold to him after it has been used for a period. Provided he pays the full market value for the car in its second-hand condition, there will be no tax charge on the difference between the cost of the car to the company and the amount at which the director purchases it. Admittedly, there is a scale benefit for the period the company owns the car, but this is often significantly less than the vehicle's depreciation during the period concerned.

Car fuel

Where an employee or director has a company car, it is clearly beneficial that he should have as much free petrol as possible as the scale benefit does not vary according to how much private petrol is provided.

Interest-free loans

There is a *de minimis* limit so that, if an individual has a beneficial loan from his company, no income tax charge arises unless the loan exceeds £5,000.

Company accommodation

It may be possible to secure a reduction in the taxable benefit that arises when a director or employee occupies a company property. This is a complex area where you should take professional advice.

4.17.6 Golden handshakes are not always taxable

A termination payment can still be treated favourably, either because of the £30,000 exemption or because it qualifies for total exemption (see 4.16).

5

SHARE INCENTIVES

ANNE-MARIE BODEN

Shares are seen as an especially attractive form of employee compensation. Share incentive schemes are often a way in which an employee can acquire a capital asset and an opportunity to make gains that are based on the increase in value of shares and which can vastly exceed his salary. Unfortunately, legislators have focused on this. Lengthy and complex legislation contains many wide-ranging anti-avoidance provisions, which may apply if the share incentive arrangements do not form part of an approved scheme. On the other hand, many employers prefer to establish unapproved schemes because of the extra flexibility in the way schemes can be operated.

In this chapter we look at:

(1) Gifts of shares.
(2) Profit-sharing schemes.
(3) Non-approved share options.
(4) Approved share option schemes.
(5) Enterprise Management Incentives.
(6) Special shares, etc.
(7) The employer's perspective.
(8) Some tax planning ideas.

5.1 GIFTS OF SHARES

A gift of shares to an employee is normally a taxable benefit, the charge being based on the shares' market value. Much the same applies when an employee buys shares for less than their real market value. If the shares are given to the employee by a shareholder, he is normally treated as if he had made a disposal of the shares at their market value, and therefore may be liable for CGT.

The tax position where an employee is allowed to subscribe for new shares at an undervalue is broadly the same. The employee is taxed on the difference between the amount he pays to subscribe for the shares and their market value. However, dealing with matters in this way usually avoids any CGT problems for the shareholders (because there is no disposal by the existing shareholders or the company, merely an issue of new shares).

A company must report the acquisition of shares by an employee as a 'reportable event' on form 42. This return must be submitted to the Revenue by 6 July following the end of the tax year.

Tax notes

You should take advice on your CGT position if you are considering making a gift of some of your shares to an employee.

PAYE must be accounted for if either the shares are marketable securities (see 20.1) or trading arrangements are in place. There is then a further liability for PAYE if the individual does not reimburse the company within 90 days of its having paid the tax.

5.2 PROFIT-SHARING SCHEMES
(TA 1988, ss 186–187)

These schemes were effectively phased-out in 2002–03. They operated by means of a trust, with the trustees receiving payments from the company's profits to enable them to buy shares, which they then 'appropriated' to employees. The amount that could be appropriated to an employee under the scheme could be between £3,000 and £8,000. No appropriation of shares under such a plan has been possible since 31 December 2002 but employees may still be receiving shares appropriated to them before that date. For details of the tax treatment, see Zurich Tax Handbook 2006–07 at 5.2.

5.3 NON-APPROVED SHARE OPTIONS
(IT(E&P)A 2003, s 471)

5.3.1 Introduction

An income tax charge may arise on the exercise of a share option that was granted by reason of the individual's office or employment. The legislation was introduced in a piecemeal way and it is often difficult to discern any clear or logical structure or principles that underlie it.

5.3.2 Non-approved share options
(IT(E&P)A 2003, s 471)

A tax charge may arise on the exercise of the option. The grant of the option is not an event that gives rise to an income tax charge.

Exercise of the option

A person who is subject to tax under section 15 IT(E&P)A 2003 (formerly Schedule E Case I) (see 4.1.1) may be subject to an income tax charge when he exercises a non-approved share option that has been granted by reason of an office or employment. The charge is not dependent on his selling the shares but arises on any profit or gain that he is deemed to have made by exercising the option. Normally the profit is simply the difference between the shares' market value at the time he exercises his option and the price payable under the option.

Example – exercise of share options

A was granted an option to acquire 1,000 shares in XYZ Ltd at a price of £2 per share. After five years have elapsed, he exercises the option and pays £2,000 to acquire the 1,000 shares. By this time the shares have grown in value to £5 per share. *A* will be assessed for the year in which he exercises the option. His profit will be assessed as £3,000, ie:

	£
Market value of 1,000 shares	5,000
Less: amount paid	(2,000)
	3,000

If the employee agrees to pay the employer's NICs on the profit from exercising the option, the NICs are deducted in arriving at the taxable amount.

5.3.3 Employee's residence status

Before 6 April 2008, no charge arose under s471 unless the employee was resident and ordinarily resident in the UK at the date the option was granted. However, a charge can now arise on the exercise of an option granted on or after 6 April 2008 to an individual who was resident but not ordinarily resident in the UK.

The charge still applies where an individual who was resident and ordinarily resident when the option was granted exercised his option after he had ceased to be resident in the UK. In some cases, the income tax charge may be reduced because of relief due under a double taxation agreement. There is a helpful article on the way the Revenue applies these rules to internationally mobile employees in *Tax Bulletin* 76 April 2005.

5.3.4 Other employee share options
(IT(E&P)A 2003, ss 193–197)

Where an individual exercises an option that was granted to him as an employee at a time when he was either not resident in the UK or not ordinarily resident, and he retains the shares, an income tax charge may arise on their eventual disposal. The legislation on beneficial loans contains deeming provisions that treat the difference between the shares' market value at the time the option is exercised and the amount payable to exercise the option as if it were a loan. On a subsequent sale or disposal of the shares, the loan is deemed to be written off and an income tax charge arises if the individual is UK-resident at that time. If you think you may be in this situation, you should seek professional advice.

5.3.5 Reporting requirements

The grant or exercise of options must be notified on form 42 by 6 July following the end of the tax year.

PAYE must be accounted for on profits from options where the shares are marketable securities or trading arrangements are in place. A further charge can arise unless the employee reimburses his employer within 90 days (see 20.1.4).

5.3.6 Capital gains tax

See 12.10.3 on the CGT consequences of disposing of shares acquired under an unapproved share option.

5.3.7 Retrospective legislation on options that form part of tax schemes

The FA 2006 contains legislation that imposes a charge on certain options granted on or after 2 December 2004.

The legislation contains a 'purpose test' – basically, special rules apply where the right or opportunity to acquire a securities option was granted mainly to avoid tax or NIC. Options caught by this rule are taken out of the tax regime described in 5.3.1–5.3.6 and are taxed under a different part of IT(E&P) A 2003. This is achieved by the securities option being taxed under legislation that applies to convertible securities (see the last part of 5.7.10), which would not otherwise be applicable to options

HMRC has published the following example of the tax consequences where an option after 1 December 2004 fails the purpose test.

Example of the charge under FA 2006

> An option to purchase securities is used as part of an avoidance scheme. This brings into play anti-avoidance legislation enacted in F(No 2)A 2005 that applies where convertible securities are acquired under an avoidance scheme. The application of this legislation means that the individual is taxed on the acquisition of the convertible security and the measure of the tax charge is based on a notional market value which assumes that the entitlement to convert is immediate and unconditional. The effect is to bring into charge the maximum possible gain.

5.4 APPROVED SHARE OPTION SCHEMES

(IT(E&P)A 2003, ss 517–526)

5.4.1 Introduction

The main types of approved share option schemes for employees are:

(1) schemes linked to save as you earn (SAYE);
(2) Share Incentive Plan (SIP)
(3) Company Share Option Plan (CSOP); and
(4) Enterprise Management Incentives (EMI) (see 5.5).

Approved SAYE-linked schemes were introduced in 1980. Their main features are that there is a limit on the value of the shares that may be allocated to an employee, and participation in the scheme must be open to all full-time employees who have completed five years' service.

In 1984 the Government introduced another category of approved share options intended to cover special arrangements for senior executives. The maximum amounts involved are much more generous and there is no requirement that the option be granted to all employees.

It is possible for an employer to establish both types of scheme and, indeed, to grant non-approved share options as well.

5.4.2 Approved SAYE-linked share option schemes

These schemes entail the grant of an option for employees to purchase company shares at a price that must not be 'manifestly less' than 80% of their market value at the time the options are granted. The employee is required to take out an SAYE-linked savings scheme (maximum £250 pm) and may use the proceeds to exercise the share option three, five or seven years later, depending on the rules of the particular scheme. No income tax liability arises on the grant or exercise of the options. CGT is charged on an eventual disposal of the shares.

5.4.3 Reporting requirements

The grant or exercise of options must be notified on Form 34 by 6 July following the end of the tax year.

For more details obtain a copy of Revenue leaflet IR97.

Tax notes

SAYE schemes are a 'one way bet'. If the share price goes up, exercise the option. If the share price goes down, take your cash from the SAYE scheme instead.

5.4.4 Share Incentive Plan (SIP)
(IT(E&P)A 2003, ss 488–515)

These schemes may involve one or more of the following elements:

- Free shares.
- Partnership shares.
- Matching shares.

The principle behind this scheme is that all employees should participate on similar terms. However, if an employer awards free shares, the award may be partly or wholly by reference to performance targets. Under the scheme, trustees acquire shares in the employing or holding company of a group. No income tax or NICs are payable on the award of shares. All income and capital growth that arises while the trustees hold shares will normally be tax-free. The shares must be fully paid-up ordinary shares in a company that is not controlled by another company or shares in a quoted subsidiary of a company that is not a close company (see 17.13).

5.4.5 Free shares

An employee may be awarded free shares with a value of up to £3,000 pa. The shares may be awarded partly by reference to criteria based on salary, length of service, etc. In such a case, other employees may be awarded shares by reference to performance provided the highest performance-linked award does not exceed four times the highest award by reference to non-performance linked criteria. In other cases (eg where all awards are by reference to performance), the employer must demonstrate to the Revenue's satisfaction that the performance targets are broadly comparable.

Wherever awards are to be made by reference to performance, the targets and other criteria must be communicated to employees in advance. Performance criteria may be linked to individual, team, divisional or corporate performance.

Free shares must be held by the trustees for a period of between three and five years. Shares can, at the employer's discretion, be awarded so that they will be forfeited if the employee leaves within three years.

Tax notes

If you participate in one of these schemes it will generally be best not to take out your free shares during the first three years. If you do so, you will be liable for income tax.

5.4.6 **Partnership shares**

Employees may relinquish up to £1,500 of their pay in return for 'partnership' shares being acquired by the trustees on their behalf. No income tax or NICs arise on salary foregone in this way, but the employing company receives a deduction in arriving at its taxable profits equal to the amount relinquished. The partnership shares cannot be subject to forfeiture, but the scheme rules can require the trustees to pay out on the employee leaving.

Where an employee withdraws from the scheme within three years, income tax and NICs are payable on the shares' market value at the date of withdrawal. Where he withdraws after three but before five years have elapsed, the employee is charged on the lower of the shares' initial value or their market value at the time that he withdraws.

Where an employment comes to an end because of disability or redundancy, the shares may be withdrawn tax free even if this occurs within the three-year period.

Tax notes

It will generally be best (from a tax point of view) if you keep partnership shares within the scheme for five years to avoid the income tax charge completely.

5.4.7 **Matching shares**

If an employer so wishes, matching shares can be awarded to employees on a basis of up to 2:1 (ie shares worth £3,000 for an employee who relinquished salary of £1,500 in order to 'buy' partnership shares worth £1,500). An award of matching shares may be made on the basis that they are forfeited if the employee leaves within three years or withdraws his partnership shares during that period.

5.4.8 **Dividends**

The legislation gives employers a choice of whether to offer dividend reinvestment. If dividends are paid out they are taxable income for the employees. However, dividends may be reinvested tax-free up to £1,500 pa.

5.4.9 **Reporting requirements**

Each year, a Form 39 return is required for each approved scheme. The trustees will also receive a Trust SA Return for completion.

5.4.10 Company Share Option Plan (CSOP)

The general principle is that an income tax charge may arise on the exercise of a share option, but certain approved share option schemes may be established that avoid such an income tax liability. CGT may still apply, but only on a subsequent disposal of the shares concerned.

5.4.11 Conditions for approval

To receive Revenue approval, the following conditions must be satisfied:

(1) Participation in the scheme must be open only to full-time directors or employees or to part-time employees working at least 20 hours pw. Part-time directors may not participate in this scheme: the Revenue has indicated that it regards a director who works 25 hours pw as full-time. The employer may choose which employees are to be permitted to participate in the scheme.

(2) Where the employer is a close company, no participant must own (or be entitled to acquire as a result of the grant of the option) more than 10% of the company's shares. Furthermore, no individual who has owned more than 10% of the company's shares within the previous 12 months can participate.

(3) The price at which the option is to be exercised must not be 'manifestly less' than the shares' value at the time the option is granted.

(4) There is a limit on the number of shares over which a particular employee may be granted options. The scheme must limit the employee's options to shares with a market value at the time the options are granted that does not exceed £30,000.

(5) The shares issued under the scheme must be fully paid ordinary shares of the company or its parent company. They must be shares either quoted on a recognised stock exchange, or in a non-close company controlled by a quoted company, or in a company not under the control of another company.

(6) Options must not be transferable.

(7) The exemption from income tax applies only to options exercised between three and ten years after they are granted or where the option is exercised within three years because of the individual's employment coming to an end by reason of retirement, redundancy, injury or disability (the rules were more restrictive prior to 9 April 2003).

(8) There has been an income tax charge on individuals who exercise options under the scheme more than once every three years. This three-year time limit was waived if a director or employee died and the option was exercised by the personal representatives within one year of death. The charge was removed altogether by FA 2003 in relation to options exercised after 8 April 2003.

5.4.12 Reporting requirements

The grant or exercise of options must be notified on Form 35 by 6 July following the end of the tax year.

You may find it helpful to obtain a copy of Revenue leaflet IR101.

Tax notes

These approved options mean that you are not subject to an income tax charge unless you exercise the option within the first three years. You are subject to CGT but only when you sell the shares. If you transfer some to your spouse (and you have no other capital gains in the year), you can each realise tax-free capital gains of £9,600.

5.5 ENTERPRISE MANAGEMENT INCENTIVES (EMI)
(IT(E&P)A 2003, ss 527–541)

The main aspects of the EMI option scheme are as follows:

(1) Share options can be issued to employees (pre-FA 2001, there was a limit of 15 employees).

(2) The shares over which options are granted can have a value of up to £120,000 per employee (£100,000 before 6 April 2008). This refers to the value at the time the options are granted. The total value of shares over which options can be granted is £3m (£1.5m before FA 2001).

(3) The price at which options may be exercised may be more or less than market value at the time the options are granted.

(4) The only income tax charge is on exercise of the options and is equal to the difference between the shares' market value at the time of grant less the exercise price. If the options are granted at the market value, no tax is payable.

(5) If the shares are readily convertible assets at the time the option is exercised, NICs are charged on the same basis as the income tax charge described above. If the options were issued at market value, there is no charge. There are also significant CGT benefits for the employees.

(6) The shares acquired by the employees qualified for the business asset rate of taper relief. For disposals before 6 April 2008, taper relief provided relief for CGT for individuals based on the length of ownership. Under the EMI rules, the period of ownership was deemed to start from when the share options are granted (the rules for other share option schemes are that the period starts when the shares are acquired). Overall this meant that, provided the shares were sold two years after the options were granted, the maximum CGT rate was 10%. This particular aspect has been overtaken by the abolition of taper relief from 6 April 2008.

(6) Where the conditions for entrepreneurs relief are satisfied, see 16.8, the rate of capital gains tax may be 10%. However, among other conditions, there is a 12-month ownership requirement and this period runs from the date that the EMI option is exercised.

Only certain companies can operate the scheme, and certain employees may be ineligible. A summary of the rules is as follows:

(a) the company must be independent and not under the control of another company;
(b) it must be carrying on a qualifying trade defined as for EIS purposes (see 18.3.4) – this trade must be carried on mainly in the UK;
(c) its gross assets cannot exceed £30m at the time the options are granted. The £30m test is applied on a consolidated basis where the company is the parent of a group of companies. The FA 2007 contains a relieving provision that prevents a company from failing the £30m test simply by reason of its transferring an intangible asset within the group;
(d) the company must have fewer than 250 employees (new condition from the date the Finance Act received Royal assent.);
(e) the employee must be employed for at least 25 hours pw or, if less, 75% of his working time;
(f) the option ceases to qualify once the employee no longer meets the 25 hours per week requirement (this rule was relaxed for reservists who were required to serve in the Iraq war);
(g) the employee must not own more than 30% of the shares in the company.

The grant of an EMI option must be notified to the Revenue within 92 days.

Where an individual exercises an EMI option, the shares may be restricted shares (see 5.5.6 below). He is regarded as automatically making the election described at 5.6.7 if there is no income tax charge under (4) above (as this will always be to his advantage).

Where a company is taken over by another company which itself is able to establish an EMI scheme, an individual can surrender his options for replacement options in an EMI scheme set up by the new parent company. The value of the shares over which the new options are granted must not exceed the value at the time of the takeover of the shares to which the original options related.

5.5.1 Reporting requirements

The grant of share options should be notified for EMI no more than 92 days from the date of grant. Adjustments or exercise of options should be notified on form 40 by 6 July following the end of the tax year.

> **Tax notes**
>
> EMI options are the most favourable type of options because they are flexible in that there is no minimum holding period and the share valuation can be agreed with HMRC before the grant of the options. Where the conditions for entrepeneurs relief are satisfied, the rate of capital gains tax may be 10%.

5.6 SPECIAL SHARES, ETC
(IT(E&P)A 2003, ss 417–470)

5.6.1 Background

The legislation on employee shares (also called 'employment-related securities') was substantially amended by Schedule 22 FA 2003, which focused on special shares such as restricted shares and convertible shares. It also dealt with situations where employee shareholders are treated in an especially favourable way.

In the main, Schedule 22 applies only to securities acquired on or after 16 April 2003 (but note the exception to this for conversion of employment-related securities (see 5.6.10 below).

Sections 5.6.2–5.6.7 below will not apply to events that occur more than seven years after the individual has ceased to be an employee of the company awarding the shares.

Further information is available on the Revenue's website (www.hmrc.gov.uk/shareschemes).

5.6.2 Restricted securities

Until 5 April 2008, the charge on restricted securities applied only if the securities were acquired at a time when the employee was resident and ordinarily resident in the UK. It now also applies to restricted securities acquired by employees who are resident but not ordinarily resident in the UK where the securities are awarded on or after 6 April 2008.

Sometimes shares or other securities are given (ie 'awarded') to employees and the shares are subject to special restrictions, eg in relation to voting rights. The shares may become much more valuable once the restrictions cease to apply. Similarly, shares may be awarded on the basis that they will be forfeited if a target is not met or if the employee leaves within a certain period. In such a situation, the employee only acquires full ownership of the shares when the forfeiture provisions fall away. Forfeiture provisions are really just a special type of restriction on the individual's ownership of his shares.

5.6.3 Meaning of 'restrictions'

Restrictions include the following:

- restrictions on dividend rights;
- restrictions on voting rights;
- restrictions on transferability.

The legislation provides that shares are not to be treated as restricted if the only restrictions are that:

- partly-paid shares will be forfeited if outstanding calls are not paid;
- the shares have to be sold if the employee is dismissed for misconduct;
- the shares are redeemable for payment.

For further details, see Figure 5.1.

5.6.4 Charge depends on whether the restrictions can apply for more than five years

Schedule 22 made a significant distinction on restrictions that might last for more than five years.

5.6.5 Restrictions capable of lasting more than five years

If the shares or securities are subject to longer-term restrictions, an income tax charge will arise on the award of the shares and a further charge on the restrictions ceasing to apply. This is not a double charge; the amount taxed on the award of the shares is the market value of those shares, taking into account the effect of the restrictions, less anything paid by the employee for the shares. When these restrictions are lifted, the amount taxed is the market value of the shares at that time less the value used to calculate the tax charge on the award of the shares.

Example

Mr T was given shares on 1 June 2007 that had an open market value of £1,000. However, Mr T would forfeit them if he leaves his employer before 1 July 2013. The effect of this restriction is to depress the value on acquisition to £650 (ie a 35% discount). When the forfeiture provisions cease to apply on 1 July 2013, the shares are worth £5,000.

A tax charge arose for 2007–08 on £650 and will arise for 2013–14 on £1,750, ie 35% of £5,000.

Figure 5.1 – Does removal of restrictions mean there is an income tax charge?

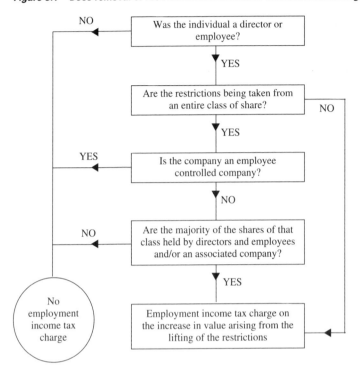

5.6.6 Restrictions not capable of lasting five years

Where the restrictions involve forfeiture provisions that can apply only for a period of five years or less, there will normally be no income tax charge on the shares or securities being awarded. The charge will normally be triggered by the release of the restrictions or the forfeiture provisions coming to an end and will be based on the market value at that time. Thus, if in the previous example the restrictions had been due to expire within five years, Mr *T* would not have been taxed on £650 for 2007–08 but he would have been taxed on £5,000 for the year in which the restrictions ceased to be operative.

However, if the employee and employer jointly elect within 14 days, the employee can be subject to an income tax charge on the value of his shares, taking into account the effect of the restrictions. If he accepts this charge, there will be a reduction in the charge which will apply on the restrictions ceasing to apply. For example, if the value of the restricted shares is only 30% of the market value of shares which are free from restrictions, the effect of making the election will be that the employee pays income tax on

30% of the full value for the year in which the shares are awarded and on 70% of the market value when the restrictions cease to apply (ie similar treatment to that in the example at 5.6.5 above).

5.6.7 Election to accept the tax charge upfront
(ss 430–431 IT(E&P)A 2003)

There is a further election that is available. The employee can choose to accept a tax charge on the full value, leaving the restrictions out of account. If he adopts this course of action, there will be no further income tax charge on the restrictions being lifted, the employee will have 'taken his medicine' upfront.

This election is available regardless of whether the restrictions are capable of remaining in force for more than five years. It must be made within 14 days of the shares being awarded.

Tax notes

Take advice on the value of shares at the time you receive them because it may be better to accept a modest upfront tax charge to avoid having to pay tax when the forfeiture provisions expire.

5.6.8 Charge where value is extracted before the restrictions are lifted
(s 446A IT(E&P)A 2003)

In the past, an employee could acquire shares that were subject to forfeiture. The income tax charge would have arisen by reference to the value on acquisition and would normally have been trivial. Before the forfeiture period came to an end, the company might pay a substantial dividend. When the forfeiture period expired, the market value of the shares was substantially reduced by the payment of that dividend and the amount charged under Schedule E would have been limited to this much reduced value. The overall effect was that the employee received his profit as a dividend that was subject to income tax at a more favourable rate. Schedule 22 imposed an income tax charge based on the market value before reduction by reason of the dividend.

5.6.9 Special rules where restrictions are part of a tax avoidance scheme

The FA 2004 varied Schedule 22. There is an exception to the general rule that no employment income tax charge arises on the acquisition of shares which are subject to forfeiture for up to five years (see 5.6.6 above). As from 7 May 2004, the legislation imposes a charge where the market value of the shares at the date that the restrictions are lifted has been artificially decreased by things done other than for genuine commercial purposes.

The new legislation was purposely drafted in wide terms and can apply where transactions are part of a scheme or arrangement designed to avoid tax or NICs. A charge can also arise where the market value of shares is artificially increased as part of such a scheme or arrangement.

Further anti-avoidance rules were unveiled by the December 2004 mini-Budget. Also, the Minister gave notice of the Government's intention to counteract future avoidance schemes by bringing in retrospective legislation. The FA 2006 contains such retrospective provisions.

5.6.10 Convertible securities
(s 439 IT(E&P)A 2003)

It is not necessary for this legislation to apply that the individual was resident and ordinarily resident in the UK at the time that he acquired the securities.

An income tax charge can arise on the value of any new shares received when a share conversion takes place and the original shares were employment-related securities. It can also arise on an employee selling convertible securities to a third-party or on his receiving a payment for relinquishing the conversion rights. The amount charged takes account of any amount already charged on the acquisition of the original shares.

This charge is intended to catch schemes where an employee receives shares with a low value that are later converted to shares with a much higher value. The charge does not normally arise where the event is triggered by the employee being disabled.

Section 439 can apply where employment-related securities were held before the 2003 Budget but are converted after 1 September 2003. There has been concern that s 439 could apply to a gain realised by a former owner of a company on the completion of an earn-out satisfied by the issue of loan notes or other securities. This is likely to be a problem where the individual is required to remain with the company after selling out and he is receiving more than other vendors or where the earn-out is closely linked with his personal performance.

The F(No 2)A 2005 introduced special rules where convertible securities are acquired as part of a tax avoidance scheme. Income tax may be charged on a notional market value of the option at acquisition, with this value being arrived at on the assumption that the right to convert is immediate and unconditional. The effect is to bring into charge the maximum possible gain.

Tax notes

Make sure that HMRC will not regard an issue of convertible securities to you as being part of a tax avoidance scheme because the consequences of a tax charge under the 2005 legislation can be dire.

5.6.11 Addition of additional rights
(s 446K IT(E&P)A 2003)

An income tax charge can arise where the value of employment-related securities is enhanced by means of non-commercial transactions. Once again, this charge can apply even where the individual was not resident and ordinarily resident at the time that he acquired the securities in question.

For the charge to apply, the market value of the employment-related securities must be increased by at least 10% by transactions carried out other than for genuine commercial purposes.

The taxable amount is the increase in value and this is charged as employment-related income for the year in which the transactions take place.

5.6.12 Purchase of shares from an employee at an overvalue
(s 446Y IT(E&P)A 2003)

An income tax charge arises where an employer or connected person purchases employment-related securities for more than market value. The amount taxed as income is the over-value. Again this is not limited to situations where the employee was resident and ordinarily resident at the time that he acquired the securities in question.

5.6.13 Employee can elect to pay employer's NIC

The FA 2004 provides tax relief if an employee bears his employer's NIC on a charge relating to restricted or convertible shares. This works in a similar way to the relief where an employer pays the NIC on exercising a non-approved option over readily convertible assets (see 5.3.2).

5.6.14 Partly-paid shares or shares acquired by borrowing from the employer
(s 446Q–U IT(E&P)A 2003)

Where an employee acquires partly-paid shares, he is treated as if he had received a notional loan. An annual charge may arise on the interest that would have been payable if the 'loan' had carried interest at the official rate (see 4.7).

Where the employer lifts the obligation to pay up the outstanding amount, the employee is deemed to have received employment income for that year (s 446U). Furthermore, a sale of the shares will also normally be treated as a discharge of the obligation so that once again a tax charge arises on the amount of the notional loan.

These provisions could also apply where there is an actual loan, eg a loan from an EBT or a major shareholder.

Section 446U can apply even though the individual was neither resident nor ordinarily resident at the time that he acquired the partly-paid shares if he subsequently carried on his employment whilst resident in the UK.

> **Tax notes**
>
> In many cases, it may be better for you to make shares fully paid before you sell them to avoid a tax charge under s446U. This is a situation where you should take professional advice.

5.7 THE EMPLOYER'S PERSPECTIVE

An employer will often be concerned about the 'democratic' aspects of many of the approved schemes, ie the principle that all employees must be allowed to participate on a similar basis (see 5.2 and 5.4). The managing director will generally want to reserve the incentive for 'key employees' whose input to the business is likely to make a significant difference to its profitability. The Enterprise Management Incentives are one type of approved scheme that is aimed primarily at such people but there are limits, both to the equity available and the types of companies that can operate EMI schemes (eg a company that is a subsidiary of another company cannot operate an EMI scheme). Other approved schemes contain a much lower ceiling for the value of shares that can be provided without a tax charge (see 5.4 on the £30,000 limit for approved share option schemes).

Employers will also be concerned that additional costs such as Employer's NIC are kept to the minimum (see 5.3.2 on one way of achieving this). Even more objectionable is anything that requires the employer to operate and account for PAYE without it being able to recover this tax from the employee (see 20.1.4 on the need to account for PAYE where shares are readily convertible assets).

If the company is going to receive a corporation tax deduction for the costs of establishing and operating a share scheme, this will reduce the net cost for the employer. See 17.3.2 on the circumstances in which the company may qualify for such relief.

5.8 SOME TAX PLANNING IDEAS

5.8.1 Subscription for shares

In some cases, it may be possible to keep things simple. Instead of having an option, the company pays a cash bonus and the amount that is left after PAYE and NIC is used by the individual to subscribe for new shares. This would make a lot of sense where a company has been set up relatively recently and the shares do not have a great deal of value (even though they are seen as capable of becoming very valuable if the business takes off).

Example

A company pays a bonus of £16,950 to a key employee. After 40% income tax and 1% NIC, he is left with £10,000 and uses this to subscribe for shares.

There will generally be some timing differences but overall the company's position could work out as follows:

	£
Bonus	16,950
Employer's NIC	2,000
	18,950
Cash returned to company as subscription for shares	10,000
	8,950
Corporation tax relief	3,979*
Effective net cost	4,971

* received nine months after company's year-end

This example assumes corporation tax relief at 21%, ie the small companies rate

However, if we were to assume that the employee paid only basic rate tax and 11% national insurance contributions, and the company enjoyed relief at the maximum rate (29.75% marginal small companies rate), the figures could be:

Bonus	16,950
Employer's NIC	2,000
	18,950
Cash returned to company as	11,695
	7,255
Corporation tax relief	5,637
Effective net cost	1,618

5.8.2 Make the election within 14 days

When this method is adopted, it will often be the case that the employee's shares are subject to restrictions and it will therefore be important that the individual and company make an election under s 431 IT(E&P)A 2003 (see 5.6.7) so as to ensure that any future growth in value is subject only to CGT.

This election has to be made within 14 days of the shares being issued to the employee.

5.8.3 Use approved schemes where possible

In cases where the shares have significant value, it is generally thought advisable to use approved schemes provided these fit in with the commercial objectives. For example, it may be that the controlling shareholders of a long-established company believe that a key manager will be tied into staying with the company in the medium term by being given 5% of the equity. Simply giving him the shares would give rise to an immediate income tax charge. Giving him an option may therefore be a better idea, especially if the option can be granted under an approved share option scheme (see 5.5). Such options can be granted over shares worth up to £30,000. Subject to the various conditions being satisfied, the individual need then have no income tax liability on acquiring his shares. In due course it may be appropriate for the employee to be given a cash bonus to give him sufficient cash to exercise his option. Where this happens, the overall effect is exactly the same as if the manager had been given the shares except that he will suffer no tax beyond the PAYE on his cash bonus.

If the shares being offered to the manager are worth more than £30,000, it may be possible to grant him an option under the Enterprise Management Incentives scheme, which can apply for shares worth up to £120,000 (see 5.5). Indeed, from the individual's point of view, an EMI option will often be more attractive because of its flexibility, there is no minimum holding period and, where the conditions for entrepreneurs relief are satisfied, the rate of capital gains tax may be 10%.

Approved share options and EMI options can be granted selectively, ie the legislation does not require similar options to be offered to other employees.

The company will qualify for a corporation tax deduction for the difference between the amount payable on exercising the option and the market value of the shares at the date of exercise (see 17.3.2).

5.8.4 Consider making loans or issuing partly-paid shares

Suppose that the employing company's shares are not eligible for approved share options or EMI schemes (eg the company may be a subsidiary of another company).

One possible way of designing a tax-efficient share scheme would be for a loan to be made to the employee (possibly from a parent company or a substantial shareholder) and for the employee to use this to buy shares, whether by subscribing for new shares or in purchasing existing shares.

No income tax charge will normally arise at the outset provided the shares are not acquired at an undervalue.

Once again, an election under s 431 may well be appropriate so that any profit on an eventual sale should be subject only to CGT (see 5.6.7).

No income tax charge will normally be payable on the loan provided it attracts interest at a rate not below the official rate (see 4.7) or the company is a close company and the employee meets either of the tests set out in 10.5 (ie the employee has a material interest or is engaged full-time in the management of the company's business).

The employee may be better off subscribing for new shares if this will mean that he can secure income tax relief under s 574 ICTA 1988 in the event of suffering a capital loss (see 16.2).

On a disposal of the shares, an income tax charge may arise on the amount of the loan unless the loan is repaid beforehand (see 5.6.14 on this).

6

SELF-EMPLOYMENT

GORDON HOPKINS

If you are self-employed, either in business on your own or in a partnership, you will be taxed under section 5 of the Income Tax (Trading and Other Income) Act 2005. Until 6 April 2005, income was charged under Schedule D Case I (trades) and Case II (professions) ICTA 1988. The introduction of IT(T&OI)A 2005 was really no more than a consolidation and re-write of the legislation in plain English. The substance has not changed.

In practice, the rules for determining taxable profits of trades and professions are almost the same and therefore all references in this chapter to a person carrying on a trade apply equally to a person who is engaged in a profession.

The following aspects of taxation of the self-employed are covered in this chapter:

(1) How self-employed individuals pay tax.
(2) Are you really self-employed?
(3) Basis of assessment.
(4) Partnerships.
(5) Limited liability partnerships (LLPs).
(6) Partnerships controlled outside the UK.
(7) Relief for trading losses.

We cover the detailed rules governing the computation of profits for tax purposes in Chapter 15. This chapter focuses on the way in which a self-employed individual should deal with his tax affairs once the amount of the taxable profit or loss has been ascertained, usually by an accountant.

6.1 HOW SELF-EMPLOYED INDIVIDUALS PAY TAX

6.1.1 Payment of tax

Unlike employees who suffer deduction of tax from their earnings under PAYE, self-employed individuals pay tax directly to the Revenue. Tax payable by them for 2008–09 needs to be paid in two instalments, on 31 January 2009 and 31 July 2009. The amount payable for each instalment is normally half the income tax liability for 2007–08. Any balance of tax for 2008–09 is then payable on 31 January 2010.

If you started self-employment fairly recently, and previously almost all your tax was collected under PAYE, you may find that you do not have to make instalment payments for 2008–09. However, the system will catch up with you on 31 January 2010 as you will then have to settle the whole of your 2008–09 tax and make the first payment on account for 2009–10.

> **Tax notes**
>
> Bear in mind that self-employed individuals have to pay instalments on account of their tax liability for the year, the first instalment falling due on 31 January.

6.1.2 Completing your tax return

You will need to complete a special schedule as part of your SA tax return; this asks for details of the type of business you are carrying on. If your sales did not exceed £64,000 pa, you can complete a self-employment (short) schedule.

Very small businesses

If your sales are less than £30,000 pa you can simply file your tax return on the basis of four entries: sales, expenses, capital allowances and profit. There is no obligation to prepare accounts, although it may be advisable to do so for other reasons. You do not need to submit a balance sheet.

6.1.3 Ascertaining taxable profits based on accounts

If your sales (or turnover) exceed £29,999 but are less than £64,001 you can still use the short form but you need to break down your expenses and put them in separate boxes. To do this, you need accounts for your business. It is advisable to send in accounts with the SA return, whether or not the Revenue wants them, as this limits the scope for the Revenue to reopen back years by making 'discovery assessments'.

Very often, accounts are drawn up for other reasons as well (eg for production to banks and other lenders) and it is important to bear in mind that there may need to be adjustments for tax purposes. There are also specific rules that govern the amount of 'capital allowances' that a trader may claim – in broad terms, capital allowances are an adjustment for depreciation or wear and tear on equipment, etc used in the business.

6.1.4 Self-assessment tax return

The full tax return for a self-employed individual with a turnover of more than £64,000 contains a schedule, which consists of boxes designed to adjust account figures for tax purposes.

Example – Profit and loss account

Z's profit and loss account for the year ended 31 December 2007 shows the following:

	£	£
Income		97,500
Expenses		
Wages	27,500	
Rent	6,000	
Insurance	1,650	
Utilities	1,060	
Repairs	2,100	
Telephone	980	
Accountancy	500	
VAT surcharge	400	
Depreciation	1,400	
Entertaining	1,200	
Miscellaneous	250	
		(43,040)
Net profit		54,460

Notes:
(1) Goods taken out for personal use: £600 without payment (at selling price).
(2) Telephone costs not relating to business: £200.
(3) Non-staff entertaining: £565.
(4) He is due capital allowances of £1,900.

The way the information has to be entered on the HMRC form is shown on pp 142–144. The computation of profits is dealt with in greater detail in Chapter 15 along with capital allowances because the principles that apply to a self-employed individual also apply to partnerships and companies.

The return directs you to submit a balance sheet if your business accounts include this.

HM Revenue & Customs

Self-employment (full)

Tax year 6 April 2007 to 5 April 2008

Your name	Your unique taxpayer reference (UTR)

Business details

1 Business name – *unless it is in your own name*

2 Description of business

3 First line of your business address – *unless you work from home*

4 Postcode of your business address

5 If the details in boxes 1, 2, 3 or 4 have changed in the last 12 months put 'X' in the box and give details in the 'Any other information' box

6 If your business started after 5 April 2007, enter the start date *DD MM YYYY*

7 If your business ceased before 6 April 2008, enter the final date of trading

8 Date your books or accounts start – *the beginning of your accounting period*

9 Date your books or accounts are made up to or the end of your accounting period – *read page SEFN 3 of the notes if you have filled in box 6 or 7*

Other information

10 If your accounting date has changed permanently, put 'X' in the box

11 If your accounting date has changed more than once since 2002, put 'X' in the box

12 If special arrangements apply, put 'X' in the box – *read page SEFN 3 of the notes*

13 If you provided the information about your 2007-08 profit on last year's Tax Return, put 'X' in the box – *read page SEFN 3 of the notes*

Business income

14 Your turnover – *the takings, fees, sales or money earned by your business*

£ 97500 · 00

15 Any other business income not included in box 14 – *excluding Business Start-up Allowance*

£ · 0 0

Business expenses

Read pages SEFN 5 to SEFN 7 of the *notes* to see what expenses are allowable for tax purposes.

	Total expenses If your annual turnover was below £30,000 you may just put your total expenses in box 30		Disallowable expenses Use this column if the figures in boxes 16 to 29 include disallowable amounts
16	Cost of goods bought for re-sale or goods used £ · 0 0	31	£ · 0 0
17	Construction industry – *payments to subcontractors* £ · 0 0	32	£ · 0 0
18	Wages, salaries and other staff costs £ 2 7 5 0 0 · 0 0	33	£ · 0 0
19	Car, van and travel expenses £ · 0 0	34	£ · 0 0
20	Rent, rates, power and insurance costs £ 8 7 1 0 · 0 0	35	£ · 0 0
21	Repairs and renewals of property and equipment £ 2 1 0 0 · 0 0	36	£ · 0 0
22	Telephone, fax, stationery and other office costs £ 9 8 0 · 0 0	37	£ 2 0 0 · 0 0
23	Advertising and business entertainment costs £ 1 2 0 0 · 0 0	38	£ 5 6 5 · 0 0
24	Interest on bank and other loans £ · 0 0	39	£ · 0 0
25	Bank, credit card and other financial charges £ · 0 0	40	£ · 0 0
26	Irrecoverable debts written off £ · 0 0	41	£ · 0 0
27	Accountancy, legal and other professional fees £ 5 0 0 · 0 0	42	£ · 0 0
28	Depreciation and loss/profit on sale of assets £ 1 4 0 0 · 0 0	43	£ 1 4 0 0 · 0 0
29	Other business expenses £ 6 5 0 · 0 0	44	£ 4 0 0 · 0 0
30	Total expenses in boxes 16 to 29 £ 4 3 0 4 0 · 0 0	45	Total disallowable expenses in boxes 31 to 44 £ 2 5 6 5 · 0 0

Tax Return: Self-employment (full): Page SEF 2

Net profit or loss

46 Net profit – *if your business income is more than your expenses (box 14 + box 15 minus box 30)* £ 5 4 4 6 0 · 0 0	**47** Or, net loss – *if your expenses exceed your business income (box 14 + box 15 minus box 30 is negative)* £ · 0 0

Tax allowances for vehicles and equipment (capital allowances)

There are 'capital' tax allowances for vehicles, equipment and certain buildings used in your business (you should not have included the cost of these in your business expenses). Read pages SEFN 8 to SEFN 11 of the *notes* and use the example and Working Sheets to work out your capital allowances.

48 Annual allowances at 25% on cars costing £12,000 or less, and equipment £ 1 9 0 0 · 0 0	**53** Enhanced 100% and other capital allowances – *read page SEFN 9 of the notes* £ · 0 0
49 First year allowances at 40% or 50% £ · 0 0	**54** Allowances on sale or cessation of business use (where you have disposed of assets for less than their tax value) £ · 0 0
50 Restricted annual allowances for cars costing more than £12,000 £ · 0 0	**55** Total allowances (total of boxes 48 to 54) £ 1 9 0 0 · 0 0
51 Agricultural or Industrial Buildings Allowance £ · 0 0	**56** Charges on cessation of business use (only where Business Premises Renovation Allowance has been claimed before) £ · 0 0
52 Business Premises Renovation Allowance (Assisted Areas only) – *read page SEFN 9 of the notes* £ · 0 0	**57** Other charges on sale or cessation of business use (where you have disposed of assets for more than their tax value) £ · 0 0

Calculating your taxable profit or loss

You may have to adjust your net profit or loss for disallowable expenses or capital allowances to arrive at your taxable profit or your loss for tax purposes. Read page SEFN 12 of the *notes* and fill in the boxes below that apply.

58 Goods and services for your own use – *read page SEFN 12 of the notes* £ 6 0 0 · 0 0	**61** Total deductions from net profit or additions to net loss (box 55 + box 60) £ 1 9 0 0 · 0 0
59 Total additions to net profit or deductions from net loss (box 45 + box 56 + box 57 + box 58) £ 3 1 6 5 · 0 0	**62** Net business profit for tax purposes (box 46 or box 47 + box 59 minus box 61) £ 5 5 7 2 5 · 0 0
60 Income, receipts and other profits included in business income or expenses but not taxable as business profits £ · 0 0	**63** Net business loss for tax purposes (if box 46 or box 47 + box 59 minus box 61 is negative) £ · 0 0

6.2 ARE YOU REALLY SELF-EMPLOYED?

6.2.1 Introduction

It is not possible to elect to be self-employed; whether you are self-employed is a matter of fact. However, since the Taxes Acts do not define 'self-employment', the rules have evolved through decisions handed down by the courts.

The real distinction between being self-employed and an employee is that there is no 'master-servant' relationship. Yet in practice it is often difficult to discern the dividing line and the Revenue may take a different view from the parties concerned. For example, freelance workers may not necessarily be recognised as being self-employed and salaried partners may be classified as employees. At one time, the position could be complicated further in that the Contributions Agency was responsible for assessing liability for NICs and occasionally reached a different conclusion from the Revenue. Such grey areas can sometimes result in companies treating freelance workers as if they were employees and deducting tax and NICs under PAYE accordingly. This reflects the Revenue's practice of seeking unpaid tax from employers in cases where a company has not operated PAYE. As a result, it is very difficult, for example, for workers in the computer industry to secure payment as being self-employed. Similar problems are often experienced by workers in the TV industry, journalists, actors and artistes, and many other industries where freelance workers are required to work 'on-site'.

The Revenue has addressed this issue by the introduction of legislation in April 2000, known colloquially as IR35. These rules are covered in more detail at 20.3 as they deal primarily with individuals who offer their services through a service company. During the consultation period leading up to the introduction of this legislation, the Revenue consolidated its statements on the dividing line between being employed and self-employed: see *Tax Bulletin* 45, available at www.hmrc.gov.uk/bulletins/tb45.htm, and www.hmrc.gov.uk/ir35/index.htm.

6.2.2 The Revenue's criteria

Guidelines issued by the Revenue to clarify employment status (leaflet IR56, *Employed or self-employed?*) included the following points:

(1) An employee generally does the work in person (and does not hire someone else to do it), working at times and places and in the way specified by the firm for whom the work is done and normally paid at hourly, weekly or monthly rates, possibly including overtime.

(2) A self-employed person may hire and pay others to do the work, or do it personally, in either case specifying the time and the way it is done, providing major items of equipment, being responsible for losses as well as profits and correcting unsatisfactory work in his own time and at his own expense.

These criteria are only for guidance and in some cases the Commissioners and the courts have held that a person who did not fulfil the requirements in (2) above was nevertheless self-employed. Thus, a journalist who worked as a freelance sub-editor at various national newspapers was held by the Commissioners to be self-employed even though she carried out all the work at the newspapers' offices. Similarly, a test case sponsored by Equity resulted in the Special Commissioners finding that actors engaged in London West End theatre work were not employees.

Commissioners' decisions, unlike court decisions, do not set binding legal precedents. It was therefore even more important that the Court of Appeal held in *Hall* v *Lorimer* [1994] STC 23 that a TV vision mixer was self-employed even though he failed to satisfy virtually all of the above tests. The taxpayer used extremely expensive equipment provided by the TV companies concerned and his work was controlled rigorously.

Tax notes

Take professional advice if you are a borderline case rather than simply accept a 'ruling' from the Revenue. The borders shift constantly; for example FA 2000 contains provisions that can treat certain partnership income as if it were employment income subject to PAYE.

6.3 BASIS OF ASSESSMENT

6.3.1 The way in which residence status affects liability
(IT(T&OI)A 2005, s 5)

A person is taxed on the profits of a trade carried on by him if he is resident in the UK regardless of where that trade is carried on. If he is not resident in the UK, he is taxed on the profits of the trade if it is carried on in the UK. If part of a trade is carried on in the UK, a non-resident person is taxed on the profits of that part of the trade.

6.3.2 Basis of assessment

The same rules apply for both trades and professions. A self-employed person may draw up accounts to any date he chooses; there is no requirement that accounts be made up to 5 April to fit in with the fiscal year, although the Revenue will encourage him to do so. All self-employed individuals are now taxed on the 'current year' (CY) basis.

6.3.3 Current year (CY) basis

A business's assessable profits are dealt with on the CY basis. This means that the assessment is determined by the profits for the accounting year that ends in the year of assessment. Thus a business with a 31 May year end will be assessed for 2007–08 on its profits for the year ended 31 May 2007. Taxable profits for these purposes are after deducting capital allowances (see 15.2).

Special rules govern the first tax year since there are normally no accounts that end in that tax year (see below).

Opening years

Special rules apply for the first two tax years:

(1) The first tax year's assessment is made by reference to profits actually earned during that year.
(2) The second tax year's assessment is normally determined by the profits of the first 12 months.
(3) The third tax year's assessment is on the CY basis.

Example – Opening years rules under the CY basis

A started in business on 6 October 2005. Accounts for the year to 5 October 2006 showed profits of £48,000. Profits for the year ending 5 October 2007 are £72,000. A will be assessed as follows:

	£
2005–06 'actual' basis ($\frac{6}{12} \times$ £48,000)	24,000
2006–07 first 12 months' profits	48,000
2007–08 CY basis	72,000

Example – Position where first accounts not drawn up for 12-month period

The precise way in which the opening year rules work is slightly more complicated when there are no accounts for a period of 12 months ending in the second tax year. This is covered by the following examples:

(1) B started in business on 1 January 2007. The first set of accounts was made up to 30 April 2007, then to 30 April 2008. B will be assessed on profits computed as follows:

2006–07	Profits of period 1 January to 5 April 2007.
2007–08	Profits of first 12 months, ie $\frac{1}{4}$ profits of period 1 January to 30 April 2007 Plus $\frac{8}{12}$ of profits for year ended 30 April 2008.

(2) C started up on 1 March 2006 and the first set of accounts was made up to 30 April 2007, ie there are no accounts ending in the second year. C's assessable profits are:

2005–06	$\frac{1}{12}$ × profits for 14 months ended 30 April 2007.
2006–07	Profits of first 12 months, ie
	$\frac{12}{14}$ profits for 14 months ended 30 April 2007.
2007–08	$\frac{12}{14}$ × profits for 14 months ended 30 April 2007.

6.3.4 Final year of trading

An individual who ceases to carry on a business is taxed under the CY basis on the profits for a notional period that starts immediately after the basis period for the previous tax year and ends on the date that he ceases. This can be illustrated by a case where a person makes up accounts to 30 April. Assume the profits for the year ended 30 April 2008 are £80,000. He ceases business on 30 November 2008 and profits for the final seven months amount to £50,000. The assessable income for 2008–09 is his share of profits for the period 1 May 2007 to 30 November 2008, ie £80,000 plus £50,000 (but subject to either overlap or transitional relief: see below).

6.3.5 Overlap relief

Because of the way a new business is assessed under the CY basis for the first two tax years, some profits may be taxed more than once. To compensate for this, and to ensure that over the life of the business tax is paid only on the actual amount of profits, overlap relief is given when the business is discontinued or, in the case of partners, when they leave the firm.

If the overlap relief exceeds the taxable profits for the final year, the balance may be treated as an allowable loss and either set against the individual's other income for that year or the preceding year, or carried back against profits of the last three years as terminal loss relief (see 6.7.7).

Example – Overlap relief

In the first example at 6.3.3, in which A's first accounts end on 5 October 2006, $\frac{6}{12}$ of the first 12 months' profits are assessed twice. Accordingly, a figure of £24,000 is carried forward and is deducted from A's profits for the final year of trading. Thus, if A retires on 5 October 2009 and the final year's profits are £60,000, the assessment for 2009–10 will be as follows:

	£
CY basis	60,000
Less: overlap relief	24,000
Taxable profits	36,000

Change of accounting dates

Unless a business from the date of commencement draws up annual accounts ending in the period 31 March to 5 April, there will be overlap relief.

Example – Change of accounting dates (1)

G started trading on 1 October 2006. The profit for the first year of trading was £45,000. The basis of assessment for the opening years would be:

2006–07	1 Oct 2006 to 5 Apr 2007
2007–08	12 months to 30 Sept 2007
2008–09	12 months to 30 Sept 2008

The overlap period is the 187 days to 5 April 2007 that will be assessed both in 2006–07 and 2007–08. The overlap profit is £23,055.

If during the business's lifetime the accounting date were extended to bring it nearer to 5 April, the overlap relief would be utilised. The intention of the legislation is to give relief in full when accounts are drawn up on a fiscal year basis, ie for the year to 5 April. If the accounting period is shortened, additional overlap relief is created.

Example – Change of accounting dates (2)

G changes his accounting date to 30 April 2008. The profit in the year to 30 September 2007 is £90,000.

2007–08	12 months to 30 September 2007
2008–09	12 months to 30 April 2008

The period of overlap is 1 May 2007 to 30 September 2007. The overlap profit is therefore £37,726 over 153 days, which is combined with the earlier overlap profit to give an overlap profit of £60,781 over 340 days.

If G extends his basis period towards 5 April, the overlap relief is used: logically, if G were to extend the accounting date to 5 April, all of the relief would be used.

Tax notes

Give consideration to the fact that the value of the relief will diminish in real terms with time. Professional advice should be taken in respect of using this relief during the course of the business by advancing the accounting date towards the following 5 April.

6.3.6 Transitional relief

The basis of assessment for a pre-6 April 1994 business changed to the CY basis in 1997–98. This meant that a businessman with a year end of 5 May was assessed for 1997–98 on the whole of his profits for the year ended 5 May 1997 even though he had already been assessed for 1996–97 on a full year's profits, albeit profits that were computed in a different way. Thus, if a business made up accounts to 5 May, the 1997–98 assessment was based on profits for the year ended 5 May 1997 and the transitional relief is $\frac{1}{12}$ of those profits.

Tax notes

HMRC is content to split years in these situations by either months or days providing there is consistency. Transitional relief will be enjoyed when the accounting date is moved to a point later in the tax year, or the individual ceases to carry on business.

Example – Transitional relief

J makes up his accounts to 5 June and has been in business for many years prior to 1994. His 1996–97 assessment was made on 50% of the profits for the two years ended 5 June 1996. Assume that this computation produced an assessment for 1996–97 of £100,000.

For 1997–98, *J* was assessed on the CY basis, ie his assessment was made on the profits for the year ending in 1997–98. Thus, if *J*'s profits for the year ended 5 June 1997 amounted to £180,000, that was his assessable income for 1997–98.

If *J* ceases to carry on the business in 2008–09, he is entitled to transitional relief equal to $\frac{10}{12}$ of £180,000, ie £150,000. This amount will be allowed as a deduction in arriving at his assessable profits for 2008–09.

Tax notes

Transitional relief is eroded by inflation, so discuss with your accountant the possibility of taking a sabbatical from your business so as to bring about a cessation of trading.

6.4 PARTNERSHIPS

A partnership's profits are computed in the same way as a sole trader's (see 6.3). However, there are complications.

6.4.1 Salaried partners

A salaried partner is engaged under a contract of employment. His profits are normally taxed as employment income. His remuneration is treated as a normal employee cost in arriving at the firm's profits. Sometimes partners have a fixed share of profits. It is not always easy to determine whether they are self-employed or salaried partners. The main indicators that a partner is self-employed are that the individual has capital at risk and that he is not subject to the control and direction of the other partners.

6.4.2 Treatment of partners under CY basis

Partners assessed individually

Assessments under the CY basis have always been made on individual partners rather than on the firm itself. Each partner is responsible for settling his own tax liabilities and is not jointly and severally liable for the total amount of tax payable by the partners. There may be a minor exception to this where there are non-resident partners in the firm.

Application of CY basis to partners

Basically, each partner is treated separately and the rules described at 6.3.1–6.3.3 are applied.

Example – How partners' taxable income is computed

> K and L start a firm on 6 October 2005. They share profits equally. On 6 January 2007, M joins them and takes a one-third entitlement to profits. Accounts to 5 October 2006 show a profit of £132,000. The accounts for the years to 5 October 2007 and 5 October 2008 show a profit of £240,000 and £300,000 respectively. The position is as follows:
>
> 2005–06 K and L are each assessed on the actual basis, ie the firm's profits of £66,000 for 2005–06 ($\frac{6}{12} \times$ £132,000 profits for the year ended 5 October 2006) are divided equally between them, so K and L are each assessed on £33,000.
>
> 2006–07 K and L are assessed on their share of the firm's profits for the first 12 months, ie profits of £132,000 are divided equally and each is assessed on £66,000. M is assessed on the actual basis, because 2006–07 is her first tax year as a partner in this firm, so she is assessed on £20,000 ($\frac{3}{12} \times$ her one-third share of the profits for the year ended 5 October 2007).
>
> 2007–08 K and L are assessed on the CY basis on their share of the firm's profits for the year ended 5 October 2007, ie £80,000 each. M is assessed on the profits for her first 12 months (ie $\frac{9}{12} \times$ £80,000 plus $\frac{3}{12} \times$ £100,000).
>
> 2008–09 All three partners are assessed on the CY basis, ie their one-third share of the firm's profits for the year ended 5 October 2008 of £300,000.

Similarly, the provisions on overlap relief are applied separately in relation to each partner. Thus, in the above example, if K retired on 5 October 2008, he would be entitled to overlap relief in arriving at his taxable profits for 2008–09. The other ongoing partners would get their overlap relief only when they retire or the firm changes its accounting date (see below). Their overlap relief is as follows:

	£
K	33,000
L	33,000
M	45,000 ($\frac{3}{12}$ × £80,000 + $\frac{9}{12}$ × £100,000).

6.4.3 Partnership interest and other investment income

A partner may be entitled to a share of interest earned by the firm on surplus cash – or indeed any other investment income.

Each partner is assessed on his share of such income, but it is assessed on the CY basis. Thus, if a firm makes up accounts to 31 May, the partners will be assessed for 2008–09 on their share of investment income in the firm's accounts for the year ended 31 May 2008 – even though the relevant income may actually have been received during the tax year 2007–08. The exception to this is investment income taxed at source, which is assessable on a tax-year basis, ie bank interest received net.

6.4.4 Catching-up charge: Partnerships formerly on cash basis

The catching-up charge for businesses taxed on the cash basis up to 1998–99 is described at 15.1.11.

The total catching-up charge for partnerships is based on the first accounting period starting on or after 6 April 1999. This charge has been spread over ten years as if there were annual instalments. The first year's instalment was allocated to the persons who were members of the partnership during that year, according to the way that they shared profits.

The same method has been used for instalments taxed in the following nine years, with the instalment being allocated to individual partners according to the profit-sharing arrangements for the 12 months ending on the anniversary of the catching-up charge that falls into the tax year. This applies irrespective of any change in accounting date.

6.4.5 Limits and changes in partners

The one-tenth and 10% limits operate at partnership level for the first nine years as they do for individuals. A partner remains liable for his share of the catching-up charge only for the period up to the date he leaves the partnership. Similarly, anyone joining the partnership during the ten-year spreading period becomes liable for his share of the charge in the future.

6.4.6 Partnership tax returns

As well as requiring returns from individual partners, the Revenue issues a partnership tax return to the 'nominated partner'. The return requires full details of the firm's profits and capital gains and the way profits (and losses) are divided between the partners. A partner needs to refer to the self-assessment reference under which the partnership return has been filed.

6.4.7 Expenditure incurred personally by a partner

The legislation means that all business expenses must be claimed on the partnership return, even where the expenditure is borne by an individual partner (eg his car expenses or the purchase of a fax machine for business use at home). The Revenue states in Helpsheet IR231 that:

> the only legal basis for giving relief for expenditure that qualifies for capital allowances is as a deduction in the calculation of the profits of the partnership business (unless there is a formal leasing agreement between the partner and the partnership, when the allowances will be due against the leasing income).

However, this does not mean that any legitimate expenditure incurred by a partner – that is any expense that would be allowable if met from partnership funds – can only be relieved if it is formally included in the partnership accounts. Nor does it mean that capital allowances can only be claimed on vehicles, or other assets, that feature in the partnership accounts. Provided that:

- any expenditure, or claim to capital allowances, is correctly calculated for tax purposes; and
- records relevant to those calculations are made and kept as if the expenditure, or assets, were part of the partnership accounts.

The Revenue will accept entries in the relevant sections of the Partnership Tax Return that, although based on the partnership accounts, include adjustments for such expenditure, or allowances. But once the adjustments have been made the expenditure will be treated, for all practical purposes, as if it had been included in the partnership's accounts.

6.4.8 Interest paid by partners on personal loans

Where a partner has taken a personal loan to finance his buying into the firm or to provide part of its working capital, he can claim relief for the interest paid by him on such borrowings. However, this relief is given by way of a deduction from his total taxable income rather than as an expense in computing his trading profits (see 10.4).

6.5 LIMITED LIABILITY PARTNERSHIPS (LLPs)

6.5.1 Background

The legislation on limited liability partnerships (LLPs) came into effect on 6 April 2001. In essence, an LLP is a hybrid. Legally, it takes the form of a body corporate (a company) with its own legal personality, but for tax purposes it may be treated as transparent. Provided the LLP is carrying on a lawful business with a view to profit, its members are taxed as if they were partners in a partnership.

Members are assessed on their share of the LLP's profits and capital gains. Unlike a conventional partnership, there is no joint and several liability between the members. Their liability, in most cases, is limited to the capital contributed to the LLP, together with any further capital they may have agreed to contribute in the event of winding up the LLP. Undrawn profits do not automatically become part of a member's capital contributed (unless otherwise agreed). The member ranks equally with other unsecured creditors for repayment of his current account balance. This contrasts with conventional partnerships where the partner is jointly and severally liable to the full extent of his personal assets. An LLP may therefore have attractions as compared with conventional partnerships, but there can also be drawbacks. For example, the LLP is technically a company and has to file accounts and disclose certain financial information, broadly in line with companies of a similar size.

6.5.2 Restriction of loss relief

If a loss arises, there may be a restriction on the member's ability to set the loss against his other income. The limit is the amount of capital contributed by the member.

This restriction does not apply where the LLP carries on a profession. Guidance notes on LLP can be obtained from Companies House (www.companieshouse.gov.uk).

6.6 PARTNERSHIPS CONTROLLED OUTSIDE THE UK
(IT(T&OI)A 2005, ss 857–858)

A UK resident may be a partner in a partnership controlled outside the UK. His earnings from such a partnership are taxable in the same way as if they arose from a partnership controlled in the UK unless he is not domiciled in the UK. A foreign domiciled partner's share of profits from a trade (or part of a trade) carried on outside the UK are taxed on the remittance basis.

6.6.1 Current year basis

A partner in a foreign partnership is assessable on the CY basis (see 6.3.3).

6.6.2 Classification of overseas entities

In practice, it is often not clear whether an overseas legal entity will be treated as a partnership or a company for UK tax purposes. This is so especially where an entity combines some of the characteristics of UK partnerships and companies. The Revenue set out its opinion of the correct tax treatment of various US and European entities in *Tax Bulletin*, Issue 83 in June 2006.

6.7 RELIEF FOR TRADING LOSSES

Relief may be available for a loss incurred by an individual in a trade or profession. Relief may also be due for pre-trading expenditure treated as a loss incurred when the trade was commenced (see 15.3). The provisions that govern the relief for trading losses are complex and there are several ways in which you may claim that losses be utilised.

6.7.1 Carry forward relief against subsequent assessments
(ITA 2007, s 23)

A loss incurred by a sole trader or a partner's share of his firm's trading loss may be carried forward and deducted in assessments for later years in respect of the same trade or profession. With the introduction of the CY basis of assessment (see 6.3.3), capital allowances are treated as trading expenses and can therefore increase or create a loss. Where losses are carried forward in this way, they must be used against the assessable profits for the first subsequent year in which profits arise. The loss carried forward in this way may also be relieved against certain income connected with the trade even though it is assessed under a different schedule (eg interest earned on temporary investment of trade receipts and dividends from trade investments). There is no limit on the number of years for which a loss may be carried forward provided the same trade is carried on.

The loss must be claimed within five years of the filing date (ie for a loss arising in 2002–03, by 31 January 2009).

Table 6.2 – Losses under self-assessment for 2007–08

Reference	Description	Deadline
ITA 2007, s 64 TCGA 1992, ss 261B and 261C	Deduction from income or gains for 2007–08	31 Jan 2010
ITA 2007, s 64	Deduction from income or gains for 2006–07	31 Jan 2010
ITA 2007, s 72	Loss in first four years of trade carried back	31 Jan 2010
ITA 2007, s 83	Carry forward against future profits	31 Jan 2014
ITA 2007, s 89	Terminal loss relief	31 Jan 2014

6.7.2 Relief against general income
(ITA 2007, s 64)

Where a sole trader or partner incurs a loss and the trade was carried on with a view to profit, the loss may be relieved against his general income for the year of assessment in which it was incurred (ie his total income for the year). Relief may also be claimed against his general income for the preceding tax year. The claim for a loss to be set against his general income for the preceding tax year is an alternative to the claim for the loss to be relieved against income of the year of loss. In other words, either the loss may be set against income of the current year (with any balance being set against income of the following year) or the individual may forgo the chance to set the loss against his income for the current year and set the full amount against income of the preceding year.

Where an individual takes relief for trading losses against his general income, he must use up the losses to the extent to which he has taxable income. It is not possible for a claim to be made to restrict the amount of losses so as to enable sufficient income to be left to make use of his personal allowances. On the other hand, the legislation permits him to deduct certain items before arriving at his general income against which trading losses can be offset. These items include relief for allowable expenses for employment income purposes, retirement annuity and personal pension contributions, interest relief and relief for donations to charities by deed of covenant or Gift Aid.

Relief for losses against other income must be claimed within 22 months of the end of the tax year in which the loss arises (ie one year after the filing date for the return relating to that year of assessment) so that a 2007–08 loss must be claimed by 31 January 2010.

6.7.3 Relief by aggregation

Where the profits of different accounting periods are time apportioned (eg on commencement of a business), a loss may be relieved by aggregation with a profit. This situation could arise if a first period of trading were less than 12 months.

Example – Loss relief by aggregation

W started business on 1 January 2008. She made a loss of £6,000 for the period ended 30 September 2008 and a profit of £24,000 for the year ended 30 September 2009. Relief by aggregation would produce the following result:

Profits assessable 2007–08	Nil
Profits assessable 2008–09	Nil
Profits assessable 2009–10	£24,000

This is because the first 12 months' trading would be deemed to produce a net loss computed as follows:

	£
Loss for period 1 Jan to 30 Sept 2008	(6,000)
$\frac{3}{12}$ of profit for year ended 30 Sept 2009	6,000
	Nil

If a loss is set against other income, it cannot also be relieved by aggregation. Thus, if W had claimed relief for the £3,000 loss that she had incurred in 2007–08, only the balance of the loss for the period ended 30 September 2008 which relates to the period 6 April to 30 September 2008 could be taken into account in arriving at the profits of the first 12 months' trading. The 2008–09 assessment would then be £3,000.

Example – Loss set against other income

Y commenced trading on 1 August 2007. He has a loss during the nine months ended 30 April 2008 of £36,000. He has profits for the year ended 30 April 2009 of £60,000.

If the 2007–08 and 2008–09 losses were used by being set against Y's other income, the taxable income would be:

		£
2007–08		Nil
2008–09	Profits of first 12 months:	
	9 months ended 30 April 2008	Nil
	³⁄₁₂ × profits for year ended 30 April 2009	<u>15,000</u>
		<u>15,000</u>
2009–10	CY basis profits for year ended 30 April 2009	<u>60,000</u>

Contrast this with the situation where relief for the loss is obtained by aggregation:

		£
2007–08		Nil
2008–09	Loss for 9 months to 30 April 2008	(36,000)
	Profits for year ended 30 April 2009	<u>15,000</u>
	Loss carried forward	<u>(21,000)</u>
2009–10	Profits assessed on CY basis	60,000
	Less: loss brought forward	<u>(21,000)</u>
		<u>39,000</u>

6.7.4 Losses arising from a business taxed under CY basis

Under the CY basis (see 6.3.3), losses are attributed to a tax year in the same way as profits are assessed. This means that once the business has got past the opening years, a loss will be treated as arising in the tax year in which the trader's accounting period ends. Losses for the opening years are computed on exactly the same basis as profits.

6.7.5 Losses in early years of a trade
(ITA 2007, s 72)

In certain circumstances, relief may be claimed against an individual's general income for the three years of assessment preceding the year in which the loss is incurred. Relief is given against income for the earliest year first. There are certain preconditions for a loss to be claimed in this way:

(1) The loss must arise during the first four tax years in which the business is carried on.
(2) Where a trade is acquired from a spouse, the four years run from the date the spouse first commenced trading (unless the trade is taken over on the spouse's death).
(3) The trade must be carried on, on a commercial basis and with a reasonable expectation of profits.

A claim for a 2007–08 loss to be relieved in this way must be made by 31 January 2010.

Tax notes

Many new businesses take time before generating substantial profits. In the past you might have been in a job that paid well and a large part of your earnings was taxed at 40%. Carrying back losses in this way could enable you to recover tax paid at 40% whereas setting the losses against your income for the current year or carrying them forward may give you only limited benefit.

6.7.6 Relief for trading losses against capital gains
(TCGA 1992, ss 261B and 261C)

An individual who has incurred a trading loss may have it set against any capital gains that arise in the same or preceding year. It is not possible to claim relief for losses in this way without first having made a claim for relief for the loss to be set against the individual's general income for the year (see 6.7.2 for the time limit for making such a claim).

Tax notes

If you have a significant loss, you should look into the possibilities for relieving it against capital gains. However, this is generally a 'last resort', especially as trading losses are set against capital gains for years up to 2007–08 before allowing for taper relief (see 12.5) and before entrepreneurs relief for 2008–09 (see 16.8).

6.7.7 Terminal loss relief
(ITA 2007, s 89)

Where a trade, profession or vocation is permanently discontinued, a loss incurred during the last 12 months can be deducted from the profits charged to tax in the three tax years before the final year. The relief can include a claim for the loss arising in the tax year in which the cessation takes place as well as a proportion of the loss for the previous tax year.

Capital allowances for the final tax year may also be claimed, as can an appropriate proportion of the preceding year's capital allowances, representing the allowances due for the period beginning twelve months before the cessation.

The terminal loss may be carried back against profits from the same trade for the three tax years preceding the year of cessation. The relief is given against the latest year's profits first.

If interest and dividends would have been included as trading profits (except that they were subject to deduction of tax at source), the terminal loss may be set against such income.

6.7.8 Anti-avoidance provisions

Losses from limited partnerships
(ITA 2007, ss 104 to 106)

Limited partnerships were widely used in tax avoidance arrangements. The House of Lords decided in *Reed* v *Young* [1986] STC 285 that a limited partner could be entitled to loss relief for an amount that exceeded his actual liability under the Limited Partnership Act. This led to specific legislation to limit the amount of loss relief to the capital that is 'at risk'. Any losses incurred beyond this amount must be carried forward to be set against any future share of profits received by the limited partner from the firm. The s 104 provisions apply to individuals who are limited partners or members of a joint venture arrangement under which their liability is limited to a contract, agreement, guarantee, etc.

'Non-active partners'

A partner who devotes less than ten hours a week to the partnership business cannot secure relief against other income for losses that exceed the capital he has contributed to the firm. Losses that exceed this capital must be carried forward and used only to offset profits from the firm for a later year. This rule came into effect on 10 February 2004.

Legislation that came into effect on 2 March 2007 prevents any sideways relief where participation in the partnership formed part of tax avoidance arrangements. Furthermore, even where no such avoidance arrangements are present, FA 2007 restricts the tax relief available to non-active partners to £25,000 a year. The perceived abuse was where a non-active partner contributed capital to a partnership to take advantage of tax losses. The restriction does not apply to qualifying film expenditure.

'Non-active sole traders'

Similar provisions were introduced from 12 March 2008 for sole traders who devoted less than ten hours to a loss-making business. Once again, loss relief against other income is restricted to £25,000 (and sideways relief is excluded altogether where the business forms part of tax avoidance arrangements). These provisions do not apply to Lloyd's Names or a film business.

Loss relief for film partnerships, etc

FA 2004 contained anti-avoidance provisions aimed at individuals who participate in partnerships only for tax planning purposes. We deal with these provisions at 24.8.

6.7.9 Loss relief where business transferred to a company
(ITA 2007, s 86)

Where a business has been carried on by an individual (either as a sole trader or in partnership) and is transferred to a company, it is possible for any unused trading losses to be relieved against his income from the company in subsequent years. This relief is available only if the business is transferred to a company wholly or mainly in return for an allotment of shares and then only if the individual has retained ownership of those shares throughout the tax year concerned. In practice, the Revenue does not withhold relief provided he has retained at least 80% of the shares.

6.7.10 Losses from an overseas partnership
(ITA 2007, s 95)

A UK resident partner's share of profits from a trading partnership that is managed or controlled abroad are taxed under s 852 IT(T&OI)A 2005 (formerly Schedule D Case V). If a loss should arise, relief is calculated in the same way as for a loss incurred in a UK trade, profession or vocation. Relief for such losses is then given in the same way as relief is given for UK trading losses, except that where a loss is to be set against other income, the loss can be deducted only from:

(1) profits from other foreign trades;
(2) foreign pensions and annuities where a 10% deduction is available;
(3) foreign emoluments taxed as employment income.

7

INCOME FROM UK PROPERTY

VIRAN DE SILVA

This chapter deals with rental income from land or property in the UK. Such income was taxed under Schedule A for years up to 2004–05 but is now taxed under s 264 IT(T&OI)A 2005. Rents received from letting an overseas property were formerly taxed under Schedule D Case V and are now taxed under s 265 IT(T&OI)A 2005 – the tax treatment of such income is covered in 9.1.

The following matters are covered in this chapter:

(1) Basis of assessment and administration.
(2) How to calculate your taxable profit.
(3) Lump sums deemed to be rent (premiums).
(4) 'Rent-a-room' relief.
(5) Furnished holiday accommodation.
(6) 'Buy to let' investments.
(7) Capital allowances on investment properties.
(8) Mineral royalties.
(9) Woodlands.
(10) Property investment company.
(11) VAT considerations.
(12) Interest earned on trust funds for service charges and sinking funds.

7.1 BASIS OF ASSESSMENT AND ADMINISTRATION

7.1.1 All rental activities treated as single business

All rental income received by an individual from UK properties is now assessed under s 264, whether the property is let unfurnished or furnished. All income and expenses are brought together in a single business of letting UK property. Income and expenses on overseas properties are totally excluded when computing the profits of an individual's UK property business and deficits on one cannot be offset against profits that fall into the other category.

The income from a UK property business is determined by using normal commercial accountancy principles. Expenses are allowed if they satisfy the test that the expense is incurred wholly and exclusively for business purposes

161

and this rule applies to interest (including overdraft interest) just as for any other expense.

You will need to complete a UK Property Schedule in your tax return for each property from which you receive rental income.

7.1.2 Exceptional types of rental income

Rental income includes ground rents. It also includes 'other receipts from an estate' in land such as charges levied by a landlord in return for maintaining a block of flats and payments made to a landowner for sporting rights. It does not include admission charges made by hotels, boarding houses, theatres, etc, since the profits of such businesses are chargeable to tax as trading income.

Income from taking in lodgers is generally treated as trading income rather than UK property business income. However, see 7.4 on 'rent-a-room' relief.

7.1.3 Property income assessed on fiscal year basis

An individual must report income on a tax-year basis, ie accounts must be drawn up to 5 April.

7.1.4 Partnership income dealt with separately

Rental income received by a partnership is treated as a separate source. If the partnership does not have any trading income, the rental income is assessed on a fiscal-year basis, irrespective of the date to which the partnership draws up accounts. In contrast, if the partnership also has some trading income, its UK property income is assessed on the same basis. Thus, if a trading partnership has a 30 April year end, the partners will be assessed for 2007–08 on their share of the partnership's UK property income for the year ended 30 April 2007.

7.1.5 UK property income is investment income

Although all UK rental income is treated as arising from a single business of letting property, the income is still treated as investment income. Any losses can only be carried forward for offset against UK property income and cannot be set against the individual's other income for the year (there is an exception to this for deficits arising from letting agricultural properties where the deficit may be set against other income: see below).

UK property income is not 'income from savings' (see 8.1.5).

7.1.6 Deficiency on agricultural property
(TA 1988, s 33)

Where an estate consists of or includes agricultural land, a deficiency may be set against any UK property income. Any balance that cannot be relieved in this way may be set against the individual's other income for the year, or the following tax year.

'Agricultural land' is defined as land, houses or other buildings in the UK occupied wholly or mainly for husbandry purposes. 'Estate' means any land and buildings managed as one estate. Where only part of the estate is used for husbandry, only a proportion of any deficiency can be relieved in this way.

7.2 HOW TO CALCULATE YOUR TAXABLE PROFIT

The legislation requires that landlords should calculate their income and expenses in accordance with normal accountancy principles but subject to the same specific rules that apply for computing trading profits (see Chapter 15).

You should study the notes and helpsheets issued by the Revenue to enable landlords to complete their SA tax returns. The Revenue's guide to the SA return sets out the normal treatment of certain common expenses.

7.2.1 Rent receivable

The Revenue confirms in its booklet that you do not bring rent into a year's tax computation merely because you receive it in, or it is due to be paid to you in, the year. Equally, you do not exclude rent merely because you receive it outside, or it is due outside, the tax year. You bring in the proportion of rent earned in the year from the tenants' use of the property in the year. You exclude the proportion earned from the tenant's right to use the property outside the year. So, you may need to make an adjustment where rent is receivable, say, quarterly, either in advance or in arrears. Incidentally, the Revenue's notes to the SA return point out that rental income includes receipts in kind as well as in cash.

7.2.2 Bad debts

A landlord can claim a deduction for rent that is due to him but has not been paid where the debt is clearly irrecoverable. A deduction can also be claimed for doubtful debts. Such a deduction is available only where the landlord has taken all reasonable steps to recover the debt. Furthermore, if the outstanding rent is collected in a later tax year, he should bring the recovery into his accounts as a receipt for his rental income for that year.

No deduction is available for a general bad debt reserve (ie a landlord cannot deduct 5% of the outstanding rents due to him at the year end just to be on the safe side). Tax relief is available for provisions for doubtful debts only if the provisions relate to specific debts and the facts relating to each debtor have been taken into account. Furthermore, as the Revenue literature makes clear, you cannot deduct a bad or doubtful debt merely because the tenant is always a slow payer. There has to be good reason for thinking the debt is likely to be bad.

7.2.3 **Rent-free periods**

The Revenue approach follows the accounting principles set out in SSAP21. If the landlord, for example, grants a lease for a five-year period with no rent being payable in Year 1 and rent of £10,000 being payable in Years 2–5, the landlord should spread the total amount of rent receivable over the five years (ie £40,000) and bring into his accounts one-fifth of that total income for each year of the lease. In other words, the treatment reflects the substance of the transaction; in essence there is not really a rent-free year at all since the £40,000 payable over the first five years is rent for the whole of that period.

7.2.4 **Expenses**

Expenses should also be brought into account on normal accountancy principles. This means that a landlord should deduct any allowable expenses that relate to work done, or goods or services supplied to him, for a particular year. There is no requirement that the supplier should have been paid during the tax year. Thus if you have raised a loan for the purchase or improvement of repairs of properties that are let out, you can claim relief for interest that has accrued up to 5 April even though the bank or building society may debit interest on a different basis (eg at 30 June and 31 December).

Expenses are deductible only if they meet the 'wholly and exclusively' rule (ie expenditure that is part business/part private is not allowable). For example, the cost of travelling to Wales to supervise repairs to a holiday cottage is not an allowable deduction for tax purposes if the landlord also takes a holiday while there (ie the visit had a dual purpose). But where a definite part or proportion of an expense is wholly incurred for business purposes, that part may be deducted. This may well arise where a landlord lives in part of the property that is rented out: here, a proportion of the insurance premium relating to the property as a whole may be deducted in arriving at the landlord's UK property income. Remember that where expenditure is partly for business and partly for personal use, you have to complete a specific box on the SA return.

7.2.5 **Repairs, maintenance and renewals**

Examples of common repairs normally deductible in computing income for tax purposes are:

- Exterior and interior painting and decorating;
- Stone cleaning;
- Damp and rot treatment;
- Mending broken windows, doors, furniture and machines such as cookers or lifts;
- Re-pointing;
- Replacing roof slates, flashing and gutters.

The Revenue has confirmed that the cost of replacing worn out single-glazed windows with double glazing may be an allowable expense in computing UK property income (see *Tax Bulletin* 59).

Substantial repairs carried out shortly after a landlord has occupied a property to put it into a fit state are generally disallowed as constituting capital expenditure.

The *Jenners* case (see 15.1.9) means that a specific and scientifically calculated provision for the cost of repair work to be carried out in the future might be allowable. You need to take specialist advice on whether making such a provision accords with the generally accepted accountancy principles set out in FRS12.

Expenditure on improvements that obviated the need for repairs used to be allowed by concession, but is no longer allowed in relation to expenditure incurred after 5 April 2001.

7.2.6 Energy saving allowance

Landlords are allowed a deduction for expenditure of up to £1,500 on or after 6 April 2004 on the installation of loft or cavity wall insulation. From 7 April 2005, expenditure on solid wall insulation also qualifies for this relief.

The allowance is due to last until 5 April 2009.

7.2.7 Refurbishing business premises in disadvantaged areas

Business Premises Renovation Allowances (BPRA) became available on 11 April 2007 and are intended to bring in a relief for the costs of renovating business property that has been empty for a year in designated 'disadvantaged areas'. The whole of Northern Ireland qualifies. Go to www.dtistats.net/regional-aa/aa2007.asp to see whether an area in England, Wales or Scotland qualifies. The capital costs of such rennovations would normally not be relieved immediately, but the intention is that a 100% allowance should be available. This relief to some extent offsets the withdrawal of the Stamp Duty Land Tax exemption for acquisition of property in disadvantaged areas. Relief is claimed on page 2 of the 'UK Property' supplementary SA form in Box 31 with any balancing charge shown in Box 29. For details on the computation of capital allowances and balancing charges generally see 15.2.

7.2.8 Renewals

The landlord can claim the cost of replacing furniture, furnishings and machinery. However, expenditure on renewals is not available where the landlord claims a standard 10% wear and tear allowance (see 7.2.11).

Where expenditure on renewals is claimed, the landlord should bring into account of his income any amounts received for items that have been scrapped or sold. Also, expenditure on renewals should not normally include the cost of items that represent a significant improvement or addition to the furniture and furnishings, etc previously made available to the tenant.

7.2.9 Legal and professional costs

The Revenue view is as follows:

Non-allowable expenses

(1) Expenses in connection with the first letting or subletting of a property for more than one year (including eg legal expenses, such as the cost of drawing up a lease, agents' and surveyors' fees and commission).
(2) Any proportion of the legal, etc costs that relate to the payment of a premium on the renewal of a lease.
(3) Fees incurred in obtaining planning permission or on the registration of title when buying a property.

Allowable expenses

(1) Expenses for granting a lease of a year or less.
(2) The normal legal and professional fees incurred on the renewal of a lease, provided it is for less than 50 years (the Revenue confirmed in its *Tax Bulletin* that the costs of granting a lease to a new tenant are normally allowable provided the replacement lease follows closely on the previous one and is broadly similar in terms).
(3) Professional fees incurred:
    (a) in evicting an unsatisfactory tenant, with a view to re-letting;
    (b) on an appeal against a compulsory purchase order; and
    (c) in drawing up accounts.

7.2.10 Costs of services provided, including wages

A landlord who provides any service to a tenant (eg gardening, the provision of a porter, cleaning, etc) can claim the cost of these services, provided they are incurred wholly and exclusively for the purposes of the letting.

7.2.11 10% wear and tear allowance

A landlord who lets a dwelling-house as furnished accommodation can claim (instead of claims on a renewals basis) an allowance amounting to 10% of the rent received after deducting charges or services that would normally be borne by the tenant but are, in fact, borne by the landlord (eg council tax). This allowance, known as 'wear and tear allowance', is accepted by the Revenue as broadly covering the cost of normal renewals of furniture.

A landlord who lets non-residential property (eg offices) can normally claim capital allowances for any items provided (eg furniture).

Table 7.1 – Computing your 2007–08 property income (straightforward situation)

Table 7.1 – Computing your 2007–08 property income (straightforward situation)

> For each property, bring in the rental income that relates to the tax year (ie if rent is receivable on 25 March 2008 for the quarter ending 24 June 2008, include a proportion for the period 25 March to 5 April 2008).
>
> **Deduct**
>
> - Charges made by an agent for rent collection and management;
> - Any rent you have to pay on the property (eg ground rent);
> - Any service charges you have to pay (particularly likely to apply if you are letting out a flat);
> - Insurance premiums paid for the period covered by the tax year: if you pay insurance for a calendar year, include $\frac{3}{12}$ of the premium for 2008 + $\frac{9}{12}$ of the premium for 2007;
> - Repairs and similar expenses (eg gardening) incurred in the tax year. Note that the expense need not actually have been incurred in the tax year so long as it is clear that it relates to the tax year;
> - Interest on borrowings used to finance the original purchase of a property, improvements or repairs or against the value of the property at the time that it was brought into the UK property business.
>
> Aggregate all the income and expenses for your different properties except for properties not let on a commercial basis (any deficit on such properties will almost certainly not be allowable). Add in any lump sums taxable as premiums (see 7.3).

7.2.12 Interest

Until fairly recently, it was understood by most tax advisers, and indeed most Revenue inspectors, that relief for mortgage interest could only be set against rental income to the extent that it related to interest paid on loans used to *purchase* the property that was being let. It was previously thought relief was not available on any subsequent borrowings except to the extent that the money was borrowed to finance capital improvements.

However, the *Business Income Manual*, which was published by the Revenue in 2004, rather surprisingly contradicted this. The relevant section states:

> Mr A owns a flat in central London, which he bought ten years ago for £125,000. He has a mortgage of £80,000 on the property. He has been offered a job in Holland and is moving there to live and work. He intends to come back to the UK at some time. He decides to keep his flat and rent it out while he is away. His London flat now has a market value of £375,000.
>
> The opening balance sheet of his rental business shows

Mortgage	£80,000	Property at MV	£375,000
Capital account	£295,000		

> He renegotiates his mortgage on the flat to convert it to a buy-to-let mortgage and borrows a further £125,000. He withdraws the £125,000, which he then uses to buy a flat in Rotterdam.

The balance sheet at the end of Year 1 shows

Mortgage		£205,000	Property at MV £375,000
Capital account			
brought forward	£295,000		
Less Drawings	£125,000		
carried forward		£170,000	

Although he has withdrawn capital from the business, the interest on the mortgage loan is allowable in full because it is funding the transfer of the property to the business at its open market value at the time the business started. The capital account is not overdrawn.

Source: HMRC

7.3 LUMP SUMS DEEMED TO BE RENT (PREMIUMS)
(IT(T&OI)A 2005, s 277)

7.3.1 Introduction

A landlord faced with the choice of letting a property for five years at £10,000 pa, or taking a lump sum in return for granting a lease for five years at an annual rent of £100, would regard the two transactions as very similar in their overall consequences. The purpose behind the tax legislation that deals with lump sums (or 'premiums') is to ensure that the tax treatment of both transaction types is similar in nature. The principle is that a proportion of a premium received by a landlord for granting a lease of less than 50 years should be taxed as if it were rent.

The following sections apply only where the person who receives the premium is the landlord, ie a person who continues to hold a superior interest in the property. An outgoing tenant who assigns the whole of his interest in the property is not regarded as receiving a premium for income tax purposes.

7.3.2 How premiums are apportioned between income and capital
(IT(T&OI)A 2005, s 277)

The rule is that the full amount of the premium is treated as rent except for 2% for every complete year of the lease after the first year. For example, if a ten-year lease is granted for a premium of £25,000, the amount subject to tax as income is 82% of £25,000, ie £20,500. See Table 7.2.

Table 7.2 – Extract from Revenue helpsheet

Working sheet for chargeable premiums – leases up to 50 years		
Premium	**A**	£
Number of complete periods of 12 months in the lease, ignore the first 12 months	**B**	£
50 minus box B	**C**	£
Box C divided by 50	**D**	£
Box A multiplied by Box D	**E**	£
Copy box E to box 20.		

Source: HMRC

7.3.3 Payments in kind
(IT(T&OI)A 2005, s 278)

It is provided that if a tenant is required to carry out work as a term of his lease, the whole of the benefit accruing to the landlord is deemed to be a premium receivable at the commencement of the lease.

7.3.4 Deemed premiums
(IT(T&OI)A 2005, s 281)

Any lump sum paid by a tenant to vary the lease can be treated as a premium receivable at the time the contract for the variation is entered into.

Example – Deemed premium

A is the landlord of a property used as offices and let on a 15-year lease. It is a term of the lease that the tenant should not use the premises for any other purpose.

The tenant secures planning consent to use the property for light industrial use. He makes a payment to A of £12,000 in Year 4 to induce him to vary the lease so that the property can be used for industrial purposes. *A* is deemed to receive a premium in Year 4. The taxable amount is:

	£
	12,000
Less: (10 × 2%)	(2,400)
	9,600

Similarly, if A had received a lump sum to induce him to waive the relevant term in the lease, the lump sum would be treated as a premium.

7.3.5 **Sale with right to repurchase the property**
(IT(T&OI)A 2005 s 284)

Where the freehold or leasehold of a property is sold subject to a condition that at a future date the purchaser may be required to sell it back to the vendor at a lower price, the vendor must treat the excess of the sale price over the repurchase price as a premium. The excess, or notional premium, is reduced by 2% for each complete year between the date of sale and the date of resale less one year, the balance is taxed as income from property.

A similar rule applies where a vendor sells a property but retains an option to repurchase it.

7.3.6 **Which year?**

The SA return pack and the Revenue's internal guidance indicate that the taxable amount of any premiums should be taxed as income for the year in which the landlord becomes entitled to them. This could be challenged on the grounds that the income for granting, say, a five-year lease should be spread evenly over the period, with part of the premium being taxed for each of the years to which it relates. Seek professional advice if substantial amounts are involved.

7.4 'RENT-A-ROOM' RELIEF
(IT(T&OI)A 2005, s 309)

Special relief is available to an individual who receives payment for letting furnished accommodation in a qualifying residence. The relief provides total exemption from income of £4,250 unless sums accrue to another person in respect of lettings of furnished accommodation in the same property, in which case the exemption is reduced to £2,125, regardless of the number of other people (ie if three people qualified in respect of the same property, the limit for all three would be £2,125 each).

A qualifying residence is a residence that is the individual's only or main residence at some time in the basis period for the year of assessment in relation to the lettings. 'Residence' means a building (or part of a building) occupied or intended to be occupied as a separate residence.

Rent-a-room relief is available automatically unless the taxpayer elects otherwise or the gross sums received exceed the £4,250 limit.

Where the gross sums received exceed the £4,250 limit for the year of assessment (or the £2,125 limit where some other person receives income from furnished lettings within the same property), the taxpayer may elect for his profits or gains for the basis period to be treated as equal to the excess. For example, if a taxpayer has gross rent of £5,000, he may compute his taxable income as £750 or he can compute it in the normal way by reference to the expenses actually incurred.

Need for caution

The Revenue has commented on the suggestion that rent-a-room relief might be available where part of an individual's residence is let to a company for use as an office (or for some other trade or business purpose). The Revenue's view is that the relief is available only where the person paying rent uses the premises for residential purposes.

7.4.1 Revenue leaflets

For further information on rent-a-room relief, obtain leaflets IR87, *Rooms to let*, and IR223, *Rent-a-Room for Traders*.

7.5 FURNISHED HOLIDAY ACCOMMODATION
(IT(T&OI)A 2005 s 322)

7.5.1 Definition

Where a person lets furnished holiday accommodation (including caravans), it may be treated as a trade provided the following conditions are satisfied:

(1) The property must be situated in the UK.
(2) It must be let commercially.
(3) It must be let as furnished accommodation.
(4) It must be available for commercial letting to the public as holiday accommodation for at least 140 days in a 12-month period.
(5) It must be let for at least 70 such days.
(6) It must not normally be occupied by the same person for more than 31 consecutive days at any time during a seven-month period within the 12-month period.

Where a person lets more than one such property, the 70-day test may be satisfied by averaging any or all of the accommodation let by that person. A claim for averaging must be made within 22 months of the end of the tax year (ie for 2006–07, by 31 January 2009).

7.5.2 Lettings classified as furnished holiday lettings

The following consequences will follow if a property is treated as being let as furnished holiday accommodation.

Relief for interest

Interest on loans used to purchase the property and to finance the lettings should qualify as an expense incurred in the trade. In some cases, the inclusion of such interest will give rise to a loss for tax purposes.

Capital allowances for plant and machinery

Equipment, furniture and furnishings may attract capital allowances: see 15.2.

Relief for pre-trading expenditure

Expenditure incurred before the business of letting such properties actually commences may be allowed as a loss incurred at the point in time when the lettings commence as pre-trading expenditure (see 15.3).

Relief for losses

Because the activity of letting such property is regarded as a trade, relief can be obtained for losses against the individual's other income (see 6.7). This applies whether the loss arises from interest, capital allowances or pre- trading expenditure or for other reasons provided it can be shown that the activity was carried on, on a commercial basis.

Profits classified as earned income

The legislation provides that profits arising from letting such property should be treated as earned income. This is not dependent on the owner taking any active involvement in the lettings: the whole activity can be dealt with by an agent where desired. This is of less significance following the changes to registered pension schemes from 'A' Day (see 25.1).

Capital gains tax

Roll-over relief may be available: see 16.4.

The property was regarded as a business asset for taper relief (see 12.11).

7.6 'BUY TO LET' INVESTMENTS

7.6.1 General principles

The tax legislation does not recognise the term 'buy to let' investments but in practice the tax treatment of such investments falls within certain clearly defined rules:

(1) Interest paid on a buy to let mortgage can be offset against other UK property income if it exceeds the rent from the property.
(2) A buy to let investment will not attract roll-over relief unless it is to be let as furnished holiday accommodation (see 7.5 above).

7.6.2 Cash backs

A feature over the past two years has been the receipt by buy to let investors of cashbacks from developers. Sometimes the cashbacks have been conditional on the purchase going through by a given date. There are instances where the lender was not advised of the cashbacks and SDLT has been paid on the full price. In such cases, the cashback might have covered the purchaser's deposit so that the lender had effectively made a 100% loan against the discounted price.

No tax charge should arise on the receipt of the cashback (see SP4/97) as this is an ordinary discount to a retail customer.

7.6.3 Deficit situations

In the current market, with initial fixed-rate mortgage periods coming to an end, many over-stretched buy to let investors may face a situation where their borrowing costs exceed their rental income. Income tax legislation gives no sideways relief for such losses against the investor's other income (unless the properties are let as furnished holiday accommodation).

A possible solution would be for the investor to sell some or all of the properties to a company and raise new loans, which he lends on to the company to enable it to pay for the properties. The money received from the company could then be used to clear all or some of the investor's original borrowings. Interest paid on the individual's new loans could be relieved against his other income (see 10.5). The company would generally pay tax at the small companies rate (currently 21%). However, the main problem with this strategy will be if the properties have fallen in value and their current value is substantially less than the investor's outstanding borrowings. Also, SDLT may be payable and the long term CGT implications may not be attractive (the company's acquisition cost will be the market value of the properties at the time that it bought them).

There is no easy solution or 'quick fix' for this situation. If you find yourself in this boat, seek advice from an accountant.

7.7 CAPITAL ALLOWANCES ON INVESTMENT PROPERTIES

7.7.1 Introduction

Capital allowances are usually given when the Revenue assesses the profits of a trade. It is also possible to qualify for capital allowances in respect of expenditure on investment properties, for example where a landlord installs a lift, air-conditioning, electrical equipment, etc, or incurs capital expenditure on a flat over a shop (see 15.2.13). Plant or machinery provided for use in residential property is otherwise excluded. The allowances must first be set against the income of a defined class (see below), but any surplus of allowances may be set against the individual's other income for that year or the following tax year.

7.7.2 Expenditure that may attract allowances

The following are often installed by landlords and generally qualify as plant:

- Electrical, cold water, gas and sewerage systems designed to meet the particular requirements of a trader to whom the building is let;
- Water-heating systems;
- Powered systems of ventilation, air cooling or air purification;
- Lifts, hoists and moving walkways;
- Sprinkler systems and fire alarms;
- Burglar alarm systems;
- Thermal insulation (deduction of £1,500 per dwelling house or capital allowances on all other buildings used for any qualifying business purpose).

7.7.3 Purchase of second-hand buildings

A landlord who acquires a building can often claim capital allowances for the plant contained in it (see 15.2.17).

7.7.4 Changes from April 2008

- Integral fixtures. The writing down allowances for plant that is contained in a building (ie a fixture) have been reduced to 10%.
- Annual investment allowance. The first £50,000 of expenditure each year by businesses on most plant and machinery will attract tax relief in full.
- General plant and machinery. From April 2008, the main rate of writing down allowances has been reduced from 25% to 20%.

7.7.5 Agricultural buildings allowances
(CAA 1990, ss 132(3) and 141)

Agricultural buildings allowances (see 15.2.20) are available for relief by 'discharge or repayment of tax' if the landlord does not carry on a farming trade. The allowances must first be set against agricultural or forestry rental income.

It is necessary to make a claim under CAA 1990, s 141 within two years of the end of the year of assessment in order that agricultural buildings allowances may be set against other income rather than carried forward. If the individual wishes, the surplus allowances may be set against income of the following tax year.

Agricultural buildings allowances are being phased out, with the rate of the allowance being reduced as follows:

2008–09	3%
2009–10	2%
2010–11	1%
2011–12 onwards	nil

7.7.6 Industrial buildings allowances
(CAA 1990, ss 9 and 141)

An individual who owns the relevant interest in an industrial building may qualify for industrial buildings allowances (see 15.2.21) because the property is occupied and used for a qualifying trade. Similarly, an individual who owns a property in an enterprise zone generally qualifies for allowances where the building is occupied for commercial purposes.

The allowances on such buildings must first be set against rental income from the buildings and then against any balancing charge that arises on the disposal of an interest in an industrial building. Any surplus of allowances may then be set against the individual's income for the year, or the following tax year. Again, a formal claim is required under s 141.

Industrial buildings allowances are being phased out, with the rate of the allowance being reduced as follows:

2008–09	3%
2009–10	2%
2010–11	1%
2011–12 onwards	nil

7.7.7 Enterprise zone trust

It is still possible to invest in properties in enterprise zones through a syndicate or 'enterprise zone property trust'. An individual who invests in the trust is treated as if he had incurred a proportion of the trust's expenditure on enterprise zone properties and the allowances may be set against his other income in the same way as described at 7.7.5. In some cases, there may be a delay in that an individual invests in a trust at the end of one tax year and becomes entitled to allowances only for the following year (because that is the year in which the trust acquires the relevant properties). Enterprise zone allowances will be withdrawn from April 2011, but without the phasing out rules applying to industrial and agricultural buildings allowances.

7.8 MINERAL ROYALTIES
(TA 1988, s 122 and Sched 6)

Mineral royalties are normally received net of tax at the basic rate. However, only part of the royalties is taxable as income. Where the recipient is resident or ordinarily resident in the UK, one-half of the mineral royalties is treated as capital gains rather than income. Similarly, only 50% of any management expenses or other sums normally deductible in computing property income may be set against the part of the mineral royalties treated as income.

When the mineral lease comes to an end, the person may claim a capital loss as if he had disposed of the land at its market value at that time. The loss may be set against capital gains for the year in which the mineral lease expires or against capital gains taxed on mineral royalties during the preceding 15 years.

Mineral royalties is defined as including rents, tolls, royalties and other periodic payments relating to the winning and working of minerals (other than water, peat and topsoil) under a lease, licence or other agreement.

7.9 WOODLANDS
(FA 1988, s 65 and Sched 6)

At one time, profits arising from the occupation of woodlands in the UK were taxed under Schedule B. This charge was abolished some years ago. Profits or gains arising from the occupation of woodlands are now exempt and woodlands are not chargeable as UK property income.

7.10 PROPERTY INVESTMENT COMPANY

This is covered in Chapter 26.

7.11 VAT CONSIDERATIONS

Do not overlook VAT: it is possible to register many rental businesses for VAT purposes and this can mean you will recover input tax. However, doing this will mean you will have to charge VAT on the rent (see 21.3.6). Also, VAT will have to be charged when you sell the property.

7.12 INTEREST EARNED ON TRUST FUNDS FOR SERVICE CHARGES AND SINKING FUNDS

Many landlords, or their agents, are required to hold service charges and sinking fund payments made by tenants and leaseholders. In general, these monies are held on trust, ie if the building were destroyed or for some other reason the money never had to be used, it would have to be returned to the tenants.

Interest earned on these funds ought in the past to have been taxed at the 40% trust rate.

Since 6 April 2007 the rate of tax on such interest will normally be only 20%.

8

SAVINGS INCOME

This chapter deals with the types of income from savings that need to be reported on page 3 of the SA tax return (reproduced on p. 42). Apart from dividends, income from savings is always taxed at 20% for 2007–08 unless the taxpayer is liable for higher rate tax (or has insufficient income to come within the basic rate band). Dividends are subject to their own rates of tax of 10% for basic rate taxpayers and 32.5% for higher rate taxpayers.

The types of savings income are:

Interest income received gross

(1) Bank and building society interest.
(2) Other interest income.
(3) Loans to individuals and other private loans.
(4) Gilts and loan stocks.

Interest received net of tax

(5) Rate of tax deducted at source.

Interest-type income traditionally taxed under Schedule D Case VI

(6) Accrued income scheme.

Other interest-type income

(7) Deeply discounted securities.

Dividends from UK companies

(8) Dividends.
(9) Sundry receipts treated as dividends.

Overseas interest and dividend income

(10) Foreign interest and dividends.

Exchange-traded funds

(11) Tax treatment of exchange-traded funds.

INTEREST INCOME RECEIVED GROSS

8.1 BANK AND BUILDING SOCIETY INTEREST

8.1.1 Interest receivable without tax deducted at source

The National Savings Bank (NSB) always pays interest without deduction of tax. The first £70 interest paid on an ordinary NSB account is exempt, but interest on an NSB investment account or from deposit bonds, income bonds or capital bonds is taxable in full.

Interest payments by UK banks or building societies on deposit accounts are normally subject to deduction of tax at source unless the depositor completes form R85. This form requires the depositor's full name, address, date of birth and national insurance number and contains a declaration that the depositor is unlikely to be liable for income tax.

Banks are permitted to pay interest without deduction on non-transferable fixed deposits for amounts of £50,000+ and where the deposit is for a fixed period not exceeding five years.

Interest payments may be made without deduction of tax on certificates of deposit provided the deposit is for at least £50,000 and the bank or building society takes the deposit for a fixed period (which must not exceed five years). Interest may also be paid without deduction of tax on deposits where no certificate of deposit has been issued, but the depositor would be entitled to a certificate if he called for one to be issued.

Interest may also be received without tax being deducted at source from loans to individuals, deposits held by a solicitor and on certificates of tax deposit (see 8.2).

8.1.2 How taxable amount is arrived at

The assessable income is the actual income that arises during the tax year, ie the CY basis. This means that for the current tax year 2008–09 the assessable income is the income receivable for the year ending 5 April 2009. Likewise for the 2007–08 SA form, the income declared is that received in the year ended 5 April 2008.

8.1.3 Date of receipt

Interest is regarded as received when it is credited to the account. Occasionally, cases arise where an individual is required to make a deposit with a bank as a condition of the bank advancing money to a company. In some situations, he is precluded from making withdrawals from the deposit account as long as the company's borrowings are outstanding. The courts have held that an individual who has a deposit account subject to such a block may nevertheless be taxed on interest credited to that account. Furthermore, there is no relief if he never receives the interest because the company goes into liquidation and the bank appropriates the money outstanding to his credit on the deposit account.

8.1.4 Minor children's accounts

A parent who gifts the capital to his unmarried minor child's account is generally charged tax on interest credited to it, unless the total income from that gift does not exceed £100 (see 32.5.4 on aggregation of minor children's income in general).

8.1.5 Rate of tax on income from savings

All interest income counts as income from savings. Tax is charged at 20% unless the recipient is liable for the 40% higher rate or is only liable for tax at the lower rate.

Example

B received untaxed interest of £15,000 in the year ended 5 April 2008. She is single and has other income of £12,000, so she is not subject to higher rate tax. She will pay tax on the interest as follows:

	£
Non-savings income	12,000
Savings income	15,000
	27,000
Less: allowance	(5,225)
	21,775
Non-savings income	
Covered by personal allowance £5,035	Nil
Starting rate £2,230 @ 10%	223.00
Basic rate £4,545 @ 22%	999.90
Savings income	
Lower rate £15,000 @ 20%	3,000.00
Tax due	4,222.90

8.1.6 Holocaust victims' bank accounts: compensation

Compensation paid by banks on dormant accounts opened by Holocaust victims and frozen during World War II is exempt from tax. See the Revenue Press Release dated 8 May 2000.

8.2 OTHER INTEREST INCOME

8.2.1 Interest payable by a solicitor

Interest may be received without deduction of tax from client's accounts held by a firm of solicitors or accountants. Such income was taxable under Schedule D Case III for 2004–05 and earlier years. It is now taxed under ITTOIA 2005 s 369.

8.2.2 Interest receivable on compulsory purchase monies

Where a property is the subject of a compulsory purchase order (CPO) that goes to appeal, and the amount payable is increased, interest is generally payable on the increase. This is regarded as income for the year in which the entitlement arises, ie when the CPO appeal is settled by agreement or on appeal and the interest is received. This principle is not affected by the fact that the interest may have accrued over several years and may be calculated using six-monthly rests.

8.2.3 Certificates of tax deposit

Interest is credited to an individual who has invested in certificates of tax deposit that are either applied to cover tax payable by assessments or are encashed. The interest is taxable and is income for the year of receipt.

8.2.4 Exempt interest

Interest paid by HMRC on over-payments of tax (called 'repayment supplement') is not subject to tax. However, interest paid by Customs in respect of official error is taxable.

8.2.5 Interest awarded by the courts

This may be exempt. The treatment turns on whether the court order or arbitration award provides for payment of interest as such (taxable) or is merely an element taken into account in arriving at the amount to be awarded (which is capital and not taxable income).

Where an investor receives compensation for being mis-sold an investment, part of what he receives may be interest (see *Tax Bulletin* August 2004).

8.3 LOANS TO INDIVIDUALS AND OTHER PRIVATE LOANS

Interest on a private loan to an individual or trust is generally received without deduction of tax. Interest paid by cheque is received when the sum is credited to the recipient's account, not when the cheque is received.

Interest is not assessable where an individual waives the interest before it falls due for payment, provided he receives no consideration for the waiver.

8.4 GILTS AND LOAN STOCKS

Interest payments on British Government Securities ('gilts') will usually be received gross, although this must be requested where interest has previously been received net. There are two exceptions:

(1) Interest on 3$\frac{1}{2}$% War Loan is always paid without deduction.
(2) Where interest is paid on gilts held on the NSB register, interest is also automatically paid without deduction.

Interest payments on loan stocks issued by companies are normally subject to deduction of tax at source.

Again, interest from gilts and loan stocks is regarded as income from savings and so qualifies for the 20% rate (see 8.1.5).

INTEREST RECEIVED NET OF TAX

8.5 RATE OF TAX DEDUCTED AT SOURCE
(TA 1988, ss 480A–482)

Interest payments made by UK banks and building societies are normally subject to deduction of tax at source (for exceptions see 8.1.1).

Interest paid on gilts may also be paid net of tax except in the case of 3½% War Loan and stocks held on the NSB register. Interest paid on local authority loan stocks and company loan stocks and debentures is subject to deduction of tax, as indeed is all interest paid by UK companies to persons other than group companies.

Because such income is income from savings, tax is deducted at 20%.

Certain unit trusts that invest only in bank deposits or gilts are treated as 'transparent' so that distributions of income are treated as interest rather than dividends. Once again, 20% tax is withheld at source.

INTEREST-TYPE INCOME TRADITIONALLY TAXED UNDER SCHEDULE D CASE VI

8.6 ACCRUED INCOME SCHEME
(TA 1988, ss 710–728)

8.6.1 Introduction

An individual who sells a gilt or fixed-interest loan stock may sell either cum- or ex-interest. In the former case, the buyer receives the next interest payment; in the latter, the seller receives the next interest payment even though it is paid after he has sold the gilt or loan stock. In practice, gilts, etc, are quoted on an ex-interest basis from six weeks or so before interest is due for payment.

The price at which a gilt or loan stock is sold generally reflects an adjustment for accrued interest. For example, if a gilt pays interest every six months, a person who sells at the end of Month 4 will receive a price that reflects four months' accrued interest. Conversely, a person who sells at the end of Month 5 would normally sell on an ex-interest basis and the purchaser would take a deduction for one month's interest (as the seller would receive this).

8.6.2 Accrued income taxable

The accrued income scheme may apply where the nominal value of gilts or loan stocks held at any point in the year exceeds £5,000. It brings into charge the interest credited to sellers of gilts and loan stocks. The interest deemed to accrue on a daily basis is treated for tax purposes as if it had been received by the seller. The amount of any adjustments in the other direction (interest received but not earned over the period of ownership) is deducted and the net amount charged to tax on the CY basis.

Example

> C subscribes £30,000 for a new Government Stock, 5% Treasury Stock 2050 issued on 1 August 2007. He holds the stock for 86 days and then sells it to D, who holds the stock at 1 February 2008 when the first six months' interest is payable. C will be assessable for income tax purposes on £353, ie $^{86}/_{183}$ 3 £750 (the half-yearly interest payable on stock). D will be entitled to a deduction of the same amount in computing his taxable income. His position will therefore be as follows:
>
> | | £ |
> |---|---|
> | D receives six months' interest of | 750 |
> | He deducts 'rebate interest' | 353 |
> | Taxable income | 397 |

8.6.3 Types of securities within accrued income scheme
(TA 1988, s 710)

The scheme applies to acquisitions and disposals of virtually all types of fixed interest securities by UK-resident individuals. The securities must be loan stock and not shares, but the scheme may apply to foreign securities as well as to UK loan stocks.

Savings certificates, certificates of deposit and zero coupon bonds are excluded. Bills of exchange and Treasury bills are not regarded as securities because they are within the definition of certificates of deposit (see 8.2.3), which are also excluded.

8.6.4 Types of disposal that may be caught
(TA 1988, s 710)

The scheme applies to transfers. This term is widely defined in TA 1988 and includes:

(1) a sale (s 710(5));
(2) an exchange (s 710(5)) or a conversion of securities (s 710(13));
(3) a gift (s 710(5));
(4) any transfer other than under (1)–(3) above (s 710(5));
(5) death (s 721(1));
(6) a change in the true ownership where a person entitled to securities becomes a trustee in relation to them (s 720(4)).

8.6.5 Year of assessment
(TA 1988, s 714)

The assessment is made for the tax year in which the interest period ends, ie if a loan stock pays interest on 30 April, a disposal of the stock on a cum-interest basis on 5 April 2008 produces taxable income for 2008–09.

8.6.6 Income from savings

Amounts of accrued income taxed under ITTOIA 2005 count as income from savings (see 8.1.5).

8.6.7 Calculation of accrued amount and rebate amount
(TA 1988, ss 710, 713 and 714)

Where transactions go through the London Stock Exchange, the accrued and rebate amounts are calculated by the broker and appear on the contract note. Where the transaction does not go through the market, the calculation is made in the same way.

If there is more than one transaction in 'securities of the same kind', the accrued and rebate amounts can be netted off. This term is interpreted strictly: £5,000 9% Treasury Stock 2020 is 'of the same kind' as £10,000 9% Treasury Stock 2020, but is not 'of the same kind' as some other issue of Treasury stock.

Separate calculation is necessary of all accrued and rebate amounts. Relief is given for a rebate amount against the next interest received on that security or, if a transfer intervenes, against the accrued amount. Thus it is possible for a rebate amount in one tax year to be set against interest received in the next.

OTHER INTEREST-TYPE INCOME

8.7 DEEPLY DISCOUNTED SECURITIES
(ITTOIA 2005 s 427)

8.7.1 Introduction

The legislation may also bring sums deemed to be interest income into charge.

A loan stock may be issued at a discount, or be redeemable at a premium. In either case, the borrower undertakes that when the loan is repaid the borrower will receive more than the amount originally paid on the issue of the stock. A typical situation is where a loan stock is issued at £80 for every £100 nominal and when the loan stock is redeemed the investor is entitled to receive £100. There are no provisions for the payer to deduct tax from discount.

The discount or premium is charged to tax where the loan stock is within the definition of a deeply discounted security and the company that issues the bond is a UK company. If the issuer is an overseas company, the discount is treated as foreign interest income.

8.7.2 Definition of 'deeply discounted security'
(ITTOIA 2005 s 430)

A loan stock is not a deeply discounted security just because it is issued at a discount; it must be issued at a deep discount. A discount is regarded as a deep discount only where it exceeds 0.5% for every year of the loan stock's intended life, or where the discount exceeds 15% in total.

The following types of loan stock cannot be a deeply discounted security:

(1) index-linked gilts.
(2) gilts issued prior to 14 March 1989;
(3) a loan stock that is convertible into shares; and
(4) certain corporate loan stocks the redemption price of which is linked to shares or other assets.

Examples – Deeply discounted security

> (1) A five-year loan stock is issued at £95 for every £100 nominal. This is a deeply discounted security because the discount exceeds 0.5% pa.
> (2) A 35-year loan stock is issued at £80 for every £100 nominal. This is a deeply discounted security, even though the discount is less than 0.5% pa, because it exceeds 15% in total.

8.7.3 Events that give rise to a tax charge
(ITTOIA 2005 s 437-439)

A disposal of a deeply discounted security can give rise to a tax charge. The whole of the profit is taxable as if it were interest.

Example – Disposal of deep discount security

> A bond is issued at £82, redeemable at £100 after two years. This reflects a compound interest rate of approximately 10% since 82 * $(^{110}\!/_{100})^2$ = 100. If the holder sells for £93 after 12 months, he will be assessed on the difference between £82 and £93, ie £11. If the purchaser holds the bond until it is redeemed in Year 2 he will be chargeable on the redemption profit of £18 as income for that year.

8.7.4 Stripped gilts

There is one exception to the general rule that individuals and trustees are taxed on discounted securities only when a disposal takes place. Where a stripped gilt is held, it is necessary to revalue it at the end of each tax year and the owner must pay tax on any increase in value as if it were income. These rules were extended with effect from 27 March 2003 so that they now also apply to strips of non-UK government securities.

8.7.5 Income from savings

Discounts taxed as interest-type income count as income from savings (see 8.1.5).

8.7.6 Losses

An individual who realised a loss on the disposal of a deeply discounted security was allowed to deduct this from his taxable income for the year. However, the loss could not be carried back or forward to a future year. This loss relief was withdrawn by FA 2003 in relation to most losses realised on disposals made on or after 27 March 2003. Loss relief can still be available for quoted securities acquired before that date.

DIVIDENDS FROM UK COMPANIES

8.8 DIVIDENDS

8.8.1 Taxable for year in which they fall due for payment
(ITTOIA 2005, ss 383-385)

The dividends that need to be reported on a tax return, and that are income for a tax year, are the dividends that were due for payment in the year. If you have shares in a company that declared a dividend that was payable on

5 April 2008, you must report the dividend as 2007–08 income. This is not affected by the fact that you may not have received the dividend cheque until early in the next tax year.

The period for which the dividend is paid is not relevant. A final dividend for a company's year that ended on 31 December 2007 would be income for 2008–09 if it was paid in, say, June 2008.

A dividend from a UK company carries a tax credit (see 8.8.2).

8.8.2 Rate of tax on dividends received from UK companies

A shareholder is entitled to a tax credit of one-ninth of the dividend. This credit is non-refundable.

An individual whose income is within the basic rate band does not have to pay any additional tax on a UK dividend; the tax credit is treated as covering his liability. Higher rate taxpayers pay a special 32.5% rate on dividends and are able to set the tax credit against this. In practice, this means that the effective rate of higher rate tax is one-quarter of the actual dividend receipt.

8.8.3 Dividends paid by unit trusts

Dividends from unit trusts are normally treated in the same way as dividends from companies except in regard to 'equalisation'. This is an amount paid to holders of units who have acquired them since the last dividend was paid. The equalisation payment is not taxable as income but is instead treated as a return of capital.

Unit trusts that invest in gilts and corporate bonds are treated differently (see 8.5).

8.8.4 Dividends paid by Real Estate Investment Trusts

REIT distributions should not be included in the figure entered in a tax return for UK dividends because they are treated as rental income. Basic rate tax is withheld at source and this tax can be reclaimed by any recipient who is not liable for tax.

8.8.5 Stock dividends
(ITTOIA 2005, s 409)

A company may make a 'scrip' or bonus issue so that shareholders receive new shares in proportion to their existing shareholdings. This is not taxable income because in reality all that has happened is that the company has subdivided its share capital by issuing new shares.

In contrast to this, a company may offer shareholders the choice between a cash dividend and additional shares to a similar value. This is called a 'stock dividend' and is taxable income.

'Enhanced scrip dividends' are a special type of stock dividend where the company offers a premium to shareholders who take stock rather than cash and makes prior arrangements to enable the shareholders to dispose of the shares that they have acquired by taking the stock alternative.

8.8.6 How stock dividends are assessed
(SP A8)

A shareholder who accepts extra shares in lieu of a cash dividend is normally treated as if he had received a dividend equal to the cash that he could have taken. Tax is deemed to have been paid at the lower rate.

A slightly different treatment applies where the value of the shares taken as the stock dividend differs from the cash dividend by 15% or more. In such a case, the shareholder is deemed to have received a dividend equal to the shares' value at the date of issue. The shareholder may therefore be required to pay higher rate tax on the 'grossed up' value of the dividend or the shares.

Example – Taxation of dividends

> E was entitled to a dividend of £2,100 or extra shares in X plc. He took the shares. If the shares were worth £1,900, he will nevertheless be charged higher rate tax on £2,100 plus an amount equal to the tax credit; the amount charged to higher rate tax for 2007–08 is £2,333 (£2,100 grossed up for the 10% tax credit).
>
> If the shares were worth £2,600 when they were issued, he would be charged higher rate tax on £2,600 'grossed up', ie £2,889.

8.8.7 Consequences for CGT of taking a stock dividend

In the example in 8.8.6, the shareholder's acquisition value for CGT purposes of the shares that he acquires through the stock dividend is the amount on which he is assessed for higher rate purposes less basic rate tax.

8.8.8 Demerger dividends
(TA 1988, s 213)

A dividend may take the form of an issue of shares formerly held by the company in a subsidiary. Where the necessary Revenue clearances have been obtained, such a dividend is treated as capital and not as taxable income. The documentation issued by the company normally states that clearance has been obtained from the Revenue and that the demerger is an exempt distribution.

8.8.9 Other dividend income

See 8.9 on sundry receipts from UK companies that are treated as distributions. See also 8.10.1 on dividends paid by foreign companies that are treated as income from savings.

8.9 SUNDRY RECEIPTS TREATED AS DIVIDENDS

8.9.1 Deemed dividends
(TA 1988, s 209)

There are various transactions that can count as a distribution, particularly where a person holds shares in a close company (see 17.13). From the recipient's point of view, a distribution is for all practical purposes the same as a dividend.

8.9.2 Interest at more than commercial rate
(TA 1988, s 209)

Interest paid to a shareholder may constitute a distribution in so far as it exceeds a normal commercial rate.

8.9.3 Issue of redeemable shares
(TA 1988, s 209(2)(c))

An issue to shareholders of redeemable preference shares (or other redeemable shares) counts as a distribution. The redeemable shares' value at the date they are issued is treated as if it were a dividend paid in cash at that time. This rule does not apply where the redeemable shares are issued for new consideration.

8.9.4 Bonus issue following repayment of share capital
(TA 1988, s 210)

Where a company has repaid share capital in the past, a subsequent bonus issue is treated as a dividend paid to the shareholders who receive the bonus shares. These shareholders may not be the same people whose shares were previously bought back by the company, but this does not make any difference to the way in which the current shareholders are taxed on receipt of a bonus issue of shares in these circumstances.

8.9.5 Benefits-in-kind provided to shareholders
(TA 1988, s 418)

Where shareholders in a close company (see 17.13) are provided with benefits-in-kind, they may be assessed as employment income. If they are not employed by the company, it is not possible for the Revenue to assess benefits-in-kind in this way. In these circumstances, the company may be deemed to have made a distribution equal to the value of the benefits-in-kind concerned.

8.9.6 Assets transferred by or to close company
(TA 1988, s 209(4))

A deemed distribution may arise where assets are transferred from the members of a company to the company at a price that exceeds their market value, or company assets are transferred to shareholders at a price that is less than market value.

8.9.7 Purchase by company of its own shares
(TA 1988, s 209)

The general rule is that where a company buys back its shares, the amount paid by the company is treated as a distribution in so far as it exceeds the shares' original issue price.

The amount treated as a distribution is not affected by the shares' value at the time they were acquired by an individual. Consequently, where a person has acquired shares by inheritance or bought them from an existing shareholder, his acquisition value may exceed the original issue price (ie the amount paid to the company in return for the shares being issued). In the event of a purchase of own shares by a company, it is the issue price that is important.

Example – Purchase by company of own shares

> *F* acquires 1,000 shares in *Y* Ltd for £10,000. The shares were originally issued at their par value of £1 per share. It subsequently transpires that *F* cannot get on with the company's directors. If her shares are bought back by the company at £9 per share, *F* is deemed to have received a distribution of £8,000, even though she had actually made a capital loss.

8.9.8 Relief under TA 1988, s 219

In certain circumstances it may be possible for a company to purchase its own shares without the transaction being treated as giving rise to a distribution. Clearance must be obtained from the Revenue that the purchase of own shares is for the benefit of the company's trade. The conditions that must be satisfied are:

(1) the company must be unquoted;
(2) it must be a trading company or the holding company of a trading group;
(3) the seller must be resident and ordinarily resident in the UK;
(4) the seller must have owned the shares for at least five years;
(5) the seller's interest in the company must be 'substantially reduced'; and
(6) the purchase must be undertaken to benefit the company's trade.

Alternatively, s 219 may apply where shares are being bought back within two years of the shareholder's death and the reason for this is that the personal representatives would not otherwise be able to pay the IHT due on the estate.

OVERSEAS INTEREST AND DIVIDEND INCOME

8.10 FOREIGN INTEREST AND DIVIDENDS

Interest on bonds issued by overseas governments or companies used to be received via a 'paying agent'. This system was abolished in 2001. All such income is now received without deduction of UK tax.

8.10.1 Foreign interest and dividends

Prior to the enactment of ITTOIA 2005, non-UK income was generally assessable under Schedule D, Cases IV and V. ITTOIA 2005 takes a different approach to charging such income to tax, so that for 2005/06 onwards each type of non-UK income previously within Case IV or V is charged to tax under the provisions charging the equivalent type of UK income.

8.10.2 How the taxable amount is computed

Income is taxed on the CY basis.

A point to watch with all foreign investments is that income tax is charged on the interest credited or dividends received, without reference to any exchange gain or loss on the money deposited or invested.

Tax notes

With foreign investments, income tax is charged on the interest credited or dividends received, without taking into account any exchange gain or loss.

Example – Foreign currency deposit account

In June 2006, *F* deposited £10,000 with a foreign bank. At the then exchange rate of £1 = 20 units of foreign currency, that sum was credited as 200,000 units. In June 2007, when the exchange rate was £1 = 25 units, interest of 30,000 units was credited to the account. In June 2008, *F* closed the account, receiving back his original capital, the interest credited in June 2007 and a further 20,000 foreign currency units as interest to close. By then the exchange rate was £1 = 30 units, so the sterling equivalent of the 250,000 units was only £8,333.

In commercial terms, *F* has suffered a loss of £1,667, but for tax purposes he received interest of £1,200 in June 2007 (30,000 units at £1 = 25) and £667 in June 2008 (20,000 units at £1 = 30) and income tax must be paid on that interest. He has also made a capital loss of £3,534, calculated as follows:

		£	£
Proceeds of	250,000 units	8,333	
	200,000 units cost (June 2006)	10,000	
	30,000 units cost (June 2007)	1,200	
	20,000 units cost (June 2008)	667	
Capital loss		11,867	
			(3,534)

Unfortunately, that capital loss may only be used by set-off against capital gains on the disposal of other assets. If F has no such gains, he cannot utilise the loss and so has paid tax on a profit of £1,867 when he has in fact made an overall loss of £1,667.

8.10.3 Double tax relief

Relief may be claimed for foreign tax withheld from the interest or dividends. This credit will be restricted to the amount of UK tax due on the income source, and if the foreign tax does not meet the full amount of tax due this shortfall will be payable.

Example – Relief by Credit

G has UK earnings of £17,500 in 2007–08 and foreign income from property of £3,000 on which foreign tax of £750 has been paid. She is entitled to a personal allowance of £5,225.

(a) Tax on total income	£	
Earnings	17,500	
Income from property	3,000	(foreign tax £500)
	20,500	
Personal allowance	5,225	
Taxable income	15,275	
Tax on £15,275 @ 10/22%	3,092.90	

(b) Tax on total income less foreign income	£
Earnings	17,500
Personal allowance	5,225
Taxable income	12,275
Tax on £12,275 @ 10/22%	2,432.90

The difference in tax between (a) and (b) is £660. The foreign tax is less than this and the full credit of £500 is available against the UK tax payable. If the foreign tax had been £750, the credit would be limited to £660 and the balance of £90 would be unrelieved.

8.10.4 Retention tax

Countries in the EU, and most offshore territories, introduced a system during 2005 whereby a person who is not resident there and who is in receipt of interest must either agree to his identity being revealed to the revenue authorities of the country where he resides or have 15% retention tax withheld at source. The retention tax was then paid over to the revenue authority of the country in which the person is resident but without the person's identity being disclosed.

The fact that interest has suffered retention tax does not alter the person's obligation to include the income on his tax return. Conversely, a person is allowed a credit for tax withheld in this way. If, exceptionally, he is not liable for the 15% tax, HMRC will repay this. The rate of retention tax is increased to 20% from 1 July 2008.

8.10.5 Some income taxable on the remittance basis is not income from savings

Foreign interest taxed under the remittance basis (see 34.12) does not count as income from savings. This meant that foreign domiciliaries paid tax at 22% for 2007–08 on income that would have been taxed at 20% if they had been UK domiciled.

8.10.6 Foreign dividends treated as savings income for 2007–08

It was not formerly the case but for the tax years 2006–07 and 2007–08, a foreign domiciled individual who remitted an overseas dividend was taxed at 10% if he was a basic rate taxpayer and at 32.5% if he was a higher rate taxpayer.

8.10.7 Foreign dividends not treated as savings income for 2008–09

FA 2008 has reversed the change described at 8.10.6 for 2008–09 onwards. This means that remittance basis users who bring foreign dividends into the UK may be taxed at 40% and not at the 32.5% rate.

However, see 8.10.10 regarding the possible availability of a 10% tax credit.

8.10.8 Stock dividends and other peculiarities
(TA 1988, s 249)

As explained in 8.8.5, an investor who opts to take a stock dividend (ie additional shares in lieu of a cash dividend) from a UK company is taxed as if he had received an equivalent amount in cash. This rule does not apply where a non-UK resident company declares a stock dividend.

A higher rate taxpayer offered the choice between a stock and a cash dividend is therefore usually better off taking the stock dividend. However, this assumes that the additional shares offered are worth at least as much as the cash option and that they are readily saleable. As always, the 'tax-saving' tail must not be allowed to wag the 'sensible investment policy' dog. Moreover, in one court case it was suggested that, if stock dividends are taken year after year, and the shares so obtained are sold to provide the shareholder with an income, then income tax may be charged on that income. The Revenue is unlikely to take this view unless a substantial amount of money is at stake.

In some situations, payments by an overseas company may escape income tax where an equivalent payment by a UK company would be taxable as a dividend. The most common situation where this occurs is where a payment by an overseas company is treated under the relevant foreign law as a partial return of the shareholders' original investment. Such distributions are treated as capital even though a similar payment by a UK company would be treated as taxable income. This is an area where you may need professional advice.

8.10.9 Reporting untaxed income from abroad

If you have foreign dividends or interest, you will need to tick the box at Q5 on the second page of your tax return and complete a special schedule for foreign income.

8.10.10 Taxation of foreign dividends from 2007–08

From 6 April 2008, owners of foreign shares are entitled to a non-repayable tax credit of one ninth of the dividend to align the treatment with that of dividends paid by UK companies. The notional tax credit will cover any basic rate liability. Higher rate taxpayers will be charged at a rate of 32.5% on the dividend and tax credit in the same way as if they had received a UK dividend.

This treatment will not apply where an individual owns 10% or more of the shares in the foreign company.

EXCHANGE-TRADED FUNDS

8.11 TAX TREATMENT OF EXCHANGE-TRADED FUNDS

These are a type of collective investment scheme that have become increasingly popular. An investor in such a fund gets an income and capital return that exactly match the index chosen, whether that be the FTSE100 share index, an index based on an overseas stock exchange or an index that reflects all the Investment Grade $ Corporate Bonds etc. Furthermore, the charges are usually rather less than those charged by managers of tracker unit trusts.

However, the tax treatment will normally follow the legal structure. Many exchange-traded funds are Luxembourg or Irish open-ended companies. As such, distributions of income are treated as dividends and a realisation of the investment may produce a capital gain (or loss). No tax will normally be withheld from such dividends.

Bear in mind that a UK-domiciled investor in an exchange-traded fund invested in qualifying corporate bonds may have a capital gain on realising his investment whereas no capital gain would have arisen if he had realised direct investments in such bonds.

9

OTHER INCOME

This chapter deals with other income received that will need to be reported on your tax return but does not fall easily into the 'fill the box category' of more standard investments and may require the filing of supporting SA schedules. Most of the various types of income from sources covered in this chapter are received without deduction of tax at source. The exceptions where basic tax will generally be deducted are covered at 9.10.

The following are covered:

Untaxed income from abroad

(1) Foreign real estate income.
(2) Alimony and maintenance payments.
(3) Investment in overseas partnerships.
(4) Double tax relief.
(5) Foreign pensions.

Miscellaneous investment income

(6) Sale of certificates of deposit.
(7) Gains from roll-up, and other offshore, funds.

Miscellaneous income

(8) Miscellaneous income.
(9) Taxation of commission, cashbacks and discounts.

Income received net of tax

(10) Annuities, trust income, etc.

UNTAXED INCOME FROM ABROAD

9.1 FOREIGN REAL ESTATE INCOME
(IT(T&OI)A 2005, s 265)

It is not unusual for a UK resident to have bought – or inherited – a villa or flat abroad. It is less usual to own commercial premises, but the tax rules are the same. In addition, the same rules apply to properties bought under 'timeshare' arrangements.

> **Tax notes**
>
> If you have untaxed income from abroad, a special schedule of your SA tax return must be completed. Advice on which form needs to be completed can be obtained by calling the number on the front of your tax form or by consulting a practising tax accountant.

9.1.1 How income is computed

In calculating the assessable rent, the landlord may deduct expenses paid: for example, repairs, redecoration, insurance, maid service, gardening, management fees and advertising. If the landlord sometimes uses the property himself, then an apportionment of these expenses must be made in the same way as for a UK property (see 7.2).

There are three important differences between the tax treatment of rent from real property in the UK and rent from property abroad:

(1) The 'rent-a-room' scheme (see 7.4) applies only to properties in the UK; this exemption cannot be claimed against rents from an overseas property.
(2) Similarly, the special rules allowing the provision of furnished holiday accommodation to be treated as a trade (see 7.5) apply only where the relevant property is situated in the UK.
(3) If the rental income statement for an overseas property shows a deficit for a year (ie if expenses excluding interest paid exceed rent received), that deficit may be carried forward and deducted from the rent received in respect of the same property in the next year (and the deduction may be rolled forward indefinitely until there is rental income against which it can be set). However, no other form of loss relief is available. In particular, the deficit may not be set against rents received from other properties, whether in the UK or abroad. Interest payments can be deducted even if the interest is paid overseas.

9.1.2 Accounts

In the past, rental income statements should have been drawn up to 5 April, but in practice the Revenue often accepted statements drawn up to any convenient date. For example, the rental statement for the calendar year will often have been taken as the measure of the income for the tax year. This is no longer acceptable and it is necessary to report the income that has actually arisen in the tax year.

One possible complication is that income may be received, and expenses incurred, in either UK or local currency. In practice, the Revenue accepts any reasonable basis of currency conversion. For example, if a local agent collects the rents, disburses local expenses and remits a net sum to the landlord, that net amount may be converted at the spot rate for the day it was remitted. However, the Revenue expects the same basis of conversion to be retained from one year to the next.

9.2 ALIMONY AND MAINTENANCE PAYMENTS
(IT(T & OI)A 2005, s 727)

A UK resident may receive maintenance or alimony payments from a spouse, former spouse or parent resident abroad. This income is almost always exempt from tax.

It used to be that the tax treatment was dependent on whether the maintenance or alimony payments counted as an 'existing obligation'. Broadly, an existing obligation was one created by a court order or agreement made before 15 March 1988 either in the UK or abroad. Even payments under existing obligations were taken out of charge from 6 April 2000.

9.3 INVESTMENT IN OVERSEAS PARTNERSHIPS
(TA 1988, s 391)

A UK resident may be a sleeping partner in a business carried on abroad. For example, a man might provide the finance for his son to set up in business abroad in return for a share of the profits. It may be difficult to tell whether the father has become a sleeping partner in the son's business or has made a loan at interest to the son. If the father is entitled to a stated proportion of profits (say, one-quarter), then he is certainly a sleeping partner; if he is entitled to a fixed annual sum, he may be a sleeping partner or may simply have made a loan. In practice, since both interest and a sleeping partner's profit share are taxed in the same way, it will not normally be necessary to decide this.

The important question is whether the UK resident is a sleeping or an active partner. If he is an active partner, the partnership business is likely to be carried on at least partly within the UK, in which case complex questions arise that are outside the scope of this book and specialist advice should be sought.

If the sleeping partner is entitled to a fixed sum, at annual or other intervals, and that sum is stated in a foreign currency, then each instalment must, for tax purposes, be converted into sterling at the spot rate for the date it falls due. If he is entitled to a stated proportion of profits, and the business accounts are prepared in a foreign currency, the appropriate profit figure must be converted into sterling at the spot rate for the last day of the accounting period. If the sleeping partner is obliged to bear a share of a trading loss, that loss may be relieved against overseas trading and pension income, but not against overseas investment income or any UK income. In most cases, therefore, it is relieved by deducting the loss amount from the partnership profit share assessable for a later year.

9.4 DOUBLE TAX RELIEF
(TA 1988, s 790)

Foreign tax paid can be deducted from the UK tax charged on the same income.

Example – Double tax relief

D, a basic rate taxpayer, receives an interest payment of £1,000 from abroad, on which the foreign tax is £150. The UK tax position is:

	£
Gross interest	1,000
Foreign tax deducted or paid	(150)
Net receipt	850
UK tax at 20% of £1,000	200
Less: foreign tax paid	(150)
UK tax to be paid	50
After-tax income	800

If D were liable for tax at only 10%, the foreign tax would bring his UK tax liability down to nil, but he would not be entitled to reclaim the difference of £50.

9.4.1 An important practical point

Relief for overseas tax is not given unless the individual can prove that he has indeed paid the tax. It is not sufficient simply to demonstrate that tax is payable under foreign law: the claimant must be able to show that he has indeed paid that tax by producing an official receipt or tax deduction certificate.

9.4.2 Foreign tax adjustments

The Revenue must be notified if an amount of foreign tax paid is later adjusted and this means that too much credit has been allowed as double taxation relief. Failure to notify the Revenue within one year of an adjustment results in a taxpayer becoming liable to a penalty (not exceeding the tax underpaid) because of the claim that has proved to be excessive.

If a foreign tax adjustment means that you have not claimed enough you are under no statutory duty to report this, but it is clearly in your own interests to do so.

9.5 FOREIGN PENSIONS
(ITEPA 2003, s 573)

Certain foreign pensions are taxable as foreign income:

(1) Pensions paid by a person outside the UK.
(2) Pensions paid on behalf of a person outside the UK.
(3) Voluntary pensions paid by a person outside the UK.

Foreign pensions are taxed as follows:

(a) pensioner is resident, ordinarily resident and domiciled in the UK – 90% of the pension is charged to tax;

(b) pensioner is resident but not ordinarily resident in the UK – the pension is assessed on the remittance basis by reference to sums brought into the UK;

(c) pensioner is resident and ordinarily resident, but not domiciled, in the UK – the pension was automatically taxed on the remittance basis in 2007–08 and may be assessed on the remittance basis in 2008–09 and subsequent years if the individual makes a claim to be taxed on this basis.

Foreign pensions are taxed on the CY basis.

Nazi compensation pensions
(ITEPA 2003, s 642)

Annuities and premiums paid under German or Austrian law to victims of Nazi persecution are exempt from income tax. These are pensions paid because of serious damage to the individual's health; they are also exempt from tax in Germany and Austria.

In addition, some payments to victims or their heirs from dormant bank accounts will also be exempted from tax.

MISCELLANEOUS INVESTMENT INCOME

9.6 SALE OF CERTIFICATES OF DEPOSIT
(IT(T&OI)A 2005, s 551)

A certificate of deposit is a document that entitles the holder to receive the amount held on deposit. An owner of such a deposit can assign it to someone else. Where this is done for valuable consideration, the profit is taxable as income.

At one time it was possible to avoid having taxable income by assigning ownership of a deposit without there being a certificate of deposit. Profits on such transactions are now also caught as income taxable under s 551. They are not treated as income from savings.

This income should be reported on the SA form as part of the answer to Q15 on page 3.

9.7 GAINS FROM ROLL-UP, AND OTHER OFFSHORE, FUNDS
(TA 1988, ss 757–763)

An income tax charge may arise on gains from disposals of certain offshore funds. The types of funds concerned are generally collective investment schemes similar to unit trusts. In many cases the fund earns bank interest that is accumulated within the fund rather than distributed as dividend. When the shareholder disposes of his investment he receives the benefit of this accumulated interest in the price that he obtains for his shares.

The charge arises on the gain as it would be computed for CGT purposes, but with no allowance for indexation.

Example – Tax on offshore funds

A has held shares in an offshore fund since June 1993. The shares cost £14,000 and are worth £17,000 when sold in August 2006. If the offshore fund does not have distributor status, the gain of £3,000 is taxable income for 2006–07.

If the offshore fund had distributor status, the gain would have been charged to CGT rather than as income. The amount charged would have been less than £3,000 because of indexation allowance and the gain may have been covered by *A*'s annual exemption for CGT purposes (see 12.1.1).

9.7.1 No charge on distributor funds
(TA 1988, s 760 and Sched 27)

Gains from distributor funds are generally exempt from the charge under s 757. Offshore funds qualified for distributor status up to 2007–08 where at least 85% of investment income received by the fund was distributed as dividend. In the case of commodity funds, the 85% distribution requirement was reduced to 42.5%.

Where a fund did not qualify as a distributor fund, an income tax charge arose on a disposal. This includes certain disposals not taken into account for CGT purposes, for example a share exchange on a takeover of a fund. It also includes a deemed disposal on the shareholder's death.

It is necessary for the fund to have had distributor status for the whole period of an individual's ownership if the gain is to be taxed as capital gain rather than miscellaneous income, ie it is an 'all or nothing' test.

From 6 April 2008, a fund can be treated as a distributor fund where it reports income to investors who will then be liable for tax on this income whether they actually receive it or not.

9.7.2 Equalisation arrangements
(TA 1988, s 758)

Where an overseas fund has distributor status and there are equalisation arrangements, any sum paid to a shareholder on the sale of his shares or units and treated as equalisation is taxed as income. There is no income tax charge on the balance of the disposal proceeds.

9.7.3 Gains realised by foreign domiciliaries
(TA 1988, s 762)

A gain from a disposal of an offshore fund by a person of foreign domicile is taxed on the remittance basis (see 34.12).

9.7.4 Gains not income from savings

Gains realised from the disposal of offshore funds do not count as income from savings (see Chapter 8).

MISCELLANEOUS INCOME

9.8 MISCELLANEOUS INCOME
(IT(T&OI)A 2005, ss 261,575,579,609,614,687)

Tax was charged under Schedule D Case VI for 2004–05 and earlier years in respect of any annual profits or gains that did not fall under any other Schedule D case and was not charged by virtue of any other schedule. Such income has been taxed under IT(T&OI)A 2005 since 2005–06.

Post-cessation receipts (see 15.4) are charged as miscellaneous income, as are gains from roll-up funds, profits under the accrued income scheme and gains on foreign life policies. Furthermore, where tax is charged under various anti-avoidance provisions (see Chapter 32) the amounts charged to tax are normally miscellaneous income.

In addition, profits from certain 'one-off' or isolated business activities in the nature of a trade have been charged as miscellaneous income. Thus, the following were held by the courts to be this type of income:

(1) commission for guaranteeing overdrafts;
(2) underwriting commission on share issues;
(3) insurance commission;
(4) receipts for the use of copyright material;
(5) payments made to the wife of a train robber for their life story;
(6) profits realised by an 'angel', ie a person who sponsored a play and was entitled to a share of the profits.

Miscellaneous income can be earned income or investment income.

9.8.1 Miscellaneous income losses
(IT(T&OI)A 2005, s 872)

Losses from activities that would be taxed as miscellaneous income can be set against any profits assessable as miscellaneous income, whether or not the profits arise from the same activity. However, they cannot be set against other types of income such as employment income or savings income.

9.9 TAXATION OF COMMISSION, CASHBACKS AND DISCOUNTS

9.9.1 Commission on insurance products, etc

The Revenue published SP4/97 on the taxation of commission, cashbacks and discounts, further commenting on this subject in *Tax Bulletin* issue 33. The Revenue has offered its assurances to the 'ordinary retail customer' that there normally will be no tax liabilities on rebated commissions or discounts. However, the position is more complex with regard to insurance products. SP4/97 states:

Life insurance and personal pensions

Qualifying life insurance policies
36 Where commission in respect of a policy holder's own qualifying life insurance policy is received, netted off or invested, that policy will not be disqualified as a result of entitlement to that commission if the contract under which commission arises is separate from the contract of insurance. In practice, the Revenue will not seek to read two contracts as one in a way that would lead to the loss of qualifying policy status.

37 Where a policy holder pays a discounted premium in respect of his or her own policy, the premium payable under the policy will be the discounted premium. It is this amount that must be used for the purposes of establishing whether the relevant qualifying rules are met.

Calculation of chargeable event gains in respect of life policies, capital redemption policies and life annuity contracts
38 Chargeable event gains are computed by reference to the premiums or lump sum consideration paid. The amount paid will be interpreted as follows –
–   where a policy holder pays a gross premium and receives commission in respect of that policy, the chargeable event gain is calculated using the gross amount paid without taking the commission received into account;
–   where an amount of commission is received or due under an enforceable legal right and subsequently invested in the policy, that amount is included as a premium paid when calculating the chargeable event gain (but see 9.9.2 below);
–   where a policy holder nets off commission from an insurer in respect of his or her own policy from the gross amount of premium payable and the commission is not taxable as income on the policy holder, the chargeable event gain is calculated using the net amount paid to the insurer;
–   where a policy holder pays a discounted premium, the chargeable event gain is calculated using the discounted amount of premium paid;
–   where extra value is added to the policy by the insurer (for example by allocation of bonus units), the premium for the purpose of calculating the chargeable event is the amount paid by the policy holder without taking the extra value into account.

Tax relief in respect of personal pension contributions

39 Tax relief for contributions to personal pension schemes is due in respect of 'a contribution paid by an individual'. The amount of the contribution will be interpreted as follows where the contract under which the commission arises is separate from the personal pension scheme contract –

- where a contributor pays a gross contribution and receives commission in respect of that contribution, tax relief is given on the gross amount paid without taking the commission received into account;
- where an amount of commission is received by, or is due under an enforceable legal right to, the contributor and subsequently invested in the personal pension that gave rise to the commission, tax relief is given on that amount;
- where a contributor deducts commission in respect of his or her own pension contribution from the gross amount payable, relief is due on the net amount paid;
- where a contributor pays discounted contributions, tax relief is due on the discounted amount paid;
- where extra value is added to the policy by the insurer (for example by allocation of bonus units), relief is due on the amount paid by the contributor without taking the extra value into account.

40 If commission were to be rebated to the contributor under the same contract as the personal pension contract, this would be an unapprovable benefit (since it would involve leakage of the pension fund to the member) which would jeopardise the tax-approved status of the arrangement.

41 The consequences of paying commission on transfers between tax-approved pension schemes may be different from those outlined if such payment is effectively a benefit not authorised by the rules of the pension scheme.

The statement also encompasses the Revenue's two previous press releases by stating that:

(1) other commission rebates to ordinary customers will not be taxed; and
(2) cashbacks offered by banks and building societies as an inducement to take out a mortgage will not be regarded as chargeable to CGT.

Source: HMRC

9.9.2 Limit imposed by Finance Act 2007

Since 21 March 2007, certain commission rebates on insurance bonds (single premium insurance policies) have had to be taken into account in computing chargeable gains on the encashment of the bond. This treatment is required where:

(1) premiums paid to the insurance company exceed £100,000 in a given year; and
(2) the bond is surrendered, matures or is assigned before three tax years have elapsed.

9.9.3 Payments arising from trade or employment

If a cashback is received in the course of either the recipient's business or employment, the cashback may be chargeable as income.

The income tax consequences of the statement of practice are that employees who receive commission arising from, and discounts in connection with, goods, investments or services sold to third parties are assessable regardless of whether the commission is passed on by them to the customer and whether the commission is paid by the employer or anyone else.

The Revenue takes the view that PAYE will apply in any situation where the commission, etc falls to be taxed as employment income.

INCOME RECEIVED NET OF TAX

9.10 ANNUITIES, TRUST INCOME, ETC

9.10.1 Annuities
(IT(T&OI)A 2005, s 422)

Annuities paid by an insurance company are dealt with at 27.5. Where an annuity is payable by an individual or a private company, the payer must deduct tax at basic rate. Note that such income is not treated as savings income and therefore tax is still deducted at basic rate and not at 20% where payment is made.

Example – Annuity income received net of basic rate tax: 2007–08

M sells his business to N for a cash sum plus an annuity of £10,000 a year payable by N out of the business profits. In 2007–08, N paid M only £7,800 (£10,000 less tax at 22%).

(1) M may set any available personal allowances against the annuity, so that if he is aged 67, is single and has no other income, the position will be:

	£	£
Annuity (gross amount)		10,000
Personal allowance (over-65 rate)		(7,550)
		2,450
Tax payable		
£2,230 charged at 10%	223.00	
£220 charged at 22%	48.40	
Total tax due	271.40	
Less: tax paid by deduction	(2,200.00)	
Revenue will repay	1,928.60	

(2) If *M*'s other income is sufficient to utilise both his personal allowances and the lower rate band, there will be no repayment. If he is a higher rate tax-payer, he will have to pay additional tax on the annuity, as follows:

	£
Higher rate tax on annuity (40% of £10,000)	4,000
Less: Already paid by deduction	(2,200)
Additional tax payable by assessment	1,800

(3) The buyer, *N*, can obtain relief for the annuity paid to *M* not as a trading expense, but as a deduction in computing total taxable income.

    (a) If he is only a basic rate taxpayer, he obtains the relief to which he is entitled by keeping for himself the £2,200 difference between the gross amount of the annuity and the £7,800 actually paid to *M*.

    (b) If he is a higher rate taxpayer, additional relief is given by not charging higher rate tax on an amount equal to the gross annuity paid – a process usually referred to as 'extending the basic rate band'.

(4) Suppose *N*'s profits are £50,000, he has no other income and is entitled only to the basic personal allowance of £5,225. If he did not have to pay the annuity, his tax position would be:

		£
Income		50,000
Personal allowance		(5,225)
Tax payable on		44,775
£2,230	charged at 10%	223.00
£34,600	charged at 22%	7,612.00
£7,945	charged at 40%	3,178.00
£44,775		11,013.00

(5) As he does have to pay the annuity, the basic rate band is extended by the gross amount of that annuity (£10,000), so the position becomes:

		£
£2,230	charged at 10%	223.00
£42,545	charged at 22%	9,359.90
£44,775		9,582.90

This is a reduction of £1,430.10 and so overall the position is:

	£
Gross annuity	10,000
Net payment to *M*	(7,800)
Basic rate tax relief	2,200
Reduction in tax payable by assessment	1,430
Total tax relief	3,630

If *M* had more income within the 40% band, the total tax relief might have been £4,000 (ie 40% of £10,000

9.10.2 Income from trusts

Income paid to a beneficiary of a fixed interest trust is normally taxed at source at 20%. However, tax will sometimes have been charged on the trustees at basic rate on income received by them that is not income from savings. For example, rental income falls into this category. In such a situation, the beneficiary will have a credit for basic rate tax on that element of his income from the trust that represents income that is not income from savings.

Income payments to discretionary beneficiary carry a credit of 40%. In practice, a beneficiary will normally receive a form R185, which sets out his income from the trust and the tax withheld.

9.10.3 Estates of deceased persons
(IT(T&OI)A 2005, s649–656)

When someone dies, it takes time for his executors or personal representatives to identify all his assets, pay all his debts, settle any IHT liability and work out the best way of dividing the estate between those entitled (eg one beneficiary may want to take specific investments, another may prefer cash). During this time, known as 'the administration period', it is quite likely that income will be received by the executors or personal representatives, both on the deceased's existing investments and, for example, as interest on a bank account into which the executors have paid money collected on behalf of the estate.

The executors or personal representatives must pay tax on all income received. Items such as share dividends and bond interest are received net of tax and this tax will cover the executors' liability. Income from savings is taxed at 20%. Other income is subject to tax at the basic rate and, where no tax has been withheld at source (eg rental income), the executors will need to go through the self-assessment procedures.

The executors or personal representatives must therefore pool income on which tax has been paid. That pool must be divided between the beneficiaries in accordance with the terms of the deceased's will, or of the laws of intestacy if he left no will.

Example – Tax treatment of estate income

The gross income from an estate for 2007–08 is £200, on which the executors have paid tax of £44. The deceased's son is, under the will, entitled to half that income. He will receive a cheque for £78 plus a certificate, signed by the executors, confirming that tax of £22 has been paid to the Revenue. The son's income for tax purposes is £100, but he is treated as having already paid basic rate tax on that £100. If he has personal allowances or other reliefs available, he can obtain (from the Revenue) a repayment of some or all of the £22 tax paid; if he is a higher rate taxpayer, he will have to pay over to the Revenue the difference between basic and higher rate tax.

In some cases, the executors will have suffered tax at only 20%, rather than at basic rate, and the certificate issued by them to the beneficiary must make this clear.

9.10.4 Allocation of estate income to particular tax years

Payments made to beneficiaries out of the income of the residue of an estate are taxable as income for the year of payment.

10

ALLOWABLE DEDUCTIONS

PETER JUN TAI

In this chapter, we look at the deductions you may claim on page 2 of the Additional Information Schedule to the SA tax return.

(1) Alimony and maintenance.
(2) Loans used to purchase an annuity from an insurance company.
(3) Loans to purchase investment property.
(4) Loans to invest in partnerships.
(5) Loans to invest in close companies.
(6) Loans to invest in employee-controlled companies.
(7) Loans to purchase plant and machinery.
(8) Alternative finance 'products'.
(9) Gift Aid.
(10) Gift of listed shares and securities.
(11) Gift of land and buildings.
(12) Annuities, etc.
(13) Trade union and friendly society subscriptions.
(14) Life assurance premiums.
(15) Community Investment Tax Credit.

10.1 ALIMONY AND MAINTENANCE

No relief is normally given whatsoever for payments made after 5 April 2000.

If the payer or recipient was born before 6 April 1934, an allowance of up to £2,440 can be claimed for 2007–08 (relief given at only 10%).

10.2 LOANS USED TO PURCHASE AN ANNUITY FROM AN INSURANCE COMPANY

MIRAS relief, abolished from 6 April 2000, was given for interest on loans secured on the borrower's main residence if he was aged 65+ and at least 90% of the loan on which the interest was payable was used to buy an annuity for the remainder of his life. Interest payable on these types of loan continues to attract relief at 23% despite the general abolition of MIRAS and the reduction in the basic rate to 22%.

10.3 LOANS TO PURCHASE INVESTMENT PROPERTY

Interest on loans used to acquire a property that is let out may be allowed in computing the rental income assessable for tax purposes (see Chapter 7).

10.4 LOANS TO INVEST IN PARTNERSHIPS
(TA 1988, s 362)

Tax relief may be obtained on loan interest where the money is used to invest in a partnership that is not an investment LLP. Interest on qualifying loans may be set against the individual's general income, ie relief is not confined to an offset against income from the partnership.

10.4.1 Conditions for relief

It does not matter that such loans may be secured by way of a mortgage against the partner's main residence; the availability of relief depends on the purpose for which the loan is raised, not the way in which the lender secures its position. Relief is basically available where the loan is applied:

(1) in purchasing a share in a partnership; or
(2) in contributing capital to a partnership or advancing money to a partnership where the money advanced is used wholly for the purposes of the partnership's trade, profession or vocation; or
(3) in paying off another loan the interest on which would have been eligible for tax relief.

However, there are further conditions that must be satisfied. The borrower must be a member of the partnership throughout the period in which the interest accrues (and not just as a limited partner). Also, he must not have recovered any capital from the partnership since raising the qualifying loan.

10.4.2 Recovery of capital
(TA 1988, s 363)

If, at any time after the application of the proceeds of the loan, a partner recovers capital from the partnership, he is deemed to have used the money he has withdrawn to repay the qualifying loan on which he is claiming interest relief. This applies whether or not he actually uses the proceeds in this manner. It is therefore advisable to segregate the partners' capital and current accounts in the partnership's books so that any withdrawal can be clearly identified.

Tax notes

Relief is due for interest which is paid in a year. Interest that is 'rolled-up' will not normally be eligible for relief until it is actually paid.

10.4.3 Property occupied rent-free by partnership

Where a partner takes out a loan to purchase property occupied by the partnership for business purposes and the interest is paid by the partnership, technically no deduction is due to the partnership because the interest is not its liability but the partner's. However, SP4/85 states that the interest paid can be treated as rent so that it then becomes allowable as a deduction. In the partner's hands, the rent is taxable but the interest paid is allowed as a deduction in arriving at the amount taxable as income from property.

10.4.4 Incorporation of partnership
(ESC A43)

Where a partnership business is transferred to a limited company in return for shares, any qualifying loan in existence at the time continues to attract tax relief provided the conditions for relief in 10.5 below would be met if a new loan was taken out.

10.4.5 Tax planning: withdrawing partnership monies and replacing working capital by raising qualifying loans

Where a partner has a surplus balance on either his current or capital account with a partnership and he does not already have a qualifying loan, he may withdraw the balance due to him (with his partners' consent), use the money to pay off non-qualifying borrowings and then borrow further funds to introduce capital into the partnership with tax relief.

Example – Replacement capital

B is a partner in the XYZ partnership. He has a credit balance of £100,000 in his capital account. Outside the partnership, he has bought a yacht for his private use with the help of a £40,000 loan from his bank and he has a house mortgage of £20,000. *B* would withdraw £60,000 from his capital account in the partnership and use the money to make the following repayments:

	£
Yacht bank loan	40,000
Building society	20,000
	60,000

Once these transactions have been completed, *B* would borrow £60,000 as a loan (not overdraft) and use the funds to reintroduce capital into the partnership with full tax relief on the interest payable. Professional advice should be sought well in advance before setting up this sort of loan.

10.4.6 Raising qualifying loans to replace partnership borrowings

Another situation where it may be appropriate to restructure existing borrowings is where the partnership has taken a loan, typically to purchase another business or the property from which the business is carried on. In this situation, each partner is normally required to borrow privately his share of the partnership loan and introduce the monies raised into the partnership. The partner can then personally claim tax relief on the interest paid as a charge on his income.

The partnership collects the monies raised by each partner's loan and uses the funds to redeem the partnership loan. As a result, each partner's share of profits becomes correspondingly higher because no interest is now payable by the partnership. However, the situation redresses itself because the higher profits must be used to finance the private borrowing.

Rearranging matters in this way can provide significant cash-flow benefits because relief is available for interest up to one year earlier than where the borrowings remain within the partnership. For example, if the partnership makes up its accounts to 30 April, interest paid on partnership borrowings in the year to 5 April 2009 will normally attract tax relief in 2009–10 (ie as an expense in arriving at the partnership profits for its year falling in 2009–10), whereas replacing these borrowings with qualifying loans raised by the partners will mean that the interest attracts tax relief against their income for the tax year 2008–09.

10.5 LOANS TO INVEST IN CLOSE COMPANIES
(TA 1988, s 360)

Where interest is paid on a loan used to purchase ordinary shares in a close company, or in lending money to such a company that is used for the close company's business purposes, the interest may be eligible for tax relief. For the definition of a close company, see 17.13.1. Once again, relief is dependent on the way the loan is used, not on the way it is secured; the borrower may therefore have a qualifying loan that is secured by way of a mortgage on his home.

Interest on such a loan may be set against the individual's general income, ie relief is not restricted to an offset against income from the close company.

Tax notes

Interest on a qualifying loan may be set against any of your taxable income; it does not have to be set against the income from the close company first.

10.5.1 Conditions for relief where the loan is used to buy shares

Relief is dependent upon conditions being satisfied by the borrower, the company and in relation to the shares that are acquired.

Conditions applicable to the borrower

(1) The borrower, either alone or together with certain associates, owns a material interest in the close company (defined broadly as more than 5% of the ordinary share capital).

(2) The borrower holds less than 5% of the ordinary share capital, but works for the greater part of his time in the actual management or conduct of the company or an associated company (a works manager, a production manager or a company secretary would normally satisfy this condition).

Conditions applicable to the company

The company must exist wholly or mainly for one of the following purposes:

(a) To carry on a trade or trades on a commercial basis.

(b) To make investments in land or property let commercially to unconnected parties.

(c) To hold shares or securities or make loans to 'qualifying companies' or an intermediate company, all of which are under its control. A qualifying company is one that is under the close company's control and satisfies the conditions at (a) and (b) above.

(d) To co-ordinate the administration of two or more qualifying companies.

If the company holds property, the individual must not reside in it unless he has worked for the greater part of his time in the actual management or conduct of the company.

Conditions applicable to the shares being acquired

A loan used to buy shares is a qualifying loan only if the shares are ordinary share capital. 'Ordinary share capital' includes any shares in the company other than fixed rate preference shares.

10.5.2 Close EIS companies
(TA 1988, s 360(3A); FA 1989, s 47)

Loan interest relief is not available in respect of shares issued under the Enterprise Investment Scheme. Similar rules apply where an individual has used a loan to acquire shares on which relief was due under the Business Expansion Scheme.

10.5.3 Company ceases to be close after loan taken out

Relief can continue to be due for interest paid on a loan even though the company has ceased to be a close company provided the other conditions remain satisfied. For example, the individual must either have a material interest or be employed full-time in the management of the company or an associated company. This is often relevant where management form a company in a management buy-out (MBO) and it ceases to be close after outside institutions inject further share capital.

10.5.4 Close company taken over on share-for-share basis

Where an individual has borrowed to invest in a close company and that company is taken over by another close company on a share-for-share basis, his loan can continue to be a qualifying loan provided all the other conditions are satisfied.

10.5.5 Close company shares sold

If you sell the shares in a close company, and you have a loan that was used to finance the purchase of the shares, the loan interest ceases to qualify for relief from the date of disposal. Interest charged by a bank on the subsequent redemption of the loan does not attract income tax relief.

Furthermore, if you give away shares, you may also be regarded as having 'recovered capital'. This means you may cease to be eligible for relief on interest paid on your borrowings.

10.5.6 Borrowing to lend money to a close company

Relief is also available under s 360 if you borrow to lend money to a close company in which you have a material interest, or are a full-time director or manager, and the company uses the money in its business.

Once again, the loan ceases to be a qualifying loan to the extent that you recover capital from the company. There is a trap here in that a gift or other disposal of shares may constitute a 'recovery of capital' even though the money you have lent to the company has not been withdrawn.

Tax notes

You should make sure that your bank debits you for accrued interest just before you sell or give away the shares because interest charged after that date will not attract tax relief.

10.6 LOANS TO INVEST IN EMPLOYEE-CONTROLLED COMPANIES
(TA 1988, s 361)

It is also possible for an individual to establish a qualifying loan where he uses it to buy shares in an employee-controlled company, even if it is not a close company. The conditions that need to be satisfied for a loan to qualify under this provision are:

(1) during the year of assessment in which the interest is paid, the company must either become employee-controlled for the first time or be employee-controlled for at least nine months;

(2) the individual or his spouse must be a full-time employee throughout the period commencing with the application of the loan and ending with the date on which the interest is paid. He can also continue to obtain relief for interest paid within 12 months of his having ceased to be an employee;

(3) the shares must be acquired before, or not later than 12 months after, the date on which the company first becomes an employee-controlled company; and

(4) the individual must not have recovered any capital from the company during the period from applying the loan proceeds to pay interest.

The legislation requires that the company be unquoted and resident only in the UK and either a trading company or the holding company of a trading group. A company is 'employee-controlled' if more than 50% of its ordinary share capital and voting power is owned by full-time employees or their spouses. If a full-time employee owns more than 10%, the excess is disregarded. For this purpose, a spouse's holding is attributed to the employee unless the spouse is also a full-time employee.

10.7 LOANS TO PURCHASE PLANT AND MACHINERY
(TA 1988, s 359)

Where a partner incurs capital expenditure in the purchase of plant and machinery used for the partnership's business purposes and eligible for capital allowances, he can claim tax relief on interest paid if the plant is financed by a loan. The relief is available only in the tax year in which the loan is taken out and the following three tax years.

Example – Use of loans to purchase plant and machinery

A partner borrowed £10,000 at 10% pa on 6 October 2006 to buy a van that is used for the partnership's business. His private use is agreed at 25%.

Interest relief is available on £375 in 2006–07 and on £750 for the ensuing three tax years.

Similar relief is available for employees who are required to purchase plant for use in carrying out their duties but the relief is not available for loans used to buy a car, van or motor cycle.

Tax notes

If you have realised some capital and are in a position to clear some of your borrowings, it will generally be best to repay non-qualifying loans where you get no tax relief for the interest.

10.8 ALTERNATIVE FINANCE 'PRODUCTS'

Where an individual enters into a contract with an Islamic bank or financial institution, he will not pay interest. However, the tax legislation provides for relief to be obtained in respect of the bank's charges as if those charges were interest.

10.9 GIFT AID

(FA 1990, s 25; F(No2)A 1992, s 26)

10.9.1 Introduction

Gift Aid is a way in which the Government seeks to encourage taxpayers to support charities. The scheme originally gave income tax relief only for substantial donations to charity. Before 6 April 2000 there was a minimum limit for gifts to qualify under this scheme of £250. This limit was abolished from 6 April 2000.

Example – Gift aid donation

In 2007–08, A gave £780 to a recognised charity. Under the Gift Aid scheme, that will be treated as a donation of £1,000, from which basic rate tax of £220 has been deducted. The charity can claim that tax from the Revenue, so it will receive a total of £1,000.

If A is a basic rate taxpayer, that is the end of the story: he has paid over £780 that the Revenue has 'topped up' to £1,000. If A is a higher rate taxpayer, he may claim higher rate relief on the gift, calculated as follows:

	£
Gross donation made	1,000
Tax relief at 40%	400
Less: deducted when gift made	(220)
Reduction in A's own tax liability	180

If *A* is not a taxpayer at all, the Revenue will require him to make good the £220 it has paid to the charity, but if he has paid sufficient tax at the lower rates to cover the £220 this is sufficient.

Relief can also be obtained against tax on an individual's capital gains.

If *A* made the £780 donation in 2008–09, the reduction in the basic rate means that the gross donation would be £975. *A*'s higher rate tax relief would be £195.

10.9.2 Carrying back relief

Since 5 April 2003 it has been possible to carry back Gift Aid donations made and this has been added to the tax form for 2004 and later years. The amount that may be carried back is the amount of donations made by 31 January following the tax year, ie payments made by 31 January 2009 can be set against the 2008 tax liability.

An individual will need to make a formal carry-back election either on the tax return when filing or as a stand alone claim. The deadline for making this election is the date that he files his tax return or (if earlier) 31 January following the year to which the donations are being carried back.

Tax notes

Carrying back Gift Aid donations will mean that you get the benefit of the higher-rate relief 12 months earlier than if you simply take the relief for the year of payment. It could also be beneficial if you were a higher rate taxpayer for the previous year but only a basic rate taxpayer for the year of payment.

10.9.3 Giving a tax refund to charity

Individuals can nominate any tax repayment, in full or part, to charity. Such donations can be under Gift Aid and, if made by 31 January 2009, can be set against an individual's tax liability as a carry back in computing 2007–08 tax. This relief is claimed by completing the *Giving your tax repayment to charity* form in the Tax Return pack. A list of charities that you can nominate can be found at the HMRC website, www.hmrc.gov.uk, or by calling the Revenue on 0845 9000 444.

It is not possible for the taxpayer to elect for a donation made in this way to be carried back under the procedure described in 10.9.2 above.

Where it transpires that an error has arisen, and a repayment sent to a charity was not in fact due, the Revenue procedure will depend upon who has made the error. If the taxpayer has made a mistake and a repayment is not due, the Revenue will seek reimbursement from him. If the error arose at the Revenue end, the Revenue will seek reimbursement from the charity.

10.9.4 **Qualifying donations**

Several conditions must be satisfied before a donation can qualify under the Gift Aid scheme:

(1) The recipient must be a recognised charity established in the UK or a community amateur sports club (see 37.2). Many appeal funds and societies established for the public benefit are not technically charities. In case of doubt, intending donors should ask for evidence of charitable status or should consult:

> The Charity Commission
> 57–60 Haymarket
> London SW1Y 4QX

By way of exception, four bodies that technically are not charities are deemed to be charities for Gift Aid purposes: the British Museum, the National History Museum, the National Heritage Memorial Fund and the Historic Buildings and Monuments Commission for England.

(2) The gift must be of money: it is not possible to claim Gift Aid relief for donated works of art, or even for goods (eg clothing or blankets) to be used to assist distressed people. Also, it is not possible to give money on condition that it is used to buy something from the donor, a member of his family or a company in which he has an interest.

(3) The gift may be made in cash, by cheque or bank transfer, or by credit card. However, the Revenue does not accept that writing-off an existing loan to the charity is equivalent to a gift of money.

(4) There is no minimum or maximum donation.

(5) Any reciprocal benefit received from the charity (by the donor or a member of his family) must fall within prescribed limits (see 10.9.6–10.9.8).

10.9.5 **Payments under deeds of covenant**

Where an individual still makes payments under a deed of covenant in favour of a charity that was entered into before 6 April 2000, the payments are now treated as Gift Aid donations.

10.9.6 **Permissible benefits for Gift Aid donors**

A charity may wish to give a token of its appreciation to donors for their donations. Modest benefits received in consequence of making a donation will not stop the donation from qualifying as a Gift Aid donation, provided their value does not exceed certain limits. If they exceed the limits, the membership subscriptions cannot qualify as Gift Aid donations.

If a charity wishes to provide benefits to donors it should consider whether the proposed benefits fall within the limits in the donor benefit rules. We deal with this at 37.1.14.

10.9.7 Substantial donors

See 37.1.20 for the new rules on donors who give more than £25,000 pa to a charity.

10.10 GIFT OF LISTED SHARES AND SECURITIES

Individuals who make gifts to charity of listed shares and securities are able to claim relief in calculating their taxable income. The relief applies where listed shares or securities are given or sold at undervalue to a charity. The shares must be listed on a recognised stock exchange in the UK or overseas. A gift of AIM shares can qualify.

The deduction is equal to the market value of the shares or securities on the date of the gift (inclusive of the incidental cost of disposal) less any consideration received for or in consequence of the gift.

Example – Giving shares to charity

> C gives listed shares with a market value of £10,000 to a charity. The shares show an unrealised gain of £9,000. C obtains income tax relief on £10,000 and CGT relief of £9,000 at 18%. If C is a higher rate taxpayer, this adds up to tax relief of £5,620.

Note that the deduction is given only against income, not against capital gains.

Anti-Avoidance

The Finance Act 2004 introduced anti-avoidance legislation to prevent the abuse of this relief by the donor having a right to repurchase the shares at less than market value.

Income Tax Relief In Addition To CGT Exemption

No CGT arises on a gift of shares to charity, so the donor's 40% income tax relief may be in addition to a significant saving of CGT that would apply if he were to sell the shares.

Tax notes

Bear in mind that in the same way that no capital gain is recognised on a gift to charity, no loss is allowed. Therefore, if you are making a gift of shares ensure first that there would be a chargeable gain if you actually disposed of the shares. If not, then a better option would be to actually sell the shares and realise the capital loss. You can then make a cash donation to the charity. This would be especially beneficial if you had other chargeable gains arising during the tax year.

10.11 GIFT OF LAND AND BUILDINGS

Provisions enacted in 2002 give tax relief to a person who makes a charitable donation in kind by transferring land or buildings to the charity as gift or sale at an undervalue. The donor is allowed to deduct the value of land or buildings in arriving at his taxable income. The relief is basically the same as that for gifts of listed shares; therefore, the same considerations apply.

10.12 ANNUITIES, ETC
(TA 1988, ss 347A, 663 and 683; FA 1988, s 36)

10.12.1 Introduction

Most annuities are payments under deed of covenant, ie a written promise to pay another person a certain sum of money each year (or each week, month, quarter, etc), either for a fixed number of years or for a period determined by events (eg until the payer's or the payee's death).

At one time, all deeds of covenant operated so as to transfer taxable income from the payer to the payee, so that the payer's taxable income was reduced by the amount of the covenanted payment and the payee's similarly increased. This could save a great deal of money where (as would usually be the case) the payee was subject to a lower rate of tax than the payer. As a result, deeds of covenant were often used to redistribute income around a family. Inevitably this has led to anti-avoidance legislation that has gradually become all-embracing.

Payments under deed of covenant are now deductible only where the covenant represents:

(1) part of the purchase price of a business; or
(2) a payment made by a partnership to a retired partner, or to a former partner's widow or other dependant.

10.12.2 Business purchase and partnership annuities

Business purchase and partnership annuities attract higher rate relief as well as basic rate. The payer can deduct basic rate only at source, and must claim the higher rate relief from the Revenue. For details of such annuities, see 9.10.1.

10.13 TRADE UNION AND FRIENDLY SOCIETY SUBSCRIPTIONS
(TA 1988, s 266(6) and (7))

Some trade unions provide pensions and/or death benefits (often called 'funeral benefits') for their members. Each member is entitled to tax relief on half of that part of his subscription that relates to the provision of such benefits (up to a maximum of £100). However, this relief is sometimes given by the Revenue making a block payment to the union and the union then charging reduced subscriptions to its members.

The members of some friendly societies also pay a subscription that covers both a death benefit and a sickness benefit (ie a 'mixed policy'). Half of the amount referable to the death benefit qualifies for tax relief.

There is a distinction between relief under the special arrangements for trade union subscriptions and mixed friendly society policies and the general relief for life assurance premiums (see 10.14). Relief under the special arrangements is available only in the exact circumstances described – and not, for example, for a premium paid under a simple life assurance policy issued by a friendly society. Relief under the special arrangements is, however, available irrespective of the date the insurance came into force, whereas the general relief for life assurance premiums is available only for policies entered into force before 14 March 1984.

10.14 LIFE ASSURANCE PREMIUMS
(TA 1988, s 266)

Most life assurance polices that came into force before 14 March 1984 qualify for a form of tax relief. (The operative date is the day the policyholder's proposal was accepted by the insurance company, not the day the policy was issued.) The Revenue makes a block payment to the insurance company, equal to half the basic rate of tax on the premiums payable on qualifying policies, and the insurance company correspondingly reduces the amount actually paid by the policyholder. For example, if the standard premium was £100, the Revenue would pay £12.50 and the policyholder only £87.50. That £12.50 is the sum total of the relief available: no additional relief may be claimed if the policyholder is a higher rate taxpayer. Relief is lost completely if any material change is made to the policy – for example, if a term policy is converted into an endowment or if the insurance company makes a loan to the policyholder without charging a commercial interest rate.

No tax relief is available for the premiums on life assurance policies that came into force on or after 14 March 1984.

10.15 COMMUNITY INVESTMENT TAX CREDIT (CITC)

The Community Investment Tax Credit (CITC) scheme was announced in July 2001 and the legislation included within Finance Act 2002. The scheme came into effect on 23 January 2003 and applies to investments in accredited Community Development Finance Institutions (CDFIs) made on or after 17 April 2002. The relief is intended to stimulate private investment in disadvantaged communities by providing a tax incentive to individuals and companies investing in not-for-profit and profit-seeking enterprises in or for those communities.

The tax relief is worth up to 25% of the value of the investment in the CDFI and is spread over five years, starting with the year in which the investment is made: for example, for 2008–09 the tax relief given on a qualifying investment of £100 will be the lower of £5 or that which reduces the tax liability to nil.

The relief for a year should normally be claimed on the tax return for that year, page 2 of the Additional Information schedule to the SA form. However individual investors having received a tax relief certificate may also request a change to their PAYE code number, or claim a reduction in their self-assessment payments on account.

ALLOWANCES AND TAX CREDITS

DALE BUTCHER

This chapter looks at allowances and tax credits that may be claimed by tax-payers. The following topics are covered:

(1) Personal allowances.
(2) The basic personal allowance.
(3) Married couple's allowance.
(4) Pensioner couples.
(5) Allowances recently abolished.
(6) Blind persons.
(7) Time limits.
(8) Tax credits from 6 April 2003.

11.1 PERSONAL ALLOWANCES
(TA 1988, ss 256–278)

Income tax is not charged on the whole of a person's taxable income. In calculating the amount on which tax must be paid, he may claim a personal allowance that depends on his individual circumstances (eg age).

Personal allowances may be claimed by anyone resident in the UK. There is no minimum age requirement so that, for example, a newborn baby is entitled to a personal allowance. Sometimes it is possible, through the use of trusts or settlements, to redirect part of a family's income to a child, so that it may (being covered by his personal allowance) be enjoyed tax free (although the scope for transferring taxable income in this way has been whittled down by a succession of complex anti-avoidance provisions: see 32.5.4).

British subjects and certain other categories of people not resident in the UK may also claim personal allowances.

11.2 THE BASIC PERSONAL ALLOWANCE
(TA 1988, s 257)

Every individual resident in the UK is entitled to the basic personal allowance – often called the 'single person's allowance', a throwback to the days when there was also a 'married man's allowance'. The allowance for the current year is £6,035. If the individual is born or dies halfway through a year of assessment, the allowance is not scaled down.

Example – Death during tax year

Suppose *D* died at the end of September 2008, by which time he had earned only half his annual salary. His tax bill for 2008–09 would be:

	£
Salary	10,000
Professional subscription paid	(135)
	9,865
Personal allowance	(6,035)
Tax payable on	3,830
£3,830 charged at 20%	766.00

Because the PAYE scheme assumes that personal allowances will be used in equal monthly (or weekly) instalments over the year, about £1,400 will have been deducted from *D*'s salary while he was alive. On request, the Revenue will therefore repay his executors the excess tax deducted.

11.2.1 Higher allowances for the over-65s

Higher allowances are given to those who have attained age 65 and are of limited means. The allowance is £9,030 for 2008–09 for those between ages 65 and 74 and £9,180 for those aged 75+ (£7,550 and £7,690 for 2007–08). If an individual attains age 65 or 75 during a year of assessment, he is entitled to the appropriate allowance for the whole of that year. For example, a man born on 1 June 1943 attained age 65 on 1 June 2008 and is entitled to the higher allowance of £9,030 for the 2008–09 tax year.

The higher allowance is also given where the individual was alive on the first day of the tax year and would have achieved age 65 or 75 within the tax year had he not died.

The allowance is designed to assist only those of limited means. The allowance is reduced by £1 for every £2 by which the individual's 'total income' exceeds £21,800, until it falls back to the standard allowance for the under-65s.

Within this band, every £2 of income can cost 60p in tax (40p on the £2 itself, plus 20p on the £1 of allowances withdrawn). This is an effective percentage rate of 30%. For 2007–08, the £1-for-£2 reduction operated between 'total incomes' of £20,900 and £25,550 for those between the ages of 65 and 74 and between £20,900 and £25,830 for those aged 75+.

Example – Reduced higher allowances

In 2007–08, *E* was aged 70. He received a state pension of £5,500 pa, an occupational pension of £16,500 and rental income of £1,000. His 'total income' was £21,000; his overall income tax liability for 2007–08 is therefore:

	£	£	£
Total income			23,000
Higher personal allowance		7,550	
Total income	23,000		
Income limit	20,900		
Excess	2,100		
Half of excess		1,050	
Reduced higher personal allowance[1]			6,500
Tax payable on			16,500

[1]This cannot be reduced below the standard personal allowance of £5,225

2,230	charged at 10%	223.00
14,270	charged at 22%	3,139.40
16,500		3,362.40

The definition of 'total income' is, accordingly, very important, especially as in certain circumstances it is possible for an individual to rearrange his investments so that his 'total income', as defined by the Taxes Acts, is less than his real income. This is explained in 11.2.2.

11.2.2 Calculating 'total income'
(TA 1988, s 835)

A person's 'total income', as defined by the Taxes Acts, differs from his real income, first because not all receipts count towards total income and secondly because certain deductions can be made from real income in calculating total income.

The first step in calculating total income is to add together all the income that is assessable to tax. Income not assessable to tax is excluded. Examples include letting income exempt under the 'rent-a-room' scheme (see 7.4), the interest credited to an ISA, the dividends earned by a PEP (see 24.2) or a Venture Capital Trust (see 24.6), the growth in value of National Savings certificates (see 24.3.1) and amounts withdrawn from insurance bonds up to the 5% limit (see 27.3.3). A person whose income falls within the marginal age relief band would, therefore, clearly do well to consider placing his money in tax-exempt investments.

The second step is to deduct, from the sum of assessable income, the following outgoings:

(1) Interest paid, insofar as it qualifies for tax relief under the usual rules.
(2) All of the 'other outgoings' listed in Chapter 10, insofar as each qualifies for tax relief under the normal rules. (The 'other outgoings' that may qualify are Gift Aid donations.)

(3) Contributions paid to an occupational or personal pension scheme.
(4) Any surplus capital allowances arising from investment in enterprise zone property (see 24.7).

Example – Total income

Suppose that *E* in the example above received a windfall of £5,000. He invested £1,800 in an enterprise zone property trust and the balance in National Savings certificates. To celebrate his good fortune, he makes a Gift Aid donation of £200 (gross) in favour of his local church. His tax liability for the year 2007–08 will in fact fall to £2,702.40, as follows:

	£	£	£
Total income received			23,000
Enterprise zone property investment		1,800	
Gift Aid payment (gross)		200	
			(2,000)
'Total income'			21,000
Higher personal allowance		7,550	
Total income	21,000		
Income limit	20,900		
Excess	100		
Half of excess		(50)	
			(7,500)
Tax payable on			13,500
£2,230 charged at 10%			223.00
£11,270 charged at 22%			2,479.40
£13,500			2,702.40

Tax notes

If your income for the past year means that you don't get the full benefit from the increased personal allowance, and you are effectively subject to the 33% marginal rate (see above), it may pay for you to relate back Gift Aid donations (see 10.9.2). Another idea is to invest surplus cash in a way that does not produce taxable income as you go along (eg a roll-up fund, an insurance bond or National Savings certificates).

In some cases, a married couple may be able to 'fine tune' their position by putting more of the investments into the name of the spouse or civil partner who has the least other income.

11.3 MARRIED COUPLE'S ALLOWANCE
(TA 1988, s 257A)

This relief was abolished with effect from 6 April 2000, though it still exists for married couples and civil partners where either spouse or civil partner was born before 6 April 1935. See the *Tax Handbook 2000–01* at 7.5.

11.4 PENSIONER COUPLES
(TA 1988, s 257A)

A higher married couple's allowance is still available if either spouse or civil partner was born before 6 April 1935. The allowance for 2008–09 is £6,535 if the elder spouse or civil partner is aged between 65 and 74, and £6,625 if he or she is aged 75+. Relief is restricted to 10%. The allowance is subject to claw-back if the individual's income exceeds £21,800 (see 11.2.1). However, a minimum allowance of £2,540 (£2,440 for 2007–08) is due even where the income exceeds the limit.

11.4.1 Pensioner couples: transfer of excess allowances
(TA 1988, s 257B; F(No 2)A 1992, s 20 and Sched 5)

The whole of a higher, age-related married couple's allowance may be transferred to the wife if the husband has insufficient income to use it himself. An election to do this must be lodged with the Revenue within five years and ten months from the end of the tax year. Civil partners can also make such an election.

11.5 ALLOWANCES RECENTLY ABOLISHED

The widow's bereavement allowance under TA 1988, s 262 was abolished from 2001–02. The additional personal allowance under TA 1988, ss 259–261A was abolished with effect from 6 April 2000.

11.6 BLIND PERSONS
(TA 1988, s 265)

A person who is blind may claim a special, additional personal allowance of £1,800 for 2008–09 (£1,730 for 2007–08). A person counts as 'blind' if:

(1) he lives in England or Wales and his name appears on the local authority's register of blind persons; or
(2) he lives in Scotland or Northern Ireland and is so blind that he cannot perform any work for which eyesight is essential.

This definition means that a person resident abroad can never, for tax purposes, count as blind – an odd rule strictly enforced by the Revenue.

A person who becomes blind during a year of assessment may claim the full blind person's allowance for that year.

11.6.1 Married couples

If husband and wife are both blind, each may claim a separate blind person's allowance.

A blind husband with insufficient income to use all his personal allowances may be able to transfer the whole or part of his blind person's allowance to his wife (whether or not she also is blind). However, the transfer of the married couple's allowance took priority, so a transfer of blind person's allowance was only possible where the husband's income was insufficient to use his basic personal allowance and the blind person's allowance itself. Similarly, a wife may transfer her unused blind person's allowance to her husband (whether or not he also is blind). An individual can also transfer the unused blind person's allowance to his or her civil partner.

A claim to transfer a blind person's allowance to a spouse must be made, on Revenue Form 575, within five years of the 31 January following the end of the relevant year of assessment.

Example – Blind married couple

G, who is sighted, earns £10,000 a year. His wife, H, who is blind, has a pension of £6,000. The position for 2007–08 is:		
H	£	£
Pension		6,000
Basic personal allowance	5,225	
Blind person's allowance	1,730	
		(6,955)
Excess, transferable to husband		955
G		
Salary		10,000
Basic personal allowance	5,225	
Transferred excess from wife	955	
		(6,180)
Tax payable on		3,820
£2,230 charged at 10%		223.00
£1,590 charged at 22%		349.80
£3,820		572.80

11.7 TIME LIMITS

As noted at 11.2, every individual resident in the UK is automatically entitled to the basic personal allowance.

Other allowances must be claimed within five years and ten months of the year to which they relate, for example a claim in respect of blind person's allowance relating to the year ended 5 April 2003 must be made by 31 January 2009.

In general, most claims for allowances are made annually in the tax return. However, where a claim is overlooked or a formal return is not issued, a claim can be made to the taxpayer's tax office, normally in writing, though in certain circumstances phone claims will be accepted.

11.8 TAX CREDITS FROM 6 APRIL 2003

From 6 April 2003, various tax credits were consolidated in to the child tax credit and the working tax credit.

11.8.1 Child tax credit

As its name suggests, the child tax credit is meant to support families with children and can be claimed if you have responsibility for a child.

The credit, which can be claimed in addition to any child benefit or working tax credit, is available for the support of:

- a child until 1 September following their 16th birthday;
- a person aged 16–18 who
  - is in full time education, up to and inclusive of A levels or their equivalent (NVQ3/Scottish Highers); or
  - if not in education has no job/training place and has registered with the Careers or Connexions Service.

The 'child' must not be claiming income support or tax credits and must not be serving a custodial sentence of more than four months.

Table 11.1 is a guide to how much child credit can be claimed in the tax year 2008–09 by an individual who is not claiming working tax credit.

Table 11.1 – Child tax credit for the year 2008–09 (£)

Gross annual joint income	One Child		Two Children		Three Children	
	Annual	*Weekly*	*Annual*	*Weekly*	*Annual*	*Weekly*
5,000	2,630	50.60	4,715	90.70	6,800	130.80
10,000	2,630	50.60	4,715	90.70	6,800	130.80
15,000	2,630	50.60	4,715	90.70	6,800	130.80
20,000	904	17.40	2,990	57.50	5,075	97.60
25,000	545	10.40	1,040	20.00	3,125	60.10
30,000	545	10.40	545	10.40	1,175	22.60
40,000	545	10.40	545	10.40	545	10.40
50,000	545	10.40	545	10.40	545	10.40

11.8.2 Working tax credit

The working tax credit is available as a top up for individuals in low paid jobs, with additional payments being available for working households in which an individual has a severe disability.

In general, a qualifying individual is:

- aged 16 or over, works 16 hours a week and is responsible for a child; or
- aged 25 or over and works at least 30 hours a week; or
- aged 16 and over, has a disability that puts him at a disadvantage in getting a job and works at least 16 hours a week; or
- the individual or their partner is aged over 50 and is returning to work for at least 16 hours a week after time spent on qualifying benefits.

Table 11.2 offers a guide as to the amounts that could be receivable in 2008–09.

Table 11.2 – Working tax credit for the year 2008–09

Working tax credit (£) if you are responsible for at least one child or young person				
Gross annual joint income (£)	*Couple or lone parent working between 16 and 30 hours a week*		*Couple or lone parent working 30 hours or more a week*	
	Annual	*Weekly*	*Annual*	*Weekly*
5,000	3,570	68.65	4,305	82.80
7,500	3,150	60.60	3,885	74.70
10,000	2,175	41.80	2,910	55.95
12,500	1,200	23.10	1,935	37.20
15,000	225	4.30	960	18.45
Working tax credit (£) if you are not responsible for at least one child or young person				
Gross annual joint income (£)	*Single person aged 25 or over working 30 hours or more a week*		*Couple (working adult aged 25 or over) working 30 hours or more a week*	
	Annual	*Weekly*	*Annual*	*Weekly*
5,000	2,535	48.75	4,305	82.80
7,500	2,115	40.65	3,885	74.70
10,000	1,140	21.90	2,910	55.95
12,500	165	3.15	1,935	37.20
15,000	0	0.00	960	18.45

In addition to the amounts in Table 11.2, a qualifying individual can claim up to 80% of eligible childcare costs subject to a maximum eligible weekly cost of £300 for those with two or more children and a maximum eligible cost of £175 for one child.

The general rule is that to qualify for tax credits you must be aged 16 or over and usually live in the UK (see Figure 11.1). You may also qualify if you do not live in the UK but you are:

- A citizen of another country in the European Economic Area (EEA) and you work in the UK, or
- A Crown Servant posted overseas, or
- A citizen of a country in the EEA (including the UK) living abroad and you receive a UK state pension or contributions-based Jobseeker's Allowance.

If you feel that you meet the requirements for tax credits then you should phone the Revenue helpline 0800 500 222. Details on tax credits and an assessment of whether you qualify can be found at www.taxcredits. inlandrevenue.gov.uk.

11.8.3 Renewal of tax credits claim

It is necessary to renew tax credits annually and the Revenue will send out review packs between April and July 2009. This is an annual process of reviewing credits given for the previous year and ensuring that you have the correct entitlement for the current year.

If you require help renewing your tax credits claim, the contact details for the Tax Credits Helpline are as follows:

By phone:
GB: 0845 300 3900
NI: 0845 603 2000

By text phone:
GB: 0845 300 3909
NI: 0845 607 6078

The Tax Credits Helpline is available from 8am to 8pm, every day including weekends (except Christmas Day, Boxing Day, New Year's Day and Easter Sunday).

11.8.4 Overpayments may be viewed

The March 2006 Budget changed the rules for clawing back credits when a claimant's income goes up. For 2006–07 and years thereafter, an increase of up to £25,000 is ignored (in previous years the limit was £2,500).

Figure 11.1 Are you entitled to working tax credit?

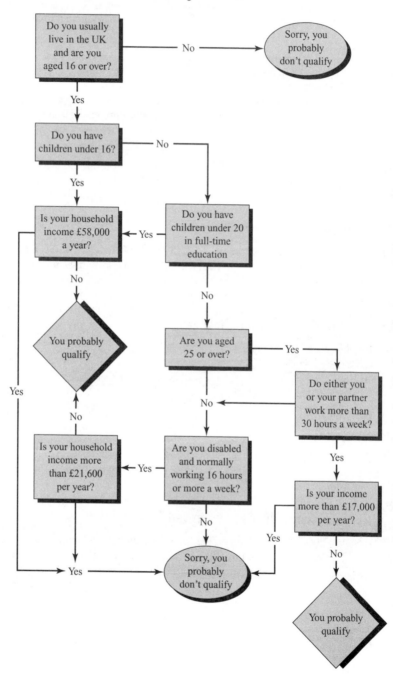

12

CAPITAL GAINS TAX

This chapter deals with the following aspects of capital gains tax:

Basic principles

(1) Outline of CGT.
(2) CGT and the self-assessment form.
(3) Who is subject to CGT?
(4) What assets are chargeable assets?
(5) Which types of transaction may produce a chargeable gain?
(6) Hold-over relief where a gift is a chargeable transfer for IHT purposes.

Computing capital gains

(7) Amount to be brought in as disposal value.
(8) What costs are allowable?
(9) Assets held at 31 March 1982 and 6 April 1965.
(10) Other acquisition values.
(11) Taper relief.
(12) Indexation.
(13) Working out your capital gain.

Special rules for certain assets

(14) Assets that have attracted capital allowances.
(15) How gains are computed on quoted securities.
(16) Unquoted shares.
(17) When may a chargeable gain arise on foreign currency?
(18) Special rules for disposals of chattels.
(19) Specific rules that apply to disposals of land and investment properties.
(20) Disposal of foreign property.
(21) Gains and losses on second-hand insurance policies.

Unless otherwise stated, the statutory references are to the Taxation of Chargeable Gains Act (TCGA) 1992.

BASIC PRINCIPLES

12.1 OUTLINE OF CGT

Capital gains are assessed for a tax year. Under self-assessment the due date for payment of the tax is 31 January following the tax year (ie for gains arising in the year ended 5 April 2008, tax is payable by 31 January 2009). There is no requirement to make payments on account: indeed capital gains do not form part of the payment on account calculation (see 2.1.3).

There is now an 18% uniform rate of CGT that applies across the board unless entrepreneurs relief is available (see 16.8).

The rate of CGT for years up to 2007–08 was governed by whether the individual's income and capital gains were sufficient to put him into the 40% band.

The way chargeable gains are computed is quite different from the rules that determine assessable income for tax purposes.

A range of exemptions and reliefs used to apply, and a major distinction between CGT and income tax was that capital gains could be reduced by taper relief (and by indexation relief, an adjustment for inflation up to April 1998). This ceased to be the case from 6 April 2008.

12.1.1 Annual exemption
(TCGA 1992, s 3)

You are not liable for CGT unless you make gains of more than the annual exemption, which for 2008–09 is £9,600. The exemptions for the past six years were:

Tax year	£	Tax year	£
2007–08	9,200	2004–05	8,200
2006–07	8,800	2003–04	7,900
2005–06	8,500	2002–03	7,700

12.1.2 No gain/loss on spouse or civil partner transactions

Provided a couple has not separated permanently, there can be no chargeable gains on any assets transferred from one spouse or civil partner to the other, whether by gift or sale. The asset is treated as passing across on a no-gain/no-loss basis, with the recipient acquiring it at his spouse's or civil partner's cost plus indexation to date (see 12.12 on indexation relief and 12.11 on taper relief). There is an exception to this rule in respect of the transfer of an asset that becomes part of the trading stock used in the spouse's or civil partner's business.

12.1.3 Losses

Losses may arise as well as capital gains. The normal rule is that capital losses cannot be offset against an individual's income but may be carried forward against capital gains of future years. Losses arising from transactions involving connected persons may only be set against gains arising from transactions with the same person.

Brought-forward losses do not need to be set against gains that are covered by the annual exemption. However, current year losses must be set against capital gains before using the annual exemption.

Tax notes

If you have already realised gains in the current tax year, and these will be covered by the annual exemption, it may pay to defer sales that will produce CGT losses until next tax year. You will then be able to carry the losses forward for offset against future gains.

12.1.4 Rate of tax for 2007–08
(TCGA 1992, s 4)

Once the gains for the year have been computed (net of any losses), the annual exemption is deducted. The balance is then added to the individual's taxable income and the CGT is normally ascertained by working out the additional income tax that would be payable if the capital gains had been income from savings.

Example

B has 2007–08 taxable income, after personal allowances, of £26,000. Her capital gains for the year are £19,200. After deducting the £9,200 annual exemption, this means adding in an amount of £10,000. The CGT payable would be computed as:

	£
Balance of basic rate band	
£34,600 – £26,000 = £8,600 at 20% =	1,720
£1,400 at 40% =	560
Total CGT payable	2,280

However, if B had no taxable income at all, the calculation would be slightly different. If the gains were again £19,200, the CGT payable would be:

	£
First £9,200	Nil
£2,230 at 10%	223
£7,770 at 20%	1,554
	1,777

Any unused personal allowances for income tax purposes simply go to waste.

> **Tax notes**
>
> If you can choose the year in which you realise capital gains, try to ensure that they fall into a tax year in which you are only subject to basic rate tax.

12.1.5 Trading losses

If relief for trading losses has been claimed against income from other sources for the year, any balance of loss may be set against capital gains for that year, or against income and capital gains of the preceding tax year.

A formal claim must be lodged with the Revenue by one year and ten months after the tax year of loss, ie a claim to utilise a 2006–07 trading loss must be made by 31 January 2009. Similar claims can be made for losses arising from letting furnished holiday accommodation, from post-cessation expenditure or from post-employment deductions (see 7.5 and 15.5).

12.2 CGT AND THE SELF-ASSESSMENT FORM

An individual is required to complete the CGT pages of the SA form:

- If there is CGT to pay;
- Total proceeds for the tax year are more than four times the annual CGT exemption, for example for 2007–08 £36,800;
- Chargeable gains exceed the annual exemption and are reduced by losses;
- A CGT relief (other than taper relief) is to be claimed;
- A CGT election is being made;
- CGT losses are being claimed.

12.3 WHO IS SUBJECT TO CGT?

An individual's residence and domicile status may have a crucial bearing on CGT liability.

12.3.1 Significance of residence status
(TCGA 1992, s 2)

An individual is subject to the CGT legislation only if he is either resident or ordinarily resident in the UK for the year in which relevant disposals take place. Residence and ordinary residence are determined in the same way as for income tax (see 33.2). There are two exceptions:

(1) Where a non-resident and non-ordinarily resident person carries on a trade or profession through a branch or agency in the UK, CGT may be charged on a disposal of assets used in that branch despite the fact that he would normally be outside the charge on capital gains.

(2) An individual who has been resident or ordinarily resident in the UK for any part of at least four of the seven tax years prior to his ceasing to be resident for a period of less than five complete tax years may be taxed on his return to the UK (see 12.3.2 and 33.5.4).

12.3.2 Individual non-resident for part of tax year

Technically, an individual is resident or non-resident for the whole of a tax year. The Revenue practice of treating certain individuals as resident for only part of a tax year for income tax purposes is really no more than an extra-statutory concession. The 'split year' treatment (see 33.5.1) is therefore subject to two exceptions.

The first concerns the year of departure. An individual who moves abroad is taxed on all capital gains for the year of departure, even if the gains are realised after the date he leaves the UK.

Second, the Revenue can assess capital gains where the individual has returned to the UK during the year in question and was non-resident for less than five years. In such a case, capital gains realised in the tax year in which he resumes UK residence may be charged to tax even though the disposals took place before his return.

Example – Non-residence for part of tax year

C was classified as non-resident in the UK from 1 January 2003 when she took up a job in the Middle East. She returned to the UK on 24 July 2007. For income tax purposes she is regarded as not resident and not ordinarily resident from 1 January 2003 to 23 July 2007, but she would be subject to CGT for 2002–03 on disposals made during the period 1 January to 5 April 2003.

Gains realised in the period 6 April 2003 to 5 April 2007 are not subject to CGT for the tax year concerned as C is neither resident nor ordinarily resident in those years. However, the gains will be taxed as if they were realised in 2007–08, ie the year in which C resumes residence in the UK. C will also be taxed on all her gains for 2007–08, not merely those realised after her return on 24 July 2007.

In some cases it was thought that the provisions of a double taxation agreement might override the five-year rule and prevent the Revenue from taxing gains realised in the year in which the individual resumes UK residence. This is an area where specialist advice is essential and anti-avoidance legislation was introduced in FA 2005, which is discussed at greater detail in Chapter 32.

12.3.3 Foreign domicile may make an important difference
(TCGA 1992, s 12)(See 34.1 on domicile.)

An individual who is resident (or ordinarily resident) and domiciled in the UK is subject to CGT worldwide (ie on gains realised both in the UK and abroad). By contrast, a non-UK domiciled individual can elect for a special tax treatment (he may have to pay £30,000 for this, see 34.2). Under the remittance basis, he will be charged tax on gains from disposals of foreign assets only if the proceeds are brought into (or, as the legislation puts it, the gains are 'remitted' to) the UK. There are more details on the CGT treatment of foreign domiciled individuals in 34.15. The rest of this chapter deals only with UK-domiciled people.

12.4 WHAT ASSETS ARE CHARGEABLE ASSETS?

12.4.1 Assets within the scope of CGT
(TCGA 1992, s 21)

Gains on virtually all types of assets are potentially subject to CGT, subject to certain stated exceptions. TCGA 1992, s 21(1) states:

All forms of property shall be assets for the purposes of this Act, whether situated in the UK or not, including:

(a) options, debts and incorporeal property generally, and
(b) any currency other than sterling, and
(c) any form of property created by the person disposing of it, or otherwise coming to be owned without being acquired.

The asset need not be transferable or capable of being assigned. The term 'any form of property' is all-embracing. For example, the courts have held that CGT was due on an employer's right to compensation from an employee who wished to be released from his service agreement. In another case, the right to compensation for property expropriated by the USSR in 1940 was held to be a form of property and therefore an asset for CGT purposes. Similarly, the High Court held in *Zim Properties Ltd* v *Proctor* [1985] STC 90 that the right to bring an action before the courts constitutes an asset that can be turned to account by the potential litigant negotiating a compromise and receiving a lump sum.

The conclusion therefore is that virtually all forms of property that can yield a capital sum are subject to CGT unless they are specifically exempt.

12.4.2 What assets are specifically exempt?

The following are the main categories of exempt assets:

(1) Principal private residence (see 13.1) [s 222].
(2) Chattels that are wasting assets, unless used in a business (see 12.18) [s 44].

(3) Chattels where the sale consideration is less than £6,000. There is some alleviation of the charge when more than £6,000 is received (see 12.18) [s 262].

(4) Decoration for valour as long as sold by the original recipient [s 268].

(5) Foreign currency acquired for personal expenditure outside the UK. This includes money spent on the purchase or maintenance of any property situated outside the UK [s 269].

(6) Winnings from betting (eg the pools, horses, bingo and lotteries) [s 51].

(7) Compensation or damages for wrong or injury suffered in a profession or vocation [s 51]. Certain compensation from foreign governments for property lost or confiscated by concession.

(8) Debts [s 251].

(9) National Savings certificates and non-marketable securities, ie those that cannot be transferred or are only transferable with a Minister of the Crown's or National Debt Commissioner's consent [s 121].

(10) Gilt-edged securities and qualifying corporate bonds (QCBs) and any options to acquire or dispose of such investments [s 115]. A QCB is a loan stock that is not convertible and is not a relevant discounted security (see 8.7).

(11) Shares held in ISAs (see 24.1) and PEPs (see 24.2) [s 151].

(12) Shares issued by way of business expansion schemes after 18 March 1986 provided the BES relief has not been withdrawn and the shares are sold, etc by the original subscriber or his spouse.

(13) Shares that qualified for income tax relief issued under an Enterprise Investment Scheme (see 24.5) provided the EIS relief has not been withdrawn.

(14) Shares in a Venture Capital Trust (see 24.6).

(15) Motor cars, unless not suitable for use as a private vehicle or commonly used for the carriage of passengers [s 263]. Also veteran and vintage cars.

(16) Woodlands [s 250].

(17) Gifts to charities and for national purposes to any one mentioned in the Inheritance Tax Act (IHTA) 1984, Sched 3 [s 257].

(18) Works of art where they are taken by the Revenue in lieu of death duties such as IHT (IHTA 1984, Sched 3) [s 258].

(19) Gifts to housing associations; a claim is made by both transferor and the association [s 259].

(20) Mortgage cash-backs: the Revenue conceded on 21 March 1996 that mortgagees who receive cash inducements from banks and building societies are not liable to CGT on such receipts.

(21) Compensation for missold personal pensions taken out as a result of disadvantageous advice given between 29 April 1988 and 30 June 1994.

(22) Life assurance policies, but only where the policy is disposed of by the original owner or beneficiaries or by a person who acquired it by way of a gift from a person who had not himself acquired it by purchase [s 210]. The rules were tightened by FA 2003 (see 12.21 and 27.3.10).

Where an asset is exempt, no gain is assessable. Unfortunately, it follows that no relief is normally given for losses (losses on a disposal of shares in an EIS are an exception to this general rule).

12.5 WHICH TYPES OF TRANSACTION MAY PRODUCE A CHARGEABLE GAIN?
(TCGA 1992, s 28)

12.5.1 Introduction

The most obvious type of disposal is an outright sale with immediate settlement, but there are many other transactions that count as a disposal for CGT purposes, for example:

- outright sale (possibly with payment by instalments);
- conditional sale;
- exercise of an option;
- exchange of property;
- compulsory acquisition of asset by local authority, etc;
- sums payable as compensation or proceeds under an insurance policy;
- gifts;
- asset destroyed or becoming of negligible value.

The liability to CGT is determined by the tax year in which the date of disposal falls.

12.5.2 Outright sale
(TCGA 1992, s 28)

The date of disposal is the day on which the unconditional contract is entered into, which may be different from the date the vendor receives payment.

Sale with payment by instalments

The date of disposal is fixed by the time the parties enter into an unconditional contract. It may be possible to pay CGT arising from such transactions as the instalments come in over a period of up to eight years (provided the instalments are spaced over a period of at least 18 months: TCGA 1992, s 280). The Revenue operates a concession where a vendor grants a mortgage to a purchaser who defaults and the vendor takes back the asset in satisfaction of the sums due to him. The disposal is effectively treated as if it had never happened (see ESC D18).

12.5.3 **Conditional sale**
(TCGA 1992, s 28)

A conditional sale is a contract that does not take effect until a stated condition is satisfied.

Example – Conditional sale

> D agrees to purchase E's shares in XYZ Ltd provided the local authority grants planning permission over land owned by XYZ by April 2008. Under this type of agreement, E remains the legal owner of his shares until the condition is satisfied. If the local authority does not in fact grant planning permission, D is under no obligation to buy E's shares.
>
> The date of disposal under such contracts is the day the condition is satisfied and the contract becomes unconditional, in the above example, the date planning permission is granted.

12.5.4 **Exercise of an option**
(TCGA 1992, s 144)

A 'call' option is a legally binding agreement between the owner of an asset and a third party under which the owner agrees to sell the asset if the other party decides to exercise his option. The purchase price payable upon the exercise of the option is normally fixed at the outset; this constitutes one of the terms of the option.

A 'put' option is one where the other party agrees to buy the asset if the owner decides to exercise an option requiring him to do so.

The grant of either type of option does not constitute a disposal of the asset concerned. This happens only when the option is exercised and the day on which this happens is the date of disposal.

In some cases, payment is made for the option to be granted. This is treated as a disposal of a separate asset unless the option is subsequently exercised.

> **Tax notes**
>
> Having a 'put' option may enable you to choose the tax year in which you realise a capital gain.

12.5.5 **Exchange of property**

An agreement to exchange an asset for another is a disposal of the old asset and an acquisition of the new asset. If there is any cash adjustment, this must also be brought into account. For example, if F exchanges his holding in ICI for G's shareholding in Glaxo, F is treated as if he has disposed of the ICI shares for the market value of the Glaxo shares at the time of the exchange. This type of transaction commonly occurs where an individual transfers portfolio investments to a unit trust in return for units.

There is an important exception to the rule that an exchange constitutes a disposal, which may apply where a shareholder takes securities offered to him on a company takeover (see 12.15.3 on such share exchanges). Provided certain conditions are satisfied, the exchange does not count as a disposal and the securities issued by the acquiring company are deemed to have been derived from the original shares, with the shareholder carrying forward his original acquisition value.

Example – Exchange of shares on company takeover

H holds 1,000 shares in XYZ plc that he acquired in 1998 for £9,000. Another company, ABC plc, makes a takeover bid and offers all XYZ shareholders a share exchange whereby they receive one ABC share (worth £30 each) for every two XYZ shares that they own. The offer document confirms that agreement has been obtained from the Revenue that TCGA 1992, s 136 applies.

If *H* accepts, he will receive 500 ABC shares worth £15,000, but he will be deemed to have acquired them in 1998 for £9,000. No disposal is deemed to have occurred on the share exchange.

12.5.6 Compulsory acquisition of asset
(TCGA 1992, s 22)

The transfer of land to, for example, a local authority exercising its compulsory purchase powers is a disposal for CGT purposes. In some cases, once the compulsory purchase order (CPO) has been served, contracts are drawn up and the land is transferred under the contract. The rules in relation to outright sales and conditional sales apply.

Where the CPO is disputed, the date of disposal is normally the earlier of:

(1) the date on which compensation for the acquisition is agreed or otherwise determined; and
(2) the date on which the local authority enters the land in pursuance of its powers.

12.5.7 Sums payable as compensation or proceeds under an insurance policy
(TCGA 1992, s 22)

In some cases, an asset (eg a building) may be destroyed or damaged and a capital sum received as compensation. In such cases, the asset is deemed to have been disposed of at the date the capital sum is received. Similarly, where a capital sum is received from an insurance policy following such damage, receipt of insurance monies is treated as constituting a disposal.

An ESC was issued on 19 December 1994, which covers the receipt of compensation under the Foreign Compensation Act 1950, the Ugandan Expropriated Properties Act, compensation payable by the UN Compensation Commission for property lost during the Gulf War and compensation payable under German Law. The concession may provide exemption for a person who receives compensation for property lost or confiscated, for example by the Nazis or under the East German regime.

12.5.8 Gifts
(TCGA 1992, s 17)

A gift is treated as a disposal at market value (except where it is from one civil partner or spouse to the other: see 12.1.2). At one time it was possible for assets to be transferred at cost, but this general form of hold-over relief was abolished in 1989. In some specific situations the capital gains may still be held over, for example where the gift involves business property (see 16.4) or is a lifetime chargeable transfer for IHT purposes, such as a gift to a discretionary trust (see 29.12) but not a PET (see 29.6.1). See 12.6. A gift often constitutes a transaction between connected persons: see 32.10.

12.5.9 Asset destroyed or becoming of negligible value
(TCGA 1992, s 24)

The total destruction or entire loss of an asset constitutes a disposal. This could be physical destruction (eg by fire) or legal/financial destruction (eg bankruptcy or winding-up).

The legislation also permits a person to elect that he should be treated as having disposed of an asset that has become of negligible value. Normally, a capital loss will arise on such an occasion.

'Negligible value' is interpreted by the Revenue as meaning considerably less than small. For example, the Revenue will only agree that shares, loan stock and other securities are of negligible value on being satisfied that the owner is unlikely to recover anything other than a nominal amount on the liquidation of the company. The mere fact that shares have been suspended or de-listed by a stock exchange is not regarded as sufficient.

The legislation provides that a disposal is deemed to take place in the year during which the Inspector of Taxes agrees that the asset has become of negligible value. However, the Revenue permits a claim to take effect up to two tax years prior to the claim provided the asset was of negligible value in the prior year (see ESC D28).

In practice it is not always beneficial for an individual to claim the ESC D28 benefit, or indeed for a claim to be made, until such time as there are gains against which the loss can be set (see 12.1.3).

Tax notes

Because the date of disposal is linked to the date that you submit a negligible value claim, you can choose to defer the loss to a later year if this will be beneficial.

12.6 HOLD-OVER RELIEF WHERE A GIFT IS A CHARGEABLE TRANSFER FOR IHT PURPOSES
(TCGA 1992, s 260)

Where a gift or a sale at an undervalue is a chargeable transfer for IHT purposes, and the donee is UK-resident, the donor and donee can elect for any gain to be held over. This generally means that the asset is deemed to pass across to the donee on a no gain/no loss basis but with the donee inheriting the donor's acquisition cost. This relief is not available for transfers of assets after 9 December 2003 to settlor-interested trusts. From 6 April 2006, the definition of a settlor-interested trust has been extended to include trusts under which the settlor's minor children can benefit.

Section 260 relief is not available where the gift is a potentially exempt transfer for IHT purposes (see 29.6) but another type of hold-over relief may be available if the property being transferred is business property for IHT purposes (see 16.4).

You should obtain a copy of Helpsheet IR295 if you make such a chargeable transfer.

The hold-over gain becomes chargeable if the donee ceases to be resident within six years.

Tax notes

The right to transfer shares to a family trust without having to pay CGT is crucially important. Transfers to such trusts can save IHT but without the hold-over relief the CGT consequences would often be unattractive.

COMPUTING CAPITAL GAINS

12.7 AMOUNT TO BE BROUGHT IN AS DISPOSAL VALUE

12.7.1 Market value
(TCGA 1992, s 17)

The general rule is that market value must be used unless the transaction is at arm's length. In the straightforward situation where a contract is entered into with a third party on a commercial basis, the disposal proceeds are the actual sale proceeds. An individual is not penalised because he has made a bad bargain and sold an asset for less than it is really worth. However, if the bargain is not at arm's length and the individual deliberately sells the asset for an amount less than its true value, the legislation requires market value to be substituted. If the disposal is to a connected person, for example a relative or the trustee of a family settlement or a family company, there is an automatic assumption that the bargain is not at arm's length and market value is always substituted for the actual sale proceeds if the two amounts are different. There are three exceptions:

(1) Transactions between spouses and civil partners (see 12.1.2).
(2) Gifts to charities and similar bodies (see 12.4.2).
(3) Situations where a hold-over election can be made (see 12.6 and 16.4).

Tax notes

Take advice if you are intending to give (or sell) assets to a connected person as you will not want to end up paying a lot of tax on notional sale proceeds.

12.7.2 Contingent liabilities
(TCGA 1992, s 49)

There may be occasions where the contract may require part of the proceeds to be returned at some time in the future. This is known as a sale with 'contingent liabilities'.

Suppose a vendor receives £150,000 for the disposal of a plot of land, but is under an obligation to return £60,000 in certain circumstances. Will the capital gain be charged on sale proceeds of £150,000 or £90,000? In fact, s 49 provides that in these circumstances the capital gain must be computed in the first instance without any deduction for the contingent liability, ie £150,000. However, if and when the vendor is required to refund part of the sale proceeds because the contingent liability has become an actual liability, the CGT assessment is adjusted accordingly.

12.7.3 Contingent consideration: quantifiable
(TCGA 1992, s 48)

In a similar way, it is possible that the contract may provide that additional sums may be payable if certain conditions are satisfied in the future. If it is possible to put a value on the further amount of consideration that is 'contingent' (ie payable only if certain conditions are satisfied), the full amount that may be received is brought into account at the date of disposal without any discount. If the conditions are not satisfied, so that the further amounts are never received, an adjustment is made later to the CGT assessment.

12.7.4 Contingent consideration: unquantifiable

The position is different where the contingent consideration cannot be ascertained at the date of disposal (this is normally the situation where the contingent consideration may vary and is not a fixed amount). Basically, the legislation requires that the market value of the right to receive the future consideration should be regarded as the disposal proceeds. The difference between this amount and the amount eventually received forms a separate CGT computation for the year in which the final amount of the actual contingent consideration is determined. The treatment of contingent consideration, especially variable contingent consideration, is fairly complex. It normally arises in relation to either land or shares in private companies.

See also 16.9 on earn-outs.

Tax notes

A sale for contingent consideration can be a tax minefield and it is essential to take professional advice.

12.7.5 Deduction for amounts charged as income
(TCGA 1992, s 31)

In some cases the disposal of an asset may give rise to an income tax charge. Where this happens, the amount taken into account in arriving at taxable income is deducted from the sale proceeds and only the balance is brought into account for CGT purposes. This commonly arises where a private company buys back its own shares and the transaction is treated as a distribution (see 8.9.7).

12.8 WHAT COSTS ARE ALLOWABLE?

12.8.1 Certain specific types of expenditure

The legislation permits only a limited range of expenses to be deducted in computing capital gains and losses. TCGA 1992, s 38(1) states:

> the sums allowable as a deduction from the consideration in the computation of the gain accruing to a person on the disposal of an asset shall be restricted to:
> (a) the amount of value of the consideration, in money or money's worth, given by him or on his behalf wholly and exclusively for the acquisition of the asset, together with the incidental costs to him of the acquisition or, if the asset was not acquired by him, any expenditure wholly and exclusively incurred by him in providing the asset,
> (b) the amount of any expenditure wholly and exclusively incurred on the asset by him or on his behalf for the purpose of enhancing the value of the asset, being expenditure reflected in the state or nature of the asset at the time of the disposal, and any expenditure wholly

and exclusively incurred by him in establishing, preserving or defending his title to, or to a right over, the asset,

(c) the incidental costs to him of making the disposal.

12.8.2 The cost of the asset

The asset's market value at 31 March 1982 or 6 April 1965 may be substituted for actual cost if the asset was held at those dates (see 12.9.1 and 12.9.4).

12.8.3 Incidental costs of acquisition

These are limited to:

(1) fees, commission or remuneration paid to a surveyor, valuer, auctioneer, accountant, agent or legal adviser;
(2) transfer/conveyancing charges (including stamp duty); and
(3) advertising to find a seller.

12.8.4 Enhancement expenditure

The legislation permits a deduction to be claimed in respect of expenditure incurred in order to enhance the asset's value provided such expenditure is reflected in the state or nature of the asset at the time of disposal. The latter condition excludes relief for improvements that have worn out by the time the asset is disposed of. Certain grey areas are worth mentioning:

(1) Initial expenditure by way of repairs to newly acquired property that is let may be allowable if no relief has been given in computing UK property income.
(2) Expenditure means money or money's worth; it does not include the value of personal labour or skill.

Tax notes

HMRC will charge tax on notional sale proceeds if you give an asset away but it will not give relief for notional expenditure where you carry out the improvement work yourself.

12.8.5 Expenditure incurred in establishing, preserving or defending legal title

The case law concerned with the allowable nature of this expenditure hinges on the interrelationship between the words 'incurred', 'establishing', etc. The High Court held in *IRC* v *Richards' Executors* (1971) 46 TC 626 that the cost of making an inventory and providing a valuation for a grant of probate was allowable under this head (see SP8/94).

12.8.6 Incidental costs of disposals

The following expenses may be deductible under this head:

(1) Fees, commission or remuneration for the professional services of a surveyor, valuer, auctioneer, accountant, agent or legal adviser.
(2) Transfer/conveyancing charges (including stamp duty).
(3) Advertising to find a buyer.
(4) Any other costs reasonably incurred in making any valuation or apportionment for CGT purposes, including in particular expenses reasonably incurred in ascertaining market value where this is required. Professional costs incurred in getting a valuation agreed with the Revenue are not allowable.

Tax notes

The costs of getting a valuation at 31 March 1982 are allowable in arriving at your capital gain but the valuer's charges for negotiating with HMRC and arriving at an agreed valuation are not allowable. You need to establish in advance what fees are likely to be incurred in such negotiations.

12.8.7 Part disposals
(TCGA 1992, s 42)

Where a person disposes of part of an asset, the cost is apportioned between the part disposed of and the part retained by the formula [A ÷ (A + B)] where A is the consideration received or deemed to have been received and B is the market value of the part retained.

Example – Part disposals

B holds 1,000 shares in XYZ Ltd that cost him £10,000. The company is taken over and he receives cash of £5,000 and convertible loan stock issued by the acquiring company worth £15,000 (assume that in this particular case no capital gain arises in respect of the loan stock because it is issued on the occasion of a takeover and the necessary Revenue clearances have been obtained (see 12.15.3 and 12.15.4)). *B*'s acquisition value will be apportioned as follows:

$$£10,000 \times \frac{5,000}{5,000 + 15,000} = £2,500$$

ie the proportion of acquisition value that relates to the part sold. £7,500 is treated as the acquisition value of the part retained, ie it will be taken into account in computing any gain or loss as and when the loan stock is sold.

12.8.8 Small capital receipts
(TCGA 1992, s 122)

There are occasions where the formula $[A \div (A + B)]$ does not have to be used, and the amount received is simply deducted from the owner's acquisition value. The most common situation where this arises is where a shareholder sells his entitlement under a rights issue, normally on a nil-paid basis. Provided the amount received is less than £3,000 or is small as compared with the asset's value, the receipt can be deducted from the owner's acquisition value. 'Small' in this context is interpreted by the Revenue to be an amount not exceeding 5% of the market value.

> **Tax notes**
>
> You do not have to deduct the small capital proceeds from your cost. There is no point in your doing this if any gain would be covered by the annual exemption.

12.8.9 Capital sums applied in restoring assets
(TCGA 1992, s 23)

Under normal circumstances, an asset is regarded as having been disposed of for CGT purposes if it is lost or destroyed. However, where a capital sum is received from such an asset (eg insurance policy proceeds), the owner may claim that the asset is not treated as disposed of if at least 95% of the capital sum is spent in restoring the asset.

12.9 ASSETS HELD AT 31 MARCH 1982 AND 6 APRIL 1965
(TCGA 1992, s 35 and Scheds 2–3)

12.9.1 General rebasing
(TCGA 1992, s 35)

The general rule is that where assets were held at 31 March 1982, it is to be assumed that they were sold on that date and immediately reacquired at their market value at that time. This is known as 'rebasing'.

The application of this rules differs as between 2008–09 and previous years.

2008–09

The 31 March 1982 value is taken as the cost. **There are no exceptions to this rule whatsoever.**

2007–08 and earlier years

The 31 March 1982 value is treated as if it were the cost. Unless a universal rebasing election was made (see below), the resulting gain or loss is then compared with the gain or loss calculated by reference to the original cost, with the following consequences:

Original cost	March 1982 value	For CGT
Gain	Gain	The lower gain is assessed
Loss	Loss	The lower loss is allowed
Loss	Gain	Nil assessed – no gain/loss
Gain	Loss	Nil assessed – no gain/loss

However, original cost is ignored if a universal rebasing election has been made.

12.9.2 Universal rebasing election (2007–08 and earlier years)
(TCGA 1992, s 35(5))

If a person so elected, the rebasing rule was applied to all disposals made by him of assets held on 31 March 1982. In other words, original cost was ignored completely, and regard had only for the value of the assets held at that date. In some cases, making this election meant that losses could be claimed that would not otherwise be available (because of the no gain/no loss rule).

A *universal* rebasing election was precisely that. If the election was made the rebasing rule was applied to all assets held at 31 March 1982. Furthermore, once made, the election was irrevocable.

There is a time limit for making the election. The legislation required it to be made within two years of the end of the year of assessment in which a disposal first took place of assets that were held at both 6 April 1988 and 31 March 1982. If no election has been made and assets held at 31 March 1982 have been disposed of during the period 6 April 1988 to 5 April 2006, it is now too late to make the election. There may still be time to make the election if your first relevant disposal took place in 2006–07 or 2007–08.

Married persons and civil partners

The election could be made by each spouse separately. Where an asset passed from one spouse to another and the spouse who received it subsequently disposes of it, the gain or loss on that particular asset is governed by whether the spouse who transferred the asset had made the universal rebasing election.

12.9.3 **Assets acquired via a gift made between 1 April 1982 and 5 April 1988**
(TCGA 1992, Sched 4)

This section may be relevant where all of the following conditions are satisfied:

(1) An asset was disposed of in 2007–08 or an earlier year.
(2) The asset was acquired as a gift or transfer from a trust during the period 1 April 1982 to 5 April 1988.
(3) The donor held the asset at 31 March 1982.
(4) The donor claimed hold-over relief so that the recipient was deemed to have acquired the asset at the donor's original cost.

When rebasing was introduced, it was recognised that it would be unfair not to permit some relief where an asset had been transferred prior to 6 April 1988 and the gain had been held over. The person who received such a gift cannot claim rebasing because he did not own the gifted asset at 31 March 1982. To give rough and ready compensation for this, the legislation included provisions so that when the recipient of such a gift made a disposal after 5 April 1988, half of the held-over gain could be 'forgiven' or left out of account.

Example – Transfer prior to 6 April 1988 with held-over gain

P received a gift of shares in August 1986 from his father Q. At the time of the gift, the shares were worth £180,000. Q's acquisition value was only £40,000, and indexation (see 12.7) amounted to £10,000. This would normally have meant that Q would have had a chargeable gain of £130,000. However, he made a claim under the legislation prevailing at the time that permitted the capital gain to be held over. This meant that Q did not suffer a CGT charge, but P was deemed to have acquired the assets with an acquisition value as follows:

	£
Market value at date of gift	180,000
Less: held-over gain	(130,000)
Acquisition value	50,000

When P disposes of the asset, his acquisition value is increased by 50% of £130,000 so that his acquisition value becomes £115,000.

12.9.4 **Relief not automatic**

A formal claim for the relief described in 12.9.3 must be made within one year and ten months of the end of the tax year in which the recipient makes his disposal eg for the tax year ended 5 April 2007 by 31 January 2009.

> **Tax notes**
>
> Make sure that you claim the relief within the time limits.

12.9.5 Assets held at 6 April 1965

There are various reliefs that could be relevant for disposals made in 2007–08 or an earlier year where the asset was owned at 6 April 1965. For details, see the 2007–08 *Tax Handbook* at 12.16.2.

12.10 OTHER ACQUISITION VALUES

12.10.1 Assets acquired via inheritance or family trust
(TCGA 1992, ss 62 and 71)

Where a person inherits an asset, he is generally deemed to have acquired it for its market value at the date of the testator's death (ie probate value). There is one exception to this: it is possible to claim a form of relief from IHT where quoted securities have gone down in value after the person has died (see 29.11.3). Where such relief has been claimed for IHT, a corresponding adjustment is made so that the person taking the assets concerned is deemed to have acquired them not at probate value, but at the value actually brought into account for IHT purposes after taking account of the fall in value.

Where assets have been acquired from a trust, the beneficiary's acquisition value is normally the market value at the time the asset is transferred to him. However, the acquisition value may be lower than this where the trustees have claimed hold-over relief under either the general hold-over relief provisions that prevailed up to 5 April 1989 or the more restrictive provisions that have applied subsequently (see 16.4).

12.10.2 Deemed acquisition value where income tax charged
(TCGA 1992, ss 120 and 141)

Where a person is subject to an income tax charge on earnings under IT(E&P)A 2003 when he acquires an asset (eg where he exercises a non-approved share option), he is deemed to have acquired it for an amount equal to the value taken into account in computing an income tax charge on him. Similarly, where a person acquires shares by way of a stock dividend (ie where there is a choice between a cash dividend or further shares issued by a UK company), the shares are deemed to be acquired for a consideration equal to the amount brought into account for income tax purposes by reason of the stock dividend (see further 8.8.6).

12.10.3 Share options exercised up to 9 April 2003

A 2002 decision by the Court of Appeal in the case of *Mansworth* v *Jelley* [2002] STC 1013 revealed an anomaly. The Court held that where an employee acquired shares by exercising an option, his acquisition cost was market value at that date *plus* an amount equal to the sum on which he was assessed for income tax purposes. This amounts to a form of 'double-counting' and generally meant that a CGT loss would arise on the sale of those shares.

This anomaly was corrected in relation to share options exercised after 8 April 2003 but the amending legislation was not retrospective. You should take professional advice if you exercised such options.

12.11 TAPER RELIEF

12.11.1 Introduction

This relief is not available for disposals in 2008–09 or subsequent years.

Taper relief reduced the amount of the chargeable gain according to how long the asset had been held for periods after 5 April 1998. The taper was more generous for business than for non-business assets.

Taper relief was given on the net gains that are chargeable after deduction of indexation allowance and any capital losses realised in the same tax year or brought forward from previous years. Where an individual has gains that attract no taper relief, losses are set against those first to produce the lowest tax charge.

12.11.2 Period of ownership

Taper relief operated as follows in respect of periods of ownership after 5 April 1998:

(1) where there was a transfer of an asset between spouses, the taper relief on a subsequent disposal was based on the combined period of holding by both spouses;

(2) for other no gain/no loss transfers, taper relief was given by reference to the period of ownership only of the new owner;

(3) where a shareholding was increased by a bonus issue, taper relief was given by reference to the date the original shares were acquired;

(4) where shares were acquired through a rights issue or other reorganisation, they were treated as if they were acquired when the original shares were acquired;

(5) where a relief deferred the gain on a disposal until a later occasion (eg the relief on reinvestment in a VCT), the taper relief on the deferred gain relates to the period during which the person owned the original asset (there was an exception to this where EIS shares issued after 5 April 1999 were sold for a gain and the gain was reinvested in new EIS shares); and

(6) where gains had been relieved under a provision that reduced the cost of a replacement asset (eg roll-over relief for business assets), the taper relief operated by reference to the period of ownership of the new asset.

12.11.3 Non-business assets

The rates of taper relief on non-business assets acquired after 17 March 1998 were:

Complete years of ownership	Taper relief (%)	Complete years of ownership	Taper relief (%)
Less than 3	nil	7	25
3	5	8	30
4	10	9	35
5	15	10	40
6	20		

Assets acquired before 17 March 1998 qualified for an addition of one year to the period for which they are treated as held after 5 April 1998. This addition was the same for all assets, whenever they were actually acquired. So an asset purchased on 1 January 1998 and disposed of on 1 July 2006 was treated for taper relief purposes as if it had been held for nine years (eight complete years after 5 April 1998 plus one additional year).

12.11.4 Taper relief on business assets up to 5 April 2000

The rate of taper relief was originally 7.5% for each complete year of ownership plus an extra year's relief where the asset was held on 17 March 1998.

12.11.5 Taper relief on business assets disposed of between 5 April 2000 and 5 April 2002

The rate of taper relief in respect of business assets altered significantly in FA 2000. For business assets disposed after 5 April 2000, taper relief was calculated according to the following table:

Complete years of ownership	Taper relief %	Effective tax rate for 40% taxpayer %
Less than 3	Nil	40
1	12.5	35
2	25.0	30
3	50.0	20

For these purposes, the period 17 March to 5 April 1998 no longer gave rise to a bonus year.

12.11.6 Taper relief on business assets disposed of after 5 April 2002

The Government reduced the period of ownership needed for full taper relief to two years. For business assets disposed of after 6 April 2002, taper relief was calculated according to the following table:

Complete years of ownership	Taper relief % 40% taxpayer %	Effective tax rate for
Less than 3	Nil	40
1	50	20
2	75	10

12.11.7 What is a 'business asset' for taper relief purposes?

We cover this in some detail in Chapter 16 but basically a business asset was an asset used by you in carrying on a trade or profession (alone or in partnership) or shares in an unquoted trading company or shares in certain other types of company if you satisfy certain conditions.

12.12 INDEXATION

(TCGA 1992, ss 53–57)

Indexation was a relief giving an allowance for inflation up to April 1998. Note that the relief is not available for any disposal by an individual or trustee after 5 April 2008.

A person who made a capital gain in 2007–08 or an earlier year was allowed to deduct not only his actual acquisition value, but also a proportion that represents the increase in the retail price index (RPI) between the month of acquisition and the month of disposal. The formula used is [(RD − RI) ÷ RI] where:

RD = RPI in month of disposal or April 1998, whichever is the earlier;
RI = RPI for March 1982 or month in which expenditure incurred, whichever is the later.

Note that where the date of disposal was after 30 April 1998, indexation allowance was given only by reference to the April 1998 figure.

Example – Computing indexation relief

S acquired shares in X plc on 1 June 1991 for £20,000. She sells them in June 2007 for £30,000. She has a capital gain of £10,000 before indexation, and a gain of £5,740 after taking indexation into account. The indexation relief is computed as follows:

$$\text{Cost £20,000} \times \frac{\text{RPI for April 1998} - \text{RPI for June 1991}}{\text{RPI for June 1991}}$$

That is £20,000 × (162.6 − 134.1 ÷ 134.1) = £20,000 × 0.213 = £4,260. The RPI figures are set out in Tax Table 40.7 at the end of this book.

12.12.1 Restriction to indexation relief

(FA 1994, s 93)

Indexation relief may only reduce or extinguish a gain; it cannot convert a gain into a loss or increase a loss.

12.13 WORKING OUT YOUR CAPITAL GAIN

Table 12.1 can be used as a 'pro forma' when calculating capital gains or losses.

Table 12.1 – Computing your 2007–08 capital gains

Sale proceeds (consider whether the market value provisions may apply) – see 12.7).	A	
Deduct incidental costs of disposal (see 12.8).	B	
Net sale proceeds (A – B).		C
If the asset was acquired after 31 March 1982, enter cost.	D	
Amount of any enhancement expenditure.	E	
If the asset was owned at 31 March 1982 and a universal rebasing election is in force, enter value at 31 March 1982 (see 12.9).	F	
If the asset was owned at 31 March 1982, but no universal rebasing election is in force, enter cost or value at 31 March 1982, whichever is the higher.1	G	
Enter the amount of enhancement expenditure – if 31 March 1982 value is entered at F or G, include only post-31 March 1982 enhancement expenditure.	H	
Enter the total of figures entered in any of D to H.		I
Unindexed gain (C – I).		J
Indexation relief on figure in D, F or G (see 12.12).	K	
Indexation relief on figure in E or H.2	L	
Enter total of K and L.		M
Deduct M from J. The result is the indexed gain.		N
Taper relief (see 12.11).3		O
Deduct O from N. The result is the taxable gain.		P

[1] Note that there will not be an allowable loss if there is an overall gain taking the original cost, but a loss taking the 31 March 1982 value.
[2] The figure of indexation relief cannot exceed the figure at J, except in relation to assets disposed of prior to 30 November 1993.
[3] The taper relief will be based on gains as reduced by any allowable losses on other transactions.

SPECIAL RULES FOR CERTAIN ASSETS

12.14 Assets that have attracted capital allowances

No CGT loss arises on a disposal of an asset whose cost has attracted capital allowances (see 15.2). On the other hand, the cost is fully deductible if the disposal gives rise to a gain.

The Special Commissioners have held that a loss on a disposal of units in an enterprise zone property trust is an allowable loss even though the individual had received 100% capital allowances (see 24.7). This decision is on the basis that the units are a distinct asset that is separate from the underlying properties on which the capital allowances arise. See *Smallwood* v *HMRC* 2005 SpC 509.

12.15 HOW GAINS ARE COMPUTED ON QUOTED SECURITIES

'Quoted securities' means shares, loan stock, warrants, etc that are dealt in on the London stock exchange and other similar stock exchanges recognised by the Revenue as having similar rules and procedures to the London exchange. This section deals with the tax treatment of transactions such as:

- sale of part of a shareholding;
- bonus issues and rights issues;
- takeovers and mergers.

12.15.1 Identification rules

Specific rules apply where a person sells part of his holding in securities of the same class. Securities are treated as being of the same class if they are treated as such under stock exchange practice. For example, all ICI ordinary shares are securities of the same class, whereas BP ordinary shares are not and form a different class.

Once again, the identification rules differ as between disposals in 2008–09 and disposals in 2007–08 and earlier years.

2008–09 disposals

These are dealt with so that shares sold are identified as follows:

(1) with acquisitions on the same day;
(2) with acquisitions made within 30 days;
(3) with acquisitions being treated as having come out of a pool. All acquisitions of shares of the same class are treated as forming a single pool, with shares coming out at average cost.

2007–08 disposals

The identification rules for disposals are that shares disposed of should be matched with:

(1) acquisitions made on the same day;
(2) acquisitions within the next 30 days: if more than one acquisition is made in this period they are dealt with on a FIFO basis, ie the first shares acquired are deemed to be the ones sold;
(3) acquisitions made after 5 April 1998 on a LIFO (last in first out) basis; and
(4) shares held in a 'pool' at 5 April 1998.

Special election for shares acquired under an employee share scheme

There is one exception to the 'same day' rule. Where an employee acquires shares from more than one employee share scheme and sells some of those shares all on the same day, the employee can elect as to which shares have been sold.

12.15.2 Takeovers and mergers

There is a special relief that may apply where a company issues shares or securities in order to take over another company or takes a 25% stake in the target company. The shareholders who accept this offer will not be treated as making a disposal provided they meet one of the following requirements:

(1) together with persons connected with them, they do not hold more than 5% of the company's share capital; or
(2) the Revenue is satisfied that the share exchange is a bona fide commercial transaction that is not entered into with a view to tax avoidance.

In *Snell* v *HMRC* 2006 SpC 532, it was held that an exchange of shares for loan notes had a tax avoidance motive because the taxpayer intended to take up residence in Jersey before cashing in the loan notes.

So far as quoted securities are concerned, the position is generally straightforward. The offer document forwarded to shareholders normally states whether clearance has been obtained from the Revenue under TCGA 1992, s 138 confirming that TCGA 1992, s 135 applies. Provided this is the case, no capital gain will arise on the exchange of shares for securities issued by the company making the takeovers.

What happens if there is a mixture of shares and cash?

Suppose a shareholder in X plc is offered a share in Y plc plus cash of £1 in exchange for every share that he holds in X plc. If he accepts this offer there will be a part disposal. The value of the new Y plc shares on the first day of trading is taken and the following computation is required:

Amount received via cash element	A
Take proportion of indexed cost of holding in X plc	
$\dfrac{\text{Cash received}}{\text{Cash + Value of Y plc shares}} \times \text{Indexed cost}$	B
Capital gain/(loss) on cash element	C

What happens if there is a mixture of shares and loan stock?

Suppose the shareholder in X plc had instead accepted an offer of one share in Y plc plus £1.25 loan stock. Assume that when the new Y plc shares were first traded they had a price of £2 and the loan stock was traded at £80 for every £100 nominal. The cost of the two types of new securities would be determined as follows.

Example – Takeover by mixture of shares and loan stock

Apportioned to Y plc shares:

$$\frac{\text{Value of Y shares}}{\text{Value of Y shares + Y loan stock}}$$

ie $\dfrac{£2}{£2 + £1}$ Cost of X shares = Deemed cost of Y shares

Apportioned to Y plc loan stock:

$$\frac{\text{Value of loan stock}}{\text{Value of loan stock + Shares}}$$

ie $\dfrac{£1}{£1 + £2}$ Cost of X shares = Deemed cost of Y loan stock

This division of the indexed cost of the original holding in X plc will be relevant as and when there is a disposal of either the Y plc shares or loan stock.

Tax notes

The part disposal rules can produce some unexpected results if one part of the 'package' subsequently increases in value quite substantially. This happened when BT demerged O_2: the way that a BT shareholder's cost was divided between his BT and O_2 shares reflected the respective values of the BT and O_2 shares at the time of the split. The O_2 shares then increased in value far more than the BT shares.

12.15.3 Special rules where share exchange involves qualifying corporate bonds
(TCGA 1992, s 116)

Loan stock is often a type of qualifying corporate bond (QCB), ie an exempt asset for CGT purposes (see 12.4.2). The offer document sent to shareholders on a company takeover normally draws attention to whether the loan stock falls into this category. If it does, the investor is not entitled to indexation relief for periods after the takeover. Furthermore, disposal of the loan stock creates a capital gain calculated according to values at the time of the takeover and not the loan stock's value when it is sold or redeemed.

As a matter of fact, the deferred gain is triggered by any kind of disposal of the QCBs. For example, a gift of the loan stock causes the deferred gain to become chargeable. Indeed, a chargeable gain could even arise on a deemed disposal such as would apply if the company that had issued the loan stock went into liquidation.

12.16 UNQUOTED SHARES

There are some special features to the way in which gains on unquoted shares are computed. Other aspects follow the principles already covered in this chapter. For example, the identification rules where a person disposes of part of a shareholding of unquoted shares are exactly the same as for quoted securities (see 12.15.3).

There are also practical considerations that do not arise in relation to quoted securities such as the need to negotiate a valuation of the shares at 31 March 1982.

In the case of gifts, the value used for CGT purposes is normally the value of the asset taken by the acquirer, not the reduction in value for the person making the disposal. From this point of view, CGT works differently from IHT (see 29.3.3).

12.16.1 Shares held at 31 March 1982

Inevitably, the market value of shares held at 31 March 1982 will be the subject of negotiation with the Revenue's Shares Valuation Division and professional advice should be taken. The shares' value will reflect factors such as the nature of the company, its assets and the size of the shareholding. See leaflet SVD1 *Share Valuation Division*.

The general approach adopted by the Division is to determine the value of the unquoted shares and securities by reference to a completely hypothetical market. It is assumed that any prospective purchaser will have available to him all of the information that a prudent prospective purchaser of the asset might reasonably require if he were proposing to purchase it from a willing vendor by private treaty and at arm's length. Open market value must be assumed and the yardstick is always the requirement of the willing and prudent purchaser and not the wishes, etc of the directors of the private company.

The company's underlying assets are largely irrelevant if a person has only a relatively small minority shareholding; they may be a more important consideration if he has control. Therefore, a quite different valuation might be placed on shares that form, say, a 7% shareholding from a 51% shareholding that gives the owner control. In the former case the valuers will be looking at factors such as the level of dividends paid in the past and the likelihood of such dividends being paid in the future. At the other extreme, a 51% shareholder would place great value on a 7/51 part of his shareholding as a disposal of such shares would cause him to lose voting control over the company.

On a practical aspect, it is possible to enter into negotiations with the Revenue in advance of filing your SA tax return. If you wish to reduce any uncertainty to the minimum by trying to agree 31 March 1982 values before filing your return, ask the Revenue for form CG34.

12.17 WHEN MAY A CHARGEABLE GAIN ARISE ON FOREIGN CURRENCY?

There is an exemption for foreign currency provided it was acquired for an individual's personal expenditure abroad. In all other situations, foreign currency is a chargeable asset and a gain (or loss) will arise when the currency is disposed of. A disposal may take place on the foreign currency being spent, converted into another foreign currency, or converted into sterling. In each of these situations, the sterling equivalent of the foreign currency at the date of acquisition is compared with the sterling equivalent at the date of disposal.

In theory, each separate bank account denominated in foreign currency counts as a separate asset. In practice, the Revenue permits taxpayers to treat all bank accounts containing the particular foreign currency as one account (see SP10/84).

12.18 SPECIAL RULES FOR DISPOSALS OF CHATTELS
(TCGA 1992, s 262)

A chattel is defined by the legislation as a tangible, movable asset. Examples are a picture, a silver teapot and a first edition of a famous novel.

12.18.1 Chattels that are wasting assets
(TCGA 1992, s 45)

Special rules apply for chattels that fall within the definition of 'wasting assets'. These are assets with a useful life expectancy of less than 50 years. They are exempt regardless of the amount of the sale proceeds. Equally, there is no relief for any losses realised on their disposal.

This exemption is not available for an asset on which the owner was entitled to capital allowances because it had been used in a trade.

12.18.2 **Other types of chattel**
(TCGA 1992, s 262)

A gain arising on the disposal of a chattel not covered by the exemption in 12.18.1 is exempt only if the sale proceeds do not exceed £6,000. However, there is a form of marginal relief under which, if the sale proceeds are more than £6,000, the maximum chargeable gain cannot exceed five-thirds of the excess. For example, if a picture costing £900 is sold for £6,900, the chargeable gain cannot exceed ⅗ * £900, ie £1,500.

In some cases the marginal relief will not help, for example if the sale proceeds were £6,900, but the picture had cost £5,800, the chargeable gain would be computed on normal principles.

Losses

A capital loss may arise on the disposal of a chattel. Where the sale proceeds are less than £6,000, the loss must be calculated on the basis that notional sale proceeds of £6,000 were received. For example, if an uninsured antique table costing £10,000 were destroyed by fire, the proceeds are taken to be £6,000, not nil.

Assets forming a set

Several chattels may be deemed to form a single asset, for example a set of antique chairs and a table. Where these are sold to the same person, or to persons acting in concert, they may be regarded as the disposal of a single asset. This rule may apply even though the sales take place at different times. As a consequence, gains that would otherwise be exempt because of the £6,000 limit may be brought into charge.

So, someone may own four antique chairs each worth £6,000. If they were to be sold one at a time to the same person, the total sale would be regarded as the sale of a single asset for £24,000 and the £6,000 exemption would not apply.

12.19 SPECIFIC RULES THAT APPLY TO DISPOSALS OF LAND AND INVESTMENT PROPERTIES

12.19.1 **Will the gain be subject to income tax?**

Speculative or short-term transactions in land may well give rise to a claim by the Inspector that the individual was dealing in land and therefore subject to tax as trading income. Whether a trade is being carried on is a matter of fact. The Inspector may cite the following 'badges of trade' in support of an assessment as trading income:

(1) Evidence that an asset was acquired with a view to its being resold in the short term.
(2) A large part of the purchase price being financed by borrowings, especially short-term borrowings such as an overdraft.
(3) The taxpayer has a background of similar transactions or has special expertise that assists in achieving a profit on disposal of the asset.

In *Kirkby* v *Hughes* [1993] STC 76, the court held that the taxpayer was carrying out a trade and the following were regarded as badges of trade:

(a) The properties were larger than would be expected for sole occupancy.
(b) The periods of occupancy were short.
(c) Another property was purchased while the taxpayer was still resident in the first without any clear intention of selling the first.
(d) There was no proof that the taxpayer had intended to acquire the first house as a personal asset.

Quite separately from the above, TA 1988, s 776 may enable the Inspector to assess a gain to income tax as miscellaneous income (formerly assessed under Schedule D Case VI). Section 776 may apply where a capital gain is realised and UK land:

(i) was acquired with the sole or main object of realising a gain on its disposal; or
(ii) is developed with the sole or main object of realising a gain on the disposal of it when developed.

There are also circumstances where disposal of shares in a company that owns land may give rise to an income tax charge (see 32.2.3).

Section 776 can apply whether or not the person is UK-resident. Furthermore, the capital gain may be received by a third party and yet still give rise to an assessment under s 776 if an individual has transferred the opportunity of making a gain to the third party. Moreover, s 776 can apply to one or more transactions that form a scheme and any number of transactions may be regarded as constituting a single arrangement or scheme if a common purpose can be discerned in them, or if there is other sufficient evidence of a common purpose. For a fuller account of s 776, see 32.2.

The main disadvantage for a UK resident who is assessed to income tax on gains from land is that he cannot deduct either the indexation allowance or the annual exemption. Also, the fact that gains are assessed as income may mean that he cannot make use of capital losses that have been brought forward from earlier years or have arisen during the same year on other transactions. On the other hand, where an individual has borrowed to acquire the land, he may be able to deduct the interest in calculating the gain for income tax purposes, whereas no deduction is normally available for CGT purposes.

The main circumstances where the Revenue is likely to argue that s 776 applies is where the individual concerned is a builder, developer or estate agent or has entered into a large number of land transactions or the amounts involved in a particular transaction are substantial.

12.19.2 Specific points on computation of gains on transactions involving land
(TCGA 1992, Sched 8)

Wasting assets

Where a person disposes of a wasting asset, his cost or acquisition value may need to be restricted. This applies where a person disposes of a lease-hold interest in land and the lease has less than 50 years to run at the date of disposal. Table 12.2 shows how the cost of a lease must be adjusted.

Table 12.2 – Depreciation of leases

Years	Percentage	Years	Percentage	Years	Percentage
50 (or more)	100	33	90.280	16	64.116
49	99.657	32	89.354	15	61.617
48	99.289	31	88.371	14	58.971
47	98.902	30	87.330	13	56.167
46	98.490	29	86.226	12	53.191
45	98.059	28	85.053	11	50.038
44	97.595	27	83.816	10	46.695
43	97.107	26	82.496	9	43.154
42	96.593	25	81.100	8	39.399
41	96.041	24	79.622	7	35.414
40	95.457	23	78.055	6	31.195
39	94.842	22	76.399	5	26.722
38	94.189	21	74.635	4	21.983
37	93.497	20	72.770	3	16.959
36	92.761	19	70.791	2	11.629
35	91.981	18	68.697	1	5.983
34	91.156	17	66.470	0	0

The fraction of the cost of the lease which is not allowed is given by the fraction

$$\frac{P(1)-P(3)}{P(1)}$$

where

$P(1)$ = the percentage derived from the table for the duration of the lease at acquisition

$P(3)$ = the percentage derived from the table for the duration of the lease at the time of disposal

Example – Wasting assets

> E purchases a 48-year lease in 1994 for £10,000. In 2002 she spends £2,000 on improvements that affect the value of the lease. She disposes of it with 36 years left in 2006. Her allowable expenditure is therefore as follows:
>
> $$\text{Original cost £10,000} \times \frac{(99.289 - 92.761)}{99.289} = £657$$
>
> $$\text{Additional £2,000} \times \frac{(95.457 - 92.761)}{95.457} = \underline{£56}$$
>
> $$\underline{£713}$$
>
> Total allowable expenditure = £12,000 – £713 = £11,287

Enhancement expenditure

It commonly happens that a person has spent money over the years on improvements. This expenditure can be taken into account provided the improvements are reflected in the state of the property when it is sold.

Where such enhancement expenditure occurred after 31 March 1982, the expenditure is added to the acquisition value and attracts indexation allowance from the time it is incurred.

Enhancement expenditure prior to 31 March 1982 may be taken into account only if the universal rebasing election (see 12.9.2) has not been made and the total of original cost and pre-31 March 1982 enhancement expenditure exceeds the market value at 31 March.

12.20 DISPOSAL OF FOREIGN PROPERTY

12.20.1 Gains must be computed in sterling

Just as a chargeable gain may arise on the disposal of foreign currency, there may similarly be a currency gain on the disposal of certain foreign assets, such as a house or flat in a foreign country. Where overseas assets are disposed of, it is not correct to calculate the gain or loss in terms of the foreign currency and then convert that gain or loss into sterling at the time of the disposal. Instead, the following formula should be used:

Market value of foreign currency received at sale
 (converted at exchange rate applying at that time) v
Deduct sterling equivalent of cost of asset on acquisition
 (converted at exchange rate applying at the time of acquisition) $\underline{w}$
   x
Deduct indexation relief $\underline{y}$
Chargeable gain z

Example – Disposal of foreign property

> G acquired a property in the USA in 1987 for $600,000 (exchange rate $2 = £1) and sold it in 2006 for $720,000 (exchange rate $1.6 = £1). The gain would be computed as follows:
>
> | | £ |
> |---|---|
> | Sale proceeds | 450,000 |
> | *Less*: cost | (300,000) |
> | | 150,000 |
> | *Less*: indexation on £250,000 – say | (100,000) |
> | Chargeable gain | 50,000 |
>
> This can produce some unexpected consequences. Suppose that G had borrowed the purchase price in US$. When she repaid the mortgage on selling the property, she might well be left with no cash in hand. In fact, the profit on the sale of the property in sterling terms was matched by the increase in the sterling value of her mortgage debt. However, there is no CGT relief for this increase and the gain of £50,000 would still be chargeable.

12.20.2 Relief for foreign tax
(TCGA 1992, ss 277–278)

Many overseas countries reserve the right to charge CGT on the disposal of real estate situated in that country, whether or not the owner is resident there. Where a UK resident has had to pay foreign tax in these circumstances, he may claim double tax relief. In effect, the overseas country's tax is available as a credit against the UK tax.

Example – Relief for foreign tax

> H has a property in Italy that cost 160m lire (at the time of purchase this was the equivalent of £90,000). The property is sold for 120,000 euros and there is a chargeable gain for UK tax purposes of £50,000 (assume that Italian CGT of £7,000 is payable). If H's £50,000 gain was chargeable to tax at 40%, the position would be:
>
> | | £ |
> |---|---|
> | UK CGT | 20,000 |
> | *Less*: double tax relief | (7,000) |
> | UK CGT actually payable | 13,000 |
>
> However, there is no relief for any excess. Thus, if H had unrelieved losses brought forward such that his UK tax had been only £6,500, there would be no relief for the balance.

Sometimes there will be a liability for foreign tax, but no capital gains for UK tax purposes.

Example – Foreign CGT only

> *J* disposes of a property in Sierra Leone at a £40,000 loss in sterling terms. However, there was a gain in terms of local currency and the tax bill in Sierra Leone is £10,000. *J* can claim a deduction for this amount as if it were a deduction from his sale proceeds, and this would mean that his loss for UK CGT purposes would be increased from £40,000 to £50,000.

12.20.3 Foreign gains that cannot be remitted
(TCGA 1992, s 279)

Where a person realises a gain on the disposal of assets situated abroad, but is genuinely unable to transfer that gain to the UK because of restrictions imposed abroad or because the foreign currency is not convertible, the amount of the gain may be omitted from assessment for the year in which it arose. Instead, the gain will be assessed to CGT only when it becomes remittable. Claims to this relief must be made within six years of the year in which the gain was realised.

12.21 GAINS AND LOSSES ON SECOND-HAND INSURANCE POLICIES

An insurance policy will normally be an exempt asset for CGT purposes. However, there is an exception for some second-hand policies.

12.21.1 Is a second-hand insurance policy a chargeable asset for CGT purposes?

Until recently, a second-hand insurance policy has been a chargeable asset for CGT purposes only if the person making the disposal acquired it by purchase (as opposed to receiving it as a gift). This allowed the CGT charge to be avoided in many circumstances. For example, where the person who purchased a policy gave it to his wife, she would not be regarded as disposing of a chargeable asset because she had acquired it by gift rather than purchase. This loophole has now been plugged and from 9 April 2003, a second-hand policy is also a chargeable asset where it is received as a gift from a person who acquired it by purchase.

The 2003 rules also cater for more complex situations where policies have at any stage been bought second-hand. However, these rules still allow exemption in three circumstances. The policy will not constitute a chargeable asset where consideration is given only on transfers between:

- spouses or civil partners;
- former spouses under the terms of a divorce settlement;
- two companies within a group of companies.

12.21.2 Computation of CGT losses

Where a second-hand insurance policy is sold, the amount brought into account in computing taxable income has been excluded from the consideration used in computing a CGT gain (or loss). In practice, this has produced substantial CGT losses. From 9 April 2003, the CGT loss is restricted to the economic loss, which will generally be negligible.

13

YOUR MAIN RESIDENCE

The largest capital gain that most people make comes from the sale of their main (or only) residence. This is not surprising as their home is likely to be their single largest investment. In the majority of circumstances, this gain is exempt from CGT provided certain conditions are satisfied.

In this chapter, we look at the following

(1) Main residence exemption.
(2) Possible restrictions on exemption.
(3) Living in job-related accommodation.
(4) Treatment where property not occupied throughout ownership period.
(5) Passing on the family home – CGT considerations.
(6) Anti-avoidance provisions.
(7) Stamp duty.

Civil partners

Since 5 December 2005 the same rules as apply to married couples have applied to civil partners.

13.1 MAIN RESIDENCE EXEMPTION

13.1.1 Basic conditions that must be satisfied
(TCGA 1992, s 222)

There is a total exemption from CGT where a gain is realised by an individual on the disposal of a property that has been his sole or main residence throughout his period of ownership. The legislation also provides exemption for land that forms part of the property (the garden or grounds) up to the 'permitted area'. The permitted area is always at least 0.5 of a hectare (approximately one acre), but may be more where the land is required for the reasonable enjoyment of the property (see 13.1.3).

Tax notes

Married couples or civil partners living together can have the exemption in respect of only one property for a particular period. Note that the exemption can also apply to a property outside of the UK.

13.1.2 Occupation test
(TCGA 1992, s 223(3); SP D4)

A delay of up to 12 months between a property being acquired and the owner taking up residence does not prejudice the exemption; the property is still treated as if it were his main residence. The 12-month period can be extended by up to 12 months if it can be shown that there were good reasons for the owner not taking up residence, for example, the need to carry out alterations or building work, or there was an unavoidable delay in the owner being able to dispose of his previous residence.

The last three years of ownership are treated as qualifying for the exemption, whether the owner lives in the property or not, provided the property has previously been his main residence.

13.1.3 The permitted area

The legislation also provides exemption for an area of gardens or grounds larger than 0.5 hectare if it can be shown that it was 'required for the reasonable enjoyment' of the property as a residence. If the taxpayer and the Inspector cannot agree on this, the Commissioners can determine the matter.

Relevant factors here include considerations such as the extent to which other similar properties have gardens or grounds larger than 0.5 hectare, the need for an area of land to provide either privacy or a buffer between the property and, for example, a motorway, and the need to have room for other facilities and amenities appropriate to the property.

The last-mentioned factor is often the most difficult to argue with the Revenue, which relies on a judgment by Du Parcq J in a 1937 compulsory purchase case, the so-called *Newhill* case [1938] 2 All ER 163:

> 'Required' … does not mean merely that the occupiers of the house would like to have it, or that they would miss it if they lost it, or that anyone proposing to buy the house would think less of the house without it … 'Required' means … that without it there will be such a substantial deprivation of amenities or convenience that a real injury will be done to the property owner …

The Revenue's interpretation is not free from doubt, as the CGT legislation is worded differently from the compulsory purchase legislation, but *Longson v Baker* [2001] STC 6 has lent support to the Revenue. Mr Longson had used land for equestrian pursuits, but the High Court upheld the Commissioners' decision that, while it might have been convenient for him to be able to stable his horses and exercise them on land attached to his home, the facility was not required for the reasonable enjoyment of the property.

This is an area where it is essential to take professional advice.

13.1.4 What is 'the residence'?

There have been several cases concerning property where servants occupy a part of the premises.

In *Batey* v *Wakefield* [1981] STC 521 the property consisted of the main house and a caretaker's lodge. The caretaker/gardener and his wife (who was the owner's housekeeper) occupied the lodge rent free. The main house and the lodge were separated by the width of a tennis court. The Court of Appeal upheld the taxpayer's claim that his residence consisted of the main house and all related buildings that were part and parcel of the property and were occupied for the purposes of the owner's residence.

Yet in *Lewis* v *Rook* [1992] STC 171 the Court of Appeal decided against a taxpayer who claimed the exemption should cover a gardener's cottage located some 170 metres away, as it was not within the same curtilage as the taxpayer's house. Following that decision, the Revenue, which set out its views in *Tax Bulletin* August 1994, said that the exemption could not apply to a separate building at all, regardless of how close it was to the house occupied by the owner.

Specialist advice should be taken if substantial sums are involved.

13.2 POSSIBLE RESTRICTIONS ON EXEMPTION

13.2.1 Part of property used for business purposes
(TCGA 1992, s 224(1))

If part of the property has been used exclusively for the purposes of a trade, business, profession or vocation, the exemption does not cover the part of the gain attributable to that part. This restriction does not apply where the relevant rooms are used for part business/part personal reasons. So, if a journalist's living room doubles up as a workroom from which he carries on his business, there is no restriction under this provision.

13.2.2 Part of property let out
(TCGA 1992, s 223(4))

A similar restriction may apply where the owner has let out part of his home. Thus, if the owner had let approximately one-third of his home, the exemption would normally be confined to two-thirds of the gain on disposal. This rule may be overridden if the lettings are as residential accommodation: the gain on the part of the property let out in this way may still be exempt up to the lesser of:

(1) the exemption on the part of the property occupied by the owner; and
(2) £40,000.

Tax notes

Civil partners or spouses who own a property jointly can each claim an exemption of up to £40,000 against their share of the gain.

13.2.3 **Expenditure incurred with view to gain**
(TCGA 1992, s 224(3))

The exemption is not available if a gain arises from the purchase of property made wholly or partly for the purpose of realising a gain.

Example – Expenditure with a view to gain

> *K*, a partner, lived in a flat owned by his firm. He was offered the opportunity to buy it for £75,000. He accepted because he knew he could fairly quickly find a buyer at £120,000. He sold it, and realised a gain of £45,000. The Revenue is likely to argue that the gain is a chargeable gain because of s 224(3). Similarly, a person who holds a leasehold interest and acquires the freehold because it will enable a better price to be obtained may suffer a restriction under s 224(3) if the Revenue can show that this was the only purpose of buying the freehold.

Some guidance on the circumstances in which the Revenue may seek to deny exemption on these grounds is contained in *Tax Bulletin* August 1994.

13.2.4 **Sale of part of gardens**

Special care is needed if it is decided to sell surplus land for development. In *Varty* v *Lynes* [1976] STC 508 the taxpayer had owned and occupied a house and the garden was less than one acre (the permitted area at that time). He sold the house and part of the garden in June 1971. Slightly less than 12 months later, he sold the rest of the garden to a builder and realised a substantial gain because he had secured planning permission in the meantime. He was assessed on the gain on the land sold to the builder. The High Court decided that the main residence exemption did not apply. Brightman J held that the exemption for the garden or grounds could apply only in relation to garden or grounds occupied as such by the owner at the date of sale. The Revenue subsequently stated that it would invoke this only where land was sold with development value. The following principles should be borne in mind:

(1) A sale of land out of a parcel of land greater than 0.5 hectare may be vulnerable even where the owner remains in occupation. The fact that the owner continues to live in the property suggests that the surplus land was not required for the reasonable enjoyment of the property.

(2) A sale of land with development value at the same time as the owner ceases to live in the property is not open to attack in the same way as in *Varty* v *Lynes*.

(3) A sale of land with development value after the owner has moved out is likely to result in a tax charge.

There has recently been another case, which is particularly instructive in terms of practical issues, where land adjoining an individual's home was sold off for development, see *Henke & Another* v *HMRC* SpC 550.

13.2.5 What happens where there are two homes?

An individual may live in two (or more) properties without necessarily owning both (or all) of them. The Revenue view is that a person has two residences if, for example, he owns a large house in Yorkshire and rents a modest flat in London where he lives during the week.

If necessary, the Commissioners decide which of an individual's two or more residences is his main residence. The test is not necessarily where the individual lives most of the time, and it is often not clear in a particular case what view the Commissioners might take.

13.2.6 Taxpayer's right of election
(TCGA 1992, s 222(5))

Fortunately, the owner can settle the matter by formally electing one property to be treated as his main residence. The election may be varied from time to time, but only in relation to the last two years prior to the variation.

There is a time limit for a notice under s 222(5) of two years. The Revenue's view has been that the time limit refers to the point in time the individual starts to have a second residence. This interpretation was upheld by the High Court in *Griffin* v *Craig Harvey* [1994] STC 54.

There is one circumstance where the Revenue will accept an election outside the two-year time limit. ESC D21 provides:

> Where for any period an individual has more than one residence, but his interest in each of them, or in each of them except one, is such as to have no more than a negligible capital value on the open market (eg a weekly rented flat or accommodation provided by an employer) the two-year time limit will be extended where the individual was unaware that such a nomination could be made. In such cases the nomination may be made within a reasonable time of the individual becoming aware of the possibility of so doing, and it will be regarded as effective from the date on which the individual first had more than one residence.

13.2.7 Two adjacent flats

A situation in which you should take professional advice is if you occupy two flats as a combined home. The Revenue internal manuals confirm that the two flats can sometimes be regarded as constituting a single residence where certain conditions are satisfied. One condition is that the flats are contiguous. Another condition is that the two flats are in the same block. However, even if you satisfy both these conditions you may still not qualify. Furthermore, you should be prepared for the Revenue to resist such a claim, at any rate in the first instance.

13.3 LIVING IN JOB-RELATED ACCOMMODATION

13.3.1 Meaning of job-related accommodation

Job-related accommodation is defined as accommodation provided for an individual or his spouse by reason of his employment where:

(1) it is necessary for the proper performance of his duties that he should live there; or

(2) it is provided for the better performance of his duties and the employment is one where employers customarily provide accommodation; or

(3) the accommodation is provided as part of the special security arrangements for the employee's safety.

13.3.2 Right to nominate a property
(TCGA 1992, s 222(8))

Where an individual is required to live in job-related accommodation, a house owned by him and intended to be occupied as his residence in due course is treated as if it were his residence. Such a house may therefore qualify for exemption even if the owner had let it and never actually occupied it himself before disposing of it, provided he nominates it as his only or main residence.

13.3.3 Similar provisions for self-employed individuals

A self-employed individual who is required to live at or near his place of work (eg a publican) can nominate a property under s 222(8) for eventual use as his main residence. This also applies if their spouse or civil partner is required to occupy such premises. Only periods after 5 April 1982 can qualify under this heading.

13.4 TREATMENT WHERE PROPERTY NOT OCCUPIED THROUGHOUT OWNERSHIP PERIOD

13.4.1 Proportion of gain may be exempt

The s 222 exemption is not necessarily an 'all or nothing' test. The legislation makes provision for a proportion of the capital gain to be exempt where the necessary conditions are satisfied for part of the period of ownership. The exempt proportion of the gain is normally:

$$\frac{\text{Period of qualifying use}}{\text{Total period of ownership}} \times \text{Indexed gain}$$

13.4.2 Periods prior to 31 March 1982 ignored

A period of non-qualifying use is ignored if it is prior to 31 March 1982.

Example – Incomplete period of occupation

> A property was acquired in March 1975 and let as an investment until March 1986. Thereafter it is the owner's sole residence. It is sold in March 2006 for a gain of £340,000. The exempt proportion of the gain would be:
>
> $^{20}/_{24} \times £340,000 = £283,333$

13.4.3 Last 36 months of ownership
(TCGA 1992, s 223(2))

Provided the property has at some time qualified as the owner's main residence, the last three years of ownership also qualify for exemption. This still applies if the property is let or another property is nominated as his main residence for all or part of that period. It also applies even where the period when the property was occupied as the individual's main residence was before 31 March 1982.

13.4.4 Periods spent working abroad
(TCGA 1992, s 223(3)(b))

If, during a period when his property was used as his main residence, the owner has to work abroad, the property continues to be regarded as his main residence (and therefore exempt from CGT) if he was employed abroad under a contract of employment and all the employment duties were performed overseas. The condition requiring the property to be the owner's only or main residence after working abroad is treated as satisfied if he is unable to resume residence because the terms of his new employment require him to work elsewhere (ESC D4).

13.4.5 Periods spent working elsewhere in UK

A period of up to four years during which the owner's employment necessitated his living elsewhere in the UK is also a qualifying period. A period (or periods in total) that exceeds four years is covered to the extent of four years. Again, it is normally necessary that the period be followed by a period of occupation, but ESC D4 applies if the individual cannot resume occupation because his current employment prevents this.

13.4.6 Other qualifying periods

A further period of absence of up to three years can be treated as qualifying for exemption, provided the period is both preceded and succeeded by a period of actual occupation.

13.4.7 Summary

Table 13.1 may help in computing the position in a particular case. The exempt gain is (X) + (Y).

Table 13.1 – Computation of exempt gain on main residence

Number of complete months since 31 March 1982 when the property was actually occupied as the owner's main residence. See 13.1.2	(A)
The lesser of 36 months or such part of the last 36 months which does not already fall within A (24 months for disposals prior to 19 March 1991). See 13.4.3	(B)
Months spent working abroad when the property was not occupied as the individual's main residence provided that the individual resumed residence after his overseas employment ceased or would have done so if he had not been required to take up employment elsewhere in the UK. Note: exclude any period which already falls to be included in B above. See 13.4.4	(C)
Number of months spent living elsewhere because the individual's employment required him to live in another part of the UK (subject to a maximum of 48 months). Again, exclude any period already included in B.	
Note, an entry is appropriate here only if the individual resumed occupation of the property at the end of the period. See 13.4.5	(D)
Any further period of absence which was both preceded and succeeded by the individual occupying the property as his main residence (subject to a maximum of 36 months). Again exclude any period already included in B. See 13.4.6	(E)
Apply the following fraction to the overall gain which arose on the disposal of the property: $$\frac{A+B+C+D+E}{\text{Months of ownership since 31 March 1982}}$$	(X)
A further exemption may also be due where the property has been let. The additional exemption is the lesser of X or £40,000. See 13.2.2	(Y)

13.4.8 Dependent relatives
(TCGA 1992, s 226)

In addition to the main residence exemption, an individual may qualify for exemption in respect of a property occupied by a dependent relative as his main residence provided the property was so occupied before 6 April 1988.

To qualify for this exemption, the property must have been occupied by the dependent relative rent free, and without any other consideration.

A widowed mother (or mother-in-law) is automatically regarded as a dependent relative. In other situations, the relative is regarded as dependent only if prevented by old age or infirmity from maintaining himself. The exemption is not available for a property acquired after 5 April 1988, even if the property is a replacement for another property previously occupied by a dependent relative.

In some cases, it may be appropriate to form a settlement with the trustees owning the property occupied by the dependent relative as the trustees may still qualify for exemption in respect of a property occupied by a beneficiary as his main residence (see 30.4.11).

13.5 PASSING ON THE FAMILY HOME – CGT CONSIDERATIONS

One of the main concerns that people have nowadays as far as taxation is concerned is the way in which their property will pass to their heirs. The inheritance tax issues are dealt with in Chapter 29. A gift of property in an estate planning exercise would give rise to a capital gains tax liability were it not covered by the PPR exemption. However, there is another aspect. Many IHT mitigation schemes have, as one of their consequences, the fact that the donor's children end up owning an interest in the family home that is not covered by the main residence exemption. To that extent, the family might have saved IHT only at the cost of taking on a long-term CGT liability that will crystallise as and when the property is sold.

13.6 ANTI-AVOIDANCE PROVISIONS

Bear in mind the restriction on the main residence exemption where hold-over relief has been obtained on a previous disposal (see 32.13).

13.7 STAMP DUTY

Capital gains tax is, unfortunately, not the only tax to be considered when disposing and purchasing a new main residence. The explosion in property prices now makes stamp duty (or SDLT as it is now known) a major consideration.

The current rates of SDLT are as follows:

Consideration	Rate
Up to £125,000	Nil
£125,001–£150,000	1%*
£150,001–£250,000	1%
£250,001–£500,000	3%
£500,001+	4%

*Nil in disadvantaged areas

We look at stamp duty in greater depth in Chapter 38.

14

THE TAX CALCULATION

DALE BUTCHER

'Tax doesn't have to be taxing' is the glib way in which HMRC advertises the self-assessment process to its 'customers'.

Remember you will normally only have to file a self-assessment tax form if you receive a return form or if you owe or are owed tax. However, regardless of whether you have to file a self-assessment (SA) form or not, you should carry out an annual review of how much tax you should have paid and how much you have actually paid.

This chapter covers the main steps involved in calculating your tax liability for the year.

Table 14.1 - Rates of tax on various types of income for 2007–08

Rates of tax on	Non-savings income	Savings income	UK dividends (eg earnings) and tax credits
First £2,230 of taxable income	10%	10%	10%
Next £32,370 of taxable income	22%	20%	10%
All remaining taxable income	40%	40%	32.5%

If you file your SA return online, the Revenue will work out your tax for you. HMRC will also do this if you submit a paper return by 30 September following the tax year. This chapter should help you to follow such Revenue calculations.

Example – Tax calculation

Joe Public has the following income and gains for the tax year ended 5 April 2008

	Income	Tax	
Salary	£38,000	£6,600.00	(figures taken from P60)
Private medical	£780		(figure taken from P11D)
Bank interest	£750 (net)	£187.50	
Dividends	£1200 (net)	£133.33	
Property income	£500		
Capital gain	£10,000		

In addition Joe had paid £50 a month (grossed up) into his personal pension plan and had donated £20 on his Visa card to Comic Relief during the tax year.

The tax calculation would look as follows:

	Income £	Tax £
Earned income		
Earnings per P60 and P11D	38,780.00	6,600.00
Net earned income	38,780.00	6,600.00
	£	£
Investment income		
UK land and property	500.00	
UK savings	937.50	187.50
UK dividends	1,333.33	133.33
Investment income	2,770.83	320.83
Total income		
Net earned income	38,780.00	6,600.00
Total investment income	2,770.83	320.83
Total income	41,550.83	6,920.83
Taxable income		
Total income	41,550.83	6,920.83
Basic allowance	5,225.00	
Taxable income	36,325.83	6,920.83
Basic rate band adjustments*		
Basic rate band	32,370.00	
Pension payments	600.00	
Gift aid and charitable payments	25.64	
Extended basic rate	32,995.64	

* The basic rate band is extended by grossed up payments which are made net of basic rate tax (eg pension and gift aid payments). This method ensures that where appropriate income tax relief is given only for higher rate tax purposes.

Tax payable

Non-savings income			
Starting rate	2,230.00	@10%	223.00
Basic rate	31,825.00	@22%	7,001.50
Savings income (other than dividends)			
Lower rate	937.50	@20%	187.50
Dividends			
Lower rate	233.14	@10%	23.31
Higher rate on dividends	1,100.19	@32.5%	357.56
			7,792.87

	£
Income tax after allowances and reliefs	7,792.87
Less: Tax credits	(133.33)
Income tax due	7,659.54
Tax deducted at source	(6,787.50)
Total income tax	872.04
Capital gains tax	
(£10,000 – £9,200) = £800.00 @40% = £320.00	320.00
Net tax due for 2006–07	1,192.04

Once you have arrived at the net tax due figure, consider:

(1) Do you have payments on account to make? See 2.1.3.
(2) Has any of the tax liability for this year already been included in a notice of coding? See 4.2.3.
(3) Do you owe tax for a previous year which should have been collected via the PAYE code for this tax year? See 4.2.3.

For more examples in respect of individuals with different circumstances and personal allowances, refer to Chapter 11.

The Revenue might have sent you a tax calculation guide and notes on the guide. The Revenue form often seems akin to a 16-page Sudoko puzzle. The form gets the right results but only by some entries that seem counter intuitive. Using the above calculation for your own figures should be enough to act as a ready reckoner as to whether you have tax under or overpaid.

Common sense

Once you have completed your tax calculation you need to find out how the liability or tax refund arose. If you have only income from earnings, the tax paid under PAYE should more or less equal the tax liability. If it doesn't, your tax code is wrong and probably needs adjusting. One common area is incorrect benefits in kind. A quick cross reference of your P11D with your end-year tax code should highlight any discrepancies.

Tax notes

Initial reaction to a tax refund is positive and to a tax liability the opposite. However, another view of a tax refund is that HMRC has been holding your money and paying you no interest for over a year; likewise, a tax liability may indicate good deferral planning by yourself or your tax advisor.

14.1 SOME POINTS TO LOOK OUT FOR

Bank and building society interest

(1) If you are not sure from your statements how much interest you received, ask your bank for an end of year certificate. They will supply these details to the HMRC.

(2) Remember to gross up net payments received as this is the taxable amount.

> **Tax notes**
>
> If you have bank interest taxable at the higher rate, the additional tax liability will be equal to the tax already deducted by the bank or society, ie 20%.

Dividends

(3) Tax credits on your dividends and unit trust income are not refundable, ie the credit is a notional credit. The effect of adding the tax credit to the dividend, computing tax at 32.5% thereon, and then deducting the tax credit, is that the higher rate tax comes to one quarter of the actual dividend received.

(4) Do not include equalisation as part of your dividends from unit trusts.

(5) If you received dividends from overseas companies and the total did not exceed £300, you can include these dividends with your UK dividends. You will then get a 10% tax credit. But bear in mind that some countries levy a 15% withholding tax on dividends and you could get a credit for this higher amount by completing the *Foreign* pages.

> **Tax notes**
>
> If you have dividend income and are liable to higher rate tax, the tax liability will be 25% of the dividend received.

Insurance bonds

(6) Gains are only subject to 20% higher rate tax unless the insurance company is not resident in the UK. Where gains are taxed only at higher rate, you should not 'gross-up' your profit.

Offshore roll-up funds

(7) Do not deduct your CGT annual exemption.

Pension contributions

(8) Personal pension payments were made net of basic rate tax in 2007–08 and relief is given by extending the basic rate tax band by the gross amount of these payments. The HMRC tax calculation guide requires you to enter the 'grossed-up' amount.

(9) Contributions to Free Standing AVC payments were also paid net of basic rate tax in 2007–08.

(10) Retirement annuity contributions might have been paid gross in 2007–08. It depends on the arrangement set up by the insurance company concerned.

Deductions from your income

(11) The HMRC tax return form requires you to enter the net amount of Gift Aid payments. You are entitled to gross-up the amounts that you pay and claim higher rate relief.

(12) Remember some reliefs, such as EIS and donations to charities can be carried back from the current year (see 10.9.2).

Generally

(13) Interest and penalties are not taxed so do not treat them as a tax credit in your calculation.

(14) Capital gains form the top slice of your income in calculating the tax rate on any gains.

(15) See 27.3.4 re top-slicing on gains from insurance bonds.

(16) Talk to your Inspector of Taxes about what underpayments have been included in your tax code from the tax year for which you are preparing the calculation and also for previous years.

(17) Compare this year's tax calculation with last year. The Inspector of Taxes will!

(18) Use the above calculation as a financial health check. If you are paying higher rate tax on investment income are you using tax free investments to the maximum? Is it worth transferring assets to a spouse or civil partner if they pay tax at a lower rate?

Tax notes

Don't believe the hype – tax *is* taxing!

PART 2

BUSINESS TAX AND FINANCE

This part contains the following chapters:

15

COMPUTATION OF BUSINESS PROFITS AND CAPITAL ALLOWANCES

VIRAN DE SILVA

The calculation of business profits and accounting standards applies not only to self-employed individuals but as general principle carries over to other areas where accounts are required, for example companies, partnership and landlords. The changes in law over recent years have, for better or worse, brought taxable profits more into line with accounts profits calculated by reference to generally accepted accountancy principles.

This chapter looks at the computation of profits and the closely related area of capital allowances.

(1) Computation of trading profits.
(2) Capital allowances.
(3) Pre-trading expenditure.
(4) Post-cessation receipts.
(5) Post-cessation expenses.

15.1 COMPUTATION OF TRADING PROFITS

15.1.1 The accounts profit is generally the starting point

Most tax computations start with the words 'Profits per accounts' and then consist of a number of special adjustments to those accounts, which are required by the tax legislation and case law.

15.1.2 What type of accounts is required?

The nature and complexity of accounts should be governed by the business. An individual in business as a window-cleaner can keep his accounts as simple as possible. Moreover, the Revenue allows certain 'short-cuts'. For example, if you use your car for business and have not registered for VAT, you can generally use the approved mileage allowance rates designed for employees (see 4.4.9) and merely claim, say, 4,000 miles at the appropriate rate rather than keep all the motoring bills and claim capital allowances.

Larger businesses require more complex accounting. The following covers the rules that govern the tax treatment of income and expenses and deals with adjustments to accounts that are required for tax purposes. For example, a set of accounts prepared for commercial reasons may include a provision for wear and tear to a building. Such a provision needs to be 'added back' (as no relief is available for depreciation as such, relief is due only via the capital allowances system).

See 2.6 on the types of adjustments that have been identified by the Revenue in 'enabling letters' sent to self-employed individuals. These letters reflect common shortcomings in accounts received by the Revenue.

15.1.3 Accounts should be on the 'earnings basis'

The Revenue's view is that accounts should normally be prepared to reflect a trader's earnings for a year rather than just the cash received. For example, the accounts should include debtors, ie bills that have been issued but not paid by the year end. Similarly, the accounts should include work in progress.

15.1.4 Sound commercial accountancy principles

The Master of the Rolls stated in *Gallagher* v *Jones* [1993] STC 537, CA:

> Subject to any express or implied statutory rule ... the ordinary way to ascertain the profits or losses of a business is to apply accepted principles of commercial accountancy. That is the very purpose for which such principles are formulated. As has often been pointed out, such principles are not static: they may be modified, refined and elaborated over time as circumstances change and accounting insights sharpen. But so long as such principles remain current and generally accepted they provide the surest answer.

Accountancy principles are constantly being refined and are published by the Accounting Standards Board (ASB) as Financial Reporting Standards. In particular, FRS18 brought together and updated a number of earlier statements on accounting policies. Some FRSs are mandatory only for businesses of a certain size; others apply more generally. Smaller businesses that do not require an audit are governed by the regularly updated FRSSE.

Key concepts for accountants include the 'going concern' concept, the need for consistency and the accruals principle whereby income and expenses related to earning it are matched. Until recently, the concept of prudence was also regarded as a fundamental principle, ie that income and profits should not be anticipated, but accountants now place increasing weight on accounts showing a 'realistic' position rather than an approach that might be regarded as excessively prudent.

15.1.5 Expenditure that is specifically disallowed
(IT(T&OI)A 2005, ss 33-35 and 45)

As mentioned above, certain types of expenditure are disallowed, although it may be sound accounting practice to deduct such costs in a trader's accounts. See Table 15.1 for a summary contained in the Revenue tax return guide. The rest of this section looks more closely at specific types of business expenses.

Capital expenditure
(IT(T&OI)A 2005, s 33)

The acquisition of a capital asset is not a cost that may be deducted in arriving at profits for tax purposes. This may seem obvious where an asset such as a building is acquired, but the definition of capital expenditure goes a long way beyond the acquisition of tangible assets. The generally accepted definition was given by Lord Cave in *British Insulated and Helsby Cables Ltd* v *Atherton* (1925) 10 TC 155; he stated:

> when an expenditure is made … with a view to bringing into existence an asset or an advantage for the enduring benefit of a trade there is very good reason (in the absence of special circumstances leading to the opposite conclusion) for treating such expenditure as properly attributable not to revenue but to capital.

The acquisition of, for example goodwill, is capital expenditure. Less obviously, a lump sum payment to secure release from an onerous liability (eg a lease at a high rent or a fixed rate loan) is also regarded as capital expenditure.

Entertaining
(IT(T&OI)A 2005, s 45)

Any expenses relating to entertaining customers or suppliers that are included in a set of accounts normally need to be added back. There is a modest exemption that may apply where the entertaining is provided by an hotelier, restaurateur or someone else who provides entertainment in the ordinary course of his trade. Staff entertainment is also an allowable expense, but the individual employee may be assessed on a benefit-in-kind.

Gifts to customers, etc
(IT(T&OI)A 2005, s 45)

The cost of gifts to customers and to potential customers and introducers is also disallowed unless the gift carries a conspicuous advertisement and is neither food, drink, tobacco nor a voucher exchangeable for such goods, nor an item that costs more than £50 per recipient per year (£10 for 2000–01 and earlier years).

Table 15.1 – HMRC summary of allowable and non-allowable business expenses

	Allowable	*Not allowable*
Basic costs	Light, heat and power; telephone; insurance; stationery and postage; business rates and rent; advertising; protective clothing; repairs; replacement loose tools (unless capital allowances claimed instead); transport of goods to customers or materials from suppliers; subcontractors (see Leaflet IR14/15)	Private and personal expenses; non-business part of running costs of premises used only partly for business; own insurance; ordinary, everyday clothing even if bought specially for business use; parking and other fines; buying, altering or improving fixed assets; depreciation or losses on sale of fixed assets
Employee costs	Employees' wages and salaries; employers' NICs; redundancy payments; pension contributions on employees' behalf; employees' expenses and benefits	Own wages or salary and drawings from the business; own pension payments and other benefits; own NICs
Finance costs	Interest on loans and overdrafts used solely for business purposes; costs of arranging such finance	Repayment of loan or overdraft (as opposed to the interest)
Professional	Accountancy fees; preparation of ordinary business costs agreement; debt recovery (if debt is for a taxable receipt); renewing leases of less than 50 years (where no premium is paid); defending business rights; appeals against business rates	Costs of settling tax disputes; legal costs of buying fixed assets (treated as part of the cost of fixed asset); costs and fines or penalties for breaking the law
Travel	Travel on business to meet customers, suppliers, etc; travel between business premises; accommodation and reasonable cost of meals on overnight business trips; vehicle running expenses (less proportion of private use)	Travel between home and place of business (unless agreed with the Tax Office that your home is your base); costs of buying vehicles (but capital allowances can be claimed); meals (except on overnight business trips)

Table 15.1 – Continued

Bad debts	Irrecoverable debts written off, if taxed when they arose; recovery costs; provisions against specific doubtful debts; debts recovered later should be shown in box 3.16 or 3.37 of the self-assessment return	General bad debts reserve; debts not taxed when they arose, eg because they relate to sale of a fixed asset
Subscriptions	Payments to certain professional bodies (Tax Office can tell you which)	Payments to political parties; most payments to clubs, charities or churches
Entertaining	Costs of entertaining staff; gifts (not food or drink) up to £50 per person per year that advertise your business	All other entertaining and hospitality
VAT	Any VAT that is not recoverable is an allowable expense. This does not include any input VAT paid on capital items. However, this can be included in their cost if a claim can be made to capital allowances for them. Where allowable expenses net of recoverable input VAT are shown, the turnover should be shown on the same basis, ie net of output VAT charged. Alternatively, you may prefer to show receipts and allowable expenses gross of VAT and the net payment to HMRC as an expense or the net repayment as a taxable receipt.	

Illegal payments
(IT(T&OI)A 2005, s 55)

A specific provision disallowing illegal payments such as bribes came into force on 11 June 1993 (the date the relevant clause was introduced in the committee stage of the Finance Bill 1993).

The disallowance was subsequently extended to cover payments made on or after 30 November 1993 in response to threats, menaces, blackmail and other forms of extortion. The disallowance in respect of bribes was further extended for expenditure incurred after 31 March 2002 to cover any payment that would constitute a criminal offence if made in the UK, effectively amending the law to cover bribes made outside the UK.

Lease rentals on expensive cars
(IT(T&OI)A 2005, s 48)

$$\frac{1}{2} \times \frac{(\text{Cost of car} - £12,000)}{\text{cost of car}}$$

Where a trader uses a leased car or provides a car to an employee and the original cost when new or retail price was £12,000+ (£8,000+ prior to 10 March 1992), part of the lease rentals must be added back as a disallowable expense. The amount disallowed is the following proportion of the lease rental:

$$\frac{1}{2} \times \frac{(£16,000 - £12,000)}{£16,000} \times £2,400 = £300$$

Thus, if a car costing £16,000 is leased for a rental of £2,400 pa, the amount disallowed is:

This treatment does not apply to maintenance costs included in the lease rentals provided they are identified separately under the terms of the leasing agreement. Amounts paid under an HP agreement are dealt with differently (see 15.1.6).

Provisions for bad debts
(IT(T&OI)A 2005, s 35)

A general provision against bad debts is not allowable, but provisions against specific debts are a proper deduction for tax purposes provided it can be shown the amount is a reasonable provision (see further 15.1.8).

Remuneration not paid within nine months of year end
(IT(T&OI)A 2005, s 36)

Bonus payments to employees may be made after the end of a year. If they clearly relate to a period of account, it would be normal for the trader's accounts to include a provision. However, this provision is allowable only if the remuneration is paid within nine months of the year end.

Pension contributions for employees
(FA 1993, s 113)

A deduction is due only if the contribution is paid during the course of the trader's year, whether to an approved or unapproved scheme.

Pension contributions for the trader himself are not an allowable deduction in computing profits, although relief is available as a deduction from taxable profits (see 25.1 for details of the method of dealing with personal pension contributions).

Expenditure not wholly for trade purposes
(IT(T&OI)A 2005, s 34)

In practice, s 34 imposes a double test:

The expenditure must be incurred for the purposes of the trade

Powell v *Jackman* 2004 STC 645 concerned the expenses of a self-employed milkman who had his office at home but collected milk from a depot 26 miles away. He claimed that his travel to the depot was business travel from the base of his business operations but the High Court held this could not be justified on the facts and that his base of operation (place of work) was the area that constituted his round. The travel costs were incurred in getting to his place of work rather than in carrying on his business operations and were not allowable. As Lord Denning put it in a previous case, the cost of getting to one's place of work 'is a living expense as distinct from a business expense'. This case can be distinguished from *Horton* v *Young* 49 TC 60 where the Court of Appeal held that the base of operations for a self-employed bricklayer was his home.

Tax notes

Basically, it is a matter of fact as to whether the base of the business is a trader's home.

The expenditure must be incurred wholly and exclusively for trade

The 'wholly and exclusively' test means that expenses incurred partly for trade purposes and partly for personal reasons are not allowable. For example, the cost of black dresses worn in court by a female barrister was disallowed on the grounds that the expenditure had a dual purpose (warmth and decency as well as the need to dress for court), as was the cost of meals incurred by a self-employed carpenter when he was working away from home.

Where an expense is incurred for mixed purposes the whole amount is disallowed; this rules out relief where an individual travels abroad mainly to have a holiday but carries out some work while there. However, where it can be shown that an additional cost was incurred wholly for business reasons, a deduction may be due for this. Consequently, if a person uses part of his home for business, the extra heat and light bills are an allowable expense for tax purposes. It should be noted that the Revenue's Employment Income Manual, at section 01476, suggests a guideline rate of £3 pw from 2008–09 (previously £2pw) for employers reimbursing employees working from home.

In practice, quite a number of expenses are apportioned between private (not allowable) and business (allowable) use. Phone bills and car expenses are two particular examples that arise often.

Arguments will often arise where expenses relate to preserve a trader's reputation as the Revenue will generally assume that the expenditure was at least partly incurred for personal reasons. In *McKnight* v *Sheppard HL* 1999 STC 669, a stockbroker incurred legal expenses in defending charges brought by the London Stock Exchange. He was found guilty of gross misconduct and suspended from trading. Because a suspension would have resulted in the destruction of his business, he appealed and his suspension was reduced to a fine. He was allowed tax relief for his legal expenses because these had been incurred wholly and exclusively for the purposes of the trade, but the fines imposed were disallowed.

Arguments will also arise where the expense relates to an activity that is regarded by HMRC as a hobby. However, this is a question of fact. A recent case involved expenditure by a coach company on motor rallying. It was held that this was an allowable expense even though the owner of the business was a motor sports enthusiast and he drove the company cars. See *McQueen* v *HMRC* SpC 601.

Payments of reverse premiums
(IT(T&OI)A, s 99)

Relief is due to a builder or developer who pays a reverse premium to induce a tenant to take a lease. However, no relief is due to a tenant who pays a reverse premium in order to be released from an onerous lease.

Sums recoverable from insurance policy, etc
(IT(T&OI)A, s 106)

Where a trader can get back from an insurance company the money that he has paid out, there is no deduction due for the expenditure. The same treatment applies where a trader has been indemnified against a particular cost.

Patent royalties and other annual payments
(IT(T&OI)A 2005, s 51)

Certain annual payments (eg patent royalties) generally need to be paid net of basic rate tax. The payments are not deductible in arriving at profits of the trade or profession, although they are allowed as a deduction for higher rate purposes.

15.1.6 Other expenditure where adjustments may be required

Interest

Relief for interest payments on qualifying loans taken by partners are given against the partner's general income (see 10.4). Interest paid by a sole trader or partnership may be deducted in arriving at the business's taxable profits provided it passes the 'wholly and exclusively' test (see above). See *Dixon v HMRC*, 2006 SpC 531 concerning the apportionment of interest where the loan was partly used to buy the flat over the trader's shop.

Problems may arise where overdraft interest is charged in a set of accounts and the proprietor's capital account is overdrawn. The Revenue is likely to argue that the interest (or, at any rate, part of it) was incurred not for business purposes, but to finance drawings. If you find yourself in this situation you should take advice from an accountant.

Cost of raising business finance
(IT(T&OI)A 2005, s 58)

There are often certain costs in raising long-term finance, and for many years the Revenue regarded these as capital expenditure. A statutory deduction is now available provided the costs:

(1) were incurred wholly and exclusively for the purposes of obtaining loan finance, providing security or repaying a loan; and
(2) represented expenditure on professional fees, commissions, advertising, printing or other incidental expenses in relation to raising finance.

In some cases a deduction is available even though the expenditure failed and the loan finance was not in fact obtained.

Plant and machinery lease rentals

In the past, the way that lease rentals have been treated has depended on the type of lease. If it was an 'operating lease', ie a lease for a period that is less than the asset's anticipated useful life, it was normal for rentals to be deducted in arriving at the profits for the period to which the rentals refer. In practice, most leasing agreements provide for rentals to be payable in advance. Thus, if on 1 December a trader paid lease rentals of £12,000, which covered a period of six months, and he made up accounts to the following 31 March, the amount deducted in arriving at the profits for the year ended 31 March would be:

$$\frac{4 \text{ months}}{6 \text{ months}} \times £12{,}000 = £8{,}000$$

A different accounting treatment was required where a trader paid rentals under a 'finance lease', ie a lease agreement under which the trader acquires almost all the benefits of outright ownership. The Revenue's view has been that the amount that should be deducted is that charged in the trader's accounts in accordance with SSAP 21 (ie the relevant Statement of Standard Accounting Practice that governs the accounting treatment of such leases).

Different rules apply from 1 April 2006 in respect of long funding leases for periods of at least seven years (these provisions may also apply to certain leases for periods of between five and seven years where the lease is not a finance lease). The broad effect of these changes is that a lessee will be able to claim capital allowances as if he had bought the asset he is leasing. These capital allowances will be computed on the 'straight line' basis. In addition, he will be able to claim relief for the financing charges contained in the lease as if they were interest.

The legislation also provides that a lessor and lessee may jointly elect for other post 31 March 2006 leases to be dealt with in this way.

Hire purchase

Where equipment is acquired under an HP contract, its cost counts as capital expenditure (in most cases capital allowances will be available). The 'interest' element is apportioned over the contract term and relief is given for the amount of interest that relates to the accounting period concerned.

Example – Adjustments for HP contracts

A trader acquires a computer under a three-year HP agreement. The cost of the computer was £12,000, but the trader pays 36 monthly HP payments of £420.

The interest payable over the three years totals £3,120. This would normally be allocated roughly as follows:

Year 1:	£1,715
Year 2:	£1,040
Year 3:	£365

This type of allocation reflects the amount of the HP 'loan' outstanding during each year.

Legal and professional expenses

Where an Inspector of Taxes examines a trader's business accounts, he normally asks for an analysis of any substantial amounts relating to legal and professional expenses. Legal costs in connection with the acquisition of capital assets are disallowable as capital expenditure, as are legal costs in connection with renewing a lease of more than 50 years. In contrast, legal costs incurred to protect a capital asset are generally allowable as a revenue expense.

Tax notes

Professional costs incurred in connection with tax appeals are not allowable on the grounds that such costs relate to tax on profits rather than an expense incurred in earning profits. However, in practice the costs of preparing and agreeing tax computations are usually allowed.

15.1.7 **Relief for premiums**
(IT(T&OI)A 2005, s 60)

A trader may be required to make a lump sum payment to a landlord to obtain a lease. Where the lease is for a period of less than 50 years, part of the lump sum may be treated as income in the landlord's hands (see 7.3) and the trader may claim a deduction for this amount as if it were rent payable over the period of his lease. The part taxed in the landlord's hands is 100% of the premium less 2% for each complete year of the lease other than the first year.

There is no relief if the lease is for more than 50 years or if the premium is paid to someone other than the landlord because such a third party (eg an outgoing tenant) is not subject to income tax as income from property.

Sometimes the lease will require a tenant to have certain building work carried out that will increase the value of the landlord's interest in the property. The landlord's UK property income should indicate the notional premium (see 7.3.4). Where this applies, the trader can claim a deduction just as if he had been required to pay a premium in cash. However, the notional premium is generally far less than the actual cost of carrying out the work concerned.

Example – Treatment of premiums

> *B* pays a premium of £40,000 for a lease of ten years. Of this sum, 82% (ie £32,800) is taxed in the landlord's hands as rental income for the year in which the premium is payable (see 7.3).
>
> *B* can claim a deduction in his accounts for the ten years as if he had paid rent of £3,280 pa. If it were not for s 87, the expenditure would be treated as capital expenditure and would attract no relief.

15.1.8 **Provision for bad or doubtful debts**

The Revenue has explained its approach with regard to provisions for bad or doubtful debts. Its interpretation is that a trader may be entitled to a deduction provided the following circumstances are satisfied:

(1) the debt existed at the balance sheet date; and
(2) before the accounts were finalised, the company's trader/directors discovered that the debtor's financial position at that date was such that the debt was unlikely to be paid.

The Revenue stated that a common example of this is where a debtor at the balance sheet date goes into administration or liquidation shortly after that date and before the date on which the trader approves the financial statements. Where the administration or liquidation commences after the balance sheet date, its occurrence before the accounts were finalised normally sheds light on the debtor's financial position at the balance sheet date. If the period between the balance sheet date and approval of the accounts is short, it is unlikely that a debtor would have gone from financial good health to insolvency in that period. In these circumstances it would normally be reasonable for the trader to regard the debt as doubtful. The acceptable amount of provision would depend on the information available.

The Revenue contrasts this with a situation where a debtor is an habitually slow payer and there are no grounds to believe his financial position has changed. In such a case, the Revenue argues that the length of time a debt has been outstanding is not in itself a sufficient reason to regard it as doubtful.

15.1.9 Provisions against liability to pay sums after year end

This is an aspect of a trader's accounts to which Tax Inspectors pay particular attention. The Revenue needs to be satisfied that relief is not sought for expenditure that will be incurred only in the future. Consequently, an Inspector will almost certainly withhold relief unless he is satisfied that the liability arose before the year end. For example, in the past it was not generally possible to secure a deduction for redundancy costs unless the necessary redundancy notices were served by the end of the trader's accounting period. Similarly, the Revenue will often argue that a provision for an amount that may be due to a client for professional negligence is not allowable unless the client's claim has been admitted by the year end.

This approach can be challenged where the accounts comply with generally accepted accountancy principles, but you should seek professional advice if sizeable amounts of tax are at issue.

The Revenue's rather restrictive approach was challenged successfully in *Johnston* v *Britannia Airways Ltd* [1994] STC 763. Civil Aviation Authority rules required each aeroplane to have a certificate of airworthiness. This would not be issued unless each engine was overhauled every 17,000 flying hours which, in Britannia's case, meant every three to five years. Accordingly, a provision for the overhaul costs was made in each year's accounts based on the average cost of the overhaul per hour flown and the number of hours flown in the period.

The Inspector took the view that the correct treatment was to make no provision before the cost of the overhaul was incurred, to capitalise the overhaul cost when incurred and then to write it off gradually over the period up to the next overhaul. The Special Commissioners found that the accruals method used by Britannia gave the most accurate picture of the airline's profits and was more effective in matching costs with revenue than the 'capitalise and amortise' method favoured by the Revenue. Furthermore, the company's method was in accordance with ordinary principles of commercial accountancy. Accordingly, since there was nothing in statute or case law to contradict it, the company's appeal succeeded. This decision was upheld by the High Court.

Bear in mind that accountancy principles are being refined and updated constantly and FRS12 now sets out 'best practice' on provisions for sums payable after the year end. The Revenue will resist an accounting treatment that does not comply with FRS12. The Britannia Airways decision has since been overtaken by changes in generally accepted accountancy principles.

There are sometimes circumstances where a payment will almost certainly be required in the future, although the precise amount has yet to be ascertained. An example contained in a Revenue publication concerns an insurance broker who may be required to refund commission to an insurance company if clients allow policies to lapse. The Revenue has accepted that a provision may be allowable in these circumstances provided it is arrived at scientifically by reference to past experience. A 'rough and ready' general provision is not allowable.

During 1999 the Revenue decided not to appeal against a High Court decision on provisions for sums that would be payable only in the future. *Herbert Smith* v *Honour* [1999] STC 173 concerned a firm of solicitors that had taken long leases on office premises that turned out to be surplus to requirements. The offices could only be sublet at a much lower rent and the firm's accounts made a provision for the loss that would accrue in later years. The Revenue's decision not to appeal followed from its acceptance that the accounting treatment was in accordance with generally accepted accountancy principles.

These issues also arose in the so-called *Jenners* case. The Commissioners held that a company operating a department store could make provisions for repairs that would have to be carried out in later years. Again, the Revenue decided not to appeal.

15.1.10 Valuation of stock and work in progress

A trader's accounts should include his stock in hand at his year end. Individual items of stock should be valued at the lower of cost or net realisable value. Cost should normally include a proportion of overheads.

Similarly, work in progress should be valued at the year end on the same basis. Where the accounts relate to a profession, the traditional view has been that it is not necessary to include in the cost the time value of work put in by the sole proprietor or partner, since this represents the proprietor's profit rather than a cost incurred in carrying on the profession. However, see below on UITF 40.

The treatment of long-term work in progress can involve complex issues and should be discussed with the firm's accountant.

15.1.11 UITF 40

Where the accounts relate to a profession or other service provider, the traditional approach has been changed by the ASB's guidance note on revenue recognition (UITF Abstract 40 published in March 2005), which requires accountants to adopt a different method of revenue recognition for accounting periods ending on or after 22 June 2005. The traditional method was for work on unbilled services to be accounted for as work in progress (ie at the lower of cost or realisable value). UITF 40 generally requires that revenue be recognised as the services are provided and shown on the trader's balance sheet under the general heading of debtors. The difference between the two methods of accounting is that the UITF 40 method recognises profit earlier. A business's taxable profits will normally be based on its accounting profit (subject to specific adjustments) and so UITF 40 will often mean that a business has higher taxable profits.

Changing the method of accounting may give rise to a large one-off profit in the first accounting period after 22 June 2005. The Government recognised that taxing this in full might give rise to hardship and the FA 2006 contains provisions that allow the additional tax to be spread over three years (or over six years if the business is severely affected).

A business qualifies for spreading relief if:

- it prepares accounts for the period after 22 June 2005 on the new UITF 40 basis; and
- previous accounts had been prepared on the basis of UK GAAP but did not follow the revenue recognition rules set out in UITF 40.

The spreading relief works in the following way:

Step 1 – re-state the opening balance sheet on the new basis.

Step 2 – spread this amount according to the following table.

Year	Additional profit to be taxed
Tax year in which accounting period of change ends and 2nd tax year after change, and 3rd tax year after change	The lesser of: ● one third of the additional profit, or ● one sixth of the total profits for the tax year.
4th tax year after change, and 5th tax year after change	The lesser of: ● the outstanding amount of the additional profit ● one third of additional profit, or ● one sixth of the total profits for the tax year.
6th tax year after change	The outstanding amount of the additionals profit.

The spreading provisions apply to both unincorporated businesses and companies although it will be of most benefit to individuals trading through partnerships. Businesses can opt to ignore the spreading rules by making an election within a year of the tax return filing deadline for the tax year in which the first accounting period ending after 22 June 2005 ends. However, for partnerships, all partners must make the election jointly.

15.1.12 Withdrawal of 'cash basis' practice for professions

Until the late 1990s, relatively large businesses were able to prepare accounts purely on a cash receipts basis without taking into account income from unpaid invoices or the value of work in progress. The cash basis was widely used by barristers, solicitors, surveyors, actuaries, doctors and accountants, supported by a Revenue SP that allowed such businesses to use this method subject to conditions that profits were computed on the earnings basis for the first three fiscal years and thereafter could be accounted on a purely cash basis. The cash basis also applied to expenses.

This cash basis was abolished by the FA 1999. Businesses have had to use the earnings basis for accounting periods starting on or after 6 April 1999. Furthermore, there is a one-off catching-up charge based on the value of work in progress and debtors, net of creditors, at the start of the first accounting period affected.

The catching-up charge is payable over ten years of assessment which started with the 2000–01 year of account. The amount chargeable in each year except the last is restricted to the smaller of:

(1) one-tenth of the total charge; and
(2) 10% of the 'normal' profit.

In the tenth year, the balance of the catching-up charge will be taxed.

Example – Catching-up charge

> *K* has prepared accounts on a cash basis for many years using a 31 October year end. He will have a catching-up charge based on the value of his work in progress and debtors less creditors as at 1 November 1999. Ten instalments are taxable for the years 2000–01 to 2009–10.

The relevant adjustment should be entered in box 69 of the full self-assessment form.

15.1.13 Other consequences of the catching-up charge

There are some relieving provisions:

(1) As the catching-up charge is taxed as 'miscellaneous income' (previously Schedule D Case VI), it is not income for Class 4 NICs.
(2) There is no charge in a loss-making year, unless this is the final year of the business.
(3) Losses arising from the same business can be set against the charge.

15.1.14 Cessation of trade

Where a business ceases, the ten-year spread of the charge will continue; there will be no 10% profits cap because there are no longer any profits.

15.1.15 Barristers and advocates

Barristers (in Scotland, advocates) have always been regarded as a 'special case' (see 36.2).

15.1.16 Use of 'true and fair view' approach

The 'true and fair view' approach to computing taxable profits and losses is intended merely to ensure that profits are calculated in accordance with appropriate accounting standards and that time is not wasted on immaterial amounts. The Revenue confirmed that sole traders and partnerships do not need to have an audit even though their taxable profits must now be based on accounts that would comply with the true and fair view recognised for audited accounts.

Guidance on the application of accounting principles for traders who were formerly on the cash basis is contained in *Tax Bulletin* December 1998. See also the ICAEW technical release Tax 30/98.

15.1.17 Miscellaneous matters

Own consumption

Any manufactured items or stock that is taken out of the business for your own use, or for members of your family and friends, should be treated as sales at market value. The same also applies where you have provided business services to family and/or friends. See box of the short form and box 58 of the full self-employment form.

This rule was previously based on *Sharkey* v *Werhner* 936 TC 275, but was put on a statutory rule basis by FA 2008, with effect from 12 March 2008.

Payments under the Business Start-up Scheme
(IT(T&OI)A 2005, s 207)

Where a trader has received a payment under the Business Start-up Scheme it should be included in his computation of trading profits, in box 27 of the short form or box 73 of the full self-employment form.

Class 4 NICs

No deduction is due for the trader's liability for Class 4 NIC (see 22.4) in arriving at the trader's taxable profits.

Gifts in kind to charities
(IT(T&OI)A 2005, ss 70 and 108)

Relief can be claimed by traders who donate computers or other equipment to charities. Relief is also due for the employer costs of staff seconded to educational establishments.

15.2 CAPITAL ALLOWANCES

15.2.1 Introduction

A trader is entitled to capital allowances on plant and machinery used in the trade. Capital allowances are also available on commercial buildings located in an enterprise zone, agricultural buildings, industrial buildings and hotels.

Allowances may also be claimed for expenditure on know-how and scientific research expenditure. All these are dealt with differently, and various rates of initial and annual allowances are given.

Capital allowances are treated like any other business expense. The allowances are computed on the current year basis, but once again with special rules for the first tax year. Allowances are due only if claimed within 12 months of the filing date for the relevant SA return.

Successive Finance Acts have overlaid one another during the last 50 years and this makes it difficult to see the wood for the trees. The key issues are addressed later (15.2.2–15.2.23).

15.2.2 What is plant and machinery?

Despite the introduction of specific legislation in 1994, the definition of 'plant and machinery' is unclear. The statutory definition focuses mainly on what is *not* plant as it forms part of a building, and the Revenue's practice and interpretation are still based largely on decisions handed down by the courts. The earliest judicial definition was provided in *Yarmouth* v *France* (1887) 19 QBD 647, in which Lindley LJ stated:

> in its ordinary sense, it includes whatever apparatus is used by a businessman for carrying on his business – not his stock-in-trade, which he buys or makes for sale, but all goods and chattels, fixed or movable, live or dead, which he keeps for permanent employment in his business ...

Some items are clearly within this definition (eg typewriters, dictating machines, telephone equipment, computers, manufacturing equipment, vans and other motor vehicles). What is less obvious is that a building may contain items that are plant and machinery. In some cases the plant will have become part of the building (eg a lift). Also, there may be structures that are items of plant (eg a dry dock or a grain silo, or a mezzanine floor put into a factory to create storage space). Capital allowances are also due on building work needed to enable plant and machinery to be installed (eg if a floor had to be strengthened to install a computer).

You should take professional advice if you acquire a building or adapt premises to meet the requirements of your trade to ensure that you obtain the Inspector of Taxes' agreement on the full amount eligible for capital allowances.

15.2.3 Allowances for plant and machinery
(CAA 2001, ss 11–15)

Formerly, plant and machinery qualified for a 25% writing-down allowance, but the rate has been reduced to 20% from 2008–09. The allowance is based on the balance of the 'pool' at the year end. The pool's opening balance represents the cost of plant brought forward from previous years, less capital allowances already received. A trader receives writing-down allowances based on the opening balance plus the cost of additional plant acquired during the year, less any disposal proceeds.

From 2008–09, there is a 100% Annual Investment Allowance (AIA) for the first £50,000 expenditure on plant and machinery, which replaces the 40% and 50% first year allowances discussed at 15.2.9 and 15.2.10 below.

Example – Writing-down allowances

S and T are in partnership. In their year to 31 March 2007 they had acquired plant and machinery at a cost of £30,000 and received capital allowances of £7,500. During their year ended 31 March 2008, they sell some of this plant for £2,000 and buy new plant for £20,000 (assume that this did not qualify for the 50% FYA covered at 15.2.8 below). In 2008–09, the partnership buys plant and machinery for £70,000. S and T's pool would be as follows:

	£
Written-down value brought forward at 1 April 2007	22,500
Additions during year ended 31 March 2008	20,000
	42,500
Less: disposal proceeds	(2,000)
	40,500
Writing-down allowances for 2007–08 (25%)	(10,125)
Written-down value carried forward	30,375
Additions during year ended 31 March 2009 less AIA	20,000
	50,375
Writing down allowances for 2008–09 (20%)	10,075
Written-down value carried forward	40,300

The pool is written off if it goes down to £1,000 or less.

15.2.4 Reduced rate of WDA for integral plant

The 20% writing-down allowance is reduced to 10% for expenditure after 5 April 2008 on plant consisting of fixtures that are integral to a building (unless the fixtures qualify as energy-saving or water-saving equipment, see 15.2.11 and 15.2.12 below). However, the 100% AIA for the first £50,000 expenditure on plant (see 15.2.3 above) may be allocated against integral plant.

Integral plant includes:

- electrical systems (including lighting systems);
- cold water systems;
- space or water heating systems, powered systems of ventilation, air cooling or air purification and any floor or ceiling comprised in such systems;
- lifts, escalators and moving walkways;
- external solar shading;
- thermal insulation in an industrial building;
- active facades.

Post 5 April 2008 expenditure on integral plant that does not attract the Annual Investment Allowance is kept in a separate pool.

15.2.5 Expenditure treated as incurred in a period
(CAA 2001, s 67)

Expenditure is deemed to be incurred in a period if a trader enters into an unconditional contract; it is not necessary that the trader should actually have paid for it or brought it into use by his year end. There is an exception for plant and machinery acquired under an HP contract where entitlement to allowances arises only when the plant is actually brought into use.

15.2.6 Assets brought into use part way through year
(CAA 2001, ss 55 and 67)

An asset acquired towards the end of a trader's accounting period still attracts full writing down allowances at the appropriate rate, unless the trade has not been going for 12 months. In such a case, the allowance may be scaled down.

> U commenced trading on 5 October 2006. On 5 April 2007 he acquired plant and machinery for £60,000. The capital allowances due to him for 2006–07 are:
>
> $\frac{6}{12} \times 25\% \times £60,000$, ie   <u>£7,500</u>

15.2.7 Assets kept separate from the pool
(CAA 2001, s 74)

Cars that cost £12,000+ need to be kept separate. The maximum writing-down allowance for such a car is £3,000, but a balancing allowance (or charge) arises on disposal.

Example – Writing-down allowances for cars

> V operates an advertising business. She makes up her accounts to 30 April. On 1 May 2008 she bought a car that cost £30,000 and this was used by an employee. After two years, the car was sold for £10,000.
>
> The car is deemed to be in a separate pool and the position is as follows:
>
> | | | £ |
> |---------|---------------------------------------|--------|
> | Year 1: | Cost | 30,000 |
> | | Writing-down allowances for 2008–09 | 3,000 |
> | | | 27,000 |
> | Year 2: | Writing-down allowances for 2009–10 | 3,000 |
> | | | 24,000 |
> | Year 3: | Disposal proceeds | 10,000 |
> | | Balancing allowance for 2010–11 | 14,000 |

Other assets kept separate
(CAA 2001, s 206)

Certain other assets are kept separate from the pool. One particular category is assets used partly for the purposes of the trade and partly for other purposes. For example, a van used by a sole trader for 40% business and 60% private motoring is deemed to form a separate pool. The trader is entitled to 'scaled down' allowances, ie he would receive 40% of the full writing-down allowance and 40% of any balancing allowance.

'Short-life' assets (see below) are also pooled separately.

'Long-life' assets (15.2.15), integral plant (15.2.4) and expenditure on thermal insulation are to be kept separate in a new 'special rate pool' from 6 April 2009, where the rate of writing down allowances will be 10%.

15.2.8 'Short-life' assets
(CAA 2001, ss 83–84)

Where expenditure is added to the pool, the trader receives writing-down allowances that are likely to get smaller and smaller. For example, a trader invests expenditure of £100,000 on plant in Year 1. He does not acquire any other plant and machinery for five years. His writing-down allowance in Year 1 will be £25,000 (ie 25% of £100,000); £18,750 in Year 2 (ie 25% of the residual £75,000); and so on. By the end of Year 5, the written-down value will be just under £24,000, but the equipment itself may be worn out and have a scrap value of only £2,000. To cover this type of situation, the legislation allows for a trader to designate certain assets as short-life assets. The cost of these assets is kept in a separate pool and a balancing allowance (or charge) arises on a sale within five years, or on the assets being scrapped by then. If an asset is not sold within that period, the asset's written-down value is transferred to the general pool.

(1) In the above example, if the plant were actually scrapped at the start of Year 5 and the trader received no scrap value at all, he would receive a balancing allowance of £31,640.
(2) Again using the same basic facts, if the plant and machinery were still in use at the end of Year 5, the written-down value of £23,730 would be transferred to the trader's pool of other plant.

The following cannot be short-life assets:

(1) Cars.
(2) Assets used partly for non-trade purposes.
(3) Assets originally acquired for non-trade purposes (eg assets acquired prior to the trade being commenced).
(4) Ships.
(5) Certain assets leased out in the course of a trade.

An election needs to be made for an asset to be treated as a short-life asset. This needs to be submitted to the Inspector of Taxes within two years of the accounting period in which the asset is acquired. The Inspector will require sufficient information to be able to identify the assets at a later stage (see SP1/86).

15.2.9 50% first-year allowances for small businesses in 2007–08

A 50% first-year allowance (FYA) was available for expenditure by small businesses during the year 2007–08 (year ending 31 March 2008 for companies).

A 'small enterprise' is one where two of the following three criteria are fulfilled:

(1) turnover does not exceed £5.6 million;
(2) assets do not exceed £2.8 million;
(3) there are not more than 50 employees.

The test in relation to assets is 'gross assets' rather than net assets after deducting liabilities.

15.2.10 First-year allowances for medium-sized entities
(CAA 2001, ss 47–49)

A 40% first year allowance was available to unincorporated businesses for expenditure during the two years ended 5 April 2008 provided they qualified as MEs (medium-sized businesses). A company that is an ME can secure the first-year allowance for qualifying expenditure during the two years ended 31 March 2008.

Normal rates of writing-down allowance apply for the second and subsequent years.

A business is regarded as 'medium-sized' if it meets the following conditions:

(1) turnover of not more than £22.8m:

(2) assets of not more than £11.4m; and

(3) not more than 250 employees.

Provided two of the above three conditions are satisfied for the current or previous year, the business is regarded as an ME.

Whilst these definitions are derived from legislation that refers to companies, first-year allowances apply to businesses carried on by individuals provided the business would qualify if it were carried on by a company.

There are two types of assets that do not qualify for first-year allowances:

(1) expenditure on plant and machinery for leasing, cars, sea-going ships and railway assets;

(2) expenditure on long-life assets (LLAs – plant with an expected useful life of at least 25 years). In practice, the £100,000 pa limit (see 15.2.15) means that this exclusion is academic for the majority of MEs.

15.2.11 100% allowance for energy-saving and environmentally friendly equipment
(CAA 2001, ss 45A–45E)

Expenditure after 31 March 2001 on designated energy-saving technologies and products qualifies for 100% first-year allowances. The qualifying items are set out in a list issued by the DETR: see www.eca.gov.uk. (CAA 2001, ss 45A–45C)

100% FYA is also available for the purchase of a new car with low CO_2 emissions of not more than 110g/km (up to 120g/km before 31 March 2008 and for expenditure on equipment for refuelling vehicles with natural gas or hydrogen fuel.

15.2.12 Expenditure on water technologies

Since 1 April 2003, businesses have been able to claim 100% first-year allowances for expenditure on designated plant and machinery to reduce water use and improve water quality. The designated technology classes are:

- meters and monitoring equipment;
- flow controllers;
- leakage detection;
- efficient toilets;
- efficient taps.

Qualifying technologies and products can be found at www.eca.gov.uk.

15.2.13 100% capital allowances for refurbishing flats over shops
(CAA 2001, ss 393A–393W)

Qualifying expenditure on flats over shops has attracted 100% allowances since 11 May 2001. There are various conditions:

(1) the expenditure must be incurred on the renovation or conversion of vacant or underused space above shops and other commercial premises;

(2) the property must have been built before 1980, have no more than five floors and all upper floors must have originally been constructed primarily for residential use;

(3) the upper floors must have been either unoccupied or used only for storage for at least one year before the conversion work was put in hand;

(4) the properties must be in traditional shopping areas and the whole or greater part of the ground floor must be 'authorised for business use', ie designated as such for business rates imposed by the local authority;

(5) the conversion must not be part of any scheme to extend the building;

(6) there must not be more than four rooms in each flat;

(7) each flat must have separate external access (ie not through the shop); and

(8) the flats must not have a notional weekly rent exceeding the following limits:

Number of rooms	Flats in Greater London	Elsewhere
1–2	£350	£150
3	£425	£225
4	£480	£300

No balancing charge will arise if the flats are retained for seven years and are either let or made available for letting throughout that period.

15.2.14 100% first year allowances for refurbishing business premises in disadvantaged areas

Legislation was enacted in 2005 to give relief for the costs of renovating business property that has been empty for a year in designated 'disadvantaged areas'. This required European approval for 'state aid' to the industries affected. Approval was eventually obtained and the relief applies to expenditure incurred on or after 11 April 2007.

The capital costs of such renovations attract a 100% first year allowance. The FYA is subject to a clawback on a disposal within seven years.

The allowance (also referred to as Business Premises Renovation Allowance) is not available for premises used for

- farming;
- fisheries;
- aquaculture;

- manufacture of substitute milk products or synthetic fibres;
- shipbuilding;
- steel or coal industries.

It cannot be claimed for renovation expenditure on a residential property.

It cannot be claimed for the costs of acquiring land, extending business premises or developing land next to the business premises.

15.2.15 Long-life assets (LLAs)
(CAA 2001, ss 90–104)

FA 1997 introduced the concept of long-life assets. An LLA has an expected working life of 25+ years. Where a trader incurs expenditure of more than £100,000 on an LLA, capital allowances are restricted to 6%.

This rule affects assets purchased on or after 26 November 1996, but not those purchased before 1 January 2001 where the contract was entered into before 26 November 1996. A number of categories of expenditure are specifically excluded from the general definition. Thus LLAs do not include any machinery or plant that is a fixture in, or is used in, a dwelling-house, retail shop, showroom, hotel or office or for ancillary purposes. Also there are specific exclusions for motor or hire cars.

Expenditure on LLAs is segregated into a separate pool that qualifies for writing-down allowances at 6% instead of 25%. This categorisation of an asset as long life is irrevocable and it cannot later be reclassified as non-long life. The LLA rules do not apply where second-hand plant is purchased from a person who qualified for 25% writing-down allowances. The rate of writing-down allowance will be increased to 10% from 2008–09.

15.2.16 Hybrid rate

For businesses whose chargeable period spans 6 April 2008, a hybrid rate will be given for unrelieved expenditure in any pool, including single asset pools. There will be two hybrid rates; one for any expenditure qualifying for the old 25% WDA (now 20%) and the other for any expenditure qualifying for the old 6% WDA (now 10%). The rate to use will be a hybrid of the old and new rates, apportioned pro rata to time.

15.2.17 Expenditure on landlord's fixtures
(CAA 2001, s 172)

Tenants are often required to install plant within a building such as lifts, air conditioning, etc. Where such items become part of a building they constitute landlord's fixtures. This means that the items of plant do not 'belong' to the tenant and as such would not qualify for capital allowances under the normal rules. The legislation deals with this potential anomaly by specifically providing that a tenant who incurs expenditure on such plant can receive allowances, but is subject to a balancing charge on the expiry or surrender of his lease, according to the plant's market value at that time. There are complex provisions dealing with situations where more than one person incurs expenditure on the same fixture or where expenditure is incurred by an equipment lessor.

The rate of writing-down allowance on 'integral building plant' was reduced to 10% for expenditure after 5 April 2008 (31 March 2008 in the case of companies).

15.2.18 Acquisition of second-hand buildings
(CAA 2001, ss 172–204)

There are anti-avoidance provisions that:

(1) prevent allowances being given on fixtures as plant and machinery and under some other category (eg enterprise zones or scientific research);
(2) limit allowances given on fixtures as plant in total to the fixtures' original cost (or, where capital allowances were claimed on the fixtures for periods before 24 July 1996, the cost price to the most recent claimant). This applies only where the disposal by the previous claimant took place on or after 24 July 1996;
(3) treat a fixture as sold at its tax written-down value if it is sold for less than that value to accelerate allowances (other than where the disposal is for good commercial reasons and is not part of a tax avoidance scheme).

15.2.19 Buildings located in an enterprise zone
(CAA 2001, ss 298–299)

Qualifying expenditure on a commercial building located in an enterprise zone can qualify for a 100% initial allowance. A 'commercial building' is defined as a building or structure, other than an industrial building or hotel, used for the purposes of a trade, profession or vocation or as an office. The definition specifically excludes a building wholly or partly used as a dwellinghouse. Certain conditions must be fulfilled, in that the building must:

(1) have been constructed under an unconditional contract entered into before the enterprise zone came to the end of its designated life; and
(2) be acquired unused or within two years of its having been let for the first time.

The part of the purchase price relating to the cost of the land does not qualify for capital allowances. Plant and machinery that have become an integral part of the building may also qualify for the 100% allowance. The initial allowance can be disclaimed, in whole or in part, and the remaining amount of qualifying expenditure is then available at 25%. The 25% writing-down allowances are given on a straight-line basis over four years rather than on the reducing basis that applies for plant.

Example – Capital allowances on buildings in an enterprise zone

An enterprise zone building is acquired for £200,000. The land cost is £20,000, so £180,000 qualifies for capital allowances. The purchaser disclaims the whole of the initial allowance. He receives annual allowances as follows:

Year of expenditure	£
Year 1	45,000
Year 2	45,000
Year 3	45,000
Year 4	45,000

If the purchaser had disclaimed only £80,000, the position would have been:

Year of expenditure	£
Initial allowance	100,000
Annual allowance	45,000
	145,000
Year 2 annual allowance	35,000
Year 3 annual allowance	Nil
Year 4 annual allowance	Nil
Year 4 annual allowance	Nil

The point to note is that the annual allowances are based on the total qualifying costs, not on the balance left over after deducting the initial allowance.

Enterprise zone allowances will be withdrawn from April 2011, but without the phasing out rules applying to industrial and agricultural building allowances.

Sale of a relevant interest

Readers should take advice on a sale of an enterprise zone property because such a sale may give rise to a balancing charge notwithstanding the general abolition of such charges from 21 March 2007.

15.2.20 Agricultural buildings allowances (ABAs)
(CAA 2001, ss 361 and 372)

The term 'agricultural buildings allowances' is misleading because the expenditure does not need to be on a building. The allowances are given in respect of expenditure on farmhouses, farm or forestry buildings, cottages, fences, ditches, and drainage and sewerage works. The land must be used for agricultural purposes.

Rate of annual allowances

Expenditure on agricultural buildings qualifies for a 4% annual allowance given on a straight-line basis.

ABAs to be phased out

The annual allowance for 2008–09 will be 3%; for 2009-10 2%; for 2010-11 1%; and nil for subsequent years.

Balancing charges and allowances

A balancing allowance or charge could arise on a disposal that took place before 21 March 2007 within 25 years of the expenditure having been incurred (but it was possible to make an election so that the asset passed across at tax written-down value). No charge or allowance arises on a disposal on or after 21 March 2007 unless the contract was entered into before that date.

15.2.21 Industrial building allowances (IBAs)
(CAA 2001, s 271)

An 'industrial building' is a building or structure used for the purpose of a trade consisting of:

(1) manufacturing or processing goods or materials; or
(2) maintaining or repairing goods or materials for customers; or
(3) maintaining or repairing goods or materials owned by the trader himself provided the relevant trade consists of manufacturing or processing goods or materials; or
(4) storage of:
   (a) raw materials for manufacture;
   (b) goods to be processed;
   (c) goods manufactured or processed, but not yet delivered to any purchaser;
   (d) goods on arrival by sea or air into the UK; or
(5) working mines, oil wells, etc or foreign plantations.

In addition, a sports pavilion provided for the welfare of workers employed in any trade qualifies for industrial buildings allowances. Qualifying expenditure again excludes the land element in the purchase price.

Rate of allowances

Expenditure on an industrial building brought into use for a trade by the year end qualifies for a 4% annual allowance, given on the straight-line basis.

IBAs being phased out

The annual allowance for 2008–09 will be 3%; for 2009–10 will be 2%; for 2010–11 will be 1%; and nil for subsequent years.

Balancing charges and allowances

A balancing charge or allowance could arise on a disposal before 21 March 2007 within 25 years of the date that the expenditure was incurred. No such charge arises on a disposal on or after 21 March 2007 unless the contract was entered into before that date.

15.2.22 Hotels
(CAA 2001, s 279)

A qualifying hotel attracts allowances that are calculated in the same way as industrial buildings allowances (see 15.2.21).

A qualifying hotel is one that meets the following conditions:

(1) Accommodation must be provided in a building of a permanent nature.
(2) The hotel must be open for at least four months during April to October.
(3) There must be at least ten bedrooms available for letting to the public in general that must not normally be in the same occupation for more than a month.
(4) The services provided must normally include the provision of breakfast and evening meals, making beds and cleaning rooms.

Once again, the allowances are being phased out and balancing charges or allowances do not arise on disposals on or after 21 March 2007.

15.2.23 Expenditure on know-how
(CAA 2001, s 452)

Expenditure on acquiring know-how for use in a trade attracts capital allowances. 'Know-how' means any industrial information and techniques of assistance in manufacturing or processing goods or materials, or working or searching for mineral deposits, or that may be relevant to agricultural, forestry or fishing operations. Allowances are given on 'qualifying expenditure', which is the aggregate of any capital expenditure on know-how during the basis period, together with any unused balance of expenditure brought forward from the previous basis period and less any disposal value for know-how that has been sold.

Writing-down allowances are given at the rate of 25%.

15.2.24 Expenditure on scientific research
(CAA 2001, s 437)

Any capital expenditure incurred by a trader on scientific research related to a trade attracts a 100% allowance. 'Scientific research' was traditionally defined as activities in the fields of natural or applied science for the extension of knowledge. It has been redefined in FA 2000 to make it clear that it includes scientific research:

(1) that may lead to or facilitate an extension of trade; or
(2) of a medical nature that has a special relation to the welfare of workers employed in particular industries.

15.3 PRE-TRADING EXPENDITURE
(IT(T&OI)A 2005, s 57)

A person may incur expenditure before starting to trade such as:

- rent for business premises;
- rates, insurance, heating and lighting;
- advertising wages or other payments to employees;
- bank charges and interest;
- lease rentals on plant and machinery and office equipment;
- accountancy fees.

Expenditure qualifies for relief only if it is incurred within seven years of the date trade is commenced. The expense is treated as an ordinary trading expense incurred on the day the trader starts business.

Pre-trading capital expenditure that qualifies for capital allowances is also treated as having been incurred at the date trade is commenced.

15.4 POST-CESSATION RECEIPTS
(IT(T&OI)A 2005, ss 242–243)

Where a person has been assessed on the cash basis (see 15.1.11), special rules apply if the trade or profession is discontinued. Subsequent receipts are normally taxed as income for the year in which they come in, although an election may be made for the post-cessation receipts to be treated as arising in the year of discontinuance.

Expenses may be deducted in so far as they were incurred wholly and exclusively for business and are not otherwise allowable. For example, a solicitor who had post-cessation receipts could deduct premiums paid on a professional indemnity policy where the cover related to the period after the solicitor had ceased to carry on his profession.

A similar charge may arise where a change occurs in the treatment of a trader's profits so that the cash basis ceases to apply and his profits are assessed on the earnings basis. Amounts received from customers that relate to invoices issued when the business was dealt with on the cash basis are treated as post-cessation receipts.

15.5 POST-CESSATION EXPENSES
(IT(T&OI)A 2005, s 250)

Expenditure may qualify for tax relief if it is incurred within seven years of a business ceasing. The following types of expenditure may qualify for this relief:

(1) the costs of remedying defective work done, goods supplied, or services rendered while the trade or profession was continuing and damages paid by the taxpayer in respect of such defective work, goods or services whether awarded by a court or agreed during negotiations on a claim;

(2) insurance premiums paid to insure against the above costs;

(3) legal and other professional expenses incurred in connection with the above costs;

(4) debts owed to the business that have been taken into account in computing the profits or gains of the trade or profession before discontinuance but that have subsequently become bad;

(5) the costs of collecting debts that have been taken into account in computing the profits of the trade before discontinuance.

The amount of the relief will be reduced by any expense allowed as a deduction in the final accounting period that remains unpaid at the end of the year of assessment in which the new relief is given.

Expenditure that qualifies for the relief will be set against income and capital gains of the year of assessment in which the expense is paid. Where there is insufficient income or capital gains to cover the expenditure, the unrelieved expenditure of that year cannot be carried forward under the relief arrangements against future income or capital gains. However, the unrelieved expenditure will still be available to be carried forward under the existing rules and set against subsequent post-cessation receipts from the trade or profession.

Tax notes

The legislation requires a formal claim to be made within 22 months of the end of the year of assessment in which the expense is paid.

16

CAPITAL GAINS TAX AND BUSINESS TRANSACTIONS

This chapter focuses on the CGT aspects of various business transactions. It deals with the following matters:

(1) Loans to private businesses.
(2) Losses on unquoted shares.
(3) Relief for replacement of business assets.
(4) Hold-over relief for gifts of business property.
(5) Partnerships and capital gains.
(6) Transfer of a business to a company.
(7) Business taper relief.
(8) Entrepreneurs relief.
(9) Earn-outs.
(10) Sale of shares to all-employee share trusts.

16.1 LOANS TO PRIVATE BUSINESSES

A common type of transaction is a loan to a sole trader or partnership (an 'unincorporated business') or to a private company. Almost as common are situations where a person gives a guarantee to a bank, etc that makes a loan to a business. This section deals with the CGT position if a loan becomes written off or a person is required to make a payment under a bank guarantee that he has given.

16.1.1 Loans to unincorporated businesses
(TCGA 1992, s 253)

A CGT loss may be deemed to arise if the Revenue is satisfied that a loan has become irrecoverable. There are various conditions that need to be fulfilled, ie the borrower must:

(1) not be the lender's spouse or civil partner;
(2) be resident in the UK;
(3) have used the loan wholly for the purposes of a trade carried on by him. The trade must not have consisted of (or included) money-lending.

When a claim is submitted, the Inspector must satisfy himself that any outstanding amount of the loan is irrecoverable and that the lender has not assigned or waived his right to recover the loan.

A claim must be made within one year and ten months of the end of the tax year in which the loan becomes irrecoverable (s 253(3A)).

The allowable loss is restricted to the amount of the loan that is irrecoverable, ie there was no indexation relief in these circumstances.

Tax notes

A claim for a loss on a loan must be made within one year and ten months of the end of the tax year in which the loan becomes irrecoverable.

16.1.2 Loans to companies
(TCGA 1992, ss 253 and 254)

Similar provisions apply where a person has made a loan to a company that proves to be irrecoverable. The principal conditions that need to be satisfied are:

(1) the company must be UK-resident;
(2) it must be a trading company;
(3) the lender must not be a company that is a member of the same group of companies.

In all other respects, relief normally applies exactly as described in 16.1.1.

Loan notes and debentures

There is an additional complication that may apply to a loss on a loan that constitutes a 'debt on a security', which is a special type of loan. In broad terms, the loan is usually evidenced by a debenture deed and is transferable. A typical example is a loan stock.

If a loan falls into this category, it is necessary to ascertain whether it also falls into another subclass, ie a qualifying corporate bond (QCB, see 12.4.2(10)). No loss relief is available on a disposal of a QCB. However, losses on other debts on security continue to attract relief.

16.1.3 Payments under loan guarantees
(TCGA 1992, s 253(4))

Instead of lending money to a relative or friend or his private company, a person might have given a guarantee to a bank, etc. Similarly, a company director might have had to give personal guarantees in respect of bank loans to his company.

Where the borrower cannot repay the loan, the bank will call on the guarantor to pay the amount due. In these circumstances, the guarantor may be able to claim a CGT loss as if he had made a loan that was irrecoverable. The following conditions must be satisfied for relief to be claimed:

(1) payment has been made under a guarantee;
(2) the payment should arise from a formal calling in of the guarantee – a voluntary payment attracts no relief;
(3) the original loan met the requirements listed in 16.1.1;
(4) the amount paid under the guarantee cannot be recovered either from the borrower or from a co-guarantor.

16.2 LOSSES ON UNQUOTED SHARES
(TA 1988, s 574)

From time to time, an individual may invest in a private company, either as a working director/shareholder or perhaps as a 'passive' investor with a minority shareholding. Investments may also be made in companies that, while they are technically public companies as defined by the Companies Act, are not quoted companies.

16.2.1 Special relief for subscribers

A loss may arise on a disposal of shares in such a company. If the investor acquired existing shares by purchasing them, the loss is a normal CGT loss and the only way it can be relieved is as set out in 12.1.3. However, if he acquired his shares by subscribing for new shares, it may be possible to obtain income tax relief for the loss. Subject to certain conditions, the capital loss may be offset against his income for the year in which the loss is realised.

The following conditions must be satisfied:

(1) The loss must arise from one of the following:
   (a) a sale made at arm's length for full consideration (this rules out a sale to a connected person); or
   (b) a disposal that takes place when the company is wound up; or
   (c) a deemed disposal where the shares have become of negligible value.
(2) There are conditions that attach to the company itself. In particular:
   (a) the company must not have been a quoted company at the date the individual subscribed for his shares or at any time during the period that starts with the individual's acquisition and ends with 6 March 2001. If any class of shares in the company are quoted this rules out relief under s 574 even though the loss might have arisen on another class of share that was not quoted;
   (b) the company must be a trading company, or the holding company of a trading group, at the date of disposal or it must have ceased to have been a trading company not more than three years prior to the date of disposal and it must not have been an investment company since that date;

(c) the company's trade must not have consisted wholly or mainly of dealing in shares, securities, land, trades or commodity futures (further restrictions apply in relation to shares issued after 6 April 1998 so that the company must have met the conditions necessary to qualify for EIS relief: see 24.5);

(d) the company's trade must have been carried out on a commercial basis.

16.2.2 Relief also available for subscriber's spouse

The spouse/civil partner of a person who subscribed for shares may also claim s 574 relief where he or she has acquired the shares in question through an *inter vivos* transfer from his or her spouse/civil partner. Shares acquired on a spouse's death do *not* entitle the widow(er) to s 574 relief on a subsequent disposal.

16.2.3 Nature of relief

The loss is calculated according to normal CGT principles. If the loss is eligible for s 574 relief, the individual may elect within two years for it to be set against his taxable income for either the year of the loss or the preceding year. Either claim may be made independently of the other. Where he has losses that are available for s 574 relief and he is also entitled to relief for trading losses, he can choose which losses should be relieved in priority to the others.

Any part of the capital loss that cannot be relieved under s 574 can be carried forward for offset against capital gains in the normal way.

16.2.4 Shares acquired by exercising a share option

If you acquired shares by exercising a share option, and you were taxed under the employment income legislation, your CGT acquisition cost may be much higher than you think (see 12.10.3). You may therefore have a CGT loss when you dispose of your shares. If the other conditions are satisfied, you can get income tax relief under s 574.

16.3 RELIEF FOR REPLACEMENT OF BUSINESS ASSETS
(TCGA 1992, ss 152–160)

'Roll-over' relief may be available where a person sells an asset used by him in a trade (or in certain circumstances, by his family company) and reinvests in replacement assets used for business purposes.

16.3.1 Nature of roll-over relief

A gain is said to be rolled over in that it is not charged to tax, but is deducted from the person's acquisition cost of the new assets. Note that the rolled-over gain is that which arises before taper relief.

Example – Roll-over relief

> L sells a farm for £450,000. His capital gain is £200,000. He starts up a new business and invests £500,000 in a warehouse. By claiming roll-over relief, he avoids having to pay tax on the gain of £200,000. The acquisition cost of his warehouse is reduced as follows:
>
> | | £ |
> |---|---|
> | Actual cost | 500,000 |
> | *Less*: rolled-over gain | (200,000) |
> | Deemed acquisition cost | 300,000 |
>
> The relief is really a form of deferment since a larger gain will arise on a subsequent disposal of the replacement asset.

16.3.2 Conditions that need to be satisfied

The asset disposed of must have been used in a business and must have fallen into one of the following categories:

(1) land and buildings;
(2) fixed plant and machinery;
(3) ships;
(4) goodwill (but not for companies that buy goodwill after 31 March 2002: see 17.6);
(5) milk and potato quotas;
(6) aircraft;
(7) hovercraft, satellites and spacecraft;
(8) Lloyd's syndicate rights ('capacity');
(9) ewe and suckler cow premium quotas and fish quota.

The replacement asset must also fall into one of these categories.

It is not possible to claim roll-over relief on the disposal of shares in a family company, nor is it possible to claim s 152 relief for expenditure on such shares on the basis that this is replacement expenditure.

The replacement asset must normally be acquired within a period starting one year before and ending three years after the date of the disposal of the original asset. The time limit can be extended (at the Revenue's discretion) if the acquisition of the replacement asset within three years was not possible because of circumstances outside the person's control.

Example – Full relief available only where all the sale proceeds are reinvested
(TCGA 1992, s 152(3)–(11))

> Using the same figures as in 16.3.1, L sells his farm for £450,000, making the same capital gain of £200,000. He starts up a business but invests only £400,000 in the new warehouse. The part of the £450,000 disposal consideration for the farm that is not applied in acquiring the warehouse is £50,000. This is less than the gain that arose on the disposal of the farm and the balance of the gain may be rolled over. The warehouse's acquisition value is reduced by £150,000.

16.3.3 Old assets not used for business throughout ownership

If the old asset was not used for business throughout the period of ownership, s 152 applies as if a part of the asset used for the purposes of the trade was a separate asset to that which had not been wholly used for those purposes.

Example – Old assets

In April 2007, *M* sells a warehouse for a gain, before taper relief has been calculated, of £50,000. It had originally been bought in April 1997 but had been used in his trade only since April 1999. The amount of gain that can be rolled over into the purchase of a new asset is calculated as follows:

$$\text{Chargeable gain } £50,000 \times \frac{\text{Period of trading use of old asset}}{\text{Period of ownership}}$$

This equals £50,000 × ⁸⁄₁₀, ie £40,000. The balance of £10,000 (£50,000 – £40,000) is a chargeable gain before taper relief.

16.3.4 Treatment where replacement assets are wasting assets
(TCGA 1992, s 154)

The roll-over relief is modified where the replacement expenditure consists of the purchase of a wasting asset (ie with an expected useful life of less than 50 years) or an asset that will become a wasting asset within ten years. Plant and machinery is always considered to have a useful life of less than 50 years. Furthermore, the acquisition of a lease with less than 60 years to run also constitutes the acquisition of a wasting asset. Paradoxically, the goodwill of a business is not regarded as a wasting asset.

The capital gain in these circumstances is not deferred indefinitely, but becomes chargeable on the first of the following occasions:

- the disposal of the replacement asset; or
- the asset ceasing to be used in the business; or
- the expiry of ten years.

Examples – Roll-over relief on wasting assets

(1) *N* sells a factory and reinvests in a 59-year lease of a warehouse that he uses in his business. In Year 6 the warehouse is let as an investment property. The rolled-over gain becomes chargeable in Year 6.

(2) *O* also rolls over into a 59-year lease. He is still using the property after ten years, but because it has become a wasting asset within that period, the rolled-over gain becomes chargeable in Year 10.

16.3.5 Reinvestment in non-wasting assets

If the person acquires new non-wasting replacement assets during the ten years, the capital gain that was originally rolled over into the purchase of the wasting assets can be transferred to the new replacement assets. Assume in example (1) above that *N* had bought the goodwill of a business in Year 5. He could transfer his roll-over relief claim to the new asset. No gain would then become chargeable in Year 6 when he lets the warehouse.

16.3.6 Furnished holiday lettings

A property acquired for letting as furnished holiday accommodation (see 7.5) may qualify for roll-over relief; gains from the disposal of such properties may be rolled over.

16.3.7 Assets used by partnership
(SP D11)

Roll-over relief can be secured where the replacement assets are used by a partnership in which the owner is a partner.

16.3.8 Assets used by family company
(TCGA 1992, s 157)

Relief can be obtained where an individual disposes of a property, etc used by his 'personal trading company', but only if the replacement asset is acquired by him and is used by the same company. A company is an individual's personal trading company if he personally owns at least 5% of the voting shares.

He need not be a director of the company – indeed, he need not even be employed by it. Also, roll-over relief is not lost because he has charged the company rent.

16.3.9 Assets owned by employee or office-holder

An employee or office-holder may claim roll-over relief where he disposes of an asset used in the employment. This condition may apply to, for example, a sub-postmaster who has an 'office' for tax purposes, but who generally owns the sub-post office premises. For further details, see SP 5/86.

There are circumstances where these provisions can mean that a director of a family company who has sold an asset used by one company and bought new assets used by another family company is entitled to roll-over relief: this is a difficult area where professional advice is essential.

16.4 HOLD-OVER RELIEF FOR GIFTS OF BUSINESS PROPERTY
(TCGA 1992, s 165)

16.4.1 Background and nature of hold-over relief

At one time, a UK-resident individual could transfer any asset to another UK-resident person on a no gain/no loss basis by claiming hold-over relief.

323

The relief was abolished in 1989 for gifts of most types of assets, although the same type of relief can still be claimed on gifts of business property to a UK-resident person.

16.4.2 Definition of 'business property'

Business property is defined for these purposes as:

- an asset used by the transferor in a trade, profession or vocation;
- an asset used by the transferor's family company in a trade;
- an asset used for a trade by a subsidiary of the transferor's family company;
- unquoted shares in a trading company, or holding company of a trading group, which does not to any substantial extent have investment activities;
- agricultural land that qualifies for the IHT agricultural property relief.

16.4.3 Situations where hold-over relief is not available

Hold-over relief cannot be claimed in respect of a gift of shares or securities to a UK company where the gift took place after 8 November 1999. The relief can, however, still be claimed on a gift to a company of an unincorporated business. With effect from 10 December 2003, hold-over relief is not available for transfers to settlor-interested trusts.

The rules concerning gifts of shares that qualify for hold-over relief changed with effect from 6 April 2003. Previously, a gift of shares in a trading company could qualify even if the company had investments which made up a substantial (ie 20% or more) part of its assets. The gain then had to be apportioned and the proportion found by applying the fraction

$$\frac{\text{Business chargeable assets}}{\text{Total chargeable assets}}$$

could be held-over. the position is now 'all or nothing'; if the company has substantial investment activities hold-over relief is not available at all.

16.4.4 Claiming the relief

You should obtain a copy of Helpsheet IR295, which incorporates an election that needs to be signed by the donor and donee (see opposite).

Claim for hold-over relief - Sections 165 and 260 TCGA 1992

	Transferor		Transferee
Name		Name	
Address		Address	
	Postcode		Postcode
Inland Revenue office		Inland Revenue office	
Tax reference		Tax reference	

Except in case of a gift in settlement, the claim must be made by both transferor and transferee. If the transferor or transferee has no Inland Revenue office or reference please explain why.

I/We hereby claim relief under Section 165/Section 260 TCGA 1992 in respect of the transfer of the asset specified below. The particulars given in this claim are correctly stated to the best of my/our information and belief.

Description of asset and date of disposal

√ one box

The gain held over is £ ___   A calculation is attached ☐

We apply for deferment of valuations and have completed the second page of the claim form. ☐

We qualify for relief because:

√ one box

- the asset is used for the business of ___   ☐
  Please insert name of person

- the asset consists of unlisted shares or securities of a trading company or holding company of a trading group ☐

- the asset is agricultural land ☐

- the asset consists of listed shares or securities of the transferor's personal company or, where trustees are the transferors, a company in which they had 25% of the voting rights ☐

- the disposal was a chargeable transfer, but not a Potentially Exempt Transfer, for Inheritance Tax purposes ☐

- Capital Taxes Office reference number ___

- the disposal was exempt from Inheritance Tax under IHTA Section ___   ☐
  Please insert Section number

Signed ___   Signed ___

Date / /   Date / /

16.4.5 Relief clawed back if donee emigrates

A gain that is held over under s 165 is brought into charge for the tax year in which the donee ceases to be resident if this happens within six years.

16.5 PARTNERSHIPS AND CAPITAL GAINS

How CGT affects partnership transactions can at times be complex. Partners should familiarise themselves with SP D12 and take regular professional advice. The following section describes some key aspects.

16.5.1 Partnership's acquisition value

Although individual partners' entitlement to profits may vary over the years, the partnership's acquisition value for the firm's chargeable assets is not affected unless there are cash payments from one partner to another to acquire a greater interest in the firm or unless assets are revalued as part of the arrangements for changes in profit-sharing.

16.5.2 Assets held by firm at 31 March 1982

For periods up to 5 April 2008, the partnership may make a universal rebasing election for the values at 31 March 1982 to be used instead of cost (see 12.9.2). This is quite separate from the individual partners' position in relation to their personal assets when a disposal of an asset takes place. There may be partners who were not in the partnership at 31 March 1982, but this does not affect the computation of the gain.

16.5.3 Partnership gains divisible among partners

Where a partnership asset is sold at a capital gain (or loss), the gain is divided among the partners in accordance with their profit-sharing ratios. Each partner is personally assessable on his share of the gain.

The partner's actual CGT liability depends on his own situation, ie whether he has other gains for the year, has available losses, or can claim roll-over relief.

16.5.4 Revaluations and retirement and introduction of partners

Problems may arise where a partnership has substantial assets that are chargeable assets for CGT purposes and worth more than their book value (ie the value at which they are shown in the firm's accounts). A revaluation to bring the assets' book value into line with their market value can produce a liability for individual partners if there is a reduction in their profit-sharing ratios. This commonly happens when existing partners retire or new partners are introduced.

Example – Retirement of partner

> *P* is a partner in a five-partner firm and is entitled to 20% of the profits. He retires and his colleagues then share profits on the basis of 25% each. As part of the arrangements for his retirement, the book value of the firm's office block is increased from £150,000 to its current value of £750,000. The surplus is credited to each partner's account so that *P* is credited with £120,000.
>
> *P* is treated as if he had realised a gain on the disposal of a one-fifth share of the building. This would be based on the £120,000. The remaining four partners are not treated as having made a disposal. Indeed, they each have made an acquisition of a 5% interest in the building for an outlay of £30,000.

Example – Introduction of partner

> *Q* and *R* are partners. Their premises are included in their firm's balance sheet at £200,000 (original cost), but are actually worth £500,000. *Q* and *R* agree to admit *S* as an equal partner in return for his paying new capital into the firm of £700,000. They revalue the premises before admitting *S* as a partner, and the surplus of £300,000 is credited to their accounts. In this case, *Q* and *R* are each regarded as having made a disposal of a one-sixth interest in the premises. This is because *S*'s new capital will go into the firm as a whole. After coming in, he effectively owns one-third of all the assets (and is responsible for one-third of the liabilities).
>
> The former partners' ownership of the premises has been reduced from 50% to a one-third interest.

16.5.5 Retirement and introduction of partners with no revaluation of assets

There is no such problem where partners leave or come in and there is no revaluation of assets. In such a case, the remaining or incoming partners normally take over the outgoing partners' acquisition values for the firm's asset.

Example – Change of partners with no revaluation of assets

> *T* and *U* are in partnership. They own premises that have a book value of £94,000 (equal to cost in 1980). *T* retires and is replaced by *V*. The premises are not revalued. Later the premises are sold for £244,000. *U* and *V* are assessed on their share of the gain.
>
> The gain is computed by reference to the original cost (£94,000) or the premises' market value at 31 March 1982, not their value at the time that *V* became a partner. This does not apply where the partners are connected persons (eg because they are relatives), or where cash payments are made to acquire an interest in the firm. In either of these categories you should seek specialist advice.

16.6 TRANSFER OF A BUSINESS TO A COMPANY
(TCGA 1992, s 162)

Where a person transfers a business to a company (ie he 'incorporates the business'), there is a disposal of the assets that are transferred to the company. Not all the assets necessarily become chargeable assets for CGT purposes, but a gain may arise on assets such as land, buildings and goodwill. Fortunately, there is a relief that may cover such situations.

16.6.1 Nature of relief

The main relief applies only where a business is transferred to a company in return for an issue of shares to the former proprietors of the business. Where the necessary conditions are satisfied so that s 162 relief is available, the gains that would otherwise arise on the transfer of chargeable assets are rolled-over into the cost of the shares issued.

Example – Transfer of a business to a company

> *W* transfers a business to B Ltd in return for shares worth £75,000. There are capital gains of £48,000 on the assets transferred to the company. If s 162 relief applies, *W* will not have any assessable capital gain, but her shares in B Ltd will be deemed to have an acquisition cost of £27,000 computed as follows:
>
> | | £ |
> |---|---|
> | Market value | 75,000 |
> | *Less*: rolled-over gain | (48,000) |
> | | 27,000 |

16.6.2 Conditions that must be satisfied

For s 162 relief to be available, all the business's assets other than cash must be transferred to the company. It is not acceptable to the Revenue for certain assets of the unincorporated business (eg trade debts) to be excluded, even though this might otherwise be advisable to save stamp duty.

Relief is available only in so far as shares are issued by the company instead of other forms of payment such as loan stock. The market value of the shares issued in return for the transfer of the business must be at least equal to the capital gains arising on the transfer of assets.

Tax notes

When transferring a business to a company, certain assets of the unincorporated business (eg trade debts) cannot be excluded, even though this might otherwise be advisable to save stamp duty.

Example – Limitations of s 162 relief

> *X* transfers a business with a net value of £400,000 to C Ltd, a new company specially formed for the purpose. Shares in C Ltd are issued to him, and these have a value of £400,000. However, closer examination reveals that the business's value is depressed by heavy bank borrowings. Furthermore, capital gains totalling £490,000 arise on chargeable assets transferred as part of the business.
>
> Section 162 relief would be limited to £400,000. The balance of £90,000 would be taxable in the normal way.

16.6.3 Conditions that are not required

(1) Relief is not confined to a transfer of a business to a company by a sole trader; the same relief is available where a partnership transfers its business to a company.

(2) The shares that are issued need not be ordinary shares.

(3) Relief does not seem to be confined to a business that is classified as a trade. It is arguable that the relevant business might, for example, consist of letting a group of properties.

(4) There is no requirement that the company should be incorporated or resident in the UK. It can be both of these things, but relief is not prejudiced just because a foreign company is involved.

16.6.4 Relief may be due on proportion of capital gains

Some relief will still be available if the business is transferred to the company in return for a mixture of shares and loan stock, or shares and cash. The formula to be used is:

$$\text{Chargeable gain} \times \frac{\text{Value of shares received}}{\text{Value of whole consideration received}}$$

16.6.5 Election to disapply this relief

It is possible to elect for s 162 relief not to apply. This might be appropriate where the shares are sold soon afterwards. The election must be made by 31 January following the filing date for the year in question, ie the election has to be made by 31 January 2007 for a business incorporated during 2004–05.

16.7 BUSINESS TAPER RELIEF

Taper relief does not apply to a disposal after 5 April 2008.

If an asset qualified as a business asset, the 75% taper relief could have meant that your rate of CGT on a sale in 2007–08 was 10% or less (see 12.11) rather than the full 40%. It is therefore absolutely crucial to establish whether assets qualified.

16.7.1 Basic definition of 'business assets'

A 'business asset' was defined as:

(1) Shares and securities held by the individual in a qualifying company.
(2) An asset used by a qualifying company for the purposes of its trade.
(3) An asset held for the purposes of a qualifying office or employment
(4) An asset used for the purposes of a trade carried on by the individual (whether alone or in partnership).

The areas where the legislation was most complicated relate to shares in qualifying companies and assets used by such companies, ie (1) and (2). The rules in (3)–(4) remained fairly constant during the period that taper relief applied and we deal with such assets at 16.7.10–16.7.13.

16.7.2 Definition of 'qualifying company' from 6 April 2000

Different rules applied according to whether the company is quoted.

All shares in unquoted trading companies qualified as business assets. AIM counted as unquoted. However, a company that was controlled by a quoted company was regarded as a quoted company for these purposes.

Furthermore, all shares in quoted trading companies were business assets if the individual was employed (full-time or part-time) by the company concerned.

If an individual was employed by a non-trading company and he did not have a material interest in that company (10% or more), his shares could also qualify as business assets.

Where an individual was not employed by a quoted trading company, his shares still qualified as business assets if he had at least 5% of the voting rights. This also covers trustees who held a 5% interest.

Shares in an unquoted company that exists in order to hold shares in a joint venture company could also qualify as business assets.

Table 16.2 can be used to determine whether a company was a qualifying company.

16.7.3 Definition in force up to 5 April 2000

A company was a qualifying company if it was a trading company, or a holding company of a trading group, and the individual met one of the following tests:

(1) he was a full-time officer or employee of that company and his shares gave him at least 5% of the voting rights; or
(2) where he did not meet the full-time condition, his shares gave him 25% of the voting rights in the company.

16.7.4 Shares held prior to 6 April 2000 sold after that date

Where shares did not qualify under the old rules, a capital gain may be time apportioned and business taper will apply only to the proportion of the capital gain that falls after 5 April 2000.

Table 16.2 – Defining a qualifying company up to 2007–08

Is the company a trading company or the holding company of a trading group?	Is the company listed?	Is the individual an officer or employee of the company or of a connected company?	6 April 1998 to 5 April 2000	From 6 April 2000 (per Finance Act 2000)	From 6 April 2000 (per Finance Act 2001)
Yes	Yes	Yes	Business asset – if the individual was a full-time working officer/ employee and held 5% of the voting rights	Business asset	Business asset
Yes	Yes	No	Business asset if the individual held 25% of the voting rights. Non-business asset otherwise	Business asset if the individual held 5% of the voting rights. Non-business asset otherwise	Business asset if the individual held 5% of the voting rights. Non-business asset otherwise
Yes	No	Yes	Business asset – if the individual was a full-time working officer/ employee and held 5% of the voting rights	Business asset	Business asset

Example - Applying business taper to a proportion

> *S* works for X plc and on 5 October 2007 he realises a gain of £95,000 on sell-
> ing X plc shares. These shares had been held since 1997 and did not qualify as
> business assets until 6 April 2000 as S did not meet the 5% requirement.
>
> The gain is time-apportioned and the proportion found by the following for-
> mula attracts business taper relief:
>
> $$\frac{6\ \text{April 2000} - 5\ \text{October 2004}}{6\ \text{April 1998} - 5\ \text{October 2004}} \times \text{gain of £95,000}$$
>
> *S* therefore gets 75% taper on £75,000.
>
> The remainder of the gain (ie £20,000) attracts 40% non-business taper relief
> based on ten qualifying years of ownership because of the bonus year.

16.7.5 Definition of 'trading company'

A company had to exist to carry on a trade and could not exist to any substantial extent for any other purpose, for example, holding investments. In
practice, the Revenue accepted that a trading company could invest surplus
cash while it looked for suitable opportunities to invest the money in its
trade. Where longer-term investments were held, the Revenue is likely to
regard them as substantial if they exceeded 20% of the company's net
worth. Some guidance is given in *Tax Bulletin* June 2001. This is an area
where specialist advice may be required.

16.7.6 Apportionment of gain

Where shares in a company did not qualify as business assets for the whole
period of ownership since 6 April 1998 (eg because the company infringed
the 20% test described in 16.7.5), the gain needs to be time-apportioned and
business taper relief is due for the proportion relating to the period when the
shares qualified.

16.7.7 Companies that held investments in a joint venture company

The rules changed on several occasions. Originally shares in such a company did not qualify as a business asset. From 6 April 2000, a company
could be regarded as a trading company if:

(1) it existed in order to hold shares in a joint venture company;
(2) at least 75% of the shares in the joint venture company were owned by
    five or fewer companies; and
(3) the company owned at least 30% of the joint venture company's shares.

Since 17 April 2002, the requirements have been that:

(1) the company existed to hold shares in the joint venture company;
(2) at least 75% of the shares in the joint venture company are owned by five or fewer persons (not necessarily companies); and
(3) the company owns at least 10% of the joint venture company's shares.

The changes made from 6 April 2000 and 17 April 2002 did not apply retrospectively.

16.7.8 Shares or securities may include loan notes and debentures

Where an individual held loan notes issued by a company, they could attract taper relief provided they were securities and were not qualifying corporate bonds (see 16.1.2). Furthermore, if the company was an unquoted trading company or was a quoted trading company that employed the individual, the loan notes could in certain circumstances attract taper relief at the business rate.

Bear in mind that a company that is a subsidiary of a quoted company was regarded as being a quoted company for taper relief, so the business taper relief was normally be available only if the company that had issued the loan notes was neither a quoted company nor a subsidiary of a quoted company, or if the individual was employed by the group. It is, however, possible that certain loan notes issued by subsidiaries of quoted companies might have qualified as business assets up to 17 April 2002.

FA 2002 changed the legislation retrospectively so that debentures and loan notes that are issued on company takeovers could be regarded as securities for taper relief purposes even though they might not have met the criteria for being regarded as securities for other CGT purposes. This retrospective change was beneficial as such debentures would otherwise not have attracted taper relief.

Tax notes

Debentures and loan notes are issued on company takeovers may qualify for taper relief as securities even though they may not meet the criteria for being treated as securities for other CGT purposes.

16.7.9 Assets used by an individual's qualifying company

An extremely wide range of assets could qualify. The most common example was land and buildings used in the business. Sometimes an individual owned goodwill, but the business was carried on by his company.

The status of such an asset as a business asset was not jeopardised by the owner charging rent (eg where he let premises to a qualifying company for use in its trade).

Up to 5 April 2000, the assets counted as business assets only if the individual held 5% of the voting shares and worked for the company on a full-time basis or the individual held at least 25% of the voting shares.

16.7.10 Assets used in a qualifying office or employment

Suppose that an individual owned a property, which was let to a quoted company that operated a restaurant. If the individual was employed (full-time or part-time) by the quoted company, the property was a business asset. For periods prior to 6 April 2000, the individual's employment had to be full time.

16.7.11 Assets used by an individual for his trade

This covered a situation where an individual used a property for a trade or profession carried on by him either as a sole trader or as a partner in a firm.

16.7.12 Mixed use

Where an asset had been used as a part business/part non-business asset, the gain on its disposal was apportioned pro rata. Part of the gain qualified for the business asset taper relief and the other part for the non-business asset taper relief. A switch to non-business asset use during the last ten years of ownership always adversely affected the taper.

Example – Taper relief in case of mixed use

T acquired a freehold office in 1996. The offices were rented out as an investment until 5 April 2001. The offices were then used by his qualifying company until 30 September 2006 when they were sold, realising a chargeable gain (after indexation to April 1998) of £375,000.

For taper relief the relevant period is from 6 April 1998 to 30 September 2006, ie 8.5 years. During this period the office was a non-business asset for 3 years (April 1998 to April 2001) and a business asset for the remaining 5.5 years. Therefore ⅗.₅ of the gain is charged as a non-business asset (£132,353) with the balance as a business asset. As the asset was held prior to 17 March 1998 it qualifies for the one-year addition in respect of the non-business portion.

	Non-business asset £	Business asset £	Total £
Chargeable gains	132,353	242,647	375,000
Deduct taper relief 35%/75%	46,323	181,985	228,308
Taxable gains (before annual exemption)	86,030	60,662	146,692

Note: If there were allowable losses for the year they would be set firstly against the gain attracting the lower rate of taper relief.

16.7.13 Business taper extended from 6 April 2004
(FA 2003)

Certain situations not covered by the previous rules qualified from 6 April 2004 to 5 April 2008.

These borderline situations which were not covered by the previous rules involved assets owned by individuals, trustees and personal representatives where they were used for the purposes of a trade carried on by:

- any individual, or any partnership which had an individual as a member;
- the trustees of any settlement, or any partnership whose members included any person acting in the capacity of a trustee of a settlement;
- the personal representatives of any deceased person, or any partnership whose members included any person acting in the capacity of a personal representative;
- a partnership whose members included a company which is a 'qualifying company' by reference to the owner of the asset; or
- a partnership whose members included a company which belonged to a trading group whose holding company is a qualifying company by reference to the owner of the asset.

The term 'qualifying company' included all unlisted trading companies and unlisted holding companies of trading groups.

16.8 ENTREPRENEURS RELIEF

This relief was introduced from 6 April 2008 to remove a widespread sense of disillusion on the introduction of the 18% flat rate and the abolition of taper relief. Many businessmen had come to regard the appropriate rate of CGT on the eventual sale of their business as 10%.

The relief is a reduction in qualifying capital gains of 4/9ths. If gains of £180,000 qualify, they are therefore reduced to £100,000. In summary, 18% of £100,000 = £18,000, ie an effective rate of 10% on £180,000.

The maximum amount on which relief may be claimed is £1 million.

16.8.1 Conditions relating to the individual

Entrepreneurs relief is normally available only if the individual has been in business, as a sole trader or as a partner or as an officer or employee of his personal trading company for at least 12 months ending with the relevant disposal. It is necessary for the disposal to be a material disposal of all or part of his interest in the business or of shares in his personal trading company (see below).

16.8.2 **Only some businesses qualify**

The business must be a trading business and not an investment business. Letting property or furnished holiday accommodation should qualify.

16.8.3 **Personal trading company**

A company qualifies as an individual's personal trading company only if:

- he owns at least 5% of the share capital and has at least 5% of the voting rights; and
- he is an officer (eg director) or employee of that company; and
- the company is a trading company or the holding company of a trading group or a joint venture company (see 16.7.7) and it does not exist to any substantial extent for any other purpose (this preserves the 20% test described at 16.7.5 above).

16.8.4 **Associated disposals**

Entrepreneurs relief can also be claimed on gains arising from associated disposals. An associated disposal consists of the disposal by the individual of an asset he has owned personally but which has been used in the business that has been the subject of a material disposal (see above).

The associated disposal must take place within three years of the related material disposal and must be related to the individual withdrawing from the

---

Tax notes

The relief will not normally be available for a gain on the sale of land or buildings used by a partnership or personal trading company where the individual had charged a full market rent.

---

business concerned. This may mean that the relief is withheld if the material disposal was merely a sale of part of the individual's stake in the business. If the individual does not utilise the maximum £1 million relief, it is possible that a trust in which he is the life tenant may be able to claim the balance (see 30.4.12).

16.8.5 **Worked examples provided by HMRC**

The Revenue gave the following worked examples in a press release of 12 March 2008:

(1) Miss *S* sells her trading business in 2008–09 and realises gains of £250,000 on her factory premises and £300,000 on goodwill but a loss of £100,000 on her retail shop giving net gains of £450,000 (before

entrepreneurs relief). She has made no other claims to the relief and the whole of the gains are eligible for relief.

If Miss *S* claims entrepreneurs relief, the gains of £450,000 will be reduced by 4/9ths (so reduced by £200,000, resulting in a chargeable gain of £250,000). Miss S has no allowable losses and no other gains in that year so she deducts the annual exempt amount (AEA) £9,600 giving an amount chargeable to CGT of £240,400. This amount is taxed at 18% giving tax payable of £43,272.

(2) Mr *W* sells his shares in a trading company in 2008–09 and realises a gain of £360,000. He has owned 50% of the ordinary shares of the company, which gave him 50% of the voting rights, for several years, during which time he has been a director of the company. He therefore qualifies for entrepreneurs relief on the disposal of his shares.

On making a claim, Mr *W*'s gain is reduced by 4/9ths, resulting in a chargeable gain of £200,000. He has no allowable losses or other chargeable gains, so after deduction of the annual exempt amount (AEA) £9,600 he has an amount chargeable to CGT of £190,400. This amount is taxed at 18%, giving tax payable of £34,272.

(3) Mrs *L* sells her trading business in 2008–09 and realises gains of £1,300,000 (before entrepreneurs relief). She has made no other claims for the relief, and the whole of the gains are eligible for relief. She claims entrepreneurs relief.

The maximum amount of gains on which entrepreneurs relief can be claimed is £1 million. So £1 million of Mrs *L*'s gains is reduced by 4/9ths (to £555,555), and the balance (over the £1 million) of £300,000 is chargeable in full, resulting in net chargeable gains of £855,555. She has no allowable losses or other chargeable gains, so after deduction of the annual exempt amount (AEA) £9,600 she has an amount chargeable to CGT of £845,955. This amount is taxed at 18%, giving tax payable of £152,271.90.

(4) Mrs *F* sells her trading business on 2008–09 and realises gains of £720,000. This amount qualifies in full for entrepreneurs relief, which she claims, and the gain is reduced by 4/9ths, resulting in a chargeable gain (before any deduction of losses or annual exempt amount (AEA)) of £400,000. From January 2009 to September 2013 Mrs *F* is a director of trading company P Ltd, and owns 15% of the ordinary share capital, which entitles her to exercise 15% of the votes. In September 2013 she sells her shares, realising a gain of £400,000. She claims entrepreneurs relief.

Mrs *F* has already had relief in respect of gains of £720,000, and there is a limit of £1 million in respect of which she can claim the relief. So £280,000 of the £400,000 gain qualifies for relief and is relief and is reduced by 4/9ths to £155,555, and the balance of £120,000 is chargeable in full, giving a net chargeable gain (before deduction of any allowable losses and the AEA) of £275,555.

(5) In 1995 Mr *E* purchased a buy-to-let property for £100,000 that is let out on an assured short-hold tenancy basis. In October 2008 he sells the property for £250,000. The CGT due is calculated by deducting the purchase cost from the sale proceeds giving a gain of £150,000. This gain is not eligible for entrepreneurs relief.

Mr *E* has no allowable losses or other capital gains in that year so he can deduct the full annual exempt amount (AEA) of £9,600 giving an amount chargeable to CGT of £140,400. This amount is taxed at 18% giving tax payable of £25,272.

(6) Mr *R* has been a member of a trading partnership for several years. He leaves the partnership and disposes of his interest in partnership assets to the other partners, realising gains of £125,000, all of which qualify for entrepreneurs relief. He also sells the partnership office building which he owned outright, but let to the partnership, realising a gain of £37,000. The disposal of the office building is 'associated' with Mr *R*'s withdrawal from the partnership business, and the £37,000 gain therefore also qualifies for entrepreneurs relief (assuming there is no restriction on the amount of the gain qualifying for relief as a result of non-qualifying use).

Mr *R* claims entrepreneurs relief in respect of total gains of £162,000. This amount is reduced by 4/9ths, resulting in a chargeable gain of £90,000. Mr *R* has no allowable losses or other gains, so after deduction of the annual exempt amount (AEA) £9,600 there is an amount chargeable to CGT of £80,400. This amount is taxed at 18%, giving tax payable of £14,472.

(7) Mrs *N* sells her business in 2009 and realises a gain of £99,000 that qualifies for entrepreneurs relief. She claims the relief, but also makes an investment of £80,000 in qualifying EIS shares and claims to defer the gain.

Mrs *N*'s gain of £99,000 is reduced by 4/9ths, resulting in a chargeable gain of £55,000. The investment in EIS shares exceeds £55,000, so the whole of the chargeable gain of £55,000 is deferred. This amount will come into charge at some later time under the normal EIS rules for charging deferred gains.

(8) Mr *C* sold his trading business in May 2006 and realised a gain of £270,000. He invested this amount in qualifying EIS shares in July 2006, so the gain was deferred. In September 2009 he sells the EIS shares and the deferred gain becomes chargeable to CGT.

The gain on the disposal of the business in 2006 would have qualified in full for entrepreneurs relief if the relief had been available at that time. So Mr *C* can claim entrepreneurs relief in respect of the deferred gain, and if he makes a claim the deferred gain is reduced by 4/9ths, resulting in a chargeable gain (in September 2009 when he disposes of the EIS shares) of £150,000 (before any deduction for losses and annual exempt amount (AEA)).

(9) Mrs *A* exchanges her shares in the trading company Y Ltd for qualifying corporate bonds (QCBs) in 2010. For some years she has been an employee of Y Ltd, owning 10% of the ordinary shares, which entitle her to exercise 10% of the votes in the company. She therefore meets the conditions for claiming entrepreneurs relief in respect of her shares in Y Ltd. The normal rules for share exchanges apply and there is no immediate charge to CGT in 2010 when she exchanges the shares, but the gain that would arise on a disposal of those shares for full market value at the date of the exchange is calculated. The calculation results in a gain of £63,000.

Mrs *A*'s of £63,000 will become chargeable to CGT when the QCBs are redeemed or she disposes of them in any other way. If Mrs *A* claims entrepreneurs relief in respect of the £63,000 gain it will be reduced by 4/9ths to £35,000 and that will be the amount that becomes chargeable when she disposes of the QCBs.

(10) Mr *D* exchanged his shares in trading company Z Ltd for qualifying corporate bonds (QCBs) in 2007. Before the exchange he had, for several years, been a director of Z Ltd and owned 25% of its ordinary share capital, which entitled him to exercise 25% of the votes in the company. A gain of £315,000 was deferred as a result of the exchange. In August 2010 the QCBs are redeemed, and the gain of £315,000 becomes chargeable.

At the time of the exchange Mr *D*'s gain would have qualified for entrepreneurs relief if the relief had been available in 2007. So Mr D can claim the relief, and the gain of £315,000 is reduced by 4/9ths, resulting in a chargeable gain (before deduction of any allowable losses and the annual exempt amount (AEA)) of £175,000.

(11) In August 2009 Miss K exchanges her shares in the trading company X Ltd for shares issued by a new company, H plc. For some years she has been an employee of X Ltd, owning 40% of the ordinary shares, which entitle her to exercise 40% of the votes in the company. She therefore meets the conditions for claiming entrepreneurs relief in respect of her shares in X Ltd. But in the exchange she receives shares amounting to only 2% of the ordinary shares of H plc. This is below the minimum 5% holding requirement, so Miss *K* will not be able to qualify for entrepreneurs relief on a disposal of her new shares in H plc.

Under the normal rules for share exchanges Miss *K* would be treated as making no disposal of her shares in X Ltd at the time of the exchange in August 2009 and there is no immediate charge to CGT then. These rules would therefore mean she loses all possibility of claiming entrepreneurs' relief. In order to allow a claim to the relief she can elect to display those normal rules. Disapplying the rules means that she is treated as disposing of the shares in X Ltd at the time of the exchange in August 2009. She can then claim entrepreneurs relief on the gain arising on that disposal.

16.9 EARN-OUTS

An earn-out is where a person sells shares and part of the consideration is dependent on the company's subsequent performance. For example, an individual might sell his private company for £1m cash plus an amount based on the company achieving certain profit targets for the next three years.

The right to receive more cash if profit targets are achieved is a valuable one, but its value will not normally be the maximum sum: it depends on whether the targets are achieved. The case law (*Marren* v *Ingles*) indicates that a present (discounted) value should be ascertained and this should be included as part of the sale consideration that is taxable for the year in which the sale takes place. When the earn-out period is over, and the actual amount due under the earn-out is known, a further capital gain (or loss) occurs for the year in which the entitlement is ascertained.

This has meant that a person who is entitled to receive an earn-out could be taxed on sums that are never in fact received. Fortunately, the law has recently been changed. Provided the sale contract specifies that the earn-out consideration **must** be satisfied by the acquiring company issuing securities or debentures (eg loan notes) rather than paying cash, and provided the person entitled to the earn-out does not make an election under TCGA 1992, s 138A, there is no question of anything being taxed in respect of the earn-out until the person makes a disposal of the securities that are received in satisfaction of his earn-out rights.

Tax notes

Be especially careful on this. Until recently, the effect of making an election under s 138A was beneficial in that it postponed the date of disposal for CGT purposes until the individual disposed of the securities received from the earn-out. The situation has been turned upside-down: you are now automatically treated in this way unless you positively elect under the revised version of s 138A to have a CGT assessment on the initial value of the earn-out. It is possible that such a CGT assessment could suit some people in unusual circumstances and in these cases the s 138A election needs to be made within 22 months of the end of the tax year in which the disposal giving rise to the earn-out takes place.

16.9.1 CGT treatment for earn-outs since 2003

There is now also some relief for individuals who are entitled to an earn-out that can be taken in cash. Such individuals are liable to be taxed on the initial value of the earn-out but there is now a carry-back relief. This allows a vendor who has been taxed on a higher amount than is eventually received to carry back the difference as a loss. In other words, the end result is that CGT is paid only on the amount that is actually collected.

This relief applies only to earn-out rights disposed of after 9 April 2003.

16.9.2 Earn-outs and income tax

See also 5.7 regarding a possible income tax charge on certain earn-outs.

16.10 SALES OF SHARES TO ALL-EMPLOYEE SHARE TRUSTS
(TCGA 1992, Sched 7C)

Where an individual transfers unquoted shares to trustees who hold them for employees under an approved all-employee share scheme (see 5.4), the individual may roll over any capital gain arising from this transfer provided he reinvests in chargeable assets within six months. The all-employee trust must acquire at least a 10% interest in the company. The chargeable assets into which the individual's gain is rolled over cannot consist of shares in the company concerned or a property that is exempt as the individual's main residence.

Tax notes

You will need a lot of professional advice if you seek to rely on this relief. But if you qualify, the roll-over relief rules are much more beneficial than in other situations.

TAX AND COMPANIES

PETER HARRUP

This chapter looks at the taxation of companies under the following headings:

(1) Who pays corporation tax?
(2) Self-assessment.
(3) How 'profits' are defined.
(4) Accounting periods, rates and payment of tax.
(5) Loan relationships.
(6) Intangible assets.
(7) Companies' capital gains.
(8) Dividends.
(9) Losses.
(10) Double taxation relief on foreign income.
(11) Groups of companies.
(12) Investment companies.
(13) Close companies.
(14) Real Estate Investment Trusts.
(15) Corporate venturing.
(16) Research and development (R&D) tax credits.
(17) ECA tax credits.
(18) Transfer pricing rules.
(19) Claims, elections and penalties.

17.1 WHO PAYS CORPORATION TAX?
(TA 1988, ss 11–12; FA 1988, s 66)

Corporation tax is levied on the chargeable profits of companies resident in the UK for tax purposes. A company is generally defined as meaning any body corporate or unincorporated association, but does not include a partnership, local authority or local authority association. The definition extends to authorised unit trusts, the detailed provisions for which are set out in TA 1988, s 468.

Corporation tax also extends to non-resident companies carrying on a trade in the UK through a branch or agency. Such companies are chargeable to tax on any income attributable to the branch or agency and on any capital gains arising on the disposal of assets used in the UK for the branch or agency's trade purposes. Any income of a non-resident company from sources within the UK that is not charged to corporation tax is liable to income tax.

A company that was incorporated in the UK is regarded as resident there regardless of where the directors exercise their management and control. Some of the double taxation conventions negotiated with other countries override this in practice and treat a dual resident company as if it were not UK-resident.

A company that was incorporated overseas may still be regarded as resident in the UK on the basis that its central management and control is exercised in the UK. Questions relating to a foreign incorporated company's residence status are usually determined by reference to the guidelines set out in SP1/90 dated 9 January 1990.

17.2 SELF-ASSESSMENT
(TA 1988, ss 8 and 10; FA 1989, s 102; FA 1990, ss 91–103 and Scheds 15–17)

Self-assessment has been in force since 1 July 1999. This is a similar system to that which applies to individuals and trustees.

Self-assessment for companies brings with it extensive record-keeping obligations.

A copy of the manual, *A Guide to Corporation Tax Self-assessment* (CTSA/BK2), can be obtained from the Revenue.

The SA system requires payments on account for certain companies. Where a 'large' company (as defined in 17.4.4) has taxable profits for such an accounting period, and it also had such profits in the preceding year, it must make four payments on account of its expected corporation tax liability for the year.

17.3 HOW 'PROFITS' ARE DEFINED

17.3.1 Computation of profits
(TA 1988, s 6)

The income and chargeable gains of a company, collectively termed 'chargeable profits', are chargeable to corporation tax. The computation of chargeable profits can be a very complex process bearing in mind the detailed tax legislation and extensive case law. There is also a myriad of Revenue statements of practice, press releases and extra-statutory concessions that may need to be borne in mind when calculating chargeable profits on which corporation tax is payable.

The schedular system remains in place for companies (ie Schedule A and Schedule D income). However, this is largely a matter of form. The general principles of profit adjustment closely follow the rules for income tax, and the assessment of income under the various schedules is computed on an actual or arising basis.

17.3.2 Special computational rules for companies

Rental income

All income from UK rental activities is now treated as arising from one source and taxed along the same lines as trading profits taxable under Schedule D Case I. Any losses are relieved first against other income and gains of the same period, and any excess is available for carrying forward against all future income, or may be surrendered as group relief (subject to certain restrictions).

Forex transactions

Special rules apply for foreign exchange profits and losses; professional advice should be taken if the company has significant foreign assets or borrowings in foreign currency.

Loan relationships

Specific rules govern the treatment of loan relationships such as gilts and other fixed-interest investments in relation to accounting periods ending after 31 March 1996. Basically, any profits on disposal of such assets are taxed as income and any losses are allowed against the company's income. It is necessary to revalue gilts and fixed interest investments at the end of each accounting period. Any increase compared with the market value at the start of the period (or the date of acquisition where the gilt, etc, was acquired during the course of the year) is taxable income; any reduction in value is an allowable loss. See 17.5.

Capital allowances

Although depreciation is not regarded as an allowable expense for tax purposes, tax relief is given for expenditure on qualifying capital assets by means of capital allowances. The principles follow very closely those that apply to individuals (see 6.5) and therefore the main provisions are not covered in detail here. Capital allowances for a trade carried on by a company are regarded as trading expenses for the accounting period in which they arise. They are therefore taken into account in arriving at the chargeable profits or overall tax loss for the accounting period.

Capital allowances for non-trading activities are primarily deductible from the income arising from that source. Any surplus allowances may be carried forward against similar source income arising in later accounting periods or deducted from overall chargeable profits for the accounting period in which they arise.

Contributions to employee benefit trusts

Contributions made on or after 27 November 2002 attract tax relief only if an employee receives sums within nine months of the company's year end on which PAYE and NIC are charged. If this condition is not satisfied, the company receives a deduction only for the accounting period in which sums are paid out. The Court of Appeal decision in the *Dextra* case indicates that this was also the position prior to 27 November 2002.

Employee options

A company may secure a corporation tax deduction for accounting periods commencing after 31 December 2002 if an employee exercises an option over ordinary share capital. Where the company is a subsidiary, the shares must be shares in the parent company.

The amount of the deduction is the amount taxed as employment income or that would be so taxed if the option were not an approved option.

Intangible assets

The tax treatment for expenditure on and gains from the sale of intangible assets was introduced by FA 2002. See 17.6.

Insurance policies

See 27.8 on life insurance policies held by companies.

Annual payments
(TA 1988, s 338)

Certain annual payments (termed 'charges on income') are deductible from a company's profits in arriving at the amount assessable to corporation tax. Examples of such annual payments are annuity and Gift Aid payments. The principle is that these charges on income are offset against the payer's total profits, not merely against a particular source of income with which the payment is connected.

A payment counts as a charge on income only if the following conditions are met:

(1) It has been made out of the company's profits brought into charge to corporation tax.
(2) It is made under a liability incurred for a 'valuable and sufficient consideration' (or the payment is a covenanted donation to charity).

(3) The payment must not be one charged to capital or one not ultimately borne by the company.

(4) It must not be in the nature of a dividend or distribution made by the company.

The basic rule is that payment must actually be made in the accounting period for it to count as a charge for that period. In certain restricted circumstances, some companies that are owned by charities are able to treat Gift Aid payments made within nine months of their year end as if they had been paid during the year.

Where the total profits for an accounting period are insufficient to absorb charges on income, excess charges in respect of payments made wholly and exclusively for the purposes of the company's trade may be carried forward and utilised against its future trading income. Non-trade charges may not be carried forward in this manner and no further relief is available.

Companies in partnership

An anti-avoidance provision aimed at companies operating in partnership has been introduced, with effect from 17 March 2004. Although relatively few in number, there are several situations in which such companies are commonly found, including such diverse activities as international business services, property development and the entertainment industry. The Government is concerned that the flexibility of profit sharing arrangements within partnerships has been exploited. Its intention is to challenge situations where income and capital profits are shared differently with, typically, the income being allocated to a non-resident partner and the capital profits to a UK-resident partner.

With effect from 17 March 2004, if a corporate partner withdraws capital, or receives capital in excess of its actual capital contribution, the excess may, in certain circumstances, be taxed as income. The capital 'received' may be as a result of distribution out of its partnership interest, liquidation or withdrawal of partnership equity. The approach adopted is to compare the excess with what might have been achieved had such a partner been credited partnership profits pro rata to its capital contribution.

17.4 ACCOUNTING PERIODS, RATES AND PAYMENT OF TAX

17.4.1 Accounting periods for tax purposes
(TA 1988, s 12)

Companies pay corporation tax by reference to their accounting periods and the chargeable profit included is assessed on an actual or accruals basis. Accounting periods may straddle two financial years (which for corporation tax purposes run from 1 April to 31 March and are named after the year in which the period begins). If this is the case, the chargeable profits are apportioned on a time basis for the purposes of determining the rate of tax to apply to the overall profit.

An accounting period begins for corporation tax purposes when:

(1) the company comes within the charge to corporation tax either by becoming UK-resident or acquiring a source of income; or
(2) the company's previous accounting period ends without the company ceasing to be within the charge to corporation tax.

An accounting period runs on for a maximum of 12 months from its commencement. It will end earlier if the company's own accounting date falls within the 12 months and it will also end if the company:

(a) ceases to trade;
(b) begins or ceases to be UK-resident; or
(c) ceases to be within the charge to corporation tax altogether.

Where accounts are made up for a period of more than 12 months, the income is usually apportioned on a time basis to the relevant accounting period. Where a more appropriate basis of apportionment is available, the Inspector may apply that basis instead (see *Marshall Hus & Partners Ltd* v *Bolton* [1981] STC 18). In some instances, the accounts year end may vary slightly for commercial reasons (eg where accounts are made up to the last Friday of a specified month). Provided the variation is not more than four days from the 'mean' date it is normally acceptable to treat each period of account as if it were a 12-month accounting period ending on the mean date.

17.4.2 Corporation tax rate
(TA 1988, s 6)

The corporation tax rate is fixed for each financial year, which for these purposes starts on 1 April. The rate for the financial year 2007 (ie 1 April 2007 to 31 March 2008) was 30%.

The rate for the financial year 2008 is 28%.

17.4.3 Small companies rates and associated companies
(TA 1988, s 13)

A reduced corporation tax rate (known as the 'small companies rate') applies to a company's profits that do not exceed a minimum level. That level has been £300,000 for some years. The rate was 20% for the financial year 2007 (ie 1 April 2007 to 31 March 2008). It has been increased to 21% for the financial year 2008 (ie year to 31 March 2009) and it will be further increased to 22% for the financial year 2009.

Where profits exceed the maximum profit limit for small companies rate purposes, an element of marginal relief is given for profits between £300,000 and £1.5m. This relief operates on a tapered basis by charging the profits to the full corporation tax rate but gives an element of credit for the reduced corporation tax rate that would have been applicable to the initial tranche of profit.

The profit limits applicable to small companies relief are restricted, based on the existence of any 'associated' companies that the company has during the accounting period concerned. For example, if a company has one associated company, the small companies profit limits are divided by two, ie one plus the number of associated companies.

A company is an associated company of another if they are under common control or one has control of the other. 'Control' for this purpose is defined as the ability to exercise direct or indirect control over the company's affairs and in particular:

(1) the possession or entitlement to acquire more than 50% of the share capital or voting rights in the company;
(2) entitlement to receive the greater part of income distributed among the shareholders;
(3) entitlement to receive the greater part of the company's assets in the event of a winding-up.

An associated company that has not carried on any trade or business at any time during the accounting period concerned is disregarded. On the other hand, a foreign company may be an associated company even though its profits are not subject to UK corporation tax.

Where a company's accounting period straddles more than one financial year and the marginal relief limits for each financial year differ, the 12-month period is treated as separate accounting periods for the purpose of calculating marginal relief.

17.4.4 Payment of tax
(TA 1988, s 10)

Corporation tax automatically becomes due and payable nine months and one day from the end of the accounting period. Large companies must pay corporation tax by instalments. For these purposes, a 'large' company is one that has taxable profits of over £10m in the year, or profits of £1.5m divided by the number of associated companies, for the year and the preceding year. The instalment payments commence 14 days after the first six months of the year in question, and are due in four equal quarterly instalments. A company with a year end of 31 December will pay on 14 July, 14 October, 14 January and 14 April.

Interest is charged on any unpaid tax due and is an allowable deduction. Interest is payable to the company on any overpayments; this interest is taxable.

17.5 LOAN RELATIONSHIPS

In broad terms, the tax treatment of profits and losses from loan relationships follows the accounting treatment. Rules introduced in FA 1996 affect the tax treatment of items such as interest received and paid, premiums and discounts.

17.5.1 Scope of legislation

The legislation applies to all UK-resident companies and UK branches of overseas resident companies. The commencement date for the new regime was the start of a company's first accounting period ending after 31 March 1996 for interest, and 1 April 1996 for gains and losses on debt.

17.5.2 'Loan relationships'
(FA 1996, s 81)

The legislation refers to 'loan relationships' rather than loans, and these can arise where:

(1) a company is a debtor or creditor in respect of a money debt, and this debt arose as a result of a transaction for the lending of money; or
(2) an instrument is issued for the purpose of representing security for, or the rights of a creditor in respect of, a money debt.

Loan relationships therefore include bank loans, director's loans, gilts, inter-company accounts and debentures. Even where a money debt does not fall within the definition (eg trade creditors and debtors), the interest charged on such debts falls within the regime.

17.5.3 Tax treatment
(FA 1996, s 84)

In general, income and expenditure is taxed or allowed in the year it is credited or debited to the profit and loss account or, if appropriate, reserves. The company's accounting treatment must comply with an 'authorised accruals' accounting policy. Where a company accounts for debt using normal accounting practice (as set out in FRS4, *Capital Instruments*) this should satisfy the authorised accruals accounting policy.

Banks are also permitted to use an authorised market-to-market basis where a loan relationship is brought into account in each accounting period at the fair value.

17.5.4 Taxation of corporate debt
(FA 1996, ss 82–83)

The tax treatment of corporate debt depends on whether the item arose from the trade. Debits and credits arising in an accounting period from loan relationships entered into for the company's trade purposes are treated as forming part of its trading profits or losses, whereas any debits and credits arising from activities outside the company's trade are aggregated in coming to a profit or loss on non-trading loan relationships.

Where any expenditure or income arises partly from trading and partly from non-trading, it is split on a pro rata basis.

Taxation of non-trading profits and losses
(FA 1996, s 83)

Net profits from non-trading loan relationships are taxed under Schedule D Case III. If there are net losses, these can be relieved in a number of ways, ie by:

(1) offset against the company's profits chargeable to corporation tax for that accounting period; or
(2) surrender as group relief to other group companies; or
(3) carry back against the profits from non-trading loan relationships of the preceding accounting period; or
(4) carry forward against all profits, other than trading profits, of the next period; or
(5) carry forward against future profits from non-trading loan relationships.

Claims must be made within two years of the accounting period in which the loss arose for (1)–(3), and two years of the next period for (4). No claim is required for losses carried forward under (5).

17.5.5 Connected parties
(FA 1996, s 87)

Special rules apply when the other party to a loan relationship is a connected company. A company and another party are connected for these purposes if they are under the same control, or one controls the other, in that accounting period. A person controls a company by owning the greater part of the shares, voting rights, or other capital giving entitlement to more than one-half of the assets in a winding-up.

17.5.6 Late interest
(FA 1996, s 87)

If two parties are connected, then interest is only allowable on an accruals basis when paid to a connected party where the recipient is liable to UK corporation tax on the full amount of interest received, or the interest is paid within 12 months of the end of the accounting period. Therefore, if the recipient is an individual, trustee, non-resident company or exempt body such as a charity, the interest must be paid by the anniversary of the accounting period if a deduction is to be obtained. If it is paid later then relief is given for the year it is paid.

17.5.7 **Bad debts and waivers**
(FA 1996, Sched 9)

No tax relief has been available for any bad debts on connected party loan relationships, and conversely no liability to tax arose when a debt was waived. FA 2002 modified this from 1 October 2002 so that tax relief may be available for bad debts on connected party loan relationships where the debtor company is in liquidation. This aspect of the legislation is extremely technical and specialist advice should be taken where material sums are involved.

17.5.8 **Annual charges**
(TA 1988, ss 338–339)

Apart from interest, a company may make annual payments in respect of annuities, royalties, covenanted payments, etc, that are available for offset as charges on income against the company's chargeable profits on a paid basis.

17.5.9 **Income tax deduction at source**

In the recent past, companies were required to deduct and account to the Revenue for income tax on payments of annual interest and other charges on income, with the exception of annual interest paid to a UK bank. A return form CT61 had to be submitted each quarter, detailing payments made and computing the income tax payable to the Revenue. In arriving at the income tax liability due, any income tax suffered on income received under deduction of tax could be offset. Where the income tax suffered on income received exceeded the income tax payable on annual charges, the surplus could be carried forward to the next quarterly return. If at the end of the accounting period it had not proved possible to obtain credit against income tax payable, credit could be obtained against the corporation tax liability for the accounting period (and if there was no or insufficient corporation tax liability to offset any income tax credit, a repayment could be obtained from the Revenue).

These rules were substantially changed by FA 2001, with effect from 1 April 2001. There is no longer any requirement for a company paying interest, etc, to deduct income tax provided the recipient is a UK-resident company.

A company is still required to deduct basic rate income tax where the recipient is an individual or a non-resident company.

Sometimes a company pays interest by issuing funding bonds. Basic rate tax has to be accounted for on the market value of funding bonds issued to individuals or non-resident companies.

17.6 INTANGIBLE ASSETS

The tax regime for intangible assets that has applied since 1 April 2002 is designed to achieve the following:

- provide tax relief to companies for the cost of acquired intangibles;

- give relief in line with the amortisation in the company's accounts;
- treat related sales receipts as taxable income but allow for roll-over relief where the proceeds are reinvested in new intangibles;
- provide transitional provisions that preserved the previous regime for intangibles held currently.

The legislation applies to intangible fixed assets as recognised under Generally Accepted Accounting Principles. It is specifically stated to apply to goodwill and intellectual property, which includes patents, trademarks, registered designs, copyright and design right; licensing and similar rights are also included.

Assets representing rights over real property (ie land and buildings), tangible moveable property, oil licences and financial assets are among the categories of intangibles specifically excluded from the new regime.

17.6.1 Key concepts

The structure of the legislation is similar to that relating to corporate debt in that it identifies tax-effective accounting debits and credits in respect of expenditure incurred after 31 March 2002 on intangible fixed assets.

Debits that attract tax relief for expenditure and losses include all expenditure on an intangible fixed asset charged to the profit and loss account. This includes the amortisation of capitalised costs (or, at the taxpayer's option, 4% annually of that cost) and even abortive expenditure of realisation of an intangible fixed asset. A loss on the sale of such an asset (compared against its tax written-down value) also qualifies for relief.

Taxable credits include all receipts in respect of intangible fixed assets credited to the profit and loss account, gains over the tax written down value on disposal of the asset and the total proceeds of realisation of intangible fixed assets not carried on the balance sheet. Any 'negative' goodwill arising on the acquisition of a business that is recognised in the profit and loss account is also taxable.

17.6.2 How debits and credits are given effect

Debits and credits are brought into account for corporation tax purposes as follows:

(1) Assets held for the purposes of a trade – treated as a trading expense or receipt.

(2) Assets held for the purposes of a property business – treated as an expense or receipt of the business.

(3) Any other assets – the debits and credits are described as giving rise to non-trading losses and gains and aggregated. Credits are taxed while debits may be relieved against total profits, carried forward or surrendered as group relief.

17.6.3 **Roll-over relief**

Where the proceeds of the realisation of a chargeable intangible fixed asset are reinvested in whole or in part in the purchase of other intangible fixed assets, the legislation provides for a form of roll-over relief. Entitlement to relief is subject to certain conditions being met. The amount of the relief is calculated as follows:

(1) If the expenditure on new assets exceeds the proceeds of old assets, relief is the excess of proceeds over the indexed cost of the old asset.
(2) If the expenditure on new assets is less than the proceeds of old assets, relief is the excess of expenditure over the indexed cost of the old asset.

Roll-over relief in respect of goodwill held on 31 March 2002 will be available under the new regime. In all other respects, intangibles held on 31 March are excluded from these provisions.

17.6.4 **Pre-commencement intangible assets**

It was never intended that a company should secure the tax reliefs under the new regime by buying intangible assets already in existence at 31 March 2002. The following assets are therefore excluded:

- Assets acquired from a group company that owned the asset at 31 March 2002.
- Assets acquired by a close company from a vendor who owned the asset at 31 March 2002 and who is a participator in the company.
- Assets acquired by the vendor since 31 March 2002 from such a person.

17.7 COMPANIES' CAPITAL GAINS

17.7.1 **Computation of gains**

Capital gains made by companies are included in their chargeable profits and are subject to corporation tax. CGT therefore does not apply to companies, although chargeable gains and losses are computed in accordance with the detailed provisions of CGT. The main differences between CGT and corporation tax on chargeable gains for companies are, first, that provisions that clearly apply only to individuals (eg annual exemption) have no application as far as companies are concerned and, second, that computations of chargeable gains are prepared on an accounting period basis rather than by income tax years of assessment. Furthermore, taper relief does not apply to companies, but they remain entitled to indexation allowance on increases in the retail price index (RPI) after 31 March 1998. The total chargeable gains for an accounting period less a deduction for allowable losses are brought into charge to corporation tax in the same way as any other source of income.

Capital losses can only be offset against chargeable gains; they cannot be offset against trading or other income. However, it is possible for a company that realises a loss after 31 March 2000 to surrender its loss to another group company for it to offset against its chargeable gains.

17.7.2 Roll-over relief
(TCGA 1992, ss 152–158 and 175)

Roll-over relief is available where the proceeds on the disposal of a qualifying asset are reinvested in further qualifying assets. It operates as a deferral of the corporation tax liability arising on the chargeable gain if the proceeds are fully reinvested in qualifying assets within 12 months before and three years after the date of disposal.

Where the proceeds are only partly reinvested, a proportion of the gain is deferred or 'rolled over' and the balance (equivalent to the amount of proceeds not reinvested) is brought into charge. The element of gain deferred or rolled over is deducted from the new asset's base cost for capital gains purposes. This operates to increase the potential gain on the eventual sale of the new asset acquired, hence the term 'roll-over relief'.

Qualifying assets for this purpose are freehold and leasehold land and buildings, ships, aircraft and hovercraft, fixed plant and machinery, satellite space stations and spacecraft. Expenditure on an asset acquired from a group company (see 17.11) does not rank as qualifying expenditure for roll-over relief.

17.7.3 Disposals of substantial shareholdings

With effect from 1 April 2002, a gain accruing to a company on the disposal of a substantial shareholding in another company is not taxable provided certain conditions are met. The exemption also applies to a disposal of an asset that derives its value from a substantial shareholding, including put or call options in the shares, securities that carry rights to acquire or dispose of the shares and interests in such securities.

A 'substantial shareholding' is one where the investing company is beneficially entitled to not less than 10% of:

- the ordinary share capital; and
- the profits available for distribution to equity holders of the company; and
- the assets available for distribution to equity holders of the company on a winding-up.

To qualify for this relief, several tests must have been met for different specified periods within the two years before the disposal:

(1) The 'investing company' must have been a trading company or a member of a trading group. For this purpose, a 'group' refers to a capital gains group but with a 51% ownership requirement. Non-trading activities must not be a substantial part of the vendor company/group's business, for this purpose a group company carrying on activities that contribute to the trade of another member of the group qualify. 'Substantial' is taken to be 20% or more.

(2) The company that has been invested in must have been a qualifying trading company. In practice this means that less than 20% of its assets consist of investments.

Note that this exemption can apply to disposals of shares in foreign trading companies.

In the same way that gains are exempt, losses are not normally available for offset against other chargeable gains.

See the flow charts in Figure 17.1 on the main conditions that need to be satisfied. However, this relief has complex provisions and professional advice should be taken. For example, some commentaries take the view that a company can never qualify if it is liquidated immediately after selling its only subsidiary but a contrary opinion is expressed in the leading textbook (*Bramwell on Corporation Tax*) and this interpretation is reflected in the flow charts. See also December 2002 *Tax Bulletin* for guidance generally.

17.7.4 Investment trusts and REITs

Approved investment trusts are exempt from tax on capital gains. A similar exemption is being introduced for Real Estate Investment Trusts. Both need to be quoted companies to enjoy this status.

17.8 DIVIDENDS

17.8.1 Taxation of company distributions

Company distributions are defined as any dividends, and any other distribution out of the company's assets, paid by a company in respect of shares in the company. The main exception to this is that any repayment of share capital is not regarded as a distribution of assets.

No tax is payable by a UK company on its making a distribution.

UK recipients of the distribution are entitled to a tax credit. This aggregate amount is described as a 'franked' payment and, as far as individuals are concerned, represents the gross equivalent of the dividend received. This amount is taxable income, but the shareholder may set the tax credit against his tax liability on the 'grossed-up' amount.

Dividends received by a company from another UK company are termed 'franked investment income'. This income is regarded as having already borne tax and does not form part of the chargeable profits of a company; it is therefore non-taxable.

Figure 17.1 – *Exemption for disposals of substantial shareholdings*

Conditions to be satisfied by the vendor company

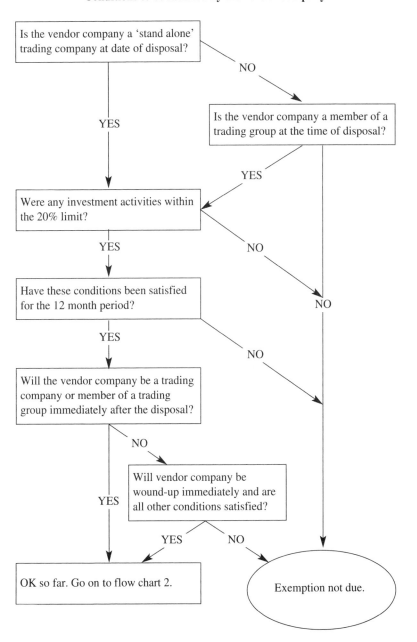

Figure 17.1 – continued

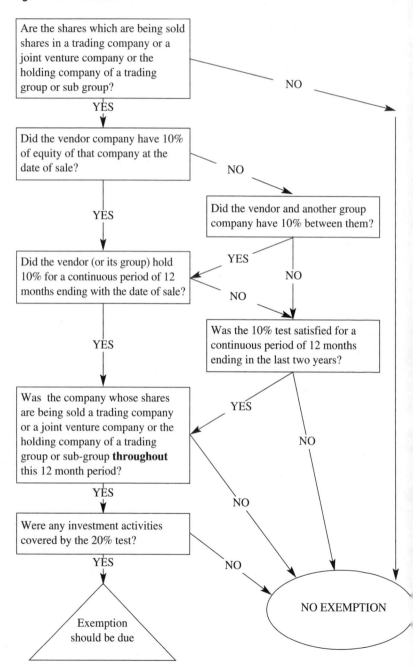

17.8.2 Advance corporation tax (abolished from 6 April 1999)

ACT was a tax that became payable when the company made distributions. This tax was then treated as a prepayment of the company's tax liability on its profits.

ACT was abolished with effect from 6 April 1999. However, it may be that a company which made substantial dividends before that date, and which has not paid out a similar proportion of its post 1999 profits, may be able to claim relief for 'shadow ACT'. If you are dealing with such a case, you should refer to the 2007–08 edition of the *Tax Handbook*.

17.9 LOSSES

17.9.1 Losses arising in accounting period
(TA 1988, s 393)

When a company makes a tax loss in respect of its trading activities for an accounting period, it may claim that the loss arising may be offset against other profits including chargeable gains arising in that accounting period. A tax loss is computed in the same manner as taxable profits, but is restricted to losses arising from trading activities carried out on a commercial basis and with a view to realising profit.

17.9.2 Utilisation of loss relief

There are several ways in which a trading loss may be relieved for tax purposes apart from being offset against other profits arising in the accounting period. The loss can be carried forward to offset against trading profits from the same trade arising in succeeding accounting periods. Losses can be carried forward indefinitely in this manner for as long as the company carries on the trading activity that generated the loss. A loss may also be carried back.

Losses can be carried back and offset against profits in the 12 months immediately preceding the accounting period in which the loss was incurred.

The company must have been carrying on the relevant trade in the earlier periods. Partial relief claims are not allowed, and relief is obtained for later years before earlier years. Relief must be obtained for the loss against other profits of the accounting period before computing the balance of the loss available for carry-back.

Tax notes

Losses can be carried back and offset against profits in the 12 months preceding the accounting period in which the loss was incurred.

17.9.3 **Capital losses**

Capital losses, like capital gains, are computed in accordance with CGT rules, although the net capital gains are subject to corporation tax as part of the overall chargeable profits for the accounting period. Capital losses may be offset against capital gains in computing net chargeable gains, and capital losses that cannot be relieved in this way may be carried forward and offset against gains arising in subsequent accounting periods without limit. The carry-forward of capital losses is not dependent on whether the company continues to carry on its trading activity, and may be offset against gains arising on trade and non-trade assets.

17.9.4 **Surplus charges on income**
(TA 1988, s 393(9))

Relief for charges on income is generally given as the last of all reliefs other than group relief (see 17.11). It is given against the total profits of the period in which the charges are paid. If profits are insufficient to absorb the charges, the amount of charges paid wholly and exclusively for the purposes of the company's trading activities may be carried forward to the next accounting period and treated as a trading loss to be offset against the company's future trading income. Non-trade charges on income may not be so carried forward and therefore relief will be lost.

17.9.5 **Terminal losses**
(TA 1988, ss 393A)

A trading loss arising in the accounting period in which the trade ceases may be carried back and offset against profits of the three years ending immediately before the commencement of the final period of trading. Charges on income paid wholly and exclusively for trade purposes are treated as trading expenses for the purpose of computing the terminal loss available for carry-back.

17.9.6 **Changes in company ownership**
(TA 1988, s 768)

There are anti-avoidance provisions designed to ensure that trading losses carried forward can only be used against future trading income from the trading activity that generated the losses. Losses may not be carried forward if:

(1) within any period of three years there is a change in the ownership of the company preceded or followed by a major change in the nature or conduct of the trade carried on by the company; or
(2) there is a change in ownership of the company at any time after the scale of activities in a trade carried on by the company has become small or negligible, and before any considerable revival in the trade.

A 'change in ownership' means a change in more than 50% of the owner-ship of the ordinary share capital in the company. A 'major change in the nature or conduct of a trade' includes a major change in the type of property dealt in, or the services or facilities provided in, the trade or in customers, outlets or markets. The Revenue issued SP10/91 on some of the factors that are relevant in determining whether there has been a major change in the nature or conduct of a trade or business.

Similar provisions apply for surplus ACT and for excess management expenses brought forward by an investment company.

17.10 DOUBLE TAXATION RELIEF ON FOREIGN INCOME
(TA 1988, ss 788–806)

17.10.1 The main reliefs

A UK-resident company may claim a credit for foreign tax paid on income or capital gains arising from any overseas source. Credit is available against the corporation tax liability payable on the same income or gains. Relief may be due either under the provisions of a double taxation agreement between the UK and the overseas country concerned, or under the general rules for 'unilateral relief' as provided in TA 1988, s 790. Where credit is due under a double taxation agreement, the relevant agreement takes prece-dence over UK domestic legislation.

For most types of income and gains, the full amount is brought into charge for the purpose of computing the corporation tax liability on charge-able profits for the accounting period. Any overseas tax suffered is then offset by way of credit against the corporation tax liability. The amount of credit available is limited to the corporation tax liability on the source of income or gain that has suffered overseas tax. No relief is due for the excess foreign tax paid.

Further relief may be available for dividends received. In addition to relief for withholding or other taxes suffered on payment of the dividend, relief may also be available for the foreign tax suffered on the profits out of which the dividend has been paid. This is known as 'underlying tax', for which relief is given automatically if the UK-recipient company controls 10% or more of the voting share capital in the overseas company paying the dividend. The dividend taxable in the UK is grossed up at the rate of under-lying tax applicable to the profits out of which the dividend has been paid. This, together with any withholding and other taxes suffered on payment of the dividend, can then be offset against the corporation tax liability arising on the grossed up equivalent of the dividend received (subject to the restric-tion that underlying tax relief cannot exceed the corporation tax liability on the same income).

Where double tax relief would be lost (eg where no corporation tax liability arises for the accounting period) it is possible to obtain relief for overseas tax paid by treating the tax as an expense in computing profits for Schedule D Case I purposes.

17.10.2 Anti-avoidance legislation

The Government introduced complex anti-avoidance legislation aimed at the use of overseas 'mixer' companies, usually resident in the Netherlands. Until 31 March 2001, the use of a mixer company enabled UK groups to average the rate of tax on dividends from overseas subsidiaries. This meant that if, for example, the Netherlands company received a dividend of £100,000 from a German company that carried credit for 50% German tax and a dividend of £100,000 from another subsidiary that carried a 20% credit, and the Netherlands company then paid a £200,000 dividend to its UK parent company, the UK company was able to claim credit for underlying tax of £97,500, as here:

	£
German dividend	100,000
Add underlying tax	100,000
	200,000
Other dividend	100,000
Add underlying tax	25,000
Total income	325,000

The corporation tax payable by the UK parent company of £97,500 (30% of £325,000) was covered by double tax relief.

If the UK company had received the dividends directly rather than via the Netherlands company, its double tax relief credit would have been limited to £85,000: the effect of FA 2000 changes is that this is the position from 1 April 2001 onwards even if the dividends come via an offshore mixer company.

17.10.3 Unremittable income

Where an overseas source of income is taxable on an arising basis but it is not possible to remit the income because of government actions in the overseas territory, it is possible to make a claim to defer the corporation tax liability until such time as sufficient funds are remitted to the UK to satisfy the liability. A claim under these circumstances may be made to the Revenue at any time within six years of the end of the accounting period in which the income arises.

17.11 GROUPS OF COMPANIES

17.11.1 Group relationships
(TA 1988, s 402)

There are special rules that apply to groups of companies. For corporation tax purposes, a group relationship exists between two companies if one company holds not less than 75% of the other's ordinary share capital, or if both companies are 75% subsidiaries of a third company. Before 1 April 2000, such companies had to be UK-resident 75% subsidiaries of a UK-resident parent company, but FA 2000 amended the rules to allow UK-resident subsidiaries of non-resident companies to constitute a group for UK tax purposes.

17.11.2 Use of losses
(TA 1988, ss 402–413)

Where one company in a group makes a tax loss for an accounting period, it may 'surrender' that loss to a member of the group for offset against that company's taxable profits. For this purpose, losses available for surrender include charges on income to the extent that they exceed profits chargeable to corporation tax. Where the accounting periods of the surrendering and claimant companies do not coincide, the amount of loss to be surrendered is restricted on a time basis reflecting the length of the accounting periods common to both companies.

For group relief purposes, the requirement for a 75% shareholding relationship is extended so that the company owning the shares must also be beneficially entitled to 75% or more of the profits available for distribution to equity shareholders, and of assets available for distribution in a winding-up.

The legislation originally required that the company seeking to surrender a loss must be UK-resident but this requirement was successfully challenged by Marks and Spencer before the European Court of Justice. The FA 2006 contains provisions that in theory allow group relief for a non UK-resident company's losses but such relief is dependent on various tests, which in practice will hardly ever be satisfied.

17.11.3 Transfers of assets between group companies

Where a trading activity is transferred from one group company to another, relief is available under TA 1988, s 343 to ensure that the company transferring the trade does not suffer balancing charges on assets that have qualified for capital allowances. The successor company merely takes over the tax residue for capital allowances purposes relating to those assets. It is also possible to elect under CAA 2001, s 569 that properties may be transferred between group companies at tax written-down value for the purpose of industrial buildings allowances. Generally, all unrelieved trade losses are also transferred with the trade to the successor company.

Section 343 can also apply where a trade is transferred to another company that is under common control, even though it is not a member of a group.

17.11.4 Capital gains
(TCGA 1992, ss 171 and 175)

For capital gains purposes, chargeable assets may be transferred from one group company to another without tax consequences. Such transfers are treated as if made at a no gain/no loss price and the recipient company will take over the assets' capital gains base cost from the transferor company. A capital gains tax group exists where at least 75% of the ordinary share capital is beneficially owned (directly or indirectly) by the principal company. This is extended to 75% subsidiaries of subsidiaries provided it is an effective 51% subsidiary of the principal company.

For assets held on 31 March 1982, it is possible for the principal company of a group (normally the holding company) to make an election on behalf of all companies in the group that assets held on 31 March 1982 should be subject to the general rebasing rule for capital gains purposes (see 16.3). Such an election is required within two years of the end of the accounting period in which the first disposal occurs after 5 April 1988 of an asset held on 31 March 1982 by a group company.

For roll-over relief purposes, all the trades carried on by group companies are treated as a single trade and therefore it is possible to roll over a gain made on qualifying assets by one group member against qualifying expenditure incurred by another group member within the appropriate timescale. Roll-over relief is generally available only for trading companies within a group although, concessionally, relief is also available for a property-holding company where the properties are used for trading purposes by the other group members.

TCGA 1992 does not allow losses of one company in a group to be set off against gains of another group company. However, since 1 April 2000, two members of a group may jointly elect that an asset that has been disposed of outside the group by one of them may be treated as if it had been transferred between them immediately before that disposal. Previously the asset had to be actually transferred to the company with the losses.

17.12 INVESTMENT COMPANIES
(TA 1988, ss 75 and 130)

An investment company is any company the business of which consists wholly or mainly of making investments and the principal part of its income arises as a result of that activity. The expenses of managing a UK-resident investment company are deductible in computing its total profits for corporation tax purposes. Where management expenses exceed the company's chargeable income and gains for an accounting period, the surplus may be carried forward and treated as management expenses incurred in the next succeeding accounting period, and may continue to be carried forward until relieved. Surplus management expenses may also be surrendered as group relief from one group company to another. Expenses brought forward from previous periods are not available for surrender as group relief.

17.13 CLOSE COMPANIES
(TA 1988, s 13A)

17.13.1 Definition
(TA 1988, ss 414–415)

Companies that are under the control of five or fewer persons, or under the control of their directors, are known as 'close companies'. There are special provisions designed to ensure that such individuals cannot take undue advantage of corporation tax legislation by virtue of their positions of influence over a company's affairs.

A person controls a company if, in fact, he is able to exercise control directly or indirectly over its affairs by owning the greater part of its share capital, voting capital, or other capital giving entitlement to more than half the assets on a winding-up. Shareholders and certain loan creditors in a close company are known as 'participators'.

17.13.2 Loans to participators
(TA 1988, s 419)

Where a close company makes a loan or advances any money to a participator, or an associate of a participator, there is a liability to account for an amount of tax equal to 25% of the loan.

This tax falls due nine months after the end of the company's accounting period in which the loan is made; no tax need be paid if the loan is repaid before the tax falls due. Where the loan is repaid after the tax falls due, the repayment of tax is not due until nine months and a day after the accounting period in which the loan is actually repaid.

Regardless of when the loan was originally made, if it is wholly or partly written off or released, the borrower is treated as receiving, as part of his total income, an amount equal to the amount so written off, grossed up at the lower rate of income tax. While no basic or lower rate tax liability arises, there may be a further liability to higher rate tax.

17.13.3 Close investment-holding companies
(TA 1988, s 13A)

These are close companies carrying on specific investment-holding activities. For this purpose, investment-holding activities do not include carrying on a trade on a commercial basis, property holding, or holding shares in companies carrying on either of these activities. An exception to this rule is a company that exists wholly or mainly for holding property rented to connected persons.

A close investment-holding company does not qualify for the small companies corporation tax rate.

17.14 REAL ESTATE INVESTMENT TRUSTS (REITs)

REITs are in essence tax-transparent collective vehicles for investment in rental property. They have been available in other countries for a number of years. The concept of UK REITs emerged a few years ago. In the 2005 Budget it was announced that this vehicle would be available in the UK from 1 January 2007.

The broad rationale is that a REIT itself should be transparent for tax purposes. This means that no tax will be payable at the company level. Instead, tax will be payable by the shareholders – this will apply to both rental profits and capital gains.

However, a withholding tax of 22% applies to most distributions by a REIT to its investors. The main exceptions are where the investors are UK-resident companies or various exempt bodies.

Qualifying distributions received from a REIT are treated as rental income rather than dividends. This means that investors can use their personal allowances to mitigate any tax charge – which would have otherwise fallen on the company at a rate of 30%.

The legislation is aimed at companies that own property as a letting investment, rather than for property trading or development. There are detailed rules on this point, which split the business between qualifying and non-qualifying activities. Other rules for REITs are as follows:

- The shares in a REIT must be listed on a recognised stock exchange.
- There can be only one class of ordinary shares, and the only other permitted class of shares is non-participating fixed-rate preference shares.
- 75% of income and asset value must be attributed to property letting business. The asset value test is calculated on the first day of each accounting period.
- 90% of all profits of the property rental business must be distributed before the filing date of the tax return of the company.
- A REIT must own at least three rental properties.
- No one property must account for more than 40% of the total value of the properties.
- A REIT must have interest cover of at least 1.25:1. The ratio compares the taxable profits of the business before financing costs and capital allowances to the financing costs. Failure to meet this test results in a tax charge.

- If any distribution is payable to a shareholder who owns more than 10% of a REIT, this will crystallise a tax charge in the REIT. This is to reflect the intention that any shareholders of a REIT should not own more than 10%.

A failure to meet these rules will result in a range of penalties, depending on which test has been failed.

These penalties may include complete removal from the REIT regime at a later stage.

There is a tax charge on conversion of an existing company into a REIT. This is 2% of the market value of the properties at the time the company converts. It will be possible to spread this charge over four years in instalments of 0.5%, 0.53%, 0.56% and 0.6%.

17.15 CORPORATE VENTURING

Companies that subscribe for new ordinary shares in EIS-type companies (see 24.5 and 18.3.3) after 31 March 2000 may qualify for tax relief at 20% on the sum invested. This relief is dependent on the shares being retained for three years. The investment may also attract a capital gains deferral so that if the company invests £50,000 it may defer £50,000 of capital gains realised during the preceding three years or the following 12 months. These gains are then brought into charge as and when the company disposes of the shares or if the qualifying conditions are breached within a three-year period.

If all or part of the investment eventually has to be written off, the loss may be set against any of the company's profits for the year in which the loss is realised or the preceding accounting period.

The company in which the investment is made must meet basically the same tests as apply under the EIS (see 24.6), ie its gross assets must not exceed £7m before the investing company subscribes for its shares, nor exceed £8m after that subscription (£15m and £16m until 22 March 2006).

The investing company must not have more than 30% of the equity. Furthermore, at least 20% of its shares must be held by individuals.

17.16 RESEARCH AND DEVELOPMENT (R&D) TAX CREDITS

Small and medium-sized enterprises (SMEs) qualify for 150% relief on sums invested in R&D after 31 March 2000. If the company eventually pays the 30% corporation tax rate, this amounts to relief at an effective rate of 45%. An increase from 150% to 175% of the sums spent on R&D is expected to take effect from 1 April 2008 (subject to EU approval).

Furthermore, an SME can surrender its right to relief for a cash sum payable by the Treasury if it does not have sufficient profits to use the relief. A company paying corporation tax at the small companies rate can receive a cash sum equal to 24.5% of the amount invested subject to this not exceeding the amount paid over to the Revenue for PAYE and NICs during the year.

An SME is defined for these purposes as a company with less than 250 employees and turnover not exceeding €50 million or a balance sheet total of not more than €43 million. Other companies with fewer than 500 employees may be entitled to the SME relief as and when EU approval is given.

The company must spend at least £10,000 to qualify for the increased rate of relief.

FA 2002 introduced credits for companies that are not SMEs. Such companies have been able to obtain 125% relief for R&D expenditure. An increase to 130% is expected to take effect from 1 April 2008 (subject to EU approval).

17.16.1 Definition of research and development

After the research and development tax credit had been in place for several years, it was recognised that take-up of the credit had not been as large as the Government expected. This was thought to be due to the difficulty in establishing in advance whether or not a particular project qualified for relief. Without such certainty, the credit had little practical effect on corporate investment decisions.

The Revenue therefore carried out a consultation exercise and published guidelines on the meaning of R&D for tax purposes.

The significant points covered in the guidelines, which have applied since 1 April 2004, are:

- R&D for tax purposes takes place when a project seeks to achieve an advance in science or technology.
- All the individual activities that directly contribute to achieving this advance in science or technology through the resolution of scientific or technological uncertainty qualify as R&D.
- Certain indirect activities related to a qualifying project also qualify. Activities other than qualifying indirect activities that do not directly contribute to the resolution of scientific or technological uncertainty in a project do not qualify as R&D.

In addition, the definition of qualifying costs has been expanded by replacing the 'consumable stores' element of qualifying costs with the following:

- materials consumed or transformed;
- water and fuel (including electricity and gas);
- specially commissioned parts for prototypes;
- software bought specifically for the R&D work.

In arriving at qualifying staff costs, expenditure on the provision of benefits in kind to staff undertaking R&D work must be excluded.

17.17 ECA TAX CREDITS

Measures were introduced in the 2008 Budget that will allow loss-making companies carrying on a qualifying activity to surrender losses in exchange for a cash payment provided:

(1) the losses are attributable to 100% first-year allowances on designated energy-saving or environmentally beneficial plant and machinery;
(2) the losses cannot be otherwise relieved by the company; and
(3) the qualifying expenditure was incurred on or after the 1 April 2008.

The amount of the first-year tax credit that will be paid to the company will be equal to 19% of the losses being surrendered, although it cannot exceed the greater of:

(1) the total of the company's PAYE and NIC for the chargeable period; or
(2) £250,000.

Any first-year tax credit will be clawed back if the qualifying plant and machinery is sold within four years of the end of the period in which the first-year tax credit was paid.

The lists for designated energy-saving or environmentally beneficial plant and machinery can be found at www.eca.gov.uk.

17.18 TRANSFER PRICING RULES

UK transfer pricing tax rules are designed to prevent related parties that are subject to different levels of taxation from entering into uncommercial transactions to move profits into a lower level of taxation. From 1 April 2004 the scope of the transfer pricing rules has been extended to include UK-to-UK related party transactions. Previously, these rules only applied to cross-border transactions.

The change has been forced on the UK Government by recent decisions of the European Court of Justice (ECJ). In a number of cases the ECJ has judged that the UK rules were invalid because, by exempting UK-to-UK related party transactions, they were discriminatory under EC law.

This means that now, for tax purposes, all related party transactions that are not carried out on an 'arm's length' basis may trigger investigations and tax adjustments. However, for UK-to-UK transactions, the Revenue will allow a compensating reduction in the profits of a party to the transactions (ie if costs are disallowed for one party, the corresponding income should not be taxed in the other).

A penalty of up to 100% of any tax lost will apply if there has been fraud or negligence by a taxpayer in self-assessing whether or not a transfer pricing adjustment should be made on his tax return. However, as a transitional measure, there is to be a relaxation of the penalty provisions in respect of poor record keeping where a taxpayer has not maintained evidence of arm's length pricing for the period to 31 March 2006.

17.18.1 Related parties

Related parties can be companies, individuals, partnerships and trusts where a control relationship exists (ie one party controls the other). A transaction can be everything from a normal sale of goods to use of one party's assets or lending arrangements.

Fortunately, many small and medium-sized businesses will be exempt from the rules. The exemption applies to all related parties in the same control relationship (including entities based outside the UK) and is based on their combined number of employees and turnover. Small groups, those that have not more than 50 employees and either total turnover and/or total assets of no more than £10 million, will not need to self-assess.

Medium-sized groups, those with not more than 250 employees and either an annual turnover of less than €50 million or net assets of less than €43 million, should maintain records of relevant transactions. The Revenue has the power to require any medium-sized business to apply an arm's length price where there has been blatant manipulation of transaction prices leading to a significant loss of UK tax.

Businesses close to the limits should watch out for seasonal staffing increases as these count, pro rata, towards the annual limits. If the staffing limits are breached at any point during an account year, transactions during the whole account year are subject to the rules and documentation requirements.

Both exemptions do not apply if the transaction is with a party resident outside the UK, unless they are in a country with which the UK has a double tax treaty that includes a non-discrimination article (visit www.hmrc.gov.uk/ international/small-medium-ent.pdf to check the list of countries at 1 April 2004).

17.18.2 Keeping up to date

If your business carries out transactions with related parties, the first thing to establish is whether or not the small enterprise exemption applies. If not, then you will need to identify what related party transactions may not be on an arm's length basis and assess what records should be maintained. Only a higher level review may be needed if the medium-sized exemption applies, but detailed records and analysis will be needed if your business is part of a larger group.

17.19 CLAIMS, ELECTIONS AND PENALTIES

Throughout the Taxes Acts there are various claims for relief from corporation tax that must be lodged with the Revenue and, in practice, are made to the Inspector dealing with the company's affairs. Unless otherwise specified by legislation, claims must be made within six years of the end of the accounting period to which they relate. The most common claims and elections are set out below, together with the time limit by which the claim or election must be made. The Inspector does not generally have discretion to accept claims made after the time limit has expired for a particular claim unless the legislation (or Revenue practice) allows otherwise.

In practice, most claims are normally made in the CTSA return form CT600.

Claim	Time limit for submission	Reference
Trading losses offset against other income of accounting period	2 years	TA 1988, s 393A
Trading losses carried back	2 years	TA 1988, s 393A
Terminal loss relief	2 years	TA 1988, s 393A
Disclaimer of capital allowances	2 years	CAA 2001, s 56
Group relief	2 years	TA 1988, s 412
Roll-over relief	6 years	TCGA 1992, s 152
CGT rebasing at 31 March 1982	2 years after the end of the accounting period in which the first relevant disposal is made after 31 March 1988	TCGA 1992, s 35

17.19.1 Error and mistake relief claims

Relief may be claimed within the normal six-year time limit against any over-assessment to corporation tax because of an error or mistake in, or an omission from, any return or statement. No relief is due where the information was not used to form the basis of an assessment, or where the assessment was made in accordance with practice generally prevailing at the time of issue. An error or mistake claim under TMA 1970, s 33 should be made to the Revenue.

17.19.2 Penalties

- Failure to notify chargeability – penalty of up to 100% of the tax not paid 12 months after the end of the accounting period.
- Filing deadline – 12 months after accounting reference date – penalty for late filing £100 (£200 where more than three months late). These flat-rate penalties increase to £500 and £1,000 respectively for the third successive failure. In addition, where the tax return is more than six months late a tax-related penalty arises, which is 10% of any unpaid tax at the date the penalty is charged, rising to 20% if the return is more than 12 months late.
- Incorrect return – tax-related penalty not to exceed the amount of tax understated by the incorrect return. These flat-rate penalties increase to £500 and £1,000 respectively for the third successive failure. In addi-

tion, where the tax return is more than six months late a tax-related penalty arises, which is 10% of any unpaid tax at the date the penalty is charged, rising to 20% if the return is more than 12 months late.

- Failure to keep proper records – penalty £3,000.
- Failure to produce documents for an enquiry – penalty £50 plus a daily fine of up to £150.

18

FINANCING YOUR BUSINESS

This chapter sets out the tax consequences of various methods of financing a business. It deals with unincorporated business ventures (sole traders and partnerships, including limited liability partnerships) and incorporated (limited liability companies). Some of the areas covered in this chapter may be covered elsewhere in the book in greater detail, but this chapter consolidates these considerations under the following headings:

(1) Financing through own resources.
(2) Financing through personal borrowing.
(3) Issuing additional shares (with and without tax incentives).
(4) Borrowing through the business.
(5) Financing assets.
(6) Cash flow management.

18.1 FINANCING THROUGH OWN RESOURCES

18.1.1 Separate funding

The establishment of a partnership or the incorporation of a limited liability company allows an individual to separate and invest funds to provide capital for a business. In the case of a partnership, funds can be made available through contribution to a partner's capital account or the subscription of quotas. In the case of limited liability companies, funding can be made through subscription to newly issued share capital. The purchase of shares in a company from an existing shareholder or a partnership interest from an existing partner does not provide additional liquid funds to the company or partnership. Further capital can be subscribed as necessary to fund the growth of the business, through additional contributions to the partner's capital account, or subscription to quotas or additional share issues.

In the case of a sole trader, funds may be put into a separate business bank account but there is no formal separation of assets between the business and its owner.

The capital accounts of partners can be either interest-bearing or free of interest. The decision lies with the partners and will be reflected in the partnership deed. The payment of interest by a partnership to partners is treated as an allocation of partnership income to the specific partner and is to be included as partnership income of that partner for tax purposes.

Limited liability companies do not pay interest on funds that have been subscribed as share capital. Preference shares can be used to give a recurrent and fixed dividend on an equity base, with preference dividends paid out in priority to ordinary dividends. For UK tax on income and capital gains, preference dividends are treated in the same way as other dividends.

An individual who is a shareholder in a company can provide funds to the company by way of a loan as well as or instead of subscribing to shares. Such loan accounts fall within the loan relationship rules and the charge in the profit and loss account for any interest charged will normally be followed for tax purposes, subject to observing the conditions applicable to connected party transactions (see 17.5.5).

18.1.2 Losses on funding a sole trader's business

Because there is no effective separation of funds paid into the business, no specific relief is given for the loss of such funds. As with partnerships, relief for losses that have arisen and resulted in the failure of a business will be under the various headings of the tax legislation (see 6.7).

18.1.3 Losses on capital investments in partnerships

No specific income tax relief is given for losses of capital invested in a partnership. A partner's share of trading losses can be relieved against his other income (see 6.7). A capital loss may arise on an individual retiring from the firm if payment has been made to acquire the partnership interest.

18.1.4 Loss on shares
(TA 1988 s 574)

If an individual acquires shares in a company through subscribing to the shares and realises a loss on those shares, subject to meeting various conditions, the loss can be set off against the income of the individual for the year in which the loss is suffered or for the previous year. The conditions placed on this relief are given at 16.2.

A qualifying loss is calculated according to normal capital gains tax principles. A claim to set the loss off against income has to be made within one year from 31 January of the year following that in which the loss arose. A loss not so used can be carried forward as a loss for CGT purposes.

Normal CGT rules apply to losses on shares in companies when the shares have not been acquired through subscribing to the shares.

18.2 FINANCING THROUGH PERSONAL BORROWING

To be able to finance a business entirely from personal resources is a rare luxury; in most cases borrowing will be required. Such borrowing can be through the business itself (see 18.4), or drawn down personally by the individual. The form of security that has to be provided as a condition of the loan being made is not significant; whether the individual obtains tax relief on the interest depends on satisfying the conditions in the tax legislation.

18.2.1 Loans to invest in partnerships
(TA 88 s 362)

An individual can claim relief against income for interest paid on eligible loans (see 10.4). Conditions are that the loan is used:

(1) To purchase a share in a partnership; or
(2) To contribute capital to a partnership or to make an advance to a partnership where the advance is used wholly for the purposes of the trade profession or vocation carried on by the partnership; or
(3) To pay off another qualifying loan.

The borrower:

(1) Must be a member of the partnership throughout the period during which the interest expense arises.
(2) Must not have recovered any capital from the partnership since the loan has been drawn down.

18.2.2 Interest on loans to invest in companies
(TA 1988 s 360)

An individual can claim relief against income for interest paid on eligible loans (see 10.5). Conditions are:

(1) The loan is used to purchase shares in a close company; or
(2) The loan is used by a close company for its business purposes; or
(3) The loan is used to pay off another loan that would have qualified for relief.
(4) The individual alone or with associates owns a material interest in the close company (material interest being defined as more than 5% of the ordinary share capital of the company or the right to receive more than 5% of the assets of the company on a winding-up of the company); or
(5) The individual holds less than 5% of the ordinary share capital but works for the greater part of the time in the management or conduct of the company or an associated company.
(6) The company is a qualifying company.

Status as a qualifying company depends on the activity. The close company must exist wholly or mainly:

(1) To carry on a trade or trades on a commercial basis;
(2) To make investments in land or property let commercially to unconnected parties;
(3) To hold shares or securities or to make loans to qualifying companies or intermediate companies that are under the control of the company (qualifying meaning that the business of the company falls under one of the two headings immediately above);
(4) To co-ordinate the administration of two or more qualifying companies.

Relief for interest expense on a loan can continue if the company ceases to be close at a time after the loan has been drawn down provided that the other conditions continue to be satisfied.

18.2.3 Definition of close company
(TA 88 s 414)

A close company is a company that is under the control of five or fewer persons (see 17.13). Interests of associates are taken into account when testing.

18.2.4 Loans to invest in employee-controlled companies
(TA 88 s 361)

Interest on qualifying loans drawn down to acquire shares in companies controlled by employees can also qualify for relief. The excess of an individual's holding over 10% of the shares of the company is treated as being owned by a person who is not an employee of the company when testing whether the company is employee controlled, so this relief is likely to be of limited use when financing a business. For the conditions to be met for a qualifying loan, see 10.6.

18.3 ISSUING ADDITIONAL SHARES (WITH AND WITHOUT TAX INCENTIVES)

A limited liability company can obtain funds through the issue of additional share capital in return for cash payment. If the additional shares are placed through a rights issue, in which the share allocation is proportional to existing shareholdings, the company will only receive additional funds to the extent that the shareholders make payment for the new shares. The share subscription can be structured as an issue to new or existing shareholders, without specific tax advantages, or to qualify as an investment under the enterprise investment scheme, the venture capital trust scheme or the corporate venturing scheme.

In all cases, the effect of the share issue in diluting the ownership interests of existing shareholders will need to be considered.

18.3.1 Share issue without tax incentives

If the share issue is not to be structured to be a qualifying investment under a tax incentive scheme:

(1) The terms and conditions of the share issue and the amount of the issue are a decision for the owner and, if applicable, the other shareholders in the company.
(2) The shares taken up in return for the new investment will be an asset for capital gains tax purposes with gain or loss on disposal being calculated according to the rules of capital gains tax.
(3) Tax relief for interest paid on qualifying loans will be available subject to the required conditions being met; see 18.2.1 above; otherwise the issue will not attract tax relief or incentives.

Share issues to venture capitalists may be structured through venture capital trusts; see 18.3.6 below, or as an issue that does not attract tax relief in which case the above three points will apply.

18.3.2 Enterprise Investment Scheme (EIS)
(FA 1994 s 135 and Sched 14)

The Enterprise Investment Scheme (EIS) provides tax incentives for individuals to encourage investment in shares in companies that meet certain conditions and carry on qualifying activities. It is intended to help small, higher risk, unquoted trading companies raise start-up and expansion finance by issuing ordinary shares. The income tax relief for individuals is 20% on investments up to £500,000 in a tax year. The investment may also qualify for CGT deferral relief.

This section provides a summary of the conditions that have to be met for the investment to qualify and continue to qualify during the required holding period (see 24.5 for a more detailed analysis). The trade-off for the current shareholder or shareholders in the company is between the ability to access funds through the share issue (investors may not be prepared to make an investment in the absence of tax relief) and the continuing commitments (which are likely to be legally enforceable through the contractual obligations required by investors) for the company to continue to comply with the conditions.

18.3.3 EIS conditions relating to the company

For EIS to apply:

(1) The issue must be of new ordinary shares in the company; the shares cannot have preference features.
(2) The company cannot have assets of more than £7 million before the share issue and £8 million after the issue.
(3) The company (or group of companies) must have fewer than 50 full-time employees or their equivalents at the time the shares are issued.

(4) The company must have raised no more than £2 million under EIS or the Corporate Venturing Scheme or as a qualifying holding for a Venture Capital Trust (see below) in the 12 months ending on the date on which the investment is made. If the limit is exceeded, none of the shares within the issue that causes the limit to be breached will qualify for EIS.

(5) The company must be unquoted (although the shares of the company can be listed on the AIM) and there must be no arrangements under which the company can become quoted.

(6) The company cannot be under the control of another company, or another company and associated persons and there must be no arrangements under which it can come under such control.

(7) The company must not control another company unless that second company is a qualifying subsidiary (see 24.5.5 for the definition) and there must be no arrangements under which such control can be established.

(8) The company must be carrying on a qualifying trade (see 18.3.4).

The company will be expected to issue certificate EIS 3 to investors claiming relief, confirming that conditions have been met in respect of the issued shares. The conditions summarised above should clearly fall within the knowledge of the company's existing shareholders and/or management who, in addition to the issue of the certificate, will be expected to give a warranty that the conditions have been met.

18.3.4 Qualifying trades

Certain trades are excluded under s 297. The company's business must not consist to any substantial extent of any of the following:

(1) dealing in land, commodities or futures, or shares, securities or other financial instruments;

(2) dealing in goods otherwise than in the course of any ordinary trade of wholesale or retail distribution;

(3) banking, insurance (but not insurance broking), money-lending, debt-factoring, HP financing or other financial activities;

(4) oil extraction activities;

(5) leasing (except for certain short-term charters of ships) or receiving royalties or licence fees. A case was recently heard by the Special Commissioners concerning a medical company called Optos, which developed eye test machines that it leased to opticians. It was held that the company was excluded from EIS relief because of this leasing;

(6) providing legal or accountancy services;

(7) providing services or facilities for any trade carried on by another person (other than a parent company) that consists to any substantial extent of activities within any of (1)–(6) above and in which a controlling interest is held by a person who also has a controlling interest in the trade carried on by the company;

(8) any of the following property-backed activities:
  (a) farming and market gardening;
  (b) forestry and timber production;
  (c) property development;
  (d) operating or managing hotels or guest houses; and
  (e) operating or managing nursing or residential care homes.

Wholesale and retail distribution trades

Wholesale and retail distribution trades qualify only if they are 'ordinary' trades. Section 297(3) states that a trade does not qualify as an ordinary trade of wholesale or retail distribution if:

(1) it consists to a substantial extent of dealing in goods of a kind that are collected or held as an investment; and
(2) a substantial proportion of those goods are held by the company for a period that is significantly longer than the period for which a vendor would reasonably be expected to hold them while endeavouring to dispose of them at their market value.

The following are taken as indications that a company's trade is a qualifying trade:

(a) The trader buys the goods in quantities larger than those in which he sells them.
(b) The trader buys and sells the goods in different markets.
(c) The company incurs expenses in the trade in addition to the costs of the goods, and employs people who are not connected with it.

The following are 'indications' that the trade is not a qualifying trade:

(i) There are purchases or sales from or to persons who are connected with the trader.
(ii) Purchases are matched with forward sales or vice versa.
(iii) The trader holds the goods for longer than is normal for such goods.
(iv) The trade is carried on otherwise than at a place or places commonly used for the type of trade.
(v) The trader does not take physical possession of the goods.

The above are only indications and are not conclusive that a company's trade is or is not a qualifying trade, but it will be difficult to persuade the Revenue that a trade qualifies if there are several indications to the contrary.

18.3.5 EIS conditions relating to the individual investor

EIS income tax relief is denied if the investor is connected with the company. This means that the individual alone or with associated parties possesses directly or indirectly more than 30% of:

(1) The share capital of the company or any of its subsidiaries.
(2) Loan capital of the company or any of its subsidiaries.
(3) Voting power in the company or any of its subsidiaries; or
(4) Rights that would give entitlement to more than 30% of assets available for distribution to shareholders in the event of the company being wound up.

While the more-than-30% test can be monitored by the company in respect of investment or rights of an individual investor, knowledge of which persons are to be treated as associated may go beyond what the existing shareholders and/or management of the company might be expected to know.

EIS income tax relief is also denied if the individual has been previously connected with the company within the two years before the issue of the EIS shares. 'Connected' in this sense means an individual who is or was:

(1) A paid director of the company or any of its subsidiaries.
(2) An employee of the company or any of its subsidiaries.
(3) A partner of the company or any of its subsidiaries.
(4) An associate of a person falling into any of these categories.

Again, while the company can be expected to have knowledge of an individual falling into any of the categories, knowledge of the associated persons may go beyond what the existing shareholders and/or management of the company might be expected to know.

18.3.6 EIS – withdrawal of relief

As detailed in 24.5, the EIS relief is withdrawn where:

(1) The company redeems share capital.
(2) The investor receives value from the company.
(3) The company ceases to be a qualifying company.
(4) The investor becomes connected with the company (withdrawal of the income tax relief).
(5) The investor disposes of the share within a three-year period (withdrawal of the income tax relief).

With the exception of the last heading, the other grounds for the withdrawal of relief should lie within the knowledge of the company's existing shareholders and/or management.

18.3.7 Venture Capital Trusts
(TA 1988 s 842 and Sched 28)

Venture Capital Trusts (VCTs) are companies that are quoted on the London Stock Exchange and derive value from investment in shares or securities. The requirements for qualification as a VCT are set out in 24.6.

At least 70% by value of the investments made by a VCT must consist of shares or securities in qualifying holdings, defined as holdings in unquoted companies that exist wholly for the purpose of carrying on one or more qualifying trades, wholly or mainly in the UK. Cash proceeds from disposals are ignored for 6 months when applying the 70% test. Qualifying trade is defined as for the EIS. The assets of the unquoted company must not exceed £7 million before the share issue and £8 million after the share issue. The company in which the investment is made must not have raised more than £2 million under EIS, the VCT legislation or the Corporate Venturing Scheme in the 12 months ending on the date on which the investment is made. If the limit is exceeded, no part of the investment that causes the limit to be breached will count as a qualifying investment for a VCT.

An individual investor in a VCT obtains income tax relief at 30% on subscription for new ordinary shares in the VCT not exceeding £200,000.

The investor also benefits from income tax relief on dividends paid on shares in a VCT to the extent that the shares acquired each year do not exceed £200,000 in value.

The minimum period for which VCT investors must hold their shares is five years.

The trade-off for the current shareholder or shareholders in the company seeking finance is between the ability to access funds through the share issue to the VCT (investors may not be prepared to make an investment in the absence of tax relief) and the continuing commitment (which is likely to be legally enforceable through the contractual obligations) for the company to continue to comply with the conditions for the relief to be obtained.

18.3.8 Corporate Venturing Scheme (CVS)
(FA 2000 S63 and Sched 15)

The Corporate Venturing Scheme (CVS) provides tax incentives for companies to encourage investment in shares in other companies meeting certain conditions and carrying on qualifying activities (see 17.15). Requirements for the investing company are that:

(1) It does not have a material interest in the issuing company at any time during the qualifying period (three years); a material interest is present if the investing company possesses directly or indirectly or is entitled to acquire more than 30% of the ordinary share capital of or voting power in the issuing company.
(2) It is not party to reciprocal arrangements with the issuing company.
(3) It does not control the issuing company at any time during the qualifying period.
(4) It is carrying on a non-financial trade.
(5) It holds the shares in the issuing company as a chargeable asset.
(6) The share issue is not tax avoidance.

At the time of issue, the issuing company must be unquoted and there can be no arrangements for it to become quoted. Gross assets of the issuing company must not exceed £7 million before the issue and £8 million immediately afterwards. The company in which the investment is made must not have raised more than £2 million under EIS, the VCT legislation or the CVS in the 12 months ending on the date on which the investment is made. If the limit is exceeded, no part of the issue of shares that causes the limit to be broken will qualify under the CVS.

Requirements to be met during the qualifying period for the issuing company are that:

(1) It is independent in the sense of not being a 51% subsidiary of another company or under the control of another company.
(2) At least 20% of the share capital is owned by one or more independent individuals.
(3) It is not a member of a partnership or a joint venture.
(4) It has no subsidiaries that are not qualifying subsidiaries and no property management subsidiaries that are not at least 90% owned.
(5) It is carrying on a qualifying trade.

Qualifying trade is defined as for the EIS scheme (see 18.3.4).

The trade-off for the current shareholder or shareholders in the company seeking finance is between the ability to access funds through the CVS (investors may not be prepared to make an investment in the absence of tax relief) and the continuing commitment (which is likely to be legally enforceable through the contractual obligations) for the company to continue to comply with the conditions for the relief to be obtained.

18.4 BORROWING THROUGH THE BUSINESS

As a business develops, its actual and projected cash flows and the assets it owns may allow it to borrow funds in its own right. As with other forms of borrowings discussed in this chapter, the deductibility of interest expense depends on satisfaction of the conditions in the tax legislation and not on the form of security given for the borrowings.

18.4.1 Loans to unincorporated businesses

Interest paid by a sole trader or partnership (as opposed to a partner in a personal capacity) and incurred wholly and exclusively for the purposes of the business can be claimed as a deduction in computing the profits of the business.

A deduction for tax is also available for costs of raising finance when these costs:

(1) were incurred wholly and exclusively for the purposes of obtaining loan finance, providing security or repaying a loan; and
(2) represented expenditure on professional fees, commissions, advertising, printing or other incidental expenses in relation to raising finance.

18.4.2 Corporate loan relationships

Since 1996, the treatment of interest expense incurred by companies for tax has depended on the loan relationship legislation; see 17.5. The legislation applies to all UK resident companies and UK branches of non UK resident companies. Loan relationships arise when:

(1) A company is a debtor or creditor in respect of a money debt and the debt arose as a result of a transaction for the lending of money; or
(2) An instrument is issued for the purpose of representing security for, or the rights of a creditor in respect of, a money debt.

In general, the tax treatment follows the accounting treatment with the expenditure on interest being allowed in the year that it is charged to the profit and loss account of the company. If the interest is payable to a connected party, a deduction for interest accrued in the accounts is only allowed where the recipient is chargeable to UK tax on the interest income or the interest is paid within 12 months of the end of the accounting period. If the 12-month limit is not met, a deduction is only allowed when the interest is actually paid (see 17.5).

18.5 FINANCING ASSETS

As a business expands, it usually will need access to more assets. Possibilities are that the assets are financed outside the business and made available to the business or that the business itself acquires the assets.

18.5.1 Loans to purchase assets

A decision to provide an asset to a business through personal funding may result from an individual having better access to credit than the business itself. There can also be efficiencies, for instance a building needed by the business owned by an individual offers the possibility of long-term capital appreciation and, if so, the possibility of realisation with one layer of tax rather than two if the property were owned by a limited liability company. Taper relief may be available to reduce the eventual gain on disposal. A property may also be a suitable investment for a self-administered pension scheme.

An asset acquired personally and let or leased to a business may attract capital allowances, depending, according to the heading under which the allowances are claimed, on the nature of the asset and demonstration that the asset is used for a qualifying activity. Capital allowances are first set off against the income generated from the asset.

As the investor and the business are likely to be connected, care will have to be taken to ensure that the terms of the transaction are justifiable as arm's length, defined as being the terms that would have been agreed in the absence of such a connection.

18.5.2 Interest on loan to acquire property

Generally, interest expense on a loan drawn down by an individual for the purchase of a property to be let to a business will attract tax relief, through set-off against the rental income received.

18.5.3 Loans drawn down by a partner
(TA 88 s 359)

A partner can claim a deduction for interest paid on a loan drawn down to finance capital expenditure on the provision of plant and machinery for the purposes of the business of the partnership. The relief is available in the year in which the loan is drawn down and the following three years.

18.5.4 Purchase of assets by business

If the business draws down a loan to finance the purchase of an asset, interest deductibility will depend on the loan relationship legislation (see 18.4.2 and 17.5).

Depreciation on fixed assets charged in the profit and loss account of a business is disallowed and added back when calculating the taxable profit. If the asset qualifies, capital expenditure will qualify for capital allowances under various headings (see 15.2). The rates of capital allowances vary and not all fixed assets will qualify for capital allowances. For tax purposes, the deductions in respect of the purchase of intangible assets generally follow the charge in the accounts of the business.

18.5.5 Leasing of assets by business

Leasing is another method for a business to obtain assets. A substantial volume of asset leasing business is written annually. In many cases, leasing is provided by the manufacturers or suppliers of assets, for example office machinery such as computer equipment and copiers, but leasing possibilities also exist for major fixed assets. The lessor is often a subsidiary of a financial institution and the cost of the lease reflects the ability to reduce taxable profits of the company itself and through group relief the profits of associated companies by the capital allowances available.

Accounting treatment of leased assets varies as to whether the lease is an operating or a financial lease. An operating lease is for a period that is less that the asset's anticipated useful life, a financial lease is written for a period that effectively equates to the expected life of an asset. When testing to determine the category of the lease transaction, an arrangement in which the net present value of the rentals is 90% or greater than the value of the asset will be treated as a finance lease.

Lease rentals under an operating lease are charged to the profit and loss account as incurred and a corresponding deduction is given when calculating taxable income of the business.

To ensure that the accounts give an accurate picture of the resources and obligations of a business, a finance-lease transaction is capitalised on the balance sheet, entries reflecting the purchase of the rights to use and enjoy the asset and the requirement to make future payments. The rental payments are apportioned between a finance charge and a reduction of the obligation to make future payments. The tax deduction in respect of payments under a finance lease is normally the amount charged to the profit and loss account in that period in respect of the finance lease. However, the tax treatment of long funding leases entered into after 1 April 2006 has been changed and the lessee may now be entitled to capital allowances (see 15.1.6).

If the lease is for a major asset, the lessee is usually required to enter into a contractual commitment to make good any reduction in the tax benefit to the lessor of the capital allowances on the leased asset through a change in tax legislation, including a reduction in the rates of tax.

18.5.6 Lease/buy analysis

When carrying out a lease/buy analysis to determine the optimum method of acquiring assets for the business, the cash flows under each of the two cases will have to be set out for the expected period of use of the asset, or a period of, say, five or ten years, if considered more appropriate to the circumstances and forecasting pattern of the business. The cash flows will include the tax effects, in the purchase case the reduction in tax for the interest costs and the capital allowances received on the asset and, in the lease case, the reduction in tax through the lease rental payments allowed for tax. Tax is only one consideration: the real point in preparing the cash flows is to ensure that the business will be able to meet the obligations under the chosen route. The effect on the profit and loss account of each route should also be determined so that a well informed decision can be taken.

18.5.7 Sale and leaseback

A business can seek to raise finance for current expenditure through selling an asset and leasing it back. This arrangement may be particularly useful if the business has an asset or series of assets that would fit within a specialist activity of the buyer. An example would be a business that sells a portfolio of properties to a pension fund or property company.

The tax effects of the disposal of the asset will need to be calculated in advance of the decision being taken. While the tax effects of the purchase is a matter for the purchaser, there are certain situations in which the capital allowances on the purchased asset will be restricted.

18.5.8 Hire purchase

When an asset is bought on hire purchase, the purchaser is entitled to capital allowances on the full purchase price from the beginning of the contract, although this sum is going to be paid by instalments. The interest element of the periodic payments charged to the profit and loss account is allowable as a tax deduction in the year when it is so charged.

18.6 CASH FLOW MANAGEMENT

Managing cash flow prudently for a growing business requires the owner/managers to avoid circumstances in which tax liabilities bear heavily on cash flow. It should also involve accelerating tax deductions wherever possible. Three points are worth noting.

18.6.1 Cash basis for VAT

Using the cash basis for VAT means that the output VAT due on invoices issued to customers does not have to be accounted for to HMRC before the money has been received from the customer. The business owner should review the turnover limits to determine whether the scheme will apply.

18.6.2 Research and development

There are specific incentives to encourage research and development, which has a wide definition. The business owner should review activity to determine whether these incentives will apply.

18.6.3 Capital expenditure

Capital expenditure incurred by the business should be reviewed to allocate as much as possible to assets qualifying for capital allowances. Although deferred tax may have to be provided on the difference between the written down values for book and tax, it is an accounting entry and not a cash movement.

19

SHOULD YOU OPERATE THROUGH A COMPANY?

There is no simple answer to this question. There are both advantages and disadvantages in carrying on business through a limited company rather than operating as an unincorporated business. Some of the considerations arise from commercial rather than tax aspects. Limited liability may be an important consideration, either for the business's proprietors or to attract finance from an outside investor. However, the apparent protection given by limited liability is often illusory because banks or other lending institutions normally require personal guarantees from directors for any bank loans made to the company. Furthermore, if limitation of liability is the main concern, you may find that having an LLP (Limited Liability Partnership) gives you the best of both worlds.

This chapter covers:

(1) Tax advantages of having a company.
(2) Possible disadvantages.
(3) Capital gains tax and IHT considerations.
(4) Limited liability partnerships (LLPs).
(5) Transferring existing business to a company or an LLP.

19.1 TAX ADVANTAGES OF HAVING A COMPANY

19.1.1 Lower rate of tax on profits

Having a company means that a lower rate of tax will apply to retained profits. The small companies rate of 21% applies to profits up to £300,000 provided there are no associated companies. If there are associated companies, the threshold at which profits attract tax at either the normal 28% rate or the marginal small companies rate is reduced. If there are no associated companies, the small companies rate can produce a very substantial saving, although the 1% increase proposed for the next financial year will eat into this.

Example – Tax saving through incorporation in 2008–09

	£
Unincorporated business	
Profits	450,000
Tax and NICs (assuming single personal allowance)	177,613
Incorporated business	£
Profits before director's remuneration	450,000
Less: director's remuneration and NICs, say	(150,000)
	300,000
Corporation tax at 21%	63,000
Tax and NICs on director's remuneration	65,576
Total tax and NICs on profits of £450,000	128,576
Annual saving in tax through operating via a company	49,037

Some of this saving may have to be handed back as and when the retained profits are extracted from the company as dividends, which attract higher rate tax.

19.1.2 Other tax considerations

Timing difference

There is a useful timing difference where a business is carried on through a company in that remuneration can be deducted from the company's profits even though it is not paid (and is not taxable income of the individuals until it is paid). Provided the remuneration is actually paid within nine months of the company's year end, the company is normally entitled to a deduction in arriving at its profits.

Example – Timing of tax payments

If a company draws up accounts to 31 March 2009, it may secure a deduction for director's remuneration of £150,000 even though the remuneration is not paid until 31 December 2009, in which case PAYE does not have to be paid over until 14 January 2010. Contrast this with an unincorporated business where tax needs to be paid on account on 31 January 2009 and on 31 July 2009, with a balancing payment on the following 31 January.

Pension contributions

With the introduction of the new regime for registered pension schemes, there is no longer any great advantage in having a company.

Payment of remuneration may prevent personal allowances going to waste

Where an unincorporated business operates at a loss, and the individuals have no other private income, the benefit of their personal allowances is lost forever. By trading through a company, it is possible to vote remuneration equal to their personal allowances and the remuneration voted in this way will increase the amount of the company's loss that can be carried forward and set against subsequent profits.

Certain reliefs are only available to companies

Companies can qualify for R&D and ECA tax credits (see 17.16 and 17.17) and get allowances for expenditure on intangibles (see 17.6). These reliefs are not available to unincorporated businesses.

19.2 POSSIBLE DISADVANTAGES

Possible disadvantages of operating through a company include the following:

19.2.1 Extra administration

There are more statutory requirements concerning book-keeping, filing annual accounts, disclosure, etc. An unincorporated business does not normally need to file annual accounts at all, whereas a company must file accounts with Companies House and make an annual return.

19.2.2 IR35 regulations

Some companies may fall foul of the regulations on personal service companies (see 20.3).

19.2.3 Admitting future partners

If profits are retained, this may make it increasingly difficult for individuals who come up through the business to become shareholder directors. For example, if a company has 100 £1 shares in issue and retains profits after tax of £15,000 pa for ten years, each share will be worth £1,500 more at the end of the ten years than at the start of the period. For an individual to acquire a 10% shareholding, he must find sufficient finance to purchase shares that reflect this. The problem does not arise in the case of a partnership, since the normal procedure is to allocate past profits to partners' capital accounts and then admit a partner on the basis that he would share in future profits at a specified percentage.

19.2.4 Tax savings may only be a deferment

The traditional analysis has been that tax generally becomes payable by the shareholders on their share of retained profits, either when they sell their shares and realise a capital gain, or as and when they extract retained profits by taking a dividend. On this analysis, the tax saving on retained profits is often little more than a deferment of tax. This is not really the end of the story as there can be a true saving because of the difference between the 18% CGT rate and the higher rates of tax payable on income. However, the saving can be less than may seem to be the case. For example, an unincorporated trader may pay tax at an effective rate of 41% on the £100,000 top slice of his earnings (40% income tax and 1% NIC). If those profits accrued to a company that paid the full rate of corporation tax, the company would retain £72,000. If the trader eventually realised his shares, he might pay 18% capital gains tax on this £72,000 and end up with around £59,000. Much of the saving is really dependent on the company paying tax at only the small companies rate.

19.2.5 Increased liability for NICs

A company must pay Class 1 NICs on all amounts paid as remuneration. There is no ceiling such as applies to the employees' own contributions. This can give rise to a substantially increased burden for a company as compared with an unincorporated business. Comparing an unincorporated business owned by four equal partners with a company that had four 25% shareholders (and it is assumed that in both cases the individuals had income of £75,000 each), the national insurance bill for 2008–09 is as follows:

	Partnership £		*Company* £
Class 2	476	Employees' Class 1 (not-contracted-out)	16,628
Class 4	12,472	Employer's contributions	38,400
	12,948		55,028

While the benefits payable to employees are better than those received by the self-employed (a larger pension because of S2P and entitlement to unemployment benefit), the higher NIC costs can be a very expensive way of financing such benefits.

19.2.6 Work in progress

In principle, a professional firm should not include partner time in arriving at the cost of work in progress. This means the figure brought into account should be lower because of this. However, if a business is carried on by a company, time put in by a director should be included when valuing work in progress.

19.2.7 Treatment of wives' earnings

If a wife is a partner in an unincorporated business, the Revenue is less likely to dispute the level of profits allocated to her. In this regard, unincorporated businesses are treated more favourably than companies where the Revenue regularly argues that a wife's remuneration is excessive and part of the remuneration should be disallowed in computing profits.

SHOULD YOU OPERATE THROUGH A COMPANY?

19.3 CAPITAL GAINS TAX AND IHT CONSIDERATIONS

19.3.1 Potential double charge for capital gains

Where a valuable asset is held within a company, a tax liability may arise at two stages before the shareholders can enjoy the sale proceeds. For example, if a company acquired a property at a cost of £100,000, and five years later it is worth £550,000, there might be a gain for the company (after indexation) of £400,000. The company will pay tax on this capital gain either at the marginal small companies rate of 29.75% or the full rate of 28%. The company will have net funds available after paying tax of £338,000, as here:

	£
Profits for accounting purposes	450,000
Less: tax on gain (£400,000 at 28%)	112,000
	338,000

If the company is then wound up and the cash distributed to the shareholders, they are likely to have a personal CGT liability on the £330,000. The maximum CGT payable by them could be £60,840 (ie £338,000 at 18%). This latter figure assumes that other assets and retained profits within the company are such that there would have been capital gains for the shareholders in any event, even if the company had not held the property concerned.

While it is not generally good policy to have appreciating assets within a company, the extent of the extra tax payable is not as great as it was in the past. While some additional tax is likely to be payable if an appreciating asset is held within a company, this is not an argument in itself against a business operating through a company. Correctly analysed, the treatment of capital gains within a company is an argument in favour of shareholder directors holding such assets in their personal capacity rather than through a company.

19.3.2 Property owned privately but used by a company

Where shareholder directors own a property used by their trading company, roll-over relief (see 16.3) should be available if they sell the property and buy another property for use by the same company.

If shareholder directors need to take a loan to buy property, they can secure relief on the interest by charging rent. Doing this will not prejudice roll-over relief but it will mean that CGT entrepreneurs relief may not be available on an eventual sale of the property (this relief is not available if the individuals have charged a market rent).

19.3.3 Inheritance tax

Where a partner owns a property that is used by the firm, he will generally qualify for 50% business property relief.

Where a controlling shareholder owns a property that is used by a trading company, he will also qualify for 50% business property relief. But no BPR is available for non-controlling shareholders who own a property used by the company. From this point of view, it is better for the property to be owned by the company because 100% business property relief will generally be due for all shareholders, controlling and non-controlling.

19.4 LIMITED LIABILITY PARTNERSHIPS (LLPs)

An option that should be borne in mind is to operate through an LLP (see 6.5). These are treated as companies for company law (and for VAT) purposes but are taxed as partnerships. Using an LLP means you can limit your personal liability towards customers, etc, while keeping the tax treatment that applies to partnerships.

19.5 TRANSFERRING EXISTING BUSINESS TO A COMPANY OR LLP

19.5.1 Transferring to a company

Some care is necessary when transferring a business to ensure that no CGT charge arises. Fortunately there is a special CGT relief intended to cover this (see 16.6). See also Chapter 38 re stamp duty. The VAT consequences should also be explored but in most cases the transfer of the business will be treated as a transfer of a going concern.

The timing of the transfer may be important. Bear in mind that if you were carrying on your unincorporated business in 1997–98, transferring it to a company may enable you to utilise your transitional relief (see 6.3.6). If your future employment income is expected to be much lower than your current self-employed profits, consider applying for a reduction in your payments on account (see 2.1.3).

If you have substantial qualifying loans used to put money into a partnership, you should take advice. But a Revenue concession will cover most situations (see 10.4.4).

See *Tax Bulletin* May 2005 regarding the tax implications if the Revenue challenges a sale of goodwill as being at an over-value. The Revenue is likely to tax the over-value as a distribution (see 8.9.6).

19.5.2 Transferring to an LLP

Transferring an existing unincorporated business to an LLP does not normally involve a disposal for CGT purposes or a cessation of your self-employed business for income tax purposes. Remember to keep your VAT office advised.

20

DEDUCTING TAX AT SOURCE AND PAYING IT OVER TO HMRC

PATRICIA GOLDIE

This chapter outlines the requirements imposed by law on employers, etc, to act as unpaid tax collectors on the Treasury's behalf. If you are caught up in this, the administrative burden can be onerous and the penalties for non-compliance severe.

The chapter covers the following:

(1) Employers.
(2) Contractors.
(3) IR35.
(4) Managed service companies.
(5) Non-resident landlord scheme.
(6) Payments to non-resident sportsmen and entertainers.
(7) Other payments to non-UK resident persons.

20.1 EMPLOYERS

An employer has an obligation to collect tax and national insurance contributions (NICs) and to operate the following schemes on HMRC's behalf in respect of the following payments:

- Pay As You Earn (PAYE)/NICs;
- Student loans.

20.1.1 Payment of PAYE to HMRC

Employers are required to withhold tax under PAYE and deduct Class 1 primary (employee's) and secondary (employer's) NICs and pay them over to HMRC each month. If the total PAYE and NIC deductions do not normally exceed £1,500 pm, the employer can account for the tax and NIC deductions quarterly. The £1,500 pm is inclusive of sums collected under the Student Loans Scheme. At the end of the year, the employer must give employees form P60 (by 31 May) showing the tax and NIC withheld from their earnings.

20.1.2 Emoluments subject to PAYE

All payments of 'emoluments' by a UK-resident employer to directors and employees are subject to PAYE. Emoluments are cash payments (salary, wages, bonus, etc) other than expense payments. *The Employer's Guide* lists the following payments as emoluments that are subject to PAYE:

- salary;
- wages;
- fees;
- overtime;
- bonus;
- commission;
- pension;
- honoraria;
- pay during sickness or other absence from work;
- holiday pay;
- Christmas boxes in cash;
- employee's income tax borne by his employer;
- payments for the cost of travelling between the employee's home and his normal place of employment;
- payments for time spent in travelling;
- cash payments for meals;
- payments in lieu of benefits-in-kind;
- certain lump sum payments made on retirement or removal from employment;
- certain sums received from the trustees of approved profit-sharing schemes;
- gratuities or service charges paid out by the employer.

As stated in the *Employer's Guide*, PAYE cannot be deducted from the following benefits even though they are regarded as taxable income of the employment:

- living accommodation provided rent free or at a reduced rent;
- gifts in kind (unless seasonal gifts considered to be minor and trivial such as Christmas turkeys, bottle of wine, etc.);
- luncheon vouchers in excess of 15p per day;
- employee's liabilities borne by the employer (even though such payments are earnings for NICs purposes) if payment is made direct to the supplier, eg school fees paid direct to the school, but under a contract between the employee and the school.

The PAYE legislation requires employers to account for PAYE when they pay staff in 'readily convertible assets' (eg gold bars, commodities, fine wine or diamonds) or with non-marketable assets where the employer has made arrangements for the employee to convert them into cash. The term 'readily convertible asset' (RCA) includes (but is not limited to):

(1) money debts;
(2) property subject to a warehousing or fiscal warehousing regime;
(3) assets that give rise to cash without the employee taking any action; and
(4) assets for which trading arrangements come into existence in accordance with other arrangements or an understanding that is in place when the assets were provided to the employee.

PAYE may also have to be accounted for on gifts of shares in the employing company or profits realised on the exercise of non-approved share options (see 5.3).

National insurance contributions

The PAYE and NICs rules have largely been aligned since 6 April 1999 and it is now unusual for a payment or benefit to be taxable as employment income but not subject to NICs. See Chapter 22.

20.1.3 Anti-avoidance of PAYE and NICs

In 1997, the PAYE legislation was amended to deal with assignments of trade debts by employers to their employees. The legislation referred to 'tradable assets' and treated such assets as if they were cash payments.

The term 'tradable assets' was subsequently replaced by 'readily convertible assets': these include assets listed in (1)–(4) in 20.1.2 above.

If an employee becomes liable to income tax on employment income on the exercise, assignment or release of an option for shares that are readily convertible assets, these provisions require the employer to operate PAYE. Similarly, PAYE will apply if the employee is rewarded by the enhancement of a readily convertible asset that he already owns. PAYE must be operated on a reasonable estimate of the amount likely to be charged to tax as employment income. Similar rules were also introduced for NICs.

20.1.4 Payment in shares

Background

Sections 698 to 702, Chapter 4 Part II of IT(E&P)A 2003 provide more guidance on PAYE on securities, PAYE on options and the meaning of 'readily convertible assets'. The guidance states that employers must account for tax under PAYE whenever an employee is provided with assessable income in the form of readily convertible assets.

Shares in an employer or company that controls the employer are not caught by this legislation if they are acquired through the exercise of options granted before 27 November 1996 or if they are acquired under a HMRC-approved share scheme (see 22.1.4 for an exception to this where approved options are exercised after 8 April 2003 in circumstances which give rise to an income tax charge).

All other cases where employees acquire shares will be subject to the rules on readily convertible assets. The meaning of readily convertible assets is provided by s 702 IT(E&P)A 2003. There are ten possibilities to consider when determining whether an asset is a readily convertible asset and only one needs to be satisfied. They are:

(a) an asset capable of being sold or otherwise realised on a recognised investment exchange;

(b) an asset capable of being sold or otherwise realised on the London Bullion Market;

(c) an asset being capable of being sold or otherwise realised on the New York Stock Exchange;

(d) an asset capable of being sold or otherwise realised for the time being specified in PAYE regulations;

(e) an asset consisting in the rights of an assignee, or any other rights, in respect of a money debt that is or may become due to the employer or any other person;

(f) an asset consisting in property that is subject to a warehouse regime, or any right in respect of property so subject;

(g) an asset consisting in anything that is likely (without anything being done by the employee) to give rise to, or to become, a right enabling a person to obtain an amount or total amount of money that is likely to be similar to the expense incurred in the provision of the asset;

(h) an asset for which trading arrangements are in existence, or are likely to come into existence in accordance with any arrangements of another description existing when the asset is provided;

(i) an asset for which trading arrangements are in existence, or are likely to come into existence in accordance with any understanding existing when the asset is provided; and

(j) an asset consisting in securities, which is not a readily convertible asset under (a) to (i), is to be treated as a readily convertible asset unless the securities are shares that are corporation tax deductible.

HMRC guidance

HMRC's *Employment Related Securities Manual* provides some examples of the tests applied in deciding whether an asset is a readily convertible asset.

Example 1 – existing trading arrangements

Ted's employer is the UK subsidiary of a French company quoted on the Paris stock exchange (not a recognised investment exchange, or RIE). Ted is awarded 1,000 shares in the parent company at a 25% discount on their £10 market value. There are no restrictions on sale.

There is a charge to income tax as earnings in respect of the money's worth to Ted of £2,500. Because the shares can be sold on an exchange, although not one that is an RIE, trading arrangements exist at the time of the award and the employer should operate PAYE and account for NIC.

Example 2 – understanding about future trading arrangements

Wendy's UK employer is not a subsidiary of any other company and is not quoted on any market. The employer gives Wendy 1,000 shares worth £5 each, as a part of her remuneration. The employer undertakes to buy the shares from Wendy at any time while she remains an employee, but only after a six-month qualifying period. There are no other conditions attached to the shares. Wendy is free to sell them, although in fact she is unlikely to find anyone prepared to buy them because the company is not listed.

The entitlement to shares represents money's worth to Wendy and there is a money's worth charge on £5,000. There are no trading arrangements at the time of the award, because the shares cannot be sold as there is no market, but there is an understanding that it is likely that the shares can be sold in the future. This satisfies subsection (i) above and the employer must operate PAYE and account for NICs.

Example 3 – corporation tax deductible shares

Bill is a manager of a small family-owned company, not being a subsidiary of any other company. He is offered the opportunity to buy 1,000 shares at par value of £1 each, but there is no market in the shares and no arrangements for repurchasing them. There is a standard pre-emption article in the Articles of Association that anyone selling shares has first to offer them to other shareholders, but there is no obligation for those other shareholders to purchase them. Shares Valuation agrees there is a money's worth value on the shares of £2,000.

There is a charge to income tax as earnings in respect of the money's worth of £1,000 to Bill (£2,000 less £1,000 paid). There are no trading arrangements that would make the shares RCAs. The charge of £1,000 on Bill will be a deductible expense to the employing company under Schedule 23 FA 2003 so the additional deeming provision in (j) above will not treat the shares as RCAs. No PAYE or NIC will be payable by the employer and Bill will pay income tax under self-assessment.

Source: HMRC

Amount on which PAYE should be operated

In simple terms, when an employer gives an employee shares for free or for less than their market value, then the amount chargeable as earnings is the difference between their market value and what the individual paid for the shares.

Refund of PAYE by employee to employer

Because the acquisition of shares is only a notional payment (the employee does not actually receive any cash) the employee may not have sufficient funds in the pay period from which the employer can deduct PAYE. The employer is therefore required to pay over to HMRC the amount he is unable to deduct. If the employee does not make good this amount to the employer within 90 days of the chargeable event (the date the individual acquires the shares) then s 222 IT(E&P)A 2003 imposes a charge to income tax on the employee.

This charge will still apply even if the employee makes good the relevant amount after the 90 days.

Payments to surrender options

FA 1998 imposed an obligation for an employer to account for PAYE where employees received a cash sum in return for surrendering options over shares that are readily convertible assets.

20.1.5 Payments to agency workers

Where the services of an individual are provided to a trader through an agency, and the manner in which he performs his work is controlled and supervised as if he were an employee, Part 2 Chapter 7 of IT(E&P)A 2003 requires the trader to operate PAYE.

There are situations where HMRC regards payments to a 'one man' company as caught by this provision so that the person paying the money to the company should deduct PAYE as if he had made payments to the individual worker concerned. This is increasingly relevant as many employers use service contracts to reduce their overheads and maximise benefits available to the worker. HMRC, however, is likely to apply the same criteria to payments made in such circumstances as those they apply to the self-employed, as covered in detail in 6.2.2.

20.1.6 Failure to operate PAYE

An employer who fails to operate PAYE (and deduct NICs) takes a substantial risk. The primary liability to account for the tax rests with the employer and the scope of PAYE does not extend simply to deducting tax from an employee's gross pay and remitting it to HMRC. Instead, an employer must remember that PAYE can also apply to all forms of casual labour, which may or may not be paid through the payroll, and to individuals considered to be self-employed (see 6.2).

Another area frequently overlooked is expenses (see 4.4.1) that constitute part of an employee's emoluments and accordingly fall within the scope of PAYE. While genuine business expenses incurred wholly, exclusively and necessarily in the course of an employee's duties may qualify for a tax deduction, there remain several areas where employers are required to operate PAYE and deduct NICs. These include the payment of all-round sum allowances that have not been approved by the Inspector in the form of a dispensation, and the payment of unauthorised or unvouched expenses. Even the payment of travel expenses may not be permitted tax free in circumstances where the place visited is deemed to be the permanent place of work. As an example, an employee living in London and permanently working on a site in Aberdeen will be taxed on all his expenses for travel between London and Aberdeen. This shows that special attention must be paid to such payments and the circumstances surrounding them. HMRC's booklet 490, Employee Travel – a Tax and NICs Guide for Employers, provides more details on the rules.

While the Collector of Taxes will invariably seek to recover any unpaid tax from the employer in the first instance, the relevant Regulations (SI 2003/2682) permit the Collector to direct that unpaid tax shall be recovered from the employee, but there is no legal requirement that he should give such a direction. The Regulations make it clear that he will make such a direction only if he is satisfied that the employer took reasonable care to comply with the PAYE regulations and the under-deduction of tax was an error made in good faith. Errors arising simply from confusion or ignorance of the rules are not considered to be a reasonable excuse: in such situations, the Collector will not only seek recovery of all duties underpaid but is likely to add interest and penalties as well.

SI 2003/2682, reg 81 provides that the Collector may pursue the employee if he has received his remuneration knowing that the employer has wilfully failed to deduct the amount of tax that should have been deducted, but HMRC will normally pursue this course of action only after it has endeavoured to collect from the employer.

All lump sum compensation payments should be considered carefully because of HMRC's attacking of termination payments for the failure to operate PAYE and deduct Class 1 NICs. It is wrong to assume that the first £30,000 of any lump sum compensation payment is exempt from income tax. Basically, if there is any contractual obligation or expectation, on the part of the employee, to receive a sum then HMRC is likely to take the view that the employer should have deducted tax and Class 1 NICs. HMRC looks specifically at the habitual making of tax-free payments such as payments in lieu of notice (autopilons).

20.1.7 Interest and penalties for late payment of PAYE

Over recent years, HMRC has progressively tightened its policing of employers operating PAYE schemes. The current position is as follows:

(1) Interest is charged on any PAYE tax and employers' and employees' NICs not remitted to the Collector of Taxes by 14 days after the end of the tax year (ie by 19 April 2009 for 2008–09).

(2) Penalties may be imposed on employers who do not submit their end-of-year returns (Forms P14, P38S and P35) by 19 May following the end of the tax year. The maximum penalty is £100 pm per unit of 50 employees (rounded up, so that 51 employees count as two units).

Electronic filing

In the 2002 Budget speech, Gordon Brown, the chancellor, announced the intention for all year-end returns to be filed electronically. The deadline for this was set out as follows:

Number of employees in PAYE scheme	First return to be filed electronically	Deadline
250 or more	2004/05	19 May 2005
50–249	2005/06	19 May 2006
Fewer than 50	2009/10	19 May 2010

Table 20.1 – Summary of year-end deadlines

Deadline		Result of missed deadline
19 October 2008	Payment date for income tax and Class 1B NICs due on any PAYE Settlement Agreement for 2007/08	Interest will be charged if payment is made late
19 May 2009	Due date for submission of forms P35	Automatic penalties
31 May 2009	Forms P60 to employees in employment as at 5 April 2009	Penalties
6 July 2009	Forms P11D and P9D to reach HMRC	Penalties of up to £300 per return
6 July 2009	Copies of P11D and P9D information to be given to employees, including any who have left the company since 5 April 2009	Penalties
6 July 2009	Deadline for third party providers of expenses or benefits to notify the recipient of the cash equivalent of the expense payment or benefit	
19 July 2009	Payment date for Class 1A NICs and final date for submission of form P11D(b) if penalties are to be avoided	Penalties
19 October 2009	Payment date for income tax and Class 1B NICs due on any PAYE Settlement Agreement for 2008–09	Interest will be charged if payment is made late

20.1.8 **Other returns required from employers**

Forms P46 (car)

These forms report details of changes in company car allocations. They are due quarterly within 28 days of the end of the periods ending 5 July, 5 October, 5 January and 5 April. Reportable events are when an employee or director:

- receives a company car for the first time;
- changes company car;
- receives an additional company car;
- gives up a company car; or
- exceeds the £8,500 threshold (see below) having been below it before.

Late returns may be liable to penalties of up to £300 per return, plus £60 a day while the failure continues.

Forms P11D and P9D

An employer must file forms P11D to report benefits and expenses for all employees earning £8,500+ pa. Directors are automatically included in this category unless they:

- are full-time working directors or directors of a not-for-profit organisation; and
- earn less than £8,500 pa; and
- do not control directly or indirectly more than 5% of the company's ordinary share capital; and
- do not have directorships in other businesses under the same control.

All benefits and expenses payments (including business expenses) must be reported, except those covered by dispensations. The amount is the cash equivalent (see 4.4–4.9 on taxation of benefits in general).

Except where special rules apply, the cash equivalent is normally the VAT-inclusive cost to the provider. Where the special rules apply, employers are responsible for calculating the cash equivalent and entering the appropriate amount on the P11D. HMRC can supply the following P11D Working Sheets to assist you:

(1) Living accommodation and associated benefits.
(2) Car and fuel benefits.
(3) Vans available for private use.
(4) Interest-free and low interest loans.
(5) Relocation expenses.
(6) Mileage allowance and passenger payments.

If an arrangement has been made for someone else to provide benefits to the employees, the cash equivalents must be reported on P11D as though the employer itself provided the benefits. If the provider cannot or will not give details of the benefits to the employer, the employer must make a best estimate of the cash equivalent and notify HMRC of this. Such arrangements are where an employer has guaranteed or facilitated provision of benefits or the benefits were part of a reciprocal arrangement with another employer.

If a third party makes any expense payments or provides benefits to someone else's employees and the employer is not involved, the third party has an obligation to notify the employees of the cash equivalent of the expense payment paid or benefit provided. The third party does not have to submit a P11D for someone else's employee and many third party providers enter into arrangements to pay the tax due through a Taxed Award Scheme. These are dealt with by HMRC's Incentive Award Unit in Manchester and guidance is available in The Employer's Further Guide to PAYE and NICs at Chapter 2.

P11D returns are due for submission to HMRC by 6 July following the end of the tax year. Filing an incorrect return can result in a penalty of up to £3,000. Further, a penalty of £300 may be imposed for each form not submitted by 6 July, with a daily penalty of £60 per return if the forms are not submitted once the initial penalty has been imposed.

Details of taxable benefits must be supplied to employees by 6 July. Forms P9D may also be required for benefits provided to employees earning less than £8,500 pa. The deadlines for submitting returns of Classes 1A and 1B NICs must also be borne in mind (see 22.1.7–22.1.8).

Returns of 'reportable events'

Certain events in relation to employment-related securities (see 5.3 and 5.6) have to be reported to HMRC within 92 days of the end of the tax year on form 42. Failure to comply can result in a fine of £300 per reportable event. The events include issue of shares, removal of restrictions, addition of special rights and purchases of securities from employees at over-value.

20.1.9 Pensions and benefits for former employees

A return must also be made of pensions and other payments to former employees, and 'relevant benefits' taxable under s 612(1) ICTA 1988 and s 393B ITEPA 2003. See 4.16.6 on this

20.1.10 Collection of student loans

Student loans are the main source of funding higher education. The Student Loans Company (SLC) administers the scheme but employers are responsible for making deductions from the former student's salary and for paying over the amounts deducted to HMRC.

The system is similar to that for working tax credits in that the employers will receive start and stop notifications from HMRC. The employer is not responsible for identifying employees who are liable to make these repayments or for answering questions from the employee on the loan. Such queries should be referred to the SLC. Only questions about operating the scheme should be referred to HMRC.

The calculation of student loan repayments is very similar to that of NICs. There is an annual limit of £15,000 pa (£1,250 pm or £288.46 pw) below which no deductions are made. This limit is non-cumulative as with NICs so an employee who earns £1,000 in one month and £2,000 in the next will only be liable to deduction in the second month. The deduction made would be as follows in respect of the latter case:

£2000 – £1,250	=	£750.00
Rate of deduction	=	9%
Student loan repaid	=	£67.50

The initial rate of repayment has been set at 9% and this will be applied to those earnings subject to secondary Class 1 NICs. For any employees not liable to NICs (eg employees working abroad in non-agreement countries) there will be no deductions due.

An employer should only begin to make deductions when a start notice (form SL1) is received from HMRC. This gives at least six weeks' notice before deductions should commence. Deductions should begin on the first pay day after this date.

If a new employee hands over a P45 with a 'Y' in the SL box, it means the previous employer had received a start notice. In this situation, deductions should be made as soon as possible. If the P45 is received some time after the employee has started work, no attempt should be made to deduct any arrears. If the employee completes box D (student loans) of the new form P46, you should make deductions. The employer collects student loan repayments by making deductions from the borrower's pay using the Student Loan Deduction Tables. These tables are available from the Employer's Orderline, on 08457 646 646. Further information is available in HMRC leaflet IR59, which is available online at www.hmrc.gov.uk.

20.2 CONTRACTORS

HMRC regards payments made by contractors to subcontractors as a high risk area because of cash payments and what it calls dubious practices. It is an obvious area in which tax is being lost to the Treasury. Subcontract workers can now be paid:

- net after the deduction of PAYE/NICs as employees;
- net under deduction of the Construction Industry Scheme standard rate of 20%;
- net under deduction of the new Construction Industry Scheme higher rate deduction of 30%;
- gross, if registered for Gross Payment under the New Construction Industry Scheme.

Agency workers

Construction workers supplied by employment agencies or other third parties were brought within the PAYE system by FA 1998. This aligned the tax and NIC treatment of such workers, who were in the past regarded as self-employed for tax purposes but as employees for NIC purposes.

Note that this change does not only apply to agencies. Companies acting as 'in-house' agencies within the construction industry that supply labour to others, and anyone else who supplies construction workers to others, fall within the legislation.

20.2.1 Payments to subcontractors in construction industry

Where a person carries on a business that includes construction work, the payments to a subcontractor in respect of 'construction operations' may be subject to a deduction of tax, as outlined above.

The contractor is normally the person making the payment for 'construction operations'. A contractor is a business or other concern that pays subcontractors for construction work. Contractors may be construction companies and building firms, but may also be Government departments, local authorities, and many other businesses that are normally known in the industry as 'clients'. Non-construction businesses or other concerns that spend more than £1 million a year (as an average over three years) on construction work, are treated as contractors and are covered by the scheme.

New regulations that took effect on 6 April 2007 have the effect of excluding from the scheme most charities, providing that they are not 'mainstream contractors' (Regulation 24 SI 2005/2045); and deemed contractors in relation to expenditure on their own premises (Regulation 22). The exclusion does not apply to premises that are let or where there is significant use by third parties.

Construction operations

'Construction operations' are defined in law in s74 Finance Act 2004 and HMRC guidance can be found in Appendix B of the booklet CIS340. As a general guide, 'construction operations' cover almost any work that is done to a permanent or temporary building or structure, a civil engineering work or installation. The work can include site preparation, alterations, dismantling, construction, repairs, decorating and demolition. Some activities on construction sites are not regarded as construction operations under the scheme, including any activity that is clearly not construction work, such as the running of a canteen, a hostel, provision of medical or safety and security services and the provision of site facilities.

Where a single contract relates to a mixture of construction and non-construction operations, all payments due under the contract are within the scheme. This is the case even if only one of the jobs is regarded as a construction operation. A typical example is where a carpet fitter is engaged to 'finish' a house, laying carpet in some rooms and wood flooring in other rooms. Unless there is a separate contract for the carpet fitting, which is not a construction operation, the scheme would have to be applied to all the works.

20.2.2 Construction Industry Scheme

The current scheme was introduced on 6 April 2007. It was designed to remove some of the administrative burden of the old scheme and provide options to the paper-based processes of CIS.

The main differences are:

- There is no longer any need for CIS cards, certificates or vouchers.
- Contractors must check or 'verify' the payment status of new subcontractors with HMRC. This requires the contractor to provide details of the subcontractor's name, national insurance number and Unique Tax Reference number (UTR); company name and registration number if a company subcontractor and partnership name and UTR, if a partnership.
- Subcontractors will be normally be paid either net of 20% tax or gross, depending on their own circumstances, with HMRC advising on the rate of tax to be deducted.
- Three tests need to be satisfied before a subcontractor can be granted gross payment status:
  (1) The business test – an individual or company needs to show that it is carrying out construction work in the UK, or supplying labour, and the business is run through a bank account.
  (2) The turnover test is based on net turnover, ie gross income from construction work excluding VAT and the cost of materials. Individuals need a net construction turnover of at least £30,000 in the 12 months preceding their application for gross payment. Partnerships and companies need net turnover either of £200,000 or of £30,000 multiplied by the number of partners or directors.
  (3) The compliance test requires that in the 12 months to the date of application for gross payment the subcontractor's tax affairs have been up to date and payment of all tax due from the subcontractor and the business, including subcontractor deductions, PAYE, NIC and any business tax have been made on time. It extends to the partners and directors affairs, where appropriate. HMRC's CIS343 fact sheet provides guidance on applying.
- Unlike the old scheme, there are no renewal applications and HMRC will police compliance by reviewing gross paid subcontractors annually and removing gross payment status if there are any significant failings at the time of the review.
- There is also a higher rate tax deduction of 30% if a subcontractor cannot be 'matched' on the HMRC system. This rate will continue to apply until the subcontractor contacts HMRC and registers or sorts out any matching problem.

- Contractors must make a return every month to HMRC showing payments made to all subcontractors. A late return gives rise to an automatic £100 penalty plus an additional penalty of £100 for every 50 subcontractors. If the penalty is incomplete or incorrect, a further penalty can be levied of up to £3,000. Furthermore, repeated non-compliance could affect the contractor's own right to receive payments without tax being deducted.
- Contractors must declare on their return that none of the workers listed on the return is an employee. This is called a status declaration.
- Nil returns must be made when there are no payments in any month. These can be made over the telephone as well as online or on paper, but they must be made – there will be financial penalties for failure to submit a return.

20.3 IR35

The revised version of the controversial rules and regulations on personal service companies came into effect as at 6 April 2000. These rules use existing case law (see Chapter 6) to determine whether an individual performs services that would be taxed as employment income were it not for the fact that his services are provided through an intermediary such as a service company. Those caught by these rules will pay approximately the same PAYE and NICs as an individual who is an employee of the end customer.

HMRC has laid out a nine-point plan for determining the deemed employment income tax charge for a tax year (see Table 20.2):

- *Step 1* determines that the starting point for the calculation is the total amount received by the intermediary during the tax year from relevant engagements. This figure includes any benefits-in-kind provided to the intermediary in respect of those engagements. This total amount is then reduced by 5%, which is an allowance for the intermediary's running costs.
- *Step 2* adds in any payments or benefits-in-kind received by the worker or his family in respect of any relevant engagements from anyone other than the intermediary, which are not otherwise taxable as employment income, but which would have been so taxable had the worker been employed by the client.
- *Step 3* deducts any amounts spent by the intermediary that could have been claimed as expenses against income tax had the worker been the client's employee and met them himself.
- *Step 4* allows a deduction for any capital allowances that could have been claimed by the worker had he been the client's employee.
- *Step 5* deducts any contributions paid by the intermediary to an approved pension scheme for the worker's benefit.

- *Step 6* deducts any employer's NICs (Classes 1 and 1A) paid by the intermediary in respect of salary or benefits-in-kind provided to the worker during the year.
- *Step 7* deducts any amount of salary and benefits-in-kind provided by the intermediary to the worker during the year, which has already been subject to income tax and Class 1 and 1A NICs (excluding any amounts that have already been deducted at Step 3). Note: if, after Step 7, the result is nil or a negative amount, there is no deemed employment income payment and no further tax or NICs are payable. If the result is positive, a deemed employment income payment must be calculated in accordance with Steps 8 and 9.
- *Step 8* allows for a deduction of the employer's NICs payable on the deemed payment. So Step 8 requires the calculation of the amount that, together with the employer's NICs due on it, equals the result of Step 7.
- *Step 9* states that the result after Step 8 is the amount of the deemed employment income payment.

Note that if the worker is within the Construction Industry Scheme (see above), it is the amount before deduction of tax under that scheme that must be brought in at Step 1 of the calculation.

Payment of tax

Tax and NICs under IR35 regulations in respect of deemed payments are due for payment by 19 April following the end of the tax year. In some situations, HMRC believes that the P35 should be filed on the basis of estimates of the deemed payment and the tax and NICs due on it. See the advice published on www.hmrc.gov.uk/ir35.

20.4 MANAGED SERVICE COMPANIES (MSCS)

Payments received after 5 April 2007 by individuals who supply their services through an MSC are subject to PAYE. Furthermore, the cost of travel from the individual's home to place of work is not a tax-free expense for workers supplied by an MSC.

This is subject to the following exclusions:

- Companies providing individuals who perform professional accountancy or legal services.
- 'Normal employment agencies' that do not influence or control the way in which payments to individual workers are made.

Collection of tax from directors of the managed service company

From 6 August 2007, where PAYE and NIC cannot be recovered from an MSC, HMRC may enforce the debt personally against a director of the MSC or from a person who has provided the MSC. There are also wider provisions due to come into force from 6 January allowing HMRC to transfer the debt to 'specified persons', ie people who 'encourage, facilitate or are otherwise actively involved in the provision of an individual's services' through an MSC.

Table 20.2 – Deemed calculation: HMRC template

Step One	Enter in this box the amount of all payments and benefits received by your company or partnership in the year for contracts to which these rules apply	1
	Enter in this box 5% of the amount in box 1	2
Step Two	Enter in this box the amount of any payments and benefits received directly by you in the year for contracts to which the rules apply and which are not already taxable	3
Step Three	Enter in this box the amount of any expenses met by your company or partnership in the year which you could have claimed personally if the worker had been an employee of the client and had paid for them yourself	4
Step Four	Enter in this box the amount of any capital allowances for purchases made by your company or partnership which you could have claimed yourself if you had been employed by your client and had made the purchases yourself	5
Step Five	Enter in this box the amount of any contributions to an approved pension scheme made by your company or partnership for your personal benefit	6
Step Six	Enter in this box the amount of any employer's Class 1 and Class 1A NICs which your company or partnership paid in the year in respect of salary or non-cash benefits which it provided to you in the year	7
Step Seven	Enter in this box the amount of any salary you received from your company or partnership in the year which is already taxable as employment income (this does not include anything for which a deduction has already been given at Step Three)	8
	Enter in this box any benefits in kind or expenses you received from your company or partnership in the year which are already taxable as employment income (this does not include anything for which a deduction has already been given at Step Three)	8a
	Add together the figures in boxes 1 and 3 and enter the total in this box	9
	Add together the figures in boxes 2, 4, 5, 6, 7, 8 and 8a and enter the total in this box	10
	Deduct the figures in box 10 from the figures in box 9 and enter the answer in this box	11
	If the answer in box 11 is nil or a negative number there is no deemed payment	

Table 20.2 – Continued

	If the answer in box 11 is a positive number you will need to process this figure to get the deemed payment and the employer's Class 1 NICs on that deemed payment	
Step Eight	Multiply the figure in box 11 by 100 and enter the answer in this box	12
	Divide the figure in box 12 by (100+12.8) and enter the answer in this box (case a), unless the figure in box 8 is less than the secondary Class 1 NICs earnings threshold, in which case complete the steps below (case b). The final figure in box 13 is the deemed payment	
	Case b: subtract the figure in box 8 from the Class 1 NICs earnings threshold and enter in this box	13a
	Case b: subtract the figure in box 13a from the figure in box 11 and enter in this box	13b
	Case b: divide the figure in box 13c by (100+12.8) (see footnote 1) and enter the answer in this box	13d
	Case b: add the figure in box 13d to the figure in box 13a and enter the answer in box 13	
Step Nine	Deduct the figure in box 13 from the figure in box 11 and enter the amount you are left with in this box. This amount is the amount of employer's Class 1 NICs due on the deemed payment	14
	Enter the figure from box 13 in this box. This amount is the deemed payment	

1. The employer's contribution rate can vary. Contracted-out or contracted-in rates are different. The figure you add to 100 at this stage should be the contributions rate that is applicable to you. See HMRC National Insurance tables CA38 and the Employer's Annual Pack for further details

Source: HMRC

20.5 NON-RESIDENT LANDLORD SCHEME

If you rent a property from a non-resident landlord, you have an obligation to withhold basic rate tax and pay this over to HMRC each quarter. There are two main exceptions to this rule, ie where:
(1) the rent paid is less than £100 pw; or
(2) you have received confirmation from HMRC that you may make the payment gross.

If you are paying rent to a non-resident landlord you should contact:

HMRC Centre for Non-Residents
St John's House
Merton Road
Bootle
Merseyside L69 9BB.

HMRC will forward you a form to complete within 30 days of the end of each quarter, explaining how the tax is calculated and how to make a payment to the Account's Office.

Example – Calculation of quarterly payment

Tax is calculated at the basic rate on the rent due in quarter less allowable expenses. Therefore, if the rent due in the quarter to 31 March 2009 is £3,000 but during the quarter you have paid £300 out of this sum to repair a broken window, then the calculation would be as follows:

	£
Rent	3,000
Less: Allowable expenses	(300)
	2,700
Tax at 20%	540

At the end of each tax year you must provide by no later than 5 July a return including details of the rent paid, allowable expenses and tax deducted. Within the same time frame you should also supply the landlord with a certificate of the tax deducted. The payments are dealt with by the Centre for Non-Residents (previously FICO) at the address above.

20.6 NON-RESIDENT SPORTSMEN AND ENTERTAINERS

Basic rate tax must be withheld from most payments made to non-UK resident sportsmen and entertainers for work performed in the UK. In addition, where benefits-in-kind are provided to them, the cost must be 'grossed up' for tax at the basic rate and accounted for. A tax voucher must be provided for each payment and the person making the payments must account for tax on a quarterly basis.

20.6.1 Payments caught by this scheme

Payments or benefits subject to these regulations include:

(1) prize money;
(2) appearance or performance fees;
(3) endorsement fees where the individual has appeared in the UK (whether or not his appearance is to promote the goods he is endorsing);
(4) payments that finance any of the above (eg commercial sponsorship).

Certain payments specifically excluded from the scheme are those:

(1) subject to deduction of tax;
(2) subject to PAYE;
(3) solely for the use of copyright in words or music;
(4) made to the Performing Rights Society;
(5) made to UK residents and ancillary to a performance (including the cost of hiring a venue and payments for the services of UK-resident performers appearing with a non-resident);

(6) that are royalties on the sale of records and tapes; and
(7) amounting to less than £1,000 in a tax year. This de minimis limit applies to all payments made in a tax year in connection with the same event. Furthermore, payments made by the same or connected persons must be aggregated and the £1,000 exemption applies only if the total is less than £1,000.

20.6.2 Special arrangements

It is possible for a payer to secure HMRC's agreement to a lower rate of withholding tax provided an application is made at least 30 days in advance. Such authorisation may be given provided that:

(1) the organiser can arrange that he is responsible for accounting for the tax; or
(2) the sponsor can apply for clearance on the grounds that the tax will be collected from someone else; or
(3) the payer can secure authority to withhold tax at a lower rate, possibly to reflect the fact that the non-resident will have certain allowable expenses or perhaps because only some members of a group are non-resident. Expenses which may be taken into account include general subsistence expenses, UK and international travelling expenses, commission, manager's and agent's fees.

20.6.3 Indirect payments also caught

The regulations provide that the withholding system should also apply to payments made to any person:

(1) who is under the control of the non-resident sportsman or entertainer;
(2) who is:
    (a) not resident in the UK; and
    (b) not liable to tax in a territory outside the UK where the rate of tax charged on profits exceeds 20%;
(3) who receives a connected payment or value transferred by a connected transfer where there is a contract or arrangement under which it is reasonable to suppose that the entertainer (or other person connected with him) is, will or may become entitled to receive amounts not substantially less than the amount paid.

The High Court held that the obligation to withhold tax applied to payments made by non-resident companies to a company owned by Andre Agassi (see *Agassi* v *Robinson* (2004) STC 610). This ruling was overturned in the Court of Appeal but has recently been upheld in the House of Lords.

20.6.4 Further information

See Revenue booklet FEU 50 *A Guide to Paying Foreign Entertainers.*

20.7 OTHER PAYMENTS TO NON-UK RESIDENT PERSONS

20.7.1 Interest paid to non-resident lender

Tax at 20% must normally be deducted where the interest is paid by a UK-resident person and the lender is not UK-resident. It may be possible for the lender to make a claim under a double taxation agreement; where such a claim has been made, HMRC may authorise payment of interest without deduction of tax.

FA 2004 contains provisions that enable a member of a group of companies to pay interest to another member of the group without deduction of tax provided that the overseas company is resident in an EU member state.

20.7.2 Patent royalties paid to non-residents

Patent royalties paid to a non-resident are normally subject to deduction of basic rate tax. Since 1 October 2002 it has been possible for a company to pay royalties without deducting tax if the recipient is a person resident in a country for which the relevant double tax treaty contains an exemption from UK tax. If it turns out that the exemption was not in fact due, the company paying the royalty would then have to account for the tax that should have been withheld.

20.7.3 Copyright royalties

Copyright royalties paid to a non-resident are also normally subject to deduction of tax. Where the payment is made via a commission agent, basic rate tax must be withheld for the net amount paid on to the non-resident. A statement made in the House of Commons in 1969 indicates that this obligation to withhold tax does not apply where copyright payments are made to professional authors who are resident abroad.

23.7.4 Purchase of British patent rights

There is an obligation for basic rate tax to be withheld where a person sells all or part of his patent rights and the vendor is not UK-resident. Once again, the provisions of a double taxation agreement may override this, but a person making payment for such rights must deduct tax unless he is authorised not to do so by the Inspector of Foreign Dividends.

21

OUTLINE OF VAT

ROBERT NEWEY

Value added tax was introduced by FA 1972 and became operational on 1 April 1973. In concept, it is a simple tax, although various exclusions from a VAT charge and the European influence have resulted in a simple concept becoming one of the most complicated taxes.

This chapter covers some of the detail of VAT under the following headings:

(1) Introduction.
(2) Legal authorities.
(3) Liability to VAT.
(4) Practical implications.
(5) Anti-avoidance measures.
(6) Special schemes.
(7) Control and enforcement procedures.
(8) Fraud.
(9) Appeals.

21.1 INTRODUCTION

The introduction of VAT was a precondition of the UK's acceptance into the then European Economic Community (EEC) which, as a result of the European Communities Act 1982, became the European Community (EC), now commonly referred to as the European Union (EU). Part of the EU philosophy is the harmonisation of taxes, particularly those that affect cross-border trading activities. One example of harmonisation is customs duty, which is payable when goods enter the EU and charged at the same rate when or wherever the goods enter the Community.

Once customs duty is paid the goods can move freely between member states without payment of any further duty or being subject to customs' controls. The legislative authority for customs duty is to be found in EC Regulations, which, once agreed by the EC Commission, have immediate direct effect in each member state.

The harmonisation of VAT has been the subject of much discussion by the EC Commission, resulting in the introduction of transitional rules with effect from 1 January 1993 and commonly referred to as The Single Market Legislation. The rules implement a degree of harmonisation on the VAT accounting requirements of the movement of goods between member states. The Commission proposed a staged work programme to introduce complete harmonisation for EC VAT, and has agreed the system will not take effect until two years after the European Council adopts the measures; the present transitional system will therefore remain for some time.

Several EC directives are the ultimate legal authority for VAT, and they must be reflected in the national legislation of each member state. To that extent, directives have direct effect. For example, if the national law is not in accordance with a directive and thereby disadvantages the taxpayer, the taxpayer can argue his case, using the directive, in the national court, which must recognise the directive, and with the ultimate right of appeal to the European Court of Justice.

The UK administration of VAT was given to HM Customs & Excise (Customs), which introduced a completely new system of tax enforcement to the majority of businesses and the accounting profession. Customs, which is steeped in the history of duty enforcement, brought with it its practical approach to controlling the taxpayer. For the first time, many businesses and their professional advisers had to justify, face to face with the enforcement agencies (the VAT control officer), what had been declared in the VAT return and the amounts shown in the annual accounts. It should be noted that Customs merged with HM Inland Revenue in April 2005 to form a new government department, HM Revenue & Customs (HMRC). This chapter will continue to refer to the administrative authority as Customs.

VAT is not, in principle, a tax on profits but a tax on transactions. VAT is a tax on the consumer that is collected in stages throughout the business chain and, eventually, by the businessperson supplying the consumer, whether that be an individual or a business that is not registered for VAT.

A business must account for VAT on its supplies ('outputs') but can deduct VAT on its expenditure ('input tax').

If a business fails to charge and account for VAT correctly, it must account for both the VAT and any penalties from its own resources and thereby, by default, VAT becomes a charge on profits. Put simply, the businessperson is a tax collector.

For VAT purposes, the UK consists of England, Scotland, Wales, Northern Ireland and the Isle of Man; the Channel Islands are not included.

21.2 LEGAL AUTHORITIES

No single piece of legislation covers the administration and collection of VAT. The VAT legislation is described briefly below.

21.2.1 The VAT Act 1994 (VATA 1994)

This consolidation Act brought together the VATA 1983 and subsequent Finance Acts amending the original legislation. It deals with the administration of the tax and provides for certain aspects to be dealt with by delegated legislation.

21.2.2 VAT Regulations 1995

This consolidates 60 sets of existing regulations and amendments introduced since 1972. It deals with a wide range of administrative procedures that must be complied with, for example the detail to be shown on tax invoices, the method of recovering VAT when a VAT-registered person is not entitled to a full recovery of VAT paid to his suppliers, and special VAT accounting procedures for particular transactions.

21.2.3 Treasury orders

Certain Treasury orders describe among other things what is or is not chargeable to VAT, and give certain organisations legal authority to recover VAT that would otherwise not be recoverable. Treasury orders are published in the *London Gazette*.

21.2.4 Customs notices and leaflets

Generally, VAT public notices are not part of the law, although certain notices are published pursuant to VATA 1994 and the VAT Regulations 1995 and, thereby, become part of the law. As such they have the same status as Acts of Parliament and are legally binding on the taxpayer. For example, Notice 700 (General Guide) is principally Customs' interpretation of the law, but the section dealing with values expressed in a foreign currency is part of the law, as is much of the Public Notice on the special VAT Retail Schemes (Notice 727).

Customs' leaflets are not strictly part of the law, but certain leaflets explaining the Commissioners' requirements for particular types of transactions are, in practical terms, legally binding. This applies to relatively few of the leaflets, the vast majority being simply the Commissioners' interpretation of the law.

21.2.5 EC directives

All VAT law has its roots in the EC Sixth VAT Directive, which has direct effect in the UK and other EU countries through their respective national laws. A number of other EC directives deal with specific aspects such as that which, on 1 January 1993, introduced VAT harmonisation in the Single Market and others that provide the right to recover VAT incurred in other countries.

21.3 LIABILITY TO VAT

VAT is chargeable on transactions made in the UK when the goods or services are supplied 'in the course or furtherance of any business'. Services supplied free of charge are not subject to VAT. Supplies made outside the UK are outside the scope of UK VAT. There are complex rules for determining the place of supply. The rules differ depending on whether the supply is one of goods or services: professional advice should be taken if you are unsure about the place of supply of a transaction.

21.3.1 Business
(VATA 1994, s 94)

'Business' is not defined in VAT legislation, but has been widely interpreted to cover all organisations that carry on an activity in a business-like way. This has resulted in a number of organisations that do not consider themselves to be carrying on a business (eg charities) having to conform to VAT legislation and, where appropriate, register and account for VAT on their business income. In addition, the VAT legislation provides that certain organisations are deemed to be businesses (eg clubs and associations). If it can be demonstrated that the activity is a hobby, there is no requirement to charge VAT on any resulting income.

An employee's services to an employer in return for a salary meets the definition of a supply of services, but the law specifically provides that they are not in the course or furtherance of a business and so are outside the scope of VAT.

There is sometimes uncertainty as to who is supplying a service. A recent case involved lap dancers who received fees from customers. It was held that the dancers were principals and not agents of the club at which they performed.

Charities

There is no automatic relief from VAT for supplies either to or by charities. A charity carrying on a business activity must register and account for VAT on its business income the same as any commercial organisation.

Certain supplies to charities are zero-rated (see 21.3.2), but these are mainly in the health and welfare area, and new commercial property used wholly for charitable non-business activities, known as 'qualifying buildings'. Customs by concession allows zero rating where there is a small amount of business use (up to 10%) by the charity concerned.

Zero rating was extended in FA 2000 to include supplies of advertising when made to charities and all costs incurred in producing the advertising material when supplied with advertising. In addition certain goods used in connection with collecting monetary donations became zero-rated by concession from 1 April 2000.

A more generous relief from VAT for fundraising by charities was introduced by FA 2000. This allows charities, in certain circumstances, to treat fundraising income as exempt from VAT.

Clubs and associations
(VATA 1994, s 94(2)(a))

Many local clubs and associations, including those formed by local residents, consider they are not carrying on a business, but this is not correct. The law specifically provides that the provision of benefits to members in return for a subscription or other payment is a business activity.

Certain trade and professional organisations consider they either are not in business or qualify for exemption as professional associations, and consequently have no requirement to register for VAT. Yet because they generally provide other benefits to their members and possibly non-members that are not within the exemption, they may be liable to register.

To avoid the risk of penalties all clubs, associations and similar organisations should review their activities to ensure they meet their VAT obligations at the correct time.

Admission to premises
(VATA 1994, s 94(2)(b))

Admitting persons to any premises in return for a payment is a business activity. Anyone carrying on such an activity must register and account for VAT if the income exceeds the registration threshold.

Under FA 2001, several national museums and galleries granting free admissions are treated in the same way as local authorities and similar organisations covered by VATA 1994, s 34. Thus, these museums and galleries can recover VAT on related costs. The museums and galleries eligible to recover VAT on costs are chosen by the Treasury. Normally free admission is a non-business activity and museums and galleries granting free admission cannot recover VAT on costs.

21.3.2 Supplies

The application of VAT differs depending on whether there is a supply of goods or a supply of services.

A supply of goods is where title to the goods is, or is to be, transferred to another person. This includes, for example, the transfer of title in land by means of a freehold sale or a lease exceeding 21 years.

Anything that is not a supply of goods and supplied for a consideration is a supply of services. The definition is deliberately wide. For VAT to be charged on a supply, it must be a taxable supply made in the UK. This means that the supply must not fall within any of the categories of exempt supply (21.4.7). A charge to VAT arises only where consideration is present, so a free supply of services is outside the scope of VAT. Care is required, because what may appear to be free is not necessarily so in real terms and a hidden VAT liability could arise.

Taxable supplies

These are supplies subject to VAT at either the zero, reduced (see below) or the standard (currently 17.5%) rate. There is no list of standard-rated goods or services. If a particular supply is not relieved from VAT by lower rating, zero rating or exemption, and is not treated as outside the scope, then the supply is by default standard-rated.

Zero-rated supplies

Zero-rated supplies include exports of goods to places outside the EU (VATA 1994, s 30(6)). Supplies of goods to VAT registered customers in other member states are zero-rated (VATA 1994, s 30(8)). Other categories of zero-rated supplies are listed in VATA 1994, Sch 8. There are 15 groups in Sch 8:

(1) Food for human consumption and animal feeding stuffs.
(2) Sewerage services and water (but not bottled water).
(3) Books and newspapers, etc.
(4) Talking books and wireless sets for the blind.
(5) Construction and sales of new dwellings (including sales of non-residential buildings converted to dwellings).
(6) Approved alteration of listed residential buildings and listed buildings used by charities for non-business purposes.
(7) International services (note that qualifying services were greatly reduced on 1 January 1993).
(8) Transport.
(9) Caravans and houseboats.
(10) Gold.
(11) Bank notes.
(12) Drugs, medicines, aids for the handicapped, etc.
(13) Imports, exports, etc.
(14) This group has been deleted – it was tax-free shops.
(15) Charities (certain supplies to or by charities).
(16) Clothing and footwear (children's and protective).

Reduced-rate supplies

VAT is charged on certain supplies of goods and services at a reduced rate, currently 5%. The categories of goods and services to which the lower rate applies are set out in VATA 1994, Sch 7A:

(1) Supplies of domestic fuel and power.
(2) Installation of energy-saving materials.
(3) Grant funded installation of heating equipment or security goods or connection of gas supply.
(4) Women's sanitary products.
(5) Children's car seats.
(6) Residential conversions.
(7) Residential renovations and alterations.
(8) Contraceptives products.
(9) Welfare advice or information.
(10) Installation of mobility aids for the elderly.
(11) Smoking cessation products.

Care is required when determining whether the zero or reduced rate applies. The group headings only are shown above and there is extensive detail to consider.

Exempt

These are supplies that are exempt from VAT by statute, ie those listed in VATA 1994, Sch 9 (see 21.4.7). The exemption rules are, in theory, the same throughout the EU whereas zero rating is a derogation from normal EU rules. Exemption and zero rating must not be confused because the overall effect on a business is totally different. As discussed below, zero rating gives entitlement to recover VAT on underlying costs whereas exemption does not.

'Outside the scope'

Certain supplies or business activities are outside the scope of VAT. For example, the supply of goods situated outside the UK, or services where the place of supply is treated as being outside the UK. There are also sundry business transactions which are not subject to VAT (eg transactions between companies in the same VAT group (see 21.4.1)).

VAT is recoverable, subject to partial exemption rules, on costs relating to supplies outside the UK (and therefore outside the scope of UK VAT) which would be taxable supplies if made in the UK.

Non-business activities are outside the scope. VAT is irrecoverable on costs relating to non-business activities. Examples of non-business activities include free supplies of services, donations, free entry to museums, etc.

21.3.3 Exports

Goods which are exported to a place outside the EU are zero-rated. This includes goods exported to the Channel Islands but not to the Isle of Man. It is only the final exporter who is allowed to zero rate his supply, although in certain cases zero rating is allowed one stage back from the last supply in the UK. Details can be found in Customs Notices 703 and 704.

Exporters must be able to satisfy Customs that the goods have been exported. Detailed records of exports must be retained. Customs requirements are contained in Notice 703, parts of which have the force of law.

21.3.4 Imports

VAT is normally charged on the importation of goods into the UK from outside the EC. Payment of VAT is due at the time of importation, but can be deferred until the 15th day of the month following importation provided a deferment number is obtained. The VAT payable can be recovered as input tax, subject to the normal rules. Security may be required for VAT and duty payable in the form of a bank guarantee. With effect from 1 December 2003, the duty deferment scheme has been relaxed. Approved importers no longer have to provide security for the full amount of VAT deferred. Customs duties must still be fully secured. Businesses can apply to Customs for approved importer status which will reduce bank charges as the guarantee will be either cancelled or reduced (if goods are liable to Customs duty).

21.3.5 European Community

The terms 'acquisitions' and 'despatches' replace 'imports' and 'exports' respectively for transactions with other member states. It is not necessary to make an import declaration on an acquisition of goods from a supplier in another EC country. Provided the customer gives his or her VAT registration number to the supplier, the supplier will not charge local VAT. However, VAT has to be declared to Customs on the acquisition of goods by calculating the VAT on the amount payable and declaring the VAT in box 2 of VAT returns. The self-generated VAT charge can be recovered as input tax in box 4 subject to the normal rules.

Subject to certain conditions (eg showing the customer's VAT number on each invoice), despatches or supplies to a customer registered for VAT in another EC country can be zero-rated. UK VAT is chargeable if the conditions cannot be met.

UK VAT is chargeable on goods provided to non-registered customers in other member states. However, where the supplier is responsible for delivery (eg mail order businesses) then distance selling rules apply. The effect of the distance selling rules is that, subject to turnover limits, suppliers have to register in the relevant member states.

21.3.6 Commercial property

The sale of the freehold of a new commercial property (ie a property less than three years old) is subject to standard rate VAT. The standard rate applies to all sales of a property within three years of completion. The grant of the freehold of old commercial property or the grant of a leasehold interest in new or old property is exempt from VAT, but the landlord has the right to elect to waive the exemption and charge VAT on the sale or on rental payments, commonly known as 'the option to tax'. The major advantage of making an election is that a landlord can recover VAT on costs relating to an elected property. The tenant can recover VAT charged on rent provided he is using the property for taxable purposes.

The election is not available for certain supplies where, at the time the interest was granted, there is an intention or expectation that the land will become 'exempt land'. In broad terms, exempt land is land or buildings used wholly or mainly for non-VATable purposes. See 21.5.6.

21.3.7 Transfers of going concerns

The sale of a business as going concern is, subject to certain conditions, outside the scope of VAT. The conditions can be found in Article 5 of the VAT (Special Provisions) Order 1995 (SI 1995/1268).

21.4 PRACTICAL IMPLICATIONS

The administration of VAT is by a system of VAT registration, the submission of regular VAT returns and control verification visits (known as 'assurance visits') by Customs.

21.4.1 VAT registration

Registration is required where a business or any other organisation makes taxable supplies over a predetermined limit. The limits, which are based on gross turnover, are increased each year, generally in line with inflation.

It is the person who is registered, not the business activity. Once registered, all business activities must be reflected in the VAT accounting records; for example, a solicitor VAT-registered as a sole proprietor must also include his farming or writing income in his VAT accounts.

Currently, registration is required when one of the following two conditions is satisfied:

(1) When, at the end of any month, the gross taxable turnover during the previous 12 months, on a rolling basis, exceeds £67,000 (£64,000 prior to 1 April 2008). Liability to VAT registration must be notified within 30 days and registration is effective from the first of the month following the month in which a liability to notify arose. For example, where taxable turnover in the 12 months to 31 May 2008 is, say, £68,000, notification must be made within 30 days and registration is effective from 1 July. There is no VAT liability on income received prior to the effective date of registration.

(2) As soon as there are reasonable grounds to believe the value of taxable supplies to be made within the following 30 days will exceed £67,000 notification has to be made immediately. This rule catches large transactions (eg property sales). Registration is effective from the first day of the month in which the large transaction will take place.

Only taxable turnover (ie goods or services liable to VAT at either the zero, reduced or standard rate) is taken into consideration when determining whether there is a liability to register for VAT. Income that is exempt or outside the scope of VAT is ignored.

Voluntary registration

There is an entitlement to voluntarily register for VAT where the taxable turnover of the business is below the VAT registration limits. This could be an advantage to an expanding or small business as VAT on costs is recoverable and, providing the VAT charge on supplies does not reduce demand for the product, will increase profitability. Businesses based in the UK that do not make any supplies in the UK but make what would be taxable supplies overseas are entitled to register and can thereby recover VAT on UK costs.

VAT groups

Incorporated companies under common control may register as a single unit – a VAT group. All supplies between the companies in the VAT group are disregarded for VAT purposes; ie no VAT charge arises. One company is nominated as the representative member and is responsible for submitting the VAT returns and accounting for VAT on all supplies to or received from persons outside the group. There is a joint and several liability on all companies within a VAT group for any VAT due to Customs. This means Customs can recover a debt by a member of a VAT group from any other member of the group. Customs has extensive powers to refuse to allow VAT grouping but in practice only uses its powers where it considers there is an avoidance motive to grouping (for further comment see 21.5.5).

21.4.2 Tax invoices

A tax invoice containing specified details must be issued by a VAT-registered person in the following circumstances:

(1) When a standard- or reduced-rated supply is made to another taxable person.
(2) A supply, other than an exempt supply, is made to a person in another member state of the EU.

The details required are set out in Regulation 14 to the VAT (General) Regulations 1995.

On 1 January 2004, the EU Invoicing Directive was implemented in the UK. The Directive removes the need to show type of supply on a tax invoice. There is an additional requirement to show unit price.

Where the value of a supply does not exceed £250, a document referred to as a 'less-detailed tax invoice' can be issued. In addition to the supplier's name, address and VAT registration number, the document need only include time of supply, description, total amount payable (including VAT) and the VAT rate in force.

21.4.3 Time of supply

VAT has to be accounted for in the VAT accounting period (21.4.4) in which the time of supply (or tax point) occurs.

The basic tax point is determined in accordance with rules set out in VAT 1994, s 6. These rules are different depending on whether the supply is goods or services (21.3.2). The basic tax point for goods is the date the goods are sent to or made available to the customer. For services, the basic tax point is the date the service is performed.

However, if an invoice is issued or any payment is received before the basic tax point, the date of issue or receipt creates a tax point that overrides the basic tax point date.

Another tax point rule allows for an invoice issued after the basic tax point to become the actual overriding tax point. This is provided the invoice is issued within 14 days of the basic tax point.

There are also rules for particular circumstances including continuous supplies of services. The tax point rules are complex and if in doubt professional advice should be sought.

21.4.4 VAT returns (VAT 100)

Once a business is registered, VAT returns must be submitted on a regular basis. Each VAT-registered person is allocated a three-monthly VAT accounting period, but it is possible to request particular VAT periods (eg to coincide with the business's financial year). It is also possible to request monthly returns if the business regularly recovers VAT from Customs.

Returns must be submitted with full payment by the end of the month following the end of the VAT accounting period. Failure to submit returns and make full payment by the due date is penalised by a default surcharge (see 21.7.2). There is an automatic seven-day extension to the due date for electronic payments. Payment of VAT by direct debit is also available (payment is taken 10 days after the due date).

The VAT chargeable on supplies made during the period (known as 'output tax') must be declared on the VAT return provided automatically each period by Customs. Output tax is due on all tax invoices issued during the period, irrespective of whether they have been paid. Special schemes are available to ease this particular requirement for certain classes of business, as explained in 21.6. In addition, VAT is also due on all monies received for supplies made during the period and for which a tax invoice has not been issued, for example scrap sales, vending machine income, emptying phone boxes, staff canteen sales, and certain deductions from salaries for supplies to staff.

For businesses that do not issue tax invoices (eg retailers), VAT is due on the gross taxable income received during the VAT period.

Payments on account

Businesses that normally pay more than £2m annually to Customs must make monthly payments on account with a balancing payment when the three-monthly VAT return is submitted; payments must be made by electronic means. Monthly payments on account are ¹⁄₂₄th of the annual VAT liability. Businesses have the option of paying their actual monthly VAT liability instead of the set amount. Unfortunately, payments on account are subject to the default surcharge (see 21.7.2) and the seven-day period of grace given to taxpayers who pay their VAT liability by electronic means does not extend to businesses that have to pay on account.

21.4.5 VAT recovery

VAT-registered businesses may offset any VAT paid to suppliers (known as 'input tax') against the output tax declared, subject to the following conditions:

(1) Goods/services have been supplied to and have been, or will be, used by the business to make taxable supplies.
(2) Documentary evidence of the supply received, ie a tax invoice, is obtained and retained. If there is no tax invoice or other documentary evidence, Customs will normally refuse claims for input tax.

However, Customs has discretion and may accept other evidence of VAT paid.

Supplies of zero-rated and reduced-rated goods or services are taxable supplies with an entitlement to recover VAT on related costs, whereas there is no such entitlement in respect of exempt supplies.

VAT is recoverable on the purchase of a motorcar used wholly for business purposes. Customs interprets 'wholly for business purposes' strictly, and in practice most businesses, with the exception of car leasing companies, cannot recover the VAT.

VAT is recoverable on buying road fuel for business purposes, but unless business mileage is logged, VAT on private use of the fuel has to be declared using the scale charge laid down. The amount of VAT to be declared depends on the engine size and type of vehicle. Since 1 May 2007, the VAT chargeable on private use of fuel has been based on the vehicle's CO_2 emissions.

SI 1992/3222 was amended with effect from 1 March 2000 to allow for the sale of items to be treated as exempt where input tax deduction on the purchase of the item had previously been blocked. This follows an ECJ decision against the Italian Government in favour of an appeal made by a taxpayer.

VAT is not recoverable on business entertainment expenses. In addition, VAT on goods or services received by the VAT-registered person and used for either a non-business activity or private use is not recoverable as input tax. Many people believe that merely because a VAT-registered person pays an invoice, there is an automatic entitlement to recover the VAT shown on it. This belief is not correct and recovery of VAT that is not input tax may give rise to penalties. Where assets are purchased and used for both business and private (non-business) purposes, taxpayers can recover VAT in full and account for output tax on non-business use over a set number of years. This is known as 'Lennartz' accounting after the case giving rise to the principle. The principle has been extended to land and buildings with output tax on non-business use to be calculated over ten years. All taxpayers can use the alternative measure of apportioning input tax at source between business and non-business use.

The recovery of VAT by businesses that make both taxable and exempt supplies is described in 21.4.7.

Bad debt relief

A claim for bad debt relief may be made for any debt that is more than six months old. A claimant used to have to notify VAT-registered debtors of his claim within seven days of making it. However, for supplies made after 1 January 2003 such notification is not required. Businesses that have not paid for supplies within six months of the due date for payment will have to repay the input tax to Customs automatically and regardless of whether the supplier has made a bad debt relief claim.

Once a debt is six months old and providing the VAT has previously been accounted for to Customs, the debt may be written off by being entered in a Refund for Bad Debt Account (ie not written off in the accounting sense, as for corporation tax). The VAT is recovered by including the sum in Box 4 (input tax recovery). Any payment received after the claim has been made is VAT inclusive and the VAT element must be repaid to Customs. VAT bad debt relief is not available for businesses that use either a retail or the cash accounting scheme; such relief is built into the scheme.

21.4.6 Three-year cap

Claims for refunds of overpaid VAT are limited to a period of three years. Customs' power to issue assessments for underdeclared VAT is also limited to the three-year period. However, there is a 20-year limit in cases of fraud. It should be noted that there is currently a series of challenges to the way the three-year cap was introduced in 1996, ie relating to the lack of a proper transitional period following a decision from the European Court of Justice in the case of *Marks & Spencer*. A number of recent cases have been won by taxpayers at both tribunal and court level and there could be a further reference to the European Court in future.

21.4.7 Partial exemption

A business that makes both exempt and taxable supplies is known as 'partly exempt' and is generally unable to recover all VAT paid to its suppliers. Partly exempt businesses have to adopt a method of calculating recoverable VAT. The only method which can be used without Customs' permission is the standard method. This method apportions VAT incurred in the ratio of taxable to total income, eg if 50% of income is taxable then 50% of VAT on costs which are not directly related to taxable or exempt supplies, i.e. general overheads, can be recovered. If any other method of calculating recoverable VAT is required the method has to be negotiated with and agreed in writing by Customs. Methods other than the standard method are known as special methods. Since 1 April 2007 businesses submitting applications for special methods have been required to declare that the proposed special method is fair and reasonable.

If the VAT on costs relating, directly and indirectly, to the exempt activities (known as 'exempt input tax') is below prescribed limits (known as 'de minimis limits'), all the VAT incurred is recoverable in full. The current limits are that the exempt input tax must not exceed £625 pm on average and 50% of the total input tax incurred. This means that a business can incur approximately £42,800 pa of costs that relate to its exempt activities without having to restrict its recovery of input tax provided the 50% qualification is not breached. Once the exempt input tax limit is exceeded in any VAT year (the VAT year ends March, April or May depending on the business's VAT return period), all the relevant VAT is irrecoverable, ie the £625 pm is not an automatic entitlement.

There are other minor limits that apply in particular circumstances. The rules are complex and it is advisable to obtain professional advice. Full details may be found in the VAT Regulations 1995 (SI No 2518), regs 99–111 and Customs VAT Notice 706.

VAT-exempt goods and services are listed in VATA 1994, Sch 9. The main headings are:

(1) Land (with a number of exceptions, and see 21.3.2).
(2) Insurance.
(3) Postal services.
(4) Betting, gaming and lotteries.
(5) Finance.
(6) Education (when provided by eligible bodies, which include youth clubs).
(7) Health and welfare.
(8) Burial and cremation.
(9) Trade unions, professional bodies and other public interest bodies.
(10) Sports competitions, sport and physical education.
(11) Works of art, etc (in limited circumstances).
(12) Fundraising events by charities and other qualifying bodies.
(13) Cultural services.
(14) Supplies of goods where input tax cannot be recovered.
(15) Investment gold.

As the headings are a general description and the rules for exemption can be complex, it is advisable to take professional advice before exempting a particular transaction.

21.5 ANTI-AVOIDANCE MEASURES

Several anti-avoidance measures are available to Customs. These include the following.

21.5.1 Business splitting

Where a business activity has been divided among a number of legal entities (eg a series of partnerships with a partner common to all) and the reason for splitting the business is to avoid accounting for VAT, Customs may issue a direction informing all the businesses that they are registered as a single unit (see 21.4.1) and that VAT must be accounted for on all taxable income. The direction can only take effect from a current or future date.

Customs is not obliged to prove the division was for VAT avoidance; it can treat connected businesses as one entity for VAT purposes, whether or not there is genuine commercial reason for the division.

21.5.2 Sales to connected parties

Where a VAT-registered business supplies goods or services at below market value to a connected party that is not entitled to a full recovery of input tax, Customs may direct at any time, during the three years following the supply, that VAT is accounted for on the open market value.

21.5.3 Self supplies, etc

In certain circumstances, an output VAT charge will arise on normal business activities that are not supplies made to third parties, ie a VAT charge arises on business expenditure (usually referred to as 'self supplies'). The value of such supplies is taken into consideration when determining a liability to register for VAT; the more important ones are described below. The reasons behind such a liability are both anti-avoidance and to reduce possible trade distortion.

Reverse charges

Certain services purchased from overseas persons give rise to an output tax liability on the recipient. The services are deemed to be both supplied and received by the UK organisation, ie there is an output tax liability, and the VAT may also be recovered under the normal rules (restricted if partly exempt). The services concerned are listed in Sch 5 to the VATA 1994 and include royalty and/or licence payments; advertising, legal, accountancy and consultancy services; the secondment of staff or hire of equipment; telecommunications services; radio and television broadcasting services; and electronically supplied services (such as the supply of software, films and music).

Customs has obtained a derogation to use the reverse charge as an anti-avoidance measure on certain business-to-business transactions (eg mobile phones and computer chips). The measure came into force on 1 June 2007. It means suppliers will not charge VAT (customers will apply the reverse charge), thereby reducing the scope for VAT fraud.

Joint and several liability

The VAT legislation provides that VAT registered purchasers of certain goods can be held jointly and severally liable for any VAT unpaid in the supply chain. This is provided the purchaser has reasonable grounds for suspecting VAT would be unpaid. This measure was first applied to mobile phones and computer chips but since 1 May 2007 has applied to electronic equipment used by individuals for leisure, amusement or entertainment purposes.

21.5.4 Transfer of a business

Where the assets of a business are transferred to another person who intends to use them to carry on the same kind of business as the vendor, the transaction is not subject to a VAT charge (21.3.7). However, where a partly exempt VAT group (ie a VAT group that is not entitled to a full recovery of input tax) acquires assets in these circumstances, there is a deemed taxable supply by the VAT group and output tax must be accounted for on its VAT return. The corresponding input tax is restricted by whatever method has been agreed with the local VAT office.

21.5.5 Group registration

Customs can direct, in exceptional circumstances, that VAT be charged on intragroup supplies, which are normally disregarded for VAT purposes. In addition, it can treat an associated company as part of a VAT group retrospectively from a particular date or remove a VAT group member from that group with effect from a particular date.

These powers are used only where the group structure will result in a loss to the Revenue; they are designed to have an effect only in cases involving VAT avoidance. Customs consulted with professional bodies and issued a statement of practice in May 1996. The statement of practice gives examples of proposed structures where the powers will be used.

Customs is also able to remove companies from a VAT group that are no longer eligible and companies presenting a revenue risk.

Overseas companies, which subject to certain conditions had been eligible to be included in VAT groups, no longer qualify unless they have a branch or substantial business establishment in the UK.

21.5.6 Election to tax commercial property

The election to tax the grant of freehold or leasehold interests in commercial property is not available in certain circumstances if the purchaser or tenant does not use the property wholly or mainly for taxable purposes. The Customs' view is that 'wholly or mainly' means more than 80%, although this has not been tested at a VAT Tribunal. This does not apply to leases granted prior to 26 November 1996. This subject is beyond the scope of this book; those entering into property transactions should seek professional advice.

Landlords and vendors of commercial property must enquire about a tenant's or purchaser's legal relationship with the vendor, the financing arrangements and likely use of the property as, if the election is disapplied, this may affect the landlord's or vendor's right to recover VAT on related costs. Indemnity clauses may therefore need to be inserted into leases and agreements.

21.5.7 Disclosure of VAT schemes

New rules were introduced with effect from 1 August 2004. The rules require users of a scheme 'designated' by Customs, to notify Customs (on the relevant VAT return) that the scheme has been used in the period concerned. Customs has published a list of the designated schemes and the list includes schemes relating to land and property, value shifting arrangements, various cash-flow saving schemes where goods are supplied on approval or sale of return, and credit card or cash handling services provided as an intermediary for a retailer.

Smaller businesses, ie those with a turnover below £600,000, will not need to report the use of designated schemes.

Businesses which have a turnover above £10m are required to report the use of any scheme where the main purpose is to save VAT and the scheme arrangements include a published list of 'designated' provisions known as 'hallmarks'. The provisions will include agreements to share tax savings with another party or adviser, where contingency fees will be paid and where consideration for a supply is given by a loan or by subscription for shares between connected parties.

Businesses that are currently considering putting VAT saving arrangements in place should take professional advice and consider the list of published schemes and provisions by Customs. Full details can be found in Public Notice 700/8.

21.6 SPECIAL SCHEMES

Several special schemes are either designed to simplify accounting for VAT or reduce the VAT liability.

21.6.1 Flat-rate scheme for small businesses

A flat-rate scheme for VAT-registered small businesses was introduced on 25 April 2002. The turnover threshold is £150,000. A business that elects to use the flat-rate scheme will simply account for VAT at a flat-rate percentage of its turnover rather than on every single transaction. The flat-rate percentage applied depends on the trade sector of the business concerned, and is calculated to include relief for input tax. Customs has published full details of the scheme in VAT Notice 733.

21.6.2 Retail schemes

These are special schemes used by retailers, ie businesses that sell, hire or repair goods direct to the general public rather than to other VAT-registered businesses and are in trade classification Groups 24 (Retail Division) and 28 (Miscellaneous Services). Generally the schemes are for those businesses which deal direct with the public on a cash basis and who do not normally issue tax invoices.

Use of retail schemes has been restricted. Taxpayers are only allowed to use a retail scheme when normal VAT accounting is not possible. Since then the measures have been implemented on an individual basis as part of Customs' normal VAT assurance visit programme.

As retailers normally account for VAT on receipt of payment, retail schemes provide automatic bad debt relief, although retailers must account for VAT on all credit sales at the time of sale.

21.6.3 Second-hand schemes

The second-hand scheme allows suppliers to charge and account for VAT on the profit, if any, as opposed to the full selling price. Before 1 January 1995, schemes were available for certain goods. The scheme is currently available for sales of the following:

(1) Supplies of works of art, antiques and collectors items.
(2) Supplies of motor vehicles.
(3) Supplies of second-hand goods.
(4) Any supply of goods through an agent acting in his own name.

Special stock recording and records are required.

It has been recognised that dealers in low-value, high-volume goods have difficulty maintaining the detailed records required, so a simplified VAT accounting method, 'Global Accounting', was introduced. Under the system 'eligible businesses' can account for VAT on the difference between total purchases and sales in each tax period rather than on individual items.

21.6.4 Cash accounting

The general principle is that VAT must be accounted for on all tax invoices issued, whether or not the customer/client has paid for the supply. Businesses that cannot use a retail scheme and with a turnover of less than £1,350,000 p.a. from 1 April 2007 (previously £600,000), excluding VAT, may use the cash accounting scheme, provided certain conditions are satisfied. The conditions are laid down in regulations as described in C&E Notice 731, which in this respect has the force of law. Output VAT is not due until payment has been received but, similarly, input tax on purchases/expenses cannot be recovered until the supplier has been paid and a receipt obtained.

21.6.5 Annual accounting

To avoid having to submit returns quarterly, businesses with an annual turnover not exceeding £1,350,000, excluding VAT, may be authorised, in writing, by Customs to use the annual accounting scheme. Nine monthly payments or three quarterly payments, in either case based on the previous year's VAT liability, are made by direct debit and a final, balancing payment is made with the VAT return at the end of the second month following the allocated VAT year.

The annual accounting scheme can be combined with the flat rate scheme, under which a business can account for VAT as a flat-rate percentage of its turnover. The applicable percentage depends on the business sector concerned. A business can apply to join the flat rate scheme if its taxable turnover in the next year will be £150,000 or less and its total business income will be £187,500 or less.

21.6.6 Tour operators' margin scheme

This scheme must be used by any VAT-registered business that supplies packaged travel/accommodation services. As the name implies, VAT is accountable on the margin, if any, on the taxable element of the package. Special record keeping and an annual calculation are required.

21.6.7 Agricultural flat-rate scheme

This is a special scheme under which farmers and other agricultural businesses need not register and submit VAT returns in order to recover VAT on overhead expenses, etc. Instead, the farmer charges VAT at a nominal 4% on all his supplies that he retains (in lieu of input tax). The recipient is entitled to recover the charge as input tax under the normal rules. The scheme requires authorisation by Customs and is not applicable to all farmers: farmers who would benefit by more than £3,000 compared with being VAT registered are not entitled to join the scheme.

21.7 CONTROL AND ENFORCEMENT PROCEDURES

21.7.1 VAT visits

Customs officers regularly visit VAT-registered businesses to verify the returns submitted. Their powers are extensive and include the right to see any documents, accounts, etc relating to the business activities, and to inspect (but not search) the business premises. The frequency of visits depends on a number of factors such as business size, types of business activity and compliance history. Visits can range from half a day every few years for smaller business to several weeks a year for multinationals.

Where errors are discovered, the visiting officer will raise an assessment for any VAT previously underdeclared and, where appropriate, impose penalty and interest charges (see 21.7.2). It is therefore advisable to have all assessments independently reviewed. Customs collects over £1,000m by way of additional assessments from approximately 450,000 visits each year, but most visits do not result in assessments being issued. If the accounting records have been well kept and independently reviewed regularly, no problem should arise at the visit.

21.7.2 Penalties

Customs may impose a number of penalty provisions automatically and arbitrarily for a failure to comply with the many complex VAT regulations. The penalty provisions were introduced with a view to improving compliance and reducing the amount of VAT outstanding at any one time.

Significant changes are occurring to the penalty regime, including the possibility of no penalty being imposed for genuine mistakes and the introduction of suspended penalties.

Late registration
(VATA 1994, s 67(1))

Failure to notify at the correct time (see 21.4.1) results in Customs imposing a financial penalty. The penalty is a percentage of between 5% and 15% (depending on the length of the delay) of the net tax due between the date notification was required and the actual date of notification.

Late returns
(FA 1994, s 59)

If one payment is submitted late in any 12-month period, Customs notifies the VAT-registered person that payments submitted late during the following 12 months will be subject to a default surcharge.

If a payment is submitted late during the 12-month surcharge period, a 2% penalty is imposed and the surcharge period extended for a further 12 months. The surcharge rises for each successive late payment to 5% and by increments of 5% to a maximum of 15%. If payments have been submitted by the due dates for 12 months, the business is removed from the default surcharge regime and the cycle starts again.

The surcharge is waived if it is assessable at the lower rate and below a minimum amount of £200.

Misdeclaration penalty
(FA 1994, s 63)

If a VAT officer discovers an underdeclaration that exceeds specified limits, he will assess a misdeclaration penalty of 15% of the additional VAT assessed. The penalty, which is based on each individual period (ie it is not accumulative), is imposed where the additional VAT assessed exceeds the lesser of:

- £1m; and
- 30% of the gross amount of tax due for the appropriate return period.

Voluntary disclosures

Errors in excess tax of £2,000 must be disclosed to Customs on form VAT 652 or by letter. Errors not exceeding £2,000 can be corrected on VAT returns.

Customs will not impose a penalty but will impose interest when an error is voluntarily disclosed. Once an attempt to arrange an assurance visit is made by an officer, Customs normally considers the point of voluntary disclosure to have passed.

New penalty ruegime for incorrect returns

A new penalty regime, relating to incorrect returns for income tax, corporation tax, PAYE, National Insurance contributions and VAT, has started to come into force. It came into force on 1 April 2008 as regards documents relating to tax periods starting on or after that date. No person shall, however, be liable to a penalty under the new regime in respect of a tax period for which a return is required to be made before 1 April 2009.

Under the new regime the penalties are as follows:

- for careless action, up to 30% of the potential lost revenue;
- for deliberate but not concealed action, up to 70% of the potential lost revenue;
- for deliberate and concealed action, up to 100% of the potential lost revenue.

Interest
(VATA 1994, s 74)

An interest charge is imposed on assessments for additional tax issued by VAT visiting officers. The interest rate is the prescribed rate as enacted by Treasury order and is not deductible for income or corporation tax. Customs has stated that interest may not be imposed where there is no overall loss of revenue, for example where a supplier has failed to charge VAT to a customer who would have been entitled to recover the VAT charge. Customs has indicated that each case will be decided on its merits, but that officers have been made aware of the need to consider whether there has been a loss of revenue.

Other penalties

There are other penalty provisions such as failure to maintain or produce records, unauthorised issue of a tax invoice (by non-registered persons), persistent incorrect returns, etc. There are, in fact, over 60 regulatory offences that could give rise to a penalty.

21.8 FRAUD

There are two forms of fraud in VAT law: civil and criminal.

21.8.1 Civil
(VATA 1994, s 60)

If, after an investigation, Customs is satisfied there has been an element of dishonesty, it may seek to impose a civil fraud penalty of 100% of the tax involved. If there has been full co-operation by the taxpayer, Customs, or (on appeal) a VAT tribunal, may reduce the penalty by whatever percentage is considered reasonable.

Despite the introduction of the new penalty regime for incorrect returns, these civil fraud provisions will remain in effect with respect to dishonest conduct which does not relate to an inaccuracy in a document or a failure to notify HMRC of an underassessment by HMRC.

21.8.2 Criminal
(VATA 1994, s 72)

The more serious cases are dealt with under the criminal law with penalties of up to three times the VAT involved, or imprisonment, or both. In these cases Customs must use the criminal rules of evidence, etc and prove beyond reasonable doubt that a fraud has been committed deliberately.

21.9 APPEALS

21.9.1 VAT tribunals

There is a right of appeal to an independent VAT tribunal on a number of matters, including:

(1) Assessments considered to be incorrect or not issued to the Commissioners' best judgement.
(2) Liability rulings by Customs in respect of a specified supply.
(3) Penalties, other than the interest charged for errors, if there is a reasonable excuse for the error. The law does not define 'reasonable excuse' but does state that the insufficiency of funds or the reliance on another is not a reasonable excuse.
(4) The amount of the reduction, if any, of a penalty for a civil fraud where the taxpayer considers he has provided full co-operation with the investigating officers.

The details of appeal procedures are outside the scope of this book. However, the procedure for lodging an appeal to a VAT tribunal (which must be made within 30 days of the notification of appealable decision) is straightforward. It is prudent to obtain professional advice before appealing and it is advisable to be represented at the tribunal hearing, which in many ways resembles a court hearing, although less formal.

A VAT tribunal decision may be appealed to a higher court on a point of law and, in limited circumstances, an appeal may be referred to the ECJ for a ruling.

21.9.2 Proposed reforms to the appeal system

It is intended that from April 2009 the tax appeal system, for VAT as well as direct taxes, will be replaced with a single system comprising a First-tier tribunal and an Upper Tribunal. The First-tier tribunal will hear most tax appeals; the Upper Tribunal will hear appeals against the decisions of the First-tier tribunal and may also hear some first instance appeals.

21.9.3 Departmental reviews

Many disputes are settled by negotiations with Customs by formally requesting a departmental review of the disputed ruling/assessment within the 30-day time limit. This allows discussions to continue without the loss of the right to appeal to an independent VAT tribunal. The departmental review may become compulsory but has not yet done so. If so, taxpayers will not be able to lodge an appeal to a VAT tribunal until a departmental review has been completed. The Commissioners, if requested, usually review an assessment after the 30-day limit has expired and, where appropriate, reduce the amount assessed. In certain circumstances it is also possible to make an application to a VAT tribunal to hear a case that is out of time.

22

NATIONAL INSURANCE CONTRIBUTIONS

This chapter covers the following topics:

(1) Class 1 contributions.
(2) Class 2 contributions.
(3) Class 3 contributions.
(4) Class 4 contributions.

Where rates are quoted, they are the 2008–09 rates; these and the 2007–08 rates can be found in Table 22.1 (see 22.4).

22.1 CLASS 1 CONTRIBUTIONS

22.1.1 Introduction

Employed individuals are liable for Class 1 NICs unless they are over the retirement age. Secondary contributions are paid by employers (see 22.1.7).

No contribution is payable unless the employee earns £105+ pw, although entitlement to benefits starts for earnings in excess of £90. If he earns £105+, contributions are calculated at 11% on the excess amount over £105 on earnings between £105 and £770 pw (eg on weekly earnings of £125, employee NICs due are £125 – £105 = £20, × 11% = £2.20). A lower rate of 9.4% contributions is payable if the employee is contracted out of the State Second Pension.

Since 2003–04, an additional 1% charge is imposed on all earnings above the upper earnings limit.

Women who married on or before 6 April 1977 and have chosen to pay a reduced rate are subject to pay NICs of only 4.85%. This right is lost if the woman is divorced, but is not lost if she is widowed. Such a woman still has to pay the 1% on earnings in excess of £770 pw.

Contributions are normally assessed by reference to weekly earnings, but if the employee is paid less frequently, contributions are calculated on the corresponding figures for a monthly basis or whatever other period is covered by the payment to him.

An individual's liability to NICs is not affected by a previous period of unemployment during the year. Each 'earnings period' is looked at in isolation and there is no principle that corresponds to the cumulative method used for income tax where a tax year is looked at as a whole. There is a slight exception to this for company directors (see 22.1.3), but this is basi-cally an anti-avoidance provision.

The Inland Revenue National Insurance Contributions Office (NICO) administers NICs, statutory sick pay (SSP) and statutory maternity pay (SMP). Before 1999, these matters were dealt with by the Department of Social Security.

Most NICs, SSP and SMP appeals can be heard by an independent tri-bunal in the same way as tax appeals. Previously, the Secretary of State was asked formally to determine one of a range of 'questions' via the Office for the Determination of Contribution Questions (ODCQ) based in Newcastle. Note, however, that appeals on contracting-out pensions issues and Working Families' Tax Credits (WFTC) are not heard by tax tribunals.

22.1.2 Deferment

An individual who has more than one job and total earnings likely to exceed the upper limit may apply for deferment so that NICO may authorise certain employers not to withhold contributions from his remuneration (form CA 2700). The deferment application is made on form CF 379. Ideally, this form should be submitted before the start of a tax year for which deferment is sought. In any event, deferment will not be granted for 2007–08 unless NICO had received the application by 14 February 2008. NICO is also reluctant to grant deferment for a year in which the individual will reach pensionable age. Where a deferment application is made, the individual cannot choose which earnings should be subject to deduction for NICs. In addition, NICO will always defer contributions at the non-contracted out rate if any of the employments is not contracted out.

The position is reviewed after the end of a tax year. It may be that the individual has not had the anticipated level of earnings from a particular employment and this may mean that the liability for the year has not been satisfied. In such a case, NICO will apply for payment of the balance and this falls due for payment within 28 days of NICO making such a demand.

There is an entitlement to a repayment of contributions withheld from the remuneration, where they exceed the maximum for the year, even if the individual has not applied for deferment.

Where deferment is granted, the second employer should deduct 1% con-tributions from all earnings above the earnings threshold and not just from the upper earnings limit. A similar principle applies if someone is employed and also has profits from self-employment. In this situation, there will gen-erally be a residual 1% on all profits above the lower profits limit.

22.1.3 Company directors

Remuneration paid to a company director is normally assessed for NICs as if it arose on a yearly basis. Therefore, a large lump sum payment of fees or a bonus could attract the maximum contributions for a year, rather than the maximum contributions for one week or one month.

Example – Assessment on lump sum payments

A weekly paid company director received remuneration of £35,000 paid in a single sum. The liability for contributions is the liability for the year, ie

52 × £665 (ie £770 upper limit – £105 lower limit) × 11% ie £3,803.80

It is not just the maximum for one week's earnings, ie 11% of £665, ie £73.15, plus 1% of the excess over £770.

Regulation 6A of the Social Security (Contributions) Regulations 1979 ensures that the earnings period is annual but it is possible to make payments on account. When the last payment is made to the director in the tax year, the employer is required to reassess the NICs due on the total earnings for the tax year on an annual, or pro rata annual, earnings period, as appropriate. To qualify for these arrangements, the following three conditions must be satisfied:

(1) the director agrees to NICs being assessed this way;
(2) he normally receives his earnings in a regular pattern; and
(3) those payments normally exceed the lower earnings limit for the pay period.

Directors (and officers) may be held liable for the employer's contributions where it has failed to pay NICs on time and the failure appears to be attributable to fraud or neglect by the culpable officers.

22.1.4 Definition of earnings

'Earnings' for NICs purposes include all cash remuneration. Contributions are also payable on sick pay, holiday pay, etc. The NICs definition of 'earnings' is quite different from that used for income tax purposes. For example, NICs are assessed on an individual's pay before pension contributions and before any charitable donations made under a payroll deduction scheme. See *Tax Bulletin* June 2005 on tips, service charges and troncs.

Where an employer settles an employee's pecuniary liability, the sum paid is treated as earnings for NIC purposes even though it is not pay for PAYE purposes. Previously, only certain types of benefits-in-kind that could easily be converted into cash were liable to NICs. For example, premium bonds and National Savings certificates are regarded as earnings for NICs purposes because they may be encashed by the holder surrendering them. With effect from 6 April 2000 the definition of earnings for NICs purposes was extended to cover all benefits-in-kind that are taxed as emoluments or deemed emoluments (see 22.1.8).

Non-cash vouchers are also treated as earnings with the following exceptions (see 4.4.7 and 4.4.8):

- transport vouchers where the employee earns less than £8,500;
- transport vouchers for the disabled;
- transport vouchers for the armed forces;
- vouchers exchangeable for the use of sports or recreational facilities;
- vouchers associated with long service awards;
- vouchers in respect of staff functions (less than £150 per person);
- vouchers exchangeable for meals provided on employer's premises or at a staff canteen;
- first 15p per working day of luncheon vouchers (maximum £1.05 pw);
- incentive awards up to £150 pa per donor;
- childcare vouchers for children up to age 16.

NICs are also due on an employer's contribution to a FURBS established specifically for an individual director or employee.

Share options

No NICs arise on the grant or exercise of approved share options, unless the shares are readily convertible assets, the exercise takes place after 8 April 2003 and it gives rise to an income tax charge, for example, where the option is exercised within three years of grant.

There is no NICs liability on the grant of an unapproved option.

The exercise of unapproved share options involving shares that are 'readily convertible assets' attracts NICs if the option was granted on or after 6 April 1999. The charge arises on the same amount as is chargeable to tax (see 5.4.2), ie it is based on the amount the shares would realise if sold on the day the option is exercised. The definition of readily convertible assets was substantially widened by FA 2003 (see 20.1.3).

No NICs liability arises on the exercise of a non-approved option over shares that are not readily convertible assets at the time of exercise. This is because TA 1988, s 135 does not deem such a profit to be an emolument, it merely states that the profit shall be charged to tax under IT(E&P)A 2003.

Employers and employees can jointly elect for employees to bear the employers' NIC. The election allows the employer to make an application to HMRC for approval of a joint election in which the liability for secondary NICs is legally transferred to the employee. The election covers securities options, conditional awards such as long-term incentive plans, cash cancellation payments made to give up a security option or restricted and convertible securities and post-acquisition gains from restricted or convertible securities.

Income tax relief will be available to the employee equal to the amount of the secondary NICs transferred from the employer to the employee under the terms of the election.

Dividends

NICs ought not to arise where a director receives a dividend, or interest on a loan made to the company, or rent for a property used by the company. Investment income of this nature is clearly not earnings but there may be borderline cases where a so-called dividend is really remuneration that has been given a misleading label. NICO may have a point if the dividend payment does not conform to company law requirements.

22.1.5 Problem areas

One major problem area concerns directors' drawings. NICO takes the view that where a director arranges for a personal liability to be settled by the employer and charged to his drawings account, the payment constitutes earnings for NICs purposes unless the drawings account is in credit.

Example – Directors' drawings

A has a drawings account with his company which is £60 in credit. The company pays a personal bill for A of £100 and debits his drawings account with £100, thus turning the credit balance into an overdrawn balance of £40.

NICO takes the view that £60 of the payment of the £100 bill is a repayment of a loan and attracts no NICs, but the balance of £40 is a payment of earnings and the grossed up amount is subject to NICs.

Another problem area surrounds tips paid to employees. Tips are exempt from Class 1 NIC if one of two conditions are satisfied:

(1) they are not paid, directly or indirectly, to the employee by the employer and do not comprise or represent monies previously paid to the employer by a customer;

(2) they are not allocated, directly or indirectly, to the employee by the employer.

Therefore, NICs are due on tips paid through a tronc if the employer decides, directly or indirectly through another person, who should receive what amount by way of tips. Thus, an independent troncmaster should be appointed who genuinely decides which employees should receive a payment and the amount of such a payment: the employer does not allocate the payments.

22.1.6 Loans from the employer

Curiously, NICO takes the view that if an individual arranges for a loan from his employer that is used to settle a personal liability, there is no NIC liability unless (and until) the employer writes off the loan. Considerable care should be taken when dealing with any documentation and the structure of such arrangements to minimise liability.

22.1.7 Employer's NICs

In addition to the 'primary' contributions paid by the employee, employers are required to pay 'secondary contributions'. There is no ceiling on the amount of an employee's earnings that attracts secondary contributions. No liability for secondary contributions can arise unless there is a liability for primary contributions, except when an employee with other employment has a deferment form CA 2700 or is a pensioner (Table C or S).

An employee can agree to pay his employer's NICs on profits from the exercise of non-approved share options after 19 May 2000. The NICs borne by the employee are then deducted in arriving at his IT(E&P)A 2003 income (see 5.4.2). The Revenue has published model agreements under which an employee can agree to pay his employer's NICs on his share option.

Employers are also liable for Class 1A NICs where the employee has benefits-in-kind (see 22.1.8). For company cars, the cash equivalent used for income tax purposes is treated as if it were additional earnings subject to secondary contributions. A further charge may arise if the employee is provided with fuel for private mileage, with the Class 1A charge again being based on the scale benefit used for income tax purposes.

Class 1A NICs on cars are also due on unremunerated employees and directors (Social Security Act 1998, s 52). This section states that the person liable to pay Class 1A NICs in these circumstances is the person who would normally have been liable to pay secondary Class 1 NICs had the benefit of the car been earnings.

NICs have been aligned with the Revenue's treatment of PAYE Settlement Agreements (PSAs). This means that Class 1B NICs are payable on PSAs and are payable at the same time as the tax (19 October). Class 1B NICs are currently payable at 12.8% on the total value of:

(1) all items covered by the PSA that would give rise to a Class 1 or 1A liability, and
(2) the tax payable by the employer under the PSA.

22.1.8 Class 1A NICs

Class 1A NICs now apply to most benefits-in-kind. The payment date of Class 1A NICs is 19 July after the end of the year of assessment.

The amount of the charge is normally equivalent to the highest rate of employer's secondary Class 1 NICs, which is currently 12.8%. The Class 1A liability is an employer's charge only and is a tax-deductible expense. The charge is not payable by employees or directors.

Class 1A NICs are not charged if:

(1) NICs are already due (eg on expense payments);
(2) the expense payment or benefit-in-kind is covered by a P11D dispensation, extra-statutory concession or specific exemption;
(3) the expenses payment or benefit-in-kind is included in a PSA (where Class 1B NICs will be payable); or
(4) the benefit-in-kind is provided to an employee earning at a rate (inclusive of benefits) of less than £8,500 pa.

To reduce the reporting requirements, the Revenue has announced an exemption from income tax and NICs for the following:

(1) tools and equipment provided for work use where there may be a small amount of private use in the home, workplace or elsewhere;
(1) qualifying beneficial loans;
(1) general welfare counselling (but not private medical treatment or consultation); and
(1) refreshments provided by employers.

Class 1A NICs reports are merged with the existing forms P11D.

22.2 CLASS 2 CONTRIBUTIONS

22.2.1 Introduction

A self-employed individual is liable to Class 2 NICs of £2.30 pw unless his earnings are less than £4,825 pa and he has applied for a Certificate of Exemption. A penalty can be charged if he has not notified NICO within three months of taking up self-employment. See Tax Bulletin June 2001.

The Class 2 NICs for sharefishermen is £2.95 pw and for volunteer development workers is £4.50 pw.

22.2.2 Earnings from employment and self-employment

Where an individual has income from both employment and self-employment, both Classes 1 and 2 NICs are payable unless he applies for deferment. The maximum he may pay for any year is an amount equal to the maximum Class 1 primary contributions on 53 weeks' earnings. A repayment may be claimed if he has paid a mixture of Classes 1 and 2 NICs in excess of this amount.

22.2.3 Small earnings exemption

A person may avoid paying Class 2 NICs by applying in advance for the small earnings exemption. The amount of the limit for small earnings exemption for 2008–09 is £4,825.

Earnings for this purpose are measured by reference to actual earnings for the tax year. For example, if a trader makes up accounts to 30 September, the small earnings exemption is available only if his earnings for 2008–09 are less than £4,825 when computed as follows:

$\frac{6}{12}$ × profits for the year ended 30 September 2008

$\frac{6}{12}$ × profits for the year ended 30 September 2009

An individual may apply for repayment if Class 2 NICs have been overpaid. The repayment claim must normally be made between 6 April and 31 January following the end of the tax year and thus the deadline for making a repayment claim for 2008–09 will be 31 January 2009.

A false economy?

In general, choosing not to pay Class 2 NICs could prove a false economy as entitlement to benefits such as pensions and sick pay may be affected.

22.3 CLASS 3 CONTRIBUTIONS

These are a type of voluntary contribution. A person who is neither employed nor self-employed (or whose earnings fall below the exemption) may pay voluntary Class 3 NICs to secure the state retirement pension. The weekly rate is set at £8.10 for 2008–09.

Class 3 weekly rates are:

2002/2003	£6.85
2003/2004	£6.95
2004/2005	£7.15
2005/2006	£7.35
2006/2007	£7.55
2007/2008	£7.80
2008/2009	£8.10

22.4 CLASS 4 CONTRIBUTIONS

These are payable by self-employed individuals according to the level of their profits as determined for income tax purposes. For 2008–09, Class 4 NICs are levied at the rate of 8% of trading profits between £5,435 and £40,040. Earnings in excess of the upper profits limit attract Class 4 NICs at the rate of 1%.

Where an individual pays interest on a business loan or has suffered trading losses, such amounts may be set against his earnings for the purposes of assessing liability for Class 4 NICs. This situation applies even where the losses have been relieved for income tax purposes by way of offset against his other income.

Table 22.1 – National Insurance contributions

Item	2006–07	2007–08	2008–09
Lower earnings limit, primary class 1	£84 per week	£87 per week	£90 per week
Upper earnings limit, primary class 1	£645 per week	£670 per week	£770 per week
Primary threshold	£97 per week	£100 per week	£105 per week
Secondary threshold	£97 per week	£100 per week	£105 per week
Employees' primary class 1 rate	11% of £97.01 to £645 per week;1% above £645 per week	11% of £100.01 to £670 per week;1% above £670 per week	11% of £105.01 to £770 per week; 1% above £770 per week
Employees' contracted-out rebate	1.6%	1.6%	1.6%
Married women's reduced rate	4.85% of £97.01 to £645 per week;1% above £645 per week	4.85% of £100.01 to £670 per week; 1% above £670 per week	4.85% of £105.01 to £770 per week 1% above £770 per week
Employers' secondary Class 1 rate	12.8% on earnings above £97 per week	12.8% on earnings above £100 per week	12.8% on earnings above £105 per week
Employers' contracted-out rebate, salary-related schemes	3.5%	3.7%	3.7%
Employers' contracted-out rebate, money-purchase schemes	1.0%	1.4%	1.4%
Class 2 rate	£2.10 per week	£2.20 per week	£2.30 per week
Class 2 small earnings exception	£4,465 per year	£4,635 per year	£4,825 per year
Special Class 2 rate for share fishermen	£2.75 per week	£2.85 per week	£2.95 per week
Special Class 2 rate for volunteer development workers	£4.20 per week	£4.35 per week	£4.50 per week
Class 3 rate	£7.55 per week	£7.80 per week	£8.10 per week

Table 22.1 – Continued

Item	2006–07	2007–08	2008–09
Class 4 rate	8% of £5,035 to £33,540 per year; 1% above £33,540 per year	8% of £5,225 to £34,840 per year, 1% above £34,840 per year	8% of £5,435 to £40,040 per year 1% above £40,040 per year
Class 4 lower profits limit	£5,035 per year	£5,225 per year	£5,435 per year
Class 4 upper profits limit	£33,540 per year	£34,840 per year	£40,040 per year

PART 3

WEALTH PLANNING

This part contains the following chapters:

23

WEALTH PLANNING BY MANAGING YOUR FINANCIAL AFFAIRS

This chapter addresses issues that are likely to come up in connection with your personal financial affairs and those of your immediate family. We all have objectives, needs and expectations that have financial implications. These may include the following:

- paying off a mortgage;
- getting married or entering into a civil partnership;
- providing for children's education;
- funding the costs of higher education;
- buying a second home;
- saving for retirement;
- children's marriages;
- providing for dependants;
- giving to charity;
- increasing spendable income in retirement;
- funding grandchildren's school fees;
- passing on capital to children;
- mitigating IHT.

Managing savings and investments should take account of these objectives. The management process should be flexible and continuous because different objectives may need to take priority as events unfold.

An important part of managing investments is making sure that particular types of investment are appropriate for your situation. A given investment's tax treatment is often a big factor in determining this.

In this chapter we look at:

(1) Your family and personal financial planning.
(2) Managing your investments.
(3) Tax deductible investments.
(4) Some special situations.
(5) Planning for retirement.
(6) Helping the next generation.
(7) Estate planning.

23.1 YOUR FAMILY AND PERSONAL FINANCIAL PLANNING

There are important personal financial planning issues to be addressed. These may include selecting a suitable type of mortgage, making sure you claim all that is due to you from child tax credits, tax implications of marriage (and separation and divorce), protecting your dependants by taking out life assurance, funding school fees, providing help to elderly dependent relatives and assisting your children in buying their first home. Looking further ahead, there are longer-term matters that need to be kept in mind, for example the way in which your (and possibly your spouse's) will should be drawn up. IHT planning also needs to be considered.

23.1.1 House purchase

When you buy a home, there are several types of mortgage available. Take advice about whether an ordinary repayment, endowment or pension mortgage is the most appropriate for you. Another option is to open an ISA and use this type of tax privileged savings to build up capital so you can clear the mortgage in due course.

Some mortgages involve an offset arrangement so that an allowance is made for a credit balance on your current account and you are charged interest only on your net indebtedness to that bank. These offset mortgages can be a way of saving interest, which far exceeds the amounts that you would retain after tax if you had a conventional mortgage and earned interest on temporary cash surpluses and the money that you would otherwise put on deposit.

23.1.2 Pay down debt before making long-term investments

If you receive a bonus, a gift or an inheritance, it will probably make more sense to use it to clear expensive debt than to make investments. For example, clearing credit card debt may save you from paying 15% interest – you would need to make 25% pa on investments to get an equivalent return.

23.1.3 If you and your partner are not married

The tax legislation does not recognise common law marriages. If your partner has not made a will, you may have no rights under the intestacy rules. The tax legislation may also be stacked against you because the CGT exemption for transfers between spouses is not available and neither is there an IHT exemption for transfers of assets to your partner. The absence of such relief could seriously damage your wealth if you and your partner have substantial assets.

If your partner is a foreign national, bear in mind that the intestacy rules that would apply on his death may be quite different from the rules that apply here.

All in all, there is a lot to be said in favour of marriage from a financial point of view. However, there may be other considerations (see below).

Tax notes

Tax legislation does not recognise common law marriages, so CGT exemption for transfers between spouses is not available and neither is there an IHT exemption for transfers of assets to your partner.

23.1.4 Marriage

There are several important tax considerations that arise in connection with marriage.

Capital gains tax

Bear in mind that if you transfer shares or other chargeable assets to your fiancé, you are deemed to have made a disposal at market value and a capital gain may therefore arise. From this point of view, it may be better to delay matters until after you marry as no capital gain arises on transfers between spouses who are living together. However, if you are thinking of transferring an asset on which a capital *loss* would arise, it may be best to crystallise this loss by making the transfer before you marry.

Something else to bear in mind is the position if each of you already owns your own home. Basically, you have three years' grace to resolve the position, but at the end of that time only one property can qualify as your main residence (see 13.2.5). The property concerned may be a new home or one of you may move into the other's existing home.

Inheritance tax

No IHT arises on transfers of assets by one spouse to another unless the transferor is UK-domiciled and the transferee is not (see 29.5.1).

23.1.5 Civil partners

The Government changed the rules for same-sex relationships with the enactment of the Civil Partnership Act 2004, which came into effect on 5 December 2005.

The most notable benefits of the Act are that registered civil partners benefit from spouse exemption for IHT and CGT. These benefits are, however, tempered by the fact that civil partners will also be subject to the same anti-avoidance provisions that affect married couples (see 32.4 on transfers of assets overseas and 32.5 on the settlement provisions).

Couples affected by the change in legislation will generally need advice on the following:

(1) Private residence (a couple can have only one main residence for CGT purposes).
(2) Pension planning.
(3) IHT and estate planning.

Civil partners who own businesses or who have a significant shareholding in a company should talk to their tax and financial advisors before registering as civil partners.

23.1.6 Pre-nuptial agreements

Divorce lawyers say that there is no certainty that the UK courts will pay any attention to pre-nuptial agreements. But they also say that if such agreements are to have any likelihood of being effective, the wealthier spouse must have made full disclosure of his (or her) assets and given the other party a proper opportunity to consider matters and take advice. Simply thrusting a bit of paper in front of your fiancé the day before the marriage will not meet these tests.

Tax notes

Divorce lawyers say there is no certainty that UK courts will pay any attention to pre-nuptial agreements.

23.1.7 Child tax credits

Remember you have to claim your entitlement, and you should bear in mind that claims cannot be backdated by more than three months (see 11.8.3).

23.1.8 Tax relief for having a nanny

The Government extended the working tax credits from April 2005 so that all or (more likely) part of the cost of a nanny can be covered by a tax credit (see 11.8).

23.1.9 Life assurance

Income tax relief is not given for life assurance premiums on policies taken out after 13 March 1984.

You may well have some death in service cover through your employer's pension scheme, or your personal pension plan will produce a lump sum in the event of your untimely death. However, this is unlikely to be sufficient if you have a young family. Consider taking out term insurance and have the policies written in trust so they will not attract IHT if you and your wife were to die in quick succession.

23.1.10 Funding school fees and higher education

Your children's school may run a prepayment scheme that effectively gives you a tax free return on money you deposit with the school. Ask the bursar about this.

If grandparents or other relatives are able to help, advantage could be taken of your children's tax allowances. One way is for your relatives to set up trusts and for the trustees to distribute income to your children. This money could then be used to pay school fees.

Bear in mind that this will not work if you make a trust for your own children, as any income that is paid out before they attain age 18 will be treated as if it were your income.

Where relatives cannot assist, matters are more difficult but not necessarily impossible. You should start saving as early as possible and take full advantage of privileged investments such as ISAs and qualifying insurance policies. Take advice from a specialist.

If your son or daughter is over 18, you may be able to save tax by assigning insurance bonds for him or her to cash in and use to cover university costs. A gift of such a bond does not trigger a tax charge (see 27.3.1). No tax will be payable on encashment unless your son or daughter is liable for higher rate tax.

Investigate the possibility of buying a property for your son or daughter to occupy while at university. They may be able to let spare rooms to fellow students and the rent can then cover some of your costs. If the house or flat is bought in your children's name, they may be able to claim CGT main residence exemption when the property is sold (see 13.1).

Another approach would be to set up a trust to hold the property with the trustees making the property available to your child for them to use as their main residence (see 30.4.11) because the CGT exemption can also be available in these circumstances. If you are a trustee, you will have some measure of control over what happens to the proceeds after that particular child has finished his course.

23.1.11 Saving for retirement

It's never too early to start making provision for retirement. A pension contribution that you make when you are 30 will benefit from tax free growth for 30 years, a contribution that you make when you are 62 will not grow to anything like the same extent.

We focus on planning for retirement at 23.5.

23.1.12 **Separation and divorce**

You may need to make the best of an event that you would rather had not arisen, the break-up of your marriage.

Relief for maintenance payments under pre-14 March 1988 court orders was abolished with effect from 6 April 2000. Furthermore, now that the married man's allowance has been phased out, there is no relief for maintenance payments whatsoever.

So far as CGT is concerned, you could find yourself in a Catch 22. The legislation provides that a man and his wife are connected persons for CGT purposes until the marriage comes to an end. The marriage comes to an end when there is a decree absolute, not a decree nisi. However, the exemption for transfers between spouses applies only if you are living together. You may therefore find yourself in a situation where a CGT charge may arise because you are required to transfer assets to your spouse as part of your divorce settlement.

It is possible to get round this problem if you plan ahead. The basic rule that transfers between spouses are not subject to CGT applies to transfers made during a tax year in which you have been living together at some time. Thus, if you and your wife separated on, say, 10 April 2008, a transfer of assets between you will not give rise to a CGT charge provided the transfer is made before 6 April 2009.

Tax notes

As far as CGT is concerned, you could find yourself in a Catch 22 when it comes to a divorce settlement.

23.1.13 **Buying a second home**

There are some tax issues with buying a second home.

If you are going to let it out when you do not want to use it yourself, it might make sense to take a mortgage because at least part of the interest that you pay will then attract income tax relief.

If you create a trust to hold your second home, you will have a more flexible situation. In due course, when your children have grown up, the trustees might allow one of them to use the property as his main residence and this could save tax when the property is eventually sold as the trustees may then escape CGT on part of their capital gain because of the main residence exemption (see 30.4.11).

The property may be overseas. If so, think twice about having an overseas company own the property because this may expose you to an income tax charge (see 35.4.4). If lawyers or other professionals in the country concerned recommend that you buy through a local company, it may be best for the property to be registered in the name of the company but held by that company on trust for you and your spouse – this is a matter where you need specialist advice.

23.1.14 Providing for dependants

Disabled children

You may have a disabled child or grandchild. If so, consider making provision for him or her, perhaps by creating a trust (see 30.7).

Elderly dependants

Many readers will be making a contribution towards the support of elderly parents or other relatives. Unfortunately, recent Chancellors have significantly reduced the scope for obtaining assistance towards these costs through tax relief. In particular, it is no longer possible to transfer income via a deed of covenant and the income tax allowance for dependent relatives has been abolished altogether.

One possibility for securing tax relief is where it is necessary to purchase a property that is used by the relative as his home. There is no tax relief for a mortgage taken out for this purpose, but it may be possible to secure CGT exemption in due course if you follow a fairly involved route.

The CGT exemption is not available if you own the property yourself (unless you owned it before 5 April 1988). However, if you form a trust and put money into it to enable the trustees to buy the dependant's home, the trustees may be entitled to an exemption as and when they eventually sell the property. Furthermore, this exemption is not affected by your being a beneficiary under the trust yourself. So the answer may be to set up a trust under which your elderly parent is entitled to occupy the property during his lifetime, with the trust coming to an end on his death and the property passing to you as a beneficiary of your own trust.

IHT could be a problem here if the property is worth more than £312,000 or if you have previously made chargeable transfers and a gift into trust takes you over the £312,000 nil rate band.

Talk this through with a specialist tax adviser to see if a trust would fit with your objectives and makes sense in your particular circumstances.

23.1.15 Helping your adult children to make tax privileged investments

If you can afford it, it may make sense for you to give or lend your adult children the money so that they can use their quota of tax exempt and tax privileged investments such as ISAs or even stakeholder pensions.

23.1.16 Giving to charity

There are many ways of getting tax relief for gifts to charities. Gift Aid means that the charity will get a tax rebate of nearly one third of what you give and you will receive higher rate relief if you pay tax at 40% (see 10.9).

If you have quoted securities that you bought for a fraction of the current price, it may be better to give these to charity rather than draw down on your cash – you will save the CGT that you would have paid if you had sold the shares and you get income tax relief at your top rate. See 10.10–10.11 on the income tax reliefs for gifts of quoted securities and land.

Some readers may be able to set up charitable trusts of their own. This can make financial sense if you are prepared to put in capital of £100,000 or make regular Gift Aid payments of £20,000 or £25,000 pa.

Tax notes

If you have quoted securities that you bought for a fraction of the current price, it may be better to give these to charity to avoid paying the CGT – and get income tax relief.

23.1.17 Increasing spendable income in retirement

There are many ways of increasing your retirement income. For example, you can invest in an insurance bond and make 5% annual withdrawals to use as income. No tax is charged on such withdrawals although they are taken into account in determining any tax charge on encashment of the policy. You may also invest in National Savings certificates, premium bonds and ISAs. See Chapter 24 on tax reliefs. If all else fails, you might consider using some of your capital to buy an annuity but hopefully you will be able to postpone such a radical step as it is by its nature irrevocable.

Remember not to just look at one tax. A wealthy individual had pensions that were taxed at 40%. He put all his shares into his (much younger) wife's name so that the dividends were declared on her return and did not attract higher rate tax. This worked fine but when he died she was left with a potential CGT charge if she sold the shares. It might have been better if they had stayed in his name so that most of the exposure to CGT would have disappeared on his death.

23.1.18 Funding grandchildren's school fees

If you are able to do so, you will make a tremendous contribution to your children's financial position by relieving them of some of the costs of educating your grandchildren.

Regular gifts out of surplus income qualify for IHT exemption (see 29.5.2).

Setting up an accumulation and maintenance settlement still works provided the beneficiaries will become entitled to the capital at age 18. Putting capital into such a trust will be a PET for IHT purposes, ie no IHT charge on your death provided you survive seven years (see 29.6 on this). The trustees will have to pay income tax at 40% on income that they receive but part or all of this tax (probably most of it) can be reclaimed on behalf of your grandchildren as income is paid out for their benefit (see 30.5.7).

23.1.19 Passing on capital to children

If you are having a prosperous retirement, it may be that you should turn your attention to IHT planning. You should consider making PETs and chargeable transfers that are covered by your £312,000 nil rate band. We go into this in more detail at 23.7.

23.2 MANAGING YOUR INVESTMENTS

23.2.1 General strategy

All investments involve a degree of risk. Investments that are apparently risk-free, such as having money on deposit, run the risk that they will not keep up with inflation. The reality is that people who concentrate all their financial resources on any one investment run some risks, albeit the nature of the risks varies according to the nature of the investments and the way they are funded.

Investments based on borrowings are inherently more risky: if you have taken a 100% mortgage to buy an investment property you are going to be under financial pressure if the tenant moves out and the property remains vacant. If you cannot cover the interest costs, you will have to liquidate your investment even though you would have preferred to wait until the property market had picked up. Even property does not increase in value every year – remember when many home owners had 'negative equity'. Increases in interest rates can change the economic climate overnight.

There are probably higher short-term risks with stock market investments. Don't assume that past performance is a guarantee to what will happen in the future, especially in the near future. All markets fluctuate in value from time to time. Stock markets tend to overshoot. They are just as liable to respond to good news by surging ahead and becoming 'over bought' as to over react to bad news or a period of uncertainty.

If you have known financial commitments (eg a tax liability falling due for payment on 31 January 2009 or your mortgage has to be redeemed in two years' time) then you should set aside funds to cover them and invest these funds conservatively. Most sound investments will come right eventually but it's much more risky to take a bet on the level of the stock market in 15 months' or two years' time. The long-term trend may be positive but the markets could give you a bumpy ride in between. When you really need things to come right, they have a nasty tendency to do the opposite.

The same applies if there are things that could happen in the next few years, eg if you can foresee being made redundant.

As you grow older, your perception of risk ought to change. Most soundly based investments will come right in time, especially if you have diversified rather than put all your savings into just two or three investments. But as retirement approaches, you are more likely to need to be able to draw on savings in the foreseeable future. This means that you are less able to sit tight and ride out the fluctuations of the markets.

It is therefore important to keep tax planning in perspective. In general, investment considerations should dictate your investment policy. Naturally, these vary according to an individual's perspective, whether it be age, need for short and medium-term liquidity, income requirements, the degree of risk acceptable, expectations for future inflation levels, perception of the economic climate, etc. Tax planning must fit in around such considerations. However, there are some simple steps that can often help you to reduce the tax payable on your investment income and gains.

23.2.2 Selecting investments that suit your requirements

Different types of investments have varying tax treatment and this needs to be taken into account. For example, advisers often say that you should try to arrange matters so that both you and your spouse/civil partner use up your CGT annual exemption every year. This is good advice but if this is your objective you should not be investing in roll-up funds or insurance bonds as these types of investments are subject to income tax rather than CGT.

Here are our thoughts on types of investment that are likely to meet a given objective:

Objective	Type of investment
Tax free returns	qualifying life policies (see 27.2)
	National Savings certificates (see 24.3)
	ISAs (see 24.1)
	VCT investments (see 24.6)
Use annual exemptions and use up past CGT losses	quoted shares
	unit trusts
	investment trust shares
	collective funds
Capital growth with no risk of loss to capital	stock market bonds (see 23.2.3)
Get entrepreneurs relief and pay CGT at only 10%	shares in private companies (see 16.7)

Objective	Type of investment
Avoid internal tax*	unit trusts
	investment trusts
	offshore insurance bonds (see 27.4)
Avoid paying tax on switching between specialised funds	insurance bonds (see 27.2)
No tax charge on transfer of investment	insurance bonds (see 27.2)
Avoid paying tax until encashment	roll-up funds (see 9.7)
	insurance bonds (27.2)
Deferring taxable income	roll-up funds
	insurance bonds
Avoid two tier CGT**	unit trusts
	investment trusts
	REITs (see 26.6)
	avoid private investment companies (see 26.2.1)
Reducing tax by making investments	VCTs (see 24.6)
	EIS investments (see 24.5)
	pension schemes (see 25.1)
IHT savings	unquoted shares (see 29.8.2)
	AIM shares

* investments are subject to internal tax where the fund is liable for tax (eg corporation tax) that is separate from the tax payable by the investor and which cannot be reclaimed by him

** investments attract a two tier tax charge where tax is charged on income and gains realised by the fund and the investor is subject to a separate tax charge, usually on realising his investment

Property investments

We look at some of the differences in the tax treatment various types of property investments in Chapter 26.

23.2.3 Further analysis

Selecting an appropriate investment involves more than just the 'tick box' approach that the above table may suggest. This is partly because some of the objectives run in opposite directions. For example, investing in a VCT may give you tax free dividends but it is also a more risky investment.

Similarly, it may well be desirable (all other things being equal) to avoid a fund that is subject to an internal tax charge but the drawback may be less than it looks. If you hold shares and unit trusts that are likely to produce capital gains, and you are subject to 40% income tax, an investment in an insurance company may have its plus points. The fund will suffer 'internal tax' of 20% and you may incur higher rate tax on cashing in the investment but the total tax is no more than the 40% that you would have paid if you had received the fund's income directly. Moreover, an insurance bond allows you to switch from one type of investment (eg equity funds) to another such as property funds without any tax charge. You can also give the investment bond to someone else without a tax charge whereas gifts of shares, units in unit trusts, etc, may attract a CGT charge. Looked at overall, the tax treatment of insurance bonds can therefore still be very attractive even though they do not score when measured against one particular criterion.

A lot depends on circumstances. If you are giving £5,000 to be set aside for your newly arrived grandson to use when he gets to age 18, it may well be best to invest in a broadly based unit trust or other managed investment rather than, for example, using the money to buy shares in one particular company. Money invested in a unit trust can grow virtually tax free whereas using an insurance bond would involve unnecessarily suffering the effects of internal tax.

What is important is to know what you are getting. If you are buying units in an offshore fund, you need to know whether it has distributor status or is classified as a roll-up fund (see 9.7). The difference is that profits realised on the sale of distributor funds are subject to CGT rather than income tax but gains from roll-up funds are always taxed as income.

Similarly, if you invest in a bond issued by a bank that gives you (say) 75% of the increase in the FTS100 index over the next five years or a minimum 10% return if the index goes down, you need to know how any profit will be taxed. In fact, most of these bonds are structured as a special type of insurance bond and the return may be subject to higher rate tax.

If you are a basic rate taxpayer and you are not likely to use your £9,600 CGT annual exemption, you might be better off if you put (say) half of your spare cash into a 'tracker fund' (a special type of unit trust) and kept the rest on deposit. It's all a question of looking at the effects of charges and the importance that you attach to guarantees (and to the fact that these bonds lock you into an investment for a fixed period). You should consult an IFA or other investment specialist on these types of issues.

23.2.4 Managing investments to take account of your personal situation

In the next section of this chapter, we look at ways in which you may be able to fine-tune your investments by taking full advantage of opportunities that arise from your own (and your family's) circumstances.

23.2.5 Take full advantage of tax efficient investments

Investments in an ISA are totally free from tax (see 24.1), so if possible you should open ISAs for yourself and your partner. National Savings certificates also offer a safe and tax-free return, albeit at a relatively low interest rate.

For longer-term investments, qualifying life insurance policies are often attractive. Once a policy has been in force for ten years, there is normally no tax charge whatsoever on the policy being cashed in.

Also consider taking out a stakeholder pension plan for a non-working spouse or partner.

23.2.6 Use all your family's allowances

There is generally scope for planning both in relation to income tax and capital gains tax.

Deposit interest

Spouses each have their own personal allowances and each spouse's income is taxed completely separately. If your spouse has little or no income, or is liable only at 20% whereas you have to pay 40% tax, there may be advantages in transferring income to him or her. A fairly straightforward way of doing this is to hold bank deposit accounts and other investments in your joint names. The basic rule is that where investments are held in this way, half of the resulting income is taxed on each spouse.

If you open a bank account in your minor child's name, the interest is treated as your income for tax purposes only if the total income arising from such potential gifts exceeds £100 pa per child (see 32.5.4), so there may be some limited opportunity for achieving tax-free savings.

Where you have adult children, it may make sense for you to lend cash to your children so that they can make tax efficient investments in ISAs (see 24.1).

Capital gains tax

Your spouse will have his or her own £9,600 CGT annual exemption and you should look for ways of using this each year, possibly by transferring investments (transfers between spouses are deemed to take place on a no gain/no loss basis) in order to put your spouse in a position to realise a gain on a sale to a third party. This is often appropriate where a gain has built up on quoted securities. A judicious transfer to your spouse of stocks and shares that show a paper gain can save significant amounts of tax even if the transfer takes place shortly before the securities are sold. But take care: the Revenue often looks very closely at the paperwork on such inter-spouse transfers and you must show that beneficial ownership of the securities actually passed to your spouse before a firm of stockbrokers was instructed to sell the shares. All other things being equal (which they seldom are), it is generally best to allow a few days to elapse between the transfer of the shares to your spouse and the sale by him or her.

There may sometimes be scope for using your children's annual CGT exemption as the £100 limit for income tax purposes does not apply for capital gains. Bear in mind that this is more difficult since a gift of shares, etc to anyone other than your spouse is normally treated as a disposal that is deemed to take place for CGT purposes at market value. However, if you hold shares in unquoted trading companies and you can see an opportunity coming up whereby you could realise those shares at a large gain, it may be worth transferring part of your shareholding to your children. Because the shares are in unquoted trading companies, it may be possible to 'hold over' any capital gain so that your child (or other relation or friend) takes over the shares at your original acquisition value (see 16.5). This means that you will have no capital gain. The recipient will have a gain on disposal of the difference between your acquisition value (as adjusted for inflation) and the sale proceeds. However, if you plan carefully you can probably ensure that the child, etc, realises a gain that is just within his £9,600 annual exemption – so no one pays tax on the capital gains.

When there is an opportunity to take up an attractive share issue, consideration should be given to subscribing in your child's name as well as your own.

For CGT planning generally, see Chapter 28.

Tax notes

When there is an opportunity to take up an attractive share issue, consideration should be given to subscribing in your child's name as well as your own.

Long-term planning

You may even take out a stakeholder pension plan for a minor child and contribute up to £2,808 (£3,600 gross) pa – but bear in mind that this is a much more long-term savings plan.

23.3 TAX DEDUCTIBLE INVESTMENTS

Basically, there are four types of investment that attract income tax relief when you make the investment: pension contributions; investment in enterprise zone properties; investments under the EIS; and investments in VCTs.

23.3.1 Pension contributions

We return to pension contributions because the tax situation is so attractive. There is no other type of investment where you can gain tax relief when you pay money in, enjoy the benefits of a fund that pays no tax on its income and gains and take part of the fund as a tax-free lump sum. The last aspect is one of the most important; contributions to pension schemes allow a person effectively to convert taxable income into a tax-free capital sum.

Personal pensions

An individual is allowed to make a payment of up to £3,600 pa even though he does not work and so has no earnings. The pension payments are made net of basic rate tax even if the individual has no taxable income.

Pension contributions generally

If you have employment or trading income, you can make contributions to a registered pension scheme equal to those earnings (subject to a limit of £235,000 pa). Your employer could (if it were so inclined) make contributions which exceed your earnings. See 25.1.4 on this.

23.3.2 Investment in enterprise zone properties

A 100% allowance is available where a person invests in a commercial building located in an enterprise zone. Basically, the building must be unused or you must make your investment within two years of it having first been let.

Enterprise zones were designated for a period of ten years and this period has now run out for many of them. Nevertheless, a number of enterprise zone property investments remain available.

Many people prefer to invest via a syndicate or fund, often called 'enterprise zone property trusts'. A person who invests in such a trust is entitled to relief for the corresponding proportion of the trust's investments in enterprise zone properties.

23.3.3 Investments under the enterprise investment scheme (EIS)

Wealthy individuals should consider making selective investments under the EIS. It is now possible to invest up to £500,000 pa under this scheme. Investors are entitled to 20% income tax relief and may also be able to claim CGT deferral relief (see 24.5). The income tax and CGT reliefs may add up to 60% of your investment. Any capital gain on a disposal of the EIS shares after three years is totally tax free.

The Government has also made the EIS more attractive in other ways. Many of the restrictions and anti-avoidance rules have been abolished. It is now possible for an investor to become a paid director and take a full part in the management of the company. If you have gains in excess of £500,000, or you have made gains in the last few years that you would like to 'roll over', you may be able to obtain CGT deferral relief by investing further amounts under the EIS. Also, one of the requirements for EIS investors to qualify for the 20% income tax relief is that they must not have more than 30% of the equity. This rule does not apply if you are investing in an EIS company only in order to secure CGT deferral relief (see 24.5).

23.3.4 Venture Capital Trusts (VCTs)

An individual is allowed to invest up to £200,000 pa in VCTs – although note that these may be relatively high-risk investments. There are significant tax advantages in that if you subscribe for new VCT shares you are entitled to 40% income tax relief, though CGT deferral relief ceased to apply from 2004–05. In addition, the dividends you receive from your investment and any capital gain when you eventually dispose of it can be tax free (see 24.6).

23.4 SOME SPECIAL SITUATIONS

23.4.1 Securing tax relief for losses on investments

If you are nursing losses on investments in shares and unit trusts, and you have realised gains on other investments during the current tax year (eg on the sale of a property that you have been letting), it may make sense to cash them in. Perhaps you hope that the investments will in time recover much of their value and you do not want to dispose of them altogether. There may be a way of having your loss relief without losing out on such a recovery. There are special rules aimed at 'bed and breakfast' transactions but it may be possible to side-step these if you sell and your spouse or partner buys back (see 28.2).

If you are the main beneficiary under the will of someone who has died in the last few months, it may be possible to reduce the IHT on your inheritance. If the executors sell quoted securities within 12 months of the death, and the proceeds are less than their value at the date of death ('probate value'), it may be possible to have IHT recalculated so that it is charged only on the lower value (see 29.11.3).

23.4.2 Planning for specific situations

Your circumstances may be special because of your residence status, or your plans for the future.

For example, it may be that you plan to work overseas for a few years and therefore cease to be UK-resident. In such a case, it makes sense to defer taxable income until after you have ceased to be resident as this means no tax will arise. A possible way of doing this is to invest in offshore roll-up funds, rather than bank deposit accounts, with a view to cashing in the roll-up investments after you have ceased to be a resident.

If you are about to return to the UK, having been resident abroad, then you should take advice on any investment bonds and insurance policies issued by foreign insurance companies (see 27.4). If you have been non-resident for five tax years there may be merit in realising capital gains before you resume UK residence (see 33.5.4).

Your circumstances may be special in another way: if you have suffered Schedule D Case VI losses in the past, look out for ways of realising miscellaneous income (ie income that used to be taxable under Schedule D Case VI). The point is that Case VI losses brought forward from previous years may be set against such income and the profits do not have to arise from the same source. This is not affected by the abolition of Schedule D under the IT(T&OI)A 2005.

It might be, for example, that you suffered losses on a property that you let out as furnished accommodation when such activities were taxed under Case VI. Perhaps you have sold the property or ceased to let it and you assumed that your losses would go to waste. However, you may be able to 'access' these Case VI losses by selling gilts shortly before they go ex-div. The point is that the sale of gilts cum-interest will normally give rise to miscellaneous income by virtue of the accrued income scheme (see 8.6). Another way of generating profits that may be offset by Case VI losses is to invest in offshore roll-up funds. In many cases, such investments are very similar to having money on a bank deposit overseas but no income is deemed to arise until the investor realises the investment. When this happens, the profit is charged as miscellaneous income.

Tax notes

Look out for ways of setting losses against miscellaneous income that used to be taxable under Schedule D Case VI – this is not affected by the abolition of Schedule D.

23.4.3 Property investments

Investments in real estate tend to be longer-term investments. For that reason, the tax planning considerations also tend to be long term in nature.

One planning point is relevant at the time you acquire an investment property. Interest on a qualifying loan may be set against any UK rental income. The planning point is therefore very simple: you should normally borrow at the outset unless you are quite sure that you will not need to borrow money to finance your property investments later on. Even if you do have sufficient capital, it may be best to borrow to make property investments and use your spare capital for other purposes. For example, it would not be good tax planning to use your capital to purchase an investment property and at the same time take a long-term non-qualifying loan to finance school fees.

Do not plan for one tax in isolation. If you let part of your home, or if you let your home for a period while you are living elsewhere, check on the

CGT implications (see 13.4.3). There are a number of reliefs and ESCs, but you must be very careful not to put your extremely valuable main residence exemption into jeopardy.

If you do let part of your home, bear in mind the special rent-a-room relief (see 7.4) that may mean that rental income of up to £4,250 is exempt from tax.

It may make sense to form a company to hold property investments. If this is your only company and its profits do not exceed £300,000, the company should only be subject to corporation tax at 21% on its rental income. But once again take advice on the long-term implications if capital gains are likely to arise when properties are sold. The VAT implications of property investment are also complex (see 21.3.6). It is worth obtaining professional advice as there are special rules (eg election to tax and capital goods scheme) that are not straightforward. There are opportunities to save VAT, but also pitfalls.

Bear in mind Stamp Duty Land Tax (SDLT), both on purchasing a property and on transferring it to a company (see Chapter 38).

23.4.4 Qualifying loans for company directors

If you work full time for a close company in a managerial capacity or hold more than 5% of the shares, and you wish to purchase more shares, you may be able to raise a qualifying loan (see 10.5). The interest attracts tax relief at your top rate and there is no upper limit.

23.4.5 Plan ahead when buying a private company

If you purchase the whole of the share capital of a private trading company and things do not go to plan, you are not normally due income tax relief for any loss. You may be able to get a loss allowed for CGT purposes, but capital losses may be set only against capital gains, not against income, and therefore it may be some years before you get effective relief.

There may be a way around this if you follow certain steps when you acquire the company. You should speak with your accountant, but basically what will be involved is for you to form a new company, subscribe cash for new shares in that company and have the company acquire the shares in the private trading company. At the end of the day, your position will be almost exactly the same, except that you will hold shares in a company with a wholly owned subsidiary rather than hold shares in the subsidiary itself. What is important is that by dealing with matters in this way, you will be entitled to s 574 relief on any capital loss (see 16.2), ie you will be able to set the loss against your income for the year of loss or the preceding tax year.

If you need to raise equity from outside investors, see if you can structure your company in a way that qualifies under the Enterprise Investment Scheme – see 24.5. Also consider Venture Capital Trusts as a potential source of equity investment (see 24.6).

If you are in the process of buying or setting up a business, we suggest that you read Chapter 18 as part of your preparation for a discussion with your professional advisors.

23.4.6 Long-term planning for foreign domiciliaries

There are significant planning possibilities if you have foreign domicile (see Chapter 34) or indeed if part of your family has always been based overseas.

23.5 PLANNING FOR RETIREMENT

We all need to put serious financial investments into provision for our retirement. There are many things to be considered and this section can only highlight possibilities and direct you to the relevant parts of this book.

The obvious way of planning for retirement is to make contributions to a registered pension scheme (see 25.1).

If you are employed by someone else, consider making contributions into a stakeholder pension scheme. If your employer is a large quoted company, it may be possible to persuade your board that additional pension benefits should be provided via a FURBS (see 25.1.3). Take full advantage of approved share schemes in order to accumulate capital for your retirement (see 5.4 and 5.5–5.6).

If you own and run a trading company, you should ensure that the company sets up the most beneficial scheme possible for both you and your spouse (assuming he or she also works for the company). There is also CGT to be considered. Putting money into an executive pension scheme may mean that you can effectively make investments in a wider class of assets without your company undertaking substantial investment activities in its own right.

If you are self-employed, you should consider setting up a SIPP.

If your spouse does not work, fund a stakeholder pension scheme for her (or him). Annual contributions can be made of £2,880 (£3,600 after the addition of tax relief).

Looking at another aspect of retirement planning: if your work requires you to occupy job-related accommodation, and you don't own a home of your own, you should probably buy a property and nominate it as your main residence for CGT purposes (see 13.3).

Tax notes

If your work requires you to occupy job-related accommodation and you don't own a home of your own, you should probably buy a property and nominate it as your main residence for CGT purposes.

23.6 HELPING THE NEXT GENERATION

Once again, the purpose of this part of the chapter is to get you thinking about possible issues and to refer you on to other parts of this book.

There are all sorts of ways in which you may help your sons and daughters. These may include loans or gifts to help with house purchase. Why not investigate the possibility of having your spare cash taken into account if your son or daughter has an offset mortgage (see 23.1.1)? They will still pay the same amount each month but by entering into this arrangement you could help them to clear their mortgage after 15 or 16 years rather than the full term.

Another situation where you might help is by making gifts or loans to fund retraining if they embark on a new career.

We have already covered tax aspects of helping your children by covering part of the costs of school fees, etc.

Another way in which you may wish to assist the next generation is by setting them up in business or passing on your family business – see Chapter 31 on this.

If they work for your family company, you will want to ensure that they can also benefit fully from your company pension scheme. If they work for an incorporated family business, you should encourage them to make regular contributions to a pension scheme.

One very important way of helping the next generation is to establish one or more family settlements – see Chapter 30 on this.

23.7 ESTATE PLANNING

Inheritance tax planning is a very technical area (see Chapter 29), but in general a person should:

(1) make a will;
(2) if you already have a will, get it reviewed in the light of recent IHT changes (see 29.5.1).
(3) use the annual exemptions as far as possible (see 29.6);
(4) preserve and maximise business property and agricultural reliefs;
(5) if you receive an inheritance, consider making exempt transfers by a deed of variation;
(6) make potentially exempt transfers that escape IHT after the donor has survived seven years; and
(7) fund insurance policies so as to provide cash to meet IHT payable on death.

If you have entered into IHT saving schemes in the past, you need to take advice on whether you could be subject to the income tax charge on pre-owned assets that started in April 2005 (see 32.7).

Making a trust can be an excellent way of putting capital outside your estate without relinquishing all control over the way that the capital is used (especially if you appoint yourself as one of the trustees); see Chapter 30 on trusts in general. You need to bear in mind the GWR (gift with reservation) rules (see 29.7) but with careful planning these rules should not apply if you are a potential beneficiary of a trust created by your spouse. There is also an exception from the GWR rule where a person gives an interest in a property to someone who also occupies the property and certain other conditions are satisfied (see 29.7).

See Chapter 31 on passing on the family business.

24

TAX EFFICIENT INVESTMENT

HILARY SHARPE

There is a range of investments where the interest and any gains are exempt from tax or the investment attracts tax relief. This chapter covers the following:

Investments providing tax exempt return

(1) Individual savings accounts (ISAs).
(2) Personal equity plans (PEPs).
(3) National Savings investments.
(4) Friendly society investments.

Investments qualifying for tax deduction

(5) Enterprise Investment Scheme (EIS).
(6) Venture Capital Trusts (VCTs).
(7) Enterprise zone trusts.
(8) Investment in film partnerships.

INVESTMENTS PROVIDING TAX EXEMPT RETURN

24.1 INDIVIDUAL SAVINGS ACCOUNTS (ISAs)

24.1.1 Basic outline of scheme

ISAs are designed to encourage new saving. They are offered by financial institutions, or 'providers' (eg banks, building societies and insurance companies). All UK-resident and ordinarily resident individuals aged 16+ can take out an ISA. The current annual limit is £7,200, of which up to £3,600 can be kept on deposit. The balance must be invested in stocks and shares, and unit trusts.

Investors in ISAs are exempt from income tax and CGT on their investments. Normally, contributions to an ISA are made in cash (but see below on shares acquired under approved schemes).

24.1.2 Transfers of shares into an ISA

It is possible to transfer into an ISA shares received from an approved profit-sharing scheme (see 5.2) or from an approved savings-related share option scheme (see 5.4). The market value of shares transferred into the ISA counts towards the £7,200 annual limit, but no CGT is payable on the transfer. The transfer must take place within three years of the shares being appropriated in the case of a profit-sharing scheme and within 90 days of acquisition under a savings-related share option scheme.

It is not possible to transfer other shares into an ISA, for example, shares acquired under a public offer or on a building society demutualisation.

24.1.3 Withdrawals

It is possible to make withdrawals from an ISA at any time without loss of tax relief, but it is not normally possible to return sums to an ISA unless the amounts fall within the annual 'allowance'. The Government has allowed a special exemption for savers who withdrew money from Northern Rock ISAs.

24.1.4 Practical aspects

The current regulations permit an individual to invest £7,200 in a 'maxi' ISA or £3,600 in a cash 'mini' ISA and £3,600 in a stocks and shares 'mini' ISA in a tax year.

A stocks and shares ISA can be invested wholly in quoted (but not AIM) shares, unit trusts, investment trusts and OEICs, gilts, and corporate bonds with a life of at least five years.

24.1.5 CAT standards

The Government introduced a system of voluntary 'CAT' (Charges Access Terms) standards. These vary according to the type of ISA. For example, the CAT for mini cash ISAs requires seven-day access and interest of no less than base minus 2%. The standards are voluntary, but providers must inform potential investors whether their products meet or exceed the standards.

24.1.6 Consequences if rules are broken

With an ISA invested in stocks and shares, if the rules are broken (eg because the individual has taken out both a maxi and a mini ISA in the same year), the individual must report any capital gains.

With a cash ISA, the provider must withhold 20% tax and the individual must include the interest on his SA return and pay any higher rate tax due. An individual who has knowingly broken the rules may also be liable for a penalty.

> **Tax notes**
>
> ISAs were originally intended to have a ten-year life but are now to be a permanent feature of the tax planning landscape.

24.2 PERSONAL EQUITY PLANS (PEPS)
(TA 1988, s 333)

PEPs held at 6 April 1999 continue to attract the same tax advantages as ISAs.

24.3 NATIONAL SAVINGS INVESTMENTS

24.3.1 National Savings certificates
(TA 1988, s 46)

These certificates pay an accumulating rate of interest over a two, three or five-year period. All returns are tax free. Index-linked certificates accumulate at a rate related to the RPI. If they are held for the full five years, a bonus is payable.

24.3.2 NSB ordinary account interest
(TA 1988, s 325)

The first £70 of interest paid on a National Savings Bank (NSB) ordinary account is exempt from tax (see 8.1.1).

24.4 FRIENDLY SOCIETY INVESTMENTS

Friendly societies issue qualifying insurance policies and there is no tax charge for investors when such policies mature. In this respect the position is no different from policies issued by insurance companies. The difference lies in the way friendly societies are treated favourably for tax purposes in that they are not normally subject to tax on life assurance business; this has generally enabled them to produce attractive returns.

Friendly society policies are essentially a long-term investment (minimum 10 years). The maximum premiums are very low: the maximum permitted is £270 pa. Some societies do permit a lump sum investment to be made to cover a full ten-year plan. Most of the larger friendly societies are governed by the same investment regulations as life assurance companies. All investment income and capital gains within the fund are free of all UK tax, which enhances the rate of return.

INVESTMENTS QUALIFYING FOR TAX DEDUCTION

24.5 ENTERPRISE INVESTMENT SCHEME (EIS)
(FA 1994, s 135 and Sched 14)

The scheme is intended to provide a 'targeted incentive' for new equity investment in unquoted trading companies and to encourage outside investors to introduce finance and expertise to a company. The reliefs allow minority investors to secure 20% income tax relief in addition to CGT deferral relief, which could be worth up to another 18% of the amount invested (or 40% if the EIS investment is used to roll-over pre 6 April 2008 capital gains).

Individuals can also secure EIS CGT deferral relief even though they do not qualify for the income tax relief (eg because they take a controlling stake in the company). Trustees can also use the EIS to secure CGT deferral relief but are not eligible for the income tax relief.

24.5.1 Summary of main aspects

Tax relief is due only if an individual subscribes for new shares in a qualifying company (see 24.5.3) which satisfies the £7m gross asset test (see 24.5.6).

Income tax relief

Income tax relief may be given at 20% on the amount invested; this relief is forfeited if there is a disposal within three years.

CGT reliefs

Shares that attract the 20% income tax relief are exempt from CGT, except to the extent that EIS relief has been withdrawn.

CGT deferral relief may also be obtained so that in some situations total tax relief of 60% can be secured.

Where EIS shares are sold at a loss, relief is available either against capital gains or against the individual's income by virtue of ITA 2007 s 131 (see 16.2) but this will not normally give additional relief where the investment has qualified for EIS CGT deferral relief.

Conditions to be satisfied

Income tax relief is not available if the individual acquires a shareholding that exceeds 30%, but CGT deferral relief can still be available.

Income tax relief is not available to an individual if he was previously connected with the company. This does not prevent a connected investor from qualifying for the CGT deferral relief.

There is a ceiling for investment by individuals who qualify for income tax relief under the EIS of £500,000 per tax year (£400,000 for 2006–07 and 2007–08). The ceiling does not apply for CGT deferral relief.

Up to one-half of the amount invested by an individual between 6 April and 5 October in any year can be carried back to the previous tax year if he did not invest the full amount during that year. This is subject to a maximum of £50,000.

The Revenue publishes a most informative booklet, IR137, *The Enterprise Investment Scheme*.

Certificate EIS 3

An investor must obtain a certificate EIS 3 from the company before claiming either type of EIS relief.

24.5.2 Conditions to be satisfied for relief to be available

Subscription for new shares in a qualifying company

Neither EIS income tax relief nor EIS CGT deferral relief are available unless an individual subscribes for shares. The shares must be ordinary shares that are not preferred in any way. EIS income tax relief is available only if he invests at least £500. The company must be a qualifying company.

24.5.3 Qualifying companies

A qualifying company can be a UK-resident or non-resident company, but it must be an unquoted company that either:

(1) exists wholly for the purpose of carrying on one or more qualifying trades (see 18.3) or 'so exists apart from purposes capable of having no significant effect (other than in relation to incidental matters) on the extent of the company's activities'; or
(2) has a business that consists wholly of:
  (a) holding shares or securities of, or making loans to, one or more qualifying subsidiaries of the company; or
  (b) both holding such shares or securities, or making such loans, and carrying on one or more qualifying trades.

Groups

A group's activities are considered as a whole, rather than on an individual company basis. The Revenue has confirmed that relief will not be withdrawn where non-qualifying activities do not form a substantial part of the group's activities as a whole. In practice, 'substantial' is understood to mean 20% or more.

Company must be unquoted

A company does not qualify if any of its shares or securities are dealt in on the London Stock Exchange. The fact that a company's shares are dealt in on the AIM does not disqualify it, but the £8m gross asset test will rule out many AIM companies (see 24.5.6).

Other conditions

There are other conditions that need to be satisfied if it is to be a qualifying company:

(1) it must not control another company apart from a qualifying subsidiary, either on its own or together with a connected person, and there must not be any arrangements in place under which the issuing company can acquire such control;
(2) it must not be under the control of another company, or of another company and persons connected with it, and again there must be no arrangements in place whereby such a company may acquire control of the issuing company; and
(3) there must be no arrangements for the company to become quoted.

Since 6 April 2007, a company is not a qualifying company if it has 50 or more full-time employees.

24.5.4 Meaning of 'qualifying trade'

This is covered at 18.3. Certain asset-based or low-risk trades are excluded, as are investment businesses.

24.5.5 Definition of 'qualifying subsidiary'
(TA 1988, s 308(2))

A qualifying subsidiary is one in which the issuing company or one of its subsidiaries holds at least 51% of the share capital. In addition, the company must meet one of the following tests:

(1) it must be carrying on a qualifying trade; or
(2) it must exist to hold and manage a property used by the parent company, or by a fellow 51% subsidiary, for qualifying trade purposes; or
(3) it must be dormant.

However, a subsidiary needs to be a 90% subsidiary if it is to be the company that uses the EIS money.

24.5.6 Gross asset test

EIS reliefs are available only where the company has gross assets of less than £7m before and no more than £8m after the EIS share issue (£15m and £16m before 22 March 2006).

24.5.7 Reliefs available to an EIS investor

There are two types of relief: income tax and CGT deferral relief (see 24.5.1). They are separate, and either can be claimed without the other. An individual who invests, say, £100,000 can claim both reliefs by reference to the same £100,000 invested. Trustees can only claim the CGT relief.

24.5.8 Income tax relief

An investor is entitled to the lower of the income tax payable by him and relief at the lower rate (20%) on the amount invested up to a limit of £500,000 (£400,000 for 2006–07 and 2007–08, £200,000 for 2004–5 and 2005–06). For this purpose, his tax liability is calculated without regard to any reliefs given as a reduction expressed in terms of tax.

His tax liability is also computed without regard to double taxation credits and basic rate tax deducted at source on annual payments.

24.5.9 Other conditions for income tax relief

Individual must not be connected with the company

The legislation provides that an individual may be treated as connected with the issuing company, and therefore not entitled to EIS income tax relief, if he directly or indirectly possesses or is entitled to acquire more than 30% of the:

(1) issued ordinary share capital of the company, or any of its subsidiaries;
(2) loan capital and issued share capital of the company or any subsidiary; or
(3) voting power in the company or any subsidiary.

A connected individual can still be eligible for CGT deferral relief.

An individual is also regarded as being connected with the issuing company if he directly or indirectly possesses, or is entitled to acquire such rights as would, in the event of the winding-up of the company (or any of its subsidiaries), mean he is entitled to receive, more than 30% of the assets available for distribution to the company's equity holders.

Rights of 'associates' need to be taken into account. For these purposes, an 'associate' means partner, spouse, parent, grandparent, great-grandparent, child, grandchild, great-grandchild and certain family trusts. The necessity to take account of partners' interests was confirmed by the decision in *Cook* v *Billings & others*.

An individual is also regarded as connected with the company if he possesses any loan capital in a subsidiary of the company.

Finally, if an investor receives a loan from a third party that would not have been made but for the EIS investment, he is disqualified. This applies where a bank makes a loan that is secured on the EIS shares.

Individual must not be previously connected with the company

An individual is deemed to be connected with the company if he is:

(1) a paid director of the issuing company or any of its subsidiaries; or
(2) an employee of the issuing company or any of its subsidiaries; or

(3) a partner of the issuing company or any subsidiary; or

(4) an associate of someone who is a director, employee or partner of the issuing company, or any of its subsidiaries.

An individual is disqualified if he falls into any of the above categories during the two years prior to the date the EIS shares are issued. Furthermore, he will not qualify for EIS relief if he is connected with the issuing company at the time the shares are issued, unless he is a business angel who qualified for EIS relief on his original investment and is now acquiring additional shares and he is connected only because he is a paid director (see Figure 24.1).

FA 2004 legislation

FA 2004 introduced two new rules. The first allowed shares to be issued to EIS investors at the same time as other investors (previously not allowed). The second made it possible for investors who had previously had loans repaid to them by the company to obtain income tax relief, provided the loan repayment was not deemed an 'arrangement'. Both of these provisions came into effect from 17 March 2004.

24.5.10 CGT deferral relief
(FA 1995, s 65 and Sched 13)

This relief involves a concept of deferred gain. Basically, an individual who has realised a gain may secure deferral relief if he invests in the EIS during the period beginning one year before and ending three years after the disposal giving rise to the chargeable gain. The CGT deferral relief can be claimed even where the investor is 'connected' with the company (see 24.5.9).

However, the deferred gain is separately identified and will come back into charge if certain events happen (see 24.5.17).

Example – EIS CGT deferral relief

N sold quoted shares for £65,000 in December 2007. The shares were originally purchased in January 2003 for £10,000. In June 2007, *N* invested £55,000 in ordinary shares in an EIS company. The CGT position for 2007–08 would then be as follows:

	£
Proceeds	65,000
Less: Cost	(10,000)
Gain before taper relief	55,000
Less: EIS CGT deferral relief	45,000
Net chargeable gain for 2007–08	10,000

Note: Although *N* invested £55,000, it is possible for him to claim CGT deferral relief of only £45,000 so as to avoid wasting the annual exemption for 2007–08 after allowing for 10% taper relief.

Figure 24.1 – Is an investment by a business 'angel' eligible for EIS relief?

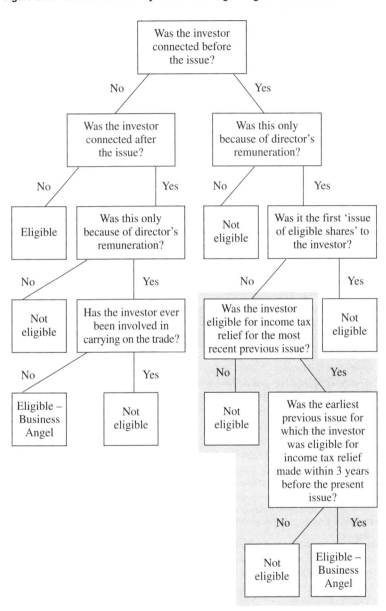

NB. The shaded area deals only with cases where there was only one issue of eligible shares to the investor before he or she became connected with the company because of director's remuneration.

24.5.11 Withdrawal of relief where company redeems share capital

All EIS investors lose a proportion of their relief if at any time during the investor's relevant period the company repays, redeems or repurchases any of its share capital which belongs to any member other than:

(1) the qualifying individual in question; or
(2) another EIS investor who thereby loses relief under the disposal of shares rule; or the total relief withdrawn from EIS investors is the greater of:
    (a) the amount receivable by the non-EIS investor; or
    (b) the nominal value of the share capital in question.

The relief so lost is apportioned between the EIS investors in proportion to the amounts of the investments that have qualified for relief.

24.5.12 Withdrawal of relief where value is received from the company

Relief is withdrawn to the extent that an investor receives value from the company within three years of making his investment. An investor is regarded as having received value where the company:

(1) repays, redeems or repurchases any part of his holding of its share capital or securities, or makes any payment to him for the cancellation of rights;
(2) repays any debt to him (other than a debt incurred by the company on or after the date on which he subscribed for the shares that are the subject of EIS relief);
(3) pays him for the cancellation of any debt owed to him other than an ordinary trade debt, ie a debt incurred for a supply of goods or services on normal trade credit terms. The legislation specifically provides that normal trade credit does not allow for payment to be left outstanding for a period that exceeds six months; or
(4) releases or waives any liability of his to the company (the liability is deemed to have been waived if the liability is outstanding for more than 12 months) or discharges or undertakes to discharge any liability of his to a third person.

Further, he is regarded as having received value where the company:

(a) makes a loan or advance to him if this includes the situation where the individual becomes indebted to the company other than by an ordinary trade debt;
(b) provides a benefit or facility for him;
(c) transfers an asset to him for no consideration or for consideration less than market value;
(d) acquires an asset from him for consideration exceeding market value; or
(e) makes any other payment to him except:

(i) one that represents payment or reimbursement of allowable expenditure;

(ii) interest at a commercial rate on a loan from the individual;

(iii) dividends representing a normal return on investment;

(iv) payment for supply of goods by the individual to the company
(provided the price does not exceed the goods' market value);

(v) reasonable and necessary remuneration for services rendered to
the company where the income is taxed as trading income (this
does not cover remuneration for secretarial or managerial services).

In addition, he may receive value from a company if it is wound up and he
receives a payment or asset in the course of the liquidation.

24.5.13 Withdrawal of relief where company ceases to be a qualifying company

(1) EIS relief is withdrawn completely where any of the following events
occurs during the three-year relevant period:

(2) the company issues shares that are not fully paid up;

(3) the company ceases to exist wholly for a qualifying trade purpose;

(4) the company comes under the control of another company, or of
another company and persons connected with it;

(5) arrangements come into being whereby another company could acquire
control.

24.5.14 Clawback of income tax relief where investor becomes connected with the company

EIS income tax relief (but not CGT deferral relief) is withdrawn completely
where an investor becomes connected with the company during his relevant
period (three years from the date that his shares are issued).

Definition of 'connected'

An individual is regarded as becoming connected with the company if he is:

(1) the owner (directly or indirectly) of more than 30% of the company's
voting shares, its issued ordinary share capital, or its loan capital and
issued share capital taken together;

(2) the owner of rights entitling him to more than 30% of the company's
assets available for distribution to equity holders;

(3) entitled to acquire more than 30% of the company's voting shares, its
issued share capital or its share and loan capital taken together;

(4) entitled to acquire rights entitling him to more than 30% of the company's assets available for distribution to the company's equity holders;

(5) the associate of a person who owns or is entitled to acquire more than a 30% interest;

(6) the owner of any loan capital in a subsidiary of the company;

(7) an employee of the company;

(8) a partner of the company;

(9) an associate of an employee or a partner of the company; or

(10) a director of the company – unless he receives only 'normal and necessary' remuneration.

24.5.15 Withdrawal of income tax relief on disposal within three years

If a disposal takes place within three years, and the disposal is not to the investor's spouse, relief is withdrawn. If the disposal is anything other than a sale to an unconnected party at an arm's length price, EIS income tax relief is withdrawn completely. Where the disposal is on an arm's length basis, relief is withdrawn only on the sale consideration received by the investor.

The grant of an option during the relevant period may be treated as a disposal, ie where the exercise of the option would bind the grantor to purchase any EIS shares.

The receipt of a loan during the relevant period may also be treated as a disposal. This applies where the loan is made to the investor or an associate of his, if 'the loan is one which would not have been made, or would not have been made on the same terms' if the EIS investment had not been made.

24.5.16 Loss relief on arm's length disposal at less than cost

Where a loss arises on disposal or the company goes into liquidation within the three-/five-year period, further income tax/CGT relief may be due to the investor. In a case where the investor receives no payment under the liquidation, the net amount of his investment may qualify as a capital loss.

Example – EIS income tax relief

> O invests £80,000 under the EIS. He receives income tax relief at 20% of £80,000, ie £16,000. If the entire investment has to be written off, he will be entitled to a capital loss of £64,000. This loss may be set against O's income or relieved against capital gains.

24.5.17 Clawback of CGT deferral relief

A gain that has been deferred is brought back into charge if any of the following events happens:

(1) the investor disposes of the shares other than to his spouse;

(2) the investor (or, where there has been a transfer between spouses, his spouse) ceases to be UK-resident at any time within three years of the issue of the EIS shares;

(3) the company ceases to be a qualifying company for EIS purposes within three years of the issue of the shares, or within three years of the date that it starts trading if this happens later.

The rule in (2) above does not apply if an individual temporarily becomes non-resident because of his employment, and he returns to the UK within three years still owning the shares.

Example – Withdrawal of CGT deferral relief

During the year 2005–06, *P* realised a capital gain of £60,000 and made an investment into an EIS company of £55,000 in August 2003. Her other income is sufficient to warrant full EIS relief.

For 2005–06 *P* received EIS relief of £55,000 * 20% = £11,000. She could also elect to defer her 2003–04 gains of £52,100 (£60,000 less the annual exemption £7,900). This would defer a potential CGT liability of £20,840.

In July 2009 *P* decides to emigrate. This causes the deferred gain of £52,100 to be reinstated as if it were a 2009–10 capital gain.

The gain is then taxed at 18%, so people with gains liable at 40% and little or no taper relief should consider making EIS investments over the next three years.

24.5.18 Taper relief

Where a capital gain arising after 5 April 1998 has been reduced by taper relief (see 12.11) and the gain is deferred by an EIS investment, the gain clawed back on disposal is the original gain (ie there is no further taper relief). Where EIS shares are issued after 5 April 1999 and sold at a gain that is reinvested in new EIS shares, extra taper relief may be due on a disposal before 6 April 2008.

24.5.19 Disposal after three years of shares that qualified for EIS income tax relief

Once shares that qualify for the 20% income tax relief have been held for three years, there is no clawback of relief on a disposal of shares. Furthermore, these shares are an exempt asset for CGT purposes so that no CGT will be payable on any gain. However, a loss realised on the disposal of the shares after the three-year period may still attract either income tax or CGT relief. Again, the loss is calculated as the difference between the net of tax cost and the disposal proceeds (see 24.5.16).

CGT may still be payable on disposal to the extent that CGT deferral relief has been obtained (see 24.5.16), even though any capital gain may be exempt.

24.6 VENTURE CAPITAL TRUSTS (VCTS)
(TA 1988, s 842 and Sched 28)

24.6.1 Qualifying trusts

Venture Capital Trusts are companies broadly similar to investment trusts. The main conditions for approval are that, in its most recent accounting period, the VCT meets the following requirements:

(1) its ordinary share capital has been quoted on the London Stock Exchange;
(2) it has not retained more than 15% of the income that it derived from shares or securities;
(3) its income must have been derived wholly or mainly from shares or securities;
(4) at least 70% by value of its investments comprise of shares or securities in qualifying holdings (see below). Securities can include medium-term loans for a period of at least five years;
(5) at least 30% by value of its qualifying holdings are made up of ordinary shares; and
(6) no holding in any one company represents more than 15% of the VCT's investments.

A VCT may be given provisional approval provided the 70% and 30% requirements are met within three years and the other conditions are met in the current or next accounting period. If the trust fails to meet the conditions within these time periods, provisional approval is withdrawn.

Qualifying holdings

'Qualifying holdings' are holdings in unquoted companies that exist wholly for the purpose of carrying on wholly or mainly in the UK one or more qualifying trades (defined as for the EIS).

VCTs may count annual investments of up to £1m in total in any one qualifying unquoted trading company as a qualifying holding. The unquoted company's gross assets must not exceed £8m immediately after the VCT's investment.

VCTs can treat certain quoted investments as qualifying holdings where the companies were unquoted at the time the VCT made its investment, and no more than five years have elapsed since the company became quoted.

The rules that govern the types of companies in which VCTs may invest are very similar to the EIS rules (see 24.5).

It is permissible for a VCT to exchange its shares in an unquoted company for shares in a new holding company where that holding company has a 100% interest in the original company and the share exchange is being carried out to facilitate a flotation. In broad terms, the VCT may treat its shares in the new holding company as a qualifying investment provided the VCT has the same interest in the holding company and the VCT's shares in the original company were a qualifying investment.

Similarly, where a VCT holds convertible loan stock or preference shares, and it exercises its conversion rights, the resulting shareholding can be a qualifying investment.

Mergers and liquidations

The legislation was amended by FA 2002 to enable VCTs to retain their approved status where they merged with another VCT. The rules were also relaxed to enable VCTs to maintain their approved status during a winding-up. These changes mean that investors do not forfeit their tax reliefs simply because of a merger or the appointment of a liquidator.

24.6.2 Income tax reliefs

There are two kinds of income tax relief available for investments in VCTs:

(1) Individuals aged 18+ are exempt from income tax on dividends from ordinary shares in VCTs to the extent that the shares acquired each year do not exceed £200,000 in value (£100,000 for 2003–04 and earlier years). This relief can be withheld if the Revenue can show that the VCT shares were acquired to avoid tax (eg where they were acquired shortly before the VCT paid a dividend and sold shortly afterwards).
(2) Individuals aged 18+ who subscribe for new ordinary shares in VCTs are, in addition, entitled to claim income tax relief at 30%, subject to the amount subscribed in any one year not exceeding £200,000. This relief on investment will be withdrawn unless the shares are held for at least five years. The clawback period has been five years since 5 April 2006.

24.6.3 CGT reliefs

At one time, there was a CGT deferral relief for investors but this was abolished from 6 April 2004.

24.7 ENTERPRISE ZONE TRUSTS

It is possible to invest in properties in enterprise zones through a syndicate or 'enterprise zone property trust'. An individual who invests in the trust is treated as if he had incurred a proportion of the trust's expenditure on enterprise zone properties. Similarly, rents (and sometimes interest) received by the trust are apportioned among the investors, ie the Revenue looks through the trust and treats the individual as if he had acquired an interest in the underlying properties.

Where an individual is treated as having acquired such an interest in an enterprise zone property, the allowances may be set against his other income (see 7.7.6). However, an individual who invests in such a trust is entitled to capital allowances only for the year in which the trust invests in enterprise zone properties. In some cases, there may be a delay in that he invests in a trust at the end of one tax year and becomes entitled to allowances only for the following year (because that is the year in which the trust acquires the relevant properties).

24.8 INVESTMENT IN FILM PARTNERSHIPS

A number of schemes have been based on exploiting tax reliefs for films.

Films are a very specialised form of investment and, because of the amount of capital involved in making films, many of the schemes that evolved were Limited Partnerships. Under such schemes an individual could benefit from the opening year rules for new businesses (see 6.3.3) and losses might also be used under ITA 2007 s 64 (see 6.7.2). These partnerships were perceived to be abusive as the return for investors was generally not dependent in any way on whether the film was successful.

The FA 2004 removed much of the scope for artificial tax-based schemes. As from 10 February 2004, individuals who devote less than ten hours a week to the partnership business are denied tax relief for losses in excess of the capital that they have contributed to the partnership (except in so far as the partnership has profits in later years). FA 2004 also introduced an income tax charge on an individual ceasing to be a partner on an amount equal to the difference between the tax losses that he has enjoyed and the amount of his economic loss.

Yet more anti-avoidance provisions were introduced in successive Budgets. However, the Finance Act 2007 provisions that deny 'sideways loss relief' for losses in excess of £25,000 incurred by non-active partners do not apply to losses arising from expenditure on qualifying films.

25

PENSIONS

TONY MILLWARD

Pension planning is one of the most important decisions you will make during your financial life and as such it no longer pays to be an innocent bystander while others make decisions that could have such a dramatic effect upon both you and your family.

Many people hold negative views of pensions and this is not surprising given their experiences, which include low incomes in retirement, complicated legislative changes and the collapse of a prominent life office. However, pensions remain highly tax efficient vehicles and with a suitable investment strategy future return expectations have a good chance of being achieved. Pensions should typically form the core long-term financial plan for most people in the UK.

There are broadly two types of pension schemes: money purchase and defined benefit arrangements. Defined benefit (final salary schemes) are employer-sponsored schemes where the pension benefits in retirement will be known beforehand and will be paid by the pension scheme.

Money purchase schemes are more common in the private sector, however more employers are now introducing these types of schemes. Under a money purchase type arrangement the pension fund increases through contributions and from investment growth; whatever the size of the pension fund at retirement will determine the size of pension income that can be attained.

Money purchase schemes include Stakeholder, Personal Pension and Self Invested Pension Schemes (SIPPS). The investment choice within all these types of schemes is important and is a key factor when reviewing or considering pension planning.

This chapter looks at the following:

Registered pension schemes

(1) New regime that came into force on 'A' Day.
(2) Retirement benefits under the new regime.
(3) Pension scheme investments under the new regime.
(4) Tax relief for contributions.

Other retirement benefit schemes

(5) Unapproved schemes.

State benefits

(6) State pension benefits.
(7) Contracting out.

REGISTERED PENSION SCHEMES

25.1 NEW REGIME THAT CAME INTO FORCE ON 'A' DAY.

On 6 April 2006 ('A' Day), a new, unified pensions tax regime came into force replacing the existing pension tax regimes. The new rules affect pension scheme savers in all types of pension schemes, employers and the pension industry, together with financial advisers.

25.1.1 Pension scheme registration

On 6 April 2006 the whole concept of approved pension schemes and discretionary approval was replaced with the concept of registration.

To benefit from all tax privileges, a pension scheme must be registered with HMRC. All schemes are automatically registered unless they elect to be non-registered. De-registration results in a tax charge of 40% on the value of the scheme assets with the lump sum payable at retirement no longer being tax free.

No tax benefits can be enjoyed until a scheme is registered. This could be important for end of company year tax planning.

25.1.2 Statutory lifetime allowance (SLA)

Limits on retirement benefits were replaced by a single statutory lifetime allowance (SLA) covering the amount of tax-privileged pension saving. The SLA is set at £1.65m for this tax year (2008–09). It will increase each year as follows:

2009 = £1.75m
2010 = £1.8m

The SLA allowance cannot be reduced and after 2010–11 will be increased by Treasury Orders.

The value of pension benefits, whatever the type of pension scheme, is tested against the individual's lifetime allowance whenever a 'benefit crystallisation event' (BCE) occurs. BCEs include: vesting of a policy, taking a tax-free cash lump sum, death and purchase of an annuity.

A defined benefit scheme is valued for the purposes of the SLA on a 20:1 basis. If pensions benefits started before A-Day and were already in payment then these are valued by a factor of 25:1. This is applied to the annual payment when the first BCE on or after A-Day occurs.

Where the income is related to a pension income drawdown arrangement then the 25:1 factor is applied to the maximum permitted annual income at the most recent review of the member's fund.

Any excess over the SLA that is taken as income attracts a recovery charge of 25%. This is charged to the member and deducted by the scheme. The additional pension income arising from the excess is taxed at the marginal rates prevailing at the time. Alternatively, the excess can be taken as a lump sum in which case the recovery charge will be 55% (regardless of the member's tax position).

25.1.3 FURBS and UURBS

Both FURBS, and UURBS have been permitted to continue (see 25.4 below for more detail). However, they have ceased to have any tax privileges.

The value of FURBS or UURBS is not taken into account for SLA purposes.

25.1.4 Annual allowance

There are no limits on pension contributions although there is a statutory personal allowance (SPA), which qualifies for tax relief.

The SPA is £235,000 as at 6 April 2008. It will increase each year as follows and will be reviewed by the Treasury every five years thereafter:

2009 = £245,000
2010 = £255,000

Tax relief is available on a member's contributions of up to 100% of earnings, or £3,600 if earnings are below this figure.

In a defined benefit scheme, it is not the actual contributions paid into the scheme but the capital value of the increase in benefits throughout the scheme year that is tested against the SPA. A factor of 10:1 is applied to the increase in benefit in order to calculate the capital value. Therefore a member within a defined benefit scheme would be able to accrue benefits of up to £22,500 (£225,000/10) without being above the annual allowance in tax year 2007–08.

In any year in which a member wholly crystallises all the benefits in that pension scheme the maximum level of the annual allowance will not apply. However, sufficient earnings will still be required for the member to make a contribution above that of the SLA for that tax year.

Pension input periods

The annual allowance is tested against the total level of pension contributions made in a particular pension input period that ends in the relevant tax year. As input periods are not aligned to the timing of tax years the annual allowance is not therefore tested against the total pension contributions made in any particular tax year.

Pension schemes will have a scheme input period and will be specific to the particular type of scheme. The starting period will typically begin either on the first payment after A-Day or for defined benefit schemes the date that benefits start to accrue. The pension input period will end one year after the period started.

Input periods can be changed by the member or the scheme administrator within a money purchase scheme. Changing input periods within a money purchase scheme may represent a planning opportunity for some individuals to make higher pension contributions above the annual allowance in a short period of time. If an individual changed the input period during tax year 2008–09 they could potentially contribute a maximum of £480,000 (£235,000 + £245,000).

Employer pension contributions and spreading

Tax relief is potentially available without limit on all employer contributions provided that they meet the 'wholly and exclusively' test. The local tax office will determine whether a payment is appropriate for each case. Employers will also need to take into account the relevant annual allowance when considering making a larger contribution.

The employer's tax relief may have to be spread over a period of years if the contribution is over £500,000.

25.1.5 Transitional rules

The new rules apply to all pension savings after 6 April 2006. However, under transitional provisions, all rights built up before April 2006 can be protected by electing for appropriate protection. This applies to pension benefits that exceeded the SLA at 6 April 2006, or could be expected to exceed it after 6 April 2006, and tax-free cash sums, which may be greater than 25% of the value of their pension fund. There are two ways to protect a member's pre-6 April 2006 fund.

Primary protection

Primary protection is only available to those individuals whose fund value at 6 April 2006 exceeded £1.5 million. Future contributions can be made, and any growth on the fund up to the increase in the SLA each year is protected from the tax charges. However, should the fund grow at a faster rate than the SLA, a tax charge would be payable on the funds over this level.

Those people who register for primary protection will also protect any tax-free entitlement over £375,000. They will be able to take the amount of their pre-6 April 2006 lump sum rights increased in line with the increase in the standard lifetime allowance.

Enhanced protection

This allows protection of funds even if they were below the SLA at 6 April 2006. This protection effectively requires the individual to stop funding his pension, or accruing further pensionable service. However, a small level of accrual will be allowed and this is described within the 'relevant benefit accrual' rules.

Providing enhanced protection is elected and any benefit accrual is within the rules, any benefits coming in to payment after 5 April 2006 will normally be exempt from the SLA, whatever the value. For an occupational scheme member electing for enhanced protection who has earmarked funds within the pension scheme, it will require the benefits to be tested within the scheme under the old rules. If a surplus exists in the fund then this must be returned to the company and taxed at 35%.

If enhanced protection is elected and future pension contributions or accrual occurs, then it is possible to revert to primary protection if it has also been elected, otherwise you would automatically revert to 'no protection'. Protection from the recovery charge is determined by the pre-6 April 2006 pension value or the prevailing SLA for those whose pension value did not exceed £1.5m.

Should an individual wish to elect for protection, then this decision must be made by 5 April 2009 – and if enhanced protection is chosen, then no further contributions must be made from 6 April 2006.

Trustees of occupational pension schemes should review their membership to identify any individuals who should be considering protection; however, it must be the individual's decision and not the trustees.

In a defined contribution pension scheme, any tax charge which is payable on retirement will be paid to the Inland Revenue by the administrators of the scheme and the fund value reduced. The remaining fund value would then be used to provide benefits for the individual on retirement.

With defined benefit pension schemes, the situation is slightly different. The tax charge due at retirement is computed on the basis that the value of the pension rights is equal to 20 times the annual pension.

Tax notes

Trustees of occupational pension schemes should review their membership to identify any individuals who should be considering protection; however, it must be the individual's decision and not the trustees.

Points to note

It is not possible to switch from primary protection to enhanced protection at any time.

In both cases, those seeking transitional protection from pensions must register their pre-6 April 2006 pension rights, and provide all the necessary valuation information, by 5 April 2009.

25.2 RETIREMENT BENEFITS UNDER THE NEW REGIME

There is now a single set of rules governing the ways in which benefits can be drawn from a pension scheme.

25.2.1 Minimum retirement age

Benefits can be taken at any time between age 50 and 75 up until 5 April 2010. From 6 April 2010 benefits can be taken between 55 and 75.

Those with certain existing contractual rights to draw a pension earlier may have that right protected. There is special protection for members of those approved schemes in existence before April 2006 with low normal retirement ages, such as those for sports people.

It is no longer necessary for a member to leave employment in order to access an employer's occupational pension. Members of occupational pension schemes may, where the scheme rules allow it, continue working for the same employer whilst drawing retirement benefits.

25.2.2 Lump sums on death before benefits have been drawn

In the event of death before drawing benefits, the whole of the individual's pension fund is available to provide death benefits (subject to the pension scheme rules for occupational schemes). There are no limits on the size of the resulting fund and the whole of the fund can be used to provide a lump sum and/or dependants' pensions.

This applies in the event that the member dies before taking the benefits, provided he had not reached age 75. However, if a lump sum is chosen, the fund value would need to be tested against the SLA, and a recovery charge of 55% would apply to the excess over the SLA. If the fund is used to provide a dependant's pension then no tax charge will be payable regardless of the pension fund value at that time. However, any dependants' pensions will be subject to income tax. The Finance Act 2007 contains provisions that prevent a personal pension policy from only providing life assurance benefits.

The FA 2006 contains provisions that may impose IHT on the payment of a death benefit. However, the IHT treatment of a lump sum paid out in these circumstances will, as in the past, generally depend on the form in which it is paid. If it is held under an appropriate trust then it will normally be exempt from IHT. The exception where the Revenue may seek to charge IHT is where it can be shown that the individual did not take their pension because their life expectancy was seriously impaired and this resulted in an enhanced death benefit being paid. Even if these conditions are satisfied, no IHT will be payable if the lump sum is paid to a spouse, civil partner, financial dependant or a charity.

25.2.3 Tax-free lump sums

The maximum amount of pre-commencement lump sum (tax-free cash) that can be paid from all pension schemes is now a quarter of the value of the benefits subject to an overall maximum of a quarter of the SLA (2008: £1.65m * 25% = £412,500). However, for members of occupational schemes before 6 April 2006, it is possible that they are entitled to a tax-free lump sum of more than 25% in respect of their service before A-Day. If this is the case, then this entitlement to higher tax-free cash will be protected, provided the members stay in the scheme. However, any transfer away from the scheme (unless part of a bulk transfer) could result in the higher entitlement being lost.

Members of post-1987 AVC schemes, FSAVC schemes and appropriate personal pension plans can now also take tax-free cash from these arrangements. This has introduced an extra degree of flexibility, because previous rules did not allow this.

25.2.4 Trivial commutation

In cases when an individual has a small level of pension benefits the rules may allow them to be paid off as a lump sum as opposed to drawing a small pension for life – this is known as a trivial commutation lump sum.

Full commutation can be taken where all benefits are taken at the same time, and the total amount of all of the individual's pensions is not more than 1% of the SLA currently in force. One quarter can be paid tax-free with the rest paid as a lump sum, which is subject to income tax at the individual's marginal rate.

The triviality rules cannot be used before age 60 or after age 75.

25.2.5 Retirement income

There are three ways in which income can be paid to an individual on retirement: secured income; unsecured income; and alternatively secured pension.

Secured income

A secured income is a pension income in retirement that is promised to be paid until death. There are two forms of secured pensions; annuities and scheme pensions; both types will be treated as income for tax purposes.

An annuity is an income stream purchased from an insurance provider using the pension fund at retirement. An annuity could be considered as longevity insurance as it will continue to be paid until death, whenever that may happen.

Where annuities are purchased via money purchase type pension plans, the individual should use the open market option. The annuity market is competitive and this option will help to ensure that the most competitive annuity is purchased for the individual's personal requirements.

Many features can be built into an annuity. These include payment frequency, payment increases, spouse's pension and pension guarantees. Depending upon the level and whether an individual selects a spouse's pension or guarantee, options will effectively determine the death benefit position of the annuity.

In a defined benefit pension a scheme pension will be provided. This can either be paid to the member out of the scheme assets or the scheme can purchase an annuity to secure the income for the member. Death benefit options may be determined by the pension scheme rules or may offer flexibility.

Unsecured income

The alternative to securing benefits under secured income is to take income directly from the pension fund by means of income drawdown. Unsecured income can only continue until the age of 75.

Annual income must be taken of up to a maximum of 120% of the annual income payable from a single level annuity. There is no minimum level of income set. Income levels can vary between the two limits and must be reviewed every five years.

If a member dies before age 75 after taking unsecured income the fund can either be used to provide a lump sum payment or to provide a survivor's pension. If a lump sum is provided, a special lump sum death benefits tax charge will apply of 35% of the fund value. A survivor's pension can be provided by an annuity or income drawdown depending upon the individual's requirements; these pension payments will be taxed as income.

The FA 2006 contains provisions that may impose an IHT charge. However, IHT will not normally be charged on a lump sum paid out in these circumstances unless:

- the member dies within two years of taking income or within two years of a five yearly review; and
- the level of unsecured income has been kept low to enhance death benefits and the member's life expectancy was seriously impaired at the time he made this decision.

Even if these conditions are met, no IHT is charged if the lump sum is paid to a spouse, civil partner, dependant or a charity.

At age 75, income must be secured or alternatively secured (see below).

Alternatively secured pension (ASP)

Before April 2006, pension legislation forced pensioners to secure their income from age 75 using an annuity. The new rules have introduced the alternatively secured pension (ASP). This is an option to purchasing an annuity and will allow unsecured income to be drawn from age 75, however with different rules from those that applied before age 75 (unsecured income).

Alternatively secured pensions cannot start before age 75. However, unless benefits are crystallised before age 75 into an unsecured pension arrangement, the tax-free lump sum will be lost.

The income limits under ASP are different from the unsecured pension income rules:

- A minimum pension income requirement was introduced: 55% of the single life Government's Actuary's Department (GAD) rate at age 75.
- The maximum pension income requirement was increased to 90% of the single life GAD rate at age 75.

Once income withdrawal has commenced under ASP, the upper income limit must be reviewed every year.

The death benefit rules while an individual is in ASP are as follows:

- Where an individual dies with dependants, the remaining drawdown fund must be used to provide survivors' pensions.
- If an individual dies with no dependants, the remaining fund can be gifted to a charity tax free.
- The reallocation of remaining pension funds to other pension scheme members will be classified as an unauthorised payment and will therefore attract unauthorised tax payment charges. In many cases the total reallocation charges are likely to amount to 70% (40% unauthorised payment charge + 15% unauthorised payments surcharge + 15% scheme sanction charge).

Any reallocated pension funds will also remain subject to IHT on the original member's estate and this combination produces a potential effective tax rate of 82%.

25.2.6 Recycling of lump sums

Where an individual takes a pre-commencement lump sum (tax-free lump sum) from a pension and then deliberately reinvests this within another pension scheme this may be considered as recycling and pension tax law from April 2006 has specific rules in place to prevent this. Recycling applies when pre-planned and in the following circumstances:

- the individual must have received a pre-commencement lump sum (PCLS), which, when added to any other PCLS received in the previous 12-month period, exceeds 1% of the lifetime allowance.

- because of the payment of the PCLS, the amount of the contribution paid to a pension scheme is significantly greater than would otherwise be the case. This is defined as where the amount of the additional contributions are more than 30% of the contributions that might have been expected;
- the cumulative amount of the additional contributions to the registered scheme must exceed 30% of the PCLS.

If recycling is deemed to apply, the pre-commencement lump sum (tax free cash lump sum) will be considered an unauthorised payment and a tax charge of 40% of the lump sum payment will be applied.

25.3 PENSION SCHEME INVESTMENTS UNDER THE NEW REGIME

25.3.1 General rules for scheme investments

A single set of investment rules applies to all registered pension schemes. This effectively removed most of the previous restrictions on permitted investments, including residential property and connected party transactions. However, all investments must be made on a commercial basis. It is considered unlikely that all pension companies will accept the full range of investments in their schemes, and a wider choice of investments will only be made available by specialist pension companies operating either self-invested personal pensions (SIPPs) or small, self-administered schemes (SSAS).

Loans to members are not permitted.

Any investment entered into before 6 April 2006 is normally subject to the rules then in force and is not affected by the new rules. However, where a change takes place after 5 April 2006 to the terms of a loan made by the scheme before 'A' Day, the whole loan is subject to the new rules.

Scheme borrowing is limited to 50% of the value of the scheme assets and must be secured.

25.3.2 Prohibited investments

The FA 2006 contains provisions relating to 'taxable property' ie assets previously described as 'prohibited assets' in the December 2005 Pre-Budget Report.

Taxable property consists of any of the following:

- Residential property (whether in the UK or overseas).
- Chattels (ie tangible moveable property) other than gold bullion.

A registered pension scheme is not debarred from investing in taxable property but, where it does so, it and the members of the scheme are subject to punitive tax charges. In addition, the pension scheme could face de-registration if it invests in any prohibited investment, which in addition to the punitive tax charges applied, would also mean that the scheme loses all the tax privileges associated with a registered scheme for all of its assets.

There are exceptions for certain types of residential property that might be acquired as an investment, eg a nursing home.

Great care should be taken before a scheme invests in property that may constitute residential property and advice taken from a specialist.

25.3.3 Pension investment strategies

Pension strategies by their very nature are long-term and therefore even small enhancements can have a big effect at retirement.

Individuals with money purchase type arrangements (Stakeholder, Personal Pensions, Self Invested Personal Pensions) should carefully consider the underlying investment strategy employed within their pension plan. Future investment performance is a determinant of future fund value at retirement and individuals should seek to assess the appropriateness of their underlying strategy particularly in relation to their objectives and personal attitude to investment risk.

The investment choices for most money purchase pension plans will be linked to collective investment funds and typically the pension provider will offer a flexible range to suit different risk profiles. As with all investments some managers will perform more consistently than others and assessing the long-term consistency of performance of an underlying manager is an important consideration.

Individuals within money purchase type schemes should also seek to adjust their asset allocation to a more cautious position when approaching retirement, particularly within five years. Any equity focused investment strategy has the potential risk of a sudden fall in value within five years of retirement and therefore by adjusting the allocation to a more cautious position the value of the retirement fund can be protected.

Tax notes

A registered pension scheme is not debarred from investing in taxable property but, where it does so, it and the members of the scheme are subject to punitive tax charges.

25.4 TAX RELIEF FOR CONTRIBUTIONS

Employer contributions are always paid gross.

Contributions by a member into a registered scheme will normally be net of basic rate tax, ie a payment to an insurance company of £1,000 is treated as a payment of £1,250 from which £250 has been deducted. The insurance company recovers this £250 from HMRC.

There is one situation where a member's contributions may still be made in full. If the payment is in respect of an old retirement annuity policy and the insurance company has not established an arrangement for payments to be made net of tax relief.

OTHER RETIREMENT BENEFIT SCHEMES

25.5 UNAPPROVED SCHEMES

Unapproved occupational pension schemes were introduced to allow employers the flexibility to provide benefits for those employees who had earnings in excess of the salary cap. However, their use is not restricted to such employees and they may be used to provide benefits in excess of the normal two-thirds maximum pension benefit or to provide greater benefits for those with less than 20 years' service.

25.5.1 Eligibility

Any person in receipt of employment income is eligible for an unapproved scheme. There is no requirement that the employee is also a member of an approved scheme.

25.5.2 Types of plan

Such schemes may be funded (ie contributions set aside to fund the promised benefits) or unfunded (ie at retirement the benefits will be paid by the company out of current income or investments). A funded scheme is often called a FURBS. There is no requirement that funded schemes are established under trust, but this is commonly the case.

25.5.3 Contributions

Where a scheme was funded, the employer used to obtain tax relief on the contributions as a normal business expense and the employee was taxed on such contributions as if they were earnings. This ceased to be the case from 'A' Day. Contributions now attract no tax relief for the employer until the employee draws his benefits and the employee pays no tax until he draws the benefits.

In an unfunded scheme, there has never been a charge to tax on any reserves set up to provide for future benefits. Equally, the employer will not obtain any tax relief until the benefits are actually paid.

25.5.4 Taxation of scheme investments

Unapproved schemes do not benefit from 'gross roll-up'. In the past, the trustees of a FURBS paid tax at only basic rate on investment income. From 6 April 2006, income and capital gains became subject to 'the rate applicable to trusts', ie 40% on income other than dividends, 32.5% on UK dividends. Capital gains from a FURBS are now subject to 18% CGT.

25.5.5 Benefits

The scheme must be set up to provide relevant benefits, but there are no set limits on the benefits that can be provided. Pensions from unapproved schemes, whether funded or unfunded, are subject to income tax as earned income.

Where a scheme with UK resident trustees has been funded before 'A' Day, that part of the fund may be taken as a tax-free lump sum on retirement. Where an offshore scheme was funded prior to 'A' Day, the tax-free amount will usually be the aggregate of the employer contributions before 6 April 2006. Any lump sum in excess of these limits is taxable in the normal way.

Tax notes

Where a scheme with UK resident trustees has been funded before 'A' Day, that part of the fund may be taken as a tax-free lump sum on retirement.

STATE BENEFITS

25.6 STATE PENSION BENEFITS

The state provides a number of pension benefits with a range of eligibility conditions and contribution requirements. There are also additional means-tested benefits payable in retirement, which are beyond the scope of this book. The main state pension benefits are as follows.

25.6.1 The basic state pension

The basics state pension is the first part of the Government's pension provision. Individuals will be eligible to all or a part, providing they have a sufficient national insurance contribution record. Individuals with earnings above or equal to the lower earnings level (LEL) in any year will be accredited with a year's qualifying record for the basic state pension. There are also special dispensations for carers (home responsibilities protection).

At present, a man who has around 44 years of qualifying national insurance records will qualify for the full basic state pension, for a women this is around 40 years. The Pensions Act 2007 will change the qualifying time periods and from 6 April 2010 the period will reduce to 30 years to be entitled to the full basic state pension.

The state pensions age is presently 65 for a man and 60 for a woman. These will start to equalise from April 2010 in stages and by 2020 the state retirement age will be 65 for both sexes. The state pension age will also rise from 65 to 68 in stages between 2024 and 2046.

The value of the basic state pension has been linked to increases in inflation (RPI) each year in April. This level of increases has not been considered fair by many pensioners as average wages have typically risen at a higher rate and therefore the long-term value of the basic state pension has been gradually eroded. The Pensions Act 2007 will re-link increases to the average earnings level from 2012 at the earliest and by 2015 at the latest, subject to affordability.

25.6.2 State Earnings Related Pension Scheme (SERPS)

SERPS was introduced in 1978 and provides a pension that is based on earnings between the lower and upper earnings limits (for 2008, £4,680 and £40,040 pa, respectively). The earnings between these two figures are often called 'band earnings'. People who are self-employed neither contribute towards, nor benefit from, SERPS.

Benefit accrual under SERPs ended in April 2002 with the introduction of the state second pension.

SERPS provides a pension at state retirement age expressed as a percentage of band earnings. For those retiring in 2009–10 or later the percentage is currently 20%, with those retiring before then receiving a higher percentage up to a maximum of 25% of band earnings. Band earnings are based on an average over the whole of your working life.

The main benefit from the state scheme is a lifelong pension for the individual, but SERPS can also, in certain circumstances, provide a widow's pension, which will be of a reduced amount unless the widow is aged over 40 and has dependent children (or over 50 with no dependent children).

Accrual of SERPS benefits ceased from 6 April 2002, but benefits accrued continue to be calculated in accordance with the rules at that date.

25.6.3 State Second Pension (S2P)

S2P was introduced on 6 April 2002. Like SERPs, which it replaced, S2P is based on NICs made by employers and employees. However, S2P provides better benefits than SERPs for low and moderate earners, broadly those earning up to £31,100 for 2008–09.

To achieve this, earnings are divided into three bands rather than the single 'band earnings' used to calculate SERPs. In addition to the lower and upper earnings limits, there is a 'low earnings threshold' broadly equal to half of national average earnings (£13,500 for 2008–09) and a second earnings threshold (£31,100 for 2008–09).

The rate of accrual for the lowest band (ie for earnings between the lower earnings limit and the lower earnings threshold) is double that of the highest band and four times that of the middle band, as shown below based for a state pension age falling in tax year 2009/10:

	Earnings	Maximum S2P
Band 1	£4,680 – £13,500	40%
Band 2	£13,500 – £31,100	10%
Band 3	£31,100 – £40,040	20%

In addition to the improved benefits for low and moderate earners, S2P also provides coverage for some carers and people with long-term disabilities or illness. In these cases, it is possible to build up an entitlement to S2P for periods where individuals are unable to work.

State pension forecast

To obtain an illustration of potential state pension benefits and state second pension entitlement at state pension age individuals, should obtain a forecast by completing the Department of Work and Pensions form BR19 or completing an online application directly on its website (www.thepensionservice.gov.uk).

25.7 CONTRACTING OUT

Individuals are able to leave the state second pension by 'contracting out'. For any year where the individual has been contracted out they will forego their second state pension benefits at retirement for that particular tax year. Individuals have also previously been able to 'contract out' of SERPs.

There are three ways in which an employee can be contracted out. These are:

(1) contracting out via a personal type pension;
(2) membership of a contracted-out money purchase pension scheme (COMPS); or
(3) membership of an occupational scheme providing guaranteed minimum pension (GMP) or an occupational scheme that satisfies a 'Reference Scheme' test.

It is possible to leave S2P provided appropriate provision is made to replace the S2P benefits with a suitable approved alternative. To encourage this, individuals and employers who 'contract out' in this way receive benefits in the form of reduced NICs and/or a direct payment into individual personal pension schemes.

25.7.1 Contracting out via a personal type pension

Individuals are able to contract out via a personal type pension (including Stakeholder and Personal Pension plans). This requires no employer involvement and is open to all employees who are not contracted-out by another scheme, even those who are also members of an occupational scheme. To contract out, the employee and the chosen Personal Pension plan provider must complete a Joint Notice (Form APPI), which is submitted to HMRC.

An individual can use only one APPP to contract out at any time and must contract out for a complete tax year.

Once the Joint Notice is accepted by HMRC, payments are made once a year typically in September or October following the end of the tax year. These payments are called 'protected rights contributions' and consist of the national insurance rebate, but both the employee and employer continue to pay the full rate of NICs. A system of age-related rebates applies.

Although the new tax rules allow a tax-free lump sum of up to 25% of the protected rights fund to be taken, the remainder of the fund built up by protected rights contributions must be used to provide a pension benefit at state retirement age, or a widow(er) or dependant's pension or a lump sum on death.

The contracting out decision is not straightforward and individuals should assess their own personal situation and objectives when considering their contracting out position.

25.7.2 Contracted-out money purchase scheme (COMPS)

A COMPS is an occupational pension plan where the employer takes the initial decision to contract out, although the employer may allow individuals the choice of whether to contract out or not.

Both the employer and employee pay a reduced rate of NICs, but this saving is balanced by the protected rights contributions that the employer must ensure are paid into the pension scheme monthly. Normally, both the employer and the employee will contribute their respective shares of the protected rights contributions. In addition to the basic flat-rate rebates, the DWP pays an additional age-related payment after the end of the tax year.

The protected rights contributions must be used to provide benefits in the same way as those provided through a personal type pension.

25.7.3 Guaranteed minimum pension (GMP)

This method of contracting out involved an occupational pension scheme providing a guaranteed minimum level of pension equivalent to that provided by SERPS. Both the employer and the employee benefited from a reduced level of NICs, but the employer had to be prepared to provide the pension scheme with sufficient funds to enable it to meet the guarantee.

No further GMPs can accrue for periods after 5 April 1997. Since then, occupational schemes can be contracted out either on a money purchase basis (ie a COMPS) or by satisfying the 'Reference Scheme test'. The latter involves the scheme's actuary certifying that the pension benefits from the scheme are 'broadly equivalent' to the pension benefits of a standard Reference Scheme.

The future of contracting out

The Pensions Act 2007 proposes to stop contracting out both through contracted out money purchase schemes and via personal type pensions (Stakeholder and Personal Pension) from April 2012.

26

INVESTING IN REAL ESTATE

The choice of investment vehicle is now much more tax neutral. Rental income is taxable in much the same way, whether the investment is made direct or via a company. Also, the CGT position is now more straightforward in that capital gains are normally taxed at 18%. Properties that are let to quoted companies, Government departments or charities are taxed at the same rate. The one situation where gains may still be taxed at 10% is where entrepreneurs relief is available for the sale of a property used by the individual's personal trading company (see 16.8.4).

This chapter looks at the following ways of investing in property:

(1) 'Buy to let' investments.
(2) Private investment companies.
(3) Limited liability partnerships (LLPs).
(4) Investing surplus funds within a trading company.
(5) Buying overseas property.
(6) Quoted property companies.
(7) Property funds offered by insurance companies.
(8) Pension funds.

26.1 'BUY TO LET' INVESTMENTS

The subject of rental property is covered in general in Chapter 7.

The attraction of buying properties for letting is that the business should produce a reasonable return provided that the gearing (financing by loans) is not excessive, void periods are kept to the minimum and the properties are properly maintained. Problems arise from unexpectedly long periods without a tenant and the fact that it is often necessary to refurbish the property substantially after a tenant moves out. It may be time-consuming and difficult to manage a portfolio of investment properties, particularly if they are let on short leases or the properties require a lot of maintenance and are a long way from one another. Letting properties can require a lot of business and management skills and the ability to think ahead.

26.1.1 Relief for interest

The decision whether to borrow and invest in a second property involves two factors: interest rates and tax relief. A loan to invest in a rental property will attract tax relief but most financial institutions will then charge a significantly higher rate of interest. A loan to purchase your main residence or a remortgage of your main residence does not normally attract tax relief but will attract a competitive interest rate from the bank or building society. However, relief for interest is governed by the way that the borrowed money is used, not by the way the loan is secured. Relief should therefore be available for interest on a loan that is secured by way of a remortgage of your home but is used to buy an investment property.

Tax notes

When considering any investment, you need to look at how you will fund the transaction and what you think you will gain at the end of that transaction. Borrowing money to buy investment properties makes no sense if the interest charges are likely to exceed the rental income and future capital gains on the disposal of the properties. But if you can get tax relief for the interest, it is more likely that the benefits will outweigh the costs.

26.1.2 Increasing your gearing

It is not always necessary to take loans out when you purchase properties. We have explained at 7.2.12 that it may be possible to obtain tax relief for interest if you take fresh loans later on that are secured against your investment properties.

26.1.3 No IHT business property relief

Letting properties is a business but it is not normally the sort of business which will qualify for business property relief (see 29.8).

26.2 PRIVATE INVESTMENT COMPANIES

In this section, we look at UK and foreign investment companies.

26.2.1 UK investment companies

A UK investment company has certain pros and cons.

Pros

- An individual can raise qualifying loans if the borrowings are used to finance the purchase of shares or the making of a loan to a UK close company that exists to manage property investments. It is necessary that the individual holds a material interest in the company (either on his own or in conjunction with his associates) – see 10.5. Usually the individual and his immediate family hold all the shares and this condition is clearly satisfied.

  Interest on such a loan may be set against the individual's general income; relief is not confined to income from the company.

  Relief may be restricted if the individual 'recovers' capital from the company (see 10.5.5).

- The investment company will often pay corporation tax at only 21% whereas an individual who lets properties may well be subject to 40% tax because of the level of his other income.

- It will be easier for an individual to either put shares into his children's name from the outset or to transfer shares to his children later on than it would be if he needed to transfer a part interest in an investment property owned personally.

Cons

- When the individual draws money from the company, this will generally involve his taking remuneration or interest or a dividend. The receipt of such income may attract higher rate tax.

- When the company sells the properties, it will be liable for corporation tax on its gains. These gains are computed by reference to indexation relief (see 12.12).

- When the shareholders realise a capital gain on disposing of their shares (on a sale or a winding-up), they will also be liable for CGT (the 'two tier CGT charge').

Tax notes

In general, before you put any property in a company, consider the exit route. A buyer will be interested in the asset, ie the house, but may not be so keen to buy shares in a private company.

In general, the two tier CGT charge means that it is not likely to be beneficial for most landlords to operate through an investment company. Nevertheless, if you have an existing investment company and it has unrelieved losses, it may make sense for you to put an investment property into the company to generate more rental income and so use up these losses.

Putting investment properties into a company will normally result in an SDLT charge (see 38.2.10)

26.2.2 Foreign investment companies

A UK individual cannot raise a qualifying loan to finance the purchase of shares or the making of a loan to a non-UK resident company.

A non-UK resident company that receives rents from UK properties will generally be subject to basic rate income tax.

It will not be subject to tax on capital gains but the shareholders may be taxed under s 13 TCGA 1992 (see 32.16) where the company would be a close company if it were UK resident and the shareholder and his associates hold an interest in the company that amounts to at least 10%. This charge can now also apply to foreign domiciled individuals.

In practice, it may be difficult to show that an investment company owned by UK-resident individuals is not resident here for tax purposes (see 34.15.1).

26.3 LIMITED LIABILITY PARTNERSHIPS (LLPS)

An LLP is a type of body corporate (company) that has a transparent tax treatment for tax purposes.

There is no relief where an individual borrows personally to finance the purchase of an interest in an investment LLP (see 10.4). However, interest on borrowings taken by the LLP is an expense in computing the LLP's rental income for tax purposes.

An individual member's share of the income received by an LLP (computed in the normal way and after deducting loan interest) is taxed as if he had received that income personally.

When an investment property is sold by an LLP, the gain is divided among the members. Those members who are individuals or trustees enjoy the benefit of taper relief and their annual exemption. Non-resident members are not subject to CGT on their share of the LLP's capital gains.

No further income tax or capital gains tax is payable when members withdraw profits or the LLP is wound up.

A member's share in an LLP that carries on a property letting business will not qualify for IHT business property relief.

Tax notes

Both LLPs and UK limited companies have annual Companies House filing obligations, which need to be met to keep the entity in good standing. More information can be found at the Companies House website (www.companieshouse.gov.uk) or by calling 0870 33 33 636.

26.4 INVESTING SURPLUS FUNDS WITHIN A TRADING COMPANY

Many people operate a business through a limited company and, as the business prospers, start to make investments by using the company's surplus funds. This may involve direct investment in real estate or indirect investment via the purchase of quoted shares or other investments.

This may have adverse tax consequences in the long-term. See 16.8.3 on the way in which HMRC can withhold entrepreneurs relief where a company has substantial investment activities.

26.5 BUYING OVERSEAS PROPERTY

There are several aspects to be considered here.

26.5.1 Relief for financing costs

A UK individual may create a special purpose vehicle (SPV) by forming a UK limited company to make investments in overseas property. If the company is a close company, as will normally be the case, and the individual has a material interest (see 10.5), he can raise a qualifying loan to finance the investment by either subscribing for shares or making loans to the close company. The interest on such loans can be relieved against the individual's other income.

26.5.2 The company will be liable for tax on capital gains

Holding overseas property in this way will mean that the UK company may have a tax liability as and when it eventually realises the investment. There will then be a further CGT charge on getting money out of the company. However, there may be ways of minimising this if you plan sufficiently far ahead. One possibility is to hold each overseas investment in a separate SPV with a view to eventually selling shares in that company rather than having the company sell its property. It is not quite as simple as this because you may well need to be able to deal with a possible objection by a UK purchaser that this will leave him with a latent tax liability if he ever wishes to take the property out of the company. There are ways of squaring the circle and you should consult a specialist at the outset rather than only as and when you are ready to disinvest.

26.5.3 Using an overseas company

An overseas company may be treated in the same way as a UK company. If the company is centrally managed and controlled in the UK it will be treated as resident here (see 17.1). Even if you manage to surmount this obstacle, you may still suffer tax on a disposal of the property if s13 TCGA applies (see 32.17).

26.5.4 Be careful with holiday homes

Many people buy a holiday home with a view to letting it out for a few weeks and occupying it themselves for the rest of the year.

The Government has recently relaxed the rules on benefits in kind (see 4.8.6) but there are still many traps for the unwary in holding such investment through a company.

26.5.5 Make the SPV a limited liability partnership instead?

Another way of organising matters is to form a limited liability partnership to hold overseas property. The LLP could be a UK LLP or, if you were acquiring a US property, a Delaware LLP. The tax treatment is likely to be as follows:

- Interest relief against rental income provided that the borrowings are taken out by the LLP.
- Capital gains on a disposal of a property (but only a single charge, not a two-tier charge as described at 26.5.2 above).

26.6 QUOTED PROPERTY COMPANIES

26.6.1 UK quoted shares

Shares in a quoted UK property company have the following tax treatment:

- No relief for interest on loans used to buy shares unless, exceptionally, the quoted company is a close company and the individual either has a material interest or works full-time in the management of the company's business (see 10.5).
- The company pays corporation tax on rental income and capital gains.
- A shareholder pays tax in the normal way on dividends (see 8.8).
- An individual who realises a capital gain on a disposal of shares is subject to CGT if he is resident in the UK. He will not normally qualify for business taper relief unless he works for the company and he holds less than 10% of the company (see 16.7.2)

26.6.2 Real estate investment trusts (REITs)

REITs are quoted collective vehicles for investment in rental property. They have been available in other countries for a number of years. The legislation on UK REITs took effect from 1 January 2007.

The broad rationale is that a REIT itself should be transparent for tax purposes. This means that no tax is normally charged at the company level. Instead, tax will be payable by the shareholders – this applies to both rental profits and capital gains.

However, a withholding tax of 20% will apply to most distributions by a REIT to its investors. The main exceptions are UK-resident companies and various exempt bodies.

Qualifying distributions received from a REIT are treated as rental income rather than dividends.

26.6.3 Non-resident companies

Where a company is not resident in the UK (even though it may be quoted in London), the tax treatment is as follows:

- UK rental income is subject to tax at basic rate.
- Capital gains are not normally taxed at the company level.
- Distributions of income are taxed as dividends (see 8.10).
- A shareholder will not normally be subject to tax on the company's capital gains. The only circumstance where this can apply is where the foreign company is a close company and the UK individual has a 10% interest.
- A capital gain may arise for a UK shareholder on his realising his investment.

26.7 PROPERTY FUNDS OFFERED BY INSURANCE COMPANIES

Most insurance companies offer unitised funds that include funds invested in property. These funds pay corporation tax at 20% on rental income and realised capital gains.

The tax treatment of individuals who take out investment bonds that are invested in such funds is set out at 27.2.

26.8 PENSION FUNDS

See 25.3 on the fact that residential property investments are a taxable asset for pension schemes.

Other property investments and, in particular, investments in quoted property companies and REITs are regarded as normal investments.

27

LIFE ASSURANCE

This chapter covers the tax treatment of life assurance and covers the following topics:

(1) Introduction.
(2) Qualifying and non-qualifying policies.
(3) Taxation of life policy proceeds.
(4) Offshore life policies.
(5) Annuities.
(6) Permanent health insurance (PHI).
(7) Pre-owned assets charge.
(8) Life policies effected by companies.
(9) Life policies in trust affected by FA 2006 IHT changes.
(10) Discounted gift schemes.

27.1 INTRODUCTION

A life assurance policy is simply the evidence of a contract between the individual policyholder and the life assurance company. The general principle is that the company is the collecting house for pooled investments and mortality risks, offering benefits directly to policyholders based on personal contracts.

Life assurance policies can be classified in a number of ways, but the most common practical classification reflects the nature of the benefits provided under the policy and the periods for which they are provided. Types of policy are:

(1) whole of life policies, where the sum assured is payable on the death of the life assured, whenever that occurs;
(2) term policies, where the sum assured is payable on death during the policy term only; and
(3) endowment policies, where the sum assured is payable on death during the policy term, or on survival to the end of the term.

Each type of policy has its own characteristics in terms of the blend of life assurance protection and potential investment return. Term policies for a relatively short period are most likely to offer the highest sum assured for each pound of premium while, towards the other end of the spectrum, an endowment policy will have a greater investment element.

An important characteristic of life assurance policies is that they do not produce income as such, but are essentially medium-or long-term accumulators. While a policy is held intact, the income and gains arising from the underlying investments held by the life company are taxed in the hands of the life company itself. In general, the policyholder's prospective tax liability arises only when he receives payment under the policy.

This chapter deals with the tax consequences on the policyholder paying premiums or receiving benefits under a life assurance policy issued by a UK company or a foreign insurer operating through a branch in the UK (for 'foreign' life policies see 27.4).

Over the years many changes have been made to this complex and technical area.

27.1.1 The company's tax position

Taxation of life companies is extremely (and increasingly) complex. Broadly speaking, in respect of their life assurance business, companies are generally taxed on the excess of their investment income and realised capital gains over management expenses (the 'I-E' basis). For proprietary companies there is a formula to determine the proportions of the company's income and gains that should be allocated to policyholders and shareholders, respectively. Since 1 April 2003 the rate charged on the policyholder share of all life fund income has been 20%. The company's profits attributable to shareholders are, on the other hand, chargeable to corporation tax at the usual rate of 28%.

To enable UK life companies to compete more equally for the business of residents of other European Union states, companies are able to write such business in an 'overseas' life fund, broadly on a gross roll-up basis with no UK tax on the income and gains, but with no relief for expenses.

Registered friendly societies are in a different position, being exempt from corporation tax in respect of tax-exempt life or endowment business. This is life and endowment business where total premiums under contracts do not exceed £270 pa with effect from 6 April 1995. Policies that can be written on the tax-exempt basis are generally qualifying policies provided they satisfy a minimum sum assured test. Such policies can give tax-free proceeds even to higher rate taxpayers (see 24.4), but non-qualifying friendly society policies are taxable at basic and higher rates. The remainder of this chapter does not deal specifically with friendly society business.

27.1.2 Review of life assurance taxation

In recent years the Revenue has conducted a number of reviews of life assurance taxation covering taxation of both life companies and of life policy proceeds. The current I-E regime collects an aggregated tax in respect of both the company's trading profit and the bulk of the income and gains accruing to the individual's policy, but an alternative would be a gross roll-up regime (similar to those found in most EU countries). Under such a regime, life companies would be taxed on their profits with the remaining tax charge being levied directly on the individual policyholder when his policy comes to an end.

These debates have now been going on for over a decade and implementation of a new regime still appears to be some years away. However, piecemeal changes are regularly introduced and these are intended to increase the amount of corporation tax payable by life companies.

Anti-avoidance provisions have been introduced, which affect the taxation of policyholders.

In 2002, the Sandler Report proposed changes to life assurance taxation (specifically the removal of qualifying policy status and of the '5% withdrawals' from insurance bonds – see 27.2.1 and 27.3.3 respectively) and the introduction of simpler and cheaper products. However, the Sandler proposals on life policy taxation were not implemented and the Chancellor decided that the recommendations would have to be considered within a wider framework taking account of regulatory change and corporation tax reform. Sandler proposals still remain of interest to the Government and may eventually be implemented in some form in an attempt to stimulate a greater savings culture.

27.2 QUALIFYING AND NON-QUALIFYING POLICIES

For tax purposes, the main classification of policies is between qualifying and non-qualifying policies.

The distinction is only relevant to the individual. There is no differentiation between qualifying and non-qualifying policies in respect of taxation of the income and gains from the underlying assets in the life company's hands.

Each of the three types of policy already identified (whole life, endowment and term assurances) is capable of being a qualifying or non-qualifying policy depending on its initial design and the way in which it is dealt with once in force.

27.2.1 Qualifying policies
(TA 1988, s 267 and Sched 15)

These are policies that satisfy the conditions set out in TA 1988, Sched 15, and do not fall foul of the various anti-avoidance provisions. The main features of the qualifying rules are as follows.

Premiums

(1) must be payable for a period of ten years or more (though term assurances may be written for shorter periods) and must be payable annually or more frequently; and

(2) must be fairly evenly spread so that premiums payable in any one period of 12 months are neither more than twice the amount of premiums paid in any other 12-month period, nor more than 1/8 of the total amount of premiums payable over the first ten years (in the case of whole life policies) or over the term of the policy (in the case of an endowment).

Premiums payable for an exceptional risk of death have always been left out of account for these purposes. FA 2003 also provides that this is the case for premiums payable for exceptional risk of a critical illness (see 27.3.8).

The sum assured

(1) for an endowment policy must not be less than 75% of the total premiums payable during the term of the policy. This percentage is reduced by 2% for each year by which the life assured's age exceeds 55 years at the issue of the policy;
(2) for a whole of life policy must not be less than 75% of the total premiums payable if death were to occur at age 75;
(3) for a term policy that has no surrender value and ends before the life assured's 75th birthday need not satisfy any minimum requirement.

Benefits

(1) may include the right to participate in profits, the right to benefits arising because of disability or the right to a return of premiums on death under a certain specified age (not exceeding 16 years); but
(2) may not include any other benefits of a capital nature.

The rules for certain special types of policy may vary from those referred to above, for example, mortgage protection policies, family income policies and industrial assurances.

Life assurers usually submit standard policy wordings to the Revenue so that they can be certified as satisfying the qualifying rules (pre-certification). Policies in those standard forms can then be marketed as qualifying.

Where a policy contains options by which the policyholder may, for example, increase the sum assured or the premium, or extend the policy term, these options are tested at the outset to ensure that, however any options are exercised, the policy will still satisfy the qualifying rules.

27.2.2 Insurance bonds and non-qualifying policies

Non-qualifying policies are all other life policies not satisfying the qualifying rules, and those that, although they might have satisfied the qualifying rules at the outset, have been changed in some way such that they no longer satisfy those rules.

The most significant category of policies that are non-qualifying is single premium investment contracts (usually referred to as 'bonds'). These are written as whole of life contracts and provide for only a small amount of life cover, being primarily investment vehicles.

27.2.3 Taxation of premiums
(TA 1988, ss 266 et seq and Sched 14)

No specific tax relief is available to an individual in respect of premiums paid under a non-qualifying life assurance policy. Similarly, there is no specific relief for premiums paid under qualifying policies issued in respect of contracts made after 13 March 1984.

However, for qualifying policies issued before that date, Life Assurance Premium Relief (LAPR) is still available where the policy was issued on the life of the payer of the premium (or the payer's spouse) and where the payer is UK-resident at the time premiums are paid.

Relief is given currently at the rate of 12.5% on premiums up to the greater of £1,500 or one-sixth of total income, and is usually obtained by deducting the tax relief from the premiums payable to the life company. Relief is lost if the policy becomes non-qualifying or if the benefits secured by the policy are increased, or its term extended, after 13 March 1984.

Where an individual receives the benefit of LAPR but, in effect, recoups himself for his outlay in premiums by withdrawing money from the policy, there is a process by which some or all of the LAPR is 'clawed back' by deduction from the amount withdrawn by him.

27.3 TAXATION OF LIFE POLICY PROCEEDS
(TA 1988, ss 539–554)

In view of life policies' position as income accumulators, where liability for gains and income in respect of the underlying assets is dealt with by taxing the life company, the usual income tax principles are inappropriate to life policy taxation. Accordingly, the tax regime that applies to the individual policyholder has been specifically constructed for the purpose. It caters separately for qualifying and non-qualifying policies and for mortality and investment profits realised from policies.

It is first necessary to determine whether any particular action constitutes a chargeable event in respect of the policy. If it does not, no income tax consequence arises under the life policy regime from that action. If it does, it is then necessary to calculate the 'gain', to determine the rate of tax applicable to the gain and to determine who is liable to pay the resulting tax.

Despite references to 'chargeable events' and 'gains', it is the income tax regime that applies to life policies (for the CGT position, see 27.3.10).

For the taxation of personal portfolio bonds, see 27.3.12.

27.3.1 **Chargeable events**

Non-qualifying policy
(TA 1988, s 540)

For a non-qualifying policy, the five chargeable events are:

(1) the death of the life assured;
(2) the maturity of the policy;
(3) the total surrender of the policy;
(4) the assignment of the policy for money or money's worth; and
(5) excesses arising on partial surrenders or partial assignments in any policy year commencing after 13 March 1975 (see 27.3.3).

No chargeable event occurs where an assignment takes place by way of security for a debt (or on the discharge of the security). Similarly, an assignment between spouses or civil partners who are living together is not a chargeable event.

Qualifying policy

For a qualifying policy, chargeable events are subject to amendments:

(a) death or maturity are only chargeable events if the policy has previously been made paid-up (ie premiums have ceased but the policy has remained in force) within the first ten years (or three-quarters of the term of an endowment policy, if shorter);
(b) surrender, assignment for money or money's worth or an excess will only be a chargeable event if it occurs before the expiry of ten years (or three-quarters of the term of an endowment policy, if shorter) or if the policy was made paid-up within that period.

Three consequences of the chargeable event rules are that:

(i) the gift (ie assignment of the whole policy with no consideration) of qualifying or non-qualifying policies is not a chargeable event and so triggers no income tax consequence;
(ii) there is no chargeable event on death of the life assured under, or on the maturity of, a qualifying policy where all due premiums were paid prior to the event in question;
(iii) there is no chargeable event on the assignment for value or surrender (in whole or part) of a qualifying policy where premiums have been paid for the first ten years (or three-quarters of the term for an endowment policy).

Where there is no chargeable event in respect of a life policy, there is no income tax charge under the specific life policy tax regime, irrespective of the tax position of the individual policyholder. In particular, points (ii) and (iii) above illustrate the main current advantage of qualifying policies – ie their ability to provide tax-free proceeds, even for higher rate taxpayers.

27.3.2 Calculating life policy gains
(TA 1988, s 541)

Broadly speaking, where the chargeable event is either a maturity, total surrender or an assignment for consideration, the chargeable gain is the investment profit made under the policy. This is calculated by reference to the value of the benefits being received as a result of the chargeable event, plus the amount of any 'relevant capital payments' previously received under the policy (ie any sum or other benefit of a capital nature, other than one paid as a result of an individual's disability), less the amount paid by way of premiums and any taxable gains as a result of previous partial surrenders.

This principle of charging tax only on investment gains also applies where the chargeable event is the death of the life assured. The exclusion of mortality profit from the taxable gain is achieved by using the policy's surrender value immediately before death instead of the value of the benefits being received under the policy.

A policy capable of paying benefits on more than one death could have the considerable disadvantage that, on a death, lump sums paid on previous deaths were taken into account when calculating the 'investment gain' under the policy. This result was not intended and FA 2003 confirms this to be the case (both for the future and the past), subject to certain conditions.

See 9.2.2 regarding commission rebates.

27.3.3 Partial surrenders
(TA 1988, s 546)

A chargeable event occurs when a policyholder surrenders part of his policy (often referred to as making 'withdrawals' from the policy). Partial surrenders include the surrender of a right to a bonus. They also include loans to a policyholder made by (or by arrangement with) the insurance company, unless the policyholder's policy is a qualifying policy and the loan bears a commercial rate of interest, or the loan is made to a full-time employee of the insurer for the purposes of house purchase or improvement.

At the end of each policy year, the policy attracts a 'notional allowance' of 5% of the total premium then paid under the policy. This allowance is then set against the value of any partial surrenders made up to that date. If the value of those partial surrenders exceeds the current cumulative allowance, a chargeable event occurs; if the cumulative allowance is equal to or exceeds cumulative withdrawals, no chargeable event occurs. Allowances are given up to 100% of the total premiums paid so that, for a single premium investment bond, the allowances are given at the rate of 5% for 20 years.

Once an 'excess' (ie an occasion on which the cumulative partial surrenders exceed the cumulative allowances) has occurred, the cumulative withdrawals and allowances up to that date are considered to have been used and the process of accumulating allowances and withdrawals starts afresh (subject to the '100% of premiums' limit that applies to the allowances).

Example – Cumulation of allowances and withdrawals

X invests £10,000 in a single premium investment bond; £1,200 is withdrawn after four policy years, a further £4,500 after six policy years and £1,000 after eight policy years.

Policy years	A Cumulative allowances chargeable events £	B Partial surrender (C − A) £	C Cumulative surrender between £	D Taxable gain £
1	500 (1 × 500)	0	0	0
2	1,000 (2 × 500)	0	0	0
3	1,500 (3 × 500)	0	0	0
4	2,000 (4 × 500)	1,200	1,200	0
5	2,500 (5 × 500)	0	1,200	0
6	3,000 (6 × 500)	4,500	5,700	2,700
7	500 (1 × 500)	0	0	0
8	1,000 (2 × 500)	1,000	1,000	0
9	1,500 (3 × 500)	0	1,000	0
10	2,000 (4 × 500)	0	1,000	0

Note: (1) A chargeable event occurs only when C exceeds A.

(2) The value of the policy is irrelevant to these calculations so that it is possible to have a taxable gain under a policy at a time when the policy itself is worth less than the premiums paid.

When the final chargeable event occurs under the policy (ie death, maturity, final surrender or assignment for value), the total profit on the policy is brought into account. The profit is the final proceeds (excluding any mortality profit where the event is death), plus previous partial surrenders, less premiums paid and any taxable gains from previous partial withdrawals.

Example – Total surrender after partial surrenders

Using the example immediately above, if the policy were totally surrendered at the end of the tenth policy year for £10,400, the taxable gain on that final encashment would be as follows:

£10,400 + £1,200 + £4,500 + £1,000 − (£10,000 + £2,700) = £4,400

Note: If, on final termination, the 'gain' calculated in this way is a negative figure, it may be deducted from taxable income for the purposes of higher rate tax only (see 27.3.4).

Partial assignments of policies

FA 2001 clarified the position on partial assignments of policies (eg where a husband and wife jointly own a policy and want to transfer it to one of them only, such as on divorce) so that:

(1) partial assignments for no consideration are not chargeable events (but note that the Revenue believes that assignment on divorce will almost invariably be for consideration); and

(2) any tax liability will fall on the person whose interest in the policy is reducing.

27.3.4 Taxing gains on chargeable events
(TA 1988, ss 547 and 550)

In the majority of cases where the policyholder owns the policy for his own absolute benefit, the gain is treated as the top slice of his income and is taxed appropriately.

However, because the income and gains attributable to the policy's underlying assets have already been taxed in the hands of the life company, life policy gains are not chargeable to income tax at the basic rate. This applies to both qualifying and non-qualifying policies. Despite the fact that the gain is treated as having already suffered tax as if it were income from savings, there is no grossing up of the gain for higher rate tax purposes.

Accordingly, for an individual paying tax at the higher rate, the maximum rate of tax payable on life policy gains at present is 20% (40% less 20%). An individual whose income (including the gain) is taxable at the basic rate only will have no further income tax liability on the policy gain. Non-tax-payers will not be able to make any reclaim in respect of tax notionally paid by the life company.

If the individual realises a loss under the policy, that loss is only available as a deduction from taxable income for the purposes of higher rate tax. Furthermore, the loss is only eligible for such relief to the extent of amounts charged as income in respect of previous chargeable events.

FA 2004 contained anti-avoidance legislation that prevents loss relief for deficiencies on 'second-hand' insurance bonds.

Top-slicing

In view of the fact that the gain will have arisen over a period of years, the legislation recognises that it would be harsh to treat the total gain as part of the taxpayer's income in the year of receipt. A measure of relief is afforded by a process known as 'top-slicing'.

Top-slicing first requires calculation of the 'appropriate fraction' of the gain, more usually referred to as the 'slice'. Where the chargeable event in question is death, maturity, total encashment or assignment for value, the slice is calculated by dividing the gain by the number of complete policy years for which the policy has been in force. Where the chargeable event is caused by a partial surrender, the gain is divided by the number of complete policy years since the last excess caused by a partial surrender (or by the number of years for which the policy has been in force where the chargeable event is the first excess).

The slice (and not the whole of the gain) is treated as the top part of the policyholder's income, and the average rate of tax applicable to the slice (less the basic rate) is calculated. That tax rate will then apply to the whole of the gain to determine the total income tax liability on the gain. The result is that relief is given to individuals whose other income would mean that they pay the tax at no more than the basic rate, but who would be taken into the higher rates of tax if the whole of the gain were added to their income.

Example – No tax on the gain

A invests £20,000 in a single premium investment bond in May 2002 and cashes it in after five years for £27,500. The gain is therefore £7,500 and the 'slice' is £1,500 (£7,500 divided by five).

	£
Taxable income (excluding policy gain)	15,000
'Slice'	1,500
Taxable income	16,500

The tax rate applicable to the 'slice' is therefore 20% less 20% = 0%.

Example – Slice falling into basic and higher rate bands

B invests £12,000 in a single premium investment bond in May 2002. After five years he cashes it in for £17,000. The gain is £5,000 and the slice is £1,000 (£5,000 divided by five). In that year his other taxable income after reliefs is £34,100.

	£
Tax calculation on gain:	
Taxable income + 'slice'	35,100
Tax applicable to slice	
On £500 (ie £34,100 to £34,600) at 0% (20% – 20%)	Nil
On £500 (ie £34,600 to £35,100) at 20% (40% – 20%)	100
Total tax on slice	100

Average rate on slice

$$\frac{100}{1,000} \times 100 = 10\%$$

The tax payable is £5,000 × 10% = £500.

To illustrate the effect of top-slicing, if it had not been available the calculations would have been:

	£
Tax applicable to the gain	
On £500 at 0% (20%)	Nil
On £4,500 at 20% (40% – 20%)	900
Tax payable	900

Notes:

(1) The whole gain (without top-slicing) is counted as income in determining whether any age allowance or entitlement to children's tax credit should be reduced.

(2) There is no top-slicing where the taxpayer is a company.

(3) Any business expansion scheme relief is left out of account when calculating top-slicing relief.

(4) For top-slicing purposes, total income is computed without reference to amounts chargeable in respect of loss of office or lease premiums chargeable as rent.

(5) The examples given in this chapter assume no reliefs or amounts as mentioned in (3) and (4).

Age allowance for over 65s

If an individual is entitled to the higher personal allowance, the gain on a life policy can reduce (or eliminate) that additional allowance. Top-slicing relief does not apply in respect of this reduction of the additional allowance. See 11.2.1 for an example of how higher allowances can be reduced.

Children's tax credit

The gain on a life policy can affect entitlement to children's tax credit. As for age allowance, top-slicing relief does not apply.

27.3.5 Two policy gains in one tax year
(TA 1988, s 550)

Where an individual has two policies with chargeable gains in a tax year, tax is calculated as if the gains arose under only one policy, with a slice equal to the sum of the individual slices. Thus, if two policies are surrendered in the same tax year, one with a gain of £10,000 (having been in force for five years) and one with a gain of £24,000 (having been in force for eight years), tax on the gains is calculated as if one policy had been surrendered, yielding a gain of £34,000 and with a slice of £5,000.

This approach can have the effect of increasing or decreasing the total tax payable (compared with disposing of the policies in separate tax years) depending on the individual's tax position and the performance of the relevant policies.

27.3.6 Persons liable for the charge
(TA 1988, ss 547 and 551)

Where a policy is held by an individual for his own benefit, the tax charge falls on him. The same applies to an individual where the policy is held as security for a debt owed by him.

If the policy is held in trust, the charge falls on the settlor, who can recover the tax paid from the trustees. If a policy is held by a trust created by a settlor who has since died, it is possible that gains realised by trustees in these circumstances may escape tax altogether in view of the impossibility of taxing somebody who has not been alive in the appropriate year of assessment. Although somewhat anomalous, this has been very useful if an individual owned a policy that would not come to an end on his death (eg a joint life policy paying out on the second death). By declaring a suitable trust of the policy in his will, he might have been able to put future gains realised under the policy outside the income tax net.

FA 1998 included provisions to counter this by enabling the trustees, or perhaps even the trust's beneficiaries, to be taxed where the settlor is dead (or not UK-resident at the time of the chargeable event). The rules do not apply where the settlor had died before 17 March 1998 and the policy is not 'enhanced' after that date.

Where the policy is held by a company, or on a trust created by or as security for a debt owed by a company, the charge falls on the company (with the right for the company to recover the tax paid from the trustees where the policy is held on trust).

If a policy is assigned by way of gift, chargeable excesses arising during that policy year, but prior to the assignment, are taxed on the assignor. Future gains are taxed on the new beneficial owner. This can allow some scope for tax planning, eg where a husband assigns a policy to his wife who is subject to a lower rate of tax and she then surrenders the policy.

27.3.7 Timing of the taxation of gains

Where the chargeable event is death, maturity, total surrender or assignment for value, the gain is treated as arising at the time of the appropriate event.

Excesses arising from partial surrenders, on the other hand, are generally only regarded as arising at the end of the policy year in which the excess occurs. Accordingly, if the policy was taken out in June 1999 and an excess occurs as a result of a partial surrender in February 2007, the gain resulting from that partial surrender is treated as arising in June 2007 and so is taxable in 2007–08.

27.3.8 Critical illness policies

A development in the UK life assurance market in recent years has been the ability to include critical illness or 'dread disease' benefits in a variety of policies. In general, this benefit pays a capital sum if the life assured is diagnosed as suffering from any of the specified 'dread diseases or events'. The diseases or events specified vary from company to company, but usually include heart attack, stroke, cancer and heart by-pass surgery.

It is understood that the Revenue accepts that the payment of a benefit on the happening of a dread disease is not a chargeable event, so that this benefit is paid free of tax under the life policy tax regime.

27.3.9 Chargeable event certificates
(TA 1988, s 552)

When a chargeable event occurs, the life assurance company is required to provide the Revenue with a chargeable event certificate that gives the policyholder's name and address, the nature and date of the chargeable event and information required for computing the gain.

FA 2001 introduced some changes to these rules. Life companies now have to supply policyholders with chargeable event certificates to help them include the gains in their SA returns. The certificates also have to include more information about the chargeable event and the gain produced.

Chargeable event certificates only have to be sent to the Revenue where the gain exceeds a threshold (set at half the basic rate tax band).

27.3.10 Capital gains tax and life policies
(TCGA 1992, s 210)

Until FA 2003, a policyholder had no personal liability to CGT on a disposal of the policy if he was its original beneficial owner or if he was an assignee and acquired the policy other than for money or money's worth.

If a policy is in the hands of an individual who is not the original beneficial owner and who did acquire it for money or money's worth, the policy is an asset potentially liable to CGT. However, where the policy is issued in respect of an insurance made after 25 June 1982, the policy also remains subject to the income tax regime that applies to life assurance policies. This may also affect some policies issued before that date. The potential for double taxation (income tax and CGT) is resolved by TCGA 1992, s 37, which provides, broadly, that money or money's worth charged to income tax will be taken into account and excluded from the CGT calculations. FA 2003 has widened this so that now, if the policy is disposed of by a person who is not the original beneficial owner, and the policy at any time prior to that disposal changed hands for money or money's worth, the policy will be an asset potentially liable to CGT.

Where a life policy is subject to the CGT regime, the occasion of the payment of the sum(s) assured and the surrender of the policy are treated as disposals.

27.3.11 Guaranteed income bonds

In 1996, the Revenue raised questions concerning the taxation of some policies that could provide regular payments to the policyholder. Most common among these policies were guaranteed income bonds. The Revenue view was that such payments were interest or annual payments, rather than policy part surrenders. FA 1997 reinstated, with retrospective effect, the industry's understanding of the position, confirming such payments as part surrenders to be dealt with under the life policy tax rules.

27.3.12 **Personal portfolio bonds**

These are policies usually, but not exclusively, written offshore where the benefits due under the policy are (or may be) closely linked with the value of a portfolio of assets personal to the policyholder.

FA 1998 included the introduction of a new charge on such policies, which deems a gain of 15% of the total premiums paid to the end of each policy year and deemed gains from previous policy years chargeable under the new legislation. This is an additional charge but is not imposed in respect of any policy year ending before 6 April 1999. This charge does not apply to 'managed portfolio bonds', ie those that do not allow 'personalisation' by restricting the policy investment to pooled assets generally available to investors.

27.4 OFFSHORE LIFE POLICIES
(TA 1988, s 553 and Sched 15, paras 23–27; FA 1995, s 56)

In general, policies issued in respect of contracts made after 17 November 1983 cannot be qualifying unless they are issued by a UK insurance company or the UK branch of a foreign insurer. Before that date, foreign policies could be qualifying if they satisfied the normal qualifying rules.

Other ways in which the life policy tax regime gives a different tax treatment for offshore policies are as follows:

(1) The gain calculated on a chargeable event is reduced by reference to the amount of time, during the life of the policy, the policyholder was not UK-resident.

(2) In calculating the 'appropriate fraction' for top-slicing purposes, any complete years during which the policyholder was not UK-resident are excluded.

(3) Taxable gains arising under such policies are charged to basic rate as well as higher rate tax, as appropriate. An exception to this applies where the insurer is taxed on the investment income and gains accruing for the policyholder's benefit at a rate of not less than 20%. In such cases, the policy gains will not be liable to basic rate UK income tax. This exception will apply only to policies issued by EU or European Economic Area (EEA) insurers.

FA 1998 included a framework requiring certain categories of offshore life companies to appoint a fiscal representative in the UK to be responsible for reporting, to the Revenue, gains on life policies in accordance with TA 1988, s 552 (see 27.3.9). Discussions between the Revenue and the offshore insurers have resulted in regulations that enable insurers to comply with local secrecy laws while giving the insurers time to develop systems to comply with the reporting requirements.

At one time there was an advantage in holding offshore insurance bonds through a non-UK resident company but FA 2006 contained provisions that enabled HMRC to tax profits from the surrender of such policies under s 739 (see 32.4) from 5 December 2005.

Gains arising from offshore policies are taxed as miscellaneous income (previously Schedule D Case VI income). This means that a UK resident policyholder is taxed on the arising basis even if he is domiciled overseas. Put another way, the remittance basis does not apply.

27.5 ANNUITIES
(TA 1988, ss 656 and 685)

An annuity is an arrangement under which one person agrees to pay another a sum of money for a known period, or a period to be determined by some specified contingency.

Annuities may be immediate (ie the payment will start straightaway) or deferred (where payments will start at some predetermined point in the future). Many annuities are established to continue for the lifetime of the annuitant, but temporary annuities cease at the end of a fixed period or on the annuitant's death, whichever comes earlier. Annuities may be effected on the lives of two or more individuals and, for example, continue until the death of the last survivor. Annuities may be paid monthly, quarterly or annually, and may be of a fixed amount or subject to some sort of index-linking. Annuities may also be written with a guaranteed minimum period so as to reduce the loss that might otherwise be suffered by an individual who dies shortly after purchasing an annuity.

There are four main types of annuity:

(1) Purchased life annuities, where an individual pays a lump sum to an insurance company in return for the annuity.
(2) Annuities received as a gift (eg at one time it was common for testators to direct that annuities be paid out of their estates).
(3) Annuities paid as part of the purchase price of a business or by continuing members of a partnership to a former partner who has retired.
(4) Compulsory purchase annuities, for example, those purchased out of pension funds.

Significant changes were made in FA 1991 to the taxation of life companies in respect of general annuity business, with effect for accounting periods commencing after 31 December 1991. The changes apply to existing business, subject to transitional relief.

These changes brought the taxation of life company general annuity funds broadly into line with the regime that applies to ordinary life business. Previously, a general annuity fund was not taxed on its income and gains if annuities paid by the company during the tax year equalled or exceeded the fund's investment income and realised gains.

For the annuitant, a purchased life annuity attracts a special relief in that amounts received by him are treated in part as a return of the money paid for by the annuity (the capital element) and in part as interest on that purchase price. The capital element of each payment is calculated by reference to actuarial tables and is not taxable. This tax exemption applies even where the annuitant lives long enough for the capital element of annuity payments he receives to exceed the original purchase price of the annuity.

Other types of annuity do not receive this favourable treatment in respect of the capital element of annuity payments.

Purchased life annuities are also subject to an income tax regime similar to that previously described as applying to life policies (see 27.3.4).

Chargeable events for life annuities are total surrender, assignment for money or money's worth and 'excesses' (calculated in much the same way as in respect of life policy partial surrenders).

Where a gain arises on a chargeable event, the gain is not charged to basic rate tax where the company offering the annuity has been taxed under the new life company tax regime described above because of the 'credit' that is, in effect, given in respect of tax paid by the life company on the income and gains of its general annuity fund.

For CGT purposes, deferred annuities are also treated in a similar way to life policies, with the effect that no chargeable gain accrues on the disposal of such a contract except where the person making the disposal is not the original beneficial owner and acquired the rights for consideration in money or money's worth or, following FA 2003, the person making the disposal is not the original beneficial owner and the annuity at any time changed hands for money or money's worth.

27.6 PERMANENT HEALTH INSURANCE (PHI)

27.6.1 Introduction

Permanent health insurance (PHI) policies provide a replacement income for an individual who is unable to work through illness or disability. Contracts are usually available to those aged between 16 and 60 but terminate on the insured reaching his normal retirement date.

Once the disability or illness arises, benefits commence on expiry of a deferred period, typically between one and 12 months, selected by the policyholder. The longer the deferred period, the fewer claims the insurer will expect to pay and so the lower the premium will be per £ of benefit.

PHI contracts can be written as life assurance policies – typically as non-qualifying policies to avoid provision of substantial sums assured payable on death. If structured as a life policy, payment of disability benefits is not treated as a surrender of rights for the purposes of life policy taxation.

27.6.2 Tax consequences

If an individual effects a PHI contract for himself, premiums are not deductible for tax purposes. If an employer effects a policy on an employee to enable him to continue to pay the employee's salary during a period of disability or illness, or if the policy covers a revenue loss during such a period, the employer may be able to claim the premiums as a business expense.

Benefits from most individually owned PHI policies are tax-free.

If the contract is effected by an employer to maintain the employee's salary during the period of illness or disability, the income is taxable in the individual's hands, in the same way as salary would have been.

27.7 PRE-OWNED ASSETS CHARGE

A problem may arise from 2005–06 where individuals have taken out a policy that is written in trust so the proceeds on death would be paid to their business partners/fellow shareholders but the individual remains entitled to the amount paid out on the maturity of the policy. This type of arrangement may be wholly commercial and yet still be caught by the FA 2004 legislation (see 32.7), which imposes a charge on an annual benefit that will normally be 5% of the capital involved (in this context, the surrender value of the policy).

The pre-owned assets legislation is extremely complex and this is an area where you should seek advice from a specialist.

27.8 LIFE POLICIES EFFECTED BY COMPANIES
(TA 1988, s 540)

There are circumstances in which a company can effect a life policy. For example, it may do so on the life of a director or other key executive to provide the company with compensation for the death of that individual. Similarly, policies may be effected to provide funds to repay loans.

In general, if a company effects a term assurance for a short period (usually not more than five years), which does not acquire a surrender value and is effected solely to provide protection against the loss of profits resulting from the death of a key person, the premiums are tax deductible and the proceeds taxable in the hands of the company.

If, on the other hand, the policy is for a longer term, may acquire a surrender value, is effected for a capital purpose, or where the life assured has a material shareholding in the company, the premiums are not tax-deductible but the proceeds are unlikely to be charged to corporation tax in the company's hands, other than by virtue of the life assurance chargeable event rules.

Prior to FA 1989, policies owned by companies could be qualifying policies (provided they satisfied the qualifying rules) and so could provide tax-free proceeds to the company in the same way as for individuals. Gains from non-qualifying policies were also tax-free in the hands of the company, except where the company was a close company.

The rules changed for policies effected after 13 March 1989 (or those effected before that date but subsequently varied to increase the benefits or the policy term). Such policies cannot be qualifying policies (irrespective of their compliance with the qualifying rules) if, immediately prior to the chargeable event, the policy was owned by a company or was held on trusts created, or as security for a debt owed, by the company. Gains from such policies are treated as the company's income and are chargeable under Schedule D Case VI.

There is an exception to this denial of qualifying status where policies are used to secure company debts incurred in purchasing land to be occupied by the company for the purposes of its trade (or in constructing, extending or improving buildings occupied in that way). Broadly speaking, provided the policy has been used for this purpose since its inception, the chargeable gain will only be the amount by which the policy proceeds exceed the lowest amount of the loan that has been secured by the policy.

27.9 LIFE POLICIES IN TRUST AFFECTED BY FA 2006 IHT CHANGES

The 2006 Budget changed the way in which certain trusts are taxed. The main change was bringing the IHT treatment of 'interest in possession' trusts into line with the regime that was previously confined to discretionary trusts. This means the creation of such trusts will normally be taxed as a chargeable lifetime transfer whereas such gifts were previously treated as PETs (potentially exempt transfers), which attracted IHT only if the donor died within seven years.

Interest in possession trusts have been used for protection policies written in trust, principally because of the flexibility of beneficiaries that this type of trust provides. However, the change in rules means a more complex and potentially more highly taxed regime for policies now written in these types of trust.

For any protection plan written in an interest in possession trust after 22 March 2006, the premiums will potentially be subject to an immediate IHT tax charge of 20% (taxed as a chargeable lifetime transfer, see 29.2). The trust itself will be subject to a 'periodic' charge on the value of the trust assets every 10 years (maximum 6%) and there will also be an exit charge on any capital distributions from the trust (see 30.4.23).

However, most regular premium plans written into interest in possession trusts should escape theses tax charges. If the premiums are below £3,000, they will be exempted by the annual IHT exemption. For premiums above this level, providing they are regular and meet the relevant rules, they should be exempted from the tax charge, as they will be considered 'normal expenditure out of income'. Where neither of these situations arises there will be no immediate tax charge provided they do not exceed the IHT nil rate band (currently £312,000).

Protection policies established in trust before 22 March 2006 will not normally be caught by the new IHT regime, however care should be taken when any changes are made to these policies.

Absolute trusts or, to use their proper name, bare trusts, continue to fall within the PET rules and therefore do not attract tax as a chargeable lifetime transfer. Clearly, there will now be a temptation to write more policies under bare trusts. However, the disadvantage of these types of trust is that, by definition, it is extremely difficult to change the beneficiary and, should an individual's personal circumstances change in the future, they may be left with a policy written in a trust that is no longer appropriate.

27.10 DISCOUNTED GIFT SCHEMES

A discounted gift scheme involves a gift of an investment bond (see 27.2.2) where certain rights are retained, typically the right to take annual withdrawals. For example, a couple aged 70 may give a bond to their children whilst retaining the right to take 5% pa for the rest of their lives. In such a situation, the gift is not £100,000 but the discounted value of the right to receive what value is left in the bond when the couple have died.

HMRC published a technical note on discounted gift schemes on 1 May 2007. See also the recent 'test case' decision by the Special Commissioners in *Executors of Mrs Marjorie Bower* v *HMRC*.

28

CAPITAL GAINS TAX PLANNING

Where a capital gain arises, the transaction tends to be an exceptional or 'one-off' event. Instead of being spread evenly over the whole period of ownership, the capital growth on an investment that might have been held for many years falls entirely into the tax year in which the disposal takes place. This can often mean that a large amount of tax is involved. In broad terms you have to view the bigger picture when it comes to capital gains tax in that having a problem generally means you have made (or are about to make) a profit on your investment. It is important that you do not let tax considerations dominate to the exclusion of investment decisions.

There are ways of mitigating tax and it is usually a good idea to take professional advice. The following should be borne in mind – but they are only suggestions rather than definitive advice:

(1) Make use of annual exemptions for both spouses/civil partners.
(2) Realise gains to avoid wasting the annual exemption.
(3) Make sure you get relief for capital losses.
(4) Save tax by making gifts to relatives.
(5) Claim roll-over relief on furnished holiday accommodation.
(6) Make the most of entrepreneurs relief.
(7) Selling the family company.

Important note on civil partners

The FA 2005 put the CGT treatment of married couples and civil partners on to the same footing from 5 December 2005.

28.1 MAKE USE OF ANNUAL EXEMPTIONS FOR BOTH SPOUSES/CIVIL PARTNERS

28.1.1 Inter-spouse transfer can be a way of saving tax

All individuals are allowed to realise capital gains of £9,600 in 2008–09 before they become liable for CGT. This applies to spouses and civil partners, but there are no provisions under which any unused amount may be transferred to the other spouse or partner.

Example – Inter-spouse/civil partner transfers

If *A* has gains of £7,000 and his wife *B* has gains of £12,200, the position is as follows:

	A	B
	£	
Gains	7,000	12,200
Less: exemption	(9,600)	(9,600)
Taxable	Nil	1,600

There is often a way of avoiding this type of mismatch. If *B* had transferred assets to *A* and he then sold them, she could effectively transfer her gain to him. A transfer between spouses does not count as a disposal for tax purposes and *A* would take over *B*'s base cost. So, with a little forethought, the position could have been:

	A	B
	£	
Gains	9,600	9,600
Less: exemption	(9,600)	(9,600)
Taxable	Nil	Nil

28.2 REALISE GAINS TO AVOID WASTING THE ANNUAL EXEMPTION

Any unused annual exemption cannot be carried forward for use in a future tax year. Dealing costs may be a disincentive but, provided you expect to sell shares, etc, at some time, it can make sense to 'top up' any net gains to make full use of the £9,600 exemption.

The rules for matching sales and purchases within a 30-day period mean that 'bed and breakfast' transactions will not achieve this. However, you may be able to realise gains and then have your ISA buy the same shares (ie 'bed and ISA'). Alternatively, your spouse, civil partner or family trust can buy the shares.

28.3 MAKE SURE YOU GET RELIEF FOR CAPITAL LOSSES

It may be possible to save tax in a different way by a transfer of an asset between spouses or civil partners before it is sold to an outsider. Capital losses for previous years attach to each spouse and civil partner separately and can be set only against that spouse's or civil partner's gain.

Example – Relief for capital losses

If C's wife D has losses of £35,000 and C has an asset that has appreciated by £50,400, it will make sense for him to transfer it to D before it is sold. Instead of the position being like this:

	£
C's gains	50,400
Less: exemption	(9,600)
Taxable	40,800

the position will be:

D's gains	50,400
Less: capital losses	(35,000)
	15,400
Less: exemption	(9,600)
Taxable	5,800

Of course, the ideal position would be achieved by C transferring part of the asset to D, so that they eventually make a joint disposal, use D's losses and take full advantage of both of their annual exemptions.

28.3.1 Negligible value claims

You may have made an investment in the past that has gone badly. Indeed, you may have written it off in your own mind but, if you have not sold it, the loss is normally only a paper loss that is not allowable for CGT purposes. There is an exception to this rule: you may be able to establish an allowable loss even though there has been no disposal. If the Revenue can be persuaded that the asset has become of 'negligible value' (ie virtually worthless), you can claim a loss (see 12.5.9). In practice, the Revenue issues lists of quoted shares that have been suspended and are recognised to be of negligible value, so you should ask your Inspector whether your defunct investments are on list or alternatively view the list on line at www.hmrc.gov.uk/cgt/negvalist.htm. It may also be possible to establish losses on unquoted shares and other investments.

In some situations, it may be best to defer making a negligible value claim. If you have made capital gains that are covered by the annual exemption you will waste part of your CGT loss by making a negligible value claim for that year.

28.3.2 Review your holdings

If you find yourself holding shares that have failed to live up to your expectations when you purchased them and, worse, made a loss, consider selling these shares to crystallise a loss to offset against your capital gains. By taking positive action before the end of the tax year, you may be able to save 18% on your CGT bill and recoup in part the loss you suffered on a disappointing investment. An experienced stockbroker, IFA or investment adviser working in conjunction with a good accountant should be able to more than cover their professional fees with proactive advice.

28.4 SAVE TAX BY MAKING GIFTS TO RELATIVES

If you are planning to sell unquoted shares it may be possible to save tax.

Example – Sale of unquoted shares

G holds all the shares in a private trading company. He has reached broad agreement with a potential purchaser to sell his shares for £1,000 each, which will produce a gain of £650 per share.

If *G* so wishes, he could transfer some shares to his son *H* to enable him to use his annual exemption, ie *G* would give *H* 15 shares in the company and claim holdover relief. No capital gain need arise for *G* on his gift to *H* who would then dispose of the shares to the ultimate purchaser. *H*'s capital gain would then be as follows:

	£
Capital gain: 15 × £650 =	9,750
Less: annual exemption	(9,600)
Taxable	150

The overall effect is that *G*'s family saves tax of £1,728.

If *G* had four children, he could make gifts to all of them and save up to £6,912.

Gifts of listed shares and securities

It is sometimes possible to achieve a similar saving by transferring shares that do not attract s 165 hold-over relief, for example shares in a quoted trading company where the owner has less than 5% of the voting shares, or shares in a private investment company. But you have to plan some way ahead.

The important point is that it is possible to claim hold-over relief under a different part of the legislation where you make a chargeable transfer for IHT purposes, normally on your putting assets into a trust (see 12.6, 30.4.23 and 30.5). The first thing to do is to either create such a trust or add the shares to an existing family trust and then make a hold-over election under TCGA 1992, s 260 so that you do not have to pay any CGT (bear in mind that s 260 relief is not available if the trust is a settlor-interested trust, see 32.14.7). If the trustees subsequently appoint property in favour of the trust beneficiaries (eg your children, grandchildren, etc), they can make a similar hold-over election to avoid any CGT charge on them. The overall effect will be that the trust beneficiaries will have taken the property that you put into trust at a value equal to your original acquisition cost plus indexation; if they do not have very much income or gains, a large part of the proceeds from their eventually selling the assets will have escaped CGT.

You will need to take professional advice. In particular, bear in mind that if transfers into trusts take your cumulative transfers over the nil rate band (at present £312,000), you may have to pay IHT at the rate of 20% on the excess (see 29.2, 29.10 and 30.4.23). And do not try to do all this in rapid succession because the Revenue may well attack the transactions as a pre-ordained scheme (see 32.19 on *Ramsay*).

28.5 CLAIM ROLL-OVER RELIEF ON FURNISHED HOLIDAY ACCOMMODATION

Where a person has realised a capital gain on the disposal of a business, or has sold a property used by a firm in which they are a partner, the gain may be rolled-over (see 16.3). This normally involves the person continuing to be in business. However, if he does not wish to carry on trading, roll-over relief may still be available. A particular type of property investment qualifies in this way because where a property is acquired for letting as furnished holiday accommodation, the owner is deemed to have acquired an asset for a trade and roll-over relief may therefore be obtained.

Two points are of particular interest:

(1) The property need not be located at the seaside. A property in, for example, Central London could qualify provided it is let for at least part of the year on a short-term basis (see 7.5 and 16.3.6).
(2) Roll-over relief may be obtained provided the property is let as furnished holiday accommodation for a period. If the property is subsequently let for a longer-term or used for some other purpose (eg as a second home) the relief is not normally withdrawn. The one exception to this would be if the owner had acquired a leasehold interest on the property and the lease had less than 60 years to run at the time it was acquired. Taking such a property out of use as furnished holiday accommodation would mean that the deferred gain would become chargeable (see 16.3.4).

28.6 MAKE THE MOST OF ENTREPRENEURS RELIEF

Entrepreneurs relief is available on capital gains of up to £1 million. The tax rate is 10% rather than 18% so the relief is potentially worth £80,000.

In principle, both husband and wife can qualify for relief on gains of up to £1 million.

A gain on the sale of a property let as furnished accommodation should, in principle, qualify for entrepreneurs relief.

Conditions

(1) The vendor must either be an individual who is employed by his personal trading company or, in certain circumstances, the trustees of a life interest trust where the life tenant is employed by the company. This means that an individual who has retired completely may not qualify.

(2) A company is an individual's personal trading company only if he holds at least 5% of the voting rights. Relief is therefore not available if the individual holds only 4.9% of the ordinary shares.

A gain on an associated disposal may also attract relief. Such a disposal may include the sale of a property used by the individual's personal company if (and only if) he has not been charging the company rent (see 16.8.4).

The relevant conditions need to be satisfied for the 12 months ending with the date of sale.

28.7 SELLING THE FAMILY COMPANY

The sale of a family company may involve complex tax issues. Much will depend on the facts and circumstances. However, the vendors' advisers should generally address the following points.

28.7.1 Get clearance or you may end up paying income tax rather than CGT

It is advisable to obtain advance clearance from the Revenue that it accepts that s 703 ICTA 1988 does not apply in relation to the sale (see 32.3). If s 703 were applicable, the vendors might have to pay higher rate income tax rather than 18% CGT.

Another situation where vendors may have to pay income tax rather than capital gains tax is where they hold employment-related securities (see 5.6). Bear in mind that the tax liability will often then fall on the company (see 20.1.4) but if the company gets a deduction under Schedule 23 FA 2003 (see 17.3.2) the extra tax cost may be rather less than one would expect.

28.7.2 Checklist

Relevant questions include:

(1) Should the company make large pension contributions for the benefit of shareholder directors? This will lead to a reduction in the sale price and to a corresponding reduction in CGT.

(2) Should shareholder directors receive termination payments (exempt up to £30,000)? Again, this will lead to a reduction both in the sale price and the shareholders' CGT.

(3) If the purchaser really wants some specific parts of the company's business, would it make better sense for the company to sell those business operations rather than the shareholders sell their shares? Could the company secure roll-over relief (see 17.7.2).

(4) If the company is a holding company, would it make better sense for it to sell its trading subsidiary? A crucially important aspect here is whether such a sale would qualify for the Substantial Shareholding Exemption (see 17.7.3).

(5) Do any of the shareholder's family have substantial unrelieved capital losses? If so, consider gifts of shares to him or her before the sale

(6) Are any of the shareholders not resident in the UK? Look for ways of taking full advantage of their not being liable for CGT.

(7) Are any of the shareholders themselves companies? If so, a pre-sale dividend could be attractive.

(8) Will the purchaser want to acquire premises that are used by the company but owned by some shareholders in their personal capacity? What are the CGT implications? Those shareholders may not be able to secure roll-over relief in the future as the relief is limited to situations where the old and new assets are used by the same company (see 16.3.8). However, it may be that shareholders who are directors or employees are able to claim roll-over relief under a different head by reinvesting in assets to be used by another personal trading company (see 16.3.9).

(9) Will entrepreneurs relief be available for some or all of the shareholders?

(10) Can CGT be deferred by shareholders taking shares or loan notes in the acquiring company?

(11) If there is a 'mix' of types of consideration on offer (eg cash, loan notes, preference shares, ordinary shares, warrants, rights to an earn-out), is it more appropriate for some vendors to take their entitlement in a particular form?

For example, an ambitious shareholder who has been offered a senior position by the purchaser might accept a share exchange if this will mean that he has a 5% stake in the acquiring company and should therefore qualify for entrepreneurs relief on a future sale. This would especially make sense where the sale of the shares in the existing company would not use up a substantial part of the £1 million relief.

Conversely, elderly shareholders may take loan notes on the basis that they intend to retain them for the rest of their lives (in which case the potential CGT liability will disappear) or they may take preference shares in the acquiring company on the grounds that these shares should continue to attract business property relief.

Individuals who are planning to retire abroad may take loan notes with a view to deferring their CGT disposal until they have become non-resident and are therefore not liable for CGT (but see 12.15.2 and 16.8.4).

(12) To what extent is it practical for the vendors to plough their proceeds back into a new company and defer tax under EIS CGT deferral relief.

28.7.3 **Vendors temporarily non-resident**

If you are selling your shares while you are non-resident but you expect to resume residence in the UK within five years of your departure, you may end up being liable for capital gains tax (see 12.3.2). A person who is in this position may be better off from a UK tax perspective in taking a pre-sale dividend because the five-year rule does not apply for income tax purposes. A non-resident who receives such a dividend will have no UK tax to pay at all. However, you will need to check on the tax treatment of the country in which you are resident.

28.7.4 **Treatment of loan notes**

Questions regularly arise concerning the tax treatment of loan notes issued by a company that takes over a family company.

The first point to bear in mind is that the vendor's advisers should seek clearance under s 138 TCGA 1992 to ensure the exchange of shares in company A for loan notes issued by company B will not be a disposal for CGT purposes (see 12.15.2). HMRC will normally give such clearance provided it is satisfied that the transaction is being entered into for commercial reasons and is not part of a CGT avoidance scheme. This in turn means that no CGT charge will normally arise until the loan note holder disposes of his loan notes, either by redeeming them or by selling or giving them away.

A second issue concerns the tax treatment if loan notes that are qualifying corporate bonds (QCBs) are eventually realised at less than their face value. This can leave the loan note holders with a tax charge based on the value of the loan notes at the time of the share exchange. In practice, vendors of private companies should think hard about accepting loan notes unless they are guaranteed by a bank.

You should seek professional advice if you hold loan notes that are QCBs and the company that issued them is likely to default on its obligations.

Finally, bear in mind that you may be able to secure s 165 hold-over relief on gifts of loan notes that are not QCBs. This may allow you to achieve similar savings to those that can arise from gifts of shares before a sale of the family company (see 28.4 above). Section 165 relief is available where the securities (ie the loan notes) are not quoted and the relief can therefore apply even though company B is a quoted company.

29

INHERITANCE TAX AND INDIVIDUALS

HILARY SHARPE

Inheritance tax (IHT) is a combined gift tax and death duty. It was introduced in 1974 under the name 'capital transfer tax' and much of the legislation dates back to that time. It applies to gifts and deemed gifts made during a person's lifetime and to his estate on death. The Finance Act 2006 made some radical changes in relation to the tax treatment of interest in possession trusts and accumulation and maintenance trusts.

There is a nil rate band for IHT (see 29.1), which is currently £312,000. Cumulative transfers in excess of this taking place either at or within seven years of death are taxed at 40% (though the overall effect may be reduced on transfers that take place more than three years before death). On all other occasions when IHT is payable, the rate is 20%.

This chapter covers the following topics:

(1) Who is subject to IHT?
(2) When may a charge arise?
(3) Transfers of value.
(4) Certain gifts are not transfers of value.
(5) Exempt transfers.
(6) Potentially exempt transfers.
(7) Reservation of benefit.
(8) Business property.
(9) Agricultural property and woodlands.
(10) Computation of tax payable on lifetime transfers.
(11) Tax payable on death.
(12) Life assurance and pension policies.
(13) Heritage property.
(14) Planning: the first step.

29.1 WHO IS SUBJECT TO IHT?

A UK-domiciled individual is subject to IHT on all property owned by him, whether located in the UK or overseas. By contrast, a person of foreign domicile is subject to IHT only on property in the UK. There are various specific exceptions to this. For example, with effect from 16 October 2002, UK unit trusts and open-ended investment companies (OEICs) held by non-UK domiciled individuals have been excluded from any UK IHT charge. Also, transfers of exempt gilts are excluded from any IHT charge if the transferor is not resident or ordinarily resident in the UK even though he may be domiciled in the UK.

See Chapters 33 and 34 on domicile, residence, etc.

Section 267 of the Inheritance Tax Act (IHTA) 1984 contains a special rule that applies for IHT purposes whereby an individual may be deemed to be UK-domiciled for a tax year if he has been resident in the UK for 17 out of the 20 tax years that end with the current year. However, this is overruled by provisions contained in a few of the UK's double taxation agreements.

29.1.1 Nil rate band

The first £312,000 of chargeable transfers (the 'nil rate band') is free of IHT. The nil rate band will be £325,000 for 2009–10.

There are circumstances where an additional amount can be claimed in respect of a spouse's unused nil rate band (see 29.11.7).

29.2 WHEN MAY A CHARGE ARISE?

IHT can apply in the following circumstances:

(1) On a gift made by an individual during his lifetime.
(2) On a lifetime transfer of value regarded as a 'chargeable transfer'.
(3) On an individual's death.

A person who had an interest in possession under a trust or settlement at 22 March 2006 is normally regarded as if he were entitled to the capital. When the beneficiary dies, the trust property's full value is treated as part of his estate for IHT purposes (see 30.4.15). The position is quite different where an individual has acquired his interest in possession after that date (see 30.4.17). In general, the capital in such trusts will not be subject to IHT on the death of the individual who has the interest in possession but instead the trust will be subject to the ten-year periodic charge (see 30.5.15). There are, however, special rules that cover an individual who acquires an interest in possession on the death of his or her spouse or where the interest in possession arises before 6 October 2008 and replaces an interest in possession held by someone else at 22 March 2006.

Figure 29.1 indicates the circumstances under which a gift may be a chargeable transfer for IHT purposes.

Figure 29.1 – Is a gift a chargeable transfer?

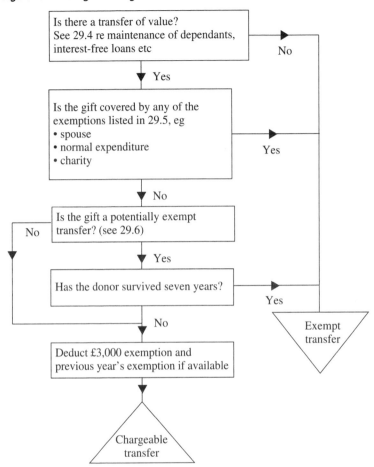

29.3 TRANSFERS OF VALUE

29.3.1 Not all transfers are gifts
(IHTA 1984, s 3)

The legislation refers mainly to transfers rather than gifts. The reason for this is that all gifts are transfers of value, but not all transfers of value are gifts. For example, where a person deliberately sells an asset at less than market value he may not be making a gift, but he is certainly making a transfer of value. Similarly, deliberately omitting to exercise a right can be a transfer of value, but this is not a gift in the normal sense of the word. To give a third example, a transfer can even involve property not owned by the person since the IHT legislation deems a person to make a gift if his interest in possession under a trust comes to an end.

29.3.2 There must be gratuitous intent
(IHTA 1984, s 10)

IHT does not normally apply to a gift unless there is an element of 'bounty', ie there is a deliberate intention to make a gift. An unintentional loss of value (eg a loss made on a bad business deal) is not subject to IHT because there was no intention to pass value to another person.

29.3.3 How a transfer is measured
(IHTA 1984, s 3)

The amount of any transfer of value is determined by the reduction in the donor's wealth. This is not necessarily the same as the increase in the recipient's wealth.

This can be shown by considering the situation where a person owns 51 out of 100 shares in a company. He has control because he has the majority of the shares. If he were to give two shares to his son, he would relinquish control of the company and his remaining 49 shares might be worth considerably less because of this. The two shares given to his son might not be worth very much in isolation, and the son might not have acquired a very valuable asset, but the father's estate would have gone down in value by the difference between the value of a 51% shareholding and that of a 49% shareholding.

29.4 CERTAIN GIFTS ARE NOT TRANSFERS OF VALUE

Certain gifts and other transactions are not regarded as transfers of value, so the issue of whether they are chargeable transfers simply does not arise. These include:

- maintenance of dependants, family, etc;
- waivers of dividends;
- waivers of remuneration;
- interest-free loans;
- disclaimers of legacies;
- deeds of variation;
- transfers involving trusts where the settlor has retained powers of appointment.

29.4.1 Maintenance of dependants, family, etc
(IHTA 1984, s 11)

The legislation specifically provides that the following lifetime payments are not transfers of value:

(1) Payments for the maintenance of a spouse or former spouse.

(2) Payments for the maintenance, education or training of a child or stepchild under age 18.

(3) Payments made to maintain a child over age 18 who is in full-time education or training.

(4) Reasonable provision for the care or maintenance of a dependent relative, ie someone who is incapacitated by old age or infirmity from maintaining himself, or a widow or a separated or divorced mother or mother-in-law.

29.4.2 Waivers of dividends
(IHTA 1984, s 15)

A waiver of a dividend is not regarded as a transfer of value provided certain conditions are satisfied:

(1) The dividend must be waived by deed.

(2) The deed must not be executed more than 12 months before the right to the dividend has accrued.

(3) The deed waiving the dividend must be executed before any legal entitlement to the dividend arises.

The position is slightly different for interim and final dividends as the point in time at which entitlement may arise can be different.

Interim dividends

A shareholder has no enforceable right to payment before the date on which a board resolution has declared that a dividend shall be payable. However, the directors can declare an interim dividend that is payable immediately without having to first seek shareholders' approval. Therefore, a deed waiving a dividend should be executed in good time before any board resolution is passed.

Final dividends

A company may declare a dividend without stipulating any date for payment. In such circumstances, the declaration of the dividend creates an immediate debt and it is therefore too late to execute a waiver.

In other cases where a final dividend is declared as being payable at a later date, a shareholder may waive his entitlement provided he does so before the due date for payment.

In practice, a final dividend will require the shareholders' approval and an individual shareholder may therefore waive a dividend provided the deed is executed before the company's annual meeting.

29.4.3 Waivers of remuneration
(IHTA 1984, s 14)

There is a specific provision whereby a waiver of remuneration does not constitute a transfer of value. The terms of this exemption were based on the income tax treatment. In practice, the Revenue certainly used to accept that remuneration was not subject to income tax if it was waived and the assessment on earnings had not become final and conclusive, and:

(1) the remuneration was formally waived (usually by deed); and
(2) the employer's assessable profits were adjusted accordingly.

The taxation of employment income has changed over the past 30 years and you would be well advised to check in advance with your Inspector of Taxes that this treatment will apply in your particular circumstances, especially where substantial amounts are involved.

29.4.4 Interest-free loans
(IHTA 1984, s 29)

The IHT legislation specifically provides that an interest-free loan is not to be treated as a transfer of value provided the loan is repayable on demand.

This exemption would not cover a situation where a loan was made for a specific period, with the lender having no legal right to call for repayment before that time. The grant of such a loan could be a transfer of value, with the Revenue assessing the transfer as the difference between the loan amount and its present market value if it were to be assigned.

29.4.5 Disclaimer of legacies
(IHTA 1984, s 142)

If a person becomes entitled to property under a will or an intestacy or under a trust (eg on a life tenant's death), he may disclaim his entitlement. Such a disclaimer is normally effective for IHT purposes and is not treated as a transfer of value provided that:

(1) no payment or other consideration is given for the disclaimer; and
(2) the person has not already accepted his entitlement, either expressly or by implication.

29.4.6 Deeds of variation
(IHTA 1984, s 142)

A deed of variation may be entered into where a person has died leaving property to a beneficiary, the effect being to redirect property. Where the necessary conditions are fulfilled, the revised disposition is treated as having taken place on the deceased person's death. Once again, a person who gives up an entitlement is not treated as making a transfer of value.

The following conditions need to be satisfied:

(1) The deed of variation must be executed within two years of a death.

(2) It must be in writing and must specifically refer to the provisions of the will, etc that are to be varied.

(3) It must be signed by the person who would otherwise have, and anyone else who might have, benefited.

(4) Only one deed of variation in respect of a particular piece of property can be effective for IHT purposes.

(5) No payment or other consideration may pass between beneficiaries to induce them to enter into the deed of variation (except that a variation is permitted that consists of an exchange of inheritances and a cash adjustment).

(6) For deeds executed before 1 August 2002, a formal election had to be submitted to the Revenue within six months of execution.

(7) For deeds of variation executed on or after 1 August 2002, there is no need for a formal election provided that the deed refers to the relevant legislation.

The Revenue's booklet IHT8, *Alterations to an inheritance following a death*, can be obtained by calling 08459 000 404.

29.4.7 Powers of appointment over settled property

Legislation was amended from 17 April 2002 to ensure that such rights and powers are not treated as being part of an individual's estate for IHT purposes. The relief applies retrospectively in relation to IHT charges that otherwise might have applied on death.

The change followed the decision in *IRC* v *Melville* CA [2001] STC 1297. This case concerned an individual who transferred property to a new discretionary settlement but had power to direct the trustees to return the property to him after three months. The Court of Appeal held that the chargeable transfer was only a modest amount as the settlor had retained a valuable right. Although this suited the taxpayer in *Melville*, it had caused concern for settlors who had retained such powers, particularly individuals who had created settlements while domiciled abroad (see 34.15.2).

29.5 EXEMPT TRANSFERS

Even if a transfer takes place, it will not attract IHT if it is an exempt transfer. The full list of exempt transfers is as follows:

(1) Gifts to spouse.

(2) Normal expenditure out of income.

(3) £250 small gifts exemption.

(4) Annual £3,000 exemption.

(5) Exemption for marriage gifts.
(6) Gifts to charities.
(7) Gifts for national purposes.
(8) Gifts to political parties.
(9) Gifts to housing associations.
(10) Certain transfers to employee trusts.
(11) Compensation paid to former prisoners of war and Holocaust victims.

29.5.1 Gifts to spouse
(IHTA 1984, s 18)

There is normally an unlimited exemption for transfers between husband and wife and, since December 2005, between civil partners. For this purpose, a couple is regarded as husband and wife until a decree absolute has been obtained. The exemption covers outright gifts, legacies and a transfer of property on death to a trust under which the widow or widower has an interest in possession.

The exemption is restricted where a UK-domiciled spouse makes transfers to a foreign domiciled spouse. In this situation, the exemption is limited to £55,000. However, the 'deemed domicile' rule (ie UK-resident for 17 out of 20 years: see 29.1) applies for all IHT legislation purposes except where expressly excluded. Consequently, a gift by a UK-domiciled individual to a spouse who has a foreign domicile, but who is treated as UK-domiciled for IHT purposes under the 17-year rule, qualifies for the unlimited exemption.

In the past, the exemption has also applied for settled property in which a surviving spouse has an interest in possession. This could arise in one of two situations. First, the deceased might have been the life tenant of a settlement and his widow stepped into his shoes and acquired a life interest on his death. Alternatively, the deceased might have drawn his will so as to create a will trust under which his widow had an interest in possession.

Spouse exemption applies in both cases where the deceased died before 22 March 2006. For an individual who died on or after that date, the spouse exemption is still available in respect of a transfer under a will trust. But where the trust is a lifetime trust, spouse exemption is now generally available only where the deceased held his interest at 22 March 2006 and his widow takes a similar interest on his death.

29.5.2 Normal expenditure out of income
(IHTA 1984, s 21)

A lifetime gift is exempt if it is shown that the gift was made as part of the donor's normal expenditure and comes out of income. The legislation requires that the gift should be normal, ie the donor had a habit of making such gifts. The legislation also requires that by taking one year with another, the pattern of such gifts must have left the donor with sufficient income to maintain his normal standard of living.

Gifts that take the form of payments under deed of covenant or the payment of premiums on life assurance policies written in trust frequently qualify as exempt because of this rule.

29.5.3 £250 small gifts exemption
(IHTA 1984, s 20)

Any number of individual gifts of up to £250 in any one tax year are exempt. If a person wanted to, he could make 100 separate gifts of £250 a time. However, where gifts to a particular individual exceed £250, the exemption does not apply.

29.5.4 Annual £3,000 exemption
(IHTA 1984, s 19)

This exemption is available to cover part of a larger gift. The exemption is £3,000 for each tax year. Furthermore, both husband and wife have separate annual exemptions.

If the full £3,000 is not used in a given year, the balance can be carried forward for one year only and is then allowable only if the exemption for the second year is fully utilised.

Example – Carry forward

Situation 1	£	£
Gifts made in Year 1		1,000
Balance of exemption carried to Year 2		2,000
Gifts made in Year 2		4,000
Annual exemption for Year 2	3,000	
Part of unused exemption for Year 1	1,000	(4,000)
Chargeable gifts		Nil

The balance of exemption from Year 1 of £1,000 may not be carried forward to Year 3.

Situation 2	£	£
Year 1 as in Situation 1 – unused exemption		2,000
Exemption for Year 2	3,000	
Gifts in Year 2	2,000	
Balance of Year 2 exemption to be carried forward to Year 3	1,000	

The balance of the Year 1 exemption of £2,000 may not be carried forward to Year 3.

29.5.5 Gifts in consideration of marriage
(IHTA 1984, s 22)

Gifts made to the bride or groom in consideration of their marriage are exempt up to the following amounts:

Gifts made by	Maximum exemption
Each parent	£5,000
Grandparents (or great grandparents)	£2,500
Bride or groom	£2,500
Any other person	£1,000

Parents may make gifts to either party to the marriage: their exemption is not restricted to gifts made to their own child but covers gifts made to both parties rather than £5,000 for each recipient. This means that in relation to the groom, for example, each of the bride's parents may give up to £5,000. The gifts should be made so that they are conditional upon the marriage taking place.

The exemption also applies for civil partnerships.

29.5.6 Gifts to charities
(IHTA 1984, s 23)

Gifts to charities established in the UK are exempt regardless of the amount. A charity may be established or registered in the UK even though it carries out its work overseas, and the exemption covers gifts to such charities. Donations made to a foreign charity established abroad do not normally qualify.

29.5.7 Gifts for national purposes
(IHTA 1984, s 25)

Gifts to certain national bodies are totally exempt. These include colleges and universities, the National Trust, the National Gallery, the British Museum and other galleries and museums run by local authorities or universities.

29.5.8 Gifts to political parties
(IHTA 1984, s 24)

Gifts to 'qualifying political parties' are exempt only if certain conditions are satisfied. A political party qualifies if it had at least two MPs returned at the last general election, or if it had at least one MP and more than 150,000 votes were cast for its candidates.

29.5.9 Gifts to housing associations
(IHTA 1984, s 24A)

Gifts of UK land to registered housing associations are exempt.

29.5.10 Certain transfers to employee trusts
(IHTA 1984, s 28)

Transfers by an individual to an employee trust of shares in a company can be exempt provided the following conditions are satisfied:

(1) The trust's beneficiaries include all or most of the persons employed by or holding office with the company.

(2) Within one year of the transfer:
    (a) the trustees must hold more than 50% of the company's ordinary share capital and have voting control on all questions that affect the company as a whole; and
    (b) the trustees' control is not fettered by some other provision or agreement between the shareholders.

(3) The trust deed must not permit any of the trust property to be applied at any time for the benefit of:
    (a) a participator in the company (ie a person who holds a 5% or greater interest);
    (b) any person who has been a participator at any time during the ten years prior to the transfer;
    (c) any person connected with a participator or former participator.

A further restriction may apply where a company makes a transfer to an employee trust.

29.5.11 *Ex-gratia* payments to POWs

There is an exemption for compensation and *ex-gratia* payments made to former prisoners of war by the Japanese Government. This has recently been extended to cover compensation received by prisoners of war from the German Government. Ask for a copy of ESC F20.

29.5.12 Holocaust compensation

Compensation paid to Holocaust victims or their families is exempt.

29.6 POTENTIALLY EXEMPT TRANSFERS
(IHTA 1984, s 3A)

29.6.1 Definition of 'potentially exempt transfer (PET)'

Irrevocable gifts made during an individual's lifetime may, provided certain conditions are satisfied, be potentially exempt transfers (PETs). These gifts become actually exempt only if the donor survives seven years. If he dies during that period, the PET becomes a chargeable transfer. The tax payable depends on the IHT rates in force at the date of death. The donee is liable to pay the tax.

The main conditions to be satisfied for a gift to be a PET are that the gift is made to:

(1) an individual; or
(2) (for transfers up to 21 March 2006) a trust under which an individual has an interest in possession (see 30.4.18); or
(3) a trust for the disabled (see 30.7); or
(4) an accumulation and maintenance trust (see 30.6). Note that from 22 March 2006, a lifetime trust qualifies as an accumulation and maintenance trust only if the beneficiaries will become absolutely entitled to the trust capital on attaining age 18 – this is a new condition and transfers to trusts before that date might have constituted PETs even though the beneficiaries did not have an entitlement to anything other than income from age 25.

A gift that is subject to a reservation of benefit (see 29.7) cannot be a PET. Furthermore, a gift to a discretionary or (after 21 March 2006) an interest in possession trust is a chargeable transfer.

29.6.2 Taper relief
(IHTA 1984, s 7)

Where an individual makes a PET or chargeable transfer and dies within the seven-year period, taper relief may reduce the amount of tax payable. The tax payable on the transfer that has become chargeable is reduced so that only a proportion is charged. The proportion is as follows:

Years between gift and death	Percentage of full charge
Three to four	80
Four to five	60
Five to six	40
Six to seven	20

Taper relief cannot reduce the tax on a lifetime chargeable transfer below the tax payable at the time the transfer was made. If a gift falls within the nil rate band, the taper relief is of no real benefit and does not reduce the tax that arises on other property that passes on the donor's death.

29.7 RESERVATION OF BENEFIT
(FA 1986, s 102 and Sched 20)

29.7.1 Introduction

Property that has been given away may still be deemed to form part of a deceased person's estate unless:

(1) possession and enjoyment of the property was bona fide assumed by the donee; and
(2) the property was enjoyed virtually to the entire exclusion of the donor and of any benefit to him by contract or otherwise.

The reference to the property being enjoyed 'virtually to the entire exclusion' of the donor means that for all practical purposes this is an 'all or nothing' test. The Revenue's view is that the exception is intended to cover trivial benefits such as might arise where, for example, the donor of a picture enjoyed the chance to view it when making occasional visits to the donee's home.

The Act refers to a benefit reserved 'by contract or otherwise' and this is meant to refer to arrangements that are not legally binding but amount to an honourable understanding. This may arise where a person gifts away a house but remains in occupation. A reservation of benefit would arise even if there were no legal tenancy and the donee could, in law, require the donor to vacate the property at any time.

For the purposes of the gift with reservation (GWR) legislation, property includes property bought with the proceeds of the original gift. However, the Revenue has confirmed that there is no such tracing where the original gift was cash.

29.7.2 Starting date

The reservation of benefit rules apply to gifts made on or after 18 March 1986. Where a gift or transfer was made before that date, and the donor reserved a benefit, the gift is effective for IHT purposes and the capital does not form part of that person's estate.

29.7.3 Two cases where the taxpayer succeeded (and the Government changed the rules)

The rules on gifts of land and buildings were tightened up in FA 1999 to block the type of arrangements upheld by the House of Lords in *IRC* v *Ingram* [1999] STC 37. Here, the late Lady Ingram carved out a 20-year lease that entitled her to occupy the property rent free and then gave away the freehold. It was decided that this did not constitute a gift with reservation, but the law has been amended with effect from 9 March 1999 to block this loophole.

The Court of Appeal held in *IRC* v *Eversden* [2003] STC 822 that the reservation of benefit rules did not apply where a woman transferred property into a trust under which her husband had an interest in possession even though that interest subsequently came to an end and the settlor was then able to benefit. The point was that the original transfer (gift into settlement) was covered by spouse exemption and the gift with reservation (GWR) rules were therefore not applicable. The subsequent termination of the spouse's interest in possession was not caught by the GWR rules because it was a transfer of value and not a gift (the GWR legislation applies only to gifts). However, this loophole was closed with effect from 20 June 2003.

29.7.4 Retrospective legislation

The Government can act like a very bad loser. FA 2004 contained legislation on pre-owned assets that imposed an income tax liability from 6 April 2005 on many people who had used (entirely lawful) ways of sidestepping the GWR rules in the past. If Lady Ingram were still alive, she might well be caught by this legislation. These provisions can catch transactions that took place as long ago as 19 March 1986. See 32.7 for more details.

29.7.5 Three specific exemptions to the GWR rule

Donor pays a market rent

FA 1986 specifically provided that occupation of property or use of chattels does not count as a benefit provided the donor pays a market rent.

Benefit enjoyed after major change in circumstances

The legislation also provides that a benefit enjoyed by a donor occupying property can be ignored where the donor's financial circumstances have changed drastically for the worse after the gift has been made.

Joint occupiers

FA 1999 introduced a further exemption whereby an individual who transfers an interest in a residence to another individual who also occupies the property is not regarded as reserving a benefit provided that he continues to meet his share of all expenses and outgoings. This can be a very important let-out where parents wish to give a half-share in the family home to children who live with them. However, it is not confined to such situations (eg there is no requirement that the children occupy the property as their main residence). Also, a donor can give (say) a 60% interest in the property to a donee who occupies only (say) 40% of the property.

You should take expert advice before taking action that relies on this let-out.

29.7.6 Position where reservation of benefit ceases

Where a person makes a gift and initially reserves a benefit, but then relinquishes that reservation, he is normally treated as making a PET at the time he gives up the reserved benefit. The amount of the PET is governed by the property's market value at that time.

Example – Giving up reservation of benefit

A gives away property worth £150,000 in July 1997 but reserves a benefit. The benefit is relinquished in July 2003 when the property is worth £220,000. A dies in October 2007.

> If no benefit had been reserved, the gift would have been completely exempt by August 2004 (ie seven years after the gift), but because a benefit was retained until July 2003 the seven-year period starts only from that date. The full £220,000 (ie the value at July 2003 when the reservation of benefit came to an end) would form part of A's estate for IHT purposes.

29.7.7 Settlements and trusts

The position is less clear cut where a person has sought to reserve the possibility of a benefit, for example, where he has created a settlement and is a potential beneficiary. It is the Revenue's opinion that a benefit is reserved where the settlor creates a discretionary trust and is a member of a class of potential beneficiaries. This would also apply where the settlor may be added to a class of potential beneficiaries.

In contrast to this, the Revenue has confirmed that no reservation of benefit arises where a person creates a settlement and is a contingent or default beneficiary. This may apply, for example, where property is put into trust for the settlor's children but the property would revert to the settlor in the event of the children dying or becoming bankrupt.

The legislation does not require that the donor's spouse should be excluded from benefit, and where a discretionary settlement is created it would be possible to include his spouse, any future spouse or widow(er) as a potential beneficiary. However, if property were to be distributed to the donor's spouse from the trust and that property were then to be applied for the benefit of the settlor, the Revenue might well take the view that, looked at as a whole, there had been a reservation of benefit.

The Revenue has confirmed that a settlor may be a trustee of a settlement created by him without this constituting a reservation of benefit. Also, where the settled property includes shares in a family company, the settlor/trustee may also be a director of the company and may be permitted under the trust deed to retain his remuneration provided it is reasonable in relation to the services rendered.

29.8 BUSINESS PROPERTY
(IHTA 1984, ss 103–114)

29.8.1 Basic requirements

A special deduction is given against the value of business property where the following conditions are satisfied:

(1) The property must have been owned during the previous two years or have been inherited from a spouse and, when the spouse's period of ownership is taken into account, the combined period of ownership exceeds two years.

(2) The property must not be subject to a binding contract for sale.

(See also 29.11.10 on replacement property.)

Figure 29.2 – Is there reservation of benefit?

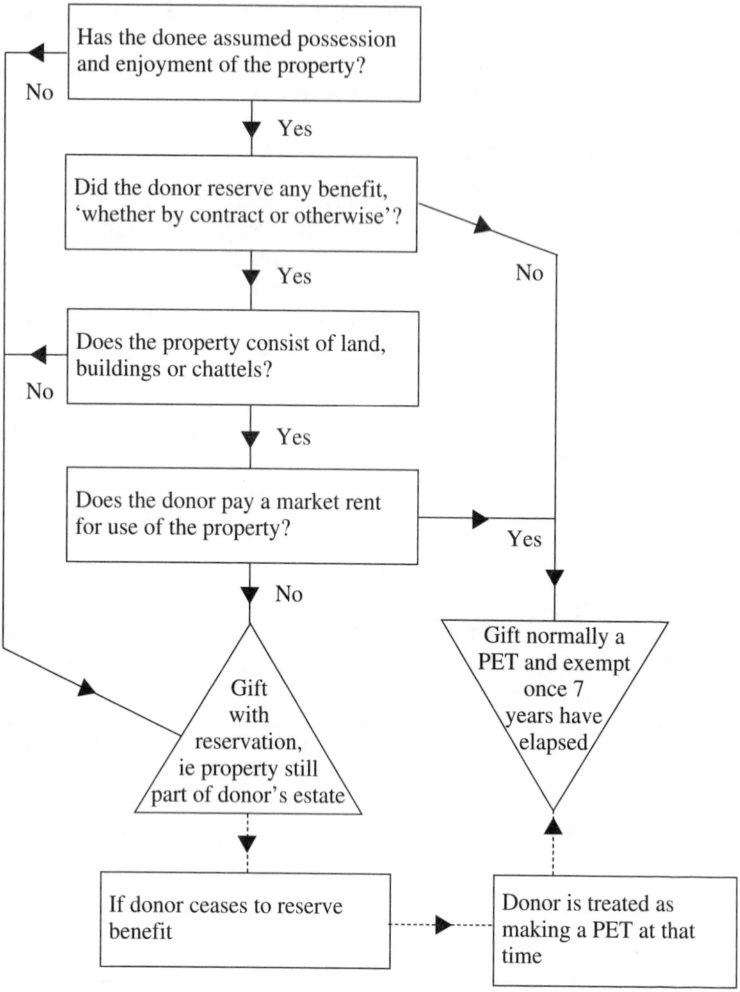

29.8.2 Rates of business property relief (BPR)
(IHTA 1984, s 103)

Unincorporated businesses

A sole proprietor's interest in his business qualifies for a 100% deduction, as does a partner's interest in his firm.

A 50% deduction is available for an asset owned by a partner but used by his firm.

Shares and debentures

Business relief is available on shares only where the company concerned is a trading company or the holding company of a trading group. The 100% relief is available on shares and debentures in an unquoted company. Where the company is a quoted company, 50% relief is due if (and only if) the person making the capital transfer had voting control before the transfer.

Shares dealt in on the AIM are treated as unquoted.

A 50% deduction was given for smaller shareholdings in unquoted trading companies. Where a controlling shareholder transfers an asset used by his trading company, or where such an asset passes on his death, 50% relief is available.

29.8.3 Businesses that do not qualify

Business relief is not normally available where the business carried on consists wholly or mainly of dealing in securities, stocks or shares, land or buildings or in holding or making investments.

Where a transfer involves shares, business relief may be restricted if the company owns investments. The legislation refers to such investments as 'excepted assets', which are defined as assets that are neither:

(1) used wholly or mainly for the purposes of the business, nor
(2) required for the future use of the business.

Where a company has subsidiaries, it is necessary to look at the group situation (ie shares in subsidiaries may have to be treated as excepted assets if the subsidiaries are investment companies).

29.9 AGRICULTURAL PROPERTY AND WOODLANDS
(IHTA 1984, ss 115–124B)

Agricultural relief is available on the agricultural value of farmland in the UK, Channel Islands or Isle of Man.

29.9.1 Land occupied by the transferor

A 100% deduction is available where the individual has occupied the farmland for the two years prior to the transfer date. Where a farm has been sold and another acquired, the replacement farm normally qualifies for agricultural property relief provided the owner has occupied the two farms for a combined period of at least two years in the last five years. Agricultural property relief is also available for land owned by an individual but occupied by a firm of which he is a partner or a company of which he is the controlling shareholder for the two years preceding the transfer date.

29.9.2 Relief for other land

A 100% deduction is also available on land not occupied by the owner provided he has (or had) the legal right to regain vacant possession within a period not exceeding 12 months. To qualify under this head, the individual must normally have owned the land for at least seven years.

29.9.3 Relief for tenanted farmland

A 50% deduction is available for farmland let on a tenancy granted before 1 September 1995 and where the owner cannot obtain vacant possession within 12 months. This would generally be the case where the land is let under an agricultural tenancy. Once again, the land must normally have been owned for seven years.

The 50% deduction is increased to 100% for land under a tenancy granted on or after 1 September 1995. This also includes a tenancy over property in Scotland acquired after that date by right of succession.

29.9.4 Woodlands
(IHTA 1984, ss 125–130)

The tax treatment of UK woodlands is largely beneficial as business relief is normally available after two years of ownership. In very unusual circumstances where business relief is not available, alternative relief may be due under s 125 after five years of ownership.

29.10 COMPUTATION OF TAX PAYABLE ON LIFETIME TRANSFERS

In practice, IHT is likely only to be paid during a person's lifetime for chargeable transfers made by him to a trust. The tax payable is calculated as follows:

Initial calculation

Chargeable transfers made during the preceding seven years		A
Add	Amount of chargeable transfer	$\underline{B}$
		C
Deduct	Nil rate band	$\underline{D}$
		$\underline{E}$
	IHT thereon at 20%	X
Deduct	IHT on a notional transfer of A minus D as if it took place at the same time	$\underline{Y}$
	IHT payable in respect of the chargeable transfer	$\underline{Z}$

Position if the donor dies within three years

Chargeable transfers made during the previous seven years		A
Add	PETs caught by the seven-year rule	$\dfrac{B}{C}$
Add	amount of chargeable transfer	$\dfrac{D}{E}$
Deduct	Nil rate band	$\dfrac{F}{G}$
	IHT thereon at 40%	H
Deduct	IHT at 40% on a notional transfer of C minus F	$\dfrac{I}{J}$

The donee is liable to pay additional IHT of J minus the amount Z above already paid.

Position if the donor dies during years four to seven

The above will be liable for additional IHT computed as J above, but subject to the IHT on PETs caught by the seven-year rule being reduced by taper relief (see 29.6.2).

29.11 TAX PAYABLE ON DEATH

29.11.1 Normal basis of computation

The charge on death is normally computed as shown in the flowchart shown in Figure 29.3. The IHT will be the tax on the figure in Box 6 minus the tax payable on a normal transfer equal to the amount in Box 4 as if the notional transfer took place immediately before the death. Some taper relief may be due on the PETs caught by the seven-year rule (see 29.6.2).

However, special reliefs may be available.

29.11.2 Death on active service
(IHTA 1984, s 154)

Since World War II death duty legislation has contained an exemption for a person who dies from wounds suffered while on active service. The exemption applies to the estates of those killed in the Falklands conflict and the Gulf War, and of members of the RUC killed by terrorists in Northern Ireland.

The exemption may well apply more often than people think. Death does not have to be immediate, nor need the wound be the only cause of death. The High Court held in 1978 that the exemption was owed to the estate of the fourth Duke of Westminster because serious wounds that he had suffered in 1944 contributed to his death in 1967.

29.11.3 Sales of quoted securities at a loss
(IHTA 1984, ss 178–189, as extended by FA 1993, s 198)

Relief is given where quoted securities or unit trusts are sold at a loss within 12 months of death. Where shares are suspended, FA 1993, s 198 permits similar relief to be claimed by reference to the shares' value when they return from suspension. It is not possible to pick and choose: the relief is confined to the amount of any overall loss. Executors must, in effect, elect that the total proceeds of any sales should be substituted for the value at date of death.

Example – Sale of quoted securities at a loss

> *B* died on 1 October 2007. His estate included a portfolio worth £70,000. The executors had to sell all of the securities in December 2007 and realised an overall loss of £25,000. The estate can be reduced by this amount so that, in effect, only £45,000 is taken into account.
>
> The overall loss of £25,000 may have been made up of a gain of £5,000 and losses of £30,000. Relief is, however, limited to the net figure.

29.11.4 Relief restricted where executors purchase quoted securities

Furthermore, the relief is restricted where the executors repurchase quoted securities within two months of the last sale.

Example – Restriction of relief on quoted securities

> *B*'s executors sold the securities in December 2007. On 10 January 2008, they reinvested £10,000 in new securities. The £25,000 loss cannot be claimed in full, it has to be reduced by
>
> $$\frac{10,000}{45,000} \times £25,000 = £5,556$$

29.11.5 Sales of land at a loss
(IHTA 1984, ss 190–198, as amended by FA 1993, s 199)

Relief is due where land and buildings are sold at a loss within four years of death, provided the loss is at least £1,000 or 5% of probate value (whichever is less). The net proceeds are substituted for the value at the date of death and the IHT is recomputed. This relief applies only where the property is sold to an arm's length purchaser, and not to a connected person.

29.11.6 Debts that may be disallowed
(FA 1986, s 103)

There is a general rule that debts are not deductible where the deceased has made a capital transfer to the person who subsequently made a loan back to the deceased. This rule applies only to loans made after 18 March 1986, but

Figure 29.3 – Charge on death computation

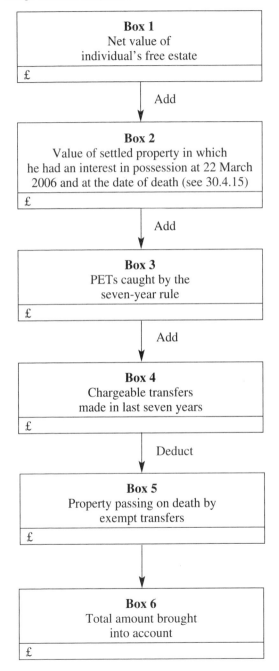

there is no such time limit on the capital transfers. A debt may be disallowed because the deceased had made a capital transfer to the lender even though that capital transfer took place before 18 March 1986. It is also of no help that the loan was made on normal commercial terms and a market rate of interest was payable.

This legislation was successfully invoked by the Revenue to deny a deduction for a debt incurred by a widower where the debt arose from his buying an interest in the matrimonial home from his late wife's executors. He had given his wife her interest in the property eight years before her death. See *Phizackerley* v *HMRC* (SpC 591). This seems a very harsh decision, especially if s 103 would not have been in point if Mr Phizackerley had died first and his wife had incurred a similar debt in buying a similar interest in the property from his executors.

29.11.7 Using the balance of the nil rate band of a former spouse or civil partner

Schedule 4 FA 2008 provides that where an individual dies after 8 October 2007, he or she may also be entitled to an additional nil rate band based on the proportion of his or her spouse's nil rate band which remained unused on the earlier death of that spouse (or civil partner).

The additional relief has to be claimed.

The maximum relief is an amount equal to the full nil rate band (in other words, a person who has been widowed twice cannot claim the full unused nil rate band in respect of both his or her previous spouses).

There is no time limit and the relief may therefore be claimed for cases where the spouse had died 30 years ago, in fact right back to the introduction of IHT on 26 March 1974.

There is also no restriction by reference to the size of the spouse's estate. In principle, the additional nil rate can be claimed in respect of a spouse who had no assets at all on his death.

29.11.8 Legitim: special rules for Scotland
(IHTA 1984, s 147)

Scottish law provides that a person must leave a set part of his estate to his children: their entitlement is called 'legitim'. If a person makes a will that does not take account of this, the children can have it set aside. In practice, children often decide to renounce their right to legitim, especially where a person's will bequeaths all his property to his widow. The legislation provides that children who renounce their entitlement within two years of the death are not treated as making a chargeable transfer and the property is treated as passing to the widow in accordance with the will.

The deed renouncing the rights must satisfy the provisions as to variations: see 29.4.6.

Practical problems arise where minor children are involved. The IHT legislation provides that children under age 18 (at the date of death) may renounce their entitlement within two years of attaining age 18 without this constituting a chargeable transfer by them. The property is then treated (for IHT purposes) as passing to the widow in accordance with the will. As a child under age 18 does not have the legal capacity to renounce his entitlement, the executors have a difficult choice: they can either account for IHT on the basis that the child takes his entitlement or on the assumption that the child will renounce his rights when he reaches 18.

Position where executors assume legitim rights are taken

IHT will have to be paid to the extent that the property that passes to the children exceeds the nil rate band. When each child attains 18, he may elect to renounce his rights so that the widow benefits. The spouse exemption will then mean that no tax should have been paid. The Revenue will then repay the IHT paid and pay interest.

Position where executors assume that legitim will be renounced

No IHT will be paid in the first instance. However, if it turns out that one of the children decides not to renounce his entitlement, IHT on the death is recomputed and the tax payable attracts interest from the date it should have been paid.

29.11.9 Quick succession relief
(IHTA 1984, s 141)

Suppose a person has recently inherited property from someone else. If he were to die and the full rate of IHT applied, the same property would have been subject to IHT twice within a relatively short period of time.

Quick succession relief is intended to alleviate this. The relief works by giving credit for a proportion of the tax charged on the first occasion against the tax payable on the second death. The proportion is set out below:

Both deaths occur	Proportion
within one year	100%
within two years	80%
within three years	60%
within four years	40%
within five years	20%

Example – Quick succession relief

D inherited property worth £150,000 in October 2003. IHT was paid on that estate at an average rate of 25%, so the grossed-up amount was £200,000 (£150,000 × 100/75) and the tax suffered was £50,000. *D* dies in August 2006. The maximum amount on which quick succession relief can be claimed is:

$$\frac{150,000}{200,000} \times £50,000 = £37,500$$

This has to be reduced to 60% of £37,500 (ie £22,500) as three complete years have elapsed. The relief is not affected by the fact that property has been sold or given away before the second death takes place.

29.11.10 Treatment of gifts caught by seven-year rule
(IHTA 1984, s 113A)

Tax on a PET that becomes a chargeable transfer because of the transferor's death is payable by the recipient of the gift. Business relief is available on a PET that becomes a chargeable transfer only if the conditions in 29.8 are satisfied both at the time of the gift and at the time of death.

Examples – Business relief on PETs

(1) *E* owns all the shares in a family company. He gives his son *F* a 24% shareholding. Three years later, the company is sold and *F* receives cash for his shares. One year after that *E* dies.

Business relief will not normally be available as the necessary conditions are not satisfied by the donee at the time of *E*'s death. If *F* had reinvested the proceeds in another private company, business relief might have been available after all.

(2) The basic position is as in (1) (ie *E*'s gift to *F* of a 24% shareholding). This time, *F* retains his shares, but by the time *E* dies the shares are quoted. No relief is due as *F* does not control the company and his shares are quoted shares.

The basic position is as in (1), but *F* retains the shares and they are still unquoted at the time of *E*'s death. The shares attract the 100% relief and this is not lost even if *F* disposes of the shares shortly after *E*'s death.

29.11.11 Replacement property
(IHTA 1984, s 107)

Where a donee has disposed of business property, but acquires replacement property, the PET may still attract business relief provided the replacement property is acquired within three years of the disposal. Similar rules apply for agricultural property.

29.11.12 Reduction in value

Where the value at date of death of property transferred by a PET is lower than the value at date of gift, the chargeable transfer is based on the value at death.

29.11.13 Acceptance of property in lieu of IHT

The Revenue has power to accept certain types of property in satisfaction of IHT liabilities. Such property includes pictures, prints, books, manuscripts, works of art, scientific objects and other items regarded as being of national, scientific, artistic and historic interest. The Revenue has to clear such arrangements with Heritage ministers and in practice only property regarded as of 'pre-eminent interest' is accepted.

Taxpayers who own such items that have been acknowledged as being first rate can find out more about these arrangements by obtaining a copy of *Capital Taxation and The National Heritage* from:

The Revenue Reference Room
Room 8, New Wing
Somerset House
London WC2R 1LB

29.11.14 Double taxation agreements

The UK has only a handful of tax treaties that cover inheritance tax. There are treaties with France, India, Italy, Netherlands, Pakistan, Ireland, South Africa, Sweden, Switzerland and the USA.

Where no double taxation arrangement exists, unilateral relief will normally be available by way of a foreign tax credit against the UK IHT charge.

29.11.15 Payment of IHT by instalments

It is possible to defer payment of IHT on certain types of property. IHT on assets that attract 50% business property relief or agricultural property relief, or IHT payable on other business/agricultural property because the two-year period of ownership is not satisfied, can be paid by instalments over ten years, with interest being charged only on instalments that are paid late. IHT on other land and buildings can also be paid by instalments but interest is charged from the normal due date.

Outstanding instalments generally become payable as and when the property is sold.

29.12 LIFE ASSURANCE AND PENSION POLICIES

29.12.1 Life assurance

Life assurance is one of the best ways of providing for the payment of IHT, but the tax treatment of policies needs to be watched carefully. The following is only a summary of a complex area.

29.12.2 Death of policyholder

A life assurance policy beneficially owned by the deceased is property subject to IHT in the same way as any other property owned by him.

29.12.3 **Gifts of policies**

Gifts of policies may generally be made in two ways:

(1) Writing the policy in trust or making a subsequent declaration of trust.
(2) Assignment of the policy.

In either case, subsequent premiums may be paid:

(1) by the donor direct;
(2) by the beneficiary out of cash gifts from the donor;
(3) by the beneficiary out of his resources;
(4) by a combination of the above.

In general, if the gift is an outright gift to an individual or a trust for the disabled, it will constitute a PET and will only be taxable if the donor dies within seven years of making the gift. Gifts to other trusts such as discretionary trusts may attract lifetime IHT.

If any of the usual IHT exemptions applies (see 29.5), neither the gift of the policy nor any gifts of premiums that have been made will be taxable, for example:

(1) The gift of the premium or policy falls within the annual exemption – currently £3,000 (note that if the policy is a qualifying policy and premiums are payable net of life assurance relief, it is the net premium that constitutes the gift; if the premiums are paid gross, it is the gross premium that constitutes the gift).
(2) The premiums come within the donor's normal expenditure out of income exemption (note that this applies to payment of premiums, not to the gift of an existing policy).
(3) The gifts fall within the marriage settlement exemption.
(4) The gifts fall within the small gifts exemption – outright gifts of not more than £250 per donee (eg a premium on a policy written in trust for the absolute benefit of a child).
(5) Policies written by husband or wife for the absolute benefit of the other.

If none of the exemptions applies, IHT may be payable in respect of the gift of the policy or the payment of subsequent premiums (unless they fall within the nil rate band). However, payment of premiums on policies written under interest in possession trusts before 22 March 2006 will often constitute PETs under transitional provisions contained in Finance Act 2006.

If IHT is payable, the chargeable transfers are the premiums paid by the donor; or, if a gift of an existing policy is made by assignment or declaration of trust, the chargeable transfer is generally the greater of the total gross premiums paid or the policy's market value (usually the surrender value).

If cash gifts have been made to enable the premiums to be paid by the beneficiary, the amount of the cash gifts will usually be PETs. The proceeds of the policy on death, maturity or surrender will not be subject to IHT in the hands of the recipient of the assignment or a beneficiary having an interest in possession in the trusts.

29.12.4 Life of another policies

On the death of the life assured the proceeds are totally free of IHT. Clearly they do not form part of the life assured's estate, as the policy is not owned by him. The surrender value will, however, be potentially chargeable in the policyholder's estate if he dies before the life assured.

If the donor makes cash gifts to the policyholder to help him pay the premiums, the cash gifts will be taxable for the donor, unless the exemptions mentioned above apply, but the proceeds will be free of IHT in the policyholder's hands.

29.12.5 Use of policies

Life assurance policies can be used in two main ways in IHT planning:

(1) as a vehicle for making gifts to beneficiaries; and
(2) to create a fund for the eventual payment of the tax.

Thus they may help to both minimise the amount of tax payable and offer a means of paying any unavoidable liability whenever it arises.

29.12.6 IHT and pension plans

Although the legislation does not permit a policyholder to alienate his right to a retirement pension, it is possible to assign any death benefits provided under retirement annuity or personal pension plans, whether provided as a sum assured or as a return of the retirement fund. The IHT rules are broadly similar to those applicable to life policy assignments except that:

(1) discretionary trusts of these assignable benefits will not be subject to the usual IHT charging regime of ten-yearly and exit charges provided the benefits are distributed within two years of the individual's death;
(2) the right to a pension is not treated as giving rise to an interest in possession in the pension fund;
(3) the gift of a 'return of fund' death benefit will usually be regarded as having no value, provided the individual is in good health. Similarly, subsequent contributions to the pension will be treated as being attributable to the provision of the pension benefits and not the death benefit, provided the individual is in good health at the time the contribution is made.
(4) an IHT charge may arise on the death after age 75 of a person who has an alternatively secured pension (see 25.2.5).

Occupational schemes are usually written under discretionary trusts and also achieve the same IHT exemptions on payment of contributions and distribution of benefits.

29.13 HERITAGE PROPERTY

It is possible to claim exemption for transfers of qualifying heritage assets, for example chattels of museum quality, land of outstanding natural beauty or of historic or scientific interest, and buildings and amenity land deemed to be of outstanding historic or architectural interest. The exemption is currently conditional on the new owner undertaking to maintain and preserve the asset and to provide reasonable public access to it. It is no longer possible to restrict access by requiring an appointment with the asset's owner.

The rules for defining qualifying chattels have also been made more restrictive by FA 1998. There used to be no time limit for claiming heritage tax exemptions, but for tax charges arising after 16 March 1998 a claim for exemption normally has to be made within two years of the date of the relevant chargeable event. In addition, transfers made after 16 March 1998 no longer qualify for the special exemption previously available for gifts and bequests to certain non-profit making bodies.

29.14 PLANNING: THE FIRST STEP

Planning for IHT is something that many people would rather not think about. The first step should be to sit down and work out the value of your estate: it is something that your next of kin may already have done if you've ever argued! If the net value of your estate is close to the IHT threshold, then perhaps the time has come to talk with your financial or tax adviser to discuss ways in which you can ensure the people you would like to benefit from your estate are provided for. As part of this process you should review your existing will, especially given the changes introduced by FA 2006 (see 29.1.2, 29.5.1 and 29.6.1). If you do not have a will, this should be the starting point for any planning.

30

THE TAXATION OF TRUSTS

MARK FRANCIS

This chapter covers the taxation of trusts under the following headings:

(1) When are trustees liable to pay income tax?
(2) When are trustees liable for UK capital gains tax?
(3) Bare trusts.
(4) Fixed-interest trusts.
(5) Discretionary trusts.
(6) Accumulation and maintenance trusts.
(7) Trusts for the disabled.
(8) Protective trusts.
(9) Trusts for the most vulnerable.
(10) Charitable trusts.
(11) Miscellaneous aspects.
(12) Executors and personal representatives.
(13) Some planning points.

30.1 WHEN ARE TRUSTEES LIABLE TO PAY INCOME TAX?
(FA 1989, s 110)

30.1.1 General rules

UK-resident trusts are liable to pay income tax on both UK and overseas income; trusts that are not UK resident are liable only in respect of UK source income.

In the main, trustees are liable for tax at 20% on income from savings, with other income being taxed at the basic rate, but trustees of discretionary and accumulation trusts are subject to additional tax so that in total they have been subject to 40% since 2004–05.

A non-resident trust is subject to tax on UK income, for example interest taxed at source and dividends. Where the non-resident trust receives untaxed interest, there is in theory a tax liability, but in practice the trustees may escape tax because of ESC B13.

Trustees are not entitled to personal allowances.

Where the settlor or spouse can benefit, the trust income may be deemed to be that of the settlor for higher rate purposes (see 32.5) but any income received gross by the trustees still needs to be reported in the trust return.

30.1.2 Trusts and self-assessment

The same general rules apply to trustees as they do to individuals under self-assessment (SA). If a trust has UK chargeable income and gains, then the trustees have to file a self-assessment form by 31 January following the relevant tax year.

30.1.3 Rules for determining the residence status of a trust from 2007–08

From 6 April 2007, a single set of rules has applied for determining the income tax and CGT residence of a trust:

- If all the trustees are UK resident, the trust is UK resident.
- If none of the trustees is UK resident, the trust is not UK resident.
- If only some of the trustees are UK resident, and the settlor was not domiciled or ordinarily resident or resident in the UK at the time that the trust was created, the trust is not UK resident.

Where a non-UK resident trustee acts as a trustee in the course of a business carried on through a branch, agency or permanent establishment in the UK, he will be treated as UK resident.

30.1.4 Different residence rules applied up to 2006–07

There were different criteria before 2007–08, and the residence status of a trust for income tax could be different from that for CGT purposes. See the 2006–07 edition of the *Tax Handbook* at 32.1.1 and 32.2.1.

30.2 WHEN ARE TRUSTEES LIABLE FOR UK CAPITAL GAINS TAX?
(TCGA 1992, ss 2 and 69)

30.2.1 General rules

Trustees are subject to CGT only if the trust is resident in the UK, or if they realise capital gains from the disposal of assets used by them in carrying on a business in the UK through a branch or permanent establishment.

In general, trustees are responsible for reporting gains and paying tax.

From 2008–09, gains realised by a UK resident settlement will be taxed as the trustees' gains even where the settlor has retained an interest (contrast the treatment for earlier years, see below). This means that losses realised by the settlor cannot be set against the trustees' capital gains.

Position for 2007–08 and earlier years

Where either the settlor or his spouse could receive a benefit under the trust, and the settlor was UK-resident, capital gains were generally taxed as if they were personal gains of the settlor up to 2007–08 (see 32.12). However, such gains still need to be reported in the trust tax return, but any tax payable was paid, initially, by the settler, who could recover it from the trustees. Where a trust was caught by this rule, any surplus capital losses realised by the trustees was carried forward to cover future gains of the trustees and could not be set against the settlor's personal capital gains.

A settlor could set a personal capital loss against a capital gain attributed to him for the years 2003–04 to 2007–08. During these years, the gain attributed to the settlor was computed before taper relief and the settlor could set personal losses first against his personal gains and then against attributed gains. The net attributed gains were then reduced by taper relief if appropriate. In this way, taper relief was effectively given to the settlor as opposed to the trustees when calculating the net gains taxable on the settlor.

Taper relief was also restricted in certain cases where the settlor had been non-UK resident for less than five years before returning to the UK. In this situation, the attributed gains were taxed under s 10A TCGA 1992 as gains of the year in which he resumed UK residence (see 12.3.2) but any taper relief was calculated by reference to the date that the trustees realised the gains in question.

30.2.2 Annual exemption
(TCGA 1992, Sched 1)

For a number of years the annual CGT exemption available to trustees has been half the individual exemption, for example for 2008–09, £4,800 (half of £9,600).

Where a settlor has created a number of settlements since 6 June 1978, the annual exemption is shared equally. The minimum annual exemption for each settlement is currently £960 (ie one-tenth of the annual individual exemption). An unused part of the exemption for one settlement cannot be used by another settlement.

Consequently, if a person created three trusts in 1975 and four in 1989, the 2008–09 exemption for the 1975 trusts would be £4,800 each, and the four trusts created after 6 June 1978 would each have an exemption of £1,200. If all seven trusts had been created after 6 June 1978, each would have an annual exemption of £960.

30.2.3 Taper relief

For years up to 2007–08, trustees could qualify for the business rate of taper relief for business assets if they owned shares in an unquoted trading company or had at least 5% of the voting rights in a quoted trading company.

Certain fixed-interest trusts could also qualify where the trustees' shares are in a company that is the life tenant's qualifying company (see below).

The requirements were stricter until 5 April 2000 in that trustees were eligible for business taper only if they held 25% of the voting rights in a trading company (quoted or unquoted) or an eligible beneficiary worked full-time for the company and held 5% of the voting rights.

30.2.4 Entrepreneurs relief

There is a relief of up to £1 million for gains realised by an individual on the sale of an interest in an unincorporated business or in his personal trading company (see 16.8). This relief means that gains are taxed only at 10%.

Where the individual has not used up the maximum relief, trustees of a trust in which he is a life tenant can use the balance of the £1 million to cover gains realised from the sale of an interest in an unincorporated business or of shares in the life tenant's personal trading company (ie a company where the life tenant is a director and he holds at least 5% of the voting rights). It is necessary for the trustees to have owned the asset for at least 12 months.

The trustees may also be able to claim entrepreneurs relief on gains realised from associated disposals, ie sales by the trustees of land and buildings that were used by the unincorporated business or by the life tenant's personal trading company. Relief will not normally be available where the trustees have always charged a full market rent.

30.3 BARE TRUSTS

A bare trust is one where trustees hold property on behalf of someone who is absolutely entitled to that property, or would be absolutely entitled if he were not a minor. Income and capital gains received by trustees of a bare trust belong to the person who is absolutely entitled to the property concerned. The trustees normally have no liability to tax.

Trustees of bare trusts are not normally required to complete SA tax returns, or to make any payments on account. Beneficiaries are required to give details of all their income and gains from bare trusts in their own tax returns, and in addition are required to account to the Revenue for the full amount of any tax due.

Under self-assessment, bare trustees cannot deduct tax from income arising to them. Any income received gross by the trustees must be paid gross to the beneficiaries. The only exception to this rule is that UK-resident trustees may be required, under the non-resident landlords scheme, to deduct and account for tax on the rental income of beneficiaries whose usual place of abode is outside the UK (see 33.6).

See 32.5.4 on the position where a parent gives money to a bare trust for his minor child.

30.4 FIXED-INTEREST TRUSTS

A fixed-interest trust is one where a beneficiary is entitled to receive income as it arises, either during his lifetime or for a specific period. A simple type of fixed-interest trust would be where the beneficiary is entitled to receive all the income during his lifetime with the trust coming to an end on his death, perhaps with the capital then passing to his children. A beneficiary who is entitled to receive trust income in this way during his lifetime is called a 'life tenant'.

There may also be a situation where a life tenant is entitled to receive a proportion of the trust income, say half, with the other half being held on different types of trust. Additionally, it is possible to have an entitlement to income (an 'interest in possession') for a specific period, so that a trust under which someone had a right to all of the income for a fixed period of ten years would be a fixed-interest trust until the end of that period.

30.4.1 Settlor-interested settlements are subject to a special tax treatment

The following analysis is on the basis that the settlor and spouse (or a civil partner) are excluded from benefiting. See 32.5.2 on the tax situation where a settlor can benefit. The definition of a settlor-interested trust changed on 6 April 2006 and can now include a trust under which the settlor's minor unmarried children can benefit even though he and his spouse are wholly excluded.

30.4.2 Income tax

From 2008–09, where property is held on fixed-interest trusts, income tax is charged on the trustees at the following rates:

- dividend income at 10%;
- all other income at basic rate (20%).

For 2007–08, the position was:

- UK dividend income taxed at 10%;
- other income from savings taxed at 20%;
- all other income taxed at basic rate (22%).

There is no deduction for personal allowances (only individuals are entitled to them), but if a trust owns investment properties on which an entitlement to capital allowances arises, such allowances may be set against the trustees' income in the same way as for individuals. Similarly, if the trustees carry on a trade, any losses may be relieved against other income. Subject to this, the trustees will either suffer tax at source or be assessed for tax on all untaxed income arising to them.

30.4.3 **Ascertaining the beneficiary's income**

It will not generally be possible for the trustees to pay over to a beneficiary the full amount of the income left to him after tax. Inevitably, there will be some expenses (eg bank charges, interest, professional fees) that are properly charged to income, and there may also be the trustees' own fees. Such expenses may not be deducted in arriving at the trustees' taxable income, but they need to be taken into account in determining the amount of the beneficiary's income. See 30.11.2 regarding a Revenue statement on expenses that may be taken into account in this way.

In broad terms, the proper procedure is to ascertain the trustees' taxable income for a year. The tax paid by the trustees for the year should then be deducted, and a further deduction made for expenses that are properly charged against income. The net amount must then be 'grossed up' and this is the amount the beneficiary will need to declare on his tax return.

Example – Tax treatment of income from a fixed-interest trust

The trustees of a fixed-interest trust have taxable deposit interest of £20,000 for 2008–09. They pay tax of £4,000 (20%). There are expenses of £1,700 that are properly chargeable against the income. The balance belongs to the life tenant, whose gross income will be ascertained as follows:

	£
Trustees' taxable income	20,000
Less: basic rate tax	(4,000)
	16,000
Less: expenses	(1,700)
	14,300
£14,300 grossed up lower rate (20%)	17,875

This income forms part of the life tenant's income for the year whether or not it is actually paid out to him. If the life tenant is subject to higher rate tax, he must pay the difference between the 40% rate and the rate paid by the trustees.

30.4.4 **Income from savings**
(FA 1993, s 79 and Sched 6)

For 2007–08, it is necessary to distinguish savings income from UK dividends and income from other sources. Dividend income was taxable at 10% as opposed to 20% on other savings income. For 2008–09, it is only necessary to distinguish between dividends and all other income. Trustees' expenses are deemed to be set first against UK dividend income, so as to minimise the restriction of the tax deemed to be withheld from the trust income.

30.4.5 **Tax returns**

The returns usually completed for trusts are forms SA900 and additional pages as necessary. For fixed-interest trusts a tax deduction certificate

(Form R185 (Non-discretionary)) should also be completed by the trustees or their professional advisers, showing the appropriate gross, tax and net figures in respect of the beneficiary's income. It is necessary to show the different types of income separately on the certificate.

30.4.6 Income mandated to a beneficiary

Trustees sometimes take the view that it is simpler to mandate dividends and other income to the beneficiary so that such income does not pass through the trustees' hands. This does not alter the fact that the trustees are still the legal owners of the assets that produce the income.

Although this income can be entered directly in the beneficiary's personal tax return, care should be taken to ensure that it is entered in the correct section for trust income so as to avoid any confusion with his personal income. Where this happens, the Revenue will assess the beneficiary rather than the trustees. If the trustees incur expenses, these may not be deducted as in 30.4.2; this applies even where the beneficiary reimburses the trustees for such expenses later on.

30.4.7 Beneficiary's exempt income

It is sometimes possible for UK-resident trustees to take advantage of a beneficiary's tax exemption to avoid paying tax that he would then have to claim back. For example, where a beneficiary is entitled to all the income of the trust and he is resident outside the UK, the trustees can agree with the Revenue that the income that arises outside the UK (and any other income that is exempt for a non-resident, for example, interest from exempt gilts: see 33.6.3) should not be taxed in the trustees' hands.

This treatment is not normally available where a non-resident beneficiary is entitled to only a proportion of the trustees' income.

> **Tax notes**
>
> Where a beneficiary is entitled to all the income of the trust and is resident outside the UK, the trustees can agree with the Revenue that the income that arises outside the UK should not be taxed in the trustees' hands.

30.4.8 Where taxable income is not income for trust purposes

Difficulties can arise where the trustees receive something that constitutes income for tax, but not for trust, purposes. For example, if trustees of a fixed-interest trust receive a lump sum premium that is taxable income from property (see 7.3), this is not income that belongs to the life tenant. Similarly, a distribution such as may arise on a company buying back its own shares may be income for income tax purposes (see 8.9.7), but is capital for trust purposes. In both these situations, the trustees must pay tax on such deemed income, but the amounts must be excluded when calculating the life tenant's income for tax purposes.

Another situation where taxable, but not trust, income may arise is where trustees have acquired an enterprise zone building (or indeed any type of industrial building) and a balancing charge arises on a disposal. Such a charge is taxed at basic rate only. Because it is a capital receipt, it is not normally possible for the trustees to pay it to a life tenant and it therefore does not constitute part of his income for tax purposes. In the past, this has meant that the tax payable has been limited to basic rate (but see below for 2006–07 and future years).

There are certain situations where the legislation makes special provision. Where trustees dispose of a loan stock cum-interest, the trustees will generally be subject to assessment under the accrued income scheme (see 8.6) in respect of the interest that has arisen on the loan stock during their period of ownership. However, this is not income that the trustees will be able to pay out to a beneficiary because a life tenant will be entitled only to actual, not deemed, income. In this specific case, the legislation has provided since 2004–05 that trustees should be taxed at 40% on income assessed under the accrued income scheme.

A similar rule applies where trustees realise gains on the disposal of shares in an offshore roll-up fund (see 9.7) and also income distributions from a purchase of own shares on or after 7 December 1996.

Enhanced scrip dividends can give rise to special problems, because the tax treatment depends on the way that the dividend is treated for trust purposes (this may be affected by the way that the trust deed is worded). You should obtain a copy of SP4/94.

The FA 2006 contained new provisions that apply in relation to 2006–07 and subsequent years. The effect of these provisions is that the trustees are now subject to a 40% tax on any amounts that are taxed as if they were income but are not income of the life tenant for trust purposes. However, these provisions do not mean that the income is deemed to be that of the life tenant.

30.4.9 Exempt receipts that are income for trust purposes

The converse may happen. For example, a trustee may receive income in the form of a repayment supplement that is exempt. This will still constitute income for trust law purposes and the life tenant will generally be entitled to receive the full amount, but it is not taxable income for him.

The treatment of dividends arising from demergers (see 8.8.8) also gave rise to concern, but a test case involving the ICI demerger established that such receipts by trustees were generally capital rather than income from the point of view of trust law, so in this particular case the treatment for trust law and taxation will normally be the same. It is important to take professional advice where significant sums of money are involved as the Revenue distinguishes between different types of demergers (remind your accountant to refer to *Tax Bulletin* October 1994).

30.4.10 Capital gains tax

From 2004–05 to 2007–08, trustees of fixed-interest trusts were subject to tax at 40% on any capital gains (after deducting taper relief where applicable). The rate was 34% for gains realised before 6 April 2004.

The rate of capital gains tax for 2008–09 and future years will normally be 18%.

No further CGT (or income tax) liability will normally arise on the trustees distributing cash to a beneficiary after they have realised a capital gain by selling an asset.

30.4.11 Exemption for property occupied by a beneficiary
(TCGA 1992, s 225)

There is an exemption for trustees in respect of a property owned by them, but occupied by a beneficiary as his main residence (provided he is entitled to do so under the terms of the trust deed). The beneficiary may not also claim exemption for a property owned by him. Where an individual has more than one residence, and it is desired to elect that a property owned by trustees be treated as his main residence, a joint notice must be given by the trustees and that individual.

Anti-avoidance legislation came into force from December 2003 (see 32.13).

30.4.12 Disposals of business assets

A major change took effect from 6 April 2008.

Position for 2008–09

For 2008–09 and future years, trustees' capital gains will normally be taxed at 18%.

Taper relief is no longer available but entrepreneurs relief may be claimed for gains arising from the sale of an interest in an unincorporated business or from the sale of shares in the eligible beneficiary's personal company. Entrepreneurs relief may also be claimed on gains arising from disposals of assets used by the business/personal company where the disposal is associated with a disposal of an interest in an unincorporated business or of shares in the beneficiary's personal company.

See further at 30.2.4.

Position for 2007–08 and earlier years

Where, during 2007–08 or an earlier year, trustees of a fixed-interest trust disposed of an asset that had been used by an 'eligible beneficiary' for the purposes of a trade carried on by him, or by a firm in which he is a partner, the asset could be treated as a business asset for taper relief purposes (see 12.11.5). Similar provisions applied where trustees sold an asset used in a business carried on by an eligible beneficiary's qualifying company, or where they sold shares in the company itself.

An 'eligible beneficiary' was a beneficiary entitled to an interest in possession over the whole of the settled property or over a part of the settled property that included the asset concerned.

A company was the eligible beneficiary's qualifying company if he was employed by it.

Relief may be restricted where the eligible beneficiary had rights to only part of the income from the settled property. Professional advice should therefore be sought if the trust fund had more than one life tenant and one or more beneficiaries were not employed by the company.

If the trustees owned shares in an unquoted trading company or held 5% of the voting shares in a quoted company, they could qualify for taper relief as business assets even though the life tenant was not employed by the company.

30.4.13 Liability may also arise on deemed disposals

A capital gain may arise on a deemed disposal such as where the trustees distribute assets to a beneficiary, or where a beneficiary becomes absolutely entitled to capital under the terms of a trust. Hold-over relief is available only if the disposal involves business property (see 16.4).

30.4.14 Transfer of capital losses to a trust beneficiary

Where a beneficiary becomes absolutely entitled to settled property, losses realised in the past by the trustees do not pass across. Furthermore, if a loss arises for the trustees on an asset passing across to the beneficiary, he may use this only against a capital gain that he may subsequently realise on a disposal of that asset.

30.4.15 Death of the life tenant
(TCGA 1992, s 73)

There is one type of deemed disposal that does not give rise to a CGT charge. Where an interest in possession ceases on a death, the assets are treated as having been disposed of and reacquired at their value at that date, but there is no chargeable gain for the trustees. This does not apply where the trustees hold assets that were subject to a hold-over claim by the settlor at the time he transferred the assets to the trustees.

30.4.16 Inheritance tax
(IHTA 1984, s 49)

Where a beneficiary has an interest in possession, and he had that interest at 22 March 2006, he is treated for IHT purposes as if he owned the trust capital. On death, the value of the trust capital is brought into account as part of the individual's estate and IHT is charged accordingly. However, the trustees are responsible for paying the IHT on the proportion of the tax attributable to the trust property.

Example – IHT liability on a fixed-interest trust

A died on 1 December 2007 owning property in his personal capacity worth £205,000 (this is called his 'free estate') and he is also the life tenant of a trust that has a capital value of £350,000. The total IHT payable is:

	£
Free estate	205,000
Trust	350,000
	555,000
Less: nil rate band	(300,000)
	250,000
IHT thereon at 40%	100,000

IHT is payable as follows:

Executors $\dfrac{205,000}{555,000} \times 100,000 = 36,937$

Trustees $\dfrac{350,000}{555,000} \times 100,000 = 63,063$

30.4.17 Fixed interest trusts where the interest in possession did not exist at 22 March 2006

The FA 2006 introduced a new IHT regime for such trusts (see 30.4.23).

30.4.18 Exemption where settled property reverts to settlor

The treatment described in 30.4.16 does not apply where the trust assets pass back to the settlor on the death of the life tenant who had his interest at 22 March 2006. No IHT charge arises on the property that reverts to the settlor. There is a similar exemption where property reverts to the settlor's spouse but this is conditional on the spouse being domiciled in the UK.

The revertor to settlor exemption does not apply if the settlor (or spouse) had purchased a reversionary interest.

30.4.19 Exempt pre-13 November 1974 will trusts
(IHTA 1984, Sched 6, para 2)

These are trusts created by the will of a person who died before 13 November 1974 and left property in trust on the following terms:

(1) his surviving spouse was entitled to an interest in possession;
(2) the surviving spouse was not entitled to demand that the capital should be paid out to her.

These trusts are exempt from the normal charge that arises when the surviving spouse's interest in possession comes to an end. The reason for this is that before 13 November 1974, estate duty was levied on an individual's death even if he left property in trust for his spouse. However, the estate duty legislation then provided an exemption on the death of the surviving spouse and this has been carried over to IHT.

Will trusts that came into being after 12 November 1974 are treated differently because of the exemption that applies for IHT purposes where property passes to a surviving spouse. Property held in a post-12 November 1974 will trust is subject to IHT on the life tenant's death.

30.4.20 No charge where life tenant becomes absolutely entitled to trust property
(IHTA 1984, s 53(2))

There are no IHT implications where a life tenant (or any other beneficiary entitled to an interest in possession) who had his interest at 22 March 2006 becomes absolutely entitled to the trust property. This is because the beneficiary was already regarded for IHT purposes as if he owned the capital concerned. All that has happened is that the beneficiary's interest has been enlarged and, while this may have CGT consequences, it does not give rise to an IHT charge.

Tax notes

There are no IHT implications where a life tenant who had his interest at 22 March 2006 becomes absolutely entitled to the trust property because he was already regarded for IHT purposes as owning the capital concerned.

30.4.21 Consequences of interest in possession terminating during a person's lifetime
(IHTA 1984, ss 3A, 23 and 52)

Where a beneficiary's interest in possession comes to an end during his lifetime, he had that interest at 22 March 2006 and he does not personally become entitled to the trust property, he is treated as making a transfer of value. The transfer is normally either a PET (see 29.6) or a chargeable transfer, according to what happens as a result of the interest in possession coming to an end. However, if an individual's spouse becomes absolutely entitled on his interest in possession terminating, the transfer will normally be an exempt transfer because of spouse exemption (see 29.5.1). Until 5 October 2008, spouse exemption should also be available if the spouse acquires an interest in possession as opposed to acquiring the trust property absolutely.

Potentially exempt transfer

If the effect of the beneficiary's interest coming to an end is that:

(1) another individual becomes entitled to an interest in possession; or
(2) another person becomes absolutely entitled to the trust property; or
(3) the trust becomes an accumulation and maintenance trust,

The person whose interest in possession has terminated is treated as having made a PET. In such instances, IHT is charged if (and only if) the person dies within the following seven years. If this should happen, the trustees are liable to pay the IHT unless the settled property passes to a beneficiary through his becoming absolutely entitled on the termination of the interest in possession. In such a situation the person who becomes absolutely entitled is liable to pay any such IHT.

Exempt transfer

Occasionally, the effect of a person's interest in possession coming to an end is that the spouse becomes entitled to an interest in possession. Where this happens, the person whose interest in possession has come to an end is treated as having made an exempt transfer. This treatment also applies if a trust becomes a charitable trust as a result of a beneficiary's interest in possession coming to an end.

Chargeable transfer

Where a person's interest in possession comes to an end and the trust thereby becomes a discretionary trust, he is treated as having made a chargeable transfer. If his cumulative chargeable transfers bring him over the nil rate band, IHT is payable right away at the lifetime rate of 20%. If he should then die within three years, the rate increases to 40% (see 30.11).

30.4.22 How transfer of value is computed on lifetime transfer

The legislation contains an anomaly. Where an individual makes a gift in his personal capacity, the transfer of value is deemed to be the amount by which his estate is reduced in value (see 29.3.3). This rule does not apply where a person's interest in possession comes to an end because, in this case, the amount of the transfer of value is taken as the value of the property in which the interest in possession has terminated.

Example – Calculation of value of lifetime transfer

> B owns 90% of a company in his personal capacity and is the life tenant of a trust that owns the remaining 10%. The value of a 100% shareholding in the company is worth £500,000. The value of a 90% shareholding is £450,000, but a 10% shareholding valued in isolation is worth only £20,000. If B had made a gift of 10% out of his personal shareholding, his transfer of value would be taken to be:
>
> | | £ |
> |---|---:|
> | Value of a 100% shareholding | 500,000 |
> | *Less*: value of remaining 90% shareholding | |
> | (taking his own shares and the trust together) | (450,000) |
> | Reduction in value of his estate | 50,000 |
>
> However, if B surrenders his life interest in the trust so that his interest in possession comes to an end, the value transferred is taken as £20,000.

30.4.23 Regime for fixed interest trusts

The FA 2006 introduced a new regime for lifetime trusts where an interest in possession comes into existence on or after 22 March 2006.

New fixed interest trusts and existing trusts where an interest in possession is created on or after 22 March 2006 will normally be subject to the IHT regime that was formerly confined to discretionary trusts (see 30.5 below), ie the creation of such a trust will be a chargeable transfer for IHT and the trust will be subject to the periodic charge (see 30.5.13) and the exit charge (see 30.5.18). On the other hand, no IHT charge will normally arise on the termination of an interest in possession, whether on death or during the beneficiary's lifetime (contrast the treatment of pre-22 March 2006 trusts described in 30.4.22 above).

Where a fixed interest trust is caught by the FA 2006 provisions, there will not be a CGT disposal and re-acquisition at the date of the life tenant's death (see 30.4.15). On the other hand, CGT hold-over relief will generally be available under s 260 TCGA 1992 (see 30.6.2) when property is put into a UK trust or comes out of the trust to a UK resident beneficiary.

30.4.24 Some situations where the pre-22 March treatment continues to apply

The new regime will not apply where:

- An individual acquires an interest in possession before 6 October 2008 that replaces an interest in possession held by another individual at 22 March 2006 (the deadline was extended by six months by FA 2008).
- The trust is created as part of arrangement dealing with a relationship breakdown.
- An interest in possession trust was in being at 22 March 2006 to hold life policies and money is only added to the trust by additional premiums being paid.

- The trust is for the benefit of a disabled person (see 30.7 for definition). In this case, the let-out can apply both to lifetime trusts and trusts created on death.
- An individual who is in the early stages of a degenerative disease creates a settlement under which he has a life interest.
- A trust is created on death (by will or intestacy) for the benefit of the deceased's minor child and the child will become absolutely entitled at age 18.
- Life interest trusts are created on death (by will or intestacy).
- The life tenant is the deceased's widow or widower – spouse exemption is available (see 29.5.1)

30.5 DISCRETIONARY TRUSTS

In contrast to a fixed-interest trust, a discretionary trust is one where the trustees can control the way the income is used. In most cases, they have power to accumulate income, in which case it may be retained by them either with a view to its being paid out in later years or as an addition to the trust capital.

In other cases, they have no legal right to accumulate income, but the trust is regarded as discretionary because no beneficiary has a fixed entitlement (ie the trustees must distribute the income, but they can choose how it is distributed and which particular beneficiary should receive it).

30.5.1 Special tax treatment for certain trusts

The following analysis is on the basis that the settlor and spouse are excluded from benefiting under the settlement. The tax treatment where a settlor can benefit is covered in more detail at 32.14 but it should be noted that trustees of settlor-interested discretionary trusts are now liable for 40% tax on the income received by them.

Employee share ownership trusts may also be exempt from the rate applicable to trusts (see 30.5.2 below) on certain types of income.

30.5.2 Rate applicable to trusts
(TA 1988, s 686)

Subject to the £1,000 band (see below), trustees of discretionary trusts are liable for tax on income that is not dividend income at 40%. (This is called 'the rate applicable to trusts' although, as we have seen, it is not applicable to all trusts.) The rate was 34% up to 2003–04.

Where part of the trust income is subject to a fixed-interest trust and the balance is held on discretionary trust, the 40% rate is charged only on the income held on discretionary trusts.

Exemption for the first £1,000 of trust income

There is an exemption for the first £1,000 of the trustees' income and only the balance is taxed at the rate applicable to trusts (£500 for 2005–06). However, this exemption is reduced according to the number of discretionary trusts created on or after 6 June 1978. In cases where the settlor has created less than ten discretionary trusts, each trust is entitled to an exemption of £1,000 divided by the number of post 5 July 1978 discretionary trusts. Where the settlor has created ten or more discretionary trusts, each gets a minimum exemption of £100.

Calculation of the tax payable

In most cases, the trustees suffer lower or basic rate tax at source and then pay additional tax to bring the total up to the required amount.

Notional income that was left out of account

Certain types of income have not been taken into account for additional rate purposes, ie sums that are capital profits under trust law, for example:

(1) Premiums treated as rent (see 7.3).
(2) Profits on sale of certificates of deposit (see 9.6).
(3) Gains from disposals of offshore funds (see 9.7).

This income was subject to tax at only 22% for 2005–06. However, the FA 2006 amended the position here and these types of income are now subject to the rate applicable to trusts (ie 40%) for 2006–07 and subsequent years.

Accrued income scheme

Income taxed under the accrued income scheme is also taxed at the rate applicable to trusts (regardless of whether the trust is a fixed-interest or discretionary trust).

30.5.3 Computing the trustees' liability to the rate applicable to trusts

The trustees' liability for basic and lower rate taxes on income from savings is calculated in exactly the same way as for trustees of fixed-interest trusts. A separate computation is then required for the purposes of the rates applicable to trusts (also called the 'special trust rates').

Expenses paid out of net income are 'grossed up' and the resulting amount is then deducted. Examples of such expenses are:

(1) Bank charges.
(2) Interest that does not qualify for tax relief.

(3) The costs of administering the trust.

(4) Charges made by professional trustees.

(5) Deficits on properties where the deficiency cannot be relieved against other UK property income.

Costs such as premiums on an insurance policy (excluding fire insurance), or property expenses such as the cost of maintenance or insurance of a property or charges made for collecting rents, cannot be included directly as a deduction in computing liability for additional rate tax. Expenses are set off first against basic rate/savings income with any balance being set against dividend income.

Example – Calculating the additional tax on discretionary trusts for 2007–08

A discretionary trust receives income from savings of £15,000 in 2007–08. It has no other income. Expenses that are not allowable in computing income for basic rate tax purposes, but are properly chargeable to income, amount to £960. The trustees' liability for tax at the 40% rate was computed as follows:

	£
Income from savings	15,000
Less: expenses – grossed up: £960 × $^{100}/_{80}$	(1,200)
	13,800
Less exempt	1,000
	12,800
Tax at additional 20%	2,560

If the trustees had also received non-savings income which had been subject to basic rate, this would normally be taxed at 18%, ie 40% less tax withheld at source. Administrative expenses are set off against income from savings first. Any balance is then grossed up at the rate of $^{100}/_{78}$ and set against other income for the purposes of calculating the additional rate.

30.5.4 Special rate on dividend income

Trustees of discretionary trusts are taxed on dividend income at 32.5% (25% up to 2003–04). Dividends received from UK companies carry a 10% tax credit.

Example – Calculating the additional tax on dividend income for 2007–08

A discretionary trust receives cash dividend income of £90 in a tax year. The trustees' tax liability on that income is computed is follows:

	£
Cash dividend received	90.00
Tax credit ($^{1}/_{9}$)	10.00
Taxable income	100.00
Rate applicable to trusts (32.5%)	32.50
Less: tax credit	(10.00)
Tax payable	22.50

Furthermore, when the trustees distribute income to beneficiaries, they will be required to pay additional tax unless the distribution can be shown to have come out of a 'pool' that has suffered the rate applicable to trusts.

Example – Situation where dividend income distributed between beneficiaries

In the above example, the trustees had dividend income of £90.00 on which they paid tax of £22.50, leaving them with £67.50. If they distributed the whole of this income to the beneficiaries in 2008–09, the trustees will have to pay further tax. The calculation is complicated and is as follows:

	£
Maximum distribution	54.00
Tax thereon (£90 × 40%)	36.00
Gross income for beneficiary	90.00

This income is regarded as having suffered 40% tax. The trustees then pay tax of £13.50 over to the Revenue so that they have paid a total of £36.00, ie:

	£
Tax payable on the dividend	22.50
Tax payable on the distribution to bring payment up to tax of 40% of £90	13.50
	36.00

Trustees may refer to *Tax Bulletin* (June 2004), which covers all this in detail.

30.5.5 Income distributions in excess of trustees' taxable income
(TA 1988, s 687)

There may be situations where trustees make distributions in excess of their taxable income. Such distributions also give rise to a liability for the trustees to account for tax at the rate applicable to trusts. There are several situations in which such a liability can arise:

(1) A trust may have income on which income tax does not have to be paid. If such income is paid out to a beneficiary as an income distribution, the trustees must account for tax at the rate applicable to trusts.

(2) Similarly, trustees may make payments of an income nature that are subject to tax as income in the hands of the beneficiary even though they come out of the trust capital. In practice, the Revenue would not normally assess such distributions unless they were made regularly.

If the income is fully distributed each year and foreign securities are held, there will be an additional liability to tax when the foreign income is distributed to beneficiaries. The liability is equal to the credit allowed against basic rate tax for double taxation relief.

30.5.6 Tax returns

One tax return (form SA900) is now completed whether the trust is fixed-interest or discretionary. There are supplementary forms to be completed for various types of income, for capital gains, and where the trust is a non-resident or charitable trust.

The Revenue provides a tax calculation guide for trusts and estates, but as the calculation layout is of Byzantine complexity the form is generally not used.

Where payments are made to beneficiaries during a particular tax year, a tax deduction certificate form R185 should be completed by the trustees or their professional advisers, showing the appropriate gross, tax and net figures.

> **Tax notes**
>
> The Revenue provides a tax calculation guide for trusts and estates, but as the calculation layout is of Byzantine complexity the form is generally not used.

30.5.7 The beneficiary's position

A beneficiary needs to include on his tax return the grossed up amount of any income distributed to him by the trustees during the tax year. Since the trustees are subject to the additional rate, the beneficiary's income is treated as net of tax withheld at the rate applicable to trusts (ie at 40% if the trustees made the payment to the beneficiary in 2004–05 or a later year).

30.5.8 Accumulated income subsequently distributed as capital

A distribution of capital that represents income that has been accumulated is not normally taxable income for the beneficiary. Such a distribution is treated as a capital distribution, though this presupposes that the trustees have power to accumulate income. In cases where they have no such power, any distributions will remain as income.

30.5.9 Capital gains tax
(TCGA 1992, s 5)

From 2008–09, the rate of capital gains tax is normally 18%.

All the capital gains of a discretionary trust (as reduced by taper relief) were taxed at 40% for 2004–05 to 2007–08 except for the amount covered by the annual exemption. The rate was 34% up to 2003–04.

As with a fixed-interest trust, no further CGT (or income tax) liability will normally arise on the trustees' distributing cash to a beneficiary after they have realised a capital gain by selling an asset.

30.5.10 Exemption for property occupied by beneficiary
(TCGA 1992, s 225)

The courts have held that trustees of a discretionary trust are entitled to this exemption where they permit a beneficiary to occupy a property as his main residence under the terms of the trust, even though the trust deed did not confer a right for him to require the trustees to provide such a property (but see SP8/79). The Revenue will resist this exemption where the trustees do not have a power to allow a beneficiary to occupy a property but such a power need not be contained in the trust deed, for example it may be a power given to the trustees under the Trustee Act 2000.

See anti-avoidance provisions introduced by FA 2004 that apply where hold-over relief is claimed on a transfer of a property to the trustees (see 32.13).

30.5.11 Business taper relief

Trustees of a discretionary settlement were entitled to business taper on gains realised before 6 April 2008 from the sale of shares in an unquoted trading company or shares in a quoted trading company in which they held at least 5% of the voting rights.

30.5.12 Entrepreneurs relief

This relief is not available for trustees of discretionary settlements.

30.5.13 Deemed disposals/hold-over relief
(TCGA 1992, s 71)

A capital gain may arise on a deemed disposal such as where the trustees distribute assets to a beneficiary, or where a beneficiary becomes absolutely entitled to capital under the terms of a trust. Hold-over relief is normally available under TCGA 1992, s 260 where a disposal of the property arises on a capital distribution to a UK-resident beneficiary (see 12.6 on s 260 relief).

30.5.14 Inheritance tax
(IHTA 1984, ss 64–65)

By definition, no beneficiary has an interest in possession in a discretionary trust and it follows that the trust capital is not treated as forming part of his estate. Therefore, no IHT charge arises on his death.

To make up for the absence of such a charge, the legislation imposes a lower charge every ten years (the 'periodic charge'). The theory is that a generation is approximately 30 years and the tax charged on three separate occasions by reason of the periodic charge will approximate to the tax payable on property passing down to the next generation.

There is also an 'exit charge' that applies where property leaves a discretionary trust or where (before 22 March 2006) the trust becomes a fixed interest trust.

There are different rules for discretionary trusts created before and after 26 March 1974.

30.5.15 Trusts created after 26 March 1974

Periodic charge
(IHTA 1984, s 66)

The periodic charge arises on the tenth anniversary of the creation of the trust and on every subsequent tenth anniversary. The maximum rate is currently 6%, computed as follows:

$$\text{Tax payable at lifetime rate } (20\%) \times 30\%.$$

The computation is actually more complex and involves the following process:

Amount of chargeable transfers made by settlor in the seven years prior to creation of the trust	A
Value of trust property at tenth anniversary	B
Add A and B	C
Deduct nil rate band	D
	E

The next step is to compute the IHT payable on E and on A − D. The tax payable by the trustees on the periodic charge is 30% of the difference.

Example – Periodic charge

C created a discretionary trust in June 1997. He had previously made chargeable transfers of £194,000. In June 2007 the trust is worth £160,000. The periodic charge is therefore computed as follows:

		£
Amount of previous chargeable transfers	(A)	194,000
Value of trust property in 2007	(B)	160,000
	(C)	354,000
Deduct nil rate band	(D)	300,000
	(E)	54,000
IHT on E		10,800
IHT at lifetime rates on A – D		Nil
		10,800

Periodic charge is 30% of £10,800, ie £3,240.

30.5.16 Trusts created before 26 March 1974

This type of trust is simpler in that there cannot have been any chargeable transfers made by the settlor before the creation of the trust. The computation is therefore:

Value of trust property at tenth anniversary	X
Deduct nil rate band	$\dfrac{Y}{Z}$

IHT at lifetime rates on Z

Periodic charge is 30% of this amount.

30.5.17 Position where trustees have made capital distributions during preceding ten years

Where the trustees have made a capital distribution within the previous ten years or property has otherwise ceased to be held upon discretionary trusts (eg by reason of a beneficiary being entitled to an interest in possession), the capital distribution value must also be brought into account in arriving at the periodic charge. The computation is as follows:

Amount of chargeable transfers made by settlor in the seven years prior to creation of the trust and capital distributions since last periodic charge	A
Value of trust property at tenth anniversary	B
Add A and B	C
Deduct nil rate band	$\dfrac{D}{E}$

The next step is to compute the IHT payable on E and on A – D. The tax payable by the trustees on the period charge is 30% of the difference.

30.5.18 Treatment of undistributed income

The Revenue accepts that undistributed income that has not been accumulated should be excluded in arriving at the value of the trust capital at the tenth anniversary. The reason for this is that such income remains income held for the benefit of beneficiaries and is not capital.

Where income has been formally accumulated, it must be brought into account for the purposes of the periodic charge. However, such accumulated income is treated as if it were additional capital added to the trust at the date the trustees resolved to accumulate it.

30.5.19 Exit charge (also known as 'proportionate charge')

The way in which the exit charge is computed varies according to whether capital leaves a discretionary trust within the first ten years or only after there has been a periodic charge.

30.5.20 Exit charge during first ten years
(IHTA 1984, s 68)

The position here is that a notional rate of charge should be computed. This is the average rate of IHT that would have been payable had the settlor made a chargeable transfer at the time he created the trust equal to the trust property's value at that time.

Example – Exit charge during first ten years

> *D* created a trust in February 1997 and the original trust property was worth £300,000. The entry charge would have been computed as follows:
>
> | | £ |
> |---|---:|
> | Value of trust property in February 1997 | 300,000 |
> | *Less*: nil rate band at that time | (200,000) |
> | | 100,000 |
> | £100,000 at 20% = | £20,000 |
>
> $$\text{Effective rate} = \frac{20,000}{300,000} \times 100$$
>
> The entry charge would therefore have been 11.47% and the tax payable if property leaves a discretionary trust within the first ten years is levied as a proportion of this rate. The exact proportion is determined by the number of complete periods of three months (or quarters) during which the trust has been in existence. Thus, if the exit charge occurred after the trust had existed for six years and seven months, the charge would be at the rate of:
>
> $$\frac{26}{40} \times 30\% \text{ of } 11.47\%$$

30.5.21 Exit charge after a periodic charge
(IHTA 1984, s 69)

The position here is that the charge applies only to the proportion of the property that leaves the discretionary trust, with the proportion being determined by the following formula:

$$\frac{\text{Number of complete quarters since the periodic charge}}{40}$$

A distribution during the first quarter following the ten-year charge is entirely free of IHT.

The tax rate charged is normally fixed by the effective rate charged on the previous periodic charge. However, the effective rate is calculated by using the scale of rates in force at the time the exit charge arises. Thus, the notional effective rate may be slightly lower than the effective rate of IHT that actually applied on the last periodic charge.

30.6 ACCUMULATION AND MAINTENANCE TRUSTS
(IHTA 1984, s 71)

An accumulation and maintenance trust is a special form of discretionary trust that has been set up for a stated class of beneficiaries. The following conditions needed to be satisfied up to 22 March 2006:

(1) One or more beneficiaries would become entitled to an interest in possession in the trust property on attaining a specified age that could not exceed age 25.
(2) Until one of the beneficiaries became beneficially entitled, the trust income had to be held on a discretionary basis with income being applied only for the maintenance, education or benefit of the beneficiaries or accumulated for their benefit.
(3) The trust could have a life of not more than 25 years or it had to be a trust for the benefit of grandchildren of a common grandparent.

From 22 March 2006, a trust can normally be an accumulation and maintenance trust only if the beneficiaries will become absolutely entitled to the settled property at age 18. The trustees have until 5 April 2008 to vary an existing trust so that it satisfies this condition. If the trust is a will trust for bereaved minor children, it can qualify as an accumulation and maintenance trust provided that the beneficiaries will become absolutely entitled by the time that they attain age 25.

30.6.1 Taxation

The same rules apply, and the same returns and certificates need to be completed, for income tax and CGT as for discretionary trusts. There are, however, different rules for CGT hold-over relief and IHT.

30.6.2 Hold-over relief for trustees
(TCGA 1992, s 260)

Where trustees dispose of assets to a beneficiary, there may be a CGT charge.

Section 260 hold-over relief is available for accumulation and maintenance trusts only if the disposal takes place when a beneficiary becomes absolutely entitled to capital and income at the same date.

This condition can be satisfied if trustees vary a trust before 6 April 2008 so that beneficiaries become absolutely entitled at age 18. If the trustees do not vary the trust in this way before 6 April 2008, the accumulation and maintenance trust will be brought within the IHT discretionary trust regime and, while this may have adverse IHT consequences, it will normally mean that IHT hold-over relief is available when the asset's beneficiary subsequently becomes absolutely entitled to the settled property.

On the other hand, there is a problem area for trustees of accumulation and maintenance trusts where a beneficiary became entitled to income on reaching age 18 before 22 March 2006, but capital vests only at age 25. If the beneficiary had become entitled to the capital at age 18, there would have been no problem but, because there is a gap in time between the accumulation period coming to an end and the beneficiary becoming absolutely entitled to the capital, it is not possible for trustees to claim s 260 hold-over relief. However, s 165 hold-over relief may be available where the settled property consists of business assets (see 16.4).

30.6.3 IHT privileges

An accumulation and maintenance trust that satisfies the conditions imposed by FA 2006 is not subject to the periodic charge described at 30.5.14. Furthermore, there is no exit charge on a beneficiary becoming entitled to an interest in possession under the trust or becoming absolutely entitled to trust property.

Pre-22 March 2006 trusts that do not meet the FA 2006 rules attract an IHT exit charge when the beneficiaries become absolutely entitled at age 25. However, provided that the beneficiaries become absolutely entitled no later than at age 25, this charge is limited to 7/10 of the exit charge that would otherwise arise, ie the maximum rate of the exit charge is 4.2%. Also, this rate will not apply for some years because of a further relief which recognises that the settled property will not become relevant property before 5 April 2008 (see example below). Indeed, the charge will not arise at all on beneficiaries becoming absolutely entitled before 6 April 2008.

Example – An accumulation and maintenance trust coming to an end in 2011

An accumulation and maintenance settlement set up on 9 April 2001 comes to an end on 9 April 2011 on the beneficiary attaining age 25. The settlement is worth £400,000.

The basic rate of the exit charge is ascertained as follows:

(1) Take the tax rate as described in 30.5.15 (maximum rate is 6%).
(2) Reduce this rate for the part of the ten-year period ending in April 2011 that falls before 6 April 2008, ie 28/40ths: this reduces the maximum rate to 1.8%.

30.7 TRUSTS FOR THE DISABLED
(TCGA 1992, Sched 1; IHTA 1984, ss 74 and 89)

A trust for a disabled person is a type of discretionary trust that enjoys certain tax privileges. The trustees are entitled to the full CGT exemption of £9,200 for individuals and there is no liability for the IHT periodic and exit charges.

The terms of the trust must be such that not less than half of the settled property and income must be applied for the benefit of a disabled person who is treated as if he had an interest in possession. A disabled person is one who, at the time the trust was created, was:

(1) incapable by reason of mental disorder within the meaning of the Mental Health Act 1983 of administering his property or managing his affairs; or

(2) in receipt of an attendance allowance under the Social Security Contributions and Benefits Act 1992, s 64; or

(3) in receipt of a disability living allowance under s 71 of the 1992 Act.

The two conditions that need to be satisfied are as follows:

(1) not less than half of the property within the trust should be applied for the benefit of the beneficiary concerned; and

(2) the person should be entitled to not less than 50% of the income arising from the property (this condition is regarded as satisfied where the trust provides that no income may be applied for the benefit of any other person).

Income is deemed to be applied for the benefit of a person where it is held by the trustees for that person on protective trusts.

30.8 PROTECTIVE TRUSTS

This is a term under the Trustee Act 1925, s 33. A protective trust is one under which a person (known as the principal beneficiary) is entitled to an interest in possession in the trust unless he forfeits his interest, for example, by assigning it or by becoming bankrupt. Protective trusts are normally worded so that if a principal beneficiary forfeits his interest, the trust property is held on discretionary trusts for a class of beneficiaries that includes the principal beneficiary.

30.8.1 IHT position where principal beneficiary dies

The periodic charge does not apply while property is held on protective trusts because the principal beneficiary has forfeited his interest under a trust where he had an interest in possession before 22 March 2006 or which met one of the conditions set out in 30.4.24. However, an IHT charge arises on the beneficiary's death. The charge varies according to whether he forfeited his interest before or after 12 April 1978.

Where forfeited before 12 April 1978, the tax charged on his eventual death is calculated at a fixed rate on the trust property's value according to the following formula:

	Cumulative total
0.25% for each of the first 40 quarters	10%
0.20% for each of the next 40 quarters	8%
0.15% for each of the next 40 quarters	6%
0.10% for each of the next 40 quarters	4%
0.05% for each of the next 40 quarters	2%
Maximum rate chargeable after 50 years	30%

The nil rate band is not available.

Where the interest is forfeited after 11 April 1978, the trustees are subject to a charge on the principal beneficiary's death as if he had an interest in possession at the date of his death.

30.9 TRUSTS FOR THE MOST VULNERABLE

The FA 2005 introduced a special tax regime that could apply from 6 April 2004.

A trust can qualify for this only if it has beneficiaries who are under 18 and have lost at least one of their parents, or who are incapable of managing their affairs because of mental disorder, or who are in receipt of attendance allowance or of a disability living allowance at the middle or highest rate.

The trustees must make an election (by 31 January 2007 for 2004–05). Once the election has been made, it applies until the beneficiary ceases to be a vulnerable person (eg by attaining age 18), or the trustees no longer hold the settled property for the benefit of that individual, or the trust is wound-up.

The broad effect of the relief is that the tax on the trustees' income and gains is limited to the tax that would have been payable if those income and gains had been personal income and gains of the vulnerable person.

30.10 CHARITABLE TRUSTS

Provided property is held for charitable purposes only, income and capital gains received by the trustees are normally exempt from tax.

Exemption from income tax
(TA 1988, s 505)

There is total exemption from income tax for all income other than trading profits. The exemption is dependent on income being applied for charitable purposes.

Exemption from CGT
(TCGA 1992, s 256)

There is also total exemption from CGT provided the charitable trust applies the capital gains for charitable purposes.

30.10.1 Application for charitable purposes
(TA 1988, s 505)

A charity's exemption from tax may be restricted where income is not applied for charitable purposes. In particular, where a charity has income and capital gains that exceed £10,000 in a tax year, exemption is restricted where the following two conditions are satisfied:

(1) The charity's relevant income and gains exceed the amount of its qualifying expenditure.
(2) The trust incurs or is treated as incurring non-qualifying expenditure.

'Qualifying expenditure' for these purposes means expenditure actually made during the year for charitable purposes and commitments for such expenditure entered into during the year.

Payments made to bodies outside the UK count as qualifying expenditure only to the extent that the charity can show that it has taken such steps that are reasonable in the circumstances to ensure the payments will be applied for charitable purposes. Expenditure for charitable purposes also includes reasonable administrative and fund-raising expenses.

Non-qualifying expenditure includes, for example, political activities, trading expenses and excessive administration costs. Furthermore, the legislation specifically mentions certain types of investments or loans that are to be regarded as not being qualifying expenditure. This is intended to catch investments in a company controlled by a connected person (eg, the settlor) or loans to such a company. Indirect arrangements may also be caught such as where a charity makes loans or investments used as security for borrowings by a connected person.

Where a charitable trust makes a payment to another connected charitable trust, this does not count as application of the income for charitable purposes unless the trust that receives the payment actually applies it for charitable purposes.

30.10.2 IHT position

Property held on charitable trusts is exempt from the periodic and exit charges. If the property is held on temporary charitable trusts, a charge arises on those charitable trusts coming to an end with tax being charged according to the same formula in 30.8.1.

30.11 MISCELLANEOUS ASPECTS

30.11.1 Trusts with sub funds

Where a trust has a number of separate sub funds, it may be possible for the trustees to elect that a sub fund should be treated as if it were a separate trust. This could be advantageous if a sub fund has trustees who are not resident in the UK. It is necessary that the sub fund's beneficiaries are not beneficiaries under the rest of the trust. An election will need to be made by 31 January 2009 for a sub fund to be treated as a separate trust for 2006–07 and by 31 January 2010 for 2007–08. Making the election will mean that the trust will be treated as if it had made a CGT disposal of the assets held within the sub fund on the first day of the year in which the election takes effect.

30.11.2 Trustees' expenses

HMRC has published a statement of practice, which indicates that many expenses incurred by trustees should be charged against capital rather than income. See guidance note issued on 31 January 2006. However, some aspects of this SP have been called into question by *Trustees of the Peter Clay Discretionary Trust* v *HMRC*. No doubt the Revenue will issue a revised SP in due course.

30.12 EXECUTORS AND PERSONAL REPRESENTATIVES

30.12.1 Being a personal representative

When a person dies leaving a valid will, his assets vest in his executors. If he does not leave a will, and so dies intestate, it is normally necessary for letters of administration to be obtained and the person who acts in this way (the 'administrator' or 'administratix' if female) is treated for most legal purposes as if he or she were an executor. The term 'personal representative' covers both executors and administrators.

Personal representatives of a deceased person are treated as a single body of persons so that there is no tax implication if an executor retires or dies. The estate is treated as a single entity for tax purposes.

You may find it useful to read the HMRC booklet IR45 *What to do when someone dies*. Also, see the Capital Taxes Office's glossary (www.hmrc.gov.uk/cto/glossary.htm).

See 30.12.7 where the deceased was not domiciled in the UK, or was not resident in the UK, at the date of death.

Tax notes

HMRC publishes a useful booklet *What to do when someone dies* (IR45). There is also an online glossary at www.hmrc.gov.uk/cto/glossary.htm.

30.12.2 Income tax
(TMA 1970, s 40)

The deceased's personal representatives are liable to pay tax on income received by the deceased up to the date of his death.

The tax is assessed in exactly the same way as if the individual were still alive, ie all the normal allowances and reliefs are due. The only difference is that the personal representatives are responsible for settling the tax (they are also entitled to any repayments).

Quite separately, personal representatives are also charged to tax on income received by them following the death. No personal allowances are given. During the administration period, dividends are taxed at 10%, and other income at basic rate. There is no higher rate liability for the personal representatives.

Although there are cases where income has to be apportioned pre- and post-death for legal purposes, for tax purposes any income received after a person's death is treated as income of the estate.

Where, under the terms of the will, a trust evolves, the executors become trustees upon the completion of the administration period. Depending on the type of trust, the trustees may become chargeable to additional rate income tax first on the balance of accumulated income at that date and secondly on receipt of subsequent income. There is no date fixed by law to determine the completion of the administration period, but it is generally agreed that it is the date on which the residue is ascertained.

30.12.3 Beneficiary's position
(TA 1988, ss 695–696)

A beneficiary of a will may receive an annuity. This income is taxable for the year in which it is payable unless, as a matter of fact, the annuity is paid out of capital in which case it is income for the year in which it is paid.

Beneficiaries of specific legacies are normally entitled from the date of death to the income that arises on the property they have inherited. Other beneficiaries will be entitled to the residue, either through a limited interest (eg a life tenant entitled to income arising from the residuary estate) or by an absolute entitlement.

During the administration period, sums paid to a beneficiary are normally treated as income for the year of payment.

Where income that has accrued to the date of death is treated as capital of the estate for IHT purposes and as residuary income, there is higher rate tax relief available to beneficiaries. Form 922 is used to calculate this relief.

30.12.4 Capital gains tax
(TCGA 1992, ss 3 and 62)

Personal representatives are liable to CGT at 18% from 6 April 2008. They are entitled to the full annual exemption due to an individual for the year of death and the following two tax years.

In computing capital gains, assets held by the deceased at the date of his death are deemed to be acquired by the personal representatives at their market value at that date (the probate value). The probate value may need to be adjusted where securities are sold at a loss within 12 months of the death and relief from IHT has been claimed (see 29.11.3). A similar rule applies where land is sold within four years of death at a loss and the sale proceeds are substituted for the probate value.

Assets transferred to beneficiaries, either during the course of or on the completion of the administration period of an estate, do not give rise to a chargeable gain because the beneficiary is regarded as having himself acquired the asset at the date of the person's death and at the probate value.

Certain expenses incurred by the personal representatives in establishing legal title to assets are allowed in computing gains on the sale of the assets (see SP8/94).

Personal representatives of an estate in the course of administration are not entitled to an annual exemption if they realise capital gains after two full tax years have elapsed since the date of death. However, if a will trust evolves upon completion of the administration period, the trustees will then become entitled to their own CGT exemption.

Losses made by personal representatives during the administration period, and not used, are not available to be transferred to residuary beneficiaries with absolute interests or trustees of a trust established by the will that takes effect on the administration of the estate being completed.

30.12.5 Property owned by the estate, but used by beneficiary as main residence

The Revenue treats the beneficiary's main residence exemption (see 30.4.11) as applying where personal representatives dispose of a property that has been used by a beneficiary of the estate as his only or main residence both before and after the deceased's death and he is entitled to at least 75% of the proceeds when the estate has been administered (see ESC D5 and *Tax Bulletin* August 1994).

30.12.6 Deeds of variation

Where the terms of a will have been varied by a deed of variation (also known as a deed of family arrangement), there are important consequences so far as IHT is concerned (see 29.4.6). Basically, the revised way in which property passes to beneficiaries is read back into the will and effectively treated as something done by the testator so far as IHT is concerned. However, the House of Lords held in *Marshall* v *Kerr* [1994] STC 813 that where the variation creates a trust, the person(s) who relinquish their original entitlement under the will are treated as the settlor for CGT purposes.

The income tax treatment is also less favourable than the IHT treatment. Even where the deed specifically provides that all income is to be paid to a beneficiary named in the deed, this has no effect for income tax purposes for income that arose before the deed's execution. If payments have been made to the original beneficiary or beneficiaries named in the will, they remain liable for any higher rate tax on such income that arose at a time when they were entitled to it. Furthermore, a person who gives up an entitlement under a will by executing such a deed is treated as a settlor for income tax purposes.

The CGT and income tax position described above has been put on to a statutory basis by FA 2006.

Tax notes

A person who gives up an entitlement under a will by executing a deed of variation is treated as a settlor for income tax purposes.

30.12.7 Acting as a personal representative for a foreign person

The fact that one or more of the personal representatives is UK-resident can mean that the estate is subject to UK tax. However, they are not subject to income tax on non-UK income if the deceased person was not domiciled in the UK. Furthermore, they are not subject to capital gains tax if the deceased was neither resident nor ordinarily resident in the UK at the date of death (except to the extent that capital gains are realised from disposals of UK assets that had been used in a trade which the deceased had carried on in this country). Even where neither of these exemptions apply, the personal representatives may not be regarded as UK-resident where the majority of them are not UK resident and the deceased was not resident, ordinarily resident or domiciled in the UK at the time of his death.

30.13 SOME PLANNING POINTS

The following are just some of the important tax planning points that arise regularly in relation to trusts and estates.

30.13.1 Settlor-interested trusts

Would there be a significant income tax saving if steps were taken to ensure that the trust was no longer regarded as a settlor-interested trust? It might be, for example, that the trust deed provides for income to be paid to A but that income is treated as taxable income of the settlor (B) because he has a reversionary interest. If A is not subject to higher rate tax, there would be an immediate saving if the trust were varied or B took some other action to disclaim his reversionary interest (eg he could settle that reversionary interest on trust for his adult children).

30.13.2 Is it better to create a discretionary or a fixed interest trust?

It all depends! A discretionary trust has often been more appropriate where there were elderly beneficiaries as the settled property did not form part of their estate on death. The IHT exposure under the regime for discretionary trusts (see 30.5.13 – 30.5.20) has always been much less than it would be for a fixed interest trust. The differences are now less given the changes brought about by FA 2006 and where the fixed interest trust was created on or after 22 March 2006, the IHT treatment will now generally be the same as that which applies to a discretionary trust (see 30.4.23). For new trusts, the deciding factors are really the settlor's wish (or otherwise) to provide a beneficiary with a fixed right to income.

The CGT position is that the settlor can generally secure hold-over relief (see 12.6) for gains on transferring assets to the trustees of most fixed interest trusts created on or after 22 March 2006 and discretionary settlements. The exceptions where hold-over relief is not available are where a fixed interest trust is not caught by the FA 2006 changes (see 30.4.24) or where the trust is a settlor-interested trust or the trust is not resident in the UK.

From an income tax point of view, the position is largely neutral. A discretionary trust pays tax at 40% (see 30.5.2) but, if the trustees make distributions to beneficiaries who are not liable for tax or who are basic rate taxpayers, the beneficiaries can make repayment claims. A fixed interest trust pays income tax at 10% on dividends and at the 20% basic rate on all other income but the life tenant has to include this income on his tax return and, if he is a higher rate taxpayer, pay further tax, which brings the combined tax up to 40%.

From the point of view of filling in forms, life is more straightforward for the trustees of a fixed interest trust.

30.13.3 Would it save tax if a discretionary trust were converted into a fixed interest trust?

From an income tax perspective, the important thing is that income is regularly distributed to beneficiaries who are able to recover some or all of the tax. Creating an interest in possession could have a similar effect in that the trustees would not be required to pay tax at the rate applicable to trusts so that less tax would be withheld in the first place.

30.13.4 Should assets be transferred to beneficiaries on a no gain/no loss basis?

Where gains are held-over (see 30.5.12), the trustees do not qualify for entrepreneurs relief and the beneficiary has to start a new ownership period from scratch. This may not matter if the beneficiaries are able to use their annual exemptions to cover gains arising on the sale of the assets, or if they can utilise capital losses.

30.13.5 Should a UK trust be exported?

Making a UK trust into a non-resident trust can precipitate a CGT exit charge (see 32.15). Also, it may not achieve very much if the settlor is going to be taxed on capital gains made by the non-resident trustees in the future (see 32.17).

30.13.6 Should a discretionary trust be converted into a fixed interest trust before or after the IHT ten-year periodic charge?

It makes no difference. The changes in FA 2006 mean that there will be an exit charge only if capital is distributed outright as opposed to the trustees creating an interest in possession. If the trustees create an interest in possession on or after 22 March 2006, the trust remains subject to the periodic charge. Creating an interest in possession used to take a trust out of the discretionary trust regime (see 30.5.13) but it no longer has this effect.

30.13.7 Should a discretionary trust make capital distributions before or after the ten-year charge?

There is no general rule here but the way in which the exit charge is computed means that the time that assets cease to be held on discretionary trusts can make a significant difference to the total tax payable (see 30.5.18 – 30.5.20).

30.13.8 Should the trustees replace an interest in possession before 6 October 2008?

If there was an individual who had an interest in possession before 22 March 2006, his interest is terminated before 6 October 2008 and another individual is given an interest in possession, the trust remains under the old regime for IHT purposes. In other words, the trust will not be subject to the periodic charge (or the exit charge) but the settled property will form part of the new life tenant's estate on his death.

Doing this could make sense if the existing life tenant wishes to make a PET in favour of a younger beneficiary.

30.13.9 Executors should take care

Suppose that the residuary legatees include a non-resident beneficiary or a charity that is exempt from capital gains tax. If the executors sell a property they will be liable for 40% CGT on any increase in value over probate value and the beneficiaries will receive their share of the amount left after tax. They cannot reclaim that tax. If the executors appropriate the property to the beneficiaries, the executors will have no capital gain. The beneficiaries will then be deemed to have acquired the property at probate value. Any gain on a sale will then be their gain, ie a non-taxable gain if the beneficiary is not subject to CGT.

31

PASSING ON YOUR FAMILY BUSINESS

There are many ways of passing on a share in a business, or transferring part of a business, to the next generation. And there are many tax aspects to be borne in mind, eg preserving relief for past trading losses, capital gains tax (CGT) for the donor, inheritance tax (IHT) and so on. Above all, the practical aspects need to be handled carefully. A factor for many proprietors is that they do not wish to relinquish control. This is why trusts often have an important role in enabling a person to hand over a business to his children.

In this chapter, we look at the following:

(1) Basic strategy.
(2) Setting up children in business.
(3) Bringing a child into partnership.
(4) Bringing a child into the family company.
(5) Outright gifts of shares.
(6) Why trusts are still often a suitable vehicle.
(7) Demergers.

31.1 BASIC STRATEGY

The most appropriate strategy will depend on your personal circumstances, objectives and the way that your assets are made up. However, some principles recur again and again when advising clients:

- The proper use of insurance policies and pension schemes can help to protect the family from any IHT charge that may arise in the short to medium term.
- Maximise the benefit of business property relief (BPR) and the facility to pay tax by instalments. Think twice about taking any action that would jeopardise these valuable reliefs.
- Draw up a will in the most tax efficient way that is compatible with what the individual wishes to happen to his assets on his death.
- The individual should take steps to secure his financial independence before making any substantial gifts.
- It may be better not to make outright gifts, especially while the individual is still making up his mind how he wants to pass on his business. In some cases, the individual will prefer to set up his children in business

on their own account, possibly by lending them money. In other cases he may prefer to bring them into his existing business as partners.

- Look for ways of making gifts that will not involve substantial CGT liabilities.
- All other things being equal, it is best for the individual to make gifts sooner rather than later, especially if the business is growing in value.
- The individual will generally wish to retain a measure of control.

31.1.1 Proper use of insurance policies and pension schemes

For an individual in his 40s, who is still building up a business, it may be advisable to take out substantial joint survivor life insurance, which would pay out on the second death. Such policies should be written in trust so that the proceeds would not form part of the estate (see 29.12.3). Similarly, it will normally be advisable for the death benefits payable under a pension scheme to be subject to discretionary trusts so that they do not form part of the estate and no IHT charge is payable on them. The maximum amount payable as a death in service benefit from a company scheme is generally four times final remuneration and this would provide the family with the necessary liquidity in the event of his untimely death.

31.1.2 Maximise the benefit of BPR

Provided that it has been owned for at least two years, a trading business carried on by an individual as a sole trader or as a partner attracts 100% BPR. This relief is also due on shares in an unquoted trading company. There are also situations where 100% agricultural property relief is due on property that does not qualify for BPR. See 29.8 and 29.9 on BPR and agricultural property relief generally.

There are many situations where these reliefs can be lost or restricted. For example, giving shares in an unquoted trading company to a spouse or civil partner means that they will have to hold those shares for two years before they qualify for BPR (the position is different if they inherits the shares). Similarly, if an individual were to secure a bank loan by giving a charge against his shares, BPR will normally be due only on the net value after the loan has been deducted.

Bear in mind that 50% BPR is available to a controlling shareholder if he owns a property that is used by his trading company, but no relief is due to minority shareholders. Once again, this rule means that BPR could be lost if a 51% shareholder were to transfer 2% of the shares to their spouse or civil partner.

Another potential trap applies if the individual has entered into buy/sell agreements with other shareholders. By entering into such an agreement, he may have forfeited BPR because the shares will be subject to a contract for sale (see 29.8.1). Cross options are a better way of achieving the same commercial objectives without losing BPR.

Certain businesses do not qualify for BPR or agricultural property relief, eg a property investment business (see 29.8.3). Such a business may still qualify for payment of IHT by instalments over ten years (see 29.11.14).

31.1.3 Draw up a will in a tax-efficient way

Property left to a spouse/civil partner is exempt from IHT (unless the spouse/civil partner is foreign domiciled). This exemption applies both to property passing to the widow/surviving civil partner absolutely and to property left in a will trust under which he or she has an interest in possession.

It would make sense from a tax perspective for assets that do not qualify for BPR to be left in a will in such a way that spouse/civil partner exemption applies. For example, the individual may have investment properties that do not qualify for BPR. One possibility would for such assets to be left to a widow/surviving civil partner and for him or her to then make gifts to the next generation. These may have to be outright gifts or gifts to an accumulation and maintenance trust given that gifts to other trusts may involve a lifetime IHT charge (see 30.4.23) although gifts that are covered by the widow's/surviving civil partner's nil rate band are still a viable option. No IHT will be payable on the widow's/civil partner's death provided he or she does not die within seven years of making the gifts.

Where an individual owns assets that qualify for BPR, such as shares in a family company, it may be more appropriate for them to pass into a discretionary will trust. This is because the assets would not then form part of the widow's/surviving civil partner's estate and so be vulnerable to IHT on their death if the business assets have been sold and the proceeds reinvested in other assets.

Tax notes

There can even be situations where a family can benefit from BPR twice. In many cases where shares in a family company have been left to a will trust, it will pay for the widow to buy the shares from the trustees, perhaps borrowing against her other assets to do so. You should consult a specialist on this but if you can arrange matters properly the widow will qualify for BPR once she has owned the property for two years and the IHT exposure on her other assets will be reduced by the borrowings secured against them.

31.1.4 Securing financial independence before making substantial gifts

A person who owns a business or shares in a private trading company would be well advised to create a separate source of income before giving away part of that business, etc. The creation and funding of a pension scheme should be a priority. Moreover, the fact that the company's profits are reduced by pension contributions may be a helpful factor in agreeing a low value of shares that are subsequently given away by the individual.

31.1.5 Would a loan be a better idea?

When the next generation are still in their 20s, their parents may prefer to set them up in business on their own account rather than bring them into the family firm. This may involve the individual making loans in his personal capacity, which will be entirely appropriate from a personal perspective but not particularly attractive from a tax point of view. Loans would not attract BPR if the lender were to die. If the loan goes bad, the lender will not be entitled to income tax relief but may qualify for CGT relief (see 16.1).

Another possibility is for the family company to make a loan to the children but this may have income tax or corporation tax consequences (see for example 17.13.2 on s 419 ICTA 1988). A half-way house that could work well enough in the right circumstances would be for the family company to inject working capital by subscribing for preference shares in a company formed by the child to carry on a business venture.

Yet another compromise is for the family company to establish a subsidiary that will carry on the son or daughter's new business.

We go into these issues in more detail at 31.2.

31.1.6 Gifts that do not involve CGT

It does not make sense to give away assets to save IHT if the gift creates a substantial liability for CGT at 40%. It is therefore necessary to be selective about what is given to the next generation. There may be certain assets that would not give rise to a substantial CGT charge if given away, perhaps because they have been acquired relatively recently. Alternatively, it may be possible to rely on s 165 hold-over relief to avoid CGT being payable on gifts of business property and shares in an unquoted trading company. See 16.4 on hold-over relief.

31.1.7 Make gifts sooner rather than later

For many people, it is a question of competing priorities. They are anxious not to give away control of the business too early. This is understandable given the way in which the economic climate, personal relationships and the income and capital that they need can change so quickly. On the other hand, the sooner wealth is passed down to the next generation, the greater the potential savings in IHT. One reason for this is the seven-year rule for IHT (see 29.6). Also, in many cases the value of the business is likely to take off (perhaps a stock market flotation is planned in the next two or three years) and the amount taxed on a PET becoming a chargeable transfer on the donor's death is limited to the market value at the date of the gift.

31.2 SETTING UP CHILDREN IN BUSINESS

As we have already touched upon, this may or may not involve bringing your son or daughter into the family firm. There are many situations where a son's business skills and mind-set mean that it makes more sense for him to set up his own business. But time and again, the problem is that he needs working capital.

31.2.1 Financing the child's unincorporated business

We have already covered the implications of a wealthy individual making a personal loan (see 31.1.5).

An alternative, which has much to commend it from a tax point of view, is for the son to form an LLP (see 6.5) and transfer his business to it. The father could then become a member of the LLP in return for injecting capital. The father need not be given any involvement in the management of the business or, indeed, in any share of the profits except for an amount corresponding to the interest that he would have received from making a loan.

The father's interest in the LLP should rank as business property for IHT.

If the son's venture is unsuccessful, the father's share of the LLP's losses can be set against his other taxable income (see 6.7).

31.2.2 Financing the child's limited company

It may be that the child has already established a company. The business may have gone well to start with but now needs more substantial working capital.

One possibility is for a parent to give a bank guarantee for the company's borrowings. From a personal perspective, this seems to be the easiest option but often gives rise to greater grief if and when the bank calls on the father or mother to honour the guarantee. This simply reflects the fact that most people who give guarantees never really face up to the possibility of having to part with money until it actually happens.

Where a person gives such a guarantee, is required to pay up and has lost the money, he can qualify for CGT relief (see 16.1). However, this is of no real benefit unless the person has capital gains.

In many cases, a more appropriate way of structuring the transactions would be for the parent to subscribe for new ordinary shares (these can be non-voting shares if required). If the company's business fails, the parent will then be able to claim a capital loss on his shares and will generally be able to use this loss by setting it against his taxable income (see 16.2).

31.3 BRINGING A CHILD INTO PARTNERSHIP

Moving on to another situation, suppose that the parent wishes to admit his son or daughter into partnership.

The section in Chapter 16 on partnerships and CGT (16.5) will be required reading in such a situation. However, the CGT aspects are manageable, especially as any deemed disposal of assets by the parent can normally be held-over under s 165 TCGA 1992 (see 16.4).

From a non-tax point of view, it may be a good idea for the new partnership to be an LLP as this will give the parties the benefit of limited liability (a new and less experienced partner may make misjudgements that could damage the business).

It may also be advisable for certain assets (eg property) to be excluded from the partnership or LLP, with the parent continuing to own them in his or her personal capacity. Assets retained by a partner but used in the business will then attract only 50% BPR but it may be preferable to accept a lower rate of BPR rather than put those assets at risk.

31.4 BRINGING A CHILD INTO THE FAMILY COMPANY

A child can become a director of the company without becoming a substantial shareholder (indeed, subject to the company's articles of association, he may not need to hold any shares).

In some situations, it may be advisable for the child to be a director of a subsidiary, especially where he is mainly involved in running the business of that subsidiary. He or she can always be appointed to the board of the parent company later, when it has become clear that the business relationship is going to work out as expected.

31.5 OUTRIGHT GIFTS OF SHARES

Sooner or later, the issue is likely to arise that the next generation who are involved in the business feel that they should own some of the equity.

The transfer of shares to the child ought not to fall within the employment related securities provisions (see Chapter 5) but the relevant legislation is drafted in such wide terms that the possibility should not be ignored. It is therefore advisable to take professional advice.

If a parent transfers shares, he will be making a disposal for CGT purposes but hold-over relief should cover this (see 16.4) provided that the company does not have substantial investment activities.

31.6 WHY TRUSTS ARE STILL OFTEN A SUITABLE VEHICLE

31.6.1 Practical considerations

As we have already mentioned, many proprietors do not wish to relinquish control. This is one aspect where trusts are especially useful, especially where your nil rate band or business property relief mean that little or no IHT is payable on their creation. For example, suppose that a person who owns all the shares in his company wishes to give a 30% stake to each of his two sons. Making an outright gift will mean that he will then be a minority shareholder and his two sons will be able to outvote him on important business decisions. If he instead puts 60% of the shares into a trust for the benefit of his sons, and he and/or his professional advisers are the trustees, he can give his sons the desired stake in the equity without ceding control to them.

Trusts can also have important non-tax benefits. Suppose you and your son are in a partnership but you own the premises. You are planning to retire. You also have a daughter. You want to treat the children equally but you are not completely sure about her husband. You may therefore decide to put the premises into a trust for your two children so that your daughter may have an income without this affecting your son's security of tenure. This may be a more satisfactory compromise than giving the premises to your two children at the present time. This might, for example, lead to conflict if your daughter wishes to sell her half-share and your son cannot raise the capital to buy her out. Problems could also arise on an outright gift if your daughter goes through a divorce. Of course, the really important thing is to choose the right trustees.

Another situation where a trust comes into its own is if you want to divest yourself of shares, and so start the seven-year period running, but you are not sure how your children will work out. Perhaps your eldest son works in the company and you want to see how he shapes up before passing over control. Putting shares into a discretionary trust may be a very good way of reconciling conflicting objectives.

31.6.2 Tax issues around trusts

It is important to bear in mind the gifts-with-reservation legislation (see 29.7). Putting shares or other property into trust will not start the seven-year period running unless you are wholly excluded from benefiting under the trust.

An IHT charge may arise on a gift of shares into a trust if the property gifted does not qualify for business property relief (see 29.8) and the settlor's cumulative chargeable transfers exceed the nil rate band (see 29.10). On the other hand, CGT hold-over relief will generally be available, provided that the settlor, spouse and the settlor's minor children are excluded from benefiting under the trust (see 12.6).

31.7 DEMERGERS

It quite often happens that the founder's children carve out a niche for themselves in a particular section of the business. For example, a company may consist of three hotels and a daughter may run one of those hotels and have little to do with the others. It is possible for the daughter to carry out a demerger (see 8.8.8). This will involve the daughter in an exchange of her shares in the present company for 100% of the shares in a new company, which will own the hotel that she runs.

Another way of facilitating a parting of the ways may be for your company to buy back some of its shares (see 8.9.8).

The detailed aspects of such transactions are beyond the scope of this book. You should consult an accountant or solicitor if you wish to break up your family business and pass part of that business down to the next generation.

PART 4

ANTI-AVOIDANCE LEGISLATION

This part contains the following chapter:

32

ANTI-AVOIDANCE

It is often said (albeit rather less often these days) that taxpayers are under no obligation to arrange their tax affairs in such a way that they maximise their tax liability. Some 70 years ago, Lord Tomlin stated in the Duke of Westminster case that:

> Every man is entitled if he can so order his affairs so that the tax attaching to them ... is less than it otherwise would be. If he succeeds in ordering them so as to secure this result, then however unappreciative the Commissioners of the Inland Revenue or his fellow taxpayers may be of his ingenuity, he cannot be compelled to pay an increased tax.

These are fine words but governments have increasingly taken the view that taxpayers must not be allowed to take this to extremes and there is a distinction between tax planning and unacceptable tax avoidance. The courts have observed that tax avoidance may be legal but often amounts to a deplorable use of the practitioner's ingenuity and technical expertise.

Successive administrations have taken the view that the answer is more and more anti-avoidance legislation. Hence the fact that more than half of all UK tax legislation consists of specific anti-avoidance provisions. These anti-avoidance provisions must be borne in mind, especially when a tax planning exercise is being carried out. They are generally intended to ensure that a person cannot reduce his tax liability by carrying out a given transaction in a roundabout way.

The present Government considered introducing a general anti-avoidance rule (GAAR), ie a rule that anything done purely for tax avoidance should be set aside by the courts, but drew back from this extreme remedy. However, the courts have effectively introduced a kind of GAAR of their own, the *Ramsay* doctrine, and this must also be taken into account. Another weapon used by the present Government is retrospective and retroactive legislation, ie moving the goal posts after the game has started.

This chapter covers:

Income tax

(1) Interest income.
(2) Transactions in land.
(3) Transactions in securities.
(4) Transfer of assets overseas.

(5) Trust income taxed on the settlor.
(6) Transactions involving loans or credit.
(7) Pre-owned assets.

Capital gains tax

(8) Bed and breakfast transactions.
(9) Disposals by a series of transactions.
(10) Transfers to a connected person.
(11) Qualifying corporate bonds.
(12) Value shifting.
(13) Trusts and main residence exemption.
(14) UK-resident settlements where settlor has retained an interest.
(15) Deemed disposal when a trust ceases to be resident.
(16) Offshore companies.
(17) Non-resident trusts.

Inheritance tax

(18) Purchased interests in excluded property settlements.

General

(19) *Ramsay* principle.
(20) Registration of tax schemes.
(21) Specific income tax avoidance schemes that have been blocked.

INCOME TAX

32.1 INTEREST INCOME

32.1.1 Background

The Taxes Acts contain extensive legislation that is designed to prevent the conversion of taxable income into capital.

32.1.2 Sale of loan stock with right to purchase
(FA 1996, s1 59(1))

At one time it was possible to enjoy the benefit of income in a capital form that was not subject to tax by selling loan stock or other interest-bearing securities and retaining a right to repurchase them. For example, a person holding £1m 3½% War Loan could sell the stock to a charity for £400,000 cum-interest while retaining the right to repurchase the War Loan once it had gone ex-interest for, say, £385,000 – an overall profit of £15,000. He had to forgo the income of £17,500 but that was taxable and worth less than £15,000. The charity, meanwhile, got the income free of tax.

There is now specific legislation designed to catch such arrangements. Using the above example, the legislation on repo contracts means that the person would be subject to income tax on the £15,000 profit or 'differential'.

32.1.3 Sale of right to income
(TA 1988, s 730)

A variation on the above scheme worked for a number of years. It was common for individuals to sell to a charity or other exempt body the right to receive interest payments for a specified period of time, while retaining legal ownership of the securities themselves. This is now caught by s 730. If the loan stock is a UK security, the arising income is assessed on the vendor. If it is a foreign loan stock, the sale proceeds are assessable as if they were income.

32.1.4 Manufactured dividends

Manufactured payments arise during a stock loan or repo transaction. They involve the person who currently holds the securities paying over to the original owner an amount equal to dividends or interest received. Individuals could deduct such payments from their total income for tax purposes. FA 2002 introduced anti-avoidance provisions to counter perceived abuses. This is a specialised area and those affected will no doubt already be aware of the changes and should have taken professional advice.

32.2 TRANSACTIONS IN LAND
(ITA 2007 s 756)

32.2.1 Introduction

Section 756 (formerly s 776 ICTA 1988) was intended to prevent tax avoidance by persons concerned with land or development of land. It may apply where a capital gain is realised and one of the following conditions applies:

(1) The gain arises from UK land (or some other asset deriving its value from land) and the land was acquired with the sole or main object of realising a gain.
(2) The gain arises from the disposal of UK land held as trading stock.
(3) The gain arises from a disposal of UK land that has been developed with the sole or main object of realising a gain on its disposal.

Where s 756 applies, all or part of the capital gain is charged as income.

The definition of land includes buildings and assets deriving their value from land (eg options). Consequently, s 756 could apply if a person received a lump sum for assigning the benefit of an option.

32.2.2 **Exemption**

There is an exemption for gains that arise on the disposal of an individual's principal private residence. This exemption continues to be available even where the CGT exemption is not due because the property was acquired with a view to realising a gain (see 13.2.3).

32.2.3 **Sales of shares**

Section 756 may apply where a person disposes of shares in a land-owning company. If a non-resident individual were to dispose of, say, a controlling shareholding in a company that itself owned a valuable UK property, he might be subject to income tax on the whole of his capital gain.

There is a let-out in the case of a land-owning company that holds land as trading stock (ie a company that is a builder or developer or deals in land as a trade). No liability arises under s 756 on a sale of shares in such a company, provided the land held by the company is disposed of in the normal course of its trade and a full commercial profit from that land is received by the company.

Despite this let-out, s 756 may still be a problem on a sale of a land-owning company since the company may be an investment company (in which case it will not hold the land as trading stock).

32.2.4 **Clearance procedure**

It is possible for a person to apply for advance clearance from the Revenue that s 756 will not apply to a particular disposal. This clearance may be sought either for a sale of land or of shares in a land-owning company. The legislation requires the person to supply full written particulars to the Inspector who must then give a decision within 30 days. Once clearance is given, the Revenue cannot subsequently charge tax under s 756 unless the clearance application was invalid because it did not accurately set out all the facts.

32.3 TRANSACTIONS IN SECURITIES
(TA 1988, s 703 now s 682 ITA 2007)

32.3.1 **Introduction**

Legislation was introduced in 1960 to enable the Revenue to counteract tax advantages obtained by transactions in securities. The legislation is often applied by the Revenue to prevent tax savings being achieved because a right to income has been converted into a capital gain. An example of the type of transaction that may be caught in this way is where a person sells shares with a right to repurchase them for a lower amount after a dividend has been received by the purchaser. The legislation also applies to more devious types of transactions where the tax advantage is less obvious at first sight.

32.3.2 Conditions to be satisfied before legislation can apply

For s 703 to apply, the following three conditions must be satisfied:

(1) there must be one or more transactions in securities; and
(2) a person must have obtained, or be in a position to obtain, a tax advantage; and
(3) one of the prescribed circumstances set out in s 704 must have occurred.

If s 703 does apply, an income tax assessment may be made to counteract the tax advantage.

32.3.3 The term 'transactions in securities'

This term is widely defined to include transactions of whatever description relating to securities. It includes in particular:

(1) the purchase, sale or exchange of securities;
(2) the issuing of new securities;
(3) alteration of rights attaching to securities.

'Securities' is, in turn, defined as including shares and loan stock.

32.3.4 Tax advantage

In general, a tax advantage is deemed to arise if there is any increased relief, or repayment of tax, arising from transactions in securities, or if the transactions result in a reduction in the amount of tax that would otherwise be assessed. The courts have taken the view that a tax advantage may arise wherever the Revenue can show that an amount received in a non-taxable form could have been received in a way that would have given rise to an income tax liability. Going back to the example given in 32.3.1, the Revenue would say that a tax advantage arises when a person sells shares and has a right to buy back at a lower price after a dividend has been paid because he could simply have retained the shares and received the dividend.

> **Tax notes**
>
> A tax advantage is deemed to arise if a transaction in securities results in a reduction in the amount of tax that would otherwise be assessed.

See the recent case of *Trevor G Lloyd* v *HMRC* SpC 672 on the meaning of 'tax advantage'.

32.3.5 Prescribed circumstances

Section 704 listed five circumstances, outlined in ss 704A–704E, and at least one of them must apply before the Revenue can invoke s 703. Section 704A has recently been taken off the statute book as the mischief at which it was aimed no longer exists. Sections 704B and 704E apply to special situations that are outside the scope of this book; the remaining two are as follows.

Section 704C

This applies where a person receives consideration without paying income tax on it as a result of a transaction whereby another person subsequently receives an abnormal amount by way of dividend. The consideration received must represent:

(1) the value of assets available for distribution by way of dividends; or
(2) future receipts of the company; or
(3) the value of trading stock of the company.

Section 704D

This subsection applies where a person receives consideration that is not subject to tax and represents:

(1) the value of assets available for distribution by way of dividends; or
(2) future receipts of the company; or
(3) the value of the trading stock of the company.

This is obviously similar to s 704C, but s 704D can apply even though there has been no abnormal dividend.

Section 704D can apply only to transactions involving specified companies, ie:

(1) companies that are under the control of not more than five persons; or
(2) transactions involving any other unquoted company.

32.3.6 Exemption for bona fide commercial transactions

If there is a transaction in securities and the prescribed circumstances apply, a taxpayer may still avoid assessment if he can show that transactions were carried out for bona fide commercial reasons or in the ordinary course of making or managing investments, and that none of them had as their main object the obtaining of a tax advantage.

32.3.7 Clearances

Section 707 provides a procedure whereby a person can give details of the proposed transactions to the Revenue and request clearance that the Board will not apply s 703.

Once a written application has been made under s 707, the Revenue has 30 days in which to request more particulars, which must then be provided within 30 days.

The Revenue must give a decision either within 30 days of receiving the original application or within 30 days of receiving the further particulars.

Where the Revenue has notified someone that it is satisfied that s 703 should not apply, it may not subsequently change its mind. Where information given in the application is incomplete or inaccurate, any clearance given by the Revenue may be void.

32.3.8 Situations where clearance should be sought

It is standard practice for vendors or their advisers to seek clearance under s 707 where a private company is being sold for a substantial amount. Quite apart from anything else, the vendor would otherwise be at the mercy of the purchaser who might extract an abnormal dividend and thus bring s 707 into consideration.

It is also advisable to seek clearance under s 707 where a company is liquidated, the reserves are extracted in a capital form and it is intended that the company's business should be carried on by a new company owned by the current shareholders.

32.4 TRANSFER OF ASSETS OVERSEAS

Legislation was introduced in 1936 to prevent tax savings for UK-resident and ordinarily resident individuals arising from their transferring assets overseas. The legislation refers to avoidance of income tax. Capital tax avoidance is not subject to counteraction by ITA 2007 ss 714-723 (formerly s 739 ICTA 1988), although separate anti-avoidance legislation also exists for CGT (see 32.21).

32.4.1 Where the individual or spouse can benefit

Section 714 applies where a UK-resident has made a transfer of assets and either he or his spouse (or, since 5 December 2005, his civil partner) may benefit as a result of it. He is deemed to meet this test if he has 'power to enjoy' income that arises overseas. Power to enjoy income exists in the following circumstances:

(1) The income accrues for his benefit.
(2) The receipt of the income increases the value to him of any assets held by him or for his benefit.
(3) He may become entitled to enjoy the income in the future.
(4) He is able in any way whatsoever, and whether directly or indirectly, to control the way the income is used.

Where s 714 applies, the transferor or spouse is assessed on the income as it arises, even if it is not actually paid out to them.

32.4.2 Exemption for bona fide transactions

Section 737 ITA 2007 contains a clearance procedure. The individual used to have to show to the Revenue's satisfaction that:

(1) the purpose of avoiding tax was not one of the purposes for which the transfer of assets was carried out; or

(2) the transfer of assets, and any associated operations, were bona fide commercial transactions and not designed for tax avoidance.

In *Carvill* v *IRC* SpC 233, the Special Commissioners held that the test was a subjective, and not an objective, one. The taxpayer also succeeded in the case of *Beneficiary* v *IRC* where a Japanese individual who was not resident in the UK established an offshore trust for the benefit of his daughter who was not capable of managing her own finances (this was a case where the Revenue sought tax under s 732 ITA 2007 (see 32.4.5 below) rather than s 714).

Unfortunately, many of the successes achieved by taxpayers have been reversed by legislation in FA 2006. The requirements for s 740 ITA 2007 exemption have been reinforced in relation to income arising on or after 5 December 2005 and the exemption is now dependent upon HMRC or, on appeal, the Special Commissioners, being satisfied that one of two conditions are satisfied. These conditions are:

- it would not be reasonable to infer from all the circumstances of the case that avoiding tax was the purpose, or one of the purposes, for which the relevant transactions were effected;
- all the relevant transactions were genuine commercial transactions and it would not be reasonable to infer from all the circumstances of the case that any one or more of those transactions was more than incidentally designed for the purpose of avoiding tax.

A relevant transaction is a commercial transaction only if it is effected in the course of a trade or business or with a view to setting up a business.

A transaction is commercial only if it is made on arm's length terms and is a transaction that would have been entered into by independent persons dealing at arm's length, eg a loan will not be commercial even if it carries a commercial rate of interest if no arm's length lender would have made a loan of that amount.

The new version of s 740 ITA 2007 specifies that the intentions and purposes of professional advisers may be taken into account as well as the transferor's own objectives. This is likely to make the test more 'objective', ie it is not sufficient to look at the transferor's intentions in a subjective way.

In practice, it is always going to extremely difficult to satisfy HMRC that the re-stated conditions are satisfied.

32.4.3 Transfer of assets by non-residents

The Revenue's view has always been that s 714 ITA 2007 could apply to income arising from a transfer of assets made by an individual at a time when he was not UK-resident. The House of Lords found against the Revenue on this in *IRC* v *Willoughby* [1997] STC 995, but FA 1997 restored the position to what the Revenue always believed to be the case in relation to income arising on or after 26 November 1996.

32.4.4 Assessment of income caught by s 714 ITA 2007

Income caught by s 714 is normally taxed as miscellaneous investment income (in the past this was taxed under Schedule D Case VI). Where it is UK dividend income, or other income that has borne tax at source, relief is given for such tax and the assessment will be for higher rate tax purposes only.

32.4.5 Liability of non-transferors
(ITA 2007, s 732)

A person may not be assessed under s 714 unless he or his spouse has made a transfer of assets. However, a UK-ordinarily resident individual may be assessed under s 732 if he receives a benefit from a transfer made by another person. This applies particularly to beneficiaries of non-resident settlements created by someone other than the individual and his spouse. It is also arguable that s 732 might apply to a person who had made a transfer of assets but was not 'caught' by s 714, perhaps because he was not resident at the time of the transfer.

In contrast to s 714, a liability may arise under s 732 only when the individual concerned receives a benefit. 'Benefit' is not specifically defined, although the legislation states it includes a payment of any kind. It is understood that the Revenue regards an interest-free loan or the provision of accommodation as constituting a benefit.

This is an area where professional advice is essential.

32.4.6 Matching income with benefits

The legislation allows benefits to be matched with income received in either earlier or later years.

Example – Matching benefits

An overseas trust receives income of £10,000 in 1994–95. In 1996–97 a capital payment of £100,000 is made to a UK-resident and ordinarily resident individual. In the year 2007–08, the trustees receive further income of £120,000. If s 740 applies, the individual will be taxed as follows:

	£
1996–97	10,000
2007–08	90,000

32.4.7 **An interest-free loan may constitute a benefit**

The High Court decided in January 2000 in *Billingham* v *Cooper* [2000] STC 122 that an interest-free loan that was repayable on demand gave rise to a benefit equal to interest at the 'official rate'.

32.4.8 **Assessment under s 732**

Where income is taxed under s 732, there is no credit for any UK tax suffered at source. This can give rise to double taxation. Thus, going back to the previous example, if the trustees' income represented interest from UK companies, the total tax suffered would really be as follows:

	£
Tax at source on interest: £100,000 × $^{25}/_{100}$ =	25,000
Tax charged on beneficiary under s 740 =	40,000
	65,000

32.4.9 **Clearances**

Once again, it is possible to obtain clearance from the Revenue that s 732 should not apply because the transfer of assets concerned was not carried out for tax avoidance purposes.

32.4.10 **Foreign domiciliaries**

Where the income arising to the non-resident trust or company is foreign source income, no liability arises for a foreign-domiciled individual who elects for the remittance basis except to the extent that he remits such income to the UK (see 34.10). However, the individual may need to pay a £30,000 special charge to get the benefit of the remittance basis (see 34.2)

32.4.11 **Reporting income taxable under s 714 or s 732**

Question 5 on page 2 of the tax return asks, among other things:

> Have you, or could you have, received (in the widest sense) income, or received a capital payment or benefit, from a person abroad as a result of any transfer of assets?

If you tick the 'yes box', you will be required to complete the Foreign pages.

Other overseas income and gains

41	Gains on disposals of holdings in offshore funds (excluding the amounts entered in box 13) and discretionary income from non-resident trusts - *enter the amount of the gain or payment*	44	Number of years
	£		
		45	Tax treated as paid - *read page FN 16 of the notes*
			£
42	If you have received a benefit from an overseas trust; company or other person abroad, enter the value or payment received - *read page FN 15 of the notes*	46	If you have omitted income from boxes 11, 13 and 42 because you are claiming an exemption in relation to a transfer of assets, enter the total amount omitted (and give full details in the 'Any other information' box)
	£		£
43	Gains on foreign life insurance policies etc. (excluding the amounts entered in box 13) - *enter the amount of the gain*		
	£		

Extracts from Revenue notes to the tax return

The notes to the Foreign pages state:

Dividends and all other income received by an overseas trust, company or other person abroad

If you have transferred, or taken any part in the transfer of assets, as a result of which income has become payable to a person abroad, you may need to complete boxes 10–13. All items chargeable as income under the transfer of assets provisions should be entered in this section only. Help Sheet 262 has more details on how you complete these boxes.

If you have received a benefit from an overseas trust, company or other person abroad, enter the value or payment received in box 42

If someone else has transferred, or taken part in the transfer of assets, as a result of which income has become payable to a person abroad, the value of the payment or any other benefit you receive may be treated as your income for tax purposes. If you think this applies to you (and you will probably know if it does) Help Sheet 262 has more detail on how to complete this box.

(In notes to previous years' tax returns, the Revenue stated that 'benefits' include, for example, loans at less than a commercial rate of interest and the occupation or use of property at less than a commercial rent, the value of the benefit being the difference between the commercial rate of interest or rental and any amount actually paid by you.)

If you have omitted income from boxes 11, 13 and 42 because you are claiming an exemption in relation to a transfer of assets, enter the total amount omitted in box 46

The provisions described at boxes 10 to 13 and 42 do not apply if you can show for all the circumstances that the purpose of the transfer and any associated operations was not to avoid tax. But if you omit income for this reason from boxes 11, 13 and 42, you must enter the total amount of income you have omitted in box 46, together with details of the assets transferred and details of the offshore trusts, companies etc involved in the 'Any other information' box on your tax return or on a separate schedule. Help Sheet 262 provides further information.

32.5 TRUST INCOME TAXED ON THE SETTLOR

32.5.1 Introduction

There are several provisions under which income on property that belongs to trustees may be taxed as if it were income that belonged to the settlor.

32.5.2 Trust where settlor may benefit
(IT(T&OI)A 2005, s 624, previously s 660A TA 1988)

Legislation may catch income that arises to a trust under which the settlor or his spouse may benefit (a 'settlor-interested trust'). The legislation provides that the settlor/spouse should be treated as capable of benefiting where they may benefit in any circumstances whatsoever except in one of the following exceptional cases:

(1) The bankruptcy of a person who is beneficially entitled under the settlement.
(2) The death under age 25 of a person who would be beneficially entitled to the trust property on attaining that age.
(3) In the case of a marriage settlement, the death of both parties to the marriage and of all or any of the children of the marriage.

The Revenue interprets this legislation rather literally. For example, if a person creates a trust for the benefit of his son, and the trust deed states that the property should revert to the settlor if the son dies before age 35, the Revenue takes the view that s 624 applies because the let-out applies only where property reverts on the death of someone before he attains age 25.

Sometimes the trust deed is silent on a matter. For example, a person creates a trust for the benefit of his three children and the deed makes no reference to the capital coming back to the settlor. In such circumstances, the Revenue is apt to say that the property could revert to the settlor if all his children died and they left no children of their own. To avoid this kind of argument, it is normal for a trust to contain a clause that provides the capital shall in no circumstances whatsoever come back to the settlor but shall be held for the benefit of, say, a charity in the event that all the named beneficiaries die before the capital is distributed.

The Revenue does not take the view that a person has reserved the benefit simply because his spouse may benefit after his death as his widow. On the other hand, cases have actually arisen where the settlor and his wife were excluded but the Revenue said that s 624 should apply because the settlor's current marriage might come to an end and he might marry someone who could benefit. Once again, it is best to make sure that the trust deed excludes such an interpretation by expressly providing that any future spouse of the settlor should be excluded from all benefit.

Where a settlor's spouse can benefit, the settlor is assessed on the trust income. This means that the benefits of independent taxation cannot be secured by putting capital into trust for a spouse.

FA 2000 introduced a concession. Where a settlor is not totally excluded but one of the beneficiaries under the trust is a charity, income arising after 5 April 2000 that is actually paid out to the charity will not be assessable on the settlor under s 624.

32.5.3 Settlements where the property given is just a right to income
(IT(T&OI)A 2005, s 624)

The legislation contains a very wide definition of 'settlement'. It can even apply to an outright gift where the property given is 'wholly or substantially' a right to income. It can also apply where there is no gift at all but there are arrangements that amount to a settlement as might apply where an individual lets someone else subscribe for shares in a new company.

The Revenue arguments seem to have a 'seasonality'. In the early 1990s, Inspectors often tried to apply these provisions where a husband had admitted his wife into partnership. The argument was that this was uncommercial and the partnership's profits should be assessed on the husband who contributed most to the business (and invariably paid tax at a higher rate). But as the Revenue met dogged resistance from tax accountants these arguments largely ceased, but without the Revenue ever conceding that the principle was incorrect.

In 2003, these arguments resurfaced in the context of small companies. The Revenue argued that where the husband was the main contributor to the company's profits, s 624 allowed the Revenue to treat dividends paid to the wife as the husband's income. The Revenue said tax avoidance arose from 'income-splitting'.

The Revenue set out its views in the April 2003 and February 2004 editions of *Tax Bulletin*. The February 2004 edition contains examples of circumstances where the Revenue believed that s 624 was applicable. The Revenue initially succeeded before the High Court in *Jones* v *Garnett* (often referred to as the *Arctic Systems Limited* case) but lost before the Court of Appeal and the House of Lords. However, the Government intends to reverse the decision of the House of Lords by bringing in specific legislation to counter 'income-splitting'. This will feature in FA 2009 and take effect from 2009–10.

Also, bear in mind s 624 if you are entering into a dividend waiver. Again, see the *Tax Bulletin* articles for guidance on the Revenue's position.

The FA 2004 contains a specific provision regarding jointly-owned shares in private companies. The gist of this provision is that if s 624 were considered applicable, the normal rule that dividends from shares which are jointly owned by husband and wife is disapplied. This provision applies only to dividends paid after 5 April 2004.

32.5.4 Settlements on minor children
(IT(T&OI)A 2005, s 629, formerly s 660B TA 1988)

Where a person gives capital to his minor children, the resulting income may be taxed as if it belonged to the parent. This treatment applies where the following three conditions are satisfied:

(1) The child is a minor.
(2) The child is unmarried.
(3) The income exceeds £100 per tax year for each child.

Similarly when a person makes a settlement under which his minor children may benefit, income distributed to the children before they are age 18 is treated as the settlor's income (subject to the £100 *de minimis* exemption). This applies even where he is separated or divorced and the children live with his former wife.

For s 629 purposes, 'child' includes an adopted child and an illegitimate child. Again, the Revenue interprets this legislation strictly and it has been known to tax a grandparent who set up a trust for his daughter's (illegitimate) child whom he subsequently adopted and brought up as his own.

There are two circumstances where s 629 does not apply:

(1) Where the child has married.
(2) Where the settlor is not resident in the UK.

The legislation does not stop here. Any capital payments made to the children are also caught so far as the capital payments may be matched with accumulated income within the trust. Since in the past trustees have normally paid 34% tax on accumulated income (see 30.5.2), this has meant that the additional tax payable was normally 6% (ie the difference between the 40% top rate and 34% paid by the trustees). The tax at issue could be more (eg in cases where non-resident trustees had not paid UK tax on income). In future, it will often be less now that the rate applicable to trusts has been increased to 40% (see 30.5.2).

Tax notes

The Revenue has been known to tax a grandparent who set up a trust for his daughter's (illegitimate) child whom he subsequently adopted and brought up as his own.

Roll-up funds

A way that remains open for achieving a tax saving may be for a parent to give capital to a minor child, with the money being invested in a roll-up fund or some other investment that does not produce taxable income. If the roll-up fund is cashed in shortly after the child's 18th birthday, the income counts as the child's income, and not the parent's. This may be a good strategy where a child is unlikely to have much income in his own right, perhaps because he will be in full-time education during the year in which he attains age 18.

Insurance bonds

Another way of achieving a tax saving is for a parent to invest in single-premium insurance bonds.

> **Tax notes**
>
> One way of saving tax may be for a parent to give capital to a minor child, with the money being invested in a roll-up fund or some other investment that does not produce taxable income.

32.5.5 Capital payments to settlor
(IT(T&OI)A 2005, s 633, formerly s 677 TA 1988)

Section 633 may apply to enable the Revenue to charge tax on income received by the trustees of the settlement under which the settlor and spouse are both totally excluded from benefit. Thus it may apply where the trustees of the settlement have accumulated income and make a capital payment to the settlor. The capital payment is then treated as if it were income for the year in which the payment was made provided there is sufficient undistributed income.

If only part of the capital payment can be 'matched', the balance is matched with income for subsequent years, and amounts matched in this way are then taxable for those years.

Example – Matching of capital payments

> In 1997–98 A received a capital payment of £18,000 from a UK trust set up by him in 1985. The trust has net undistributed income of £30,000. A will have been assessed under s 633 as if he had received gross income that after tax at the rate applicable to trusts (34%) would have left £18,000, ie £27,272.
>
> In 2001–02 A received a capital payment of £50,000. The trustees had undistributed income for that year of £20,000. The trustees made no further capital repayments but in 2002–03 and 2007–08 they had undistributed income of £10,000 and £8,000 (after tax). The following amounts are taxable under s 633:
>
> | | | | £ |
> |-------|---------------------------|-----|--------|
> | 1997–98 | £18,000 grossed up | = | 27,272 |
> | 2001–02 | £32,000[1] grossed up | = | 48,484 |
> | 2002–03 | £10,000[2] grossed up | = | 15,151 |
> | 2007–08 | £8,000[3] grossed up | = | 13,333 |
>
> [1] ie balance of the undistributed income available at the end of the year 1997–98.
> [2] grossed up for 34% tax
> [3] grossed up for 40% tax

Section 633 can also apply in relation to non-resident trusts. The tax payable may be greater in such cases because the undistributed income might not have suffered tax at the rate applicable to trusts.

32.5.6 Income may be matched with capital payments made in previous 12 years

Undistributed income can be identified with past capital payments for up to 12 years. The only way to get round this is for the whole of the capital sum to be repaid by the settlor, but even doing this does not affect the position for past years and the year in which the capital sum is repaid.

32.5.7 Loans may also be caught

A loan from the trustees to the settlor or spouse may be treated under s 633 as if it were a capital payment. Furthermore, the repayment of a loan made by the settlor to the trust can also be treated as a capital payment.

Example – treatment of loans

In 1997–98 *B* made a £150,000 loan to a trust created by him. The trustees repaid the loan in full during 2000–01. At that time, the trustees had undistributed income of £45,000 (ie this was the net income retained after 34% tax). *B* was taxed under s 677 on £45,000 grossed up at 34%, ie £68,181.

If the trustees had undistributed income of £30,000 for 2002–03 and £85,000 for 2007–08 (in both cases after tax), the position would be that assessments could be made on £30,000 grossed up for 2002–03 and £75,000 grossed up for the year 2007–08.

32.5.8 Payments by companies connected with trustees

A liability could arise under s 633 if a company connected with the trustees makes a capital payment to the settlor. There have to be three conditions here:

(1) The trustees must have undistributed income.
(2) There must be 'associated payments' by the trustees to the company. An associated payment may include a capital payment (eg a subscription for shares) or the transfer of assets at an undervalue by the trustees to the company.
(3) The company must make a capital payment to the settlor, or make a loan to him or repay a loan made by the settlor to the company. This must occur within five years of the associated payment taking place.

32.6 TRANSACTIONS INVOLVING LOANS OR CREDIT
(TA 1988, s 786)

Specific legislation exists to prevent any tax avoidance that could otherwise arise if a person who was liable to pay non-allowable interest found a way of converting his liability to pay interest into some other payment that was tax deductible. Section 786 may apply where a transaction is effected with reference to money-lending. It can apply whether the transaction is between the lender and borrower or involves other persons connected with them.

(1) Section 786(3) states that if the transaction provides for payment of any annuity or other annual payment it shall be treated as interest for all purposes of the Taxes Act.

(2) Section 786(4) states that if the borrower agrees to sell or transfer to the lender any securities or other property carrying a right to income, the borrower may be charged income tax on an amount equal to the income that arises from the property before he repays the loan.

(3) Section 786(5) refers to income being assigned, surrendered, waived or forgone and states that the person who has assigned, surrendered, etc may be charged to tax on the amount of income assigned, surrendered, etc.

In theory, s 786 could apply to interest-free loans. The Revenue has given some degree of comfort in that it has said that in the straightforward situation where one person lends money to another and then waives the interest, and there is no further transaction linked in any way to the arrangements, s 786 will not be invoked. There has been some concern in the past that s 786 could apply where, for example, a client deposited a large lump sum with his accountant on the basis that the accountant would not pay interest but would reduce his accountancy fees by the amount of interest that would have been paid at commercial rates on the client's deposit. It is possible to read s 786(5) as permitting the Revenue to make an assessment in this way even though the type of transactions described are somewhat different from those envisaged when the legislation was enacted.

32.7 PRE-OWNED ASSETS

The Government announced in December 2003 that it proposed to impose an annual income tax charge from 2005–06 where individuals have transferred assets but continue to enjoy benefits. It justified this charge as being aimed at individuals who had used artificial schemes to avoid the IHT legislation that catches gifts with reservation (the GWR rule). The relevant Press Release stated that the effect of these artificial structures was that 'people have been removing assets from their taxable estates but continuing to enjoy all the benefits of ownership'. In practice, most of these schemes were intended to save IHT on the family home.

The December 2003 announcement resulted in many representations being made on the unfairness of such a charge where the transactions were entered into many years ago. The Government took some of these representations on board.

The charge will not apply in any of the following situations where:

- the benefit enjoyed by the donor is worth less than £5,000 a year;
- the benefit enjoyed by the donor is 'consistent with' an interest retained by him (eg where an individual gives a 50% interest in his home to a child living with him);
- the transfer was a gift that took place before 18 March 1986 (the date that the GWR rule was introduced);
- the property has been transferred to the donor's spouse;
- the transfer was a sale at market value and the purchase price has been paid in full;
- the transfer was effected by a deed of variation as permitted under the IHT legislation;
- any enjoyment of the property that has been given away is no more than incidental;
- the asset given away is an intangible asset (eg an insurance policy) and the benefits retained by the donor are of a very limited nature;
- the donor was not domiciled in the UK (or deemed to be domiciled under the 17-year rule) at the time that he made the transfer and the property concerned is foreign property.

Furthermore, it was possible to make a special election by 31 January 2007 whereby the donor would renounce the IHT benefits in return for being exempt from the income tax charge. Where this election has been made, the property concerned will be treated as caught by the GWR rule.

32.7.1 Charge on occupation of a property

The charge may apply whenever a person occupies land and buildings that he does not own. The essential test is whether or not he owned the property or provided funds for its purchase, directly or otherwise, after 17 March 1986. If none of the reliefs and exemptions applies (see above) the calculation of the tax payable will be based on the rental value of the property. This will be arrived at in the same way as for employment income purposes (see 4.8).

32.7.2 Charge on use of chattels

Very similar rules can apply in respect of chattels (eg, works of art, cars, boats, etc). In this case the charge will be calculated by reference to the value of the chattel using a notional interest rate.

32.7.3 Trusts

The above charging provisions do not apply if land or chattels have been placed in an interest-in-possession trust for the benefit of either the taxpayer or his or her spouse. However, there are separate rules for settlements where the settlor retains an interest in the property of the settlement. Again, the rules ought not to apply if the settlement is for the benefit of a spouse. The charge is calculated by applying a notional interest rate to the value of settlement property in which the taxpayer has retained an interest.

Where the settlor suffers a capital gains or income tax charge under the existing settlement rules, the tax paid can be offset against this new liability. Nevertheless, there will be many circumstances were the taxpayer is being taxed twice in respect of the same source.

CAPITAL GAINS TAX

32.8 BED AND BREAKFAST TRANSACTIONS

For disposals of shares by individuals or trustees on or after 17 March 1998, any shares of the same class and in the same company that are sold and then repurchased within a 30-day period will be matched so that the gain or loss that would otherwise have arisen by reference to shares already held will not be realised. This blocks a widely used way in which individuals have realised losses and then brought back the same shares on the following day.

It would appear that it is still possible to circumvent this rule by one spouse selling and the other purchasing the same securities. However, the Revenue may attack this as an artificial transaction entered into solely for tax avoidance, especially if the purchasing spouse subsequently transfers the shares to the original owner.

32.9 DISPOSALS BY A SERIES OF TRANSACTIONS

32.9.1 Basic principle behind the legislation
(TCGA 1992, s 19)

There are certain assets that are worth more in total than the sum of their various parts. For example, a 55% shareholding in a private company will almost always be worth a great deal more than five times the value of an 11% shareholding since a 55% shareholder has control of the company. It follows from this that if there were not specific anti-avoidance legislation, a person could reduce his exposure to CGT on a gift to a relative, etc by transferring the asset in stages.

In fact, in certain circumstances, the Revenue may look at the value transferred by a series of transactions and assess that value by each separate transaction according to an appropriate part of the total value transferred.

> **Tax notes**
>
> In cases where a person has reduced his exposure to CGT on a gift by transferring an asset in stages, the Revenue may assess the value of each separate transaction as an appropriate part of the total value transferred.

32.9.2 Legislation may have wide application

The legislation can also apply in unexpected ways. Thus, if an individual with a 75% shareholding in an investment company decided to give 25% to each of his brother's three children and even arranged to make the gifts over a period of two (or more) years, the Revenue could still apply s 19 to catch the total value transferred.

32.9.3 Circumstances that cause s 19 to apply

The following circumstances may result in the Revenue applying s 19:

(1) A person disposes of assets to another person (or other persons) who falls within the definition of a connected person.
(2) There are 'linked transactions' that fall within a period of six years.
(3) The disposals have all taken place since 19 March 1985.
(4) The aggregate value transferred by the series of linked transactions is greater than the total of the values transferred by the individual transactions.

A transaction may be caught by s 19 even if it is a sale rather than a gift.

32.9.4 Section 19 can result in retrospective adjustments

If the Revenue invokes s 19, it may result in assessments for previous years being reopened. For example, *C* may have made a gift to her father in 2000–01 of a 10% shareholding in X Ltd and the shares' value may have been agreed with the Revenue as, say, £20,000. If *C* made a further gift to her brother in 2006–07 of a 70% shareholding, the position might have to be reopened. If the Revenue establishes that an 80% shareholding is worth £800,000 at the time of the gift to *C*'s brother, the effect of applying s 19 will be:

Deemed disposal proceeds on the 2000–01 gift	£100,000
Deemed disposal proceeds on the 2006–07 gift	£700,000

32.9.5 Hold-over relief may cover the position

In some circumstances, the donor may not have to pay extra tax because he and the donee have agreed that the hold-over provisions should apply (see 12.6 and 16.4). However, hold-over relief will not always be available since the asset will not always fall within the definition of business property or the donee may not be UK-resident or a settlor-interested trust (see 12.6 and 16.4.3).

Professional advice is clearly essential where a person is contemplating making a series of gifts to connected persons.

32.10 TRANSFERS TO A CONNECTED PERSON

Another potential pitfall arises from special rules that govern the way market value is to be determined when assessing a gain on a transaction between connected persons (whether the transaction is a gift or a sale).

32.10.1 Some restrictions may be taken into account
(TCGA 1992, s 18)

A gift or sale to a connected person may involve an asset over which the acquirer already has certain rights. Thus, D may own the freehold of a building and his daughter, E, may have valuable rights as a tenant. Suppose the freehold is worth £230,000 with vacant possession, but is worth only £180,000 if E's lease is taken into account. When D sells the freehold to E, will the market value be taken as £230,000 or £180,000?

The legislation states that the market value shall be taken to be the asset's market value less the lower of:

(1) the value of the interest held by the connected person who acquires the asset; or

(2) the amount by which the transferor's asset would increase in value if the connected person's rights did not exist.

Consequently, D would be deemed to make a disposal of an asset worth £180,000.

32.10.2 Some restrictions are ignored
(TCGA 1992, s 18(7))

Certain valuable rights may have to be left out of account. One example of this is an option. Suppose the facts set out in 32.10.1 had been slightly different so that D had vacant possession of a property worth £230,000, but his daughter had an option under which she could acquire it for £180,000. If D sells the property to E or if she exercises her option he will receive only £180,000, but he may be assessed as if he had received £230,000.

This is because the legislation requires options to be ignored or left out of account when computing an asset's market value. Similarly, legal rights that, if exercised, would effectively destroy or impair the asset also have to be ignored. Market value is determined as if such rights did not exist.

> **Tax notes**
>
> Options are ignored when computing an asset's market value. Similarly, legal rights that, if exercised, would effectively destroy or impair the asset also have to be ignored.

32.11 QUALIFYING CORPORATE BONDS (QCBS)
(FA 1997, s 88)

Anti-avoidance provisions took effect from 26 November 1996. They concern situations where an individual or groups of individuals dispose of their private company shares and take loan stock issued by the acquiring company as part of the sale consideration (referred to as 'rolling over' into loan stock since no capital gain normally arises until the loan stock is sold). Since 1984, legislation has made specific provision for the situation where a person receives qualifying corporate bonds (QCBs) in exchange for shares. The capital gain that would have arisen had he taken cash rather than QCBs is calculated but held over until such time as he disposes of the bonds. The legislation did not make express provision for the situation where the vendor receives loan notes that are not QCBs at the time of acquisition but become QCBs before a disposal takes place. As QCBs are normally an exempt asset for CGT purposes, the legislation seemed to allow a capital gain to escape a charge altogether, which gave rise to the term 'disappearing trick'.

The Revenue was sceptical that these arrangements succeeded in their objective. However, and without prejudice to litigation on past transactions, FA 1997 clarified the position.

The CGT legislation has been amended so that when a loan stock changes from a non-QCB into a QCB, the change is treated as a conversion of securities. This ensures that any gain that has been rolled over on an exchange of shares for loan stock is preserved and does not escape charge. The new rules apply to disposals after 25 November 1996, even where the loan stock was converted before the Budget.

32.12 VALUE SHIFTING
(TCGA 1992, s 29)

The legislation contains provisions that are intended to ensure that disguised gifts are assessed as a disposal at market value.

32.12.1 Type of transaction that may be caught

A controlling shareholder might exercise his control over a company to transfer value in an indirect way.

Example – Value shifting

> *F* owns all the shares in Y Ltd. The company has 1,000 £1 ordinary shares in issue. Assume that the value of these shares is £300,000. If *F* allowed his son *G* to be issued with 2,000 £1 shares at par, he would not have made a disposal of his own shares. However, *G* would have acquired a valuable asset in that his 2,000 shares will probably be worth in excess of £200,000 compared with the £2,000 that he had paid to acquire them. Furthermore, *F*'s 1,000 shares will have gone down in value since he will have become a minority shareholder.
>
> Where the Revenue can apply s 29, the person who has transferred value (in this example, *F*) is treated as if he had disposed of an asset.

32.12.2 Omission to exercise a right

There can be circumstances where s 29 is relevant because a person has failed to exercise a right. For example, if *H* and his grandson *J* were 50:50 shareholders in Z Ltd and the company announced a rights issue of three new shares for every one share already held and the amount payable for each share was £1 (par), s 29 would come into operation if *H* chose not to exercise his entitlement to the rights issue, as this omission would mean that after the rights issue the shares in Z Ltd would be owned as to:

H	20%
J	80%

Control would have thereby passed to *J*.

32.13 TRUSTS AND MAIN RESIDENCE EXEMPTION

Anti-avoidance legislation was introduced by FA 2004 and took effect from 10 December 2003.

32.13.1 No main residence relief for a property that has been transferred under a hold-over election

Where a property is given to a trust and the donor's gain is held over (see 12.6) the trustees are not able to claim exemption under s 225 TCGA 1992 (main residence exemption where a property is occupied by a beneficiary of a trust). Furthermore, the FA 2004 rules apply even where the property is transferred out of the trust, the trustees' gain is held over, and the property is occupied by the recipient as his main residence. When he comes to sell the property, he will not be able to claim the main residence exemption.

32.13.2 Transitional rules

The FA 2004 provisions also apply to cases where an asset was transferred to a trust under a hold-over election before 10 December 2003. However, in this situation the trustees may be able to claim a residence exemption for part of their gain, this being calculated on a time-apportionment basis with the proportion of the gain relating to the period up to 10 December 2003 being exempt.

Example – Claiming a residence exemption

A owned a second property. On 10 December 2002, it was worth £350,000. *A* transferred the property to a discretionary trust on that date and made a claim for hold-over relief under s 260 TCGA 1992. Assume that the gain held over amounted to £200,000.

The property was then occupied as the main residence of one of the beneficiaries of the trust. The property was eventually sold for £400,000 on 10 December 2007.

The trustees' gain will be calculated as follows:

Proceeds		400,000
Less cost	350,000	
Held over gain	200,000	
		150,000
		250,000

The trustees held the property for five years. The period of ownership up to 10 December 2003 was exactly one year.

The trustees would be entitled to main residence exemption on one fifth of the gain, ie £50,000.

32.14 UK-RESIDENT SETTLEMENTS WHERE SETTLOR HAS RETAINED AN INTEREST

32.14.1 Introduction
(TCGA 1992, s 77)

Capital gains realised by trustees of a UK-resident settlement before 6 April 2008 may be taxed under s 77 as if they were the settlor's own gains if he is deemed to have retained an interest in the trust. The gains were simply added to his personal gains and he is responsible for paying the CGT. He can, however, reclaim the tax from the trustees.

This does not apply unless the settlor is UK-resident or ordinarily resident for the tax year concerned.

32.14.2 Circumstances where settlor is deemed to have retained an interest

A settlor is regarded as having retained an interest if there are any circumstances whatsoever under which the property within the settlement or income arising to the trustees may become payable to him, his spouse or his civil partner. Furthermore, he may be deemed to have retained an interest if he or his spouse enjoys a benefit derived directly or indirectly from the settled property. From 6 April 2007, a settler is deemed to have retained an interest if his minor children can benefit before they marry or attain age 18.

There are some circumstances in which a settlor is not deemed to have retained a benefit even though he might receive a benefit. These exceptions relate to the possibility of the settlor or spouse benefiting in the event that a beneficiary becomes bankrupt or dies under age 25 or, in the case of a marriage settlement, the death of the married couple and their children.

32.14.3 Considerable care needed

There is no 'proportionality' here, so the retention of even a very small interest could result in the settlor being taxed on considerable gains that he did not (and perhaps never could) enjoy. There are two areas of special concern: loans by a settlor and remarriage.

Loans by a settlor

If the settlor lends money to the trustees there is a risk that he might be said to have an interest in the settled property. This situation should therefore be avoided.

Remarriage

The possibility of the settlor's current marriage coming to an end and his remarrying may be remote, but will be considered by the Revenue to bring s 77 into operation if such a future spouse is not specifically excluded from benefiting under the settlement.

32.14.4 Death of settlor

Once the settlor died, s 77 ceased to apply. His widow or civil partner could not then be charged on the trustees' gains.

32.14.5 Relief for personal CGT losses

For many years, it was not possible for a settlor to set his personal CGT losses against capital gains attributed to him under this legislation. This restriction ceased to apply from 2003–04 onwards. Furthermore, settlors could elect for this offset also to be available for any of the years 2000–01, 2001–02 and 2002–03. Such an election needed to be made by 31 January 2005.

32.14.6 Section 77 abolished from 2008–09 onwards

A settlor is no longer taxed under section 77 even if he has retained an interest. This is because the rate payable by the trustees is the same 18% rate that is payable by individuals.

32.14.7 No hold-over relief on transfers to settlor-interested trusts

See 12.6 and 16.4.3 on other legislation introduced by FA 2004.

32.15 DEEMED DISPOSAL WHEN A TRUST CEASES TO BE RESIDENT

A trust is regarded as resident or non-resident in the UK for a tax year, there is no concept of a trust in resident for only part of a year.

A UK resident trust can cease to be resident if non-resident trustees are appointed and the ordinary administration of the trust is then carried out overseas.

In such a case, there is a deemed disposal for capital gains tax purposes at the time that the trust ceases to be UK resident with market value being taken as the deemed disposal proceeds. As regards subsequent disposals, the trustees are deemed to have re-acquired all of their assets at market value.

32.16 OFFSHORE COMPANIES
(TCGA 1992, s 13)

A person who is resident and ordinarily resident in the UK (see 33.2) may be liable for a proportion of capital gains realised by a non-resident company in which he has a shareholding.

Example – Possible liability for capital gains

> *K* owns all the shares in X Ltd, a company incorporated and resident in Bermuda. The company realises a capital gain by disposing of a US property that it owns. The legislation enables the Revenue to assess *K* as if he made the capital gain himself. However, certain conditions need to be satisfied before the Revenue can assess a capital gain in this way (see 32.13.1).

32.16.1 Conditions that need to be satisfied

First, the company must be controlled by five or fewer shareholders, or shareholder directors must between them own more than 50% of the company's shares.

Second, the individual must be resident (or ordinarily resident) and, for years up to 2007–08, domiciled in the UK (see 34.1 and 34.14). For 2008–09 onwards, s 13 can apply to individuals who are resident and ordinarily resident but not domiciled in the UK.

Third, he and persons connected with him must between them have an interest in the company of at least 10%. Until 27 November 1995, the legislation could apply only if the individual was a shareholder who was entitled to at least

5% of the company's assets on a winding-up. From 27 November 1995 to 6 March 2001, the legislation applied if he had an interest of more than 5% in the company.

32.16.2 Certain gains not assessable under s 13

The legislation is really intended to catch gains on investment assets, etc held through an offshore company. There is therefore an exemption under s 13(5) for gains arising:

(1) on the disposal of foreign currency where the currency represents money in use for a trade carried on by the company outside the UK;
(2) from the disposal of 'tangible property' used for the purposes of a trade carried on by the company outside the UK;
(3) from disposals of assets used by a UK branch of the company.

32.16.3 Distribution test
(TCGA 1992, s 13(5)(d))

Where an offshore company has realised gains that are not exempt under 32.14.3, the individual may still escape assessment on gains realised before 28 November 1995 if he can show that the offshore company has distributed the gains within two years, either as a dividend or on the company being wound up. However, if he is UK-resident at the time he receives such a distribution, he will be assessed on it (either for income tax or, in the case of a liquidation, for CGT).

32.17 NON-RESIDENT TRUSTS
(TCGA 1992, s 86 and Sched 5)

32.17.1 Introduction

Trustees of a trust may be resident outside the UK and the administration of the trust may be carried out overseas. Provided both these conditions are satisfied, the trust is not resident and there will not normally be any liability for the trustees so far as UK CGT is concerned. There may be a liability for either the settlor (ie the person who set up the trust) or the beneficiaries (who may include the settlor).

32.17.2 Qualifying trusts
(TCGA 1992, s 86 and Sched 5)

The legislation refers to 'qualifying settlements'. In fact, they qualify for an adverse CGT treatment in that the trustees' gains are deemed to be the settlor's personal capital gains. The conditions under which the trust's capital gains will be treated in this way are as follows:

(1) The settlor must be UK-resident or ordinarily resident for the year concerned.
(2) The settler must be domiciled in the UK for the year in which the trustees realise capital gains.
(3) He must not have died during the course of the year.
(4) The people who benefit from the trust include one of the following:
    (a) the settlor;
    (b) his spouse;
    (c) his children (and spouses);
    (d) a company connected with him;
    (e) for trusts created after 16 March 1998, his grandchildren.

32.17.3 Relief for the settlor's personal losses

From 1998–99 to 2002–03, it was not possible for an individual who has been taxed on capital gains under s 86 to set off his personal CGT losses against these attributed gains. This restriction ceased to apply from 2003–04. Furthermore, an individual could elect for personal losses to be set against attributed gains for any of the tax years 2000–01, 2001–02 and 2002–03. Such an election needed to be made by 31 January 2005.

32.17.4 Stockpiled gains in pre-March 1991 trusts
(TCGA 1992, s 97(1))

Provided the trust did not become a qualifying settlement (see 32.14.5), there was no CGT liability for beneficiaries for years up to 1998–99 until such time as 'capital payments' were received.

UK-resident and domiciled beneficiaries may be assessed for CGT purposes under s 87 TCGA 1992 on a proportion of the trustees' pre 1998-99 capital gains ('stockpiled gains') that can be 'matched' with capital payments received.

The receipt of a benefit may count as a deemed capital payment (the rules are virtually the same as under s 740: see 32.4).

Example – Pre-19 March 1991 offshore trusts

> Trustees of an offshore trust make capital gains in 1989–90 of £200,000. In 1989–90 to 1991–92 the trustees distribute income, but their doing this does not have any CGT consequences. In 2007–08 they make a capital payment of £50,000 to L, who is UK-resident.
>
> L would be assessed as if she had personally made capital gains of £50,000 for 2007–08. The tax actually payable will depend on whether she has made other capital gains, whether she has capital losses available for offset and her rate of tax.

32.17.5 UK-resident beneficiaries of settlements that are not caught by s 86

Where a UK resident and ordinarily resident beneficiary receives a capital payment from a settlement that is not caught by s 86 (eg where the settlor has died), he may be taxed under s 87 on stockpiled capital gains that can be matched with the capital payment. This rule has been in place since 1981 as far as settlements created by UK domiciliaries are concerned.

32.17.6 Supplementary charge

A supplementary charge may be made of 10% of the tax for each complete year between 1 December following the year in which the trustees realised the gain and the time the trustees make the capital distribution. The supplementary charge cannot exceed 60%.

32.17.7 Settlements created by foreign domiciliaries

UK domiciliaries were made liable to tax on capital payments from trusts created by foreign domiciliaries by FA 1998. With effect from 17 March 1998, UK-resident and domiciled beneficiaries can be assessed where they receive capital payments from a non-resident trust created by a foreign domiciled settlor; this can apply only where payments made after 16 March 1998 can be matched with gains realised by the trustees after that date.

32.17.8 Beneficiary's capital losses

It is not possible for a beneficiary to offset personal CGT losses against gains attributed to him under s 87 TCGA 1992.

32.17.9 Finance Act 2008 changes

FA 2008 has brought foreign domiciliaries within the scope of s 87 in relation to capital gains realised by the trustees on or after 6 April 2008. However, there is a key difference in that if the beneficiary is a remittance basis user he will be subject to tax under s 87 only if he brings the capital payment into the UK (depending upon his circumstances, the foreign domiciliary may need to pay the £30,000 special charge to have the benefit of the remittance basis (see 34.2). Furthermore, the trustees can elect for all gains to be computed as if the market value of the asset at 5 April 2008 were the cost.

32.17.10 Sale of trust interest by beneficiary

A disposal of an interest in a non-resident trust has been a disposal of a chargeable asset for CGT purposes since 1981. On the other hand, a disposal of an interest in a UK resident trust has not normally been subject to CGT.

FA 1998 introduced a further rule so that if beneficiaries of UK-resident trusts dispose of their interest, and the trust has been non-resident in the past, the beneficiaries' disposal is subject to CGT.

32.17.11 Flip-flop arrangements

It was considered possible to avoid s 87 by arranging for a trust to borrow and to use the borrowed funds to make a gift to another settlement. The terms of the original trust were varied so that no UK person could benefit and any gains subsequently realised within that trust were not taxable under s 86. The settlement receiving the transfer had no capital gains and could therefore make a capital appointment to UK beneficiaries without their being liable under s 87. The legislators have made several attempts to block all such loopholes, most recently in FA 2003.

A recent case, *West* v *Trennery* and others [2005 STC 138] has suggested that some flip-flop schemes may fail because of the courts interpreting the legislation in accordance with principles established in the *Ramsay* case (see 32.19).

INHERITANCE TAX

32.18 PURCHASED INTERESTS IN EXCLUDED PROPERTY SETTLEMENTS

A trust created by an individual of foreign domicile settling foreign situs assets is excluded property for IHT purposes (see 34.16).

The Government has discovered that this has been used for avoidance by UK domiciliaries purchasing interests under such settlements. The definition of excluded property now excludes interests in such trusts where the interest was purchased on or after 5 December 2005 (whether the purchase was by the individual who owns the interest or by someone else).

GENERAL

32.19 *RAMSAY* PRINCIPLE

This chapter has concentrated so far on anti-avoidance legislation. There is another factor, ie case law, which has been developed by the courts that the Revenue can use in much the same way as anti-avoidance legislation to counter tax avoidance schemes.

The House of Lords decided in the *Ramsay case* (*IRC* v *W T Ramsay Limited* [1981] STC 174) that it should determine the tax consequences of a 'composite transaction' (i.e. a series of interlinked transactions) by looking at the overall effect. Furthermore, artificial steps that had been introduced only for tax avoidance purposes could be disregarded.

In another famous case, *Furniss* v *Dawson* 1984 STC 153, taxpayers sought to avoid capital gains tax by exchanging their shares in a UK company for shares in an Isle of Man company which on the same day (in fact immediately after lunch) sold its shares in the UK company to a third party purchaser. The House of Lords held that the interpolation of the Isle of Man company was an artificial step that could be disregarded and the UK vendors were therefore treated as if they had sold their UK company directly to the ultimate purchaser.

The *Ramsay* doctrine was summarised in another House of Lords case as applying only in the following circumstances:

- There was a pre-ordained series of transactions in mind from the outset that were intended to produce a given result.
- Certain transactions within that series of transactions had no purpose other than tax avoidance.
- At the time that the transactions were carried out, there was no practical likelihood that the pre-planned series of transactions would not take place in the order ordained. In that sense, some of the intermediate transactions were not contemplated as having a life independent from the pre-ordained series of transactions.
- The pre-ordained events did in fact take place.

Note that the courts have attached a great deal of importance to transactions being pre-ordained. This is not quite the same thing as pre-conceived. An individual might carry out a series of transactions with a view to ultimately selling a company to a third party. That series of transactions would be pre-conceived but would be pre-ordained only if the series of transactions were carried out with a particular purchaser in view. In one particular case, steps had been carried out with a view to a sale to a particular purchaser. That transaction fell through and the vendors eventually sold to a different person. It was held that a series of transactions started with the original purchaser in mind was not a single composite transaction and Ramsay therefore did not enable the Revenue to strike out those individual steps that secured a tax advantage for the vendor.

The likely application of the *Ramsay* doctrine to specific transactions carried out with tax savings in mind is fraught with uncertainty. There have been several recent court decisions. At one stage, it appeared that a distinction was being drawn between commercial concepts and legal concepts, with purely legal concepts being less susceptible to *Ramsay*. However, this appears to have been a misunderstanding and recent decisions in the *Arrowtown* and *Carreras* cases indicate a very wide interpretation of the *Ramsay* doctrine.

The House of Lords has held that conditions put into contracts merely to create some uncertainty as to the final outcome should be ignored. Their Lordships held that the creation of uncertainty by the insertion of such conditions did not prevent the final outcome from being preordained.

A recent decision by the ECJ was that a VAT avoidance scheme failed because it amounted to an 'abuse of rights'. It remains to be seen whether this can be invoked by the Revenue in areas other than VAT (*Halifax plc & others v C&E Commissioners 2006* 2 WLR 905).

> **Tax notes**
>
> Any taxpayer undertaking an artificial tax scheme should bear in mind that the Revenue may well attack it by invoking the *Ramsay* doctrine and that the courts are increasingly sympathetic to such Revenue arguments.

32.20 REGISTRATION OF TAX SCHEMES

Tax advisers and their clients can have an obligation to notify the Revenue of tax-saving arrangements implemented since 18 March 2004. The legislation also specifies that where a taxpayer uses arrangements that enable a tax advantage to be obtained, or where one of the main benefits of an arrangement is the obtaining of a tax advantage, these must be notified to the Revenue.

Furthermore, where there is any proposal for arrangements that would be notifiable (even if the arrangement is not put in place) the arrangements must be disclosed to the Revenue within five working days. Both tax advisers and taxpayers have an obligation to report such arrangements.

Penalties of up to £5,000 can be levied for non-notification of arrangements or proposals and £600 per day that non-notification continues after imposition of the penalty.

Initially, not all tax-saving schemes needed to be disclosed, only those that fell within categories that were specified by regulations issued by the Treasury. The regulations issued up to 31 March 2006 defined a notifiable arrangement as:

- an arrangement that relates to the reduction or avoidance of tax on employment income; and
- an arrangement that seeks to achieve the reduction of income tax (corporation tax) or capital gains tax through transactions involving financial instruments; and
- (from July 2005) an arrangement that is intended to achieve a reduction of SDLT.

Substantial amendments to the disclosure rules were contained in the March 2006 Budget. Since 1 August 2006 it has been necessary to disclose all arrangements that seek to avoid income tax, corporation tax, and CGT which contain any of the following 'hallmarks':

(1) 'confidentiality conditions' imposed on those who are advised of the scheme.
(2) the scheme commands a premium fee.
(3) the scheme involves 'off market terms'.
(4) the scheme is 'mass marketed' by substantially the same arrangements being sold to more than one person.
(5) a 'loss making scheme' involves an investment that generates a tax loss to offset against other income or gains.

(6) the scheme involves finance leases of plant and machinery valued at £10m or more and the arrangements involve a non resident party or a sale and lease-back on terms which remove the normal commercial risks for the lessor.

Once an arrangement has been notified to the Revenue it will in most circumstances issue a reference number and the taxpayer must report this number on his tax return. The registration does not imply any judgment on the technical merits of the scheme.

The rules on disclosing schemes have been further tightened by FA 2008. See HMRC guidance at www.hmrc.gov.uk/ria/disclosure-guidance.pdf.

Tax notes

Since 1 August 2006 it has been necessary to disclose all arrangements that seek to avoid income tax, corporation tax and CGT which contain certain 'hallmarks'.

32.21 SPECIFIC INCOME TAX AVOIDANCE SCHEMES THAT HAVE BEEN BLOCKED

The last five Finance Acts have contained provisions that blocked certain income tax avoidance schemes. These include the following:

- schemes and arrangements involving special shares and securities. Almost every Finance Act has dealt with an area of abuse. This has culminated with FA 2006 introducing retrospective legislation which takes effect from 1 December 2004;
- schemes involving the creation of a relevant discounted security and its subsequent sale to an unconnected party – FA 2003, Sched 39 applicable from 27 March 2003;
- schemes involving the abuse of reliefs for deficiencies on non-qualifying insurance policies – FA 2004, s 140 applicable from 3 March 2004;
- schemes involving stripped gilts and gilt futures – FA 2004, s 138 applicable from dates between 15 January and 17 March 2004;
- schemes involving repos and/or 'manufactured dividends' – FA 2004, Sched 24 applicable from 17 March 2004;
- schemes that sought to take advantage of the relief for gifts of quoted securities to charities – FA 2004, s 139 applicable from 2 July 2004;
- schemes involving an abuse of the reliefs due for films – FA 2004 – applicable from 10 February 2004 and further legislation in both FA 2005 and FA 2006;
- SDLT anti-avoidance provisions aimed at schemes involving foreign unit trusts – FA 2006;

- an investor who holds 10% or more of a unit trust could be subject to an annual tax charge in future (this legislation seems to be directed at 'private unit trusts') – FA (No 2) 2005;
- restrictions on trade loss relief for non-working partners or limited partnerships – these prevent sideways relief for losses against the partner's other income in so far as such losses exceed £25,000 pa. The legislation took effect from 2 March 2007;
- CGT relief is not available for artificial losses realised on or after 6 December 2006;
- legislation contained in FA 2008 seeks to prevent the abuse of double taxation agreements for UK resident beneficiaries of trusts that participate in partnerships controlled in the overseas territory concerned;
- similar legislation is likely to be introduced more frequently as the Revenue learns about schemes at an earlier stage through the registration of schemes (see 32.20).

PART 5

RESIDENCE, DOMICILE AND INTERNATIONAL MATTERS

This part contains the following chapters:

33

RESIDENCE STATUS

This chapter covers the following:

(1) Consequences of residence in the UK.
(2) Various criteria for determining residence status.
(3) Individuals who are resident but not ordinarily resident.
(4) Basis on which individuals are regarded as ordinarily resident.
(5) Ceasing to be resident in the UK.
(6) UK income and capital gains received by non-residents.
(7) Non-resident investment companies.
(8) When tax should be withheld from payments to non-residents.

33.1 CONSEQUENCES OF RESIDENCE IN THE UK

The basic principle of UK taxation is that an individual may be charged tax on his worldwide income if he is resident in the UK. If he is not, he is still liable for tax on income that arises in the UK, but not for tax on income that arises overseas.

There is an exception to this in that an individual who is UK-resident but not ordinarily resident and/or not domiciled in the UK, may have to pay tax only on UK income. The concept of domicile is different from residence (see 34.1) and this chapter proceeds on the basis that an individual has a UK domicile.

33.2 VARIOUS CRITERIA FOR DETERMINING RESIDENCE STATUS

33.2.1 Introduction

For UK taxation purposes, 'the UK' means England, Scotland, Wales and Northern Ireland. It does not include the Republic of Ireland, the Channel Islands and the Isle of Man. A person may be resident in more than one country so the fact that he is treated as resident in, for example, the US or South Africa does not necessarily mean that he is not resident in the UK.

A person is resident or not resident for a tax year. A person may also be ordinarily resident if he is habitually resident in the UK as opposed to simply being resident for one year in isolation.

Somewhat surprisingly the word 'resident' is not defined in the Taxes Acts, but there is considerable case law and the position is summarised below.

33.2.2 Two tests

An individual will always be treated as UK-resident for a tax year if he is caught under either of the following tests:

(1) The six-month rule, ie he is present in the UK for 183 days or more during the tax year.
(2) The three-month average rule, ie he is present in the UK for an average of 91 days or more pa measured over a period of four tax years.

In a case decided some years ago, fractions of a day were taken into account in applying the 183-day test. The Revenue later introduced a practice whereby days of arrival and departure were normally left out of account for these tests but this was not a universal rule. In a 2006 case ('Gaines-Cooper'), the Special Commissioners did take such days into account because, they said, omitting such days would have distorted the position. The High Court and Court of Appeal subsequently approved this treatment. The FA 2008 now contains specific rules covering part days (see 33.2.3 below).

Mobile workers may also be treated differently: see *Tax Bulletin* April 2001, which sets out the Revenue's view that individuals whose home and settled domestic life are in the UK may be regarded as remaining UK-resident despite frequent and regular trips abroad. See *Shepherd* v *HMRC*, 2006 SpC 484, for a case where the Revenue recently successfully argued this. A key factor in this decision was that Mr Shepherd spent a lot of time at the original family home in Wokingham and his Cyprus home was more in the nature of a holiday home than a main residence. For a case where the situation was the other way round, see *Grace* v *HMRC* SpC 663. In this case, the taxpayer retained a small flat near Gatwick and had his main home in Cape Town. The Commissioner was satisfied that, during the years in question, he came to the UK only in order to do his work and for no other reason. He was therefore adjudged to be neither resident nor ordinarily resident in the UK.

Tax notes

An individual will be treated as UK-resident if (a) he is present in the UK for 183 days or more during the tax year, or (b) for an average of 91 days or more pa over a period of four tax years. But there are also situations where a person who has spent fewer days in the UK may nevertheless be regarded as resident.

33.2.3 Days that are counted as UK days

The FA 2008 provides that from 6 April 2008 onwards, any day in which an individual is present in the UK at midnight shall normally be counted as a UK day. However, days spent in transit will not count as UK days even if the individual is present in the UK at midnight, provided that the individual does not engage in activities that are inconsistent with his merely being in transit.

33.2.4 Existing UK residents

So far as a person who has been resident in the UK for a number of years is concerned, he is likely to continue to be regarded as UK-resident despite temporary periods of absence from the UK unless the following conditions are satisfied:

(a) he works full-time abroad, and the period spent overseas includes a complete tax year, or
(b) he has no accommodation in the UK and he lives abroad for at least one full tax year.

The treatment of UK residents who move overseas is covered at 33.5.

33.2.5 Foreign nationals coming to the UK

The residence status of individuals who come to the UK is now governed by the six- and three-month rules set out in 33.2.2. Individuals who regularly visit the UK, and are therefore caught by the three-month rule, are normally treated as ordinarily resident only from Year 4. However, an individual may be regarded as ordinarily resident from Year 1 if it is clear he intended to spend an average of three months pa in this country.

33.2.6 Double taxation agreements

The UK has entered into many double taxation agreements (also known as double tax treaties) with other countries. Provisions of such an agreement may override UK tax law. Specifically, the agreement may provide exemption for certain income received by a person resident overseas even though the income arises in the UK. For example, most double taxation agreements provide that a resident of the foreign country concerned may claim exemption from UK tax in connection with interest income arising in the UK.

Most double taxation agreements also make provision for the situation that an individual may be resident in both the foreign country and the UK. They usually contain a clause along the following lines:

(1) If the individual has a permanent home in only one country, he is deemed to be resident there.
(2) If the position has not been resolved by (1), he is treated as resident where he has the centre of his personal and economic interests.
(3) If the above tests do not resolve the position, he is treated as resident in the country where he has an 'habitual abode'.

(4) If he has an habitual abode in both countries, he is deemed to be a resident of the country of which he is a national.

(5) If he is a national of both countries, or he is not a national of either country, the Revenue authorities of the UK and the foreign country may settle the matter by mutual agreement.

These provisions apply only for the purposes of determining residence under the agreement. They are deeming provisions and, under UK law, an individual might still be regarded as UK-resident even though he might be treated as resident in the foreign country for the purposes of the double taxation agreement. However, the terms of a double taxation agreement override UK tax law and, if an individual is deemed to be resident in a foreign country under the agreement, his liability to UK tax is then computed in accordance with other provisions of the agreement.

33.3 INDIVIDUALS WHO ARE RESIDENT BUT NOT ORDINARILY RESIDENT

An individual who is resident but not ordinarily resident in the UK has certain tax privileges.

33.3.1 Employment income

Earnings from duties performed outside the UK are taxable on the remittance basis. This applies even where the employment relates to a mixture of UK and overseas duties. Furthermore, this treatment can apply even where the employer is UK resident (contrast foreign emoluments where the employer must be non-resident: see 34.2).

IT(E&P)A 2003, s 690 allows an employer to require a direction from the Revenue as to how much of a not ordinarily resident employee's remuneration should be subject to PAYE deductions.

Table 33.1 – Basis for assessment for employment income

	Services performed			
	Wholly in UK	*Partly in UK*	*Partly abroad*	*Wholly abroad*
Non-resident	All	That part	None	None
Resident but not ordinarily resident	All	That part	Remittances	Remittances
Resident and ordinarily resident	All	All	All	All

Remuneration from a mixed employment (ie duties performed within and outside the UK) is normally allocated by the day, ie remuneration for overseas duties is found by taking the number of days substantially (ie more than half) devoted to working overseas and dividing by the total number of working days during the year.

33.3.2 Overseas investment income

This is taxable under the remittance basis.

33.4 BASIS ON WHICH INDIVIDUALS ARE REGARDED AS ORDINARILY RESIDENT

33.4.1 Intention to make a permanent home in the UK

Where an individual arrives with the intention of staying in the UK for at least three years (apart from holidays and short business trips), he is regarded as ordinarily resident from the outset. If he arrives with no definite intention but stays in the UK he will be regarded as becoming ordinarily resident for the tax year in which the third anniversary of his arrival falls (unless he decides to stay in the UK on a longer term basis during the first three years in which case he will become ordinarily resident from the start of the tax year in which he makes such a decision).

Different rules apply to an individual who spends a significant part of his time overseas (see below).

33.4.2 Accommodation in the UK

Where an individual does not spend all his time in the UK but has UK accommodation available for his use, he is normally regarded as ordinarily resident as well as resident. He does not have to own the accommodation; it is sufficient if it is made available to him. Accommodation is regarded as available if it is kept in a permanent state of readiness for his occupation. Rented accommodation is ignored if the lease is for a period of less than 12 months (unfurnished) or for a period of less than two years (furnished).

33.4.3 Regular visitors

An individual who comes to the UK with the intention of spending at least 91 days in the UK for a period of four tax years is regarded as ordinarily resident from Year 1. An individual who comes without any such clear intention becomes ordinarily resident in Year 5 unless he forms a definite intention during the intervening years (in which case he becomes ordinarily resident from 6 April of the year in which he decides to reside in the UK for at least four tax years).

33.4.4 Visits for education

A person who comes to the UK for a period of study or education expected to last more than four years is regarded as resident and ordinarily resident from the date of his arrival. If the period is not expected to exceed four years, he may be treated as not ordinarily resident, but this depends on whether he:

(1) has accommodation available in the UK, or
(2) intends to remain in the UK when his education is complete, or
(3) proposes to visit the UK in future years for average periods of three months or more per tax year.

If, despite his originally intending not to do so, he remains in the UK for more than four years, he is treated in any event as ordinarily resident from the beginning of Year 5 of his stay. This applies to both a person who comes to the UK for his own education or a parent or guardian of a child who comes in connection with the child's education.

33.5 CEASING TO BE RESIDENT IN THE UK

33.5.1 Working abroad

Up to 1992–93 there was an important distinction between individuals who worked full-time abroad and others who lived overseas in that the legislation provided specifically that, where an individual worked full-time abroad, the fact that he had accommodation available for his use was not regarded as a relevant factor in determining his residence status. As from 6 April 1993, this distinction became less important as the legislation now provides that an individual shall not be regarded as resident just because he has available accommodation in the UK. Nevertheless, it is still easier to establish non-resident status if you are working overseas.

A key Revenue publication (IR20) states that if a person goes abroad for full-time service under a contract of employment and:

(1) all the duties of his employment are performed abroad or any duties he performs in the UK are incidental to his duties abroad; and
(2) his absence from the UK and the employment itself both extend over a period covering a complete tax year; and
(3) any interim visits to the UK during the period do not amount to:
    (a) six months or more in any one tax year; or
    (b) an average of three months or more per tax year;

he is normally regarded as not resident and not ordinarily resident in the UK on the day following the date of his departure until the day preceding the date of his return. On his return, he is regarded as a new permanent resident.

The treatment whereby a person is treated as not resident for part of a tax year is called the 'split year' concession. The latest edition of IR20 indicates that this concession will also apply to self-employed people who leave the UK to work full time in a trade, profession or vocation providing they are able to meet the conditions similar to those set out above.

33.5.2 Involuntary residence
(SP2/91)

The Revenue operates a concession that covers individuals who are forced to spend time in the UK because of exceptional circumstances outside their control, for example, someone who was working abroad in a Gulf state, but who had to return to the UK prematurely at the outbreak of the Gulf War, may be allowed some leeway when the Revenue applies the three-month average test. Similarly, where an individual spends days in the UK because of illness, these may be left out of account in certain circumstances.

These concessions do not apply where an individual returns to the UK because his employer has prematurely terminated his employment contract. Also, and more fundamentally, the Revenue's concession does not affect the rule that an individual is treated as UK-resident if he spends 183 days or more in the UK during a particular tax year.

Tax notes

Concessions on residence status do not apply where an individual returns to the UK because the employer has prematurely terminated an employment contract.

33.5.3 Other individuals who live abroad

Different rules apply where a person does not work full-time abroad (eg where an individual moves to a foreign country on retirement), or where he works overseas but continues to perform duties in the UK that are not incidental to the work carried out abroad. A person who falls into this category continues to be treated as resident where he spends an average of three months pa in the UK over a four-year period.

33.5.4 Temporary non-residence

An individual who leaves the UK on or after 17 March 1998 and who:

(1) has been tax resident in the UK for any part of at least four out of the seven tax years immediately preceding the year of departure; and
(2) becomes not resident and not ordinarily resident for a period of less than five tax years; and
(3) owns assets before he leaves the UK

remains liable to tax on any gains realised on those assets after departure from the UK. Gains made by him in the year of assessment in which he leaves the UK are chargeable for that year. Gains made after that year are chargeable in the year of assessment in which he resumes residence in the UK. Losses are allowable on the same basis as gains are chargeable. Gains of non-resident trusts and companies may also be taxed if they would have been taxable had the individual been resident (see 32.17).

Any gains made in the intervening years (ie between the tax years of departure and of return) on assets acquired by the taxpayer after becoming tax resident abroad are exempt from the charge. This exemption will not apply to assets held in a non-resident trust or closely controlled non-resident company. Special rules prevent gains on assets held before departure from escaping the charge, where gains are rolled over or otherwise deferred on the acquisition of assets during the period of absence.

Until recently, it was understood that certain double taxation agreements might protect a temporary non-resident from the five-year rule. Recent statements by the Revenue have cast doubt on this and the Government gave notice in the March 2005 Budget that it would put the matter beyond doubt.

33.6 UK INCOME AND CAPITAL GAINS RECEIVED BY NON-RESIDENTS

A person who is not UK-resident for a tax year may still be subject to tax on UK source income, but is not liable to tax for income that arises abroad. The following types of income are deemed to arise within the UK and are therefore subject to tax even where the individual is not resident there:

(1) employment income that relates to duties performed in the UK;
(2) trading profits from a branch or permanent establishment in the UK;
(3) rents from UK properties;
(4) dividends from UK companies;
(5) interest paid by a person who is UK-resident;
(6) 'annual payments' made by a UK-resident person.

Tax charged on investment income of a non-resident individual is normally limited to the tax deducted at source. This does not apply to income from property in the UK or from trading in the UK through a broker or investment manager.

The provisions of a double tax agreement or extra statutory concession may also limit the tax charged on a non-resident individual.

33.6.1 Earned income

Where an individual is non-resident, profits from a trade carried on outside the UK are not subject to UK tax. Where such a person has a branch or permanent establishment in the UK, a liability to UK tax may arise from profits earned by that branch. Double taxation agreement provisions may govern what type of presence in the UK is deemed to constitute a branch or permanent establishment.

Earnings from an employment may attract UK tax where the duties are performed in the UK (see 33.6.5 on double taxation agreements).

Where an individual works full-time abroad under a contract of employment, the resulting income is not subject to UK tax even though the employer may be a UK company. However, a Crown employee or a member of the Armed Forces is regarded as performing the duties of his employment in the UK and he may therefore be subject to UK tax even though he performs all his duties overseas and is not resident in the UK.

Problems have arisen in recent years where an individual was granted a non-approved share option at a time when he was UK-resident and subject to tax under s 15 IT(E&P)A 2003 (formerly Schedule E Case I), with the option subsequently exercised after he ceased to be UK-resident. The Revenue's view is that a liability may arise in these circumstances even if he is no longer employed by the company concerned (but see *Tax Bulletin* October 2002 on the Revenue's views on treaty relief).

Pensions paid by UK residents are subject to tax unless the recipient can claim the benefit of a double taxation agreement (see 33.6.5).

33.6.2 Concession for bank and building society interest

In practice, certain income arising from a UK source is not subject to UK tax. In particular, bank deposit interest is not subject to deduction of UK tax at source provided the non-resident certifies he is not ordinarily resident in the UK (TA 1988, s 481(5)(k)). The Revenue will not assess such income unless the account is managed or controlled by a UK-resident agent. This also applies to interest or dividends paid gross by a building society, discount (eg on deep discount bonds), gains on deep gains securities and interest on certificates of tax deposit.

33.6.3 Exempt gilts

Interest paid on all British Government securities is exempt from UK tax where the person who owns the security is not UK-resident (unless the interest forms part of the profits of a trade carried on in the UK).

33.6.4 Income from property

Rental income received by an individual from a UK property is subject to UK tax even if he is not UK-resident. A tenant who pays rent exceeding £100 pw direct to a non-resident landlord should withhold basic rate tax at source unless the Revenue has authorised the tenant to pay the rent gross. Where rent is paid to a UK agent, the tenant should pay the rent without deduction, but the agent must then deduct tax from the net rental income.

The Revenue will authorise a tenant or agent to make no tax deductions if the landlord has registered for self-assessment and his tax affairs are up to date. See leaflet IR140, *Non-resident landlords, their agents and tenants.*

> **Tax notes**
>
> Rental income received by an individual from a UK property is subject to UK tax even if he is not UK-resident.

33.6.5 Double taxation agreements

Where an individual is not UK-resident but is resident in a foreign country that has a double taxation agreement, it may be possible for certain income that would normally suffer UK tax at source to be exempt from UK tax, or subject only to a lower rate.

Remuneration for work performed in the UK

Most double taxation agreements provide an exemption from UK tax for employment income, provided the following conditions are satisfied:

(1) the recipient of the remuneration is present in the UK for a period not exceeding 183 days in aggregate in the tax year concerned; and

(2) the remuneration is paid by, or on behalf of, an employer who is not UK-resident; and

(3) the remuneration is not borne by a permanent establishment or a fixed base that the employer has in the UK.

Pensions

Double taxation agreements generally provide for exemption from UK tax in respect of a pension paid by a UK company or pension scheme, although such a pension is normally subject to tax in the foreign country concerned.

Interest

In general, most double taxation agreements provide for a person resident in the foreign country concerned to be exempt from UK tax on interest. The company, etc that pays the interest can be given authorisation to pay it gross. In cases where tax has been withheld at source, the individual may be entitled to a repayment.

Dividends

A double taxation agreement usually includes a provision that the person who receives a dividend from the UK company is entitled to the benefit of a reduced tax credit and any balance should be repaid.

Royalties

Most double taxation agreements provide that where a royalty is received by a person resident in the foreign country concerned, the royalties shall be free from UK tax.

33.6.6 Allowances and reliefs

A British subject is entitled to full personal allowances for a tax year, even if he is not a UK resident.

Nationals of EU countries have been entitled to a full personal allowance from 1996–97. This also applies to nationals of the following EEA countries: Iceland, Norway and Liechtenstein.

A non-resident person is not generally entitled to a repayment supplement so it is normally important that tax should not be overpaid where this can be avoided. However, EU nationals may be entitled to such a supplement even though they are not UK-resident.

Limits on tax liability of non-residents

Section 128, FA 1995 limits the extent of the UK tax liability on non-residents so that, in general terms, it does not exceed:

- the tax due on total income less excluded income, but without relief for personal allowances, plus
- the tax deducted at source from the excluded income.

For the purposes of this section excluded income is:

- Interest from UK sources (see Chapter 8);
- Dividend income from UK companies (see 8.8);
- Profits on the disposal of certificates of deposit (see 9.6);
- Certain Social Security benefits including state pensions (see Chapter 39);
- Other trading income carried out by brokers and investments managers as defined by s 127 (1)a&b, but not Lloyd's underwriting income (see 36.7); and
- Any other income so designated by the Treasury.

Example – Alternative calculations

Mr and Mrs M live in Spain and are treated as not resident in the UK for the tax year ended 5 April 2006. They have the following UK income arising in the tax year:

Source	Mr M £	Mrs M £
Rental income	2,000	5,000
Bank interest paid gross	5,000	500
Dividends and tax credits	4,000	0
Total taxable income	11,000	5,500

UK tax liability for 2005–06		
Income	11,000	5,500
Less: Personal allowances	4,895	4,895
Taxable UK income	6,105	605
Tax calculation		
Rent/Interest £2,090/£605 at 10%	209.00	60.50
Interest £15/0 at 20%	3.00	0.00
Dividends £4,000/0 at 10%	400.00	0.00
Total	612.00	60.50
Less: Tax credits	400.00	0.00
Balance payable	212.00	60.50

The s 128 calculation produces the following results:

Source	Mr M £	Mrs M £
Total UK income	11,000	5,500
Less: Excluded income under s 128		
Bank interest	5,000	500
Dividends and tax credits	4,000	0
Net taxable UK income	2,000	5,000
Tax calculation		
Rent £2,000/£2,090 at 10%	200.00	209.00
Rent £0/2,910 at 22%	00.00	640.20
	200.00	849.20
Excluded income – tax deducted	400.00	0.00
Total	600.00	849.20
Normal tax liability (see above calculation)	612.00	60.50
Tax advantage/(disadvantage) of s 128	12.00	(788.70)

In this example, Mr *M* would consider using the alternative calculation and Mrs *M* would not as it is obviously not to her advantage.

The Revenue Helpsheet IR300 deals with this subject.

33.6.7 Capital gains

A non-UK resident is not normally subject to CGT except where capital gains arise from the disposal of assets used by a branch or permanent establishment of a business carried on by him in the UK (but see 33.5.4 on the taxation of gains realised by former UK residents who are non-resident for less than five complete tax years and the change in FA 2005 where temporary non-residents seek to rely on DTA exemption).

33.7 NON-RESIDENT INVESTMENT COMPANIES

A non-UK resident who has significant investment income arising within the UK may take certain steps to minimise his UK tax liability. In particular, where he cannot claim the benefit of a double taxation agreement, it may be advisable for UK assets such as real estate to be held through a non-UK resident company. This means that any tax liability is confined to basic rate tax and there is no question of any higher rate liability.

In such a case, it would still be sensible for some portfolio investments to be retained in his own name if he is a British subject or is otherwise entitled to claim a personal allowance. Sufficient personal income should arise to use such an allowance as this will be wasted if all income arises within an offshore company.

In some cases, a non-resident landlord should form an offshore company to acquire UK properties already owned and let by him. The offshore company may raise a qualifying loan to purchase the properties from the individual concerned and interest payable on the loan may then be offset against the non-resident company's rental income. This is a way in which an individual who already owns a property that is not subject to a mortgage may create a situation where interest is payable on a qualifying loan that is deductible in computing UK property income. However, see *Tax Bulletin* April 2000 on the possibility of the Revenue challenging a deduction for excessive interest under the transfer pricing legislation.

> **Tax notes**
>
> Where a non-UK resident cannot claim the benefit of a double taxation agreement, it may be advisable for UK assets such as real estate to be held through a non-UK resident company.

33.8 WHEN TAX SHOULD BE WITHHELD FROM PAYMENTS TO NON-RESIDENTS

33.8.1 Non-resident sportsmen and entertainers

A person paying a non-UK resident sportsman or entertainer for work carried out in the UK is liable to withhold tax at basic rate and pay this over to the Revenue (see 20.6), although it may be possible to agree an alternative withholding rate with the Inspector of Taxes at Special Compliance Office.

Olympic Games 2012

We have already seen the start of legislation in respect of the 2012 Olympic Games to be held in London. One of the measures introduced effectively takes non-UK resident Olympic athletes out of the foreign entertainer rules and consequently out of the scope of UK tax.

33.8.2 Rent payable to non-resident landlord

A person who pays rent to a non-resident landlord must withhold tax at the basic rate and account for this to the Revenue unless he has been authorised to pay gross (see 33.6.4). This obligation arises whether the payment is made within the UK or by payment out of a bank account held overseas.

Where a UK resident pays a premium to a non-resident landlord, the same requirement to withhold tax arises.

Where a tenant has failed to withhold tax, he may be required to account for it to the Revenue. In such circumstances, he may withhold sums from subsequent payments of rent to cover the amounts paid over to the Revenue.

The obligation to withhold tax does not arise where the tenant pays rent to an agent in the UK. Also, the Revenue would not normally pursue a tenant who had failed to deduct tax where he could not have known that the landlord was non-resident and nothing had happened to put him on notice.

For more details, see 20.5.

THE INCOME AND CAPITAL GAINS OF FOREIGN DOMICILIARIES

MIKE WILKES

This chapter deals with the tax treatment of individuals who are resident but not domiciled in the UK. The following subjects are discussed:

General principles

(1) Meaning of 'domicile'.
(2) £30,000 special charge for some remittance basis users from 2008–09
(3) What constitutes a remittance?

Earned income

(4) Foreign emoluments.
(5) Travelling expenses.
(6) Subsistence allowances for employees seconded to the UK.
(7) 'Corresponding payments'.
(8) Overseas pension funds.
(9) Self-employment.
(10) Partnerships controlled outside the UK.
(11) Pension benefits.

Investment income

(12) The remittance basis for investment income.
(13) Position if foreign domiciliary acquires UK domicile.
(14) Managing the remittance basis.

Capital gains tax

(15) Remittance basis for capital gains on foreign assets.
(16) Use of offshore companies and trusts.

Inheritance tax

(17) UK and foreign situs property.

34.1 MEANING OF 'DOMICILE'

Domicile is a fundamentally different concept from residence and ordinary residence. It is not the same as nationality, although an individual's nationality may be one relevant factor in determining his domicile. The basic concept is that a person is domiciled in the country he regards as his real home. The fact that he may be prevented from living in that country or may need to live elsewhere because of temporary reasons (eg business and/or employment) does not mean he is domiciled in the country in which he resides. Under English law, an individual normally acquires his father's domicile at birth and retains it unless his father changes his own domicile before the child attains age 16. The mother's domicile may apply instead where a child is illegitimate or the parents divorce. The domicile acquired in this way is called the individual's 'domicile of origin'.

An individual may change his domicile to a 'domicile of choice'. Normally this would happen by his leaving his country of origin and taking up permanent residence abroad with the intention of never returning to live in the country of origin permanently. His domicile of origin will revive if his intentions alter and he decides not to make his permanent home in the new country after all. This is a question of fact, see *Allen & another (exors of Johnston) v HMRC*, 2006 SpC 481, where a woman who had acquired a Spanish domicile of choice was held to have retained this even though she returned to the UK to be cared for by a relative.

34.1.1 Married women

A woman married before 1 January 1974 generally acquired her husband's domicile (referred to as a 'domicile of dependency'), which continued after divorce or the husband's death, although she could discard her domicile of dependency and regain her domicile of origin. A domicile of dependency in the UK may be discarded by the woman establishing that she no longer intends to remain permanently in that country and by her ceasing to be resident there. The mere intention is not itself sufficient: an Australian woman who had acquired a domicile of dependency in England was held to be domiciled in the UK, despite her intention to return to Australia, because she had not ceased to be resident.

The law is somewhat different for couples married after 31 December 1973. The Domicile and Matrimonial Proceedings Act 1973 allows a woman to retain an independent domicile on her marriage.

There may be exceptions to this rule imposed by the taxation treaty with the other state. For example, the treaty with the US treats wives as if they were married after 31 December 1973, regardless of the actual date of marriage.

34.1.2 Registration as an overseas elector

FA 1996, s 200 provides that where an individual registers as an overseas elector to vote in UK elections, this is not to be taken into account in determining his domicile status for tax purposes.

34.1.3 Remittance basis

The remittance basis means that an individual pays tax on foreign income and capital gains by reference to amounts brought into the UK. Foreign domiciliaries are eligible for this tax treatment but they have to make a claim to be taxed in this way. Up to 5 April 2008 it was only necessary to make a claim in respect of overseas investment income, as overseas earnings and capital gains were automatically taxed on a remittance basis. From 6 April 2008 the claim will cover all overseas income and capital gains.

34.2 £30,000 SPECIAL CHARGE FOR SOME REMITTANCE BASIS USERS FROM 2008–09

A special £30,000 charge applies from 2008–09 where an individual over the age of 18 elects for the remittance basis and

(1) he has been resident in the UK for seven of the preceding nine tax years; and

(2) his unremitted overseas income and capital gains are £2,000 or more.

The special charge does not apply to minors.

If an individual does not elect for the remittance basis he will be liable for UK tax on his worldwide income and capital gains (see Figure 34.1).

The payment of the £30,000 is an annual decision and it will be open for an individual to choose the remittance basis for some tax years and not others.

The £30,000 may be creditable against US tax where it is paid by US citizens, but this remains to be confirmed.

If the individual pays the £30,000 to the Revenue directly from an overseas bank account, doing so will not constitute a remittance. But if money is transferred into the individual's UK account this will be a remittance even if he then uses that money to pay the £30,000 special charge.

Figure 34.1 – New rules for non-doms for 2008–09

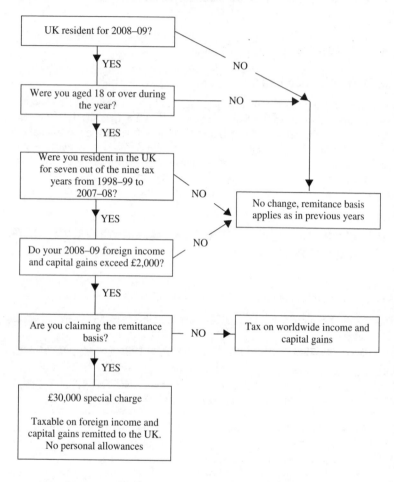

34.3 WHAT CONSTITUTES A REMITTANCE?

34.3.1 General principles

A remittance arises where an individual brings money into the UK, either in cash or by transferring money to a UK bank account.

Overseas income and capital gains are also remitted if they are brought into the UK or enjoyed there. For example, payment of the disposal proceeds into a UK bank account counts as a remittance, as does a payment into a UK bank account from an overseas bank account containing such proceeds. Less obviously, the income will be enjoyed in the UK if an individual has a large deposit account outside the UK and he formally secures a UK bank loan against this deposit account. However, if the money is spent outside the UK, it is not deemed to have been remitted.

Payment of disposal proceeds into a bank account in the Channel Islands or Isle of Man does not constitute a remittance to the UK. An outright gift that takes place outside the UK will not normally be a remittance provided a cheque, etc is paid into an overseas bank account for the recipient.

34.3.2 Constructive remittances
(ITTOIA 2005, ss 831–834 and 839)

The legislation deals with constructive remittances and states that a remittance is deemed to have occurred if an individual applies overseas income towards the satisfaction of:

(1) a debt (or interest thereon) for money lent to him in the UK;
(2) a debt for money lent to him abroad and brought to the UK;
(3) a loan incurred to satisfy such debts.

However, these rules have been substantially amended for 2008–09 and subsequent years, see 34.3.4.

Case law also indicates that a constructive remittance is deemed to have occurred if an individual borrowed from a UK bank but had his borrowings formally secured against money held in an overseas bank account.

The courts have held that a complex arrangement whereby money was transmitted between two South African companies, with the individual receiving a loan from one of them, constituted a constructive remittance of income because he had never really relinquished control of the money as it passed through various intermediaries. Since the courts are increasingly having regard for the overall consequences of a series of transactions, it would be unwise to rely on an artificial scheme that enabled an individual to enjoy sums in the UK that could be matched with overseas income.

34.3.3 Unauthorised remittances

In the Duchess of Roxburgh's case, a bank remitted untaxed overseas income by mistake. Because the bank acted contrary to its customer's instructions, it was held there was no liability under the remittance basis.

34.3.4 Extension of the definition of 'remittance' for 2008–09 onwards

The definition of 'remittance' has been extended to include bringing into the UK property that has been purchased out of overseas unremitted income. However, this does not apply to certain assets owned on 11 March 2008 or to assets acquired after that date but which were brought into the UK before 6 April 2008, or to any of the following:

(1) artwork brought into the UK for public display;
(2) personal effects, eg clothes, shoes, jewellery and watches;
(3) assets costing less than £1,000;
(4) assets brought into the UK for restoration;
(5) assets in the UK for less than 275 days.

A remittance may also be deemed to have occurred when a loan from a non-UK institution has been advanced in the UK and interest has been paid out of unremitted overseas income. However, this charge will not apply to mortgages already in existence on 11 March 2008 until 6 April 2028 (or the remaining period of the loan, if shorter) provided that the terms of the loan are not varied and no advances are made on or after 12 March 2008.

Tax notes

Be careful not to change the terms of an offshore mortgage in place on 11 March 2008 or using overseas income to pay the interest may in future count as a remittance.

34.3.5 Five-year rule

If a foreign domiciled individual ceases to be resident in the UK but resumes residence within five tax years, remittances made to the UK in years during which he was not resident may be taxed as if they were remittances made in the year that he returns to the UK.

34.3.6 Gifts of unremitted income before 6 April 2008

The safest course of action has been for a gift to take the form of a cheque to be drawn on a foreign bank account, with the recipient paying the sum into a foreign bank account. If matters were handled in this particular way, there could be no question of the gift constituting a remittance.

Where an individual made a gift of foreign income, he was not affected by what happened subsequently. The money lost its income quality once it had been given away and the recipient could bring the money into the UK without any liability under the remittance basis. In principle, this rule ought also to apply to gifts between spouses, although one should expect the Revenue to scrutinise such arrangements to ensure there are no hidden arrangements that govern the way the recipient must use the money given.

34.3.7 Gifts of unremitted income after 5 April 2008

Another extension of the concept of remittance may bite where income or gains have been alienated after 5 April 2008, ie given to another person. If that person then brings the money into the UK and it is enjoyed by the original owner or members of his immediate family, he is deemed to have made a remittance. Minor children are regarded as party of an individual's immediate family along with his spouse or civil partner. In addition, 'immediate family' now includes individuals living together as spouses or civil partners.

34.3.8 Remittances made out of mixed funds

An individual may have a 'mixed fund', eg a bank account where the money has come from a number of sources. FA 2008 provides that where a mixed fund was built up out of monies from different types of income and gains, remittances are matched with those types of income and gains in the following order:

(1) employment income;
(2) foreign self-employed earnings not subject to foreign tax;
(3) relevant foreign earnings that have not suffered foreign tax;
(4) foreign investment income that has not suffered foreign tax;
(5) foreign capital gains that have not suffered foreign tax;
(6) foreign self-employed earnings that have been subject to foreign tax;
(7) relevant foreign earnings that have suffered foreign tax;
(8) foreign investment income subject to foreign tax;
(9) foreign capital gains on which foreign tax has been charged;
(10) other income or capital.

EARNED INCOME

34.4 FOREIGN EMOLUMENTS

34.4.1 Introduction

A UK resident and ordinarily resident foreign-domiciled individual who is employed by a UK-resident employer is basically treated no differently from a UK-domiciled individual in a similar position. The earnings from such an employment are taxed in full on the arising basis under IT(E&P)A 2003 (for the taxation of such earnings, see Chapter 4).

Where a person domiciled outside the UK is employed by a non-UK resident employer, and he claims the remittance basis, the tax treatment is fundamentally different. Earnings from such an employment are called 'foreign emoluments'. Their tax treatment is as set out in Table 34.1.

Table 34.1 – Tax treatment under IT (E&P)A 2003 of earnings by foreign domiciled individual from non-UK resident employer ('foreign emoluments')

	Duties of employment performed wholly or partly in the UK		*Duties of employment performed wholly outside the UK*
	In the UK	*Outside the UK*	
Employee resident and ordinarily resident in the UK	Liable to UK tax (s 15 IT (E&P)A)	Liable to UK tax (s 15 IT (E&P)A)	Liable if remitted to the UK (s 22 IT(E&P)A)
Resident but not ordinarily resident	Liable to UK tax (s 25 IT (E&P)A)	Liable if remitted to the UK (s 26 IT (E&P)A)	Liable if remitted to the UK (s 26 IT(E&P)A)
Not resident	Liable to UK tax (s 25 IT (E&P)A)	Not liable	Not liable

34.4.2 Employer's resident status need not be same as individual's domicile

It is not necessary that the employer should be resident in the same country as that in which the individual is domiciled (although this is often the case). An individual domiciled in, for example, Switzerland and employed by a company resident in the US has foreign emoluments.

34.4.3 Earnings from employer resident in the Republic of Ireland
(ITEPA 2003, s 22)

Up to 5 April 2008, there was one exception to the general rule that foreign emoluments arise from an employment by a person not domiciled in the UK from an office or employment with a non-UK resident employer. Where the employer was resident in the Republic of Ireland, the earnings were not regarded as foreign emoluments. However, with effect from 6 April 2008 foreign emoluments will include earnings from an employer resident in the Republic of Ireland.

34.4.4 Earnings of person not ordinarily resident in UK

Where an individual has foreign emoluments and is resident in the UK, but not ordinarily resident (see 33.2.1 for meaning of ordinary residence), it is necessary to divide the emoluments between those that relate to duties performed in the UK and those performed overseas. The remuneration referable to the UK duties is taxed on an arising basis under IT(E&P)A 2003 s 25, but the remuneration for duties performed overseas is taxed on the remittance basis under IT(E&P)A 2003, s 26.

34.4.5 Split contract needed for person resident and ordinarily resident in UK

A different rule applies when an individual is both resident and ordinarily resident in the UK. The earnings from an employment with a foreign employer are all subject to tax in the UK on an arising basis where all or any part of the duties are performed there. There are no provisions whereby remuneration can be split between earnings relating to work done in the UK and work performed overseas. However, if a foreign-domiciled individual has a contract of employment under which all the duties are performed outside the UK, the earnings are taxed on the remittance basis under IT(E&P)A 2003 s 26.

It may be possible to take full advantage of this treatment by an individual having two separate contracts of employment, one covering duties performed in the UK and the other covering duties performed overseas. However, the Revenue has announced that it will be considering dual contracts much more carefully to ensure that in practice they are indeed separate contracts, and are not merely an artificial split of a single contract. See Tax Bulletin April 2005.

Where a foreign national is given a right to tax equalisation in his service contracts, the amount charged on the UK employment may be carefully scrutinised by the Revenue. This is an area where you should take advice from a specialist.

Tax notes

The Revenue has said that it will be considering dual contracts of employment much more carefully to ensure that they are indeed separate contracts, and are not merely an artificial split of a single contract.

34.5 TRAVELLING EXPENSES
(IT(E&P)A 2003, ss 373–375)

There are special provisions that apply for individuals of foreign domicile. Certain travel expenses paid or reimbursed by an employer are not assessable income where all the following conditions are satisfied:

(1) The expenses must be paid during the five-year period that begins from the date of arrival in the UK.
(2) The expenses must relate to a journey between the individual's usual place of abode and the place in the UK where he works.

(3) The expenses must relate to journeys made by the employee, unless he is in the UK for a continuous period of 60 days or more for the purposes of performing duties. In this event, the expenses of a visit by his spouse or minor child will also be allowable, although there is a limit of two visits by any such person in a tax year.

To secure this exemption it is also necessary that he must not have been resident in the UK in either of the two tax years that precede the year in which he took up his UK employment.

34.6 SUBSISTENCE ALLOWANCES FOR EMPLOYEES SECONDED TO THE UK

The Revenue accepts that an employer may bear certain costs where an employee is seconded to the UK for a period not exceeding 24 months. An article in *Tax Bulletin* December 2000 analyses what is meant by 'secondment' and outlines circumstances in which an employee of an overseas company may actually be coming to the UK to take up a new office or employment rather than be working there under a continuation of his existing employment contract.

The article also goes on to explain that if the employer provides, for example, a flat for the seconded employee to use instead of hotels, the expenditure is not regarded as a taxable benefit provided 'the total cost of the accommodation is appropriate to the business need and is reasonable and not excessive'. Examples are given of what might be regarded as not being reasonable.

34.7 'CORRESPONDING PAYMENTS'
(IT(E&P)A 2003, s 355)

Certain payments made by an individual out of foreign emoluments qualify for tax relief where they are made 'in circumstances corresponding to those in which the payments would have reduced his liability to income tax' had they been paid in the UK. The main type of payment that can be relieved under this heading are contributions to an overseas pension fund (see below). Before 2000–01, mortgage interest, alimony and maintenance could also be deducted from foreign emoluments.

34.8 OVERSEAS PENSION FUNDS

An overseas pension fund will not normally be an approved retirement benefit scheme for UK tax purposes. However, where the benefits provided by an overseas pension fund are broadly similar to those that arise from UK-approved retirement benefit schemes, the Revenue may regard the employer's contributions as not constituting remuneration for IT(E&P)A 2003 purposes and any contributions made by the employee may be deducted as corresponding payments (see above). In some situations, the Revenue will accord this treatment only where the individual's rights under his overseas pension scheme are adapted or restricted. For example, a US national who has an individual retirement plan may be required to give notice to the US administrators so as to waive his ability to take a lump sum in circumstances where this would not be permitted under the rules that govern UK-approved retirement benefit schemes. Some double taxation treaties (eg UK/US) also provide for relief to be given for foreign pension contributions.

34.9 SELF-EMPLOYMENT

Where an individual is resident in the UK, any earnings from a business carried on as a sole trader are taxed as self-employment income on the arising basis. This even applies in a situation where all the work is actually performed overseas. The basis for this interpretation by the courts is that a business is deemed to be carried on from where it is controlled and, in the case of a sole trader, control is located where the proprietor is resident.

A foreign-domiciled individual who carries on self-employment and who performs a substantial amount of work overseas should consider forming a company. In particular, if an overseas company were to be formed and the company employed him and supplied his services outside the UK to customers, the earnings from that employment would constitute foreign emoluments. Provided no work is performed in the UK under the employment contract, interposing an offshore company in this way would mean that he could take full advantage of the remittance basis for earnings taxable under IT(E&P)A 2003 ss 22–26.

> **Tax notes**
>
> A foreign-domiciled individual who carries on self-employment and who performs a substantial amount of work overseas should consider forming a company.

34.10 PARTNERSHIPS CONTROLLED OUTSIDE THE UK

Where a UK-resident but foreign domiciled individual is a partner in a firm controlled outside the UK, his earnings from that firm are taxed as follows:

(1) Profits from a UK branch: as trading income on the arising basis.
(2) Overseas profits: as foreign trading income under the remittance basis.

34.11 PENSION BENEFITS

34.11.1 Lump sums paid under overseas pension schemes
(ESC A10)

Income tax is not charged on lump sum benefits received by an employee (or by his personal representatives or any dependant) from an overseas retirement benefit scheme or overseas provident fund where the employee's overseas service comprises:

(1) not less than 75% of his total service in the employment concerned; or
(2) the whole of the last ten years of his service in that employment (subject to the total service exceeding ten years); or
(3) not less than 50% of his total service in that employment, including any ten of the last 20 years, provided the total service exceeds 20 years.

If the employee's overseas service does not meet these requirements, relief from income tax is given by reducing the amount of the lump sum that would otherwise be chargeable by the same proportion as the overseas service bears to the employee's total service in that employment.

34.11.2 Pensions

An individual who receives a pension paid by a non-UK resident person is subject to tax under the remittance basis. There is no such reduction as exists for UK-domiciled individuals taxed on only 90% of such pensions. If the whole pension is remitted, tax is charged on the full amount.

INVESTMENT INCOME

34.12 THE REMITTANCE BASIS FOR INVESTMENT INCOME

34.12.1 Remittance basis

Individuals who are not ordinarily resident or not domiciled in the UK can make a claim for their assessable income to be based on the amount of overseas income remitted to the UK (subject to paying the £30,000 special charge if they have been resident in the UK for seven of the preceding nine tax years, see 34.2).

34.12.2 Income arising within the Republic of Ireland
(IT(T&OI)A 2005, s 269)

For years up to 2007–08, where a foreign-domiciled individual had income that arose within the Republic of Ireland, it was always taxed as it arose and not on the remittance basis. It was taxed on the CY basis. This distinction was abolished by FA 2008 so that Irish income can constitute overseas income and be taxed on the remittance basis.

This brings the treatment of a foreign domiciliary's Irish income into line with the treatment of capital gains arising in Ireland, which have always been taxed on a remittance basis.

34.12.3 No assessment can be made if individual ceases to have source of income

For years up to 2007–08, an assessment on the remittance basis could be made for a tax year only if the individual had the source of investment income during that year. This rule was abolished by FA 2008 with effect from 6 April 2008.

34.12.4 Income from savings

Interest income assessed on the remittance basis cannot qualify for the 20% rate that applied to income from savings in 2007–08 (see 8.1.5). Although dividend income remitted prior to 6 April 2008 was only chargeable at the special dividend rate of 10% or 32.5%, subsequent remittances of dividend income will be taxable at the full rate.

34.12.5 Relief for foreign tax
(TA 1988, s 793)

Where overseas income has borne foreign tax, credit may be claimed for this against the UK tax assessed on the same income. Relief for foreign tax paid will, however, be restricted to the UK tax payable on the same income, and only take into account the maximum foreign tax rate permitted under the terms of a double taxation treaty.

34.13 POSITION IF FOREIGN DOMICILIARY ACQUIRES UK DOMICILE

Where an individual is assessable under the remittance basis, but then acquires a UK domicile of choice, the remittance basis ceases to apply for income tax purposes and his overseas income is taxable under the arising basis. No tax liability arises if he then remits money that would formerly have given rise to an income tax liability under the remittance basis. The Special Commissioners have held that this rule does not apply for CGT purposes and gains that are remitted after the time the individual acquired a UK domicile continue to attract a tax liability (see 34.15.5).

34.14 MANAGING THE REMITTANCE BASIS

34.14.1 Maintaining separate bank accounts

Where a foreign-domiciled individual has substantial overseas income, it i
normal for arrangements to be put in place so that remittances to the UK ma
be identified, as far as possible, with capital. The way this is normally deal
with is by arranging for him to have three separate bank accounts, as follows

(1) The first account is capital, ie the cash actually held by him at the tim
he took up residence in the UK. It is normal for further sums to be pai
into this bank account where the cash relates to the sale proceeds o
assets sold at a loss for CGT purposes or the proceeds arise from th
sale of exempt assets. The bank should be instructed that any interest o
this bank account should not be credited to the account, but paid to a
separate income account (see below).
(2) The second account should contain the sale proceeds of assets that giv
rise to capital gains.
(3) The third account should be kept for income, including interest on th
capital account and the capital gains account.

Clearly, in practice, an individual may minimise his liability under th
remittance basis by taking remittances from the capital account in (1).

In some situations, it may be sensible to go one stage further and kee
two income accounts with one account containing income that has no
borne tax at source (eg overseas bank deposit interest) and the other contain
ing income that has borne foreign tax. By organising matters in this way
remittances of income can come out of the account that contains income tha
has suffered foreign tax, and this will further minimise any UK tax liability

There may be CGT savings from having different types of capital gain
account (see 34.15.4).

34.14.2 Use overseas income accounts to fund expenditure outside UK

A foreign-domiciled individual should also organise matters so that all pos
sible expenditure outside the UK is funded out of the income account and
where relevant, out of the income account that represents income that ha
not borne any foreign tax at source.

CAPITAL GAINS TAX

34.15 REMITTANCE BASIS FOR CAPITAL GAINS ON FOREIGN ASSETS

34.15.1 Introduction
(TCGA 1992, ss 12 and 275)

A person of foreign domicile may be subject to CGT if he is either resident or ordinarily resident in the UK. Gains on UK assets are charged in the same way as gains realised by UK-domiciled individuals. Gains realised on assets situated overseas by foreign domiciled remittance basis users are subject to UK CGT only if the proceeds are remitted to the UK (the foreign domiciliary may need to pay the £30,000 special charge, see 34.2).

The following rules determine whether an asset is deemed to be situated in the UK or abroad:

(1) Real estate and rights over such property are situated in the country where the real estate is located.

(2) Tangible movable property and rights over such property are situated in the country where the property is located.

(3) Debts are normally situated in the country where the creditor is resident.

(4) Stocks, shares and securities are generally situated in the country where the company maintains its principal register. Bearer shares and securities issued by a UK incorporated company were brought within the definition of UK situs assets by FA 2005.

(5) Goodwill is treated as situated where the trade or business is carried on.

(6) Patents, trademarks and designs are situated in the country where they are registered.

Tax notes

Gains realised on assets situated overseas are subject to UK CGT only if the proceeds are remitted to the UK.

34.15.2 Losses not allowable
(TCGA 1992, s 16(4))

For 2007–08 and earlier years, where a loss arose on an overseas asset, a person of foreign domicile could not claim a capital loss. In some situations this could give rise to hardship.

Example – Losses not allowable

> *B* had 2007–08 capital gains of £90,000 on UK assets and capital losses of
> £60,000 on foreign assets. Unfortunately, there was no relief for the £60,000
> losses so he would be taxed on gains of £90,000.

This restriction was abolished by FA 2008 with effect from 6 April 2008.

34.15.3 How to take full advantage of remittance basis

In some cases it may be that there is no likelihood of the individual needing
to bring the proceeds of a sale of foreign assets into the UK. In such a situation the payment of CGT is something that he may or may not choose to do
since he can control the amount of his chargeable gains. Where it is going
to be necessary to bring money into the UK at some stage in the future, it is
advisable for him to keep separate bank accounts.

One account should receive the proceeds of assets that have been sold at
a loss when measured for UK CGT purposes. This account may be used to
fund remittances to the UK that are not going to give rise to a CGT liability. A second account should contain the sale proceeds of assets subject to
foreign CGT. Remittances out of this account will give rise to a CGT
assessment, but double tax relief will be due in respect of the foreign CGT
that has been paid. Other sales of assets that have produced a gain should be
kept in a third account, and should be remitted only as a last resort.

34.15.4 Position where foreign domiciliary acquires UK domicile

The law is not clear here. A Special Commissioners' decision indicates
that a CGT liability may arise for a UK-domiciled individual if he remits
sums that would have been subject to CGT had they been remitted before he
acquired a UK domicile of choice. Special Commissioners' decisions do not
constitute binding precedents, but caution is advisable here.

34.16 USE OF OFFSHORE COMPANIES AND TRUSTS

34.16.1 Offshore companies

The anti-avoidance legislation contained in TCGA 1992, s 13 (see 32.13)
may now apply to foreign-domiciled individuals. Provided that the individual is not caught by the IHT 17-year rule (see 29.1), it may well be advisable
for him to create a non-resident trust and transfer shares in an existing offshore investment company to the trustees. This will prevent any tax liability
arising under s 13 on the offshore company disposing of its investments.

It is also dangerous for the individual to occupy a property owned by an
offshore company as the Revenue may seek to assess him under IT(E&P)A

2003 as a 'shadow director'. The Revenue at one stage indicated that it might also raise assessments under transfer-pricing legislation introduced in FA 1998, but relented.

> **Tax notes**
>
> It is dangerous for an individual to occupy a property owned by an offshore company as the Revenue may seek to assess him as a 'shadow director'.

34.16.2 Offshore trusts

The formidable anti-avoidance provisions on offshore trusts covered in Chapter 32 do not have the same effect where a foreign-domiciled individual is concerned.

Offshore or non-resident trusts can still be extremely tax-efficient where foreign-domiciled individuals are concerned. A settlement established by a foreign-domiciled individual after 18 March 1991 cannot be a 'qualifying settlement', which means the provisions of s 86 TCGA 1992, which charge a settlor to tax on gains realised by the trustees of his non-resident settlement, do not apply. The exemption from s 86 applies even where the individual does not have the benefit of the remittance basis because he has chosen not to pay the £30,000 special charge (see 34.2) for that year.

The provisions of TCGA 1992, s 87, which charge UK resident beneficiaries when they receive capital payments are moderated where the beneficiary is a remittance basis user (he may have to pay the £30,000 special charge to qualify for this, see 34.2). Such an individual is taxed on capital payments only if he brings them into the UK (see 32.17.9).

See Figure 34.2 and Figure 34.3.

Professional advice should be taken to avoid potential pitfalls.

INHERITANCE TAX

34.17 UK AND FOREIGN SITUS PROPERTY

IHT may be charged on the death of an individual who is not deemed to be domiciled in the UK, but only to the extent that his estate consists of property situated there. No charge arises on foreign situs property as this is classified as 'excluded property'. Table 34.2 indicates the types of property that are regarded as situated in the UK.

There is a special rule for IHT whereby an individual may be deemed to be domiciled in the UK if he has been resident for 17 of the 20 tax years ending with the current year.

Foreign situs assets settled by a foreign domiciliary remain excluded property even if the individual is subsequently caught by the 17-year rule.

Figure 34.2 – Implications for a UK-resident user of the remittance basis having a shareholding in an offshore company

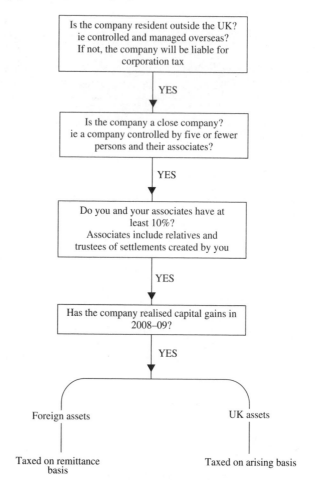

Figure 34.3 – CGT implications for a remittance basis user benefiting under an offshore trust

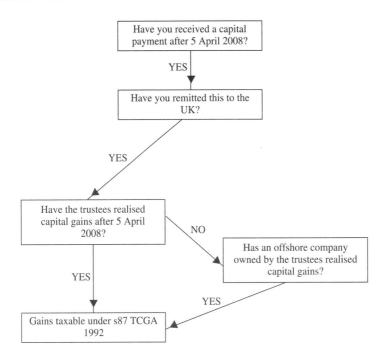

Table 34.2 – Assets chargeable to IHT

	Not chargeable	Chargeable
Channel Island property	✓	
Isle of Man property	✓	
Other foreign property	✓	
UK property		✓
Bank deposits outside the UK	✓	
UK sterling bank deposits		✓
UK foreign currency deposits	chargeable only if the owner is resident in the UK	
Shares in UK companies		✓
UK unit trusts and OEICs	✓	
Registered shares in foreign companies	✓	
Bearer securities	depends where the bearer certificates are held	
Debts owed by a UK resident person		✓ (normally)
Debts owed by foreign resident person	✓	

BEING SUBJECT TO TWO TAX REGIMES

NICHOLAS TARRANT

Increasingly, UK-resident individuals find themselves spending significant amounts of time working in another country and may even become resident in that country as well as in the UK. There are also people who are subject to two tax regimes because their country of origin will not let them go. An example of this is the USA, where a UK resident who is a US citizen or who has a 'green card' has a continuing requirement to file a US tax return and pay US tax.

We focus here on US citizens because this is one of the more extreme examples of the tax complications that arise from having a tax footing in two regimes or 'jurisdictions'.

Another common situation is for a UK resident to have a second home in another country. Some people even have a foot in three jurisdictions, for example someone might be UK resident, of French or Swedish domicile and have a second home in Portugal. If his wife is a US national, they could end up reporting to four different revenue authorities! And it is not uncommon for such people to be beneficiaries of trusts that are administered in yet another country.

This chapter covers the following:

(1) General principles.
(2) Working abroad.
(3) US citizens living in the UK.
(4) UK nationals with second homes overseas.
(5) Exchange of information.

35.1 GENERAL PRINCIPLES

As will become apparent, part of the art of managing all this is to recognise that there are aspects where no general rules apply.

35.1.1 Don't make assumptions

It is important to bear in mind that each country can have a tax system that is logically coherent but does not fit another country's set of tax rules. For example, the UK draws a distinction between employment income and self-employment income. Directors are taxed on the basis that they have employ-ment income. But in some countries the dividing line would be drawn at a different point and directors who were not full-time officers might be treated as independent contractors (ie, as if they were self-employed).

The UK has the concept of domicile (see 34.1). Other countries either do not use this term or, if they do, mean something akin to ordinary residence.

The UK system gives a tax credit for UK dividends but a Jersey or Guernsey resident may have to pay 20% tax on the dividend.

There are also different rules for capital gains. Some countries do not tax capital gains unless they are closely connected with a business (countries as diverse as Belgium, New Zealand and Singapore fall into this category). Other countries are like the UK in having a comprehensive capital gains tax regime but calculate the gain very differently – if you were to take up residence in Australia or Canada the value of an asset at the date of your arrival is treated as your 'cost' for the relevant country's CGT purposes. UK legislation does not normally tax non-residents' capital gains (unless they arise from a permanent establishment in the UK); many other countries charge CGT on gains from real estate realised by non-residents. Australia has reserved the right to assess non-residents on capital gains from sales of shares in Australian companies.

Just to make things even more confusing, countries call completely different taxes by the same name. Everywhere else in the EU, inheritance tax (IHT) means a tax charged on a person who receives an inheritance rather than, as in the UK, a tax based on the circumstances of the person who leaves a legacy to someone else. And in these EU member states, the rate of inheritance tax payable generally depends on how closely you are related to the deceased. Many EU member states also have forced heirship rules, ie legislation that governs the way in which property must pass on death. Wills that do not accord with these rules are effectively over-ridden. Some countries' legal systems do not even contain the concept of a trust, let alone provide for the way in which trusts will be taxed.

Several EU member states also have taxes that are completely different from UK taxes, for example, France and Spain have an annual net wealth tax. Most other EU member states have a much higher rate of stamp duty on property purchases.

UK IHT gives a complete exemption where an individual leaves property to their spouse or civil partner (unless one is domiciled in the UK and the other is domiciled elsewhere when the exemption is limited to £55,000). The USA allows an exemption for bequests to a non-US spouse only if the property is put into a Qualifying Domestic Trust.

The discrepancies between different tax systems are more obvious in relation to personal taxes but they also exist in business taxes. Take VAT – just because the EU has a common VAT Directive this does not mean that each country applies VAT consistently. The UK is unusual in that it zero-rates sales of books. The threshold for registration in the UK is annual turnover of £67,000 but some other member states have no threshold at all.

To sum up, tax is often worked out very differently in other countries. You need to ascertain the principles which apply to you in any other country with which you are connected and (equally important) the way in which its taxes are administered. You will also need expert advice on how the two tax regimes interact, ie which country has primary taxing rights, and the consequences of a given transaction or series of transactions in each country. If you are a beneficiary of a trust in the foreign country, you probably need to find out how this will affect your taxable income in the UK.

35.1.2 One country will not recognise another's tax incentives

Bear in mind that if you become subject to Australian or US tax, you will not be exempt for interest earned within an ISA (see 24.1). In fact, tax exempt investments such as life policies or pension schemes may not attract any special tax treatment, especially if the framework in which such investments are set up is unfamiliar to the overseas system.

A stock option can qualify for a tax exempt status in the USA but this treatment does not govern the UK treatment. The boot can just as easily be on the other foot – an IRS official will not be over-impressed when he hears that a profit has been realised from the exercise of an EMI option by a US national working in the UK.

The IRS may tax a UK-resident US national on the sale of his London home even though it is an exempt asset for UK CGT purposes. The US system does not have a main residence exemption as such, instead it has an exclusion from charge on gains of $250,000 ($500,000 for joint filers), where the property qualifies as the taxpayer's private residence for two of the last five years. With the current trend of house price inflation coupled with a strong pound, it is therefore quite conceivable for a gain to arise on the sale of a UK property by a US taxpayer.

Donations to overseas charities that are not registered in the UK will not normally attract Gift Aid relief. Gifts and legacies to such charities will be potentially subject to IHT. Likewise gifts to non-US charities will not qualify as a deduction on the US form.

> **Tax notes**
>
> With the current trend of house price inflation coupled with a strong pound, it is quite conceivable for a gain to arise for a US taxpayer – and hence a tax liability – on the sale of a UK property.

35.1.3 Business entities may be taxed differently

The UK has a special tax treatment for LLPs but a foreign tax inspector will probably treat an LLP just like any other UK company. The same can apply the other way round. The US system accords a special tax treatment for Limited Liability Corporations so that the members are treated as if they were partners. The UK Revenue will not adopt a similar treatment.

35.1.4 Double taxation agreements

Where the UK tax legislation (our 'domestic legislation') is in conflict with the provisions of a double taxation agreement (DTA), the UK domestic legislation gives way. This is not always the case with other countries!

The UK's network of double taxation agreements mean that an individual who is resident in both countries will be treated as if he were resident only in one country (see 35.3.9). This does not mean that the other country can impose no tax, it normally means that the country in which the individual is treated as resident can impose tax on his worldwide income whilst the other country can tax only income and gains arising in that country.

The UK also has some DTAs on IHT. These can have some unexpected results: for example, an individual who dies domiciled in India is not subject to the UK normal rule, which deems an individual to be UK domiciled for IHT purposes if he has been resident in the UK for 17 of the last 20 years (see 29.1).

The UK has taken some measures to reduce what it would perceive as an abuse of tax treaties. For example, the FA 2005 introduced measures aimed at stopping individuals who became temporarily non-resident for UK tax purposes from avoiding UK CGT by taking advantage of treaty relief with a country that has a low or nil rate of capital gains tax.

35.1.5 The EU dimension

There are very few Articles in the EC Treaty (the most important source of EU law) that cover direct taxes. Each member state has responsibility for setting its own domestic direct tax rules. However, these rules must not contravene fundamental principles of EU law. The EU is meant to be one large single market and any tax provisions that act as a disproportionate obstacle to the movement of workers, capital and the right for companies and individuals to establish themselves in different EU states have been held to contravene these principles.

Over the past ten years the European Court of Justice (ECJ) has heard a number of cases where aggrieved taxpayers have argued that legislation in particular member states does not accord with EU law.

Provisions that treat non-residents less favourably than residents have been struck down by the ECJ as contrary to the EC Treaty.

An ECJ case raised questions over the validity of exit charges imposed by UK domestic tax legislation. In the case of *Hughes du Lasteyrie du Saillant* v *Ministere de L'Ecomomie de Finances et de L' Industrie*, a French individual emigrated to Belgium and was subject to French tax on the unrealised gains on the shares a French company that he took with him. On 11 March

2004, the ECJ stated that such a charge was an impediment to the 'freedom of establishment' enshrined within the EU Treaty. It ruled that France could have asked the Belgian tax authorities for assistance in collecting the tax on any gains once the shares were sold and hence the exit charge was a dispro-portionate measure for collecting tax.

The UK applies an exit charge in a number of situations:

1) When a UK individual emigrates and in the last six years he has received an asset on which the donor's capital gain has been held-over (see 12.6 and 16.4.5).
2) When a UK resident trust becomes non-resident (see 32.15).
3) When a company ceases to be UK resident.

It is arguable that the ECJ decision means that these exit charges are con-trary to EU law. The Dutch and German tax authorities have already announced changes to their own exit charge rules as a result of this case. The UK may have to follow suit.

Individuals who have suffered exit charges should take professional advice on whether tax repayment claims could now be made.

Tax notes

People who have suffered exit charges on leaving a European country should take professional advice on whether tax repayment claims could now be made under EU law.

35.1.6 Enforcement of foreign taxes

Until recently, UK courts have not been prepared to enforce taxes imposed by other countries. The FA 2002 gave other EU countries the right to take out legal proceedings in the UK to collect unpaid taxes. Other countries have a more practical approach in that you may not be permitted to leave the country unless you have a 'tax clearance' certificate.

35.2 WORKING ABROAD

Bear in mind that the UK provides no exemption for UK residents' earnings from overseas employments. Unless you are domiciled abroad and have for-eign emoluments (see 34.2), you will be taxable in full.

We cover the rules on residence and non-residence in Chapter 33.

If you spend sufficient time in another country, you may become a resi-dent of that state as well as a UK resident. See 33.2 regarding provisions in the UK's double tax agreements that provide for a dual resident to be treated as being resident in only one country.

Some EU countries (eg, the Netherlands and Belgium) sometimes exempt tax investment income arising in another country where an individual is newly arrived and is expected to remain there for less than five years.

Take advice if you are being seconded overseas and you have share options that you intend to exercise while you are abroad (see 5.3).

See 13.4 regarding the tax treatment if you retain your UK home but let it while you are working overseas.

35.3 US CITIZENS LIVING IN THE UK

35.3.1 US taxation

A US citizen or green card holder is liable to US taxation regardless of where in the world this income is paid, earned or received, so it can be said that a US citizen continues to be taxed on his passport. Relief is available in respect of foreign-earned income and housing credits. This section deals in brief with these allowances and some of the filing requirements that apply to a US citizen living and working in the UK.

The examples quoted are in respect of the 2007 US calendar year, but the general principles hold true for the current year, 2008.

35.3.2 Filing requirements

The filing date for the US federal return for the calendar year to 31 December 2007 was 15 April 2007. There is an automatic extension until 16 June to the date to file, though not to pay taxes, for a US individual working outside the USA who fulfils either the foreign residence or physical residence test (see 35.3.4).

Table 35.1 shows the requirements for each filing status for the last three years. If your income was below the income limit for your filing status, you are not required to file a US federal income tax return for that year.

Filing status

When filing a US tax return, the taxpayer must first determine their filing status. This will decide the appropriate standard deduction and tax rates to apply. The choices are:

- single;
- head of household;
- married filing jointly;
- married filing separately;
- qualifying widow(er) with dependent child.

Table 35.1 – Requirements in US for each filing status

IF your filing status is:	AND at the end of the year you were	THEN file a return if your gross income for 2005 was at least:	THEN file a return if your gross income for 2006 was at least:	THEN file a return if your gross income for 2007 was at least:
Single	Under 65	$8,200	$8,450	$8,750
	65 or older	$9,450	$9,700	$10,050
Head of household	Under 65	$10,500	$10,850	$11,250
	65 or older	$11,750	$12,100	$12,550
Married filing jointly	Under 65 (both spouses)	$16,400	$16,900	$17,500
	65 or older (one spouse)	$17,400	$17,900	$18,550
	65 or older (both spouses)	$18,400	$18,900	$19,600
Married filing separately	Any age	$3,200	$3,300	$3,400
Qualifying widow(er) with dependent child	Under 65	$13,200	$13,600	$14,100
	65 or older	$14,200	$14,600	$15,150

Notes: Table 37.1 refers to 'gross income', which means all income received in the form of money, goods, property and services that is not exempt from tax. *This includes any income from sources outside the USA, even if you may exclude part or all of it.* Foreign currencies must be converted to US dollars. Do not include social security benefits unless you are married filing a separate return and you lived with your spouse at any time in 2007. If you were born on January 1, 1943 you are considered to be 65 at the end of 2007.

Filing extensions

If a US individual cannot file a return by the normal due date, he can file for an extension using the IRS Form 4868. This form should be filed by the due date of the return together with a 'good faith' estimate of the tax due.

The filing date is automatically extended by two months for US individuals living and working outside the USA or Puerto Rico on the date the return is due, ie for 2007 the normal filing date for those qualifying was 16 June 2008. Individuals relying upon this automatic extension do not need to file the extension but should reference that it applies when filing the Form 1040. For an additional four-month extension to this filing date, Form 4868 should have been filed by 16 June 2008 together with an estimated payment of the tax due.

35.3.3 Foreign earnings exclusion

A US citizen or green card holder living outside the USA may elect to exclude up to $85,700, of foreign earned income. The exclusion can only be claimed if the tax home is outside the USA and the individual meets either the foreign residence or physical presence test. If only part of the qualifying period falls within the tax year, the amount of exclusion available is scaled down proportionally.

35.3.4 The foreign residence and physical presence test

The bona fide foreign residence test applies to US citizens only and requires that a US citizen is physically present in any one or a number of foreign countries for a period that includes a complete US tax year. The physical presence test extends to resident aliens as well as US citizens and to qualify the individual must be physically present in any one or a number of foreign countries for 330 days during any consecutive 12-month period.

35.3.5 Housing costs

A US citizen can elect to exclude from his US taxable income the excess of reasonable unreimbursed housing expenses. The housing exclusion is claimed on Form 2555.

35.3.6 Foreign tax credit

A US citizen can elect to claim tax paid on his non-US earnings as a credit as opposed to a deduction. The credit is limited to the ratio of foreign source taxable income to worldwide taxable income multiplied by the US tax. The foreign tax credit available will also be scaled down if he uses the foreign earned income exclusion.

Excess credits may be carried back one year and carried forward ten years.

Tax notes

The IRS tentatively accepted in an exchange of correspondence with HMRC that the new 'non-dom' charge of £30,000 would be allowed as a foreign tax credit.

5.3.7 Coming to work in the UK

A US individual coming to work in the UK should review his residence position as discussed in Chapter 33. If he is on secondment to the UK for less than two years, all reasonable subsistence accommodation expenses can be paid tax-free. Split contracts for non-UK duties are a way of mitigating UK, but not US, tax. There are also NICs and other exemptions from UK tax included in the US/UK double taxation treaty and the reciprocal social security agreement.

Alternative Minimum Tax (AMT)

To counteract the tax savings that legislative changes have created over the years the US Congress enacted the Alternative Minimum Tax (AMT). In brief, the AMT ensures that where a taxpayer takes legitimate advantage of the tax relief available to him in the tax code, the IRS claws back part of this by use of the AMT calculation. In the past, overseas taxpayers who offset their US income tax with a substantial foreign tax credit often became liable for AMT, and the resulting calculations can be extremely complex. AMT is computed using IRS Form 6251. In effect, individuals with incomes that are offset by large deductions have those deductions and exemptions either reduced or eliminated. The remaining income is taxed at 28%. For years up to 2004, if an individual has foreign tax credits equal to or greater than 90% of the AMT figure, the credit is reduced to 90% of the AMT. This makes all of the income over the limit effectively taxed at a rate of approximately 2.8%. From 2006 this 90% restriction no longer applies. This commonly applies to US taxpayers who have income in excess and are claiming the foreign earnings and housing exclusion.

Exchange rate

The IRS, via its website, publishes an unofficial exchange rate to assist individuals with their tax filing. For 2007, this rate was $2.0018 to £1.

5.3.8 Forms and publications

The following forms and guidance notes can be found on the IRS web pages www.irs.gov or via the US Embassy website for London.

Form 1040 –   US Individual Return and supporting schedules
Form 1116 –   Foreign Tax Credit
Form 4868 –   Application for Automatic Extension of Time to File US Individual Income Tax Return
Form 5471 –   Information Return of US Persons With Respect To Certain Foreign Corporations
Form W7 –   Application for IRS Individual Taxpayer Identification Number by non-US individuals
W8-Ben –   Certificate of foreign status of beneficial owner for United States Tax Withholding.
Publn 54 –   Tax Guide for US Citizens and Resident Aliens Abroad

35.3.9 Double taxation agreement

The new UK/US double taxation treaty was ratified on 21 March 2003. The treaty took effect as follows:

UK and US withholding taxes	Payments made on or after 1 May 2003
Other US taxes	1 January 2004
UK corporation tax	1 April 2003
UK income and capital gains tax	6 April 2003

To coincide with the introduction of the treaty, the Revenue released a special *Tax Bulletin*, which can be found at www.hmrc.gov.uk/ bulletins/tbse6.pdf.

Non-resident alien

A US non-resident alien in the past needed to file a US tax form if he had earnings that were effectively connected with a US business or trade. This requirement is effectively lifted where the amount is less than the personal exemption ($3,400 for 2007).

A non-resident alien is defined in the negative as an individual who is neither a US citizen nor green cardholder and is not resident in the USA.

35.3.10 Death duties

Under normal circumstances, the estate of a US citizen will be subject to US federal estate taxes, based on the value of the worldwide assets held on the date of death. The estate may also be chargeable to US local state estate taxes, depending on the deceased's connections with, and the property held in that state.

However, UK situs assets may also be chargeable to UK IHT, although if the individual concerned had acquired a 'deemed domicile' in the UK at the date of death the potential charge to IHT is extended to the value of his worldwide assets.

For IHT purposes only, a deemed UK domicile can be acquired if the deceased had been resident in the UK for at least 17 out of the last 20 years before his death (see 29.1). This can lead to some complicated situations, but fortunately the double taxation estate treaty between the UK and the USA goes some way towards solving some of the problems. In particular, the treaty restricts the charge on the value of moveable assets to the country of domicile, and where the deceased was domiciled in both countries under domestic rules, a series of tie-breaker clauses set out to determine the country of domicile to be used for the purposes of applying the treaty.

Unfortunately, the treaty does not prevent a double charge on any immoveable real estate, and this will be subject to tax both in the country of domicile, and the country where the property is located. In these circumstances, credit for tax payable in the country where the property is located will be given in the country of domicile. This credit will, however, be limited if the rate of tax is more than in the country of domicile, and the overall rate of tax payable on real property will therefore always be at the highest rate of the two countries.

35.3.11 Potential conflict of laws

Further difficulties can arise where inter spouse transfers take place, due to the slightly different way in which the usual inter spouse exemption is applied in the UK and the USA. In the USA, the exemption is based on citizenship, whereas in the UK it is based on domicile, or deemed domicile.

For example, the estate of a US citizen husband, who has a deemed UK domicile because of his period of UK residence, will qualify for the full IHT inter spouse exemption in the UK if it passes to his UK domiciled British citizen wife. However, because the estate will not be passing to a US citizen spouse, it will not qualify for the surviving spouse marital deduction in the USA.

Similarly, the estate of US citizen husband, who has a deemed UK domicile because of his period of UK residence, which passes to a US citizen wife who does not have a deemed UK domicile will only qualify for a £55,000 IHT inter-spouse exemption, even though the full surviving spouse marital deduction will be available in the USA.

35.3.12 Useful contact details

Internal Revenue Service

The IRS in the UK can be contacted in the UK at:

United States Embassy/IRS
24/31 Grosvenor Square
London W1A 1AE
Tel: + (44) 207 408 8077 (9 am to 12 noon Monday to Friday)
Fax: + (44) 207 495 4224
Web page: www.irs.ustreas.gov

National Association of Enrolled Agents (EAs)

The IRS licenses and regulates tax preparers who have either passed exams or have experience with the IRS as Enrolled Agents (EAs). You can get details of EAs practising in your area from:

The National Association of Enrolled Agents
1120 Connecticut Avenue, NW Suite 460
Washington, DC 20036
Fax: 001 202-822-6270
E-mail: info@naeahq.org
Web page: www.naea.org

35.4 UK NATIONALS WITH SECOND HOMES OVERSEAS

It is becoming more and more common for UK residents to have a second property located outside the UK. It is beyond the scope of this book to cover this subject in depth but the following should be considered by anyone buying such a property.

35.4.1 Income tax on rental income

You may let the property when you are not using it. The tax treatment of rental income is dealt with in Chapter 8. The income will be reported on the foreign pages of your tax return. Take your obligations in the foreign country seriously – it is not worth cutting corners here. For example, a person who lets a property in Eire is required to register as a landlord. If he or she fails to do this, he forfeits the ability to offset mortgage interest against the rental income.

Tax notes

Anyone who lets a property in Eire is required to register as a landlord. Failure to do so leads to the loss of the ability to offset mortgage interest against the rental income.

35.4.2 Capital gains tax

Capital gains tax (CGT) will apply on the disposal of a foreign property in the same way that it would apply on the disposal of an investment property in the UK. In some cases, the foreign property may be treated as your main residence for CGT purposes (see 13.1).

35.4.3 Stamp duty

The purchase of a foreign property will not be subject to UK stamp duty. However, it is likely that the overseas country will impose local stamp duties.

35.4.4 Use of offshore companies to hold the property

There are often local tax reasons why it is considered advantageous for a UK purchaser to form an offshore company to hold the property. However, the UK tax aspects of this need to be very carefully considered. For example, in the past the Revenue might well have argued that the owner's occupation of the property was a benefit in kind, which gave rise to a UK tax liability as employment income (see 4.8). Even where the UK owner was not a director of the offshore company, the Revenue often argued that he was a 'shadow director' who could be treated as if he were a director. The Revenue received some support for this from the Court of Appeal decision in *Dimsey* v *Allen* (2001 STC 1520).

Tax notes

The Finance Act 2008 has addressed the problem of owning a foreign property via a company by removing the potential benefit-in-kind earnings charge. Furthermore, this relaxation is retrospective. However, the let-out applies only where the company was solely designed for the holding, maintenance and letting of a property and the company is owned and funded by an individual. This will not cover all situations (eg where the offshore company is owned by trustees). It also does not address the CGT position (see below).

The capital gains tax position on sale needs to be carefully considered. A sale of the property by an offshore company would generally give rise to a liability for a UK resident owner under s 13 TCGA 1992 (see 32.16).

Another strategy is for the property to be held in a UK LLP because the employment income point will then not arise. If you have to have a local company, investigate whether you can have the company as an undisclosed agent, which holds the property on trust for you and your wife but with this relationship being kept private. An employment income charge cannot arise in relation to property held by a company on trust in this way and arguably it will be more efficient for CGT.

35.4.5 Will you become subject to local taxes?

If you acquire a second home overseas, you should take professional advice as to the circumstances in which you may become liable to taxes in the foreign country (eg net wealth tax).

35.4.6 Inheritance tax

The property will form part of your UK estate, but normally will generally also be subject to a charge in the country in which the property is situated. Your heirs should not suffer a double charge to IHT and foreign death duties as relief should be available, either under a double tax treaty or by virtue of the IHT provisions for unilateral relief. However, you would be well advised to make proper provisions for both UK and foreign taxes by taking professional advice in both jurisdictions and ensuring that your will is recognised in both the UK and the other country.

Figure 35.1 – Flow of tax information

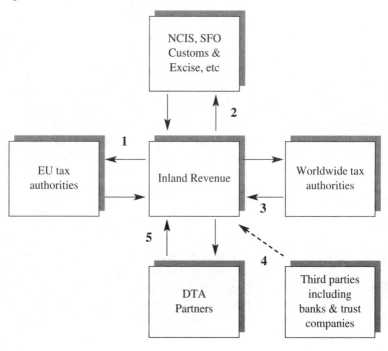

35.5 EXCHANGE OF INFORMATION

Not so long ago, providing information to a taxman was like confessing to a priest. The sinner would clear his conscience, a penance would be demanded but, where possible, the matter would be kept confidential. Now, the Revenue cannot help but share its concerns, not just with other UK Government departments, but also with other countries. It also works the other way round.

Figure 35.1 shows just how freely tax information can flow.

---

(1) All EU member states are bound by the Mutual Assistance Directive, which requires states to exchange information, either on request or spontaneously.

(2) Many parts of UK domestic legislation allow the Revenue to share information with other agencies (and vice versa), in the continuing battle against crime. For example, the National Criminal Intelligence Service (NCIS) receives a huge amount of intelligence on money laundering (including the proceeds of tax evasion) and it will pass this information on to the Revenue.

(3) The Anti Terrorism Crime and Security Act 2001 provides for a worldwide information gateway between tax authorities. The Revenue says it will pass on information spontaneously.

(4) The Revenue has the power to require third parties to provide information regarding specific or unnamed taxpayers. For example, in 2005 the Revenue asked credit card companies to provide details of UK individuals who had been issued with credit cards funded by offshore bank accounts and this request was upheld by the Special Commissioners. More recently, the Revenue has had more requests for information upheld so that UK banks are now being required to divulge information about their customers who have accounts with their overseas branches. In any event, since 1 July 2005 the European Savings Directive has required banks in any EU member state to either provide details of cross-border interest payments made to EU individuals or deduct 'retention tax'.

(5) Double tax agreements between two countries usually include an 'exchange of information' article. Increasingly, in the UK's agreements, this article requires information to be exchanged to assist in preventing tax fraud and avoidance. The Revenue and the US IRS are particularly active in exchanging information.

PART 6

OTHER TAXPAYERS AND TAXES

This part contains the following chapters:

36

SOME SPECIAL TYPES OF TAXPAYER

This chapter gathers together special tax provisions and Revenue practices that are relevant only to specific occupations. We also look at the tax treatment of Crown servants who are working overseas and the way that Irish nationals are taxed if they live in the UK.

The chapter covers:

Specific occupations and trades

(1) Authors.
(2) Barristers and advocates.
(3) Doctors.
(4) Dentists.
(5) Farmers.
(6) Independent financial advisers (IFAs) and insurance agents.
(7) Lloyd's underwriters ('Names').
(8) Ministers of religion.
(9) Members of Parliament.
(10) Sub-postmasters.
(11) University lecturers.
(12) Venture capitalists and participants in MBOs.
(13) Seafarers.
(14) Entertainers.
(15) Business economic notes.

Specific rules for certain types of individuals

(16) Crown servants working overseas.
(17) Irish nationals living in the UK.
(18) The green taxpayer.

SPECIFIC OCCUPATIONS AND TRADES

36.1 AUTHORS

36.1.1 Averaging profits

FA 2001 introduced provisions that enable authors' profits to be averaged. Authors are allowed to average the profits of two consecutive tax years provided the profits of the lower year are less than 75% of those for the higher year. The averaged amount is then taken as the taxable figure for each year.

36.2 BARRISTERS AND ADVOCATES

36.2.1 General information

Detailed notes on the requirements following FA 1998 for barristers to produce accounts on an earnings basis are available from the General Council of the Bar, 3 Bedford Row, London WC1R 4TB. Bear in mind that barristers' accounts may be produced on the cash basis for the first seven years. (See also 15.1.2)

Readers may also refer to a Bar Council publication, *Taxation and Retirement Benefits Handbook*, available at www.barcouncil.org.uk. Among other things, this handbook gives detailed guidance on the amounts to be included in respect of disputed fees.

36.2.2 Accounts on a cash basis

Whereas a person carrying on a profession must normally submit accounts that include work-in-progress (see 15.1.12), barristers going into practice are allowed to remain on the cash basis until the seventh anniversary of the start of their practice. They then have to change to the earnings basis and meet the catching-up charge at that time.

It is possible for a barrister to change to preparing accounts with work-in-progress during the seven-year period, but this decision will depend on a number of factors, including his marginal rate of income tax and the reliability of future profit projections.

36.3 DOCTORS

Medical practices are independent contractors to the NHS, and proprietors (GPs and non-GPs) are treated for tax and national insurance purposes as self-employed.

36.3.1 Practice expenses claims

GPs and non-GP proprietors are entitled to make annual claims for income tax purposes in respect of any expenditure relating to the practice that has been incurred personally and not reimbursed by the practice. The claims should be based on the accounting year-end of the partnership accounts.

These claims usually include the following items:

- motor expenses;
- home and mobile telephone;
- use of home/study allowance;
- employment costs of spouse;
- courses and conferences;
- books and journals;
- computer costs;
- locum insurance premiums;
- professional subscriptions.

Capital allowances can also be claimed on any capital items such as cars, computers, medical equipment and surgery fittings.

36.3.2 NHS superannuation contributions

GPs and non-GP proprietors are responsible for paying both the standard employee contributions at varying rates up to 8?% and also the employer's contributions at 14% on which they receive full tax relief by claiming the contributions paid during a given tax year in their annual personal tax return. GPs were, before 'A' Day, only able to claim tax relief on superannuation contributions by virtue of ESC A9 but could instead choose to forfeit tax relief on their superannuation contributions in favour of claiming tax relief on personal pension contributions. However, the ESC A9 concession was withdrawn from 6 April 2006, and normal limits now apply.

GPs and non-GP proprietors were able to pay additional contributions to buy pension rights for past years (added years) on which tax relief could be claimed. However, this facility was withdrawn from 1 April 2008 though transitional arrangements are available until 31 March 2009 for those expressing an interest before 1 April 2008. All existing arrangements will be honoured and those purchasing added years at 31 March 2009 will continue to do so until normal retirement age.

The new rules concerning the valuation of pensions are likely to affect GPs significantly because the value of a full-time GP's NHS pension may be near the lifetime limit.

The lifetime limit for 2008 is £1.65m and is set to increase each year as follows:

2009 = £1.75m
2010 = £1.80m

In the event that the total pension values from all arrangements (NHSPS and personal pensions) exceed the lifetime limit in force at retirement, a recovery charge of 55% will be applied on the excess. This will apply either at retirement or in the event of death before retirement.

36.3.3 Tax relief on personal loans

Interest paid on personal loans taken out by GPs to introduce capital into the partnership either in respect of partnership capital or to purchase a share in the surgery premises attracts tax relief when claimed on the GP's personal tax return.

36.3.4 Surgery premises

It was previously possible to claim capital allowances on the cost of plant and machinery comprised within the surgery building. However, many of the items previously qualifying for capital allowances will now fall under the integral fixtures list and join the '10% special rate pool'. The proposed integral fixtures listed are:

- lifts, escalators and moving walkways;
- electrical and cold water systems;
- space or water heating systems;
- powered systems of ventilation;
- air cooling or air purification;
- external solar shading;
- active facades;
- thermal insulation.

36.3.5 Capital gains issues

Many GPs dispose of their share of the surgery premises to an incoming partner when reducing their commitment to the practice ahead of retirement before actually leaving. However, one of the conditions of the new entrepreneurs relief is that it is only available when leaving the practice. This will therefore affect many GPs who when reducing their commitment to the practice may now need to retain their full share of the surgery premises until they actually leave the practice to ensure entitlement to entrepreneurs relief.

Tax notes

Where a GP has a surgery attached to his main residence, the surgery is not normally covered by the principal private residence exemption when it is sold.

36.3.6 **Value added tax**

The provision of health services by registered practitioners is generally exempt from VAT. Exemption only applies to practitioners included on a medical register recognised by the Department of Health. For example, clinical psychologists have no such register, so HMRC treats their services as liable to VAT, a position seen by many as restrictive and unfair.

For medical practices, VAT has become more of an issue in recent times, and more practices are becoming VAT registered.

In 2006, the Government decided that the refund of VAT incurred on the purchase of drugs for dispensing should be reclaimed via HMRC rather than the Prescription Pricing Authority (PPA). This resulted in dispensing practices becoming VAT registered from 1 April 2006, and the VAT incurred on pharmaceutical purchases being reclaimed on the VAT return. To add complexity, VAT incurred on drugs that are personally administered by a medical professional still has to be reclaimed through the PPA.

On 1 May 2007, the effects of a European Court of Justice VAT case were introduced in the UK with the result that some income streams that had been treated as VAT exempt became liable to VAT at 17.5%. Services provided by a medical practitioner on behalf of a third party in order for that party to make a decision are now subject to VAT. Common examples are pre-employment medicals, aviation medicals and HGV licences, but there are many types of income that, although relatively small, attract VAT.

As a result of these changes, many practices have to monitor their income in case receipts that are subject to VAT exceed £67,000 in any 12-month rolling period. This would mean a mandatory VAT registration for such a practice. Practices that had already registered in April 2006 should already be accounting for VAT on any income that now falls outside of the health exemption.

In summary, medical practices need to keep aware of their VAT position and responsibilities in what is an increasingly complex area.

36.4 DENTISTS

Relief is due in respect of insurance premiums paid to secure locum cover (see 36.3.1). Self-employed dentists are given tax relief for their contributions to the NHS superannuation scheme contributions (see 36.3.2); and they too could renounce relief for these in relation to 2005–06 and earlier years.

The big issue for dentists is whether to take advantage of a recent change in the rules and transfer their business to a limited company. Doing this could involve a disposal of goodwill and the considerations set out in 16.6 are therefore relevant here.

36.5 FARMERS

There are several tax provisions that are specific to farmers.

36.5.1 All farming a single trade
(ITTOIA 2005, s 9)

The legislation specifically provides that all farming activities carried on by an individual within the UK are treated as a single trade. However, where an individual is a sole trader and also a partner in a farming partnership, the two activities are regarded as separate and distinct trades for tax purposes.

36.5.2 What counts as farming income?

'Farming' is defined within the statute. For tax purposes, it can be said to be the occupation of land in the UK wholly or mainly for the purposes of husbandry. Although there has always been the inclusion of items that should strictly not be taxed as farm income, HMRC has generally not sought to tax small amounts separately. Wayleaves, income from grazing and income from coppice cultivations are examples of types income that would generally be included as farming income.

Where farmers engage in ancillary activities (eg providing B&B accommodation or self-catering facilities for holidaymakers), the Revenue normally regards the resulting profits as forming part of a separate business unless they are relatively modest, in which case they may be included in the profits of the farming business for administrative convenience.

36.5.3 Farmhouse

It was normal practice for many years to claim that one-third of the farmhouse expenses were an allowable expense in computing the farm's trading profits. The Revenue has since moved away from this practice and has emphasised that regard should be had to the actual usage of the farmhouse (see HMRC manual reference BIM55250).

36.5.4 Valuation of stock

As with any business, an annual stock take and valuation exercise is required. If you are involved with the accounts for a farming business then the HMRC booklet BEN 19 sets out the principles to be applied and provides detailed guidance. It is one of a series of Business Economic Notes produced to give Inspectors background on the commercial practice of different industries (see 36.15).

36.5.5 Herd basis
(ITTOIA 2005 Chapter 8)

The effect of a herd basis election is that the herd is treated as a fixed asset. The original cost of the herd and any additions are excluded in arriving at the farm's profit for tax purposes. If the whole herd (or a substantial part of it) is disposed of, the proceeds are not treated as a trading receipt. Advice should be sought from an accountant about the mechanics of the herd basis.

36.5.6 Treatment of set-aside payments

Where farmers receive payments under the Government's set-aside scheme, the way such payments are taxed depends on the use to which the land is put. If the farmer allows the land to become fallow, income received under the set-aside scheme is normally treated as farming income. In contrast, where the land that has been set aside is used for non-agricultural purposes, income received under the set-aside scheme is not regarded as farming income, but rather as UK property income.

36.5.7 Averaging
(ITTOIA 2005 Chapter 16)

It is possible for a farmer to make a claim under which his profits of two consecutive years of assessment are averaged. This election cannot be made where the profits of the lower year exceed three-quarters of the other year's profits.

Where the profits of one year are no more than 70% of the other year's profits, the results of the two years are simply averaged. Where the profits of the lower year are between 71% and 75% of the other year, averaging is done as follows:

Take three times the difference between the two years' profits   A
Deduct 75% of the profits for the higher year $\dfrac{B}{\overline{\overline{C}}}$

Take the resulting figure (C) away from the taxable profits for the higher year and add it to the profits for the lower year

36.5.8 Farming losses

Restrictions under ITA 2007 s 67 (previously TA 1988, s 397) may apply to losses suffered by farmers. The legislation may prevent a farming loss being set against the individual's other income where he has suffered losses for each of the preceding five tax years. This period is extended to 11 years for thoroughbred horse breeders. The restriction shall not be applied where it can be shown that no reasonably competent farmer would have expected to have made a profit until after the period end. It should be noted that the loss position is considered before being adjusted for capital allowances.

When dealing with a farming business being carried through a partnership the losses available to a non-active partner are restricted by ITA 2007 s 26.

36.5.9 CAP single payment scheme

See the special issue of *Tax Bulletin* issued in June 2005.

36.6 INDEPENDENT FINANCIAL ADVISERS (IFAS) AND INSURANCE AGENTS

IFAs and insurance agents will either be employed or self-employed. As such there are no special rules outside of those outlined in Chapters 4 and 5, and it is outside the scope of this book to examine why certain individuals in the insurance business are treated as self-employed while others in apparently similar positions are employed. The following areas have received comment from the Revenue in regard to this anomaly.

36.6.1 Commissions

The time at which commission is brought into account depends on the terms of the contract. If the agent has carried out the majority of his work when the policy is sold, the full amount of the initial commission receivable should be charged in the tax period in which the policy is sold. In such circumstances a specific provision will be allowed to take into account the contingent liability to repay the commission, should the policy lapse. *IRC* v *Gardner Mountain and D'Ambrumeni* 29 TC 69 and *Owen* v *Southern Railway of Peru* 36 TC 602 give some guidance, but specialist advice should be taken.

36.6.2 Agent's book

Agents may have a financial interest in their business, known as a 'book'. The book is a single asset for tax purposes and will give rise to a CGT charge on a material disposal. The Revenue has issued its guidance and views on how such a disposal may be treated; these can be found in the Inspector's manuals at the Revenue website. A test case was recently heard by the Special Commissioners on the purchase of an IFA's practice by an insurance company, with the Revenue unsuccessfully arguing that the amount paid was a post-cessation receipt taxable under Schedule D Case VI (see 6.7). The case is *Rafferty* v *IRC* 2005 Sp Com 484.

36.7 LLOYD'S UNDERWRITERS ('NAMES')

It is beyond the remit of this book to cover the taxation of underwriters in any depth and this may shortly become of historical reference only as Lloyd's has now ceased to accept individuals in an unlimited capacity. The following sections act as a general guide.

36.7.1 General principles

An individual who is a Name at Lloyd's is deemed to carry on a trade. All underwriting profits (including syndicate and other Lloyd's investment income and syndicate capital appreciation) are treated as earned income. Class 2 NICs are payable by all Names with effect from 5 January 1997, and Class 4 NICs from 1997–98, unless they are already paying maximum NICs on other sources of earned income.

Lloyd's profits are assessed for the year of assessment in which the results are declared and not for the year in which they arose (eg 2004 profits are assessed in 2007–08).

36.7.2 Allowable deductions

A deduction may be claimed for the following personal expenses borne by the Name strictly on a calendar year cash basis:

(1) Premiums for insurance policies (known as 'Personal Stop Loss' policies) paid to minimise a Name's exposure to underwriting losses. The premiums are allowable as a deduction for the calendar year in which they are paid. Any recovery from the insurance company will in turn be treated as additional underwriting income for the year of the loss to which the recovery relates.

(2) The annual cost of maintaining a letter of credit or bank guarantee.

(3) Interest on a loan raised to finance an underwriting loss and on money borrowed to fund the Lloyd's deposit and personal reserves (and Lloyd's expenses).

(4) Personal accountancy fees. The Revenue takes the view that only fees relating to the agreement of income tax assessments or to the earning or calculation of profits for the Name are allowable (and, therefore, those relating to the computation of transfers to the special reserve fund or the submission of loss claims are not). The deduction is on a cash basis.

(5) Premiums paid to an estate protection plan (an insurance arrangement intended to facilitate the winding-up of a Name's estate following death).

(6) Subscriptions to the Association of Lloyd's Members and certain expenses of attending meetings.

(7) Purchase of Lloyd's 'blue book' (annual listing of syndicate members), Chatset tables (Lloyd's league tables) and certain other publications.

(8) Subscriptions to Names' Action Groups (eg, Lime Street Action Group).

(9) Central Fund payments, Members Agency fees and commissions and personal run off contract premiums.

(10) Payment for EXEAT policies.

36.7.3 **The special reserve fund**
(FA 1993, Sched 20)

The purpose of the special reserve fund is to enable Names to set aside some of their Lloyd's income, free of tax, as a reserve against future liabilities. Subject to the rules set out below, the amount transferred (if any) is entirely at the Name's discretion.

Transfers to the special reserve fund

The fund operates as follows:

(1) Transfers into and withdrawals from the fund are made gross rather than net of tax at basic rate.

(2) Payments into the fund are deducted as a trading expense and withdrawals are taxed as trading receipts.

(3) A transfer into the fund is permitted of up to 50% of the profits for an underwriting year provided the fund's value at the end of the year does not exceed 50% of the Name's overall premium limit.

(4) Transfers are voluntary and must be made by the earlier of:
  (a) the date in which the balance of the Name's profit is paid to him; or
  (b) 31 October of the year of distribution.

(5) Income and gains on the investments in the fund are exempt from income tax and CGT.

(6) If an underwriting loss is sustained, a withdrawal must be made from the fund of the lower of the loss and the amount of the fund.

(7) If a cash call is made, a withdrawal must be made of the lower of the cash call and the amount of the fund and, if the cash call is greater than the ultimate loss, the excess must be transferred back.

(8) The fund is valued each year at 31 December and if the fund's value exceeds 50% of the premium limit for that year, the excess must be withdrawn.

(9) When a Name ceases to underwrite, the fund's balance is repaid to him or his estate. This repayment may take the form of money or money's worth. Where assets are transferred, the Name (or his personal representatives) acquires the assets at market value for CGT purposes.

(10) The fund managers can claim repayment of tax suffered by deduction and payment of tax credit, because it is a gross fund.

(11) Although funds accumulate tax free in the fund, there is a potential tax liability on withdrawal and this is on the fund's full value.

(12) If a withdrawal is made when a Name ceases to underwrite, the payment is treated as a trading receipt received immediately after the end of the year preceding the one in which his Lloyd's deposit is repaid to him, ie normally a receipt of their final year of underwriting.

36.7.4 Payment of tax

The 2004 Account was declared in the summer of 2007 and will form the basis of assessment for the tax year ended 5 April 2008. Names or their agents will receive form CTA1 and CTA2 to help them complete the relevant pages of the SA form. In recent years the Lloyd's Members' Service Unit has even included numbers on these forms that correspond with the boxes on the SA form.

36.7.5 Treatment of underwriting losses for UK taxation purposes
(TA 1988, ss 380–381, 385; FA 1994, Sched 1(2))

Underwriting losses for an underwriting year arise where a Name's total syndicate net claims and expenses (including reinsurance costs and personal allowable expenses) exceed his total syndicate income from premiums, investments, capital gains and personal Lloyd's income (including stop loss recoveries). A formal claim for the relief of such losses must be made by the Name to the Inspector of Taxes not later than 31 January following the end of the tax year after the year of the loss and would normally be incorporated in the SA tax return. Thus a loss arising from the 2004 underwriting account (ie a loss for the tax year 2007–08) must be claimed by 31 January 2009.

Order of set-off

Such losses are now set off against the claimant Name's income in the following order:

(1) Other income of the same, or the previous, year of assessment, for example the 2004 account, can be set against other income for 2006–07 or 2007–08.
(2) Any balance of loss can only be carried forward under TA 1988, s 385 against future underwriting income and investment income from the Lloyd's deposit, special reserve fund and personal reserves (but not personal capital gains). Consequently, if beneficial, a Name can choose to carry forward all losses against future Lloyd's income.
(3) Underwriting losses can be set off against a Name's capital gains in certain circumstances.

Names have the option, in any of their first four years of underwriting, to carry back any loss under TA 1988, s 381(1) against any income of the three years immediately preceding that in which the loss arose (see 6.9.5).

Terminal loss relief under TA 1988, s 388 can be claimed in the year that a Name ceases underwriting. Normally this is the year in which the final syndicate account closes. Run-off syndicates can therefore delay such a claim, which has led to the use of EXEAT policies to close an account.

36.7.6 **Capital gains tax**

A Name may have several sources of capital gains as a result of his participation in Lloyd's, and it is necessary to distinguish between each type in order to determine the correct tax treatment. Capital gains or losses that arise within each of the syndicates in which a Name participates are not subject to CGT, but are charged or allowed as Lloyd's syndicate income or expenses. They form part of a Name's Lloyd's trading income for the year of account in which the disposal takes place.

Capital gains or losses that arise within the new Lloyd's special reserve fund are free of all taxes while in the fund, but are effectively taxed on withdrawal as trading income.

By contrast, capital gains or losses that arise from the disposals of assets held in a Name's Lloyd's deposit or personal reserves (other than the special reserve fund) are treated as personal gains or losses for the tax year in which the disposal takes place. They are therefore added to any other personal gains or losses arising during the same fiscal year.

Similarly, the sale or transfer of syndicate capacity is treated as a personal disposal and any gain or loss arising must be included with other capital gains or losses for the tax year in which the disposal takes place. Some Names write insurance through Members' Agent Pooling Arrangements (MAPAs), which allows them to buy into a preselected portfolio of syndicates, rather than participate directly in a much smaller number of syndicates. This enables them to spread the risk of their underwriting activities. FA 1999 gave Revenue practice a statutory basis in treating a MAPA as a single asset for CGT purposes. Effectively a CGT liability will only arise when there is a distribution from the MAPA manager of surplus funds (normally at the time of the annual auctions) or if the MAPA Name withdraws from the MAPA.

FA 1999 extended the classes of assets that qualify for roll-over relief to include syndicate capacity whether held directly or through a MAPA.

Capacity is treated as a business asset for taper relief purposes; additional investment in an existing syndicate or MAPA is treated as enhancement expenditure (ie the taper will run from the date of the original purchase, not the date of the additional expenditure).

36.7.7 **Inheritance tax**

The value of a Name's underwriting interests at Lloyd's is potentially chargeable to IHT when transferred on death. The valuation of these interests is normally based on the insolvency statement for the underwriting account ending with the calendar year preceding that in which the death occurs, and includes the value of investments held as funds at Lloyd's, underwriting profits or losses for open and running off accounts, and undistributed profits or losses for closed accounts.

Normally, underwriting interests qualify for business property relief (currently 100%), but the CTO investigates all claims for relief, and may seek to reduce the relief where it believes a Name's combined reserves are excessive in relation to the amount and nature of the underwriting activities.

Tax notes

Normally, underwriting interests qualify for business property relief (currently 100%), but the Revenue investigates all claims for relief.

36.7.8 Other issues

Names should be aware that special rules apply on the cessation or death of a Name who was underwriting prior to the 1972 Account. Details can be obtained on this subject along with any other taxation points from the Lloyd's Taxation Department at the number given below.

FA 2000 also changed the rules in respect of non-UK tax credits and their availability to non-resident Names. These, in general terms, will be available to be claimed as a credit with effect from 6 April 1999 (in the past they had only been allowed as a deduction to those Names). The Revenue also announced that its treatment of EU/EEA Names had been incorrect and these Names were invited to make claims for earlier years for non-UK tax credits in respect of their Lloyd's UK income, which had only been allowed as a deduction.

Lloyd's no longer accepts new Names underwriting with an unlimited liability and FA 2004 eased the transition from limited to unlimited liability underwriting by allowing the losses of the individual to be carried over to a company in which he is the majority shareholder or into a Scottish Limited Partnership where he is the sole member in the partnership carrying on an underwriting business. In addition, Names will be able to defer gains on the transfer of their underwriting activities into a company taking over the underwriting business.

36.8 MINISTERS OF RELIGION

36.8.1 Ministers treated as office holders

For tax purposes, a minister of religion is generally treated as an employed person unless his remuneration does not consist wholly or mainly of stipend or salary. However, different rules can apply for NIC purposes, eg Elim Pentecostal ministers and Roman Catholic priests can be regarded as self-employed because of the absence to a right to remuneration.

36.8.2 No tax on rent-free accommodation

A clergyman is not normally liable for tax in respect of his occupation of a vicarage or other living accommodation provided by the church, charity or ecclesiastical body for carrying out his duties (IT(E&P)A 2003, s 99).

ESC A61 also provides exemption for payment or reimbursement of heating, lighting, cleaning and gardening expenses. This does not apply if the clergyman is a P11D employee because his earnings exceed £8,500 pa (see 4.4.1).

Where the minister's earnings exceed £8,500, any tax charge on such 'service benefits' in respect of his vicarage or manse is limited to 10% of the net emoluments (after deducting expenses).

If the clergyman pays his wife wages for cleaning the part of the house used for official duties, this may be treated as a tax deductible expense for him.

36.8.3 Allowable expenses

The following expenses commonly incurred by clergy are allowable deductions under TA 1988, s 198:

- Stationery, postage and use of telephone for clerical duties;
- Secretarial costs (including wages paid to the clergyman's wife for providing such assistance provided this is separate and distinct from work she performs as an active member of the church);
- Travelling in the course of his duties (including the 12p per mile for 'business use' of a bicycle);
- Cost of repair or replacement of robes;
- Communion expenses;
- Cost of providing a locum;
- Reasonable entertainment on official functions.

White v *Higgingbottom* [1983] STC 143 decided that a clergyman was not entitled to allowances for an overhead projector and screen that he paid for personally.

36.8.4 Capital gains tax

Where a clergyman buys a property, he can often nominate it as his main residence for CGT purposes on the grounds that his work requires him to live elsewhere (see 13.3).

For further background information, contact the Churches Main Committee, Fielden House, Little College Street, London SW1P 3JZ for a circular, *The Taxation of Ministers of Religion*.

36.9 MEMBERS OF PARLIAMENT

As one would expect, there are special rules that apply to MPs, Members of the Scottish Parliament and Members of the Welsh Assembly. MPs are dealt with by a central Revenue office in Cardiff. They complete a supplementary form SA101 (MP), which is available on the Revenue's website, together with help notes. The Revenue also publishes a leaflet, *MPs, Ministers and Tax*.

36.9.1 Additional costs allowance

MPs receive a tax-free additional costs allowance that covers the additional costs of living away from home while engaged in Parliamentary duties either in London or in their constituency (IT(E&P)A 2003, s 292). This means an MP can effectively receive tax relief on interest on a mortgage to buy a second home in London, as the allowance is calculated to allow for the payment of either rent or mortgage interest in the case of a property owned by him.

> **Tax notes**
>
> The tax-free additional costs allowance means an MP can effectively receive tax relief on interest on a mortgage to buy a second home in London.

36.9.2 Travel

MPs are issued with rail/air warrants. No taxable benefit arises where these are used to travel from Westminster to a home in the constituency. Where the MP's home is not in the constituency, the extent to which a benefit is taxable is as follows:

- Where his home is not more than 20 miles from the constituency, no amount is taxable.
- Where the home is within 20 miles of Westminster, no amount is taxable.
- In other cases, the cost of the rail/air warrant is taxable.

Where a warrant is used for travel to/from the constituency via home, only the excess cost over a direct journey from Westminster to the constituency is taxed. This treatment depends on the MP staying at home for only one night unless the journey spans a weekend.

The position of car allowances is complex because the cash mileage reimbursement that the MP receives from the Fees Office includes the cost of travel between his home and Westminster, or between home and constituency. All this ranks for tax purposes as private travel. In strictness, the car mileage allowance paid by the Fees Office is assessable as an emolument and an expenses claim should be made. However, for practical purposes the allowance is generally not taxed.

Incidental travel costs in London, for example taxi fares between London rail and air terminals and Westminster, and in visiting ministers on parliamentary business, are allowable expenses. Where an MP uses a bicycle for Parliamentary business, the Fees Office pays an allowance of only 7p per mile. The MP can claim tax relief for the difference between this and the authorised mileage rate (see 4.4.9) of 20p per mile.

Exemption is also available for travel and subsistence expenses incurred in travelling abroad to visit all EU institutions and agencies, the parliament of a country that has applied to join the EU and a parliament of an EFTA country.

36.9.3 Office costs allowance (OCA)

MPs receive an allowance for office, secretarial and research expenses, currently around £50,000 pa. This is taxable, but a deduction is made for the actual costs of any secretarial and clerical assistance, general office expenses and research assistance undertaken in the proper performance of the MP's parliamentary duties. Such expenses include the normal costs of office accommodation such as rent, heat and light, including the use of part of the home as an office and the costs of repairs and renewals of office equipment. Telephone, stationery and postage costs, if not provided free, are also allowable. An MP's secretary is paid direct by the Fees Office rather than the MP receiving the salary as part of a claim for office expenses; PAYE is operated by the Fees Office.

36.9.4 Incidental expenses

An MP can claim a deduction for the following:

- Costs of hiring a room to meet constituents;
- Costs of expenses incurred in participation in delegations organised by all-party Parliamentary organisations such as the Parliamentary Group for European Unity;
- Payments to a local agent or party organisation for assistance in constituency work;
- Extra cost of meals taken while travelling on parliamentary business.

36.9.5 Pensions and retirement lump sums

Parliamentary pensions accrue at the rate of 1/50 final remuneration for every year of service. MPs can buy extra year's pension by making regular contributions or by paying a lump sum within 12 months of election to the House of Commons.

Ministers are able to pay contributions into a personal pension scheme if their ministerial salary is not pensionable under the Parliamentary Pension Scheme. Terminal grants to a person ceasing to be an MP are regarded as tax free up to £30,000.

36.10 SUB-POSTMASTERS

Salaries paid by Post Office Counters Limited to sub-postmasters who carry on a retail trade from the same premises are in practice treated as part of their self-employment income.

Where a company operates a sub-post office from its shop, with its directors acting as nominee sub-postmasters, a salary paid to the individual can be treated as part of the company's income provided that the individual is required to pay it over to the company. However, this is not altogether satisfactory from an NIC point of view as Post Office Counters Limited will normally have deducted employees' NIC contributions.

36.11 UNIVERSITY LECTURERS

36.11.1 Allowable deductions

A lecturer may claim a deduction for annual subscriptions to a learned society such as the Royal Society of Chemistry. Annual subscriptions to bodies such as the Association of Teachers and Lecturers and the National Association of Teachers in Further and Higher Education are also allowable.

The cost of academic dress is an allowable deduction. Where a lecturer is required to demonstrate in a laboratory or do other laboratory based work, the cost of a lab coat, goggles and other protective clothing can also be claimed.

36.11.2 Study allowance

Where a lecturer is required to undertake research work, he may be able to secure a study allowance reflecting extra expenditure on light and heat and the cost of office equipment such as a photocopier or fax machine. The Revenue accepts that giving a deduction for a study does not result in any restriction of the CGT main residence exemption.

36.11.3 Shares in university spin-outs

Some university lecturers may be offered the opportunity to acquire shares in companies that exploit their research (university spin-outs). The acquisition of such shares could give rise to tax charges on employment income under the FA 2003 legislation (see 5.7). The FA 2005 contains special relieving provisions that apply where the individual acquires his shares within a period of six months before and after the date of an agreement under which the university or other research institution transfers intellectual property to the company. In such a situation, market value is calculated without taking into account value injected into the company by the transfer of the intellectual property. This will therefore take most of the sting out of the legislation originally introduced by Schedule 22 FA 2003 that would otherwise impose an income tax charge on the acquisition of shares at an undervalue or on the release of restrictions.

The FA 2005 relieving provisions apply where the individual acquires shares or the intellectual property is transferred after 1 December 2004.

36.12 VENTURE CAPITALISTS AND PARTICIPANTS IN MBOs

A concern for managers involved in MBOs (management buy-outs) is whether they may be subject to an income tax charge on their shares. Similarly, individuals who work for venture capital firms are able to participate in investments, either alongside the fund through 'co-investment schemes' or through a shareholding in the venture capital company, or by being a partner in a limited partnership.

The Revenue has published a memorandum setting out a 'safe harbour' whereby such investments will be subject only to capital gains tax rather than income tax if certain conditions are satisfied. See *The memorandum of understanding between the Revenue and the BVCA* attached to the Revenue's press release of 22 July 2003.

36.13 SEAFARERS

A 100% deduction can be claimed by seafarers where they spend a continuous period of 365 days working outside the UK and they are resident and ordinarily resident in the UK during that period. Journeys starting or ending outside the UK are treated as periods working outside the UK. A day of absence is a day when the seafarer is outside the UK at midnight. Shorter periods can be aggregated to make up a 365-day period provided that UK days in between do not make up more than one half of the combined period.

Because of the loose definition of 'seafarer', it was possible for employees who worked on particular types of oil rigs to qualify. However, following a decision by the Court of Appeal, with effect from 17 March 1998, employees who work on jack-up rigs or similar structures in the offshore oil and gas industry are not regarded as seafarers and are therefore not entitled to the 100% deduction.

Until 1998, a similar 100% deduction was available generally for individuals who worked outside the UK.

36.14 ENTERTAINERS

Individuals who are employed as entertainers are entitled to claim a deduction for fees paid to agents of up to 17.5% of their earnings (s 722 IT(E&P)A 2003).

The question is 'who is an entertainer?' In June 2006, the Special Commissioners upheld a claim by chat show hosts Richard Madeley and Judy Finnigan that they fell into this category.

36.15 BUSINESS ECONOMIC NOTES

Even if there is no special legislation that governs the way in which your particular occupation is taxed, you may well find it interesting to see the background information the Revenue provides to its staff.

The Revenue publishes a series of Business Economic Notes that are primarily intended to aid Inspectors in the examination of accounts. The notes, listed in Table 36.1, are available for purchase from the Revenue, Room 28 New Wing, Somerset House, Strand, London, WC2R 1LB, or can be viewed online at www.hmrc.gov.uk/bens.

Tax notes

The Revenue publishes Business Economic Notes to aid Inspectors in the examination of accounts. These can be seen on the Revenue's website.

Table 36.1 – Business Economic Notes

	Subject	*Date of issue*
1	Travel Agents	February 1987
2	Road Haulage	February 1987
3	Lodging Industry	February 1987
4	Hairdressers	February 1987
5	Waste Materials Reclamation and Disposal	March 1987
6	Funeral Directors	May 1987
7	Dentists	July 1987
8	Florists	September 1987
9	Licensed Victuallers	May 1988
10	Jewellery Trade	1989
11	Electrical Retailers	1989
12	Antique and Fine Art Dealers	March 1990
13	Fish and Chip Shops	October 1990
14	The Pet Industry	October 1990
15	Veterinary Surgeons	October 1990
16	Catering – General	October 1990
17	Catering – Restaurants	October 1990
18	Catering – Fast Foods, Cafes and Snack Bars	October 1990
19	Farming – Stock Valuation for Income Tax Purposes	April 1993
20	Insurance Brokers & Agents	August 1994
21	Residential Rest & Nursing Homes	November 1994
22	Dispensing Chemists	May 1995
23	Driving Instructors	June 1997
24	Independent Fishmongers	June 1997
25	Taxicabs and Private Hire Vehicles	July 1997
26	Confectioners, Tobacconists and Newsagents	November 1997

HMRC is phasing out the business economic notes and replacing them with TIPs (Tactical and Information Packages). The current TIPs were online at www.hmrc.gov.uk/tips. However, following a review of its publication policy, a decision has been made to withdraw the current TIPs from the HMRC website. However, the Business Economic Notes are still online.

Subject	Date of issue
Estate Agents	December 2006
Mortgage Brokers	September 2006
Franchises	September 2006
Confectioners, Tobacconists and Newsagents	January 2007
Waste Disposal & Landfill Sites	September 2006

SPECIFIC RULES FOR CERTAIN TYPES OF INDIVIDUALS

36.16 CROWN SERVANTS WORKING OVERSEAS

A Crown servant is an individual who is an employee of the Crown whose remuneration is payable out of UK or Northern Ireland public revenue (ie a civil servant or member of HM Forces). The remuneration is treated as arising from work performed in the UK even though all work may actually be carried out overseas.

Crown servants may receive foreign service allowances, which are intended to represent compensation for the extra cost of having to live outside the UK in order to perform the duties of the employment. These foreign service allowances are specifically exempted from UK tax. In practice, these foreign service allowances may include allowances for boarding school education for the Crown servant's children.

The value of any living accommodation occupied abroad is not subject to income tax as employment income. This is because Crown servants are regarded as representative occupiers required to live in the accommodation in order to do their job properly.

Most double taxation agreements provide an exemption from foreign tax for Crown servants living and working in the overseas country concerned.

Crown servants are allowed to take out certain tax privileged investments such as ISAs and stakeholder pension plans even though they are not resident in the UK.

A Crown servant may also be eligible to claim tax credits.

> **Tax notes**
>
> The value of any living accommodation occupied by Crown servants abroad is not subject to income tax as employment income.

36.17 IRISH NATIONALS LIVING IN THE UK

An Irish national who resides in the UK is normally subject to UK tax on overseas investment income only to the extent that he remits such income to the UK (see 34.10). Moreover, this treatment now applies to investment income received from Irish sources (the position was different for 2007–08 and earlier years).

Similarly, an Irish national who is employed by a non-resident employer, and who carries out all the duties overseas, will normally be taxed on a remittance basis. From 2008–09 this also applies to employments with Irish resident employers.

36.18 THE GREEN TAXPAYER

It would be remiss of us in a chapter dedicated to special types of taxpayers not to make reference to tax incentives that are available to individuals and businesses that are concerned with environmental issues. Of course, like any good deed, the reward is in the act and should not be reward driven.

36.18.1 Individuals

A review of reliefs and tax incentives for individuals highlights the following areas:

- cars;
- transport;
- charitable giving.

Cars

As you see from section 4.5 onwards, since 2002–03 the scale benefit that applies to cars is geared not only to the value of the car made available but also to the carbon dioxide emission. A taxpayer looking to benefit the environment by driving a car with lower CO_2 emissions will also benefit with a reduced tax charge on their company car. A reduced scale rate (9%) also applies to drivers of company provided electric cars.

On your bike!

Employees can claim a tax free allowance of 20p per mile for cycled business travel. In addition no charge will arise in respect of bikes and safety equipment for employees to cycle to work, along with a number of other tax free benefits for cyclists highlighted at 4.4.8, including the provision of shower facilities at work.

Transport

There is no taxable benefit in respect of the provision of work buses with a seating capacity of 12 or more and also on subsidies to public bus services providing the employee pays the same fare as other commuters.

Congestion charge

For those people living around a congestion area, a raft of incentives exists with the aim of exempting those from the charge who make use of 'green' transport. For more details of this in the London area see www.cclondon.com.

36.18.2 Charitable giving

The other form of relief available to an individual with environmental concerns is via the Gift Aid scheme for charitable giving (see 10.9) with many environmental groups having charitable status for UK tax purposes.

36.18.3 The green business

The entrepreneur looking to improve the environment and their business can benefit from three types of tax relief:

- VAT;
- capital allowances;
- SDLT.

VAT

There is a lower rate of 5% for installation of energy saving materials.

There is also a proposal to change the basis of the fuel scale charge from engine size to CO_2 emissions, which is waiting for derogation from the EC Commission.

Capital Allowances

- *Energy saving* – Expenditure on designated energy-saving technologies and products qualifies for 100% first-year allowances. The qualifying items are set out in a list issued by the DETR: see www.eca.gov.uk/etl/
- *Expenditure on water technologies* – All businesses can claim 100% first-year allowances for expenditure on or after 1 April 2003 on designated plant and machinery to reduce water use and improve water quality. See 17.2.12 and www.eca-water.gov.uk/ for details
- *100 per cent first-year allowances for cars with low CO_2 emissions* – Finally, there are 100% first-year allowances for cars with low carbon dioxide emissions and natural gas and hydrogen refuelling equipment: for details, go to www.hmrc.gov.uk/capital_allowances/cars

SDLT

Purchasers of new, zero carbon homes receive a stamp duty tax break from 1 October 2007 as follows:

1) Purchase price of £500,000 or less – no SDLT;
2) Purchase price above £500,000 – SDLT liability reduced by £15,000.

37

CHARITIES AND NOT FOR PROFIT ORGANISATIONS

SARAH CAMPBELL

Most of this book is concerned with paying tax. However, many organisations enjoy exemptions, and their main involvement with the Revenue is in reclaiming tax.

This chapter considers the following:

(1) Charities.
(2) Community amateur sports clubs.
(3) Mutual associations.
(4) Holiday clubs and thrift funds.
(5) Investment clubs.

37.1 CHARITIES

Charities are dealt with by:

Inland Revenue (Charities)
St John's House
Merton Road
Bootle
Merseyside L69 9BB
Tel: 08453 02 02 03

In Scotland, the address is:

Inland Revenue (Charities)
Meldrum House
15 Drumsheugh Gardens
Edinburgh EH3 7UL
Tel: 08453 02 02 03.

37.1.1 A charity must exist exclusively for charitable purposes

A charity is eligible for tax exemption only if all its income and capital may only be used for charitable purposes.

> **Tax notes**
>
> Some charities operating in Scotland have recently been told that they must amend their governing document (trust deed or articles of association) to ensure that everything they do conforms with Scottish law on charities as well as English law.

37.1.2 Exemption from income tax and CGT

Charities are exempt from income tax on all income other than trading income (see 37.1.5), provided the income is applied for charitable purposes. Similarly, charities are exempt from CGT.

The exemption can be restricted in a year in which the charity accumulates income of more than £10,000 that is not reasonably required for application for charitable purposes in the foreseeable future or if it incurs non-qualifying expenditure. In practice, the rule on non-qualifying expenditure is most likely to arise where a private charity makes loans to a company connected with the settlor, especially if the loans are not on proper commercial terms. Professional advice should be obtained in such circumstances.

The CGT exemption does not cover capital gains realised by personal representatives where the charity is a residuary legatee. In such cases, it may be more tax efficient for the executors to vest the assets in the charity before they are sold to a third party.

37.1.3 Tax credits on dividends

Tax credits on UK dividends are not reclaimable.

37.1.4 Life policies held by charitable trusts

Provisions which took effect from 9 April 2003 ensure that trustees of charitable trusts do not have to pay any tax on most UK policies and no more than basic rate tax on gains from foreign policies.

37.1.5 Trading profits

Trading income is exempt only if the trade is exercised in the course of carrying out a primary purpose of the charity or if the work is carried out mainly by its beneficiaries. This includes the sale of donated goods. A problem area in the past has been the tax treatment of profits from other types of trading.

Small fundraising events

ESC C4 has applied for many years and exempted profits from most fundraising activities. The concession used to state:

Bazaars, jumble sales, gymkhanas, carnivals, firework displays and similar activities arranged by voluntary organisations or charities for the purpose of raising funds for charity may fall within the definition of 'trade' in ICTA 1988, s 832, with the result that any profits will be liable to corporation tax. Tax is not, however, charged on such profits provided all the following conditions are satisfied:

(1)　The organisation or charity is not regularly carrying on these trading activities;
(2)　The trading is not in competition with other traders;
(3)　The activities are supported substantially because the public are aware that any profits will be devoted to charity; and
(4)　The profits are transferred to charities or otherwise applied for charitable purposes.

Profits from lotteries are exempt provided the profits are applied solely for charitable purposes and the lottery is promoted and conducted in accordance with the Lotteries and Amusements Act 1976.

(Source: HMRC)

However, it was argued that the terms of the concession were too restrictive and, since 1 April 2000, a wider exemption has applied for trading profits from fundraising events provided:

(1)　the public are aware that the purpose of the event is to raise funds for charity; and
(2)　the event does not last for more than four days; and
(3)　the charity holds no more than 15 events of a similar type in the same location each year. Small-scale events with gross takings of up to £1,000 each do not count towards this total provided they are no more frequent than weekly.

Exemption for charity's trading profits

There is also a specific tax exemption for the profits of certain small trading and other fundraising activities carried on by a charity that are not otherwise already exempt from tax. This came into effect from 1 April 2000. It means that, for tax purposes, a charity no longer has to set up a trading company to carry on these activities.

The Charity Commission has confirmed that if a charity is governed by one of the Commission's model governing documents – which contain prohibitions on 'any substantial permanent trading activity' – it may lawfully carry on the activities falling within the new tax exemption without having to set up a trading company. If the charity has some other governing document, it should check that it permits it to carry on a fundraising trade before doing so.

The new exemption will apply to the profits of all trading activities, and most other incidental fundraising activities, that are not already exempt from tax, provided:

(1) the total turnover from all of the activities does not exceed the annual turnover limit, or

(2) if the total turnover exceeds the annual turnover limit, the charity had a reasonable expectation that it would not do so, and

(3) the profits are used solely for the purposes of the charity.

The annual turnover limit is:

(1) £5,000, or

(2) if the turnover is greater than £5,000, 25% of the charity's 'incoming resources', subject to an overall limit of £50,000.

For this purpose, 'incoming resources' has a very wide meaning. It means the total receipts of the charity for the year from all sources (grants, donations, investment income, etc).

Example – Turnover limits

A charity sells Christmas cards to raise funds and the sales in the year total £4,000. Assuming this is the only taxable fundraising activity, any profits will be exempt from tax because the turnover does not exceed £5,000.

However, suppose the sales in the year total £40,000 instead of £4,000. Any profits will still be exempt from tax provided the charity's incoming resources are at least £160,000, because the turnover does not exceed either:

(1) 25% of the incoming resources (£160,000 × 25% = £40,000),

(2) or the overall limit of £50,000.

Even if, in the example above, the charity's incoming resources are below £160,000, so that the turnover exceeds the annual turnover limit, the profits will still be exempt from tax if it had a reasonable expectation at the start of the year that the turnover would not exceed the limit. Thus, suppose the sales in the year total £60,000. This exceeds the overall annual turnover limit of £50,000. Any profits will still be exempt from tax if there was a reasonable expectation at the start of the year that the turnover would not exceed the limit.

The reasonable expectation test

If the total turnover of the taxable fundraising activities for any tax year exceeds the annual turnover limit, any profits will still be exempt from tax if it can be shown that, at the start of the tax year, it was reasonable to expect that the turnover would not exceed the limit. This might be because:

(1) the turnover was expected to be lower, or

(2) the charity's incoming resources proved to be lower than expected.

The Revenue will consider any evidence the charity may have to satisfy this test. For example, if a charity has carried on an activity for a number of years, it might be able to show that the turnover increased unexpectedly compared with earlier years. If it started carrying on the fundraising activity in the year, it might be able to show that the turnover was higher than forecast when it was decided to start the activity. Also, it might be able to show that its incoming resources were lower than forecast, perhaps because a grant it was expecting to receive was not paid in the year. Evidence might include minutes of meetings at which these matters were discussed, copies of cash flow forecasts and business plans, and copies of previous years' accounts.

Trading profits not covered by the exemption

If trading profits are not likely to be covered by the above exemption, consideration should be given to the establishment of a company that would carry on the trading activities and then pay away the profits to the charity by a Gift Aid donation. Professional advice should be taken on this.

Charities and membership subscriptions

To recover VAT on its expenditure (inputs), a charity must first split its activities between business and non-business activities. Input VAT can never be recovered on non-business activities. The charity must consider at what rate VAT is charged on its business activities (standard, reduced or zero) or whether they are exempt from VAT. Input VAT cannot be recovered on expenditure that relates wholly to exempt activities. Where expenditure relates to both exempt and non-exempt business activities, it will be partially recoverable.

Customs & Excise has given examples of types of activities that are always business activities (eg admission to premises for a charge) and activities that are always non-business (eg donations, legacies or other voluntary contributions from the public). However, most activities can be either business or non-business, depending on the exact circumstances, and some may even be partly business and partly non-business.

Frequently, a membership subscription entitles the charity supporter to free magazines and newsletters or free advice. In the past, charities have been able to allocate the subscription between the various benefits and charge VAT accordingly. However, at recent tribunal cases, it was decided that the membership subscription is for the provision of one service and not for a number of individual services. In such cases the whole of the subscription is liable to standard rate VAT. This has led to unexpected VAT liabilities.

Customs has proposed an extra statutory concession, allowing charities to continue to treat their subscriptions as a mixture of supplies, unless this is done for tax avoidance purposes. This may lead to a more restrictive regime for VAT recoveries. If the main benefit is zero rated, it may also be possible to reclaim VAT for the past three years.

Any special accounting scheme must, of course, be agreed with Customs in advance.

Revenue leaflet

The Revenue and Customs have issued a leaflet jointly (CWL 4), *Fundraising events: Exemption for charities and other qualifying bodies.*

37.1.6 Gift Aid donations by companies

Companies (including those owned by a charity and unincorporated associations, such as clubs and societies) do not:

(1) deduct tax from their Gift Aid donations; or
(2) have to give charities a Gift Aid declaration.

37.1.7 Gift Aid donations by individuals

Individuals still have to deduct basic rate tax from their Gift Aid donations and provide a Gift Aid declaration. The charity can reclaim this, together with a supplement for the tax years 2008–09 to 2010–11of 2% of the grossed-up Gift Aid donation.

The guidance below regarding tax reclaims and Gift Aid declarations applies only to donations by individuals.

37.1.8 Gift Aid declarations

Before a charity can reclaim tax on a donation by an individual, it must have received a Gift Aid declaration from the donor containing certain information and confirming that the donation is to be treated as a Gift Aid donation.

Donors can give a declaration:

(1) in advance of, at the time of or at any time after their donation (subject to the normal time limit within which a charity can reclaim tax – normally around six years);
(2) to cover a single donation or any number of donations;
(3) in writing (eg by post, by fax or through a website) or orally (eg over the telephone).

The amount of information required on a Gift Aid declaration has been kept to the minimum consistent with proper administration of the tax relief and the need for the charity to be able to show an audit trail. A charity can design its own Gift Aid declaration, but must ensure that it satisfies all the requirements set out below and any other legal requirements under the Data Protection Act, the Charities Act, etc. The Revenue's approval is not needed for an own-design declaration, but Inland Revenue (Charities) (IR(C)) will be happy to approve it if required.

What a Gift Aid declaration must contain

All Gift Aid declarations must contain:

- the donor's name;
- the donor's address;
- the charity's name;
- a description of the donations to which the declaration relates;
- a declaration that the donations are to be treated as Gift Aid donations; and, except in the case of a declaration given orally:
- a note explaining the requirement that the donor must pay an amount of income tax or CGT equal to the tax deducted from his donations;
- the date of the declaration.

There is no requirement for a declaration to contain the donor's signature.

In the case of a written declaration, the charity may pre-print the information (eg the charity's name) on the declaration form. In the case of an oral declaration, the information may be recited to the donor for him to confirm it, rather than asking the donor to recite the information.

Written records of oral declarations

If a charity receives an oral declaration it must send the donor a written record of the declaration showing:

(1) all the details provided by the donor in his oral declaration;
(2) a note explaining the requirement that the donor must pay an amount of income tax or CGT equal to the tax deducted from his donations;
(3) a note explaining the donor's entitlement to cancel the declaration retrospectively;
(4) the date on which the donor gave the declaration; and
(5) the date on which the written record was sent to the donor.

An oral declaration will not be effective unless and until the donor is sent the written record. This means that a charity cannot reclaim tax in respect of a donation covered by an oral declaration until it has sent the written record. Once it has sent the written record, it can reclaim tax in respect of any donations covered by the declaration, even if it received them before sending the written record. (The Revenue reconfirmed this in January 2005 in relation to the Tsunami appeals.)

> **Tax notes**
>
> A charity cannot reclaim tax in respect of a donation covered by an oral declaration until it has sent the written record.

Cancellation of declarations

Donors are entitled to cancel their declaration at any time. They may do so by notifying the charity in any form of communication. The charity should keep a record of the cancellation, including the date of the donor's notification. Cancellation has effect only in relation to donations received by the charity on or after:

(1) the date on which the donor notifies the cancellation, or
(2) such later date as the donor may specify.

The charity must not reclaim tax in respect of such donations. Any donations received up to the date of the donor's notification still qualify as Gift Aid donations.

If a donor who has given an oral declaration cancels it within 30 days of being sent the written record, the cancellation will have retrospective effect, so that it will be as if the declaration had never been made. The charity does not have to wait for the 30-day period to expire before reclaiming tax in respect of donations received. But if it reclaims tax and the donor subsequently cancels his declaration within the 30-day period, it must pay the tax back to the Revenue. It may be possible for the charity to pay the tax back by deducting it from its next tax reclaim and it should contact IR(C) on this.

37.1.9 Gift Aid donations by partnerships

In England, Wales and Northern Ireland a partnership does not have legal personality, so a donation by a partnership is treated as made by the underlying partners. One partner may make a Gift Aid declaration on behalf of all the partners, provided he has the power to do so under the terms of the partnership agreement, in which case it will be sufficient for the declaration to show the name and address of the partnership. Otherwise, it will be necessary for each partner to make his own Gift Aid declaration, in which case he may do so on the same declaration form, provided it lists all the partners' names and addresses.

In Scotland a partnership has legal personality, so in all cases one of the partners may make a Gift Aid declaration on behalf of the partnership, showing the name and address of the partnership.

To claim higher rate relief, the partners should enter their share of the donation on their own SA returns. How the donation is apportioned between the partners is a matter for them, but normally will be in accordance with their share of the partnership profits.

37.1.10 Forms for claiming repayments

Completion of a simple claim form and schedules enable charities to reclaim tax on Gift Aid donations by individuals. IR(C) issues them automatically when it receives a tax reclaim. Charities can also obtain them from the Forms Orderline 0151 472 6293.

The charity has to enter the following details on the new schedule for each donor:

- the donor's name;
- the date of the donation or, where the claim covers more than one donation by the donor, the date of the last donation;
- the total amount of donations by the donor on which the charity is claiming in the schedule.

The charity will have to complete a separate schedule for each tax year, or part tax year, included in the claim. It is not necessary to calculate the tax relating to each donation separately. The charity can simply calculate the total tax reclaimed for all the donations shown on each schedule.

37.1.11 Keeping records

A charity must keep sufficient records to show that its tax reclaims are accurate. In other words, it must keep records that enable it to show:

(1) an audit trail linking each donation to an identifiable donor who has given a valid Gift Aid declaration; and
(2) that all the other conditions for the tax relief are satisfied.

If a charity does not keep adequate records it may be required to pay back to the Revenue tax it has reclaimed, with interest. It may also be liable to a penalty. The one area where some latitude has been introduced is in relation to small charities that reclaim less than £2,500 on Gift Aid donations. From 10 March 2008, HMRC operate a 4% *de minimis* error level.

The form of records that must be kept is not prescribed in the legislation. In practice, it will depend on the size of the charity, the number of donors and the kind of systems used.

In the event that IR(C) audits a tax reclaim, the auditor will usually ask to see in respect of a donation:

- Any written Gift Aid declaration;
- In the case of an oral Gift Aid declaration, a copy of the written record sent to the donor;
- Any correspondence to or from the donor that relates to the donation, including:
    - any notification of a change of name or change of address;
    - any notification of the cancellation of the Gift Aid declaration;
- The charity's bank statements;
- Its paying-in book stubs showing details of cheques and cash banked;
- Statements received from credit card companies showing details of credit card donations;
- A cash book recording the receipt of cash donations;
- If the charity uses envelopes to collect cash donations, a sample of the envelopes and a record of the sums enclosed;
- Any other records kept relating to the donation.

A charity does not have to keep records on paper. They may be held on the hard drive of a computer, floppy disc or CD ROM, or stored on microfiche.

Revenue COP5, *Inspection of Charities' Records*, explains how IR(C) carries out its audit inspections. In particular, it explains a charity's rights, and promises that it will be treated fairly and courteously. It also promises that IR(C) will provide help where appropriate. A copy of COP5 will be issued to the charity before any audit inspection.

Tax notes

If a charity does not keep adequate records it may be required to pay back to the Revenue tax it has reclaimed, with interest. It may also be liable to a penalty.

How long must records be kept?

If the charity is a charitable trust, it must keep records until the later of:

(1) the 31 January next but one after the end of the tax year to which the tax reclaim relates (eg if it makes a tax reclaim for the tax year 2007–08, until 31 January 2010);

(2) one year after it makes its tax reclaim, rounded to the end of the next quarter (eg in the case of a tax reclaim on 25 May 2008, until 30 June 2009); or

(3) when IR(C) completes any audit it has commenced.

If the charity is a company, it must keep records until six years after the end of the accounting period to which the tax reclaim relates.

These are the minimum periods for which a charity must keep records. In the event that IR(C) audits a tax reclaim and the auditor identifies errors, he may reopen tax reclaims for earlier years. Therefore, it may be in the charity's interests to keep records for longer than the minimum period.

Using envelopes to collect cash donations

A charity may choose to collect cash donations in envelopes (eg church stewardship envelopes) so that it can show an audit trail linking the donation to the donor. For one-off donations, it may choose to pre-print the Gift Aid declaration on the envelope for completion by the donor. If the donor is a regular supporter, the charity may already hold his Gift Aid declaration, in which case the envelope need simply contain either:

- the donor's name, or
- some other unique identifier, such as a number that can be cross-referenced to a donor register.

Where a reference number is used, this should be unique to the donor. In practice, where envelopes containing the same unique identifier are used by the donor and his spouse and minor children, a charity can assume that all the donations are from the donor.

When the envelope is opened and the contents are counted, an official of the charity should record the sum that it contained:

- on the envelope, and
- in a donor record.

A charity should retain all envelopes on which a Gift Aid declaration is printed for the periods set out above, together with a sample of other envelopes (normally for one month of the year) and the donor record.

37.1.12 Donations from joint bank accounts, etc

If a charity receives a donation drawn on a joint bank account, and it has not been given a Gift Aid declaration by all of the account-holders, it will need to determine whether the donation is from a donor who has given a Gift Aid declaration. It is normally safe to assume that the donation is from the account-holder who signs the cheque, debit card slip or direct debit/standing order mandate. In the case of a donation received over the phone or online, a charity can normally assume that the donation is from the account-holder who authorised the transaction.

Similarly, if a charity receives a credit card donation drawn on an account in respect of which there is more than one authorised signatory, it can normally assume that the donation is from the authorised signatory who signs the credit card slip. In the case of a donation received over the phone or online, it can normally assume that the donation is from the person who authorises the transaction.

If there is any doubt whether the donation is from the person who signs the cheque, etc or authorises the transaction, the charity should ask him to confirm whether the donation is from him.

37.1.13 Gift Aid donations of tax rebates

Since April 2004, self-assessment taxpayers have been able to donate their tax repayments to charities. If a charity wishes to participate in this scheme it can register with IR Charities, S-A Donate. The Revenue operates a helpline on 0845 302 0203.

37.1.14 Gifts of goods and Gift Aid

HMRC has issued guidance on the Gift Aid position where goods are donated to charity by an individual.

Gift Aid applies only to gifts of money. However, where a charity or its subsidiary company sells goods on behalf of an individual, Gift Aid relief can apply to a subsequent donation of the proceeds. HMRC prefers arrangements where the individual is asked to confirm (after the sale) that he wishes to proceed and donate the sale proceeds to the charity.

37.1.15 Permissible benefits for Gift Aid donors

A charity may wish to give a token of its appreciation to donors by way of thanks for their donations. Modest benefits received in consequence of making a donation will not stop the donation from qualifying as a Gift Aid donation, provided their value does not exceed certain limits. If a charity wishes to provide benefits to donors (eg as part of a membership scheme) it should consider whether the proposed benefits fall within the limits in the donor benefit rules. If they exceed the limits, the membership subscriptions cannot qualify as Gift Aid donations.

The following need to be determined to decide whether a donation can qualify as a Gift Aid donation:

(1) whether the donor, or a person connected with him, receives any benefits in consequence of making the donation; and

(2) if so, whether their value exceeds the limits in the donor benefit rules.

Tax notes

Modest gifts given as a token of appreciation to donors will not stop the donation from qualifying for Gift Aid donation, provided their value does not exceed certain limits.

37.1.16 The donor benefit rules

The rules contain two limits for the value of benefits that a donor, or a person connected with him, may receive in consequence of making a donation. If such value:

- exceeds the limits in 37.1.17 (the relevant value test); or
- plus the value of any benefits received in consequence of any Gift Aid donations made by the same donor to the same charity earlier in the same tax year exceeds £250 (the aggregate value test);

the donation will not qualify as a Gift Aid donation. However, there is a special exemption for heritage and conservation charities (see 37.1.20 below).

37.1.17 The relevant value test

For 2007–08, the limits for the relevant value test were:

Amount of donation	Value of benefits
£0–100	25% of the donation
£101–1,000	£25
£1,001–10,000	5% of the donation

37.1.18 The aggregate value test

In addition to satisfying the relevant value test, the value of benefits received in consequence of a donation must also satisfy the aggregate value test if the donation is to qualify as a Gift Aid donation. In other words:

(1) the value of benefits received in consequence of making the donation;
(2) plus the value of any benefits received in consequence of any Gift Aid donations by the same donor to the same charity earlier in the same tax year;
(3) must not exceed £500 (£250 up to 2006/07).

37.1.19 Application of these rules to corporate donors

These rules have applied for some years to close companies that made Gift Aid donations. As from 22 March 2006, they now also apply to non-close companies.

37.1.20 Heritage and conservation charities

Some heritage charities have allowed Gift Aid donors free admission. Or, to put it another way, they have charged the normal entry fee but invited the customer to treat his payment as a Gift Aid donation so that the charity could reclaim the tax. This practice continues but is now subject to restrictions. Since 6 April 2006, Gift Aid relief has been available only for donations amounting to at least 110% of the amount that would be charged for the right to free admission for a year or, where the right to free admission is for a period of less than one year, the payment is at least 110% of the amount normally charged for the free admission during the period in question.

37.1.21 New anti-avoidance provisions introduced by FA 2006

The FA 2006 introduced rules that may restrict a donor's tax relief and/or the charity's exemption. These took effect on 22 March 2006.

These provisions can only apply to a 'substantial donor', ie a person who gives more than £25,000 in a single 12-month period, or more than £100,000 over a six-year period (these periods can pre-date 22 March 2006). They come into effect if such a substantial donor has other transactions with the charity.

The following types of transactions can be deemed to be non-qualifying expenditure by the charity:

- Sale or letting of property, or provision of services by the substantial donor to the charity or by the charity to the substantial donor;
- An exchange of property between a charity and substantial donor;
- Provision of financial assistance (eg loan, guarantee, indemnity) to a charity by a substantial donor or by a charity to the substantial donor;

- Payment of remuneration by a charity to a substantial donor (apart from a payment for services as a trustee);
- Investment by a charity in the business of a substantial donor (unless the business is listed on a recognised stock exchange).

There is a let-out for transactions deemed to have been entered into for genuine commercial reasons, or which are on commercial terms.

Where a charity is caught by these provisions and is deemed to have non-qualifying expenditure after 22 March 2006, there is a restriction of its tax exemption equal to the amount of the non-qualifying expenditure. The

---

Tax notes

HMRC says that the FA 2006 legislation was not intended to catch the 'legitimate activities of charities or donors' but the Revenue's concept of legitimate activities may give rise to some nasty surprises.

---

donor's Gift Aid relief will be similarly restricted.

HMRC has recently issued revised guidance notes on this, see www.hmrc.gov.uk/charities/guidance-notes/annex2/annex_ii.htm.

According to HMRC, the purpose of the legislation is to restrict a charity's tax exemption where a series of transactions result in all or part of a donation being returned to the donor in cash or in kind. HMRC says that the legislation is not intended to catch the legitimate activities of charities or donors.

Nevertheless, according to HMRC the legislation would bite in the following situation.

In February 2008, a charity makes a £5,000 grant to Mr Rose, a homeless person. Mr Rose subsequently inherits a large amount of money and in December 2009 makes a single £75,000 Gift Aid donation. The application of the FA 2006 legislation is that the grant of £5,000 would be treated as non-qualifying expenditure and the charity would lose its exemption for a corresponding amount of income for the year 2008–09.

37.1.22 Payroll giving schemes
(TA 1988, s 202)

Under a payroll giving scheme an employee asks his employer to deduct an amount from his wage or salary and pay that amount over to a charity (usually a clearing house such as the Charities Aid Foundation). PAYE is then operated by the employer as if the employee's wage or salary had been the amount remaining after the charitable donation, which has the effect of granting tax relief at the highest rate paid.

An employer is not obliged to offer a payroll giving scheme and, if a scheme is offered, employees may decide individually whether they wish to participate. Usually each employee will specify particular charities to the clearing house, but in some cases the money is paid into a fund administered by a workplace committee. Such funds can cause difficulties, especially where the fund's name suggests that it was established by the generosity of the employer, rather than the employees themselves.

As part of the FA 2004, the Government introduced a grant scheme for small companies, ie those with fewer than 500 employees, who implement payroll giving schemes. The grant will be available for two years.

37.1.23 Gifts of shares and land

The reliefs due where an individual gives shares or land to a charity are covered at 10.10–10.11.

37.1.24 VAT relief for certain charities

FA 2005 allows a 5% reduced rate to apply for supplies of advice or information connected with the welfare of elderly or disabled people or children. No date has been set for the introduction of this rate.

37.1.25 Useful links

Further information on charities can be found at www.hmrc.gov.uk/charities.

37.2 COMMUNITY AMATEUR SPORTS CLUBS

A package of tax relief was introduced for community amateur sports clubs (CASCs) by FA 2002. The relief is designed for those clubs that do not wish to, or cannot, apply for charitable status. See Table 37.1.

To qualify for these reliefs, CASCs must be open to the whole community, organised on an amateur basis, and their main purpose must be to provide facilities for, and promote participation in, an eligible sport. An eligible sport is defined as one of those currently recognised by the National Sports Council.

The reliefs consist of exemption from:

- Tax on interest income;
- Tax on rental income up to £20,000 (£10,000 up to 31 March 2004);
- Tax on trading income up to £30,000 (£15,000 up to 31 March 2004);
- CGT.

Table 37.1 – Comparison of charitable status with community amateur sports clubs

	Charitable status	Community amateur sports clubs
Direct taxes	Primary purpose trading income exempt from tax	Gross income from fund raising and trading exempt from tax where turnover is less than £30,000 (all such income is taxable if the threshold is exceeded)
	All rental income exempt	Gross income from property exempt from tax where less than £20,000 (all such income is taxable if the threshold is exceeded)
	80% mandatory relief from uniform business rates	Under separate legislation to take place in 2004 mandatory rates relief at 50% for clubs with a rateable value of less than £3,000 reducing to no relief for rateable values more than £8,000
Incentives to give	Gift Aid on individual and company donations	Gift Aid on individual donations only
	Payroll giving	No payroll giving
	Income tax relief on gift of shares	No income tax relief on gift of shares
	Inheritance tax relief on gifts	Inheritance tax relief on gifts
	Gift of assets on no-gain no-loss basis for capital gains	Gift of assets on no-gain no-loss basis for capital gains
Fundraising	Business: relief on gifts or trading stock	Business: relief on gifts or trading stock
	Grants available from other charities, eg community foundations and other bodies supporting charities	Will not attract charitable sources of funding
Regulation	Charity Commission regulation and audit	Inland Revenue regulation and audit
	Public recognition of and trust in 'charity' and 'Gift Aid' concepts	Public awareness of community amateur sports clubs 'brand' to be developed
	Charity Commission definition based on health	Inland Revenue definition based on the value of sport as a factor in community cohesion
	Sports must be capable of improving physical health and fitness	Likely to adopt Sports Council's list of adopted sports
	Significant social activity to be kept separate from charitable activities	Social membership permitted

In addition, when giving to CASCs, donors are able to take advantage of the following:

- Gift Aid for individual donors;
- Relief from IHT;
- Business tax relief on the gifts of trading stock;
- Relief from CGT for gifts of assets from both individuals and businesses.

These measures are designed to provide a boost for community sport activities.

37.3 MUTUAL ASSOCIATIONS

Mutual trading arises where a company or association (eg a club) trades with its members. Profits from such trading are exempt from tax under TA 1988, s 491; thus, if a member receives a dividend paid out of profits from mutual trading, he is not liable for tax on it.

Problems are apt to arise if there is a mixture of mutual trading (exempt) and trading with non-members (which is taxable), for example, a golf club that also receives green fees from non-members and makes bar profits from them. The Revenue's views are set out in *Tax Bulletin* December 1997. You should consult an accountant if you are responsible for running a mutual company or association and the level of turnover is starting to become substantial.

If a company or association receives investment income, it will be subject to corporation tax in the normal way.

Tax notes

Problems are apt to arise if there is a mixture of mutual trading (exempt) and trading with non-members (which is taxable); for example, a golf club that receives green fees from non-members and makes bar profits from them.

37.3.1 CGT roll-over relief
(ESC D15)

Roll-over relief may be due to an unincorporated association, the activities of which are not wholly or mainly carried on for profit, if it replaces an asset (eg a hockey club that sells its ground and uses the proceeds to purchase fresh headquarters). Where an asset is owned by a company of which 90% of its shares are held by such an unincorporated association or its members, roll-over relief may be due provided the other conditions are satisfied.

37.4 HOLIDAY CLUBS AND THRIFT FUNDS

In strictness, a holiday club could be regarded as an unincorporated association. However, where the club is formed on an annual basis, income earned on deposits, etc, is simply apportioned among the members (for further particulars, see ESC C3).

37.5 INVESTMENT CLUBS

Capital gains and allowable losses are apportioned among the members and should be included in their tax returns. Provided all the following conditions are satisfied, the secretary can apply for the gains and losses to be agreed by the tax district in which he lives (Form 185-1 must be used when applying for this treatment):

- There are no more than 20 members;
- The average amount invested is not more than £5,000;
- The annual subscription does not exceed £1,000;
- Total annual gains are not more than £5,000.

The Revenue will then accept each member's share of the gains without further enquiry.

38

STAMP DUTIES

Historians tell us that stamp duty originated in Holland in 1624 as a result of a competition to discover a new form of tax. It appeared in England in 1694 and was only intended as a temporary measure. However, the tax has stayed in force. Stamp duty reserve tax (SDRT) and stamp duty land tax (SDLT) are special types of stamp duty that have replaced stamp duty in relation to transfers of UK securities, land and buildings. The original stamp duty is now just a shadow of its former self and does not normally give rise to significant tax liabilities.

SDRT was introduced in 1986 and applies to transfers of UK stocks and shares. SDLT came into force from 1 December 2003 and applies to transfers of UK land.

This chapter looks at each of these taxes.

(1) Stamp duty reserve tax (SDRT).
(2) Stamp duty land tax (SDLT).

38.1 STAMP DUTY RESERVE TAX (SDRT)

SDRT is a compulsory tax payable when there is an unconditional agreement to transfer chargeable securities for consideration in money or money's worth.

38.1.1 Basic principles of SDRT

Chargeable securities in principle include UK stocks, shares, loan capital and interests in or options over such securities (but subject to certain exemptions). Securities in a foreign company kept on a UK register are also included. Any written or oral agreement to transfer these securities gives rise to a charge to SDRT of 0.5% of the consideration given in money or money's worth.

38.1.2 Loan stock

Most forms of loan capital are exempt. FA 2008 extended the exemption to cover limited recourse loan notes issued as part of capital market arrangements where the payment of interest was dependent upon the results of a business.

38.1.3 Group relief

SDRT does not apply to transfers of securities from one member of a 75% group to another. The group can include non-UK companies.

38.1.4 Special reliefs

Various statutory 'reconstruction reliefs' are available. In each case the acquiring company must be a UK company and the transaction must be effected for a bona fide commercial purpose and must not form part of an arrangement entered into for the purpose of avoiding tax.

38.1.5 Reconstructions

A full exemption applies where the whole or part of a company's undertaking (including share capital of one or more subsidiary) is transferred to a company (the acquiring company) in pursuance of a scheme of reconstruction and where the consideration shares are issued to all shareholders of the company. For this exemption to apply, the consideration must consist of the issue of non-redeemable shares in the acquiring company to the shareholders of the target company and may include nothing other than the assumption or discharge by the acquiring company of the liabilities of the target company.

38.1.6 New holding company exemption

If a UK company acquires the entire issued share capital of another company for a consideration consisting entirely of the issue of shares in the acquiring company, this will not, in certain circumstances, be liable to stamp duty.

38.1.7 Exchange-traded funds

From 6 December 2006, transactions in overseas exchange-traded funds are exempt from SDRT.

38.2 STAMP DUTY LAND TAX (SDLT)

38.2.1 Introduction to SDLT

The Finance Act 2003 replaced stamp duty in respect of UK property transactions, with a new tax, stamp duty land tax (SDLT). This was in part to block avoidance techniques, which had become commonplace in respect of large property transactions, and in part in preparation for electronic conveyancing. Instead of being a voluntary tax on documents, SDLT became a compulsory tax on all UK property transactions and is chargeable whether or not there is a document, wherever it is executed and wherever the parties are located or resident. The tax came into effect on 1 December 2003.

38.2.2 Compliance obligations

SDLT is a compulsory tax and there are wide-ranging requirements relating to filing of SDLT land transaction returns, payment, provision of information and record-keeping. Under the new regime, the purchaser or lessee is now responsible for notifying the Revenue within 30 days of the effective date of a transaction taking place and for paying the SDLT at the same time. The Revenue has substantial powers, similar to those available in respect of income and corporation tax, to enquire into returns, to require the production of documents, to issue assessments for non or underpayment of SDLT and to charge property in the event of non or underpayment of SDLT. Interest and penalties are generally charged in the event of late payment of SDLT and the amount of the penalty can equal the amount of SDLT payable.

38.2.3 Application of SDLT

SDLT is charged upon the acquisition of any 'chargeable interest' in UK land. Chargeable interest is widely defined and includes not merely freehold and leasehold interests but easements, restrictive covenants and powers over land. The grant of options and pre-emption rights are also caught as are the surrender or release of rights such as the cancellation of restrictive covenants and the surrender of leases as well as the variation of leases.

SDLT must be paid within 30 days of the 'effective date' of the transaction. The effective date will usually be completion, when the transfer is delivered or the lease granted and payment made. However, if a contract is 'substantially performed', which is widely defined as providing a substantial amount of consideration (expected to be around 90% of the purchase price) or entering into 'possession', then SDLT must be paid within 30 days of this date.

38.2.4 Rates of SDLT

The current rates of SDLT are as follows:

Consideration	Rate
Up to £125,000	Nil
£125,001–£250,000	1%
£250,001–£500,000	3%
£500,001 +	4%

In the case of non-residential property, consideration up to £150,000, rather than £125,000, is at the nil rate. Duty is rounded down to the nearest £5. As the rates are tiered, duty is payable on the entire purchase price at the rate indicated. Thus, if the consideration for the purchase of land is £600,000 plus VAT, ie £705,000 the duty is £28,200.

If several properties are bought under a single contract or under associated transactions, the SDLT charge may be based on the aggregate consideration rather than the rate otherwise applicable to each individual purchase in isolation.

38.2.5 **Consideration**

SDLT is chargeable on the total consideration provided (monetary and non-monetary). This includes the value of services or works provided by the purchaser to the vendor (unless certain exemptions apply) and includes VAT unless the landlord has not elected at the time of the transaction. It includes deferred consideration without any discount for the period of deferral (although in some cases a postponement may be available). Land exchanges give rise to an SDLT on both transfers.

Where the consideration is contingent, SDLT is payable on the basis that the amount will become payable (or the sums will continue to be payable). Where the consideration is uncertain or unascertained, it is valued at the best current estimate. If the contingency occurs or the uncertainty is resolved, the purchaser/lessee must notify the Revenue if more SDLT would be payable and can claim a refund if SDLT has been overpaid.

38.2.6 **SDLT on rent**

SDLT is charged on the net present value of the lease – the total rent payable over the whole term of the lease, discounted by a statutory rate. The formula to calculate net present value is complex although the Revenue has provided an online facility to facilitate calculations.

The SDLT on the rent is 1% of the net present value. However, for non-residential property there is a nil rate band of £150,000.

Originally, the rent payable under a lease was taken to be the actual rent paid during the first five years of its term and thereafter equal to the highest annual rent paid in those first five years. However, this is subject to an anti-avoidance rule for 'abnormal' increases in rent, which applies to increases of more than 5% plus the retail price index annually. The FA 2006 changed the basic formula to the rent *payable* under the lease for the first five years, rather than the rent actually paid in each of those first five years.

The FA 2006 also brought in changes to the rules for determining whether or not the assignment of a lease is notifiable (that is, must be reported even though there is no apparent liability). In future, notification will only be required where there is consideration for the assignment, the lease is for a period of seven years or more, and the consideration for the assignment is charged at a rate of 1% or more, or would be so chargeable but for the availability of some relief.

Tax notes

The FA 2006 brought in changes to the rules for determining whether or not the assignment of a lease must be reported, even though there is no apparent liability.

38.2.7 Exemption for land in disadvantaged areas

Transfers and leases of non-residential property in certain 'disadvantaged areas' specified in a Treasury list were totally exempt from stamp duty up to 17 March 2005. For residential property this still applies if the value does not exceed £150,000.

38.2.8 Some transactions that do not attract SDLT

The FA 2006 took some transactions out of the charge to SDLT by providing that there is no consideration for SDLT purposes in the following situations:

- gifts of land where the donee pays any CGT or IHT on the gift;
- payment of a landlord's reasonable costs on the grant, variation or termination of a lease;
- an agricultural tenant's covenant to assign entitlement to the Single Farm Payment on the termination of the tenancy;
- transfers of assets between sub-funds under a settlement.

38.2.9 Alternative property finance

The rules here seek to collect the same amount on property finance arrangements that are compliant with Islamic law as on conventional mortgage arrangements under which interest is charged – that is, only on the original acquisition of the property by the householder. FA 2008 contained anti-avoidance legislation to counter the abuse of this exemption involving sales and lease-backs followed by the sale of the subsidiary.

38.2.10 SDLT charge on gifts of land to a company

A gift of UK land to a company or a sale at undervalue can give rise to a SDLT charge based on the land's market value.

38.2.11 Exemption for charities

No SDLT is payable by a charity on the purchase of a property used for the furtherance of the charity's objects or to hold as an investment from which the return will be used for the furtherance of the charity's objectives (Schedule 8, paragraph 1 FA 2003). The exemption does not apply if the involvement of the charity is part of an SDLT avoidance scheme.

This exemption can also apply to a unit trust that is limited to charity funds.

38.2.12 Other exemptions and reliefs

Other exemptions from stamp duty have been replicated in the SDLT regime. Thus there is a relief for intra-group transfers and for transfers that occur in the course of reconstructions and new holding companies (see below).

> **Tax notes**
>
> There are also some new reliefs such as relief from a double charge to SDLT that could otherwise apply in the context of Islamic financing arrangements and a relief for an employee who is required by his employer to relocate.

38.2.13 **Group relief**

Sales of assets between companies in the same group give rise to SDLT in the same way as sales between unconnected parties. However, group relief (called 'associated company relief') is available on intra-group transactions if

(1) one company is the beneficial owner of not less than 75% of the issued ordinary share capital of the other; or
(2) the issued ordinary share capital of both of them is beneficially owned as to not less than 75% by a third company.

In addition, various economic tests (similar to those for corporation tax group relief) requiring an entitlement to 75% of dividends and to assets on a winding-up must be satisfied.

The FA 2007 provides that shares which have been bought back by a company and which are held for re-issue are to be left out of account in applying the 75% test.

Non-UK companies can satisfy these tests provided they have a share capital. To obtain relief, the effect of the instrument must be to transfer the beneficial interest in the property. Relief is granted if the necessary conditions are satisfied at the date of execution of the document and is not subject to forfeiture if conditions later change (but see below regarding the three-year rule).

Relief is not available if certain 'offensive' arrangements are present at the time of the transaction. In practice it may be difficult to show these did not apply, in particular if it is proposed to sell the transferee company or the assets transferred to a non-group person.

Furthermore, intra-group transfers of UK land can become subject to SDLT if the transferee company ceases to be an associated company within three years of the intra-group transfer, even if there were no arrangements for this to happen at the time of the transfer.

There is an article about associated company relief in *Tax Bulletin* April 2004.

FA 2008 introduced anti-avoidance provisions that catch arrangements where the vendor company leaves the group first. Until 13 March 2008, a loophole allowed the transferee company to then leave the group without this triggering a SDLT charge. The new provisions impose a clawback charge where the vendor company leaves the group and there is then a subsequent change in control of the transferee company within a period of three years of the intra-group sale. HMRC is able to link these events and treat the transferee company as if it had left the group first. Group relief is not clawed back where only the vendor company leaves the group.

38.2.14 Reconstructions and acquisitions

A 'reconstruction' relief is available. This gives a full exemption from SDLT where the whole or part of a company's undertaking is transferred to a company (the acquiring company) in pursuance of a scheme of reconstruction and the consideration shares are issued to all shareholders of the company.

For this exemption to apply, the consideration must consist of the issue of non-redeemable shares in the acquiring company to the shareholders of the target company and may include nothing other than the assumption or discharge by the acquiring company of the liabilities of the target company. The acquiring company must be a UK company and the transaction must be effected for a bona fide commercial purpose and must not form part of an arrangement entered into for the purpose of avoiding tax.

38.2.15 FA 2004 provisions

FA 2004 included a number of measures concerning SDLT:

(1) There are detailed corrections to the administration rules.
(2) The existence of an exemption for the transfer of property under a will or intestacy rules is confirmed.
(3) The exemption for charities is extended to charitable trusts.
(4) Some detailed amendments are made concerning shared ownership leases of private houses.

38.2.16 Partnerships

The FA 2004 also made a fundamental change by introducing a SDLT charge on transfers of partnership property.

These provisions sought to impose a SDLT charge whenever an interest in land or buildings was brought into or out of a partnership, or where partners changed their individual shares in partnership property. The rules involved a special definition of a transfer of a partnership interest in land. The charge was based on the market value of the proportion of the property interest that changed hands (rather than on the consideration that actually passed between the partners).

For example, if a farming partnership were formed by two individuals, who acquired equal shares, and one of those partners brought in the farmland and buildings, half of the value of this property was subject to the SDLT charge. Equally, if one of the partners were to retire, either selling his half interest in the property to his former partner or taking the whole property with him, the charge would be on half the overall value.

Transfers of property into or out of a partnership are generally straightforward transactions. However, there were anti-avoidance rules to catch the transfer of a property to a former partner after his retirement, transfers to spouses rather than individual partners and the artificial manipulation of profit-sharing ratios.

The charge on transfers within partnerships was more complex. A transfer of an interest in a partnership that included an interest in land potentially attracted an SDLT charge. This affected many situations where profit-sharing ratios changed. It is not uncommon for a professional partnership to change profit sharing ratios each year. Under the FA 2004 regime, this could involve annual SDLT returns, and property valuing costs. No document or deed was needed to create an SDLT charge, and even the transfer of an interest in an existing lease that had been granted at full rent could create a charge in some circumstances.

Several changes and simplifications were introduced by the FA 2006:

- A transfer of property into and out of partnerships now normally only triggers a charge that is based on the market value of the proportion that changes hands. Thus, a dentist entering into partnership with an existing practitioner where the practice owns premises worth £500,000 is deemed to have acquired property worth £250,000 (if the terms state that the practice income will be shared equally). Under the pre-FA 2006 rules, the charge could be increased by a proportion of the actual consideration he had given for the right to join the partnership.

- The transfer of an interest in a property-owning partnership is now only taxed where the business of the partnership is to invest in or develop property. Furthermore, the transfer of an interest in a partnership (ie change in profit-sharing ratios) now attracts SDLT only if the partnership's main activity consists of developing or dealing in land.

- Significant anti-avoidance legislation was also brought in. This took effect from 6 December 2006 and 19 July 2007.

Although the SDLT rules for partnerships were radically simplified, complex and obscure aspects remained. In particular, many SDLT reliefs are 'notifiable' and must be specifically claimed. Furthermore, FA 2007 contained provisions that can result in a gift or transfer for no consideration of an interest in a partnership.

FA 2008 amended the FA 2007 provisions retrospectively to 19 July 2007 when those provisions took effect. The legislation now distinguishes between two types of transfers of partnership interests.

'Type A transfers' continue to attract SDLT by reference to a proportion of the market value of the UK property held by the partnership immediately before the transfer. The proportion is the income profit entitlement of the interest transferred, eg if a partnership owned land worth £5 million and A's interest in profits were 5%, a transfer of A's interest in the partnership could attract a SDLT charge on £250,000. However, this charge will normally arise only where *A* receives consideration for the transfer of his interest or where a new partner is introduced at the time that *A* retires and there is a withdrawal of money or money's worth by *A*.

A type A charge can also arise where a partner's interest is reduced and he receives payment either from the existing partners, or from an incoming partner or there is a withdrawal of money or money's worth at the time that his interest is reduced.

'Type B transfers' are basically all other transfers of partnership interests. A SDLT charge can arise in the same way as for type A transfers but there is a 'safe harbour' rule, which means that certain partnership property is ignored. This let-out applies where:

(1) the property was transferred to the partnership before 23 July 2004; or
(2) the vendor under the property transfer was not a partner or a person connected with a partner; or
(3) an appropriate election has been made (see below).

The election disapplies the special computation charging provisions for the transfer of property to the partnership from a partner or person who is connected with a partner (see 2004 changes described above). Making such an election may mean that additional SDLT becomes payable on this transfer.

38.2.17 Unit trusts

'Seeding relief' was abolished by FA 2006 with effect from 22 March 2006. This relief allowed the initial acquisition of land investments in exchange for the issue of new units in the trust to be made without payment of SDLT. This relief was the basis of many SDLT avoidance schemes involving foreign unit trusts.

38.2.18 Tax avoidance disclosure rules for commercial transactions over £5 million

Rules were introduced with effect from 1 July 2005 to ensure that promoters or users of schemes that were expected to produce an SDLT advantage must disclose details of the schemes to the Revenue. The rules apply where the scheme relates to non-residential property that has a market value of at least £5 million.

38.2.19 Anti-avoidance provisions

Changes were introduced by FA 2005 to block a number of SDLT avoidance schemes.

These schemes involved:

● use of group relief;
● use of acquisition relief;

- grants of leases by bare trustees to their principal;
- certain variations of leases to remove restrictive covenants;
- use of repayable loans or deposits as consideration;
- reduction of market value by encumbrance;
- use of 'sub-sale relief' in alternative finance transactions; and
- use of partnerships.

These changes apply to land transactions on or after 17 March 2005. However, transactions effected in pursuance of contracts entered into before 17 March 2005 are not affected unless there is a variation of the contract or assignment of rights under the contract. This let-out will therefore not apply to pre-17 March 2005 contracts where there is the exercise of any option, right of pre-emption or similar right, or any assignment, sub-sale or similar transaction.

The FA 2007 introduced more anti-avoidance provisions aimed at schemes that involved the abuse of group relief and reliefs for partnerships such as 'seeding relief'.

38.2.20 General anti-avoidance provision

With effect from 2pm on 6 December 2006, HMRC can look through a series of transactions that form part of an avoidance scheme and charge SDLT on the total consideration across the scheme as a whole. This is intended to stop schemes that complicate transactions to draw in the benefit of exemptions and reliefs that would not otherwise be available.

38.2.21 Relief for zero carbon new homes

Purchasers of new zero carbon homes will receive a stamp duty tax break from 1 October 2007 as follows:

(1) Purchase price of £500,000 or less – no SDLT.
(2) Purchase price above £500,000 – SDLT liability reduced by £15,000.

The exemption has been extended by FA 2008 to cover new zero-carbon flats bought between 1 October 2007 and 30 September 2012.

39

SOCIAL SECURITY BENEFITS

In this chapter, we look at the following:

(1) Taxable benefits.
(2) Non-taxable benefits.
(3) Tax credits.

39.1 TAXABLE BENEFITS
(TA 1988, s 617)

The following benefits are taxed as earned income under IT(E&P)A 2003:

● Bereavement Allowance* ● Incapacity benefit (not taxable for first 28 weeks) ● Income support paid to unemployed and strikers ● Industrial death benefit (if paid as pension) ● Invalid care allowance ● Invalidity addition paid with retirement pension ● Jobseeker's allowance (contributions-based) ** ● The state pension ● Statutory maternity pay ● Statutory paternity pay ● Statutory adoption pay ● Statutory sick pay ● Widowed parent's allowance*** ● Widowed mother's allowance ● Widow's pension.

Notes:

* Bereavement allowance replaced Widow's Pension from 9 April 2001
** The jobseeker's allowance was introduced from 7 October 1996. Payments are dependent on NIC records and/or the income
*** Widowed parent's allowance replaced Widowed Mother's Allowance from 9 April 2001, although WMA is still paid to widows whose entitlement arose before 9 April 2001

39.2 NON-TAXABLE BENEFITS

The following benefits are not taxable:

● Attendance allowance ● Back to work bonus ● Bereavement payment Child benefit ● Child's special allowance ● Christmas bonus for pensioners ● Cold weather payment ● Council tax benefit (administered by local authorities) ● Disability living allowance ● Employment rehabilitation allowance ● Fares to school ● Guardian's allowance ● Invalidity addition paid with invalidity pension ● Invalidity pension ● Job finders grant ● Maternity allowance ● One parent benefit ● Severe disablement allowance ● Sickness benefit ● Employment training allowance ● War orphan's pension ● War widow's pension ● Widow's payment ● Winter fuel payment

Means-tested benefits

● Child tax credit Educational maintenance allowance ● Family credit ● Hospital patients' travelling expenses ● Housing benefit ● Jobseeker's allowance (income-based) ● Income support ● Social fund payments ● Student grants ● Uniform and clothing grants ● Working tax credit

Note: The jobseeker's allowance was introduced from 7 October 1996. Payments are dependent on the NIC record and/or the income.

Armed Forces compensation scheme/War disablement benefits

● Disablement pension, including: Age allowance ● Allowance for lowered standard of occupation ● Clothing allowance ● Comforts allowance ● Constant attendance allowance ● Dependant allowance Armed Forces guaranteed income scheme ● Education allowance ● Exceptionally severe disablement allowance ● Invalidity allowance ● Medical treatment allowance ● Severe disablement occupational allowance ● Unemployability allowance.

Industrial injury benefits

● Disablement benefit, including: Constant attendance allowance ● Exceptionally severe disablement allowance ● Reduced earnings allowance ● Retirement allowance ● Unemployability supplement ● Industrial death benefit child allowance.

Adoption allowances
(ESC A40)

Sums paid under schemes approved under the Children Act 1975, s 32 are exempt from income tax.

39.3 TAX CREDITS

39.3.1 The role of employers

The role of employers in paying tax credits was removed with effect from 1 April 2006. HMRC now pays tax credits direct to all claimants whether they are employed or self-employed.

Table 39.1 – Taxable social security benefits

	2006–07	2007–08	2008–09
	£	£	£
Retirement pension			
Single	84.25	87.30	90.70
Adult dependant	50.50	52.30	54.35
Incapacity benefit*			
Long-term benefit	78.50	81.35	84.50
increase for age higher	16.50	17.10	17.75
increase for age lower	8.25	8.55	8.90
Short-term benefit			
under pension age			
lower rate	59.20	61.35	63.75
higher rate	70.05	72.55	75.40
Incapacity benefit*			
Short-term benefit			
over pension age			
lower rate	75.35	78.05	81.10
higher rate	78.50	81.35	84.50
Income support			
Single/lone parent			
– under 18	34.60	35.65	47.95
– 18 to 24	45.50	46.85	47.95
– 25 or over	57.45	59.15	60.50
Couple			
– both under 18	34.60	35.65	47.95
– both 18 or over	90.10	92.80	94.95
Statutory sick pay			
Earnings threshold	84.00	87.00	90.00
Standard rate	70.05	72.55	75.40
Statutory maternity pay			
Earnings threshold	84.00	87.00	90.00
Lower rate	108.85	112.75	117.18
Single people under 18	34.60	35.65	47.95
Single people 18–24	45.50	46.85	47.95
Single people 25 and over	57.45	59.15	60.50
Widow's payment			
Widowed parent's allowance	84.25	87.30	90.70
Widow's pension (standard)	84.25	87.30	90.70

Table 39.2 – Non-taxable social security benefits

	2006–07 £	2007–08 £	2008–09
Attendance allowance			
Higher rate	62.25	64.50	67.00
Lower rate	41.65	43.15	44.85
Child benefit			
First or only child	17.45	18.10	18.80
Each subsequent child	11.70	12.10	12.55
Severe disablement allowance			
Basic rate	47.45	49.15	51.05
Age-related addition			
higher rate	16.50	17.10	17.75
middle rate	10.60	11.00	11.40
lower rate	5.30	5.50	5.70
Bereavement payment			
Single lump sum	2,000.00	2,000.00	2,000.00
Christmas bonus			
Single annual payment	10.00	10.00	10.00

40

TAX TABLES

Table 40.1 – Rates of income tax

	Rate	Taxable income £
2008–09		
Starting rate*	10%	0–2,320
Basic rate	20%	2,321–34,800
Higher rate on dividends	32.5%	(see Note)
Higher rate	40%	Over 34,800
2007–08		
Lower rate	10%	0–2,230
Basic rate	22%	2,231–34,600
Higher rate on dividends	32.5%	(see Note)
Higher rate	40%	Over 34,600
2006–07		
Lower rate	10%	0–2,150
Basic rate	22%	2,151–33,300
Higher rate on dividends	32.5%	(see Note)
Higher rate	40%	over 33,300
2005–06		
Lower rate	10%	0–2,090
Basic rate	22%	2,091–32,400
Higher rate on dividends	32.5%	(see Note)
Higher rate	40%	over 32,400
2004–05		
Lower rate	10%	0–2,020
Basic rate	22%	2,021–31,400
Higher rate on dividends	32.5%	(see Note)
Higher rate	40%	Over 31,400

Note: Rates of tax applicable to dividends are 10% for income below the basic rate and 32.5% for income above it.
• There is a new 10% starting rate for savings income only, with a limit of £2,320. If an individual's taxable non-savings income is above this limit then the 10% savings rate will not be applicable.

Table 40.2 – Personal allowances and reliefs (see Chapter 11)

Allowances (£s)	2003–04	2004–05	2005–06	2006–07	2007–08	2008–09
– under 65	4,615	4,745	4,895	5,035	5,225	6,035
– under 65	6,610	6,830	7,090	7,280	7,550	9,030
– 75 plus	6,720	6,950	7,220	7,420	7,690	9,180
Married couple's allowance						
– either spouse 65 plus[2]	5,565	5,725	5,905	6,065	6,285	6,535
– either spouse 75 plus	5,635	5,795	5,975	6,135	6,365	6,625
– £1 in £2 for income over	18,300	18,900	19,500	20,100	20,900	21,800
Blind person's allowance	1,510	1,560	1,610	1,660	1,730	1,800
	–	–	–	–	–	

Table 40.3 – 'Official rate' of interest for beneficial loans (see 4.7)

	%
2008–09	6.25
2007–08	6.25
2006–07	5.00
2005–06	5.00
2004–05	5.00
2003–04	5.00
2002–03	5.00

Table 40.4 – Pension contributions

The pensions regime changed with effect from April 2006 and limits on contributions increased substantially, although there is an overall limit – the 'lifetime allowance' – on the total value of an individual's pension.

Maximum contribution	*2006/07* £	*2007/08* £	*2008/09* £
Individual – 100% of relevant earnings up to maximum of	215,000	225,000	235,000
Employer – unlimited but triggers benefit in kind if total pension contributions from both employee and employer are over	215,000	225,000	235,000
Individual's lifetime allowance	1,500,000	1,600,000	1,650,000

Table 40.5 – Rates of capital gains tax

	2003–04	2004–05	2005–06	2006–07	2007–08	2008–09
Annual exemptions						
Individuals	7,900	8,200	8,500	8,800	9,200	9,600
Trusts	3,950	4,100	4,250	4,400	4,600	4,800
Rates of tax						
2008–09 onwards flat rate						18%
2008–09 onwards entrepreneurs rate (available on certain disposals of business, reducing effective rate to 10% on first £1m of qualifying gains.) (£1m is a lifetime limit.)						10%
Individuals						
Gains are effectively taxed						
As top slice of taxable income:						
Gain less than lower rate limit	10%	10%	10%	10%	10%	
Gain less than basic rate limit	20%	20%	20%	20%	20%	
Gain greater than basic rate limit	40%	40%	40%	40%	40%	
Trusts						
Discretionary (including accumulation and maintenance)	34%	40%	40%	40%	40%	
Interest in possession	34%	40%	40%	40%	40%	

Table 40.6 – Taper relief to 5 April 2008

Non-business assets

Number of complete years after 5 April 1998 for which asset held*	*Percentage of gain chargeable*
0	100
1	100
2	100
3	95
4	90
5	85
6	80
7	75
8	70
9	65
10 or more	60

*Assets acquired before 17 March 1998 qualify for an addition of one year to the period for which they are treated as held after 5 April 1998. This addition will be the same for all assets, whenever they were actually acquired. So, for example, an asset purchased on 1 January 1998 and disposed of on 1 July 2000 is treated for the purposes of the taper as if it had been held for three years (two complete years after 5 April 1998 plus one additional year).

Business assets

(1) For disposals on or after 6 April 2000, a four-year taper for business assets applies for holding periods from 6 April 1998. The gains charged to tax are reduced as set out in the table:

Period asset held (years)	*Percentage of gain chargeable (%)*	*Equivalent rate for higher rate CGT payer (%)*
0–1	100	40
1–2	87.5	35
2–3	75	30
3–4	50	20

The additional year for assets held at 17 March 1998 has been consolidated into the new four-year taper so that it is not added for disposals on or after 6 April 2000.

(2) For disposals after 6 April 2002, the table is:

Period asset held (years)	*Percentage of gain chargeable (%)*	*Equivalent rate for higher rate CGT payer (%)*
0	100	40
1	50	20
2	25	10

Table 40.7 – Capital gains tax indexation allowance (see 12.12)

	RETAIL PRICE INDEX FIGURES					
	1982	*1983*	*1984*	*1985*	*1986*	*1987*
Jan		325.9	342.6	359.8	379.7	394.5/100.0
Feb		327.3	344.0	362.9	381.1	100.4
Mar	313.4	327.9	345.1	366.1	381.6	100.6
Apr	319.7	332.5	349.7	373.9	385.3	101.8
May	322.0	333.9	351.0	375.6	386.0	101.9
June	322.9	334.7	351.9	376.4	385.8	101.9
July	320.0	336.5	351.5	375.5	384.7	101.8
Aug	323.1	338.0	354.8	376.7	385.9	102.1
Sep	322.9	339.5	355.5	376.5	387.8	102.4
Oct	324.5	340.7	357.7	377.1	388.4	102.9
Nov	326.1	341.9	358.8	378.4	391.7	103.4
Dec	325.5	342.8	358.5	378.9	393.0	103.3
	1988	*1989*	*1990*	*1991*	*1992*	*1993*
Jan	103.3	111.0	119.5	130.2	135.6	137.9
Feb	103.7	111.8	120.2	130.9	136.3	138.8
Mar	104.1	112.3	121.4	131.4	136.7	139.3
Apr	105.8	114.3	125.1	133.1	138.8	140.6
May	106.2	115.0	126.2	133.5	139.3	141.1
June	106.6	115.4	126.7	134.1	139.3	141.0
July	106.7	115.5	126.8	133.8	138.8	140.7
Aug	107.9	115.8	128.1	134.1	138.9	141.3
Sep	108.4	116.6	129.3	134.6	139.4	141.9
Oct	109.5	117.5	130.3	135.1	139.9	141.8
Nov	110.0	118.5	130.0	135.6	139.7	141.6
Dec	110.3	118.8	129.9	135.7	139.2	141.9
	1994	*1995*	*1996*	*1997*	*1998*	*1999*
Jan	141.3	146.0	150.2	154.4	159.5	163.4
Feb	142.1	146.9	150.9	155.0	160.3	163.7
Mar	142.5	147.5	151.5	155.4	160.8	164.1
Apr	144.2	149.0	152.6	156.3	162.6	165.2
May	144.7	149.6	152.9	156.9	163.5	165.6
June	144.7	149.8	153.0	157.5	163.4	165.6
July	144.0	149.1	152.4	157.5	163.0	165.1
Aug	144.7	149.9	153.1	158.5	163.7	165.5
Sep	145.0	150.6	153.8	159.3	164.4	166.2
Oct	145.2	149.8	153.8	159.5	164.5	166.5
Nov	145.3	149.8	153.9	159.6	164.4	166.7
Dec	146.0	150.7	154.4	160.0	164.4	167.3

RETAIL PRICE INDEX FIGURES

	2000	2001	2002	2003	2004	2005
Jan	166.6	171.1	173.3	178.4	183.1	188.9
Feb	167.5	172.0	173.8	179.3	183.8	189.6
Mar	168.4	172.2	174.5	179.9	184.6	190.5
Apr	170.1	173.1	175.7	181.2	185.7	191.6
May	170.7	174.2	176.2	181.5	186.5	192.0
June	171.1	174.4	176.2	181.3	186.8	192.2
July	170.5	173.3	175.9	181.3	186.8	192.2
Aug	170.5	174.0	176.4	181.6	187.4	192.6
Sep	171.7	174.6	177.6	182.5	188.1	193.1
Oct	171.6	174.3	177.9	182.6	188.6	193.3
Nov	172.1	173.6	178.2	182.7	189.0	193.6
Dec	172.2	173.4	178.5	183.5	189.9	194.1

	2006	2007	2008
Jan	193.4	201.6	209.8
Feb	194.2	203.1	211.4
Mar	195.0	204.4	212.1
Apr	196.5	205.4	
May	197.7	206.2	
June	198.5	207.3	
July	198.5	206.1	
Aug	199.2	207.3	
Sept	200.1	208.0	
Oct	200.4	208.9	
Nov	201.1	209.7	
Dec	202.7	210.9	

Table 40.8 – Rates of interest on overdue tax/repayment supplement

Rates from 6 August 2002:	
For overdue income and capital gains tax	5.5%
For overpaid income and capital gains tax	1.75%
Rates from 6 December 2003:	
For overdue income and capital gains tax	6.5%
For overpaid income and capital gains tax	2.5%
Rates from 6 September 2004:	
For overdue income and capital gains tax	7.5%
For overpaid income and capital gains tax	3.0%
Rates from 6 September 2005:	
For overdue income and capital gains tax	6.5%
For overpaid income and capital gains tax	2.25%
Rates from 6 September 2006:	
For overdue income and capital gains tax	7.5%
For overpaid income and capital gains tax	3.0%
Rates from 6 August 2007:	
For overdue income and capital gains tax	8.5%
For overpaid income and capital gains tax	4.0%
Rates from 6 January 2008:	
For overdue income and capital gains tax	7.5%
For overpaid income and capital gains tax	3.0%

Note that different rates apply for late payment/repayment of inheritance tax. The current rate is 4%.

Table 40.9 – Rates of corporation tax

Financial year commencing 1 April	2002–6	2007	2008
Full rate (see 17.4.2)	30%	30%	28%
Small companies rate (see 17.4.3)	19%	20%	21%
Small companies rate – profit limit	£300,000	£300,000	£300,000
Small companies Marginal relief Profit limit	£1.5m	£1.5m	£1.5m

Table 40.10 – Rates of inheritance tax

Cumulative chargeable transfers £	TRANSFERS ON DEATH Rate on gross % age	LIFETIME TRANSFERS Rate on gross % age
from 6 April 2001		
0–242,000	nil	nil
Over 242,000	40	20
from 6 April 2002		
0–250,000	nil	nil
over 250,000	40	20
from 6 April 2003		
0–255,000	nil	nil
over 255,000	40	20
from 6 April 2004		
0–263,000	nil	nil
over 263,000	40	20
from 6 April 2005		
0–275,000	nil	nil
over 275,000	40	20
from 6 April 2006		
0–285,000	nil	nil
over 285,000	40	20
from 6 April 2007		
0–300,000	nil	nil
over 300,000	40	40
from 6 April 2008		
0–312,000	nil	nil
over 312,000	40	40

Note: for married couples and civil partners, a carry-forward of the proportion of the nil-rate band unused on first death to the death of the second spouse or civil partner on or after 9 October 2007.

GLOSSARY

Actual basis of assessment Where a person carrying on a trade or profession is assessed according to the profits that he has actually earned during the tax year concerned. See 6.3.

Accounting reference date The date to which accounts are made up for a company. In practice, when a company is formed the accounting reference date is normally the last day of the month in which the anniversary of its incorporation falls.

Accruals basis A system of bookkeeping which brings into account income when earned and expenditure when incurred. Contrast **cash basis**.

'A' Day 6 April 2006, the date that the new pensions tax regime came into force. See 25.1.

Additional voluntary contribution (AVC) A contribution by an employee to secure additional benefits under his employer's registered pension scheme.

Ad valorem duties Duties charged as a percentage of the value of the asset concerned, particularly **stamp duty**. See Chapter 38.

Agricultural buildings allowances A form of **capital allowance** given in respect of expenditure on buildings used for agricultural purposes. See 15.2.19.

Agricultural property relief A relief given for **IHT** purposes. The relief is either 50% or 100% of the value of agricultural land. To qualify, the land must be situated in the UK, Channel Islands or Isle of Man. See 29.9

All-employee share scheme An approved scheme for employees to receive shares tax free. See 5.3.

Alternative Investment Market The Stock Exchange launched the AIM in June 1995 to enable investors to deal in shares in unquoted companies.

Annual exemption Individuals are entitled to an annual exemption for CGT purposes of £9,600 for 2008–09. See 12.1.1. There are two types of annual exemption for **IHT**. An individual may give away up to £250 to any number of people in a tax year (generally called the 'small gifts exemption'). Separately from this, he is allowed to make chargeable transfers of up to £3,000 pa which are treated as exempt. See 29.5.

Approved share option schemes There are two types: SAYE-linked schemes, which are democratic in nature and must be made available to all employees; and executive share option schemes, which can be restricted to directors and senior executives. See 5.5. See also **Enterprise Management Incentives**.

Associated companies Companies controlled by the same person or groups of people. See 17.4.

Basis period The period on which an individual's profits for the tax year are based.

Bed and breakfasting A widely used way of establishing CGT losses by selling shares and repurchasing the next day. Anti-avoidance rules now prevent this. See 32.8.

767

Benefits-in-kind Perks received by a director or employee that are taxed as employment income and are generally subject to **NICs**. See 4.4.

Beneficial loans Loans to an employee at less than a commercial rate of interest. See **Official rate** and 4.7.

Body corporate Another name for company. Types of body corporate include **Limited Liability Company**, **Company Limited by Guarantee**, **Unlimited Company and Limited Liability Partnership**.

Business property relief A deduction of either 50% or 100% from the value of business property when it is assessed for **IHT** purposes. See 29.8.

Capital allowances Allowances given in respect of plant and machinery, industrial buildings and commercial property in enterprise zones. In general terms, capital allowances represent a form of relief that corresponds to depreciation. See 15.2.

Capital expenditure A 'once and for all' expense to achieve an enduring benefit for a trade. It is not a cost that may be deducted in arriving at profits for tax purposes, although **capital allowances** may be available. See 15.1.5.

Cash accounting A method of accounting to HMRC for VAT as and when payment is received rather than according to when VAT invoices are issued. See 21.6.4.

Cash basis A method of accounting that recognises income and expenditure only when paid.

Chargeable transfer A gift or other transfer of value made by an individual which is not covered by any of the various exemptions and is therefore a transfer for **IHT** purposes. See 29.2–29.5.

Charitable trust A trust where all income must be used for charitable purposes. In England and Wales, most charities have to be registered with the Charity Commissioners.

Class 1A NICs Special **NICs** charged on an employer in respect of cars made available to employees for private use. The contributions are levied on the 'scale' benefits used to arrive at the employees' taxable benefit. See 22.1.8.

Class 1B NICs Class 1B contributions were introduced from 6 April 1998 and apply where an employer settles tax in respect of employees' benefits under a **PSA**. See 22.1.7.

Close company A company where the directors control more than half of the voting shares or where such control may be exercised by five or fewer people and their associates. See 17.13.

Commutation Taking a lump sum instead of a pension.

Company Limited by Guarantee A company which does not have share capital. Usually used by a charity or not for profit organisation. The member's liability is limited to the amount of their guarantee.

Corporate venturing A relief for companies that invest in small trading companies by subscribing for ordinary shares. See 17.15.

Corporation tax A tax levied on companies' profits. The full rate is currently 30% (due to be reduced to 28%), but many companies will qualify for the **small companies rate**.

Crown servant Civil servant or member of the armed forces.

CTSA Corporation Tax Self-Assessment.

Current year basis The basis of assessment whereby a self-employed individual is assessed on his profits for the firm's year which ends in the tax year.

CY basis Current year basis.

Deeds of variation A special term for **IHT** purposes. Where the provisions of a person's will are varied by the beneficiaries' mutual consent, and the necessary deed of variation is executed within two years of the relevant death, IHT may be computed as if the deceased's will had contained the revised provisions from the outset. A similar treatment may apply where a person has died without making a valid will, and the individuals who would benefit under the intestacy rules mutually agree to vary the position. See 29.4.6.

Deregistration This occurs when a trader who has been registered for VAT purposes is permitted to deregister. Once deregistered, he must not charge VAT on any supplies subsequently made by him in the course of his business. See Chapter 21.

Discretionary trust A type of trust where the trustees can vary the way they use the trust monies and can choose how they pay out (or 'distribute') income to members of a class of potential beneficiaries. This is different to other types of trust where the trustees are bound to pay over the income to a particular beneficiary.

Dispensations An employer is required to make annual returns of payments and benefits provided to employees (**form P11D**). A dispensation may be negotiated with the Revenue whereby certain expenses and other payments need not be reported on the form.

Distribution A distribution of a company's assets to its members (ie shareholders), for example, a payment of a dividend. Distributions may also be made by a liquidator. Where assets are distributed to members of the company during the course of a liquidation, there is said to be a distribution in specie.

Dividends A cash amount paid to a member of a company according to the number of shares held by him. Dividends may only be declared out of distributable profits.

Domicile (see 34.1) A legal concept that can be very important where a person has overseas income or gains or transfers property situated outside the UK. Income tax and CGT on foreign assets may be charged only on the **remittance basis**.

A person generally has a foreign domicile if he does not regard the UK as his real home and he retains strong links with another country.

The concept of domicile is not exactly the same as that of nationality, although if you are a foreign national this will be very helpful in establishing that you are not UK-domiciled. Your domicile of origin is normally that of your father when you reached age 16 (or that of your mother if she was unmarried or your father died while you were still a minor). The relevant age is 14 for individuals domiciled in Scotland.

Your domicile of origin continues to remain in force until such time as you acquire a new domicile of choice by making a permanent home elsewhere.

Drawings Amounts taken out of a business by sole traders or partners (eg to cover general living expenses). Drawings are taken out of profits, they are not an allowable expense in arriving at those profits.

Earnings basis Accounts should be prepared so as to reflect a trader's earnings for a year, rather than just cash received. Thus, accounts should include debtors, ie bills which have been issued but which have not been paid by the year end.

Election to waive exemption A VAT term used in commercial land and property transactions. Otherwise known as the 'option to tax'. A landowner has the option to make what would otherwise be an **exempt supply** into a taxable supply. Formal notification to HMRC is required. See 21.3.6.

Enhancement expenditure A term used in the context of CGT. In computing a person's capital gain, it is possible to deduct the costs incurred in acquiring the asset and any enhancement expenditure on improvements, etc reflected in the state of the asset at the date of disposal. See 12.8.4.

Emoluments Normal remuneration, bonuses and other employment income received by a director or employee.

Employment income Income from offices or employments and pension income taxed under the Income Tax (Earnings & Pensions) Act 2003. The old term for employment income was Schedule E income.

Enterprise Investment Scheme A scheme under which individuals may receive income tax and CGT relief when investing in qualifying unquoted trading companies. See 24.5.

Enterprise Management Incentives An **approved share option scheme** that allows employees to receive options over shares worth up to £120,000 in a small trading company. See 5.6.

Enterprise zones A Government-designated area, normally lasting for a ten-year period, during which a person carrying on a business within the zone is exempt from business rates. There is also considerable freedom from planning controls.

Expenditure on commercial buildings situated in an enterprise zone qualifies for capital allowances. Acquisition of an unused commercial building, or a building that has been let only during the preceding two years, attracts a 100% allowance. See 15.2.18.

Entrepeneurs relief A CGT relief which may mean that individuals pay tax at only 10% on capital gains of up to £1m. See 16.8.

Equity partner A term used to distinguish between a salaried partner taxed as an employee and proprietors of the business or 'full partners' who are self-employed.

ESOP Employee Share Ownership Plan.

ESOT Employee Share Ownership Trust.

EU The European Union. Currently Austria, Belgium, Czech Republic, Cyprus, Denmark, Estonia, Finland, France, Germany, Greece, Hungary, Ireland, Italy, Latvia, Lithuania, Luxembourg, Malta, the Netherlands, Poland, Portugal, Slovakia, Slovenia, Spain, Sweden and the UK.

Evasion consists of illegal steps taken to pay less tax than which is properly due. Contrast **avoidance**, which seeks to achieve the same ends but does not involve the individual in breaking the law.

Exempt supplies Supplies not liable to VAT. A person who makes only exempt supplies cannot recover **input VAT** suffered by him.

Exempt transfers The following transfers are exempt from **IHT**: gifts to spouse; normal expenditure out of income; £250 small gifts exemption; annual £3,000 exemption; exemption for marriage gifts; gifts to charities; gifts for national purposes; gifts for public benefit; gifts to political parties; certain transfers to employee trusts. See 29.5.

Ex gratia A person makes an *ex gratia* payment when he does so without admitting liability, for example, a payment by an employer on terminating an employment.

Filing date An individual or trustee must file his **self-assessment** return on or before 31 January following the end of the tax year concerned. See 2.1.

Financial Reporting Standards Issued by the Accounting Standards Board, and mandatory for companies.

Foreign situs property Assets which are located (ie situated) outside the UK. See 34.16.

Form CT61 A quarterly return required for a company in respect of annual payments made under deduction of tax. See 17.5.9.

Form P11D An annual return made by employers of expenses payments and **benefits-in-kind** provided for an employee.

FURBS Funded Unapproved Retirement Benefit Scheme.

Gift Aid A tax efficient system for donations to charities which was greatly enhanced by FA 2000 and also encompasses donations made under a deed of covenant. See 10.9 and 37.1.

Gross income Income from which no tax has been deducted at source. It may still be taxable income.

Group registration for VAT purposes Companies under common control may register for VAT purposes as a single unit or VAT group. Where this happens, all supplies between those companies are disregarded for VAT purposes. VAT is charged only on supplies outside the group. See 21.4.1.

Groups of companies (See 17.11) There are various different rules under which companies may be regarded as part of a group. A parent company may have subsidiaries, ie other companies in which the parent has a majority shareholding. The companies constitute a group for company law purposes.

　　The conditions that need to be satisfied for companies to form a group for tax purposes vary, but in general the parent must have a 75% interest in its subsidiaries.

HM Revenue & Customs New Government department that incorporates the functions previously performed by the Inland Revenue and Customs & Excise.

Hold-over relief Relief given to a donor or other transferor of business assets or where the gift, etc constitutes a chargeable transfer for **IHT** purposes. Where an individual, etc is entitled to hold-over relief, his gain is not charged but is deducted from the asset's market value in determining the transferee's acquisition value for CGT purposes. See 12.6 and 16.4.

IHT Inheritance tax.

Income from savings Income taxed at only 20% unless you are a higher rate taxpayer. Income from savings includes interest, dividends and purchased life annuities.

Income received gross Income received without any tax having been deducted. See **Gross income**.

Indexation (See 12.12) An adjustment made for CGT purposes to allow for inflation up to April 1998. The adjustment is computed by reference to the increase in the retail price index between the month of acquisition (or March 1982 if later) and the month of disposal (or April 1998 if earlier). Replaced by taper relief for individuals and trustees in relation to periods after April 1998. Abolished altogether for disposals after 5 April 2008.

Individual savings account (ISA) A savings scheme that came into operation on 6 April 1999. All income and capital gains are free of tax. See 24.1.

Industrial buildings Buildings occupied for qualifying trade purposes may qualify as industrial buildings. The significance of this is that a person who incurs expenditure on an industrial building may claim industrial buildings allowances. Normally, allowances are given at the rate of 4% pa over a 25-year period. See 15.2.20

Inheritance tax (IHT) A combination of a gift tax and death duties. Tax is payable on chargeable transfers made by an individual during his lifetime and on his estate at the time of his death.

Input VAT The VAT paid to suppliers of goods and services. Where a person has paid for such goods and services and is himself VAT registered, he may recover input VAT by offsetting the tax paid by him against tax charged on his own supplies. See 21.1.

Insurance bond A common type of non-qualifying life policy (see 27.2.2) where the life cover is relatively small and the policy is really a form of investment. Holders of such bonds can make tax-free annual withdrawals of 5% of their original investment (see 27.3.3).

Interest in possession trust Where the beneficiary is entitled to income arising from the trust capital and is legally entitled to demand that the trustees pay that income to him or her. An interest in possession can also exist where the trust owns a property and the beneficiary is entitled to live there rent free.

Intestacy Where a person dies without making a valid will (ie he dies intestate), his estate passes to relatives in a set order under the intestacy provisions.

Investment companies A company that exists wholly or mainly for carrying on the business of managing investments.

IR 35 A generally used way of referring to provisions introduced in FA 2000 to combat the use of 'one man companies' to enable contractors to receive income without tax and **NICs** being withheld at source under **PAYE**. See 20.3.

Know-how Certain expenditure by a person carrying on a trade to acquire information required to carry out certain industrial or manufacturing processes may qualify for a form of **capital allowances**. See 15.2.22.

Limited liability company The proper term for a limited company (ie X Ltd or X plc)

Limited liability partnership (LLP) A type of body corporate which gives its members limited liability but is treated as a partnership for tax purposes.

Market value rule Where an asset is transferred to a person by way of a gift or some other disposal which is not an arm's length transaction, CGT may be charged as if the person making the disposal had in fact received market value.

National insurance contributions Social Security Contributions: **Class 1 NICs** are payable by an employer and employees; Class 2 and Class 4 NICs are payable by the self-employed. The national insurance system is administered by the Department of Social Security.

NCIS National Criminal Intelligence Service.

NICs National insurance contributions.

Official rate A rate of interest set by Parliament which is supposed to be a commercial rate. Loans from an employer are generally treated as a benefit-in-kind if interest is paid at less than the official rate. See 4.7.

Offshore disclosure facility A way for individuals who have evaded tax in the past to settle up with HMRC. See 3.4.3.

Opening years' rules There are special rules for the opening years under the **CY basis** for self-employed traders. See 6.3.3.

Options A legally binding contract under which one party is bound to buy or sell an asset to the other. A call option is an option under which the grantor agrees to sell an asset to the other party if he exercises his option. A put option is where a person has the right to require the other party to buy an asset from him.

Output tax (See 21.1) VAT chargeable on goods or services supplied in the UK. The trader must account for VAT charged on such supplies by completing a VAT return, normally on a quarterly basis.

Outworkers Some industries have outworkers who work on their own premises. However, depending on the circumstances, they may be regarded as employees, and not as self-employed. This means payments made by the person using outworkers' services may be subject to **PAYE** and employers NICs. See 6.2.

Overlap relief (See 6.3.5). Under the **CY basis** of assessment, there are special provisions to cover the way profits are assessed during the opening years. The general principle is that total amount of profits assessed over the life of the business should precisely equal the actual profits earned by the business. Overlap relief covers situations where a particular year's profits are assessed more than once (usually under the **opening years' rules**) and is effectively an adjustment to ensure that this does not result in excessive amounts being assessed overall. Overlap relief is given by way of a deduction from an individual's profits when he ceases to carry on his business or profession, or when the firm's accounting date is changed to a date that falls later in the tax year.

Partially exempt trader Under VAT, a person who makes a mixture of standard- or zero-rated supplies and supplies that are exempt for VAT purposes. A partially exempt trader may not be able to claim full credit for his input tax.

Pay As You Earn A compulsory system for deduction of tax at source from cash payments to employees.

PAYE Pay As You Earn.

PAYE Settlement Agreements Formerly known as Annual Voluntary Settlements (AVSs), these provide employers with the mechanism to meet tax liabilities arising on a wide range of staff costs that would otherwise be assessed to tax on the employees concerned as **benefits-in-kind**.

Payment in lieu of notice (PILON) The Revenue may argue that payments to an employee are taxable where the employment contract refers to the possibility of the employer making a PILON. See 4.16.8.

Personal pension scheme Approved pension schemes run by insurance companies, banks, building societies or unit trust groups.

Plant and machinery Plant and machinery attracts **capital allowances** if used by a person in the course of a business carried on by him. There is no statutory definition of 'plant and machinery', although certain rules have evolved through decided cases. See 15.2.

Potentially exempt transfers (PETs) An outright gift made by one individual to another. The gift will be exempt from **IHT** provided the donor survives seven years. If the donor does not survive that period, the PET becomes an actually exempt transfer and becomes chargeable to IHT. See 29.6.

Pre-owned assets charge (also called POT) An income tax charge introduced by Finance Act 2004 which can result in an individual being deemed to have income because he has the use of assets which he has given away. See 32.7.

Premium A lump sum payment to a landlord to obtain a lease is regarded as a premium for tax purposes. Where the lease is for a period of less than 50 years, part of the premium is normally treated as income for the landlord. See 7.3.

Prescribed accounting periods Periods covered by VAT returns. Normally periods are of three-month duration ending on the dates notified in the certificate of VAT registration.

Pre-trading expenditure Certain expenditure incurred in connection with a trade that is about to be carried on may qualify for tax relief once the trade is commenced. See 15.3.

Probate value The value included for an asset in a IHT return on an individual's death. This will often be the CGT acquisition value for the person who inherits.

PSA PAYE Settlement Agreement.

Purchase of own shares A company may purchase its own shares. A public company is normally permitted to do so only in so far as it has distributable profits or such purchase is being funded by the proceeds from an issue of new shares. A private company may purchase its own shares out of capital. In all situations, there is a set procedure that must be followed to comply with company law.

A special tax treatment may apply where a private trading company purchases its own shares.

Qualifying corporate bonds (QCBs) A loan stock issued by a company may be an exempt asset for CGT purposes (ie it qualifies for exemption). However, any loss realised on a disposal of a QCB is not normally allowable for CGT purposes. See 12.4.2 and 16.1.2.

Qualifying loans (See 10.5). An individual who is a partner is entitled to relief for interest paid on qualifying loans, ie loans used to acquire an interest in the firm or which have been taken to enable him to make a loan to his firm for use in the ordinary course of the firm's business.

Shareholders in a close company may also be able to raise qualifying loans to acquire shares or make loan capital available to the company.

Rate applicable to trusts The rate of tax suffered by discretionary trusts, i.e. 40% for 2004–05 onwards. See 30.5.2.

Readily convertible assets A term used for **PAYE** and **NICs** purposes. PAYE and NICs have to be paid if an employee receives readily convertible assets as part of his remuneration. See 4.2.1 and 20.1.2.

Real property Land and buildings.

Rebasing A technical term for CGT purposes whereby an individual who held an asset at 31 March 1982 may have his capital gain computed as if his cost were the market value of the asset at that date. See 12.9.

REITs Real estate investment trusts (see 17.14 and 26.6.2)

Relevant discounted security A loan stock issued at a discount of more than 0.5% for each year of its life (or more than 15% if the stock has a life of more than 30 years). A gain on the sale of a relevant discounted security is taxed as income. See 8.7.

Relevant earnings Profits from a trade or profession and earnings from a non-pensionable employment. For years up to 2005–06, an individual could only make contributions into a **personal pension scheme** based on a percentage of his relevant earnings for a tax year.

Remittance basis The rule under which foreign domiciled individuals pay tax on overseas income and gains only if they are remitted to the UK. See 34.10.

'Rent-a-room' relief A special relief for individuals who let rooms in their home.

Reservation of benefit An **IHT** term. Where a person makes a gift but reserves a benefit, the transaction is not regarded as a **potentially exempt transfer**. The asset remains part of his estate for as long as he continues to reserve a benefit. If he has not relinquished his reserved benefit by the time of his death, the asset's market value will be brought into account for **IHT** purposes just as if he still owned the asset. See 29.7.

Restrictive covenant An undertaking not to do something in the future. Where an employee receives a cash sum in return for entering into such a covenant, the cash is taxed as employment income (see 4.14).

Retention tax A kind of withholding tax which is deducted from interest paid by an overseas bank to a UK resident individual and which is eventually paid over to HMRC without the identity of the UK individual being disclosed. See 8.10.4.

Retirement annuity contracts (RACs) These were similar to **personal pension schemes**. In effect, they were approved contracts under which a person who was self-employed or in non-pensionable employment could provide for their retirement prior to the introduction of personal pension schemes in July 1988. The rules on this type of pension plan have been superceded by the single new pensions regime introduced from 'A' Day.

Retirement benefits scheme A technical term for a pension scheme.

Revenue expenditure Expenditure that is deductible in arriving at a company's profits. Cf **capital expenditure**.

Reverse charge A VAT charging mechanism that obliges the customer to account to Customs for VAT on the price charged for goods or services. The VAT charged is recoverable as **input VAT**, subject to the normal rules. See 21.5.3.

Roll-over relief A CGT relief that applies where an individual disposes of a business or an asset used in a business and spends the proceeds on acquiring replacement assets during a qualifying period (normally up to one year before and up to three years after the date of disposal of the original asset). See 16.3.

Roll-up fund A colloquial term for an offshore collective fund where the managers do not pay out income but accumulate it within the fund. See 9.7.

S2P State second pension. See 25.5.3.

Salaried partner An individual who is subject to the supervision and direction of equity partners and who is therefore no more than a very senior employee. Salaried partners are taxed as employees rather than self-employed.

Schedule A An individual's income from UK property was taxed under Schedule A up to 2004–05. It is now taxed as income from a UK property business. See Chapter 7.

Schedule D A self-employed person's profits used to be assessed under Schedule D. From 2005–06, they are taxed under IT(T&OI)A 2005. See Chapter 6.

Schedule E The old name for employment income. Directors and employees were assessed under Schedule E for 2002–03 and earlier years. The normal basis of assessment for Schedule E /employment income is the receipts basis, ie an individual is assessed according to remuneration received by him during the year. See Chapters 4–5.

Scientific research allowances Certain expenditure incurred by traders on scientific research may attract allowances. **Revenue expenditure** is allowed in full. **Capital expenditure** may attract 100% **capital allowances**.

Self-administered pension scheme A pension scheme with no more than 12 members where either the company that established the scheme or one or more of the members are trustees.

Self-assessment A system for assessing tax and payment of tax liabilities which came into force in 1996-97 for individuals and trustees. Companies moved onto a self-assessment system for accounting periods ending on or after 1 July 1999.

Settlement Another name for a trust.

Shares Valuation Division A specialist section of the Capital Taxes Office which negotiates valuations of unquoted shares where such a valuation is required for tax purposes.

Sideways loss relief Setting trading losses against an individual's other taxable income. See 6.7.2.

Small companies rate (See 17.4.3) Corporation tax is charged at only 21% unless the company concerned has profits in excess of the lower limit (presently £300,000, provided there are no associated companies). If there are associated companies, the lower limit is divided by the number of associated companies.

Sole traders An individual is a sole trader if he carries on business on his own account rather than in partnership or through a company. Similarly, an individual carrying on a profession on his own account is termed a 'sole practitioner'.

Stakeholder pensions These are a special type of personal pension plan where the insurance company or other provider's charges are subject to an upper limit.

Stamp duty Duty payable at 0.5% on transfers of shares and at 1–4% on transfers of property. See Chapter 38.

Surcharge A penalty based on the amount of tax payable which is imposed automatically if an individual has not paid the tax due on his self-assessment return by one month after the filing date. A further surcharge is normally imposed if tax remains unpaid after a further six months have elapsed.

Taper relief Capital gains could be reduced by taper relief, depending on the number of complete years of ownership after 5 April 1998, and depending on whether the asset disposed of is a business asset. See 12.11.Relief not available for disposals after 5 April 2008.

There is also a taper relief for **IHT** where an individual dies within seven years of making a **potentially exempt transfer**. See 29.6.

Tax Bulletin A newsletter issued by the Revenue for practitioners.

Tax invoice An invoice issued by a supplier which must show specific information. It is the document on which VAT accounting and control procedures are based.

Tax point The time at which a transaction is regarded as taking place for VAT purposes, and when VAT becomes payable or recoverable. See **Cash accounting**.

Time apportionment basis Where an asset was owned at 6 April 1965, and no universal **rebasing** election has been made, it is sometimes possible for a capital gain to be computed on the apportionment basis. This means that only a proportion of the gain achieved over the total period of ownership is brought into charge. See 12.9.

Trust Property is held in trust where trustees hold it for the benefit of clearly identified beneficiaries. The trustees must use the capital and income as directed by the trust deed and in accordance with trust law. See Chapter 30.

Unincorporated businesses A company is an incorporated business. Businesses carried on by a **sole trader** or partnership are unincorporated businesses.

Universal rebasing election An irrevocable election that may be made under which the 31 March 1982 value of assets held by that person is treated as if it were the original cost. See 12.9.

Venture capital loss relief Where an individual has subscribed for shares in an unquoted trading company, any losses may be set against his income for the year in which the loss is realised. See 16.2.

Venture capital trust A type of investment trust established under FA 1995 provisions. VCTs must invest in unquoted trading companies with net assets of no more than £7m. See 24.6.

Wasting assets Assets with an expected useful life of less than 50 years. See 12.4.2.

Zero-rating A sale on which no VAT is charged. A person making zero-rated supplies may nevertheless still be able to recover **input VAT**. See 21.3.2.

INDEX